THIRD EDITION

ORGANIZATION

Text, Cases, and Readings on the Management of Organizational Design and Change

Phyllis F. Schlesinger
Babson College

Vijay Sathe
The Peter F. Drucker Graduate Management Center
The Claremont Graduate School

Leonard A. Schlesinger
Graduate School of Business Administration
Harvard University

John P. Kotter
Graduate School of Business Administration
Harvard University

IRWIN

Chicago • Bogotá • Boston • Buenos Aires • Caracas
London • Madrid • Mexico City • Sydney • Toronto

© RICHARD D. IRWIN, INC., 1979, 1986, and 1992

Sponsoring editor: Kurt Strand
Project editor: Rebecca Dodson
Production manager: Bette K. Ittersagen
Designer: Jeanne M. Rivera
Cover designer: Three Communication Design
Compositor: J.M. Post Graphics Corp.
Typeface: 10/12 Times Roman
Printer: R. R. Donnelley & Sons Company

Library of Congress Cataloging-in-Publication Data

Organization: text, cases, and readings on the management of
   organizational design and change / Phyllis F. Schlesinger . . . [et
   al.].—3rd ed.
      p.   cm.
   Rev. ed. of Organization / John Kotter, Leonard A. Schlesinger,
Vijay Sathe, 2nd ed.   1986.
   Includes bibliographical references.
   ISBN 0-256-09184-6
   1. Organization.   2. Management.   I. Schlesinger, Phyllis F.
II. Kotter, John P., 1947-   Organization.
HD31.0752   1992
658.4′06—dc20   91–23122

Printed in the United States of America
      3   4   5   6   7   8   9   0   *DOC*   8   7   6   5

Preface

We have prepared this third edition both to present developments in organizational design concepts and to make available cases and readings that have appeared since the second edition. The basic concepts and analytical techniques presented in the first and second editions have been maintained and special topics such as the design of high-commitment organizations and the influence of corporate culture on organizational change have been included.

We would like to thank the many users who have provided us with feedback on the first and second editions. We also owe special thanks to students in the Organizational Design and Development Class at the Graduate School of Management at Babson College, who tested the new material. Thanks also to the Word Processing department at Babson College for their assistance in preparation of the manuscript.

We would also like to thank the following reviewers for their insightful comments and suggestions:

Dr. Rafik I. Beekun
University of Nevada

Prof. Richard N. Logozzo
Central Connecticut State University

Prof. Timothy W. Edlund
Morgan State University

Prof. Afsaneh Nahavandi
Arizona State University—West Campus

Prof. Barbara H. Hillman
Pepperdine University

Our grateful appreciation of persons who have contributed the readings and cases used in this edition is acknowledged by name where their work appears.

Phyllis F. Schlesinger
Vijay Sathe
Leonard A. Schlesinger
John P. Kotter

Contents

PART TWO   101

Chapter 4   Organizing Human Resources in a Single-Business Company   103

Interdependence: The Factor Creating a Need
for Integration   Factors that Make It Difficult to
Cope with Interdependence: *Complexity
Differentiation   Poor Informal Relationships
Size and Physical Distance*   Commonly Used
Integrating Devices: *Management Hierarchy
Staff   Rules and Procedures   Goals and Plans
Committees and Task Forces   Integrating Roles
Formal Authority   Measurement and Reward
Systems   Selection and Development Systems
Physical Setting   Departmentalization*
Selecting a Set of Integrating Mechanisms
Drawing Subunit Boundaries   Summary

PART THREE   259

Chapter 5

Organizing Human Resources for Multibusiness and Multinational Companies   261

Chapter 6

Managing Organizational Change   336

PART FOUR 339

PART FIVE   457

Chapter 8

Developing an Organization that Contributes to Long-Run Effectiveness   459

A Case of Organizational Decline Characteristics of an Effective Organization— From a Long-Range Point of View Bureaucratic Dry Rot Organizing for the Future *Organizational Development (OD)   OD Change Efforts*   Summary

Cases

Readings

PART SIX   569

C h a p t e r   1

Introduction

The real secret of the greatness of the Romans was their genius for organization.

James Mooney, Vice President
General Motors, 1931

It was on the strength of their extensive organization that the peasants went into action and within four months (in 1926) brought about a great revolution in the countryside, a revolution without parallel in history.

Mao Tse-tung, 1927

Organizing Human Resources

One important aspect of managerial work involves organizing human resources to ensure that the right people focus on the right tasks; that they have the proper information, tools, incentives, and controls to perform these tasks effectively and efficiently;[1] and that their efforts are coordinated to achieve the organization's overall objectives. Generally, the higher one's position in an organization, the greater the responsibility that person has for large numbers of employees and the more time and effort that manager will spend on this aspect of managerial work.

In a small group of people, a manager can create and maintain an appropriate organization through face-to-face interaction with his or her employees. The manager can verbally assign tasks, monitor their completion, coordinate activities, compensate people fairly, and so on. If the organization begins to break down, the manager can spot this immediately and remedy any problems. Managers only need to use their interpersonal skills to monitor the organization's functioning.

As the number of people a manager is responsible for grows, interpersonal skills become insufficient for maintaining an appropriate organization. A single manager

---

[1]Effectiveness is measured by the degree to which an organization meets its goals. Efficiency is measured by the amount of resources expended in achieving results.

Figure 1-1
The Human Organization

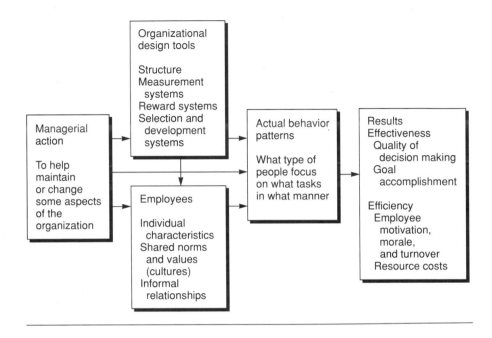

no longer can deal with everyone face-to-face, coordinate everything personally, and always be around to deal with crises. Many entrepreneurs have learned this lesson the hard way.

To organize large numbers of people, or people who are often spatially separated from one another, managers use different organization design tools. These tools include: job design, compensation systems, performance-appraisal systems, training programs, and reporting relationships. Considerable evidence suggests that the design and implementation of these tools can have a major impact on an organization's financial performance and on the quality of work life for its employees (see Figure 1–1). Furthermore, research indicates that improper design is one factor that undermines an organization's performance and generates various disruptive problems.

Organizational Problems

Inappropriate organizational designs often lead to these types of recurring problems:

- Ineffective decision-making. (Production personnel in one company continually made poor decisions about inventory levels, which created various problems throughout the company.)

- High employee turnover. (One firm's management turnover was 30 percent per year, compared with less than 5 percent for other companies in its industry.)

- Low morale. (Nearly 50 percent of the employees in one company complained that they didn't like their jobs and felt that the company was a poor place to work.)

- Expensive conflict among individuals and groups. (The production and sales personnel within one company literally plotted against one another.)

- A lack of employee motivation. (The sales employees in one firm worked, on average, a five-hour day.)

- Wasted employee energy. (Using the same equipment and working the same number of hours, the production employees in one firm produced only 60 percent of the daily output of a similar firm.)

- Lack of goal accomplishment. (The sales department in one company missed its sales objectives for 10 consecutive quarters.)

An important characteristic of these organizational problems, which differentiates them from other types of problems, is that they *recur*. They recur not because they are caused by an idiosyncratic individual, group, or environmental event, but due to the **organizational design.**

In addition, inappropriate attempts to introduce changes in organizational design also can be costly. They can disrupt a company's operations, generate resistance and hostility among employees, and lead to any of the organizational problems previously listed. Such improper strategies can simply fail to produce a needed change, or they can generate change at burdensome cost to an organization.

The Purpose and Organization of This Book

The basic purpose of this book is demonstrating how to avoid potential organizational problems through appropriate planning and how to solve existing organizational problems through organizational analysis and action planning. Specifically, our objectives are:

1. To provide examples that illustrate a variety of real situations in which managers deal with organizational issues.

2. To provide the best research-based conceptual maps to help analyze organizational design and change issues.

3. To provide a sequence of material that efficiently develops new awareness, ideas, and skills related to organizational design and change.

To achieve these objectives, the book contains text, cases, and readings. The text provides an integrated analytical framework based on recent organizational research. The readings explore questions and issues identified in the text in greater detail and from more diverse viewpoints. The cases, mostly written in the past five years, focus on common organizational problems and questions that managers face today.

The book is organized into five parts, each of which builds on the previous section. It begins by looking at organizational design questions within the basic building block of modern organizations—the specialized department. Primary issues in Part One relate to turnover and morale, personnel selection and development, performance appraisal, employee motivation, job design, career paths, and compensation. In the second part, the focus is more complex, and the material deals with multiple, interdependent departments within single-business companies. Major issues relate to coordination, interdepartmental conflict, management control systems, and organizational structure. Innovations in the structure of single-business companies are examined. In Part Three, the focus moves to another level—large multidivisional and multinational organizations, each one comprised of numerous single-business units. Primary issues at this point are coordination and control, the management of extreme diversity, cross-cultural conflict, group structures,and design problems associated with mergers and acquisitions. Part Four focuses on organizational change processes initiated to correct the types of organizational design problems dealt with in the first three parts. Important issues here relate to organizational culture, change strategies, planning change processes, questions of timing and speed, and power and influence. In Part Five, the focus shifts to the long-term horizon and to questions relating to developing an organization for long-run survival and effectiveness. The key issue here concerns the systematic development of adaptability while coping with short-run realities.

C h a p t e r   2

Organization Design Tools

Organizations as Social Systems

There are many ways to conceptualize the elements of organizations. Because we see the organization as a complex and open social system, we will begin by outlining a way to understand organizations as whole systems. Then, we will look at formal elements of organizational design.

Organizations are complex social systems with the following characteristics. First, they are *interdependent*. Changes in one part of the organization affect other parts. Ideally, the choices managers make about the characteristics of one element depend on the choices they make about other elements. (For example, decisions made about structuring salespersons' commissions will affect their performance.)

Second, organizations can use information received as *feedback* to change or to correct errors. Organizations (or managers in organizations) can choose to ignore this feedback; that does not mean they do not receive the feedback. Production people receive information about their product's quality from other areas of the organization, but they use this information as they wish.

Organizations strive to reach a *balance* or steady state. Changes in one area cause an organization to behave in ways that try to return it to balance. For example, a new manager in a hierarchically structured organization marked by a distrust of hourly employees decided to give increased shop-floor responsibility to a small group of employees. The group quickly becomes the most productive group in the company, breaking records for both quantity and quality produced. The organization misunderstood the experiment and only saw that the manager was giving responsibility to people who knew little about production. Top management quickly brought the organization back to equilibrium by releasing the manager and ending the experiment.

Finally, there is *no best way* of organizing to accomplish a task. This does not mean that there is no preferred way given certain circumstances. It simply means that how one organizes depends on the balance of the following elements.

5

A Framework for Analyzing Organizations as Systems

Managers spend most of their time designing organizations. They determine the people, the tasks, and the structures in which people work. Most of this text focuses on analyzing, problem solving, and deciding on these design elements. However, because organizations are systems, managers must understand how the organization as a system behaves—before making design decisions. Each design decision must be made with the following concepts in mind.

Each organization has a set of **key success factors,** items that it must do well to survive. These factors include maintaining product innovation in a high-tech company, maintaining quality control in a production line, and so forth. *Context factors* have some influence on key success factors. Every organization exists in a context. This is the reality in which the organization functions. It is composed of the organization's environment, physical setting, history, political and social milieu, and strategy. These contextual factors are usually not under the organization's influence, but they are influenced by the world around it. Thus, although it is important to understand and monitor the context in which an organization operates, it is usually the last place that an individual manager concentrates his or her efforts in achieving organizational effectiveness.

Organization *design factors* are the people in the jobs, the tasks they perform, and the formal organization structure and operating system (the hierarchy of authority, the pattern of reporting relationships, the formal measurement and control system, the reward system, and the selection and recruitment systems). The arrangement of these variables in a balance has a considerable effect on an organization's effectiveness. Managers have more control over design elements than any other piece of the organization as a system.

Managers spend much of their time working with design factors: they can determine the levels of hierarchy and reporting relationships, they can set the levels of performance and measurement of performance, and managers can hire people to fill tasks that they design. It is because these design factors are often established without paying attention to the consequences on the whole system that this book focuses on organization design tools.

Every organization has a *culture*. The emergent activities, attitudes, and interactions that define the organization, on which basic decisions about organizational life are made, is the organizational culture. An organization's culture reflects the behavior patterns, values, and attitudes that organizational members use to guide organizational life.

Finally, each organization has particular outputs. Organizations produce goods and/or services. Organization members have opportunities for growth and development for stagnation, and they can be satisfied or dissatisfied with their work. The outputs, productivity, satisfaction, and growth and development of individual employees can be measured and used to guide other decisions.

The choices managers make about structuring design factors influence the organization's culture and outcomes. Thus, an organization is a system of variables with individual definitions that affect each other. Contextual factors affect the nature of design factors. For example, the presence of strong affirmative-action monitoring—a contextual factor—can affect the people one hires—a design factor. If employees have the requisite skills for the work—a design factor—tasks are appropriate for their abilities and preferences, and organizational arrangements in balance—design factors—they generally will behave in ways that embody a positive value system—culture. This culture and design factor can combine to yield positive outcomes and an organization that is productive and includes people who are productive, satisfied, and have opportunities for growth and development.

There are many ways to conceptualize the formal elements of organizational design. In this book, the formal elements are: task, people, structure, measurement systems, reward systems, and selection and development systems.

Tasks

Jobs in organizations are a set of tasks assigned to an individual. These tasks either can be clearly defined, perhaps in a detailed job description, or vague. Most organizations are comprised of many different jobs. Some of these jobs contain similar tasks that either can be difficult (staff specialists) or simple (clerical and assembly-line jobs), while others require a varied set of tasks (managerial jobs).

People

People in organizations who fulfill specified tasks differ in their skills, interests, values, attitudes, preference for variety and structure, and desire for individual challenge. Formal structural measurements can be designed so that appropriate people are hired for appropriate jobs.

Structure

When a manager allocates responsibilities, activities, and authority to individuals and coordinates these individuals vertically and horizontally, they define a structure. This structure is also called an organizational design. Organizational design is best understood by starting with specialization requirements at the level of individual job design—grouping individual jobs into units, these units into larger units, and so on, ultimately coordinating the activities of jobs and units through integrating mechanisms. These designs presumably exist to support organizational goals and prioritize an organization's key success factors.

The elements of structure include subunits such as departments or divisions, a management hierarchy, rules and plans, and committees and task forces. These design tools are used to influence behavior by clearly specifying what individuals are responsible for, where in the organization they should work and with whom, what authority they have, to whom they are responsible, and how to perform their tasks.

Organizational structure groups jobs into subunits such as departments, and it groups subunits into large subunits such as divisions. This grouping is usually based on functional similarity (all marketing jobs or subunits are grouped into a marketing department). **Functional organizations** are most appropriate when the organization makes a fairly standard single product or a related line of products that are stable technologically and in a stable environment. This form offers great economies of scale, good communication among specialists, and good opportunities for professional development within each function. Product or service similarity (all jobs or subunits dealing with consulting are grouped into the consulting service department); or geographical area (all jobs or subunits dealing with Europe are grouped into the European division) are also rationales for grouping, because when environmental, product-related, or technological change occurs, more interdependence exists among the functions. Interdependence increases because it is crucial to stay informed about what happens. When more lateral communication becomes necessary, **product organizations** are formed. They can handle the increasing uncertainty, the increasing amount of information necessary, and the increasing complexity and diversity. While most organizations place a single job into one subunit, so-called **matrix organizations** group individual jobs into two or more subunits (e.g., a job may be in both the marketing and consulting services departments).

Matrix organizations coordinate different functional specialties while preserving the functional organization. This design enables them to identify and concentrate on the changes in markets, customers, technology, information, and therefore quickly respond to changes.

Divisionalized organizations produce a variety of products and service a number of markets and areas. Each division is a relatively autonomous business unit with most functions reporting to a general manager who has profit and loss responsibility. The key to establishing a divisional structure is that business volume must be large enough to support the functional organization while maintaining efficient economies of scale. While senior corporate managers set the long-run strategic direction of the firm and make resource-allocation decisions assisted by corporate staffs, separate divisions operate differently. Some divisions are independent, sending in monthly reports and having infrequent reviews. Others have extensive senior corporate involvement. The degree of involvement depends on performance, culture, and individual managers. Divisions can be more responsive to environments and markets, but they engender losses in certain economies of scale.

Closely related to such groupings is a management hierarchy that specifies reporting relationships and distributes formal authority for people and decisions to managers throughout the organization. Typically, the head of an organization has the most formal authority. The people who report to him or her, some or all of whom are in charge of the organization's largest subunits, are given less formal authority, and so on, down through the organization. Organizations are *centralized* if the formal authority is heavily concentrated in the hands of a few top people. If authority is widely distributed throughout the organization, the organization is *decentralized*. Hierarchies are sometimes described as "tall" and "flat," depending on the number of people reporting to each manager. A small span of control (few people reporting to each manager) creates relatively tall structures, and vice versa.

A fourth part of the structure of organizations includes rules, procedures, goals, and plans. Rules and procedures inform employees of how to perform their jobs. An organization with many rules and procedures is often called bureaucratic. Plans and goals are temporary rules and procedures; they also help define what people are to do for a limited period.

A final part of structure consists of committees and task forces. These devices formalize team (as opposed to individual) efforts to work on some task. The only significant difference between the two devices is that task forces are temporary in nature. Both components sometimes contain as few as 3 or as many as 20 members who often come from different organizational subunits.

Measurement Systems

Measurement systems attempt to influence human behavior by gathering, aggregating, disseminating, and evaluating information on the activities of individuals and groups within the organization. Measurement helps managers ask and answer questions such as: Are our managers achieving the organization's objectives? Do our employees perform according to the organization's expectations?

Measurement systems are either focused on the monitoring of ongoing activities or they are designed primarily to appraise past performance. Either type can be based on financial, quantitative (other than financial), and/or qualitative data. The two most common types of measurement systems are management-control systems and performance-appraisal systems.

Management-control systems ensure that the organization's (or subunits') resources are used consistently with goals and objectives. These systems focus on financial data and are usually referred to by how information is collected and assessed: standard-cost centers, revenue centers, discretionary-expense centers, profit centers, or investment centers.

Performance-appraisal systems measure factors associated with individual employees. These systems can be formal and regular or informal and irregular. These systems commonly ask a supervisor or a group of managers to rate individuals periodically on some scale regarding general characteristics of their work or personal traits. Often the individual rates his or her performance and that of his or her supervisor. Other types of performance-appraisal systems include ones wherein managers must rank all employees from best to worst performers, ones that are closely tied to predetermined mutual objectives and expectations, and ones where managers periodically write essays about employee performance.

Reward Systems

Reward systems induce people to join the organization, to work as its structure directs, and to work toward certain measured objectives. The two main characteristics of a reward system are the criteria used to allocate rewards and the nature of the rewards.

Reward systems are sometimes tied to measurement systems so that rewards are allocated primarily based on measured results. Other common criteria for the allocation of rewards include qualitative factors such as past achievements, seniority, loyalty, and other external criteria such as cost of living in the local area, family size, and education.

The most common rewards include money, fringe benefits (monetary and nonmonetary), promotions, intrinsically satisfying job assignments, and job security.

Organizations typically offer money either as a base salary or as a base plus incentives. Incentive plans can be based on individual performance, group performance, or organization-wide performance. Fringe benefits typically include an allowance for overtime work; holidays, vacations, and sick days off with pay; insurance; and special employee services (e.g., inexpensive lunches at the cafeteria). Additional fringes for managers include bigger and better offices, a company car, first-class travel on business trips, stock options, and so forth. Promotions reward an individual with more status, more power, and more responsibility. A job assignment that the individual likes can give him or her different kinds of rewards— challenge, agreeable social relations, a comfortable work pace, excitement, and so on. Job security provides a stable income and other types of rewards over time.

Selection and Development Systems

Selection and development are separate but interrelated formal organizational systems. They indirectly affect behavior patterns by influencing the knowledge, skills, values, and personalities of people who work on the organization's tasks.

Selection systems range from simple to elaborate, and the selection process can vary within an organization depending on job requirements and experience of candidates. At one extreme, new employees may be selected based on a simple form that they are asked to fill out. At the other extreme, an applicant's past work experience may be carefully examined, and he or she may be asked to take a series of tests and undergo many interviews with various managers. In either case, data on the person is sometimes compared to clear selection criteria, but often it is given to one or more individuals who make a judgment.

Development systems also range from simple to elaborate. Some organizations provide only informal on-the-job training and development, which is based entirely on the skills and interests of individual managers. At the other extreme, some organizations use information from the performance-review discussion to generate ideas for individual development. They then offer formal internal training courses or send employees to university programs. Some organizations also systematically follow the skill levels and work experience of certain employees with employee planning systems and periodically make development decisions (transfer, rotation, promotion, and training) based on that data. These organizations, through their measurement and reward systems, also systematically encourage managers to develop their subordinates' skills.

Choices

In designing the overall structure and the measurement, reward, selection, and development systems of an organization, managers face many choices. Should they use a functional structure, for example, or a product structure? How many people should report to each manager? What type of people should be hired for each subnunit? What is the best way to measure individual performance? Should people be paid for performance, their seniority, or for their future potential?

In some cases, making these choices is easy. For example, a small company that produces one product for a limited geographical area simply will adopt a functional structure. But in many cases, the best choice is not so obvious. For example, how much of a salesperson's income should depend on current sales performance—0 percent (a flat salary), 25 percent, 50 percent, 75 percent, or 100 percent (all commission)? How much money should an organization spend on management training programs—none, 1 percent of net income, or 10 percent of net? How many people should be assigned to a multibusiness company's corporate staff?

The basic purpose of the first three parts of this book is to help you develop the ability to analyze available design alternatives and to make difficult choices.

PART ONE

The first part of this book focuses on the most basic organizational building blocks: the specialized subunit that performs a limited functional task. Examples of subunits included in Part One are a corporate sales organization (Chicago Bond Sales) and a technology group (Technology Transfer at a Defense Contractor).

Managers of specialized subunits, as the cases illustrate, often face various human resource problems associated with high turnover, inadequate individual performance, and low morale. The text provides a research-based framework for analyzing these problems and for deciding how to address them successfully by using organization design tools. The readings focus on four tools that are particularly important at the subunit level—job design, reward systems, and performance-appraisal systems.

Chapter 3

Organizing Human Resources Within Specialized Subunits

In the late 18th century, Adam Smith convincingly demonstrated the significant economic advantages of applying the concept of specialization in organizations. Through specialization, he argued, people develop expertise in performing a limited set of activities and thus become highly effective at accomplishing those activities. In addition, Smith noted, specialization often produces significant economies of scale, thus helping an organization to be more efficient in using resources.

Virtually all of today's organizations consist of parts based on the Smithian notion of specialization. To understand the organizational issues that confront modern corporations, we must begin by focusing on the most basic organizational building block: the subunit that performs a limited, specialized function.

Conceptualizing Organization Design within Specialized Subunits

The logical objective of the organizational design of a specialized subunit is to select, develop, and manage a group of human resources to accomplish a limited set of assigned objectives efficiently and effectively in both the short run and long run. Recent research suggests that a useful way to conceptualize how the organization design of a subunit achieves this objective is in terms of the three-way "fit" shown in Figure 3–1.[1] The design factors presented in Chapter 2 are useful here. The design factors—an organization's structure, people, and tasks—must "fit" each other; each element must be compatible with the others. A structure that fits with

---

[1] Jay Lorsch and John Morse, *Organizations and Their Members* (New York: Harper & Row, 1974).

Figure 3–1
Conceptualization of Organization Design Function within a
Specialized Subunit

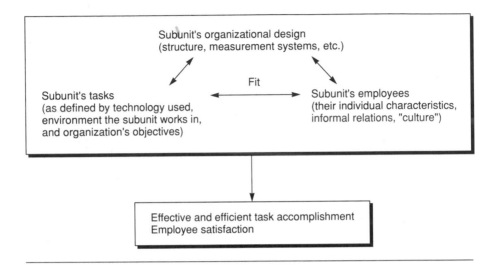

both the subunit's tasks and its employees will lead toward efficient and effective task accomplishment and satisfied employees.

Organizational designs that do not exhibit the three-way fit presented in Figure 3–1 typically generate problems. If either the design or the employees do not fit the tasks, the subunit tasks will usually not be accomplished effectively. If either the design or the tasks do not fit the employees, the subunit's employees will become dissatisfied and may exhibit corresponding negative organizational outcomes—turnover, absenteeism, lateness, and so on.

When conceptualized as in Figure 3–1, the task of organizing a specialized subunit may appear simple. In reality, it seldom is easy. Achieving an appropriate three-way fit in a specific situation is difficult because of the multiple task, human, and organizational design variables. (Figure 3–2 presents a list of such variables.) It is possible to have a situation where task, human, and organizational design variables all *fit* on dozens of dimensions, and yet organizational problems result because of a misfit on one or two additional dimensions. Since the people and the tasks in a subunit can change, even in the short run, misfits on a dimension or two and resultant organizational problems can develop easily.

Because there are so many potentially relevant variables and relationships implied in Figure 3–1, it is impossible to provide an exhaustive listing. Organization designers must try to assess this "fit" at all possible levels to minimize mismatches. It *is* possible, however, to examine some important relationships and some common mismatches that cause organizational problems.

Figure 3–2
Some Examples of Relevant Task, People, and Design Variables

Task
   Amount of diversity within the task
   Task complexity
   Routineness of task
   Time span of task completion
   Amount of personal contact involved
   Magnitude of task
   Relevant dimensions on which task
     accomplishment can be measured

People
   Age
   Education
   Expectations (re: work)
   Native ability
   Nature of special skill
   Needs/drives/motives
   Values
   Adaptability

Organizational Design
   Number of rules and procedures
   Diversity of the activities in each job
   Span of control of first-line
     supervision
   Amount of detail on job descriptions
   Dimensions measured in
     performance-evaluation system
   Frequency of appraisal reviews
   Criteria whereby people receive
     rewards
   Percent of compensation that is fixed
     or variable (due to incentive,
     bonus, and so on)
   Selection criteria
   Amount of money allocated to formal
     training programs

The Organization Design-People Relationship

A fit between a specialized subunit's organizational design and its employees implies that the subunit's structure, measurement, reward, and selection and development systems are congruent with its employees' needs, abilities, personalities, and expectations.

Structure

Perhaps the most obvious and important aspect of this relationship is the link between job design and employee skills and abilities. All jobs require some type of cognitive and interpersonal skills on the part of their incumbents. A mismatch between job requirements and employee abilities creates problems.

    Various techniques have been developed in the past 30–40 years to assist in matching job requirements with employee skills and abilities, such as systems for job-content measurements, psychological tests, and assessment centers.[2] While these techniques can help eliminate job design-people mismatches and are widely used, they have drawbacks. The more complex techniques, such as assessment centers, can be expensive to develop and to use. The simpler methods, such as tests, can be ineffective in dealing with complex jobs or with jobs where requirements change over time. As a result, managers still rely heavily on their own judgment in trying to match job design and employees. Successful managers are effective in making these judgments.

[2]Edgar Schein, *Organizational Psychology* (Englewood Cliffs, N.J.: Prentice-Hall, 1965), pp. 19–26.

Job-people mismatches typically result from insufficient analysis of a job's requirements or from inappropriate measurement of people's abilities and skills. The underlying problem in both cases is usually that managers make assumptions (that are usually a function of *past* events) about what a job demands or what certain people can provide without testing those assumptions in a serious analysis of the current situation.

Many factory jobs, for example, have been designed in extremely narrow, routine, and predictable ways. Such jobs may have fit the needs and abilities of a poor, uneducated, largely immigrant work force, but they are increasingly inconsistent with the characteristics of today's worker who is better educated, more affluent, and holds considerably higher expectations for job variety and challenge. The most widely used solutions to this type of organizational problem are called *job enlargement* and *job enrichment,* which both involve changing job designs to correct the misfit. With job enlargement, elements of several routine jobs are combined to increase work variety. With job enrichment, job designs are altered to allow for more challenge, responsibility, and autonomy.[3] Though both of these techniques have been used successfully in many situations, they have also failed numerous times.[4]

The common theme in these failures is that job designs were altered without a clear objective of matching the current tasks involved or the current employee groups. In some cases, the "enlarged" or "enriched" jobs did not fit the existing set of technologically determined tasks, and costs rose considerably. In other situations, they provided employees with more variety, ambiguity, and challenge than they wanted or could handle, and they led to poor performance and angry employees.[5]

Job design-people mismatches also are often created by changes in the subunit's task environment. These changes lead management to redesign jobs that do not fit the skills of current employees. Management subsequently is faced with either training employees to fit the new job demands or replacing them.

In growing organizations, for example, the nature of managerial jobs at the subunit level tends to change continuously. The job of an advertising manager in a company with sales of $5 million a year and an advertising department with only 2 people, for instance, differs from the job of advertising manager in a $100 million company that has an advertising department with 20 people. Constantly replacing managers because their jobs outgrow them is an expensive and demoralizing solution to this problem. But getting managers to grow or change with their jobs is also difficult, especially if the changes occur regularly.[6]

---

[3]John J. Morse, "A Contingency Look at Job Design," *California Management Review,* Fall 1973, p. 68.

[4]Ibid., p. 69.

[5]For a good discussion of the problems job enrichment programs have encountered, see J. Richard Hackman, "Is Job Enrichment Just a Fad?" *Harvard Business Review,* September–October 1975.

[6]See, for example, Peter Drucker, *The Practice of Management* (New York: Harper & Row, 1975), pp. 246–62.

Changes in an organization's size, usually due to growth, can produce various other structure-people mismatches. For example, research shows that as organizations add more people, subunit structure usually changes by adding more levels in the hierarchy, which increases the amount of specialization in jobs, increases the number of formal rules and procedures, and decentralizes decision-making authority.[7]

Many other aspects of subunit structure are occasionally mismatched with current employees. The structure, for example, might include many committees and meetings, while the employees are highly independent and not group-oriented. The management hierarchy might have a wide span of control (many people reporting to one supervisor), while many employees are new, unskilled, and need fairly close supervision. A large and old corporation might have many rules and procedures, while its newer, college-educated managers and professionals might be used to an informal, permissive environment. In all of these cases, the subunits involved will experience a continuing series of problems unless the mismatch is identified and corrected.

Measurement Systems

Another significant aspect of the organization design-people relationship that often creates problems is the type and frequency of feedback that performance appraisal and other measurement systems provide. It is possible for measurement systems to provide too little, too much, or the wrong information to fit the needs and expectations of employees.

All too often there is a mismatch between a newly-hired, college-educated employee and the almost nonexistent performance-appraisal system in some organizations. A person with a bachelor's degree has typically received concrete, often quantitative performance feedback within short and predictable intervals for most of his or her life. When such a person begins work in an organization that provides nothing equivalent to what he or she is used to receiving, one finds problems.

In contrast, where elaborate appraisal systems exist, they sometimes ignore the social and psychology research that identifies types of feedback that cause people to become defensive and angry, which creates a different kind of mismatch. Ideal feedback, research suggests, is descriptive rather than evaluative, directed at something the person can control, timely, specific rather than general (with clear and recent examples), and not given in large amounts at any one time.[8] Some performance-appraisal systems, on the other hand, are designed to provide large amounts of evaluative feedback about a person's traits (e.g., one's aggressiveness, good humor, leadership potential, and so forth) in general terms on an annual basis.

Performance-appraisal systems often are inconsistent with the objectives or skills

---

[7]See Chapters 2 and 3 in John Child, *Organization* (New York: Harper & Row, 1977). For a good discussion of the decentralization question, see Howard Carlisle, "A Contingency Approach to Decentralization," *Advanced Management Journal*, July 1974.

[8]See John Anderson, "Giving and Receiving Feedback," in *Organizational Change and Development*, ed. Gene Dalton, Paul Lawrence, and Larry Greiner (Homewood, Ill: Richard D. Irwin, 1970).

of the people who must implement them—the subunit's managers. For example, the systems sometimes require providing feedback at appraisal interviews—a skill that many managers do not possess. They sometimes generate strains in a manager's relationships with either subordinates (if the ratings seem low) or with peers (if the ratings seem high).[9] They also sometimes put supervisors in the uncomfortable dual and conflicting roles of evaluator and coach/helper.[10] As a result of one or more mismatches, many managers resist using performance-appraisal systems altogether.[11]

Virtually any aspect of a measurement system can in certain situations be out of phase with employees. A management control system, for example, might provide data on a subunit's results only once every three months, completely frustrating a group of employees whose high-achievement motivation leads them to seek more frequent feedback.[12] Or, a performance-appraisal system could force supervisors and employees to interact in appraisal interviews in ways that are completely inconsistent with their normal interaction preferences, such as scientists in a research laboratory who view each other as colleagues.

Reward Systems

Possibly the most important aspect of the organization design-people relationship deals with the fit between reward systems and people's needs and perceptions of what they deserve from the organization. Reward systems can create severe problems for a company if they do not provide both the type and the amount of rewards that employees perceive as appropriate and fair.

The *types* of rewards that an individual or group of people will find attractive are affected by many factors including: cultural backgrounds, education, age, career aspirations, off-the-job lifestyles, and work experiences.[13] Effective reward systems acknowledge these factors and attempt to offer different types of individuals and groups different reward possibilities. Pay may be stressed in some cases, while others emphasize promotion opportunities, job security, challenging assignments, or fringe benefits.[14]

A second related group of factors affects the *amount* of rewards that an employee group will perceive as fair. These variables include general economic conditions,

---

[9]Alan Patz, "Performance Appraisal: Useful but Still Resisted," *Harvard Business Review,* May–June 1975.

[10]See Herbert Meyer, Emanuel Kay, and John French, Jr., "Split Roles in Performance Appraisal," *Harvard Business Review,* January–February 1965, pp. 123–29.

[11]For a good discussion of the underlying problem and some solutions, see L. L. Cummings and Donald P. Schwab, "Designing Appraisal Systems for Different Purposes and Performance Histories," *California Management Review,* in press.

[12]See David McClelland, "That Urge to Achieve," *Think Magazine,* 1966.

[13]See Robert Suttermeister, ed., *People and Productivity* (New York: McGraw-Hill, 1976), chap. 5.

[14]Edward E. Lawler III, "Reward Systems," in *Improving Life at Work,* ed. J. Richard Hackman and J. Lloyd Suttle (Santa Monica, Calif.: Goodyear Publishing, 1977), p. 167.

the nature of different jobs, employee perceptions of their performance, seniority, and the rewards that employees in other companies receive.[15] To help match pay levels and employees' feelings of equity, many large organizations have developed elaborate personnel systems that:

1. Periodically measure the skills required for all jobs, often assigning each one a numerical score to represent its "content."

2. Assign a pay range to all jobs. The higher the content score, the higher the pay range.

3. Periodically compare the company's compensation with other companies in the same locale and/or industry.

4. Devise detailed formulas to determine a person's compensation within his or her job's pay range (usually a function of performance and/or seniority).[16]

Selection and Development Systems

The selection and development systems in a company's subunits can be inappropriate for employees if they do not provide the training people expect or need for their jobs or if they hire people who cannot get along with other employees.

In one study, for example, recently graduated MBAs reported that the largest discrepancy between their expectations of what they would receive in their first jobs and what their companies expected to offer them related to personal and professional development opportunities. The MBAs expected more than they received.[17] When this was an important expectation from the MBA's standpoint, the person often quit and moved to another employer.

Another problem many organizations face is related to environmental change and its impact on subunit tasks. For example, one company's customers began to change, which also caused the selling task to change. Management responded by hiring a different type of salesperson. When older employees realized what was happening, many actively opposed the new selection criteria. Because these criteria represented a clear signal that their skills and abilities were no longer valued as much, some employees fought long and hard against the new standards. The disruptive fighting continued for nearly two years.

The Organization Design-Task Relationship

A fit between a specialized subunit's organization design and its tasks implies a fit between the various organization design tools and the attributes of the subunit's activities.

---

[15]Ibid.

[16]For a further discussion of these types of systems, see Milton Rock, ed., *Handbook of Wage and Salary Administration* (New York: McGraw-Hill, 1972).

[17]John P. Kotter, "The Psychological Contract: Managing the Joining-Up Process," *California Management Review,* Spring 1973, p. 91.

Structure

A subunit structure that fits its assigned tasks directs employees to work on those tasks in effective and efficient ways. An important aspect of the fit between a subunit's structure and its tasks is the relationship between task certainty/uncertainty and structural formality/informality. Extensive research suggests that subunits that deal with certain, predictable tasks are most effective when they are formally structured with clear job descriptions, rules, and procedures, while subunits that deal with uncertain, unpredictable tasks are best structured informally.[18] The logic behind this relationship is simple. If a subunit's tasks are routine and predictable, careful study can determine the most efficient ways to perform them. These conclusions are then programmed into job descriptions and rules. If, on the other hand, a subunit's tasks are highly uncertain, nonroutine, and unpredictable, such an analysis would be difficult and would not identify a best way to perform the tasks. In this situation, detailed job descriptions and rules would be impossible and inappropriate. More informality and flexibility are required.

The relationship between the degree of predictability of tasks and formality of structure is seen by comparing a factory with a research laboratory. Most manufacturing plants are technologically designed to contain routine and predictable tasks; such plants typically are structured formally. Research laboratories, on the other hand, engage in uncertain and nonroutine tasks and are usually structured loosely and informally. These differences in structure are not random or accidental; rather, they are created by managers who explicitly or intuitively recognize this structure-task relationship.

A second important aspect of the subunit structure-task relationship is job design. In general, job designs that fit task requirements tend to facilitate task completion effectively at a minimum cost. For example, the vice president of sales in a clothing manufacturing firm had two options for the design of his sales force. In Option 1, each salesperson would carry one of the firm's three clothing lines (men's, women's, and juniors') and sell to about 60 customers in a geographical area. In Option 2, each salesperson would carry all three lines and sell to about 20 customers in a smaller area. In making his choice, the manager focused on three critical questions: (1) Is product knowledge or customer relations the most important factor in successful selling in our business? (2) How difficult and costly is it for a salesperson to learn a product line versus building a relationship with a customer? (3) How much more will the product-line specialization option cost in travel expenses and in coordinating the three salespeople that work together in a sales area? After analyzing the situation the vice president of sales decided that the customer relationship was more important than product knowledge. While training a salesperson in all three lines was expensive, it was not as expensive as the travel and coordination costs associated with Option 1. Therefore, he chose the second option and designed sales jobs to carry all three lines for about 20 customers.

---

[18]Paul Lawrence and Jay Lorsch, *Organization and Environment* (Boston: Harvard Business School, 1967).

Another aspect of the structure-task relationship that can cause problems for managers relates to span of control. Research shows that the number of people who can effectively report to a single manager varies—from one or two employees to three dozen—depending on different task characteristics. For example, the more complex the tasks, the more time it takes a manager to hire, train, and evaluate a single subordinate; thus, a smaller span of control is needed. Likewise, the more interdependent the tasks performed by different employees, the more time it takes to manage that interdependence; thus, a smaller span of control is required.[19]

Measurement Systems

To fit a set of subunit tasks, measurement systems must focus on the most important task-related variables and provide feedback on these variables to people who can control them. When measurement systems focus on the wrong variables, feed information to the wrong people, or provide untimely information, they can cause serious problems.[20]

A rather extreme example of a measurement system that did not fit task requirements was once created by the new director of a corporation's research laboratory. Under this system, all professional personnel received a monthly report that indicated the total number of patents the laboratory had filed that month and that year to date, as well as the number of patents attributable to each individual receiving the report. This system, intended to help motivate the scientists to work on the laboratory's tasks, created serious problems. First, the research projects that the division worked on that led to profitable ventures for the corporation tended to take 5 to 10 years to complete, while the measurement system focused on monthly accomplishments. Second, the successful research projects were accomplished by teams, yet the measurement system focused on individual accomplishment. Finally, while successful research projects usually led to patents, the patent was only a by-product. The result of the company's focus on patents as an end product was an increase in patents filed and a decrease in successful research projects.

The most common problem that organizational subunits encounter in the measurement system-task linkage is a result of utilizing "off the shelf" performance-appraisal systems. These systems (designed to be used by anybody, anywhere) sometimes measure people's personal characteristics, behavior, and the results of their efforts. But, they provide these measurements without considering the subunit's specific tasks. These systems are designed without serious attention to questions such as:

- What type of behavior and results are needed to effectively and efficiently achieve the subunit's tasks?

---

[19]For further discussion of this issue, see H. Stieglitz, "Optimizing Span of Control," *Management Record* 24 (1962).

[20]Edward E. Lawler III and John Grant Rhode, *Information and Control in Organizations* (Goodyear Publishing, 1976), chap. 8.

- How can they be measured?
- In analyzing the tasks, how often should they be measured?

Performance appraisal systems often ignore these questions, which contributes to their ineffectiveness.[21]

Reward Systems

For a reward system to fit a set of subunit tasks, it must motivate necessary behavior, and it must do so at a reasonable cost in light of the importance of those tasks.[22] The most common reward system-task misfits occur when unimportant behavior is rewarded while more important task-related behavior is not rewarded or when uncontrolled task outcomes are rewarded while outcomes under a person's control are not rewarded.

For example, the president of one organization decided to change the compensation system for marketing managers to one in which (a) the variable component in the average salary was higher and the fixed component was lower than before and (b) the variable was calculated based 25 percent on individual performance and 75 percent on corporate earnings. Three years later, he abandoned this scheme after his managers bitterly protested its unfairness. They argued that they had little control over corporate profits and that it made no sense to reward (or punish) them so heavily based on corporate profits.

In another situation, the compensation plan for the managers of a manufacturing plant was revised to provide up to a 50 percent bonus if they kept costs within a fixed annual budget. This change was made when the company's sales were flat but costs were rising. The plan worked well until the company's business changed three years later. As a result of introducing new products, its sales started to increase dramatically beyond forecasts. But, the sales increase soon died because the company could not make timely delivery on its orders. Regardless of how much the sales department pleaded with the plant to increase its output quickly, the plant managers refused until the company's president granted them a change in their expense budget.

Reward system-task mismatches sometimes occur, as in the previous example, because the subunit's tasks change. They occur even more often because some managers have a pet compensation, bonus, or commission system that they think fits all situations. Sometimes, a manager has learned about such a system from friends, books, or a consultant, but most often it is one that the manager has observed working effectively somewhere else and does not recognize that the tasks in that environment are different from his or her own subunit.

---

[21]A 1974 Bureau of National Affairs survey revealed that while 93 percent of the firms polled had performance-appraisal programs, only 10 percent of these firms' personnel executives felt that their appraisal programs were effective.

[22]Lyman Porter and Edward Lawler III, "What Job Attitude Tells about Motivation," *Harvard Business Review*, January–February 1968, pp. 118–26.

Selection and Development Systems

Selection and development systems that fit task demands help staff a subunit with the quantity and quality of people needed to perform the tasks effectively. The creation of good selection and development systems is central to facilitating a dynamic fit between a subunit's tasks and its employees.

As with many organizational problems in specialized subunits, mismatches between selection and development systems and subunit tasks are often caused by changes in the subunit's tasks. Alterations in an organization's technologies, external environment, or mission are inevitable over long periods, and these changes often cause the subunit's tasks to change. A selection and development system that is consistent with a given set of tasks can become completely inappropriate if there is a significant change in those tasks.[23]

For example, over a period of 15 years, one small company manufacturing predominantly industrial products developed a large number of consumer products. As part of a general audit of the company's human resources, a consulting firm found that its sales force had abnormally high turnover and low morale. Further investigation found that the selection process for a salesperson had changed little over the preceding 15 years, despite the shift in the company's business and despite other organizational changes such as the addition of product managers. The company still hired salespeople whose skills and expectations were better suited to the old industrial products, which accounted for only 25 percent of their total sales.

In another case, a technological change in a plant modified the nature of many tasks, including routine supervision. Job descriptions were changed, and employees received special training to help adjust to the new jobs. But no one changed the routine training and development activities that the plant had used for years. Three years later, plant management determined that many new employees and newly promoted employees were performing poorly. An investigation finally identified the mismatch between old training activities and new tasks.

Managing the Relationships among Organization Design, People, and Tasks

One of the major responsibilities of any subunit manager is to manage the relationships among organization design, employee, and task variables. While in some situations this responsibility is relatively simple, often it is not. A subunit's tasks are sometimes so complex that they are difficult to comprehend completely. But without a clear understanding, it is extremely difficult for a manager to keep task variables aligned with the subunit's organizational design and employees. When a subunit has many employees with diverse backgrounds, it can be equally difficult to comprehend the people accurately. And if either the tasks or the employees change frequently, the potential problems are even greater.

---

[23]Leonard Schlesinger and Richard Walton, "Supervisory Roles in Participative Work Systems," *Academy of Management Proceedings,* August 1978.

Over the last few decades, more managers have become convinced that they need to better manage the relationships among organization design, people, and task variables. Managing these relationships is one of the only ways that a manager can influence organizational culture. They systematically ask people throughout the organization to:

—Design jobs and plan goals and measurement systems to fit task requirements.

—Select employees with requisite skills, create employee expectations, and develop employee abilities consistent with job designs, plans, goals, and potential rewards.

No panaceas exist for managing the relationships among a subunit's organization design, tasks, and people. Managers must constantly watch the changing nature of each design element. They must continually monitor the compatibility of design factors. Ultimately, only careful attention and monitoring by managers equipped with skills in organizational analysis will do the job.

Organizational Analysis

Within the context of the specialized subunit (see Figure 3–3), the ability to analyze an organization or design factors is critical. It consists of the following steps:

1. Clearly identify and understand the subunit's tasks. To do so, one must consider:
   - The organization's and subunit's environment in terms of context, general characteristics, and key success factors.
   - The organization's overall strategy and its relationship to the subunit.
   - The subunit's technology (especially if it is a manufacturing subunit).
2. Clearly identify and understand the most relevant characteristics of a subunit's current employees, such as their:
   - Number.
   - Background.
   - Skills and abilities.
   - Values and norms.
   - Expectations—especially regarding their work and the organization.
3. Clearly identify the elements of current organizational design:
   - Structure.
   - Measurement systems.
   - Reward systems.
   - Selection and development systems.
4. Identify current performance of the subunit and any problems or symptoms of problems.

Figure 3–3
Organizational Analysis at the Subunit Level

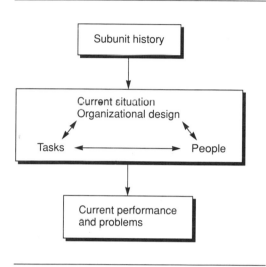

5. Trace subunit history, with special attention to important changes that have occurred in its tasks, people, or organization design. Has the subunit grown recently? Have its tasks changed due to a change in technology, business strategy, size, or the organization's environment? How has the organization design changed during this period?

6. Identify relationships between the subunit's history, its current tasks-people-organization design, and its current performance. A good analysis is characterized by intelligent inferences about these relationships.

Competent organizational analysis provides a basis for designing viable action alternatives to correct organization design-people-task misfits, and it helps decide if there is a problem and how important it is. Unlike some managerial problems, significant organizational problems are sometimes invisible to most people, while conspicuous problems may be unimportant. Under such circumstances, doing the obvious is an ineffective way to manage, and skillful organizational analysis becomes particularly important.

Case 3–1

Chicago Bond Sales Department

Anne Donnellon

It was June 1987, and through the glass walls of his office, Ed Powers, regional sales manager of the Chicago Bond Sales Department of The Welch and Rudolf Company, watched the typical early morning frenzy in his securities sales office. Like the other experienced members of his sales group, he could block out the din of the 30 ringing phones, the announcements coming over the squawk boxes from New York, and the many conversations throughout the large room. His years on the desk had taught him how to track the number of activities going on around him while consciously focusing on a particular task. Today, he thought about the presentation he was to make at the next day's meeting of the Bond Division managers, who were to consider how changes in certain of the division's systems and structures were affecting divisional sales and profitability. Attending the meeting would be the division's managing directors, the general managers for sales and for trading, the research director, and the other regional sales managers.

Powers had been asked to report on the impact of two recent changes on his Taxable Bonds sales group. One change, implemented companywide, was in the performance evaluation system. The other was in the structure of the Taxables group in Chicago.

Periodic meetings like the one scheduled for the next day had become more common recently at Welch and Rudolf, as the senior managers endeavored to adapt the organization to the complexities and strains of a growing and continuously

This case was prepared by Professor Anne Donnellon.

Copyright © 1988 by the President and Fellows of Harvard College. Harvard Business School case 488-020.

changing industry. The new evaluation process, one example of the company's commitment to maintaining effective coordination among its various divisions, was the subject of considerable debate across the firm. It involved a shift to more subjective criteria and evaluation by groups of people. The senior managers of the Bond Division were particularly interested in how the new approach to evaluation was affecting the sales of taxable securities, a very profitable product line for Welch and Rudolf.

Powers had implemented the structural change in the Chicago department four months earlier. To create a group of specialists within the Taxable Bonds group who would jointly serve the region's six largest accounts, he had changed the account assignments of some of his sales associates. Powers felt the shift was necessary because the fixed income securities business had become extremely specialized, with many large clients in the region now consisting of product specialist groups. Most of Welch and Rudolf's divisional managers expected the trend toward client-driven on product specialization to continue and they were eager to hear Powers's assessment of how the new group was functioning.

Powers had recently polled the six special accounts served by the new group. Clients from three of them indicated they were pleased with the service; the rest, however, were not yet convinced that the change was for the better. Problems had resulted from introducing new people into the long-standing relationships between taxable bonds clients and their former salespeople. Some of the new group members were not entirely satisfied with the change, either. And Powers' initial concerns that creating the specialist subgroup within the taxable bonds group might create some ill will within the department had been confirmed.

The evaluation process also was creating anxiety and resentment, which concerned Powers; he felt strongly that it was critical for the department to work well together and had labored long to develop a spirit of cooperation. Everyone seemed a bit more on edge lately, but it had been a very busy quarter. As he started to prepare for the meeting, Powers considered who would be attending. He would have to express clearly the relative advantages and disadvantages of these changes for everyone involved.

The Bond Division

Bond was one of four divisions of The Welch and Rudolf Company, a prosperous U.S. investment bank (see Exhibit 1). Founded in the early 1900s, the firm was recognized as a leading player in nearly every segment of investment banking, including corporate finance, mergers and acquisitions, block trading, and capital markets. The Bond Division had responsibility for trading and selling fixed income securities, such as corporate bonds, preferred stock, government securities, commercial paper, and money market instruments. Equity securities, such as common stock, were traded and sold by Welch and Rudolf's Equity division.

The Bond Division had been a major contributor to Welch and Rudolf's revenues and profits since 1982. Lower interest rates and changes in the federal tax law during that era had created a bullish bond market. Competition had intensified and new financial products had proliferated in the wake of the 1980s deregulation of

Exhibit 1
Chicago Bond Sales Department

Divisions of Welch & Rudolf

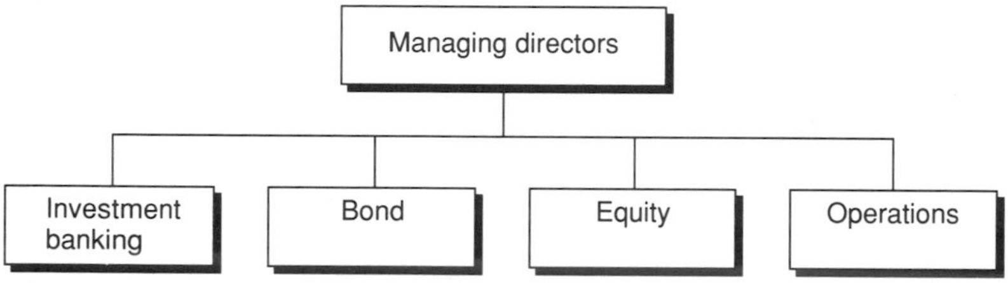

```
              ┌─────────────────────┐
              │ Managing directors  │
              └─────────────────────┘
        ┌──────────┬──────────┴──────────┬──────────┐
  ┌───────────┐ ┌────────┐        ┌────────┐  ┌────────────┐
  │Investment │ │  Bond  │        │ Equity │  │ Operations │
  │ banking   │ │        │        │        │  │            │
  └───────────┘ └────────┘        └────────┘  └────────────┘
```

the financial industry. Much of the firm's new product development was originating from the bond area, in response to a sophisticated and demanding clientele of investment fund managers.

The Bond Division at Welch and Rudolf consisted of 10 regional sales offices and headquarters in New York, where the division's trading desks, managing directors, and research operations were located. The firm's bond client base was primarily institutional, consisting of large investment funds, insurance companies, banking institutions, and corporations.

The Chicago Bond Sales Department

Several of Welch and Rudolf's largest and most important bond clients were based in Chicago. The region included many accounts that did high-volume trading in short-term securities, such as commercial paper. Large mutual fund groups based in Chicago also increasingly dominated the department's business. These clients were considered so sophisticated that product managers and new product designers from the firm's Capital Markets and Investment Banking groups in New York frequently consulted with the Chicago sales department or their clients about new products that they were developing.

The Chicago department regularly grossed second or third highest in the Bond Division, its business growing from \$6 million[1] in 1981 to a projected \$50 million for 1987. Its size had also increased considerably during that period. When Ed Powers was appointed Chicago's first regional sales manager, in 1981, his sales force consisted of eight people—seven professionals and one support person. By 1987, there were 29 people in the department: 16 professionals, including Powers, and 13 support people (Exhibit 2 summarizes the personnel data).

The department was divided into three sales groups (plus a group of support

---

[1]These figures quoted are in total volume credits, which were percentages of sales volume, weighted by profitability. Securities with lower profit margins had lower percentages applied to the sales volume.

staff members who reported directly to Powers) which were differentiated primarily by the type of product they sold:

1. Money Markets.
2. Municipal Bonds.
3. Taxable Bonds.

The Money Markets sales group of four professionals and four support staff (see Exhibit 2) sold short-term, low-risk, high-liquidity securities. Its products, known as "money market instruments," included commercial paper, repurchase finance, and banker's acceptances.

The Municipal Bonds sales group was the smallest of the three, consisting of three professionals and two assistants. It sold tax-exempt securities, such as bonds issued to raise revenue for state and local governments, hospitals, public power projects, and pollution control. The group was also actively involved in developing markets for new products, such as tax-exempt futures.

The largest of the three sales groups, *Taxable Bonds,* included eight professionals, three of whom had joined the group within the last six months, and three sales support personnel. Its products included high-yield bonds, mortgage-backed securities, futures and options, corporate bonds, and government securities.

All three groups served the same institutional accounts: insurance companies, banks, mutual funds, and pension funds. The bond business had become so specialized, however, that clients themselves had certain assigned people to deal exclusively with specific types of securities. As a result, the nature and activities of each salesperson's job depended to some degree on the type of securities that person sold.

There were, nevertheless, certain aspects of the sales job that were common to all three groups. The salesperson was responsible for distributing the bonds issued by Welch and Rudolf's clients[2] and the securities held by the firm itself; that is, securities acquired by Welch and Rudolf's traders in New York. It was not unusual for the company to have holdings of $15 billion in bonds at any given time; therefore, selling the firm's securities was a major part of the sales job.

To ensure profitability, sales efforts had to be coordinated with the traders and with product mangers. Multiple reporting lines to sales managers, traders, and product managers was one mechanism designed to achieve the necessary cooperation. (Exhibit 3 displays the reporting lines that linked the division's sales personnel, traders, and product managers.) The principal activities of the salesperson were:

1. Learning from traders what securities were available for distribution.
2. Learning from product managers about new products and how to market them.

---

[2]"Clients" refers both to the companies whose securities are issued by Welch and Rudolf's corporate finance division and to the firms that purchased these securities from the fixed-income division: insurance companies, banks, mutual funds, and pension funds.

Exhibit 2
Chicago Bond Sales Department

Personnel in the Chicago Bond Sales Department

Group/Name	Job Title	Education	Degree	Years at Welch and Rudolf	Age
Edward T. Powers	Regional Sales Manager	Harvard Business School	MBA	11	55
Laura Shipley	Secretary	Ohio State		2	48
Joyce Ivancevich	Office Manager	University of Chicago	BA	.5	35
Mimi Kran	Teletype Operator	University of Southern Illinois	AA	3	22
Meghan Meyer	Analyst	Princeton	BA	.5	23
Taxable Bonds Sales Group					
Thomas P. Connelly	High-Yield Specialist/SAG*	University of Chicago	MBA	10	34
William A. Callahan	Mortgage-backed Specialist/SAG	Columbia	MBA	4	28
Richard T. Jamison	Corporate Bonds Specialist/SAG	Brown	BA	1	40
Paul A. Weitzman	Futures and Options Specialist/SAG	Wharton	MBA	.5	28
Michael E. Pulskamp	Mortgage-backed Securities	Dartmouth	MBA	1	25
Joseph J. Mahon	Government Securities	Stanford	MBA	8	34
Alison M. Pfister	Generalist	Harvard Business School	MBA	5	33
Margaret Ciula	Generalist	Northwestern	MBA	1	26
Irene Markham	Sales Support	Syracuse	BA	.5	50

Exhibit 2 (continued)

Personnel in the Chicago Bond Sales Department

Group/Name	Job Title	Education	Degree	Years at Welch and Rudolf	Age
Janice O'Brien	Sales Support	University of Illinois	AA	5	25
Linda Faulston	Sales Support	Middlebury	BA	.5	26
Municipal Bonds Sales Group					
David L. Nesmith	Generalist	Williams	BA	1	28
Stephen P. Vinetti	Generalist	Yale	BA	12	37
Kathryn Ryan	Generalist	Bradley	BA	7	31
Sheila Mays	Registered Sales Assistant	Michigan State	BA	5	30
Amy Garner	Sales Support	Kent State	BA	2	25
Money Market Sales Group					
Donald M. Saporstein	Generalist	University of Illinois	BA	19	51
Philip Brooks	Generalist	Stanford	MBA	2	30
Joan L. Butler	Generalist	MIT	SM†	2	28
Arthur Swanson	Generalist	University of Illinois	BA	23	49
Lynn Piscor	Registered Sales Assistant	Katherine Gibbs	Trade	8	55
Jane Sullivan	Registered Sales Assistant	Joliet Junior College	AA	6	32
Maureen Hoffman	Sales Support	University of Southern Indiana	AA	4	29
Catherine Jones	Sales Support	University of Illinois	BA	.5	25

*Special Accounts Group.
†MBA equivalent.

Exhibit 3
Chicago Bond Sales Department (*Reporting Lines in Welch & Ruldolf Bond Division*)

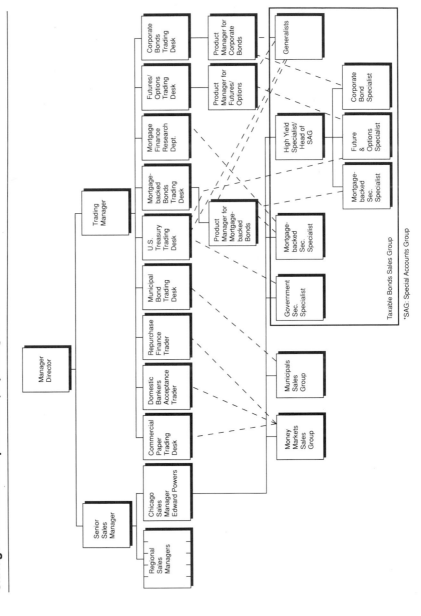

3. Calling clients to inquire about their investment needs.
4. Advising clients of investment possibilities.
5. Executing sales and swaps of securities.
6. Negotiating sales between the trader and the client.
7. Developing the client relationship through conversations, presentations, and entertaining.

Recruitment and Training

Welch and Rudolf placed high priority on finding the right people for its sales positions. The firm had developed a reputation for excellent service through its emphasis on entrepreneurial aggressiveness and teamwork and, despite the competitive labor market, was very selective. Promotional literature described the job requirements for a bond salesperson as:

> . . . *intelligence, independence, a strong desire to succeed, creativity, and an ability to quickly translate ideas into action.*

For the Chicago group, Powers added other characteristics:

> *We look for ability to deal with a breadth of types and styles. If you can't do that, you need to have outstanding technical ability.*

Formal training at Welch and Rudolf was conducted centrally. New hires spent their first six months in New York attending seminars and observing the activities on the trading desks. The more critical subtleties of selling securities, however, were learned on the job, after the formal training was completed. They were given a few small accounts to handle and were assigned a desk next to an experienced person, whom they could listen to and question. One of the newest Chicago recruits observed that bond sales was "an apprenticeship business; who you sit next to is about as important as anything."

Seating arrangements also affected how well people got to know one another. As one of the senior associates indicated:

> *You get to know best the people you sit next to, because you hear them talk all day, and because we're so busy that you really don't move around much. The person you talk to most is the person sitting next to you.*

The Daily Routine

The Chicago group worked together in the bullpen atmosphere typical of Wall Street offices. The office was a long room with three banks of connecting desks, each with a phone bank of 140 lines, three speaker phone lines ("squawk boxes") connected to the New York trading desks, two telephone receivers, and assorted computer monitors. (Exhibit 4 depicts the physical layout of the room.)

Exhibit 4
Chicago Bond Sales Department

The Physical Layout and Typical Interaction Patterns
of the Chicago Bond Sales Department

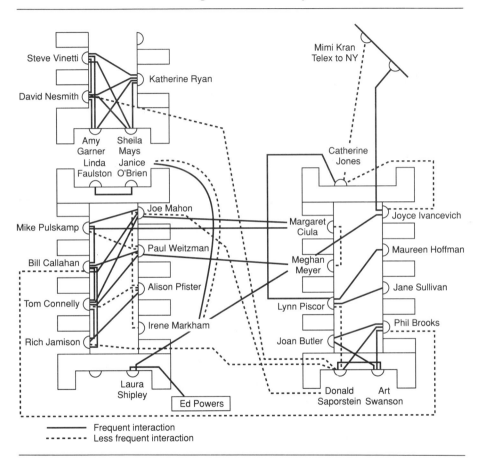

Frequent interaction
Less frequent interaction

Though business usually started with the 6:45 A.M. (7:45 Eastern Time) conference calls from the New York trading desks, all of the salespeople were at their desks between 6:15 and 6:30. Sipping coffee and perusing *The Wall Street Journal*, their conversations ranged from sports and movies to current events and trends in the financial markets. Interspersed were comments on the previous day's conversations with clients and traders and less frequently, details about their personal lives.

By 7:15 A.M., phones were ringing throughout the office and, to the uninitiated, the scene appeared utterly chaotic. At any given moment, upwards of 60 phone lines were ringing. With voices of traders speaking over each of the three channels on the squawk boxes, a cacophony resulted, decipherable only if a salesperson lowered the volume on two of his or her channels. Virtually every person in the room was on a phone; some held a receiver to each ear. Occasionally, someone would call out, "So-and-so is on line 5 for you," to be answered with either an upheld index finger (meaning "tell her to hold") or a circling finger (meaning "I'll get back to her"). Periodically, one of the sales assistants would circle the room, collecting sales tickets to be wired to New York. While the phone lines were busy, the salespeople stayed riveted to their chairs, taking and placing dozens of calls. Learning to manage the intense level of interaction was critical; as one veteran said, "It's just not acceptable to tell a client you couldn't make a bid because you had another call."

The casewriter observed that, regardless of seniority, everyone assumed responsibility for answering phones. Even when someone was already on a call, if a line was not being answered promptly, the first call would be put on hold to pick up the incoming call. Asked about this practice, one salesperson said, "We have an unwritten rule that a phone should never ring more than three times." Responses to clients always appeared to take priority over other activities. Conversations and jokes were interrupted, even at critical points, to take calls or to focus attention on something of interest coming in over the squawk boxes.

Eavesdropping on one another's conversations was not only widely practiced, but also considered a responsibility. As one person expressed it, "You need to listen to what other people are doing, so you can help them." Sharing information was one of the duties Powers demanded of his staff. It was commonplace for someone to point out new information appearing on the computer screen or to remind a colleague of a client's call not yet returned. (Typical patterns of interaction among group members are depicted in Exhibit 4.)

The intensity of the activity often remained high for several hours, especially in the morning. As the phones and activity began to abate someone often told a joke or gag that attracted everyone's attention. Frequently, it would be a mock insult issued over the intercom between the money market and the municipal sales groups. Several people said such behavior helped to relieve tension.

There were also times when little business came in. One of the sales associates described the work as being "like [that of] cops, 7 hours and 50 minutes of boredom, and 10 minutes of sheer terror." During the quiet times, the salespeople caught up on their work reading, restored order to their desks and files, called clients to chat, and joked with one another. They rarely left their desks, even during slow periods.

Unless they were entertaining customers, most of the sales professionals had lunch at their desks; each group had its own routine. In Money Market sales, everyone picked up his or her own lunch and they ate at different times. One of the support staff in Municipals usually picked up lunch for everyone in that group. In the Taxables, one of the sales associates—typically, a more junior one—took orders from all the other associates and picked up the lunches. Occasionally, the Taxable Bonds support staff was included in the ordering.

The members of the Chicago sales department obviously liked one another and enjoyed working together. Their camaraderie was evident—from the frequent exchange of kudos for deals well done and the acknowledgments of assistance to the joking and mutual teasing. One of the newer associates said he had come to Welch and Rudolf because he wanted "to work with people who are smart, energetic, and fun—and these people are."

The Chicago sales department did much of its client entertaining by group, often at lunch on slower days or in the evenings after the work day. Occasionally, sales associates and some of the support staff hosted client groups at special entertainments, which might include concerts or sports events. However, other than at these work-related functions, there was little social interaction outside the office. Many of the staff expressed regret about this lack to the casewriter. One person explained, "I think it's because we all work so many hours and give up so much time to entertaining and recruiting; people just want to spend what free time they have with their families."

Morale

For the most part, members of the Chicago sales department seemed quite satisfied with their work, although there were some trouble spots. Those who had been with the firm for several years were experiencing considerable pressure to adapt their behavior to the numerous changes occurring in rapid succession in the business. Newer associates faced adjustment problems as well. In Powers's view, his staff treated new people better than most groups do. But here, as across the industry, new people had to pay their dues. Often, they were assigned tedious tasks, such as tearing and distributing the overnight telex messages from New York and picking up lunches. Usually, they were assigned the smaller accounts, which frequently were more difficult to serve. In a business in which interpersonal relationships were often the paramount factor in determining the flow of information and business, new associates had to struggle to establish their own identities within the group and with clients.

Though each of the three sales groups operated somewhat independently, there were important flows of information between, as well as within, each of them. For example, salespeople in the money market sales group often received information from their accounts about impending shifts in a client's investment portfolio. Powers not only encouraged them to share that information with the other sales groups but also expected follow-up on such leads. Cooperation of this kind had produced considerable new business for the department. Product specialists in taxable bonds served also as a source of information for the other groups. For example, as municipal bond clients became more interested in the new tax-exempt futures, the municipals salespeople had to interact more frequently with Paul Weitzman, Taxables' futures and options specialist. His responsibilities included assisting them with transactions and negotiations for such securities. Most sales associates valued such cooperation. As one person put it:

. . . the group works well because we have a team attitude. We're about as organized as any group. There are no stars here. Well, there are, but nobody talks about it.

Several people expressed the opinion that the climate of cooperation and the sharing of information were direct results of leadership in the department:

A lot of why we work well together is that we are compensated to do that, but it also has to do with Ed. He's a good manager. He's reasonable, he understands people, he knows what motivates them.

The sales associates with experience at other investment banks contrasted Powers's leadership style favorably with the "management through fear" approach they had experienced elsewhere. One described his former office as a place where "people nearly broke out in fist fights . . . [and] you really got chewed out if you made a mistake." Powers's approach to managing the group seemed quite subtle. He was considered to be demanding but fair, with a low-key and friendly demeanor. His door was always open, and he was visible in his office, but he limited his presence on the floor to occasional strolls, usually to ask someone a question.

Powers said that he frequently mediated the inevitable conflicts that developed in this line of business.

We have fewer blowups than most groups. We have them. I'm the one who tries to solve, ameliorate them. It's harder now that I have an office. Being out there on the desk, I could always tell when something was wrong, just from the way people were talking. Now I ask people how things are going and listen hard for the answer . . . when there's a conflict, I get people in here, usually one at a time, and in calm tones, get them to talk about it. I try to make it unemotional. But sometimes that hasn't worked, I get people in here together and just let the fur fly . . . I guess most of the conflict is handled through me. It's easier for a third party to handle.

Powers downplayed his contribution to the group's success:

. . . the group's done well, not so much because of me. We started out small, worked very closely, and got to know each other well. Until 18 months ago, I had a desk on the floor . . . I've mentored [them], sat at a desk with them, raised them in the Welch and Rudolf culture, and I have a lot of loyalty from them.

The Taxable Bonds Sales Group

In June 1987, taxable bonds were the most profitable of the Bond Division's products. In Chicago, the Taxable Bonds sales group produced 66 percent of the volume credits produced by that office.

Because of the size of the Chicago taxable bonds market and the product's complexity, Taxables was more differentiated than the other two groups in the Chicago sales department. The group included generalists, who sold the full range of taxable securities, and product specialists, each of whom sold different types of securities, such as high-yield bonds, mortgage-backed securities, government securities, futures, and options. It also included the special accounts group.

Four months earlier, Powers had created a special accounts group (SAG) as a subgroup of product specialists within Taxables to serve the office's six largest accounts. Several factors had led to his decision, a major one being that one salesperson (Tom Connelly) had been handling five of the largest clients in the region for several years, and the recent growth made them too big for one person to handle. Another important factor was that, as financial products proliferated, the large accounts were becoming more specialized. Portfolio managers directed staff specialists who traded and acquired only certain types of securities. As Connelly began to develop a specialty in high-yield bonds, he was less able to meet his clients' needs for immediate, specialized information on other securities.

Powers decided to address these problems by creating SAG, which assumed its new responsibilities in February 1987. Connelly served as head of the group, as senior relationship manager, and as the specialist on high-yield securities. Rich Jamison and Bill Callahan were the corporate bond and the mortgage-backed securities specialists, respectively. Paul Weitzman, the specialist in futures and options, had a less formal role within the group; of the four, he was the only one who handled other accounts.

In the 12 years Connelly had worked in the Chicago sales department, he had developed very positive and strong relationships with his clients, who were among the best in the industry regarding profitability, commitment to Welch and Rudolf, and business standards. The company hoped that, with Connelly heading SAG, all of the large clients would receive the degree of specialized attention they needed as well as continued high-quality service. Another potential benefit of the new arrangement was that it put Connelly, the second-highest producer at Welch and Rudolf and, in Powers's words "the norm-setter in the office," in the position of coaching and developing the other SAG members while serving his clients.

Despite these possible advantages, both the creation of SAG and the shift toward specialization were controversial. Half of the special accounts felt that they were getting better service from the new group; more specialized product information was available to them faster than it had been previously. The other three clients did not yet agree that service was better. Powers believed that some people from these companies felt slighted at having to deal with a salesperson less experienced than Connelly. From this perspective, the advantage of more specialized product information might be outweighed by the disadvantage of being represented in trades by someone not as familiar with the client's special interests and preferences.

Several of the Welch and Rudolf traders also were dissatisfied with the performance of the SAG members who could not yet predict as readily or confidently as Connelly how clients would react to a proposed deal. When a trader or product manager wanted to propose an unusual deal or a novel Taxable Bond product to a particular client, the salesperson's skill in articulating both the client's interests and the proposal's relative value was vital. The quality of the relationship with the client was paramount to closing the deal. Whereas some traders recognized the benefits of having sales specialists deal with client specialists, Powers found that others "don't want to hear that we're working out the bugs in a new structure—they want information and they want it fast."

A number of people in the Chicago Bond Sales Department felt some ambivalence about SAG and the trend toward specialization. Some worried that creating a group of specialists who shared a set of accounts would reduce their interaction with the rest of the department, making them less accessible to the generalists. Others speculated that the creation of another small group would make teamwork more difficult.

Teamwork was considered very important. The salespeople who had been with the Chicago office for several years were particularly emphatic about this and Joe Mahon exemplified the commitment to it. Though not a SAG member, he was a specialist in government securities. And because government securities were the bellwether of change throughout the bond market, virtually everyone in the department depended on Mahon to keep him or her informed in that area. He interacted more often than most in the Taxable Bonds group with the sales professionals in the other groups and offered suggestions and advice to the newer associates, who seemed appreciative. On occasion, he even performed the unpopular task of distributing telex messages from New York.

The casewriter observed that interaction among the generalists and specialists of the Taxable Bonds group was most frequent between Alison Pfister and Rich Jamison. Jamison was SAG's corporate bond specialist, and Pfister was a generalist with 25 large accounts. Though she sold the full range of bond products to her clients, most of Pfister's volume was in corporate bonds. The 6:45 A.M. conference call from the New York corporate bond-trading desk provided a common focus for these two. During the day, they frequently discussed the relative values of various bonds available, generally at Pfister's initiation; she often sought Jamison's reaction to trades she planned to propose to clients and pointed out to him new developments in the taxable bonds market. Though such information could occasionally prove useful to Jamison in dealing with his current accounts, it had been more relevant before his assignment to SAG, when he was a generalist, like Pfister, and selling a wide variety of products.

Jamison also interacted often with others in the office, frequently participating in the intercom joking, reminding people of calls to be returned, and offering to help inform his colleagues' clients of newly announced pricings. Jamison had been with Welch and Rudolf for 15 months having previously worked for one of the firm's major competitors and also for one of the clients, a large mutual fund. Powers described him as "the most seasoned person in corporate debt issues in the office."

At 40, Jamison was the oldest professional in the taxables group and the only one who did not have an MBA. An experienced bond salesperson, he was unaccustomed to sharing responsibility for a client with others. And he worried that the new structure emphasized his specialization to a degree that could potentially become too restrictive if the market were to change, leaving him with little or no business. Even if business were to remain good, specialists like Jamison feared becoming bored with selling a single product line.

For the generalists, Pfister and Margaret Ciula, the problems involved being "jack of all trades, master of none," which could result in their customers feeling they were not getting current or specific enough information. The generalists worried also that the company's traders might focus their attention on the specialists selling their products and neglect other salespeople. The uncertainty created by a possible shift in the interdependence within the Chicago Bond Sales Department was being compounded further by the new evaluation system.

Performance Evaluation System

At Welch and Rudolf, the new performance evaluation included consideration of both quantitative and qualitative measures. The quantitative were the volume credits that the individual generated;[3] the qualitative factors included product knowledge, account penetration, sales skills, teamwork (especially cooperation with other sales-people, traders, and product managers), and professionalism. Consideration was given also to the quality of both the business the salesperson generated, and his or her responsiveness to the traders.

Before the change in the evaluation process, compensation had more closely resembled a commission system. Salespeople could expect to receive roughly 5 percent to 12 percent of commission payouts on their gross sales, depending on the regional manager's assessment of their efforts with clients and traders.

The new evaluation process provided more input on performance, particularly as it related to behavior affecting firm's profitability: assisting the traders in dis-tributing the firm's securities and utilizing the firm's research resources.

The New York traders now had the opportunity to evaluate the salespeople formally on distribution efforts and responsiveness to their priorities. Previously, traders' evaluations occurred informally; a common scenario was a complaint to the sales manager about a specific problem or an ongoing argument with a particular salesperson. Including the traders in performance evaluations reinforced the dual responsibility salespeople had to both sales management and trading. In their re-views, traders indicated how aggressively salespeople marketed their products, how effectively they negotiated, and how responsive they were to their needs.

Product managers, who translated research into specialized information about financial instruments and marketed them internally to sales personnel, were also involved in the new evaluation process. Because the regional sales manager solicited evaluations of salespeople's product knowledge, their sales personnel were moti-vated to learn about new and more profitable products, and thus utilize the research capacity the firm had developed at considerable expense.

Also, under the new evaluation system, regional sales managers were given greater discretion in assessing and rewarding the sales force. Considering factors such as teamwork, professionalism, and product knowledge enabled them to reward people for working in a manner that was conducive, in the long term, to better

---

[3]The schedule of volume credits was revised periodically by the division's managers to reflect changes in the market and in the firm's priorities.

business. Thus, a salesperson could earn a higher salary by cooperating with colleagues and focusing on relationship-building with a high-margin client than by focusing exclusively on producing maximum volume credits.

Formal evaluations were to be conducted every six months. The procedure started with the salesperson reviewing his or her own performance over the last period, describing current accounts and prospects and reporting the sales and entertainment activities undertaken for each client. Each salesperson then evaluated the role of others in the company in helping to build business—including traders, product managers, and research staff. Traders and product managers in New York who dealt with the salesperson also evaluated him or her.

After written evaluations of each salesperson were collected, the sales manager scheduled an evaluation meeting for each one. In these meetings, the product managers and traders elaborated on their views. The sales generalists, who dealt with numerous traders and product managers, might have as many as eight people offering feedback in this meeting.

The evaluation process was very time-consuming, and quite costly regarding hours spent by the numbers of people involved. Most of the firm's managers believed, however, that the process was contributing to the integration of the sales and trading efforts. Powers described the problem it addressed:

Sales here is the middleman between the trader and the client. Sales and traders are in a natural adversarial position, salespeople going for volume, traders for profit. (The salespeople) have to maintain credibility with both the client and the trader.

Soon after the evaluation meetings, the regional sales manager proposed to the appropriate managing directors specific compensation figures for each salesperson. Once agreement was reached, the sales manager submitted to the divisional and senior managers the recommended figures, which were then reviewed in the context of divisional and company profits for the period.

Concern about the subjectivity of the evaluation process and its impact on their earnings was expressed by several of the Chicago group members. One presented this view of the situation:

. . . we work well together because we're compensated to. But a problem now is the uncertainty in the system . . . most of us are aggressive, goal-driven, and, frankly, interested in money . . . not knowing how well we're doing is hard to take . . . I believe it's important to know that your performance is related to your rewards . . . to see the connection between your effort and what pay you get . . . some of this work is unpleasant and it's hard to get motivated to do it, to make another call if you're not sure whether it's worth it. This job has very little intrinsic reward . . . I mean, I like the people here a lot and it can be intellectually very challenging, but . . . I mean it's not the Peace Corps.

The evaluation system presented special problems for both the generalist and the specialist. Both were evaluated by every trader and product manager with whom he or she dealt. But the number of contacts the generalist had with these people was inevitably fewer than the number the specialist had, because, as a rule the specialist dealt repeatedly with one or two traders and product managers. Consequently, most of the people evaluating the generalists did not know them very well. The generalists worried that this unfamiliarity would make their evaluators less understanding and more critical. And the specialists, despite the advantage of closer relationships, were extremely vulnerable if they did not get along well with their primary trading partners. In Powers's opinion, it was the responsibility of the regional sales manager to correct such biases in the new system.

Preparation for the Meeting

As Powers prepared for the meeting, he considered the uncertainty and resentment about the evaluation process some of his staff had expressed. Many were concerned that the new process made the connection between their efforts and the compensation less obvious. It was difficult to predict to what extent their feelings would affect their performances.

Among the attendees at the meeting would be Arnie Berenson, the Philadelphia sales manager, who also was considering how to address the problems of growth and specialization with his clientele. But Powers, having heard that Berenson was skeptical about the special accounts group approach, knew he would need a very compelling argument to convince him and others that the change had been effective. The mixed response from the clients served by the SAG was difficult to interpret. Was it an instinctive negative reaction to change? If the clients' opinions did not improve, could the change still be justified on the basis of its advantages outweighing its disadvantages?

Powers also pondered the implications of the most recent developments in the bond market, which had just experienced its worst quarter in many years. He wondered how this downturn would affect his staff and whether his comments at tomorrow's meeting should take such contingencies into consideration.

C a s e   3–2

Technology Transfer at a Defense Contractor

Linda Hill and Jaan Elias

Larry Yoshino, a lab manager at Parsons Controls Corporation, gazed out his office window and let out a short sigh. Dealing with manufacturing, he thought, had to be one of the biggest headaches of his job.

The 90 engineers of Yoshino's lab at the Sonar Division (SD) in Gaithersburg, Maryland had spent three years designing and building a prototype of the control unit for the S2 sonobuoy. (See Exhibits 1 through 4 for description of corporate organization, sonobuoy, and Defense Department development process.) In order to complete the development contract, the blueprints and prototypes created in Gaithersburg had to be translated into easily replicable procedures for production in SD's Charleston, South Carolina manufacturing facility. However, the "transition" (as this process was called) was never easy; not only did the work represent a technical challenge, but also a seemingly endless series of minor skirmishes between the engineers in Gaithersburg and those in Charleston.

This morning, Yoshino's mind was on Peter Scalia and the soldering problem. Scalia was responsible for the control unit's motherboard. Three months earlier, Charleston engineers spotted a problem with the motherboard's solders, and Scalia's team had launched a series of experiments designed to identify an optimal soldering procedure. Progress on the experiments had been slow, and Scalia had complained

This case was prepared by Research Assistant Jaan Elias under the supervision of Assistant Professor Linda Hill as the basis for class discussion rather than to illustrate either effective or ineffective handling of an administrative situation. Some names, products, and places have been disguised to protect confidentiality.

Exhibit 1
Technology Transfer at a Defense Contractor

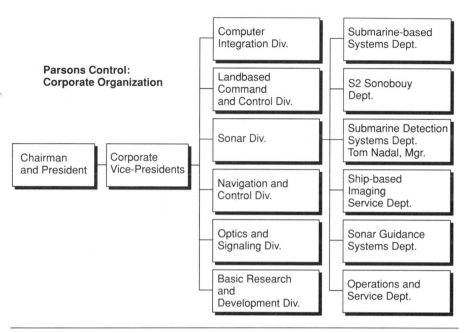

Source: Parsons Corporate Document

a number of times that he was not getting the cooperation he needed from the Charleston engineers.

Yoshino wondered what, if anything, he should do to help ease the motherboard's transition. Even a minor technical hitch could become a major problem if it halted the development and testing of the entire project and became a "show-stopper." Although the soldering problem was not a show-stopper yet, time was running short.

Yoshino also wondered what should be done in the future to avoid these problems. The changing competitive environment had forced many managers at Parsons to reassess the way the company had typically conducted its business. Yoshino knew that cost-efficient production and greater integration of design and manufacturing would be important issues for the future. The transition had become a critical step in all projects.

Parsons's Organization and Culture

Technical Excellence

Robert Parsons founded Parsons Control in 1947 and guided its early growth as a designer of large technical systems primarily for the Department of Defense (DoD).

Exhibit 2
Technology Transfer at a Defense Contractor

Titles and Responsibilities

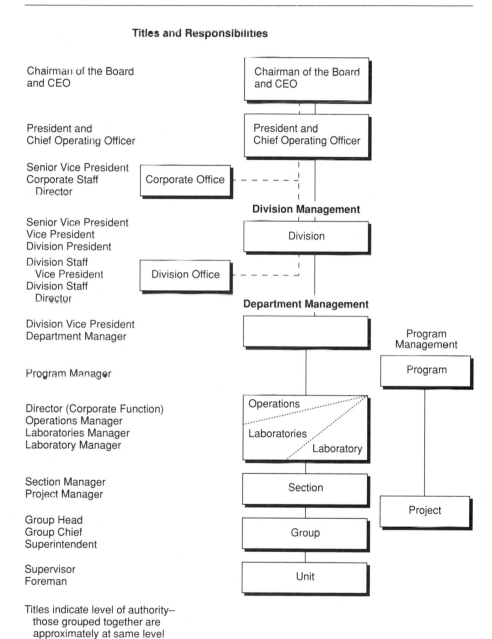

Chairman of the Board
and CEO

President and
Chief Operating Officer

Senior Vice President
Corporate Staff
   Director

Senior Vice President
Vice President
Division President

Division Staff
   Vice President
Division Staff
   Director

Division Vice President
Department Manager

Program Manager

Director (Corporate Function)
Operations Manager
Laboratories Manager
Laboratory Manager

Section Manager
Project Manager

Group Head
Group Chief
Superintendent

Supervisor
Foreman

Titles indicate level of authority—
   those grouped together are
   approximately at same level

Source: Parsons Corporate Document

Exhibit 3
Technology Transfer at a Defense Contractor

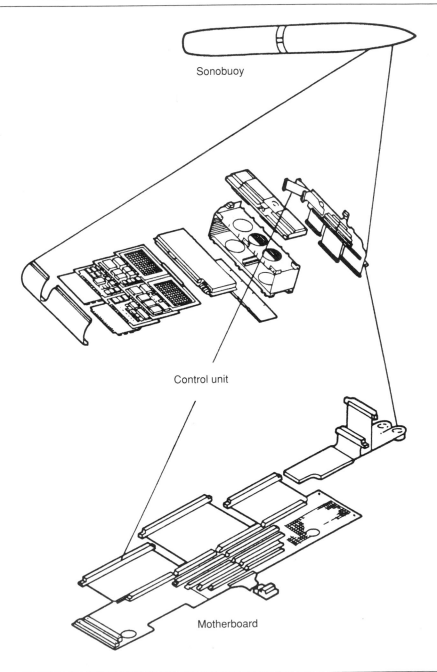

Sonobuoy

Control unit

Motherboard

Exhibit 4
Technology Transfer at a Defense Contractor
DOD Procurement Process

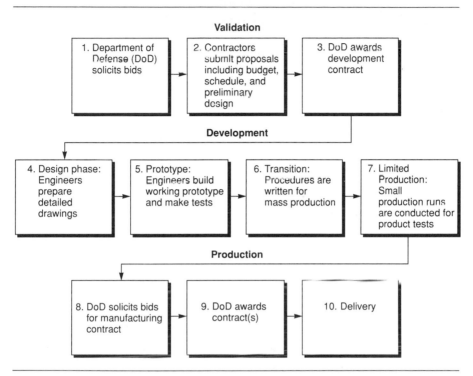

A prolific inventor, Parsons stressed the importance of scientific innovation and encouraged his staff to strive toward technical excellence. Even as his company grew, Parsons remained in the laboratory, maintaining an active research program until his death in 1962.

After Parsons's death, his family retained control of the company, leaving management in the hands of a team of senior engineers. The family supported the new management's long-term investments in building technical capacity. Over the next two decades, Parsons's substantial technical staff attained a string of scientific breakthroughs and created a number of important systems for the military. Parsons was acknowledged as the technological leader in most fields it entered. Revenues had grown from $75 million in 1962 to over $3 billion in 1983.

Beyond gaining defense contracts, Parsons's reputation as "an engineer's company" was important in attracting and retaining key specialists. Engineers accounted for over one third of Parsons's 33,000-member work force, and all senior management positions were held by engineers with strong technical reputations. At all levels in Parsons, the ability to make sound engineering decisions was considered crucial. Word of an engineer's track record circulated widely and was the most important factor in determining an engineer's access to resources and future assignments.

Parsons gave its engineers wide latitude to pursue technical excellence according to their own vision. Autonomy was a cornerstone of Parsons's corporate culture. The management structure was designed to concentrate decision making close to operations, distributing both technical and administrative responsibilities to all levels. Through a program of decentralization and diversification, Parsons had developed expertise in a wide range of fields (reflected in its growing number of divisions) allowing the company to maintain a large slate of projects. The large number of projects gave Parsons the opportunity to provide an unusual amount of job security for a defense contractor and also maintained a healthy level of internal competition. One senior executive observed:

> *Decentralization has always been a major strength for us. Internal entrepreneurship has been the rule; the company is not paternalistic. Things have been left relatively unstructured. At times, it seems as if you have thousands of anarchists running around defining their own jobs . . . Overall, our structure depends on "hyper-interactive" systems, with the exceptional performer carrying the responsibility.*

This loose structure and entrepreneurial culture were well-entrenched. Most management training at Parsons was informal. Yoshino described it as "learning through osmosis." One manager commented, "We just throw people into situations and find out what happens . . . A lot of what we do at Parsons comes naturally now. We don't talk about team building, for example, we just go and do."

Changes in the Competitive Environment

The large defense budgets of the 1980s had attracted additional competitors into the defense field and allowed the DoD to drive harder bargains. Fixed-price contracts for development had replaced cost-plus contracts, and the DoD had begun to second source the manufacture of military hardware. Previously, the company that won the development contract for a system could expect to be the manufacturer of the system. One senior Parsons executive observed: "The design of the product tends to be costlier to the company, while the profit is in sales from production. So competitors who couldn't out-design Parsons can underbid us on the manufacturing contracts and, using Parsons's drawings, take away the more profitable end of Parsons's business."

Parsons was responding to changes in the defense industry by launching a major initiative to upgrade its production capacity. Though the company had made its mark in design, in 1981 Parsons began a three-year, $450 million improvement program for manufacturing.

Government specifications on defense projects also had increased enormously. The sharp rise in the number of standards was driven by the enormous complexity of defense hardware coupled with tighter parameters written to ensure standardization across contractors. "At one time the specifications for an assembly could be held in a couple of loose-leaf notebooks." One production engineer observed, "Now it takes an entire bank of file cabinets to hold the specifications for the same assembly."

Design engineers grumbled that contract interpretation and negotiation were replacing technical skill as the most important elements of their jobs. Many expressed concern about the way their technical freedom was ebbing away under the increased pressures from the government and competitors. "I have never been managed," one senior engineer noted with pride. "If this is the way Parsons is going, sometimes I think I'd rather go and design washing machines for a living."

Further adding to the worries of engineers was the 1983 sale of the company to Providence Machine Tool Corporation (PMT), a Rhode Island manufacturer of sophisticated machine tools. PMT management bought Parsons from the founder's family in an effort to expand and diversify PMT's technical base and markets. Although PMT kept Parsons's corporate structure intact, most engineers believed that the change in ownership would eventually lead to a greater short-term profit orientation. A senior executive remarked:

> *Perceptions are changing. Maybe there may be a time of cultural change, a reassessment of who we are . . . This undoubtedly creates anxiety; this is not the same comfortable atmosphere there once was. We have to ask: Is Parsons becoming a different place? How can we build on our old strengths to take on some new realities?*

The Sonar Division

Organization

The SD was formally organized as a group in 1968, with research and design facilities in Gaithersburg, Maryland, and a manufacturing plant in Charleston, South Carolina. The research and design center consisted of a number of low-slung buildings, an hour's drive from Parsons corporate headquarters in Alexandria, Virginia. (Both Gaithersburg and Alexandria were suburbs of Washington, D.C.) The grounds were well landscaped and the overall physical appearance of the center resembled a modern community college campus. Most designers worked in private offices or in a number of small prototype laboratories sprinkled throughout the grounds.

Parsons located its manufacturing facility for sonar in Charleston near a naval shipyard. The small South Carolina city (population 69,100) was just over an hour away from Washington, D.C. by air. Since opening in 1968, the Charleston plant had manufactured more than 75,000 mobile sonar sensors of various types. Charleston engineers from all levels spent a large portion of their time on the plant floor. Besides its production engineers, the plant's labor force consisted of unionized machine operators and material handlers. Military personnel were also present, inspecting and testing devices as they rolled off the line.

Dixie Blockade/Foggy Bottom

Sharp differences existed between engineers in Gaithersburg and those in Charleston. Manufacturing engineers and design engineers faced different tasks, employed different approaches to problems and valued different outcomes. Each function claimed that the other failed to recognize their problems; Gaithersburg engineers designated the divide the "dixie blockade"; in turn, Charleston engineers called

Gaithersburg, "foggy bottom." (Foggy Bottom is the name of a neighborhood in Washington, D.C.)

SD's management was looking for ways to bridge the gulf and better integrate design and manufacturing. Engineers were urged to give greater attention to "producibility" of their designs. According to a Parsons publication, producibility problems occurred when "(1) designs were released without enough attention to existing production capabilities; and (2) production processes and equipment are inadequate to meet new engineering requirements."[1]

Gaithersburg engineers felt that better integration could be achieved by creating more producible designs during the design phase. Charleston engineers, while acknowledging the importance of producible designs, felt that design engineers often held onto projects for too long. A production engineer commented, "The sooner I get a design, the farther down the learning curve I can get. If the design engineers spend too long with a design, making it 'clean,' there is little recovery time for us in Charleston if something should go wrong."

To ease the transition from the designer's table to the factory floor, management had sought to bring together production and design engineers earlier in development. However, when engineers from Gaithersburg went to live in Charleston for the duration of a transfer, the move often presented a considerable hardship to their families. Transitions could stretch out many months, sometimes years. Rather than choose reassignment, some lab managers rotated different Gaithersburg engineers through Charleston, but this hurt continuity of effort. Alternately, Charleston engineers were assigned to Gaithersburg during design. Most, however, who were willing to leave Charleston for that amount of time were younger and had fewer ties to the company. By the time the design had been completed, many of them had left the company or had transferred to other projects.

Some of the cooperative efforts were successful. One engineer reported that on his project, Charleston and Gaithersburg engineers had worked well together during the design phase and later had an exceedingly smooth transition. The engineer described the camaraderie as "fortuitous": both design and production engineers had been approximately the same age and single. Had the engineers' backgrounds been less similar, he speculated, the ties which facilitated the transition would not have been as tight.

One engineer observed, "Each time we do a transition, we start from scratch and tend to make the same mistakes over again." Transitions of major systems did not occur often, and during any given transition the focus was on specific technical issues. Formally, the transition was the last step of the development process, and Gaithersburg engineers remained responsible for a design until both sides signed papers certifying the design as producible. Informally, manufacturing engineers were necessary to complete development, and design engineers felt responsible for their designs well after manufacturing had begun.

A production engineer from Charleston noted that building bridges between Gaithersburg and Charleston took time and required a great deal of personal ini-

---

[1]"Design Policy," *Parsons Corporate Manual*, 1984.

tiative. "Initially when I went to Gaithersburg, it was hard to get a hearing from the design engineers. But over time, they get to know you and you get to know them. Now, they will go out of their way to ask me what I think of a design. I guess you just have to be persistent."

Problems With Workmanship

In 1982, following inspections by the military, concern had been raised over the workmanship in the Charleston plant. In response, Parsons shut down a number of manufacturing lines and instituted a schedule of periodic audits of all manufacturing procedures. Many production engineers likened the experience to an inquisition, and most agreed that it had adversely affected morale. They felt that they had been scapegoated to appease government critics. In their view, SD management had reacted to calls to "do something" by laying blame entirely at the feet of the production engineers.

Despite the funds expended on the production process and the increased attention to manufacturing procedures, some production engineers felt that real progress would come only if the basic perceptions of the company changed. Parsons's reputation as a "design shop" permeated the culture of the company. "When you look at all the literature the company puts out," noted one senior production engineer, "it's all about what a great place Parsons is to work on design. I think that says something about management's priorities."

The S2 Sonobuoy Project

Making of a Lab Manager

In his 24 years at Parsons Controls, Yoshino had built an enviable reputation for technical virtuosity and organizational ability. Peers praised his ability to complete difficult design problems and coordinate the work of other engineers. A senior executive noted of Yoshino, "The bottom line is he turns out products and delivers on promises."

In 1981, Yoshino was brought in to oversee the development of the control unit for the S2 sonobuoy. A sonobuoy is a device deployed by ships to search for enemy submarines. After being launched, the proposed S2 would descend to a designated depth, emit sonar waves, and transmit back data to a shipboard computer. In submarine-infested waters, sonobuoys could be placed around the perimeter of a convoy or towed in an array behind a single ship. The S2 represented the next generation of sonobuoys for the U.S. Navy. Since Parsons had attained a strong position in submarine detection equipment, the company fought hard to win the contract and remain preeminent in this area.

Most engineers felt that the development contract had been underbid but hoped that losses in development could be recouped in manufacturing. The U.S. Navy estimated that it would need upwards of 3,500 sonobuoys a year over the next seven years. Parsons also hoped to sell the technology to other allied navies.

Yoshino became involved with the project after the development contract had been won. His laboratory was to develop the control unit—the electronic equipment inside the buoy which controlled the sonar sensors and transmitted information. Meeting the performance standards for the sonobuoy was a leap into the unknown; many of the technologies outlined in the proposal were untried. The financial and time parameters were tight. And all military contracts were proving to be more politically controversial as the U.S. Congress increased its scrutiny of "big ticket" defense systems. "S2 was the biggest challenge of my career," Yoshino noted. "It's not the type of project that people line up to do."

Yoshino divided the work on the control unit into nine separate components (or chassis). The development of each chassis was assigned to an accountable engineer (AE) who selected a design team, supervised the work, and was responsible for the budget and schedule. Sonar was Parsons's forte; many of its scientists and engineers had worked on previous sonar devices. In making his selection of AEs, Yoshino took great care to match individuals with their assignments; he chose people he trusted and had worked with on previous projects.

Setting the schedule for completion of the control unit was one of Yoshino's first tasks. Initially, Yoshino met with each AE to get an assessment of the time to complete his chassis. Then he met with the program office that had made the initial bid. Over a number of months, Yoshino went back and forth between the program office and his AEs, attempting to finalize a schedule agreeable to both sides. Once the schedule was set, it remained fixed for the duration of the project.

Yoshino acted as mediator between the program office and his engineers on numerous other occasions. "Unlike some other managers, Larry wouldn't agree to anything without first consulting with his engineers," an engineer in the program office noted with some frustration. Yoshino believed program managers had to understand the concerns of his engineers before he would commit the resources of his lab. He noted that honesty and a track record of delivering on commitments were essential elements in building a good relationship between program and line managers. On this aspect of their relationship, the program office gave Yoshino high marks: "Once Larry gives his word, you know you can trust it."

Project Management

The schedule and budget set, the work of developing the control unit began in earnest. A large amount of Yoshino's time was spent with the client: standards and requirements needed frequent updating. Given the uncertainty surrounding inter-pretation of the contract and developing a new detection system, Yoshino had to constantly revise and update projections, developing contingency plans for each step of the project.

Managing the development of the control unit required long hours for planning and frequent meetings with other managers. Administratively, Yoshino had to document the work that had been done for the government and the program office. He also stayed in touch with other line managers to ensure that the control unit could be properly integrated with the rest of the buoy. From time to time, he met with managers of other programs to initiate planning of the work his lab would do as they completed the S2. To maintain good relations, Yoshino always followed the chain of command and responded quickly to those with whom he had a direct reporting relationship. Despite an often hectic schedule of meetings with clients and subordinates, Yoshino made sure to return phone calls the same day.

In monitoring the progress of his AEs, Yoshino said he did not believe in "micromanaging" a project. Although he met informally with engineers in their labs and offices and maintained an open door policy, he got his best sense of the "pulse" of the work from twice-monthly design review meetings and monthly budget and schedule reports.

During the design review, each AE would present a 20-minute summary of the progress made during the previous two weeks. The meetings were attended by all of the AEs, people from the program office, Yoshino, and other members of Yoshino's staff. AEs were questioned, potential trouble spots identified and solutions proposed. Yoshino pushed his AEs to meet the schedule and budget commitments they had made. Engineers described the meetings as "intense." According to one engineer, there was always pressure to present "solutions, not problems. You never really wanted to be the bearer of bad news."

Avoiding delays meant avoiding "major surprises during the course of a project," Yoshino explained. "I tell the engineers to do it right the first time. It's important to invest time early to spot problems that could occur down the road. As the design gets closer to completion, it gets more difficult and expensive to change things."

Motivating engineers to put in extra work in order to complete an assignment quickly was one of Yoshino's biggest concerns. He felt it was important to make his engineers "feel special" by getting them the best possible resources—be it more computer time, lab space, or personnel. Despite Parsons's extensive facilities at Gaithersburg, the competition between programs and labs created substantial jousting for the prime resources. Yoshino's engineers gave him high marks in coming through on their requests.

Yoshino's approach to decision making was distinguished by the meticulousness characteristic of precise engineering. He noted that other managers made quicker decisions, but that he preferred to lay out all of the facts and decide issues on their technical merits. Colleagues observed that once Yoshino reached a decision, he was very persistent. "Larry will come back to you again and again. He's very polite—but firm; and in the end he'll generally get what he wants."

Transitioning the Motherboard
Design

Yoshino asked Peter Scalia to be the AE for the control unit's motherboard. Scalia had been with Parsons for 10 years. He had a strong design background, and he had been an AE for Yoshino on a previous sonar project. Scalia assembled a team of designers, negotiating to get engineers he knew and trusted. The motherboard development team consisted of a nucleus of five designers. A dozen other individuals (such as draftspeople, process engineers, and others) also contributed in other capacities.

The motherboard provided the connections between all of the other chassis as well as shielding and anchoring the entire control unit. Due to the large number of operations the sonobuoy had to perform, the total number of circuits in S2's control unit were an order of magnitude greater than any previous sonobuoy. However, because of physical constraints, S2's motherboard could not be larger than previous units.

Scalia's team began development of the motherboard in the summer of 1981. Early on, it became apparent that the design specified in the bid was infeasible. In order to meet performance standards, Scalia and his team had to create a motherboard that was quite different than any Parsons had manufactured before. It was, according to an engineer of another assembly, a rather "nifty" piece of engineering.

In the summer of 1982, the motherboard's basic design had been completed and Scalia's team began the construction and testing of a prototype. In order to build a working unit, the delicate interconnections between the motherboard and the other chassis had to be precisely fitted. The prototype was built by hand in a Gaithersburg workshop, allowing Scalia and his team to make quick alterations in the design and immediately incorporate them. The complex and time-consuming process took over a year.

Running the Dixie Blockade

Preparation for the transition had begun early in the project; Yoshino had asked that production engineers from Charleston be assigned to Gaithersburg to assist with design. Two production engineers had joined Scalia's team in the summer of 1981 and stayed with the group until the basic design was completed in the summer of 1982. During the subsequent year and a half period of building the prototype, the Charleston engineers who had been with Scalia's unit left the company or were assigned to other units. Scalia observed:

> They [the Charleston engineers] were good people, but they were young and inexperienced with manufacturing. They didn't understand how design decisions in Gaithersburg would prove important later on in Charleston . . . The Charleston people really did not have much impact on the actual design, but I had hoped that by observing what we did, the transition would be easier. There was a lot of lost training when the individuals who were here did not stay with the project in Charleston.

The task of seeing the motherboard through manufacturing in Charleston fell to James Pastore. Pastore joined Parsons-SD in 1979 and came to the S2 program in 1983 after a six-month international assignment. Acknowledged to be energetic and hardworking by engineers in both Gaithersburg and Charleston, Pastore put in long hours on the floor of the manufacturing facility. Pastore noted:

> In order to be successful in manufacturing, you have to be dynamic and take charge of the situation. The deadlines are tight, forcing you to get down on the floor and roll up your sleeves. The pressures we face in Charleston do not allow you to sit back and be a deep thinker.

Most engineers agreed that both Pastore and Scalia were confident of their own abilities and tended to be forceful personalities, although they did differ in temperament and style. One observer described it as the difference between "beer [Pastore] and wine [Scalia]." Pastore was thought to be aggressive and "quick on the draw." Some Gaithersburg engineers claimed "he had his finger in every pie" and was spread too thinly to be effective. Scalia, on the other hand, was thought to be a careful decision maker—much more "laid back" than Pastore. However, some Charleston engineers complained privately that he was aloof and inordinately interested in maintaining "good appearances" with superiors.

The Soldering Problem

In the beginning of 1984, the design of the motherboard and manufacturing specifications were sent to Charleston to begin production trials. In one step of the manufacturing procedure, five flex/cable connectors and six large connectors had to be soldered to a 16-layer printed wiring board. To solder the hundreds of joints at one time, the motherboard had to be placed through a wave-soldering machine (so-called because the motherboard travels over "waves" of molten solder on a conveyor). With a printed wiring board of 16 layers, significantly thicker than previous motherboards built by Parsons, Charleston engineers suspected that there might be problems wave-soldering joints which were up to military specifications. Military specifications dictated precise standards for solder formation on-and-around the plated holes and connector pins of the motherboard.

When tests on the wave-soldering machine began in March 1984, visual inspection of the solder joints seemed to confirm the suspicions of the Charleston engineers. The solder joints were not "wicking" up through the holes as required by military specs. Before notifying Gaithersburg of the problem, Pastore wanted additional evidence. He had the boards x-rayed, cross-sectioned, and examined microscopically. Pastore felt the tests supported the Charleston engineers' identification of the problem and he fired off a letter to Gaithersburg, sending copies not only to Scalia, but also to Yoshino (see Exhibit 5). The letter laid out the technical problem and presented the test results (performed by quality control) in graphic detail, complete with photographs. Pastore also made recommendations about the manufacturing procedures and suggestions about modifying the design to make it more producible in the long term.

Yoshino was surprised by the letter and doubly surprised that a copy of the letter had also come to the attention of Yoshino's supervisor, Tom Nadal. While he did not feel it appropriate to respond directly to Pastore, Yoshino contacted Scalia and reviewed Pastore's findings. Scalia and Yoshino requested their own set of tests on the boards.

In examining the problem, Gaithersburg concluded that while the basic design of the motherboard was sound, a new soldering procedure was required to ensure quality. Scalia noted, "The real problem was recognized by our management . . . We did a valid design; the wave soldering was the problem. But the first reaction out of Charleston is always 'redesign it for us.' " Scalia added that he did not understand why Pastore had sent the letter to Yoshino and others, "I thought I had good rapport with James. He just told me he didn't think he was getting my attention." Another Gaithersburg engineer attributed the letter to Pastore's style,

---

Exhibit 5
Technology Transfer at a Defense Contractor
                        Chain of Command for S2 Sonobuoy

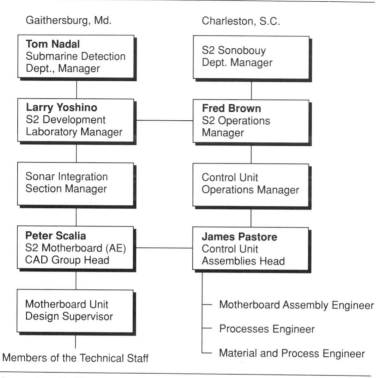

Gaithersburg, Md.   Charleston, S.C.

Tom Nadal
Submarine Detection
Dept., Manager

S2 Sonobouy
Dept. Manager

Larry Yoshino
S2 Development
Laboratory Manager

Fred Brown
S2 Operations
Manager

Sonar Integration
Section Manager

Control Unit
Operations Manager

Peter Scalia
S2 Motherboard (AE)
CAD Group Head

James Pastore
Control Unit
Assemblies Head

Motherboard Unit
Design Supervisor

Members of the Technical Staff

— Motherboard Assembly Engineer

— Processes Engineer

— Material and Process Engineer

Source: Larry Yoshino

"James has a flair for the dramatic." Discussing the letter with the casewriter, Pastore explained:

> There is a strong, "not invented here," syndrome in Gaithersburg which keeps them from listening to Charleston. . . . We needed to get the x-rays and photos to get their [Gaithersburg's] attention; otherwise they wouldn't believe us. They would have come back and told us that we were crazy. We went to Larry when we felt it might become an us versus them thing. Conflict happens when there is a lot of finger pointing and scapegoating.

Throughout the transition, Pastore worried that Yoshino might not have an accurate picture of the difficulties manufacturing the motherboard presented. Once Gaithersburg engineers gave a detailed explanation of the rationale for their design of the motherboard, Charleston engineers withdrew their redesign proposals and concentrated their efforts on revising the procedure. "It would have been a lot easier if we had known this from the start," one noted.

Finding the Proper Procedure

Because there was no wave-soldering machine in Gaithersburg, all of the tests to find a new procedure had to be run in Charleston. In correspondence with Charleston, Scalia's team outlined a systematic approach to the problem. They proposed varying the time and temperature of the machine and the ways of preparing the motherboard before soldering in a series of experiments on other layered boards. The complicated procedure for testing each run of layered boards took over a week to complete.

The Charleston engineers felt many of the experiments tested procedures unsuited to manufacturing. Working from their knowledge of wave soldering, the production engineers tried their own approaches. "If this had been some new process or product, then fine, Gaithersburg might have a better handle on it. But I had been working with wave soldering for years. Each week we had to spend time trying to convince them that we knew what we were doing," one Charleston engineer noted.

For Gaithersburg, the engineers in Charleston were too "cut-and-try." For example, one of the few available prototypes of the motherboard was burned in Charleston. "It was simply because they were not following directions," Yoshino noted with some chagrin. "That should have never happened, it was simply careless." (Charleston engineers told the casewriter that they felt they were performing an essential experiment.) With three years of work on the motherboard design behind them, Scalia believed Gaithersburg had the most applicable knowledge. "We understand the complexities of the design. Without knowing, Charleston's rework of the procedure could invalidate the rest of the design. We take care of any changes."

Resource Problems

To oversee the transition, a Gaithersburg engineer spent one or two days a week in Charleston on rotation. However, when Gaithersburg engineers went down to Charleston, they often found that they could not get on the soldering machine to run the tests, or that materials necessary for running the experiments were not set up. Progress on the tests seemed unnecessarily slow. Scalia described his team's frustration:

> We were having problems getting them [Charleston] to even set up desks for us. We didn't have direct access to the floor of the plant, so we couldn't work directly on the machines. In order to get the operator to run a test, we had to go to a supervisor to get authorization . . . It was like playing a game of telephone.

Even as the soldering problem dragged on, Scalia and his team had other pieces of the motherboard to worry about. For example, an important part of the motherboard was being manufactured for Parsons by a small Pennsylvania company that was having trouble delivering a quality product. Scalia's team had to work with this company in addition to overseeing the transition in Charleston.

All of the Charleston engineers assigned to the motherboard had between 10 to

20 other projects. Each project had its own deadline; there was no strict list of priorities. They felt they were devoting as much time as they could to wave soldering, and had made progress toward writing a new procedure. Many of them expressed frustration that Scalia's team was not utilizing the work they had been doing. One engineer noted: "Production engineers are oriented toward getting physical results. Results are measured in the number of finished products that roll off the line."

The Charleston engineers were also disappointed in the effort Scalia's team was placing into the soldering problem. "You can't work on production problems from an office," one Charleston engineer explained. "You have got to get on the floor." Another felt that the rotation of different engineers was disrupting the continuity of effort. "You just can't get to know the problems in a couple of days a week . . . You have to be at the plant for a couple of days a week straight so that you really get to know the manufacturing problems." Another said simply, "You can't engineer through IDC (interdepartmental correspondence)."

By April 1984, an engineer from Scalia's team was spending most of his days in Charleston. "If we weren't there, it [the experiments on the wave soldering machine] wasn't getting done," Scalia explained. "Charleston did not take responsibility for the problem . . . They seemed to feel that it just wasn't their job."

Privately, both Gaithersburg and Charleston were commenting that the other team seemed to be "in over their heads technically" and were unwilling to admit it.

Yoshino's Role in the Motherboard Transition

Yoshino had conferred frequently with Scalia (though not with Pastore, who was not under his direct authority) about the soldering problem. Yoshino trusted Scalia's technical judgments and felt that Scalia's approach to finding the right soldering procedure was sound. When Scalia had complained of Charleston's lack of cooperation, Yoshino had brought the issue up with his Charleston counterpart, Fred Brown, during their twice-monthly meetings. Yoshino enjoyed a good rapport with Brown and was respected by a number of manufacturing engineers in Charleston. Each time after he "rattled the cage" to get the resources, Yoshino had received reports that access for members of Scalia's team had improved for a time.

Even under the best of circumstances, writing a manufacturing procedure could be time consuming. Creating new technologies often involved a great deal of uncertainty and debate over proper approaches. Though Pastore had tried to involve him, Yoshino felt that it was best to "let the engineers slug it out for themselves in the trenches"; the role of the lab manager was to "set the tone of the transition and spread goodwill whenever he could."

Over the long-term, Yoshino felt that learning how to get along with production was part of the maturation of a design engineer. Scalia was known to be hardheaded, and like many technically proficient design engineers, he could be touchy about his work. Yoshino explained:

Since they spend so long developing their designs, some designers see their own work so clearly that they have trouble explaining it to others, and trouble in accepting any changes. They get accused of trying to steamroller their ideas through . . . I tell them, "You aren't just selling the design, you are selling your-self." You have to develop a level of trust to be effective.

But now (June 1984) time on the soldering problem was running short. The problem was not a show-stopper, but Yoshino realized that if a procedure could not be ironed out quickly, costly delays would result. However, he knew that the goal was not only to finish development on time, but also to create a high-performance sonar device that could be manufactured cost-efficiently and with high quality.

Yoshino wondered: What, if anything should he do now to help the motherboard transition? And what should be done in the future to assure effective transitioning of technology?

Reading 3–1

Performance Appraisal: Dilemmas and Possibilities*

Michael Beer

It completely refused to run (a) when the waves were high, (b) when the wind blew, (c) at night, early in the morning, and evening, (d) in rain, dew, or fog, (e) when the distance to be covered was more than 200 yards. But on warm, sunny days when the weather was calm and the white beach close by—in a word, on days when it would have been a pleasure to row, it [the outboard motor] started at a touch and would not stop.

John Steinbeck

Steinbeck's description of an outboard motor is a very apt introduction to an article on performance appraisal. When performance and potential are good, when superior and subordinates have an open relationship, when promotions or salary increases are abundant, when there is plenty of time for preparation and discussion—in short, whenever it's a pleasure—performance appraisal is easy to do. Most of the time, however, and particularly at the times when it is most needed and most difficult to do, performance appraisal refuses to run properly.

The difficulties managers and subordinates experience in the appraisal interview may be traced to the quality of their relationship, to the manner and skill with which the interview is conducted, and to the appraisal system itself—that is, the objectives the organization has for it, the administrative system in which it is embedded, and the forms and procedures that make up the system. This article will explore the difficulties, the many causes of these difficulties, and what might be done about them.

*Reprinted, by permission of the publisher, from *Organizational Dynamics*, Winter 1981 © 1981 AMACOM, a division of American Management Associations, New York. All rights reserved.

Goals of Performance Appraisal

Both the organization and the individual employee want the performance appraisal to meet particular objectives. In some cases these objectives or goals are compatible, but in many cases they are not. The potential for conflict between the employee's goals and the organization's objectives for performance appraisal has been discussed by Lyman W. Porter, Edward E. Lawler III, and Richard J. Hackman, and the subject will be reviewed and expanded in this article.

The Organization's Goals

Performance evaluation is an important element in the information and control system of most complex organizations. It can be used to obtain information about the performance of employees—so that decisions about placement, promotions, terminations, and pay can be made.

Performance appraisal systems and, more important, discussions between supervisor and subordinate about performance, can also influence the employee's behavior and performance. This is true of management by objectives (MBO) systems, as well as various performance rating systems. The process of influencing behavior is an important part of the organization's efforts to develop future human resources, and it is of utmost importance to managers in their attempts to obtain the results for which they are accountable. From the manager's and the organization's points of view, the performance appraisal process is a major tool for changing individual behavior.

The following lists summarize the organization's objectives for performance appraisal. First, the *evaluation goals:*

1. To provide feedback for subordinates so that they will know where they stand.
2. To develop valid data for pay (salary and bonus) and promotion decisions and to provide a means for communicating these decisions.
3. To help the manager in making discharge and retention decisions and to provide a means for warning subordinates about unsatisfactory performance.

Next, the *coaching and development goals:*

1. To counsel and coach subordinates so they will improve their performance and develop future potential.
2. To develop commitment to the larger organization through discussion with subordinates of career opportunities and career planning.
3. To motivate subordinates through recognition and support.
4. To strengthen supervisor-subordinate relations.
5. To diagnose individual and organizational problems.

Note that this list includes many goals and, as the vertical arrow on the left of Exhibit 1 shows, they are in conflict. When the performance appraisal is being

Exhibit 1
Conflicts in Performance Appraisal

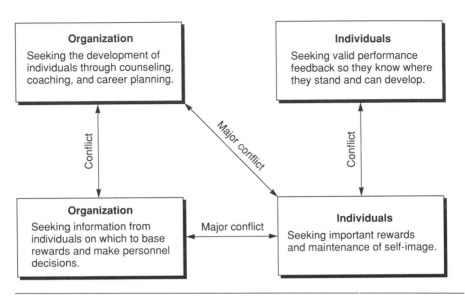

Adapted from Porter, Lawler, and Hackman, 1975.

conducted to meet evaluation goals, the system is a tool by which managers make difficult judgments that affect their subordinates' futures. When they communicate these judgments, they may well have to justify their appraisal in response to, or in anticipation of, subordinates' disagreement. The result can be an adversary relationship, faulty listening, and low trust. None of these are conducive to the coaching and development objectives of performance appraisal. When coaching and development are the goals, managers must play the role of helper. If they are to help, they must draw out subordinates, listen to their problems, and get them to understand their own weaknesses. The different communication processes required to achieve the conflicting goals of performance appraisal create difficult problems for the manager involved.

The Individual's Goals

As the vertical arrow on the right of Exhibit 1 shows, the employee also has conflicting goals for the performance appraisal. Employees want and desire feedback about their performance because it helps them learn about themselves, how they are doing, and what management values. If this information is favorable, it helps satisfy their psychological needs for competence and success; if it is not, they tend to experience failure, and the feedback may be difficult to accept. Thus, even when people in organizations ask for or demand feedback, they are really looking for favorable feedback that will affirm their concept of themselves. When rewards, such as pay and promotion, are tied to the evaluation, employees have even more reason for wanting to avoid unfavorable evaluations.

An employee's self-development goals require him or her to be willing to accept feedback and ideas for alternative approaches to the job. Subordinates must be willing to drop their defenses and consider accepting the manager's view of their performance. They need an inquisitive attitude about their performance and what might be done to improve it. However, to protect their self-image or to obtain valued rewards, subordinates may gloss over, if not deny, problems. Often without realizing it, individuals may present themselves in a more favorable light than warranted by the facts. The simultaneous needs to be open and to be protective create difficult problems for the individual.

Conflicting Individual and Organizational Goals

The biggest conflict, however, is between individual and organizational goals or objectives. The individual desires to confirm a positive self-image and to obtain organizational rewards, such as promotion or pay. The organization wants individuals to be receptive to negative information about themselves in order to improve their performance and promotability. It also wants individuals to be helpful in supplying necessary information. The conflict is over the exchange of valid information. As long as individual employees see the appraisal process as having an important influence on their reward (pay, recognition), on their career (promotions and reputation), and on their self-image, there will be a reluctance to engage in the kind of open dialogue required for valid evaluation and personal development. The poorer the employee's performance, the worse the potential conflict, and the less likely that there'll be an exchange of valid information. Major conflicts between the individual and the organization are shown by the diagonal and horizontal arrows in Exhibit 1 and are the reasons why performance appraisals run like Steinbeck's outboard motor.

Problems with Performance Appraisal

Several identifiable problems develop around the performance appraisal process. Some of the most troublesome follow.

Ambivalence and Avoidance

Given the conflicts that are present in the performance appraisal process, it is not surprising that supervisors and subordinates are often ambivalent about participating in it.

Supervisors are uncomfortable because their organizational role places them in the position of being both judge and jury. They must make decisions that affect people's careers and lives in significant ways. Furthermore, most managers are not trained to handle the difficult interpersonal situations that are likely to arise when feedback is negative. This is a problem particularly because managers must maintain good relations with their subordinates to perform their own jobs effectively. All this leads to uncertainty about their subjective judgments and anxiety about meeting with subordinates to discuss performance. Yet supervisors also know they must have performance discussions because the organization expects it and subordinates want it. Finally, supervisors often feel personally and legally bound to let people know where they stand. If they are not open with their subordinates, mutual trust suffers because subordinates usually sense when supervisors have been less than truthful. Then, too, there's the growing threat that supervisor's actions can lead to legal action against the organization if an individual feels he or she has been treated unfairly. Furthermore, as I have already pointed out, subordinates usually want constructive feedback, but they're very ambivalent about receiving negative feedback.

The ambivalence of both superiors and subordinates has led to what some behavioral scientists have called the "vanishing performance appraisal." In many organizations, supervisors report that they hold periodic appraisal interviews and give honest feedback, while their subordinates report they have not had a performance appraisal for many years or that they heard nothing negative. The appraisals conducted by the supervisors seem to "vanish." What probably happens is that supervisors, fearful of the appraisal process, have talked in very general terms to the subordinates, alluding only vaguely to problems. There are many ways this can occur. One of the most common is the "sandwich approach"—that is, the supervisor provides negative feedback between heavy doses of positive feedback. He or she may choose to conduct an appraisal on an airplane or during a car ride where the setting blurs its serious purpose. There are other ways, too, to obscure the process— for example, the supervisor makes very general statements and doesn't refer to specific problems. Or when the supervisor's own anxiety or the subordinate's defensiveness signals potential problems, the supervisor does provide negative feedback, but immediately counterbalances it with positive statements.

The subordinate's fear of learning things that will diminish his or her self-image often leads to the lack of initiative in seeking negative feedback and an unconscious collusion with the supervisor that results in avoidance. Thus the supervisor and subordinate engage in long conversations that are only marginally related to the purpose of the appraisal interview. Or they may engage in small talk or humor that conveys an oblique message, or they may develop a pattern of communication in which phrases do not convey a clear meaning to either of them. Thus there is no in-depth exploration of negative feedback, and it is not fully understood and internalized by the subordinate.

Defensiveness and Resistance

The conflict between the organization's evaluation objectives and its coaching and development objectives tends to place the manager in the incompatible roles of judge and helper during the appraisal interview. Some managers feel obligated to fulfill their organizational role as judge by explaining to the employee all facets of his or her evaluation. They want to be sure they fulfill their obligation to let the subordinate know where he or she stands by going down a rating form or discussing all "shortfalls" in performance. This tactic can naturally elicit appraisees' resistance as they defend against threats to their self-esteem.

Defensiveness may come in a variety of forms. Subordinates may try to explain away their "shortfalls" by blaming others or uncontrollable events; they may question the appraisal system itself; they may minimize the importance of the appraisal process; they may demean the source of the data; they may insincerely apologize and say they will not do it again, just to cut short their exposure to negative feedback; or they may seem to agree readily to the information while inwardly denying its validity or accuracy.

The core of the problem is that the supervisors' organizational role as judge can lead them into communicating and defending their evaluation to subordinates at the very time they are trying to develop an open two-way dialogue for a valid information exchange and development. The defensiveness that results may take the form of open hostility and denials, but it may also take the form of passivity and "surface" compliance. In either case, the subordinate doesn't really accept or understand the feedback. Thus, those subordinates who may need development the most may learn the least.

The Worst of All Interviews: Avoidance and Defensiveness Combined

The problems created by ambivalence and avoidance can combine with the problems of defensiveness and resistance in the same appraisal interview. For example, when managers go through a perfunctory performance appraisal to fulfill their supervisory duty, ambivalence leads them to avoid direct and meaningful talk about performance, while the need to fulfill the judge's role leads them to a complete but mechanical review of the evaluation form. Thus even though they avoid delving into subordinates' performance problems, they elicit defensive behavior from subordinates by going through the evaluation form in detail. Thus neither the benefits of avoidance (that is, maintenance of good relations and personal comfort) nor the benefits of accurate feedback (that is, clear understanding and development) are reaped, and none of the problems of avoidance and resistance are resolved.

Nonevaluative Evaluation

The basic dilemma of the appraisal process is how to have an open discussion of performance that meets the employee's need for feedback and the organization's need to develop employees, yet prevents damage to the employee's self-esteem and to his or her security about organizational rewards. This is, of course, a paradox, and thus both goals are not fully achievable. In the rest of this article, I will offer some ideas and suggestions on dealing with this paradox.

Potential Solutions to Appraisal Problems

There are three major ways in which the problems I have outlined can be dealt with. First, the appraisal system can be designed to minimize the negative dynamics outlined above. (The manager often has only marginal control over these matters.) Second, more attention can be paid to the ongoing relationship between supervisors and subordinates. Third, the interview process itself—that is, the quality of communication between supervisor and subordinate—can be improved. Let's look at how these approaches can be directed toward solving appraisal problems.

Designing the Appraisal System

The following corrective steps can improve performance appraisal systems.

Uncoupling Evaluation and Development.   Herbert Meyer and his associates have suggested that less defensiveness and an open dialogue result when the manager splits her or his role as helper from that as judge. This can be done by having two separate performance appraisal interviews: one that focuses on evaluation and the other that focuses on coaching and development. The open problem-solving dialogue required for building a relationship and developing subordinates should be scheduled at a different time of the year than the meeting in which the supervisor informs the subordinate about her or his overall evaluation and its implications for retention, pay, and promotion. Such a split recognizes that managers cannot help and judge at the same time without the behavior required by one role interfering with the behavior required by the other.

Many performance appraisal systems inadvertently encourage managers to mix the role of judge and helper by providing only one evaluation form that ends up in the subordinate's personnel record. What is needed are two distinct forms and procedures. The evaluation form becomes part of the personnel record while the form that guides the development discussion does not.

Choosing Appropriate Performance Data.   A manager can minimize defensiveness and avoidance by narrowly focusing feedback on specific behaviors or specific performance goals. For example, rating a person as unsatisfactory on a characteristic as broad as motivation is likely to be perceived as a broadside attack and as a threat to self-esteem. Feedback about specific incidents or aspects of "how" a person is performing the job is more likely to be heard than broad generalizations, and it will be more helpful to the individual who wants to improve performance. Thus an appraisal discussion that relies on a report card rating of traits or performance is doomed to failure because it leads the supervisor into general evaluative statements that threaten the subordinate.

Fortunately, some appraisal techniques are available to guide the supervisor toward more specific behavioral observations. One example is the behavioral rating scale that asks supervisors to indicate the degree to which subordinates fulfill certain behavioral requirements of their job (for example, participating actively in meetings or communicating sufficiently with other departments). Another technique is the critical-incident method in which the supervisor records important examples of effective or ineffective performance.

Similarly, there are various management by objectives (MBO) techniques that can be used to guide the appraisal discussion toward reviewing specific accomplishments.

Robert Ruh and I have suggested elsewhere that a comprehensive performance management system include both MBO and behavioral ratings. MBO is a means of managing *what* the individual should do, while behavioral ratings are a means for helping employees examine *how* they should do it. They are different but complementary tools in managing and appraising performance. A behavioral rating form might very well be the tool an organization can provide to managers as a guide for the developmental interview.

Separating Evaluations of Performance and Potential. Current performance, as measured by the attainment of results, is not necessarily correlated with potential for promotion. Yet many appraisal systems do not adequately provide for separate evaluations of these dimensions. In the case of a subordinate who rates high in current performance and low in potential for advancement (or vice versa), a manager is placed in the situation of averaging his or her unconscious assessment of these qualities and then defending an evaluation that may be inconsistent with his or her perception and the subordinate's self-perception of either performance or potential alone. Even if separate evaluations of these dimensions do not reduce subordinate defensiveness, they can reduce the manager's need to defend a composite rating that he or she cannot justify. Systems that separate assessments of performance and potential increase the likelihood of a constructive dialogue and therefore reduce the likelihood of avoidance.

Recognizing Individual Differences in System Design. Individuals differ in their needs for performance evaluation and development. Upwardly mobile employees may desire and need more feedback about performance and promotability than less upwardly mobile employees. They will also need longer and more frequent developmental discussions. Similarly, more confident and open employees will be able to handle these discussions better than will employees who lack self-esteem and are defensive. Performance appraisal policies should permit managers to use different methods depending on the particular employee being appraised. An appraisal every two or three years may be enough for an employee who has reached the peak of his or her capabilities. Such an appraisal could be limited to a rating and discussion of current performance, but omit any discussion of promotion potential. Uniform systems and procedures stand in the way of such differential treatment.

Upward Appraisal.   The appraisal dynamic that contributes most to defensiveness and/or avoidance is the authoritarian character of the supervisor-subordinate relationship. The simple fact that one person is the boss and responsible for evaluation places him or her in a dominant role and induces submissive behavior on the part of the subordinate. Furthermore, the boss holds and controls rewards. In order to develop the open, two-way dialogue required in the coaching and developmental interview, power must be equalized or at least brought into better balance during the interview. One way to achieve this is to ask subordinates to appraise their supervisor.

An upward appraisal can help a supervisor create the conditions needed for an effective performance appraisal interview for several reasons. It gives subordinates a real stake in the appraisal interview and an opportunity to influence a part of their environment that ultimately influences their performance. Thus it makes them more equal and less dependent, increasing their motivation to enter the appraisal process with an open frame of mind. It also offers the supervisor an opportunity to demonstrate nondefensive behavior and a willingness to engage in a real two-way dialogue (assuming the supervisor is capable of behaving nondefensively).

Organizations can encourage the use of upward appraisals by providing forms and developing policies that support this approach. If the organization doesn't do so, the supervisor can develop his or her own form or seek informal feedback sometime during the appraisal interviews.

Self-Appraisal.   Experience with self-appraisal suggests that it often results in lower ratings than the supervisor would have given. Subordinates appraising themselves before an interview do so with the knowledge that an unrealistic or obviously self-serving rating will affect their manager's perception of them. Thus performance appraisal systems that include self-appraisal before either the coaching or evaluation interview are likely to result in a more realistic rating and a greater acceptance of the final rating by subordinates and supervisors.

Some or all of the system design elements described in this section can be used to minimize manager avoidance and subordinate resistance. But by themselves they are not sufficient. Good relationships and interpersonal competence are also required.

Improving Supervisor-Subordinate Relationship

Not surprisingly, the quality of the appraisal process depends on the nature of the day-to-day supervisor-subordinate relationship. First, an effective relationship means that the supervisor is providing feedback and coaching on an ongoing basis. Thus the appraisal interview is merely a review of issues that have already been discussed. Second, the appraisal interview is only a small segment of the broader supervisor-subordinate relationship, and expectations for it are likely to be shaped by the broader relationship. If a relationship of mutual trust and supportiveness exists, subordinates are more apt to be open in discussing performance problems and less defensive in response to negative feedback.

There is no substitute for a good supervisor-subordinate relationship. Without such a relationship, no performance appraisal system can be effective. Although the development of such a relationship is not the subject of this article, it is important to understand that the appraisal interview itself can be used to build a relationship of mutual trust, provided the interview is modeled after some of the ideas discussed in the next section.

Improving the Appraisal Interview

The appraisal interview has multiple objectives. Therefore, it isn't surprising that different objectives are best met by somewhat different interview methods.

Directive Interviews.   If the interview's objective is to communicate a performance evaluation or pay decision that has already been made, the interview should take a more directive form. The manager tells the subordinate what the evaluation is and, to assure the subordinate about its fairness, the process by which it was determined. The manager then listens actively, accepting and trying to understand the employee's reactions and feelings without signaling that the performance evaluation is open to change.

If the manager has already evaluated the subordinate, any attempt to conduct an open and participative dialogue to motivate the subordinate will fail. Such an approach encourages the subordinate to try to influence the manager's rating—a move that puts the manager in the position of defending a final decision. In this situation, the subordinate not only has to accept an evaluation that may be inconsistent with his or her self-perception, but may also have to leave the interview frustrated by unsuccessful attempts to influence the manager.

As stated earlier, managers may be drawn into this situation by systems that provide only one form for evaluation. An open dialogue cannot occur, because the manager follows the form mechanically in an effort to communicate accurately judgments that he or she has already committed to paper. Corporate procedures that require the manager's boss to review the evaluation before the appraisal interview only increase the manager's need to defend the rating and reduce even further the likelihood of an open dialogue.

Participative Problem-Solving Interview.   If the interview's objective is to motivate subordinates to change their behavior or improve their performance, an open process that includes mutual participation is required. This approach takes the manager out of the role of judge and puts him or her into the role of helper. The objective is to help subordinates discover their own performance deficiencies and help them take the initiative to develop a joint plan for improvement. The problem-solving interview makes no provision for communicating the supervisor's unilateral evaluation. The assumption underlying this type of interview is that self-understanding by subordinates and motivation to improve performance cannot occur in a setting where the manager has already made judgments and psychologically separates her- or himself from the subordinate to avoid being swayed. The problem-

---

Exhibit 2
Mixed-Model Interview

Interview Begins

1. Open-ended discussion and exploration of problems, in which the subordinate leads and the supervisor listens.

2. Problem-solving discussion, in which the subordinate leads, but supervisor takes somewhat stronger role.

3. Agreement between supervisor and subordinate on performance problems and a plan for improvements.

4. Closing evaluation, in which the supervisor gives his or her views and final evaluation if the subordinate has not dealt with important issues.

Interview Ends

---

solving interview is therefore less structured, relies on the subordinate to lead the discussion into problem areas, and relies on the manager to listen, reflect, care, guide, and coach.

Individual Differences and the Interview.   The subordinate's characteristics should also determine the interview method. Subordinates differ in their age, experience, sensitivity about negative feedback, attitude toward the supervisor, and desire for influence and control over their destiny. For example, if the subordinate is young, inexperienced, and dependent and looks up to the supervisor, a more directive interview in which the supervisor does most of the talking may be appropriate—unless, of course, it is the supervisor's objective to help the subordinate become more independent. On the other hand, if the subordinate is older, more experienced, and sensitive about negative feedback, and has a high need for controlling his or her destiny, the same objective is best met by a less directive approach.

Mixed-Model Interviews.   When situational factors such as corporate policies, practices and forms, available time, and subordinate expectations prevent separate evaluation and developmental interviews, it is possible to design one interview to achieve both purposes. The most effective way of implementing a mixed-model appraisal interview is to start the appraisal process with the open-ended problem-solving approach and end with the more directive approach. If the supervisor starts off with one-way communication, real two-way communication and in-depth exploration of personal and job performance issues are unlikely to occur. Thus, as Exhibit 2 shows, the interview should start with an open-ended exploration of perceptions and concerns, with the subordinate taking the lead, and it should finish with a more closed-ended agreement on what performance improvements are expected. Performance problems and improvements are agreed to jointly, but if such agreement is not possible, ultimate responsibility rests with the supervisor. The supervisor may choose to tell the subordinate what is expected if crucial problems have not been discussed or solutions agreed on.

There are many ways in which a mixed-model interview can be implemented. I have outlined one possible pattern for an effective appraisal interview with multiple purposes below. The following assumptions underlie the recommended interview process:

1. It is possible to defuse the potential negative effects of corporate systems and traditional expectations through joint supervisor-subordinate agreement on interview content and process before the interview.

2. Joint planning of the interview enhances the probability that the interview goals and process will be compatible.

3. Joint supervisor-subordinate agreement on ground rules for effective communication before the interview increases control over the process.

4. It is necessary to equalize the power of the appraiser and appraisee to achieve developmental objectives and maintain good relations. However, this should not prevent the supervisor from taking a more directive role later in the interview if it is necessary.

5. A good appraisal interview can occur only in a context of good supervisor-subordinate relations or when both parties are motivated to use the interview as a means of improving relations.

6. Managers can mix the inherently incompatible judging and helping roles only if the latter is the primary role and goal.

7. A mixed interview requires the manager to assume a substantial range of styles and to have the ability to shift between them quickly and appropriately.

The following proposed interview sequence is only illustrative:

1. *Scheduling.* Notify the subordinate well in advance when the appraisal discussion is scheduled. The interview should be set at a time when both parties are alert and undisturbed by external organizational or personal matters. The discussion should be scheduled as long after the salary review as possible.

2. *Agreeing on content.* Before the interview, discuss the nature of the interview with the subordinate and work toward agreement on the goals of the interview and what will be discussed (for example, rating forms to be used or performance issues to be discussed). This gives the subordinate a chance to prepare for the interview (including self-rating or rating the supervisor if this is to be part of the session), and to come to the interview on a more equal footing with the supervisor. If necessary, it also permits supervisor and subordinate to devise a form and procedure compatible with their goals for the interview.

3. *Agreeing on process.* Agree on the process for the appraisal discussion with the subordinate before the interview. For example, agreement should be reached on the sequencing of interview phases. If an open, exploratory discussion is to come first, followed by problem solving, action planning, and upward appraisal, this is the time to tell the subordinate about these phases. Similarly, ground rules for communications can be established that will ensure constructive feedback and good listening. (See Step 7.)

4. *Setting location and space.* If possible, meet on neutral territory or in the subordinate's office. In this way, a relationship of more equal power that's so crucial to open communication can be established.

5. *Opening the interview.* Review the objectives of the appraisal interview that were previously agreed to. This review sets the stage and allows supervisor and subordinate to prepare themselves psychologically.

6. *Starting the discussion.* Give the initiative to the subordinate in the discussion that follows the opening statement. Specifically start the discussion by asking, "How do you feel things are going on the job? What's going well and what problems are you experiencing? How do you see your performance?" Such general questions will stimulate the subordinate to take the initiative in the problem identification and solving discussion. To facilitate this, a subordinate may be asked to appraise his or her own performance. If the manager starts by expressing views about the employee's performance, the interview inevitably becomes directive.

7. *Exchanging feedback.* Follow well-accepted ground rules for giving and receiving feedback. A supervisor who sets up these methods for effective communication encourages the exchange of valid information.

In giving feedback, a supervisor can reduce employee's defensiveness by being specific about the performance and behavior-causing problems (that is, what was said and done?). Citing specific examples of observed behavior and describing the consequences of that behavior in terms of effects on others, on the supervisor's feelings, and on the department's performance can help an employee identify what needs to be changed. To prevent defensive reactions, the supervisor should avoid making general statements, imputing motives to behavior (that is, you are lazy or you aren't committed), blaming, or accusing.

The supervisor should set up ground rules for receiving feedback and encourage the subordinate to follow them. Defensiveness should be avoided at all costs; negative feedback is usually cut off by the giver when signs of defensiveness appear in the receiver, and this reduces the amount of information transmitted. Active listening can encourage receptiveness to and understanding of negative feedback. The receiver should paraphase what is being said, request clarification, and summarize the discussion periodically. The receiver can maintain openness and keep information coming by exploring the negative feedback and showing a willingness to examine him- or herself critically. On the other hand, feedback is usually cut off and understanding reduced by justifying actions, apologizing, blaming others, explaining, and "building a case."

The ground rules for receiving feedback are not meant to imply that supervisors and subordinates should not help each other understand why they are doing what they are doing. However, the timing of explanations is critical in stimulating openness instead of defensiveness. Active listening first, followed by explanations later, is a better sequence than the reverse.

8. *Presenting the supervisor's views.* The supervisor should provide a summary of the subordinate's major improvement needs based on the previous discussion. This summary sets the agenda for the next phase of the discussion in which plans for improvement are developed jointly. However, the summary should also include the subordinate's strengths—those things that should be continued.

9. *Developing a plan for improvement.* Let subordinates lead with what they think is an adequate plan for improvement on the basis of the previous discussion and summary. It is much easier to prevent defensiveness if the supervisor reacts to and perhaps expands on the subordinate's plans for changing instead of making such suggestions directly. A problem-solving rather than blame-placing approach should be maintained. However, if subordinates cannot formulate good action plans, or seem to be unmotivated to do so, the supervisor can take a more directive approach at this point. It is critical that the interview end in a concrete plan for performance improvement or else no change is likely to occur.

10. *Closing the discussion.* Close the discussion with a view of the individual's future. However, this is relevant only in organizations where opportunities for promotion exist and for individuals who clearly have potential—unless, of course, the individual brings it up and wants to know. If the individual needs to be told what his or her evaluation is, this should be done at the very end of the interview if it cannot take place in a separate interview.

Summary

This article attempts to summarize what is known about the underlying causes of problems experienced with performance appraisal and to suggest some means for overcoming these. The central thrust has been to find means for dealing with the main barrier to effective appraisals—that is, avoidance by the supervisor and defensiveness from the subordinate. We have suggested a number of ways in which supervisors and subordinates might negotiate the difficult dilemma of discussing an evaluation of performance in a nonevaluative manner.

Selected Bibliography

A discussion of the many organizational and contextual factors affecting performance appraisal can be found in Morgan W. McCall and David L. DeVries's "Appraisal in Context: Clashing with Organizational Realities," presented in symposium "Performance Appraisal and Feedback: Fleas in the Ointment," David DeVries, Chair, *84th Annual Convention of the American Psychological Association,* Washington, D.C., September 5, 1976.

The section on performance appraisal goals draws extensively on discussions of this subject in Lyman W. Porter, Edward E. Lawler III, and Richard J. Hackman's *Behavior in Organizations* (McGraw-Hill, 1975).

An example of a performance appraisal system designed to deal with some of the dilemmas discussed in this article can be found in Michael Beer and Robert A. Ruh's "Employee

Growth through Performance Management," *Harvard Business Review*, July–August 1976.

The phenomenon of the "vanishing performance appraisal" was first discussed by Douglas T. Hall and Edward E. Lawler III in "Job Characteristics and Pressures and Organizational Integration of Professionals," *Administrative Science Quarterly*, Third Quarter 1970.

The effects of performance feedback on a person's self-esteem were discussed by Alvin Zander in "Research on Self-Esteem, Feedback and Threats to Self-Esteem," in A. Zander, ed., *Performance Appraisals: Effects on Employees and Their Performance* (Foundation for Research in Human Behavior, 1963).

The classic study of performance appraisal that first posited the importance of splitting evaluation from developmental interviews is Herbert H. Meyer, Emanuel Kay, and John R. P. French, Jr.'s "Split Roles in Performance Appraisal," *Harvard Business Review*, January–February 1965.

The critical-incident technique in which managers record incidents of effective or ineffective performance by subordinates as data for appraisals was first discussed by John C. Flanagan and Robert K. Burns in "The Employee Performance Record," *Harvard Business Review*, September–October 1955.

The idea that different types of individuals have different performance appraisal purposes was articulated by Norman R. F. Maier in "Three Types of Appraisal Interviews," *Personnel*, March–April 1958.

Problem-solving performance appraisal interviews that rely heavily on non-directive counseling were first discussed by Carl R. Rogers in "Releasing Expression," *Counseling and Psychotherapy* (Houghton Mifflin, 1942).

A number of ideas in this article about methods for improving the performance appraisal interviews were discussed by Herbert H. Meyer in "The Annual Performance Review Discussion—Making It Constructive" (University of South Florida, unpublished and undated paper).

Guidelines for giving and receiving feedback are cited in this article as important in guiding a constructive dialogue between boss and subordinate. This was discussed in more detail in John Anderson's "Giving and Receiving Feedback," in G. W. Dalton, P. R. Lawrence, and L. E. Greiner, Eds., *Organizational Change and Development* (Richard D. Irwin and Dorsey Press, 1970).

Reading 3–2

Designing the Innovating Organization*

Jay R. Galbraith

Innovation is in. New workable, marketable ideas are being sought and promoted these days as never before in the effort to restore U.S. leadership in technology, in productivity growth, and in the ability to compete in the world marketplace. Innovative methods for conserving energy and adapting to new energy sources are also in demand.

The popular press uses words like *revitalization* to capture the essence of the issue. The primary culprit of our undoing, up until now, has been management's short-run earnings focus. However, even some patient managers with long-term views are finding that they cannot buy innovation. They cannot exhort their operating organizations to be more innovative and creative. Patience, money, and a supportive leadership are not enough. It takes more than these things to achieve innovation.

It is my contention that innovation requires an organization specifically designed for that purpose—that is, such an organization's structure, processes, rewards, and people must be combined in a special way to create an innovating organization, one that is designed to do something for the first time. The point to be emphasized here is that the innovating organization's components are completely different from and often contrary to those of existing organizations, which are generally operating organizations. The latter are designed to efficiently process the millionth loan, produce the millionth automobile, or serve the millionth client. An organization that is designed to do something well for the millionth time is not good at doing something for the first time. Therefore, organizations that want to innovate or revitalize themselves need two organizations, an operating organization and an innovating organization. In addition, if the ideas produced by the innovating

*Reprinted by permission of the author.

organization are to be implemented by the operating organization, they need a transition process to transfer ideas from the innovating organization to the operating organization.

This article will describe the components of an organization geared to producing innovative ideas. Specifically, in the next section of this article, I describe a case history that illustrates the components required for successful innovation. Then I will explore the lessons to be learned from this case history by describing the role structure, the key processes, the reward systems, and the people practices that characterize an innovating organization.

The Innovating Process

Before I describe the typical process by which innovations occur in organizations, we must understand what we are discussing. What is innovation? How do we distinguish between invention and innovation? Invention is the creation of a new idea. Innovation is the process of applying a new idea to create a new process or product. Invention occurs more frequently than innovation. In addition, the kind of innovation in which we are interested here is the kind that becomes necessary to implement a new idea that is not consistent with the current concept of the organization's business. Many new ideas that are consistent with an organization's current business concept are routinely generated in some companies. Those are not our current concern; here we are concerned with implementing inventions that are good ideas but do not quite fit into the organization's current mold. Industry has a poor track record with this type of innovation. Most major technological changes come from outside an industry. The mechanical typewriter manufacturers did not introduce the electric typewriter; the electric typewriter people did not invent the electronic typewriter; vacuum tube companies did not introduce the transistor, and so on. Our objective is to describe an organization that will increase the odds that such nonroutine innovations can be made. The following case history of a nonroutine innovation presents a number of lessons that illustrate how we can design an innovating organization.

The Case History

The organization in question is a venture that was started in the early 70s. While working for one of our fairly innovative electronics firms, a group of engineers developed a new electronics product. However, they were in a division that did not have the charter for their product. The ensuing political battle caused the engineers to leave and form their own company. They successfully found venture capital and introduced their new product. Initial acceptance was good, and within several years their company was growing rapidly and had become the industry leader.

However, in the early 1970s Intel invented the microprocessor, and by the mid-to late 70s, this innovation had spread through the electronics industries. Manufacturers of previously "dumb" products now had the capability of incorporating intelligence into their product lines. A competitor who understood computers and software introduced just such a product into our new venture firm's market, and it met with high acceptance. The firm's president responded by hiring someone who knew something about microcomputers and some software people and instructing the engineering department to respond to the need for a competing product.

The president spent most of his time raising capital to finance the venture's growth. But when he suddenly realized that the engineers had not made much progress, he instructed them to get a product out quickly. They did, but it was a half-hearted effort. The new product incorporated a microprocessor but was less than the second-generation product that was called for.

Even though the president developed markets in Europe and Singapore, he noticed that the competitor continued to grow faster than his company and had started to steal a share of his company's market. When the competitor became the industry leader, the president decided to take charge of the product development effort. However, he found that the hardware proponents and software proponents in the engineering department were locked in a political battle. Each group felt that its "magic" was the more powerful. Unfortunately, the lead engineer (who was a cofounder of the firm) was a hardware proponent, and the hardware establishment prevailed. However, they then clashed head-on with the marketing department, which agreed with the software proponents. The conflict resulted in studies and presentations, but no new product. So here was a young, small (1,200 people) entrepreneurial firm that could not innovate even though the president wanted innovation and provided resources to produce it. The lesson is that more was needed.

As the president became more deeply involved in the problem, he received a call from his New England sales manager, who wanted him to meet a field engineer who had modified the company's product and programmed it in a way that met customer demands. The sales manager suggested, "We may have something here."

Indeed, the president was impressed with what he saw. When the engineer had wanted to use the company's product to track his own inventory, he wrote to company headquarters for programming instructions. The response had been: It's against company policy to send instructional materials to field engineers. Undaunted, the engineer bought a home computer and taught himself to program. He then modified the product in the field and programmed it to solve his problem. When the sales manager happened to see what was done, he recognized its significance and immediately called the president.

The field engineer accompanied the president back to headquarters and presented his work to the engineers who had been working on the second-generation product for so long. They brushed off his efforts as idiosyncratic, and the field engineer was thanked and returned to the field.

A couple of weeks later the sales manager called the president again. He said that the company would lose this talented guy if something wasn't done. Besides, he thought that the field engineer, not engineering, was right. While he was considering what to do with this ingenious engineer, who on his own had produced more than the entire engineering department, the president received a request from the European sales manager to have the engineer assigned to him.

The European sales manager had heard about the field engineer when he visited headquarters, and had sought him out and listened to his story. The sales manager knew that a French bank wanted the type of application that the field engineer had created for himself; a successful application would be worth an order for several hundred machines. The president gave the go-ahead and sent the field engineer to Europe. The engineering department persisted in their view that the program wouldn't work. Three months later, the field engineer successfully developed the application, and the bank signed the order.

When the field engineer returned, the president assigned him to a trusted marketing manager who was told to protect him and get a product out. The engineers were told to support the manager and reluctantly did so. Soon they created some applications software and a printed circuit board that could easily be installed in all existing machines in the field. The addition of this board and the software temporarily saved the company and made its current product slightly superior to that of the competitor.

Elated, the president congratulated the young field engineer and gave him a good staff position working on special assignments to develop software. Then problems arose. When the president tried to get the personnel department to give the engineer a special cash award, they were reluctant. "After all," they said, "other people worked on the effort, too. It will set a precedent." And so it went. The finance department wanted to withhold $500 from the engineer's pay because he had received a $1,000 advance for his European trip, but had turned in vouchers for only $500.

The engineer didn't help himself very much either; he was hard to get along with and refused to accept supervision from anyone except the European sales manager. When the president arranged to have him permanently transferred to Europe on three occasions, the engineer changed his mind about going at the last minute. The president is still wondering what to do with him.

There are a number of lessons about the needs of an innovative organization in this not uncommon story. The next section elaborates on these lessons.

The Innovating Organization

Before we can draw upon the case history's lessons, it is important to note that the basic components of the innovating organization are no different from those of an operating organization. That is, both include a task, a structure, processes, reward systems, and people, as shown in Exhibit 1. Exhibit 2 compares the design parameters of the operating organization's components with those of the innovating organization's components.

This figure shows that each component must fit with each of the other components and with the task. A basic premise of this article is that the task of the innovating organization is fundamentally different from that of the operating organization. The

Exhibit 1
Organization Design Components

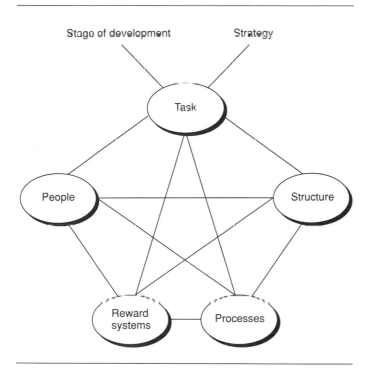

innovating task is more uncertain and risky, takes place over longer time periods, assumes that failure in the early stages may be desirable, and so on. Therefore, the organization that performs the innovative task should also be different. Obviously, a firm that wishes to innovate needs both an operating organization and an innovating organization. Let's look at the latter.

Structure of the Innovating Organization

The structure of the innovating organization encompasses these elements: (1) people to fill three vital roles—idea generators, sponsors, and orchestrators; (2) differentiation, a process that differentiates or separates the innovating organization's activities from those of the operating organization; and (3) "reservations," the means by which the separation occurs—and this may be accomplished physically, financially, or organizationally.

The part that each of these elements plays in the commercialization of a new idea can be illustrated by referring to the case history.

Exhibit 2
Comparison of Components of Operating and Innovating Organizations

	Operating Organization	*Innovating Organization*

Structure	Division of labor
	Departmentalization
	Span of control
	Distribution of power
		Roles:
		  Orchestrator
		  Sponsor
		  Idea generator (champion)
		Differentiation
		Reservations

Processes	Providing information and communication Planning and budgeting Measuring performance Linking departments	Planning/funding Getting ideas Blending ideas Transitioning Managing programs
Reward systems	Compensation Promotion Leader style Job design	Opportunity/autonomy Promotion/recognition Special compensation
People	Selection/recruitment Promotion/transfer Training/development	Selection/self-selection Training/development

Roles

Like any organized phenomenon, innovation is brought about through the efforts of people who interact in a combination of roles. Innovation is not an individual phenomenon. People who must interact to produce a commercial product—that is, to innovate in the sense we are discussing—play their roles as follows:

- Every innovation starts with an *idea generator* or idea champion. In the above example, the field engineer was the person who generated the new idea—that is, the inventor, the entrepreneur, or risk taker on whom much of our attention has been focused. The case history showed that an idea champion is needed at each stage of an idea's or an invention's development into an innovation. That is, at each stage there must be a dedicated, full-time individual whose success or failure depends on developing the idea. The idea generator is usually a low-level person who experiences a problem and develops a new response to it. The lesson here is that many ideas originate down where "the rubber meets the road." The low status and authority level of the idea generator creates a need for someone to play the next role.

- Every idea needs at least one *sponsor* to promote it. To carry an idea through to implementation, someone has to discover it and fund the increasingly disruptive and expensive development and testing efforts that shape it. Thus idea generators need to find sponsors for their ideas so they can perfect them. In our example, the New England sales manager, the European sales manager, and finally the marketing manager all sponsored the field engineer's idea. Thus one of the sponsor's functions is to lend his or her authority and resources to an idea to carry the idea closer to commercialization.

The sponsor must also recognize the business significance of an idea. In any organization, there are hundreds of ideas being promoted at any one time. The sponsor must select from among these ideas those that might become marketable. Thus it is best that sponsors be generalists. (However, that is not always the case, as our case history illustrates.)

Sponsors are usually middle managers who may be anywhere in the organization and who usually work for both the operating and the innovating organization. Some sponsors run divisions or departments. They must be able to balance the operating and innovating needs of their business or function. On the other hand, when the firm can afford the creation of venture groups, new-product development departments, and the like, sponsors may work full time for the innovating organization. In the case history, the two sales managers spontaneously became sponsors, and the marketing manager was formally designated as a sponsor by the president. The point here is that by formally designating the role or recognizing it, funding it with monies earmarked for innovation, creating innovating incentives, and developing and selecting sponsorship skills, the organization can improve its odds of coming up with successful innovations. Not much attention has been given to sponsors, but they need equal attention because innovation will not occur unless there are people in the company who will fill all three roles.

■ The third role illustrated in the case history is that of the *orchestrator*. The president played this role. An orchestrator is necessary because new ideas are never neutral. Innovative ideas are destructive; they destroy investments in capital equipment and people's careers. The management of ideas is a political process. The problem is that the political struggle is biased toward those in the establishment who have authority and control of resources. The orchestrator must balance the power to give the new idea of a chance to be tested in the face of a negative establishment. The orchestrator must protect idea people, promote the opportunity to try out new ideas, and back those whose ideas prove effective. This person must legitimize the whole process. That is what the president did with the field engineer; before he became involved, the hardware establishment had prevailed. Without an orchestrator, there can be no innovation.

To play their roles successfully, orchestrators use the processes and rewards to be described in the following sections. That is, a person orchestrates by funding innovating activities and creating incentives for middle managers to sponsor innovating ideas. Orchestrators are the organization's top managers, and they must design the innovating organization.

The typical operating role structure of a divisionalized firm is shown in Exhibit 3. The hierarchy is one of the operating functions reporting to division general managers who are, in turn, grouped under group executives. The group executives report to the chief executive officer (CEO). Some of these people play roles in both the operating and the innovating organization.

Exhibit 3
Typical Operating Structure of Divisionalized Firm

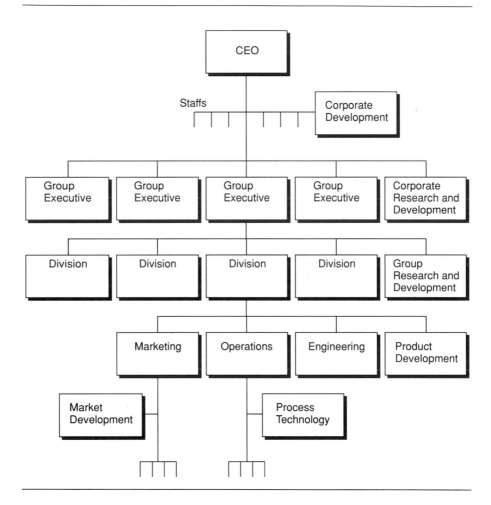

The innovating organization's role structure is shown in Exhibit 4. The chief executive and a group executive function as orchestrators. Division managers are the sponsors who work in both the operating and the innovating organizations. In addition, several reservations are created in which managers of research and development (R&D), corporate development, product development, market development, and new-process technology function as full-time sponsors. These reservations allow the separation of innovating activity from the operating activity. This separation is an organizing choice called differentiation. It is described next.

Exhibit 4
An Innovating Role Structure (Differentiation)

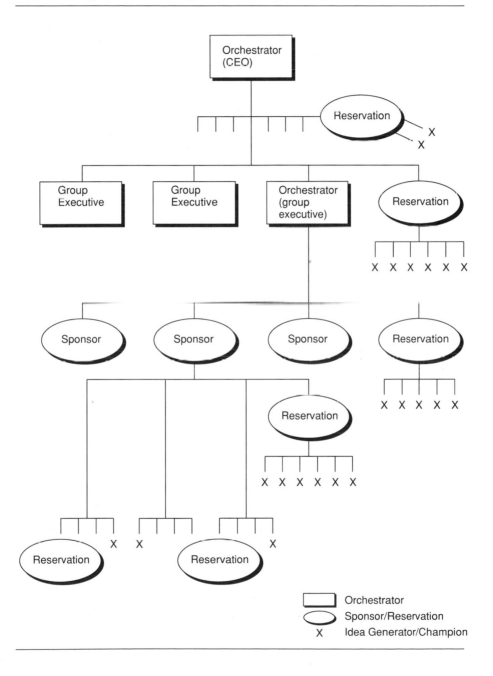

Differentiation

In the case history, we saw that the innovative idea perfected at a remote site was relatively advanced before it was discovered by management. The lesson to be learned from this is that if one wants to stimulate new ideas, the odds are better if early efforts to perfect and test new "crazy" ideas are differentiated—that is, separated—from the functions of the operating organization. Such differentiation occurs when an effort is separated physically, financially, and/or organizationally from the day-to-day activities that are likely to disrupt it. If the field engineer had worked within the engineering department or at company headquarters, his idea probably would have been snuffed out prematurely.

Another kind of differentiation can be accomplished by freeing initial idea tests from staff controls designed for the operating organization. The effect of too much control is illustrated by one company in which a decision on whether to buy an oscilloscope took about 15 to 30 minutes (with a shout across the room) before the company was acquired by a larger organization. After the acquisition, that same type of decision took 12 to 18 months because the purchase required a capital appropriation request. Controls based on operating logic reduce the innovating organization's ability to rapidly, cheaply, and frequently test and modify new ideas. Thus, the more differentiated an initial effort is, the greater the likelihood of innovation.

The problem with differentiation, however, is that it decreases the likelihood that a new proven ideal will be transferred back to the operating organization. Herein lies the differentiation/transfer dilemma: The more differentiated the effort, the greater the likelihood of producing a new business idea, but the less likelihood of transferring the new idea into the operating organization for implementation. The dilemma occurs only when the organization needs both invention and transfer. That is, some organizations may not need to transfer new ideas to the operating organization. For example, when Exxon started its information systems business, there was no intention to have the petroleum company run this area of business. Exxon innovators had to grow their own operating organizations; therefore, they could maximize differentiation in the early phases. Alternatively, when Intel started work on the 64K RAM (the next generation of semiconductor memories, this random-access memory holds roughly 64,000 bits of information), the effort was consistent with their current business and the transfer into fabrication and sales was critical. Therefore, the development effort was only minimally separated from the operating division that was producing the 16K RAM. The problem becomes particularly difficult when a new product or process differs from current ones, but must be implemented through the current manufacturing and sales organizations. The greater the need for invention and the greater the difference between the new idea and the existing business concept, the greater the degree of differentiation required to perfect the idea. The only way to accomplish both invention and transfer is to proceed stagewise. That is, differentiate in the early phases and then start the transition process before development is completed so that only a little differentiation is left when the product is ready for implementation. The transition process is described below in the section on key processes.

In summary, invention occurs best when initial efforts are separated from the operating organization and its controls—because innovating and operating are fundamentally opposing logics. This kind of separation allows both to be performed simultaneously and prevents the establishment from prematurely snuffing out a new idea. The less the dominant culture of the organization supports innovation, the greater is the need for separation. Often this separation occurs naturally as in the case history, or clandestinely as in "bootlegging." If a firm wants to foster innovation, it can create reservations where innovating activity can occur as a matter of course. Let us now turn to this last structural parameter.

Reservations

Reservations are organizational units, such as R&D groups, that are totally devoted to creating new ideas for future business. The intention is to reproduce a garagelike atmosphere where people can rapidly and frequently test their ideas. Reservations are havens for "safe learning." When innovating, one wants to maximize early failure to promote learning. On reservations that are separated from operations, this cheap, rapid screening can take place.

Reservations permit differentiation to occur by housing people who work solely for the innovating organization and by having a reservation manager who works full time as a sponsor. They may be located within divisions and/or at corporate headquarters to permit various degrees of differentiation.

Reservations can be internal or external. Internal reservations may include some staff and research groups, product and process development labs, and groups that are devoted to market development, new ventures, and/or corporate development. They are organizational homes where idea generators can contribute without becoming managers. Originally, this was the purpose of staff groups, but staff groups now frequently assume control responsibilities or are narrow specialists who contribute to the current business idea. Because such internal groups can be expensive, outside reservations like universities, consulting firms, and advertising agencies are often used to tap nonmanagerial idea generators.

Reservations can be permanent or temporary. The internal reservations described above, such as R&D units, are reasonably permanent entities. Others can be temporary. Members of the operating organization may be relieved of operating duties to develop a new program, a new process, or a new product. When developed, they take the idea into the operating organization and resume their operating responsibilities. But for a period of time they are differentiated from operating functions to varying degrees in order to innovate, fail, learn, and ultimately perfect a new idea.

Collectively the roles of orchestrators, sponsors, and idea generators working with and on reservations constitute the structure of the innovating organization. Some of the people, such as sponsors and orchestrators, play roles in both organizations; reservation managers and idea generators work only for the innovating organization. Virtually everyone in the organization can be an idea generator, and all middle managers are potential sponsors. However not all choose to play these roles. People vary considerably in their innovating skills. By recognizing the need for these roles, developing people to fill them, giving them opportunity to use their skills in key processes, and rewarding innovating accomplishments, the organization can do considerably better than just allowing a spontaneous process to work. Several key processes are part and parcel of this innovating organizational structure. These are described in the next section.

Key Processes

In our case history, the idea generator and the first two sponsors found each other through happenstance. The odds of such propitious matchups can be significantly improved through the explicit design of processes that help sponsors and idea generators find each other. The chances of successful matchups can be improved by such funding, getting ideas, and blending ideas. In addition, the processes of transitioning and program management move ideas from reservations into operations. Each of these is described below.

Funding

A key process that increases our ability to innovate is a funding process that is explicitly earmarked for the innovating organization. A leader in this field is Texas Instruments (TI), a company that budgets and allocates funds for both operating and innovating. In essence the orchestrators make the short-run/long-run trade-off at this point. They then orchestrate by choosing where to place the innovating funds—with division sponsors or corporate reservations. The funding process is a key tool for orchestration.

Another lesson to be learned from the case history is that it frequently takes more than one sponsor to launch a new idea. The field engineer's idea would never have been brought to management's attention without the New England sales manager. It would never have been tested in the market without the European sales manager. Multiple sponsors keep fragile ideas alive. If engineering had been the only available sponsor for technical ideas, there would have been no innovation.

Some organizations purposely create a multiple sponsoring system and make it legitimate for an idea generator to go to any sponsor who has funding for new ideas. Multiple sponsors duplicate the market system of multiple bankers for entrepreneurs. At Minnesota Mining & Manufacturing (3M), for example, an idea generator can go to his or her division sponsor for funding. If refused, the idea generator can then go to any other division sponsor or even to corporate R&D. If the idea is outside current business lines, the idea generator can go to the new-ventures group for support. If the idea is rejected by all possible sponsors, it probably isn't a very good idea. However, the idea is kept alive and given several opportunities to be tested. Multiple sponsors keep fragile young ideas alive.

Getting Ideas

The process of getting ideas occurs by happenstance as it did in the case history. The premise of this section is that the odds of matchups between idea generators and sponsors can be improved by organization design. First, the natural process can be improved by network-building actions such as multidivision or multireservation careers or companywide seminars and conferences. All of these practices plus a common physical location facilitate matching at 3M.

The matching process is formalized at TI, where there is an elaborate planning process called the objectives, strategies, and tactics (or OST) system, which is an annual harvest of new ideas. Innovating funds are distributed to managers of objectives (sponsors) who fund projects based on ideas formulated by idea generators, and these then become tactical action programs. Ideas that are not funded go into a creative backlog to be tapped throughout the year. Whether formal, as at TI, or informal, as at 3M, it is noteworthy that these are known systems for matching ideas with sponsors.

Ideas can also be acquired by aggressive sponsors. Sponsors sit at the crossroads of many ideas and often arrive at a better idea by putting two or more together. They can then pursue an idea generator to champion it. Good sponsors know where the proven idea people are located and how to attract such people to come to perfect an idea on their reservation. Sponsors can go inside or outside the organization to pursue these idea people.

And finally, formal events for matching purposes can be scheduled. At 3M, for example, there's an annual fair at which idea generators can set up booths to be viewed by shopping sponsors. Exxon Enterprises held a "shake the tree" event at which idea people could throw out ideas to be pursued by attending sponsors. The variations of such events are endless. The point is that by devoting time to ideas and making innovation legitimate, the odds that sponsors will find new ideas are increased.

Blending Ideas

An important lesson to be derived from our scenario is that it is no accident that a field engineer produced the new product idea. Why? Because the field engineer spent all day working on customer problems and also knew the technology. Therefore, one person knew the need and the means by which to satisfy that need. (An added plus: The field engineer had a personal need to design the appropriate technology.) The premise here is that innovation is more likely to occur when knowledge of technologies and user requirements are combined in the minds of as few people as possible—preferably in that of one person.

The question of whether innovations need stimulated or means stimulated is debatable. Do you start with the disease and look for a cure, or start with a cure and find a disease for it? Research indicates that two thirds of innovations are need stimulated. But this argument misses the point. As shown in Exhibit 5A the debate

Exhibit 5
Linear Sequential Coupling Compared with Simultaneous Coupling of Knowledge

A. Linear Sequential Coupling

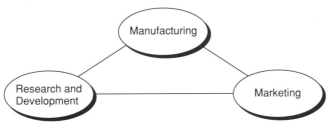

B. Simultaneous Coupling

is over whether use or means drives the downstream efforts. This thinking is linear and sequential. Instead, the model suggested here is shown in Exhibit 5B. That is, for innovation to occur, knowledge of all key components is simultaneously coupled. And the best way to maximize communication among the components is to have the communication occur intrapersonally—that is, within one person's mind. If this is impossible, then as few people as possible should have to communicate or interact. The point is that innovative ideas occur when knowledge of the essential specialties is coupled in as few heads as possible. To encourage such coupling, the organization can grow or select individuals with the essential skills, or it can encourage interaction between those with meshing skills. These practices will be discussed in a "People" section.

A variety of processes are employed by organizations to match knowledge of need and of means. At IBM they place marketing people directly in the R&D labs where they can readily interpret the market requirement documents for researchers. People are rotated through this unit, and a network is created. Wang holds an annual users' conference at which customers and product designers interact and discuss the use of Wang products. Lanier insists that all top managers, including R&D

Exhibit 6
Transitioning Ideas by Stages

| | Stages | | | |
Choices	I	II	Nth	Implementation
Sponsor	Corporate	Corporate	. . .	Division
Champion	Corporate	Corporate	. . .	Division
Staffing	Corporate	Corporate-division	. . .	Division
Location	Corporate	Corporate	. . .	Division
Funding	Corporate	Corporate	. . .	Division
Autonomy	Complete	Complete	. . .	Minimal

management, spend one day a month selling in the field. It is reported that British scientists made remarkable progress on developing radar after actually flying missions with the Royal Air Force. In all these cases there is an explicit matching of the use and the user with knowledge of a technology to meet the use. Again these processes are explicitly designed to get a user orientation among the idea generators and sponsors. They increase the likelihood that inventions will be innovations. The more complete a new idea or invention is at its inception, the greater the likelihood of its being transferred into the operating organization.

Transitioning

Perhaps the most crucial process in getting an innovation product to market is the transitioning of an idea from a reservation to an operating organization for implementation. This process occurs in stages, as illustrated in the case history. First, the idea was formulated in the field before management knew about it. Then it was tested with a customer, the French bank. And finally, at the third stage, development and full-scale implementation took place. In other cases, several additional stages of testing and scale-up may be necessary. In any case, transitioning should be planned in such stages. At each stage the orchestrator has several choices that balance the need for further invention with the need for transfer. The choices and typical stages of idea development are shown in Exhibit 6.

At each stage these choices face the orchestrator: Who will be the sponsor? Who will be the champion? Where can staff be secured for the effort? At what physical location will work be performed? Who will fund the effort? How much autonomy should the effort have, or how differentiated should it be? For example, at the initial new-idea formulation stage the sponsor could be the corporate ventures group with the champion working on the corporate reservation. The effort could be staffed with other corporate reservation types and funded at the corporate level. The activity would be fully separate and autonomous. If the results were positive, the process could proceed to the next stage. If the idea needed further development, some division people could be brought in to round out the needed specialties. If the data

were still positive after the second stage, then the effort could be transferred physically to the division, but the champion, sponsor, and funding might remain at the
corporate level. In this manner, by orchestrating through choices of sponsor, champion, staff, location, funding, and autonomy, the orchestrator balances the need
for innovation and protection with the need for testing against reality and transfer.

The above is an all too brief outline of the transition process; entire books have
been written on the subject of technology transfer. The goal here is to highlight
the stagewise nature of the process and the decisions to be made by the orchestrator
at each stage. The process is crucial because it is the link between the two organizations. Thus to consistently innovate, the firm needs an innovating organization,
an operating organization, and a process for transitioning ideas from the former to
the latter.

Managing Programs

Program management is necessary to implement new products and processes within
divisions. At this stage of the process, the idea generator usually hands the idea
off to a product/project/program manager. The product or process is then implemented across the functional organization within the division. The systems and
organizational processes for managing projects have been discussed elsewhere
and will not be discussed here. The point is that a program management process
and skill is needed.

In summary, several key processes—that is, funding, getting ideas, blending
ideas, transitioning, and managing programs—are basic components of the innovating structure. Even though many of these occur naturally in all organizations,
our implicit hypothesis is that the odds for successful innovation can be increased
by explicitly designing these processes and by earmarking corporate resources for
them. Hundreds of people in organizations choose to innovate voluntarily, as did
the field engineer in the case history. However, if there were a reward system for
people like these, more would choose to innovate, and more would choose to stay
in the organization to do their innovating. The reward system is the next component
to be described.

Reward System

The innovating organization, like the operating organization, needs an incentive
system to motivate innovating behavior. Because the task of innovating is different
from that of operating, the innovating organization needs a different reward system.
The innovating task is riskier, more difficult, and takes place over longer time
frames. These factors call for some adjustment of the operating organization's
reward system, the amount of adjustment depending on how innovative the operating
organization is and how attractive outside alternatives are.

The functions of the reward system are threefold: First, the rewards must attract
idea people to the company and the reservations and retain them. Because various
firms have different attraction and retention problems, their reward systems must

vary. Second, the rewards provide motivation for the extra effort needed to innovate. After 19 failures, for example, something has to motivate the idea generator to make the 20th attempt. And, finally, successful performance deserves a reward. These rewards are primarily for idea generators. However, a reward measurement system for sponsors is equally important. Various reward systems will be discussed in the next sections.

Rewards for Idea Generators

Reward systems mix several types of internal motivators, such as the opportunity to pursue one's ideas, promotions, recognition, systems, and special compensation. First, people can be attracted and motivated intrinsically by simply giving them the opportunity and autonomy to pursue their own ideas. A reservation can provide such opportunity and autonomy. Idea people—who are internally driven—such as the field engineer in our story can come to a reservation, pursue their own ideas, and be guided and evaluated by a reservation manager. This is a reward in itself, albeit a minimal reward. If that minimal level attracts and motivates idea people, the innovating organization need go no further in creating a separate reward system.

However, if necessary, motivational leverage can be obtained by promotion and recognition for innovating performance. The dual ladder—that is, a system whereby an individual contributor can be promoted and given increased salary without taking on managerial responsibilities—is the best example of such a system. At 3M a contributor can rise in both status and salary to the equivalent of a group executive without becoming a manager. The dual ladder has always existed in R&D, but it is now being extended to some other functions as well.

Some firms grant special recognition for high career performance. IBM has its IBM fellows program in which the person selected as a fellow can work on projects of his or her own choosing for five years. At 3M, there is the Carlton Award, which is described as an internal Nobel Prize. Such promotion and recognition systems reward innovation and help create an innovating culture.

When greater motivation is needed, and/or the organization wants to signal the importance of innovation, special compensation is added to the aforementioned systems. Different special compensation systems will be discussed in the order of increasing motivational impact and of increasing dysfunctional ripple effects. The implication is that the firm should use special compensation only to the degree that the need for attraction and for motivation dictates.

Some companies reward successful idea generators with one-time cash awards. For example, International Harvester's share of the combine market jumped from 12 percent to 17 percent because of the introduction of the axial flow combine. The scientist whose six patents contributed to the product development was given $10,000. If the product continues to succeed, he may be given another award. IBM uses the "Chairman's Outstanding Contribution Award." The current program manager on the 4300 series was given a $5,000 award for her breakthrough in coding. These awards are made after the idea is successful and primarily serve to reward achievement rather than to attract innovators and provide incentive for future efforts.

Programs that give a "percentage of the take" to the idea generator and early team members provide even stronger motivation. Toy and game companies give a royalty to inventors—both internal and external—of toys and games they produce. Apple Computer claims to give royalties to employees who write software programs that will run on Apple equipment. A chemical company created a pool by putting aside 4 percent of the first five years' earnings from a new business venture, which was to be distributed to the initial venture team. Other companies create pools from percentages that range from 2 to 20 percent of cost savings created by process innovations. In any case, a predetermined contract is created to motivate the idea generator and those who join a risky effort at an early stage.

The most controversial efforts to date are attempts to duplicate free-market rewards within the firm. For example, a couple of years ago, ITT bought a small company named Qume that made high-speed printers. The founder became a millionaire from the sale; he had to quit his previous employer to found the venture capital effort to start Qume. If ITT can make an outsider a millionaire, why not give the same chance to entrepreneurial insiders? Many people advocate such a system but have not found an appropriate formula to implement the idea. For example, one firm created five-year milestones for a venture, the accomplishment of which would result in a cash award of $6 million to the idea generator. However, the business climate changed after two years, and the idea generator, not surprisingly, tried to make the plan work rather than adapt to the new, unforeseen reality.

Another scheme is to give the generator and the initial team some phantom stock, which gets evaluated at sale time in the same way that any acquisition would be evaluated. This process duplicates the free-market process and gives internal people the same venture capital opportunities and risks as they would have on the outside.

The special compensation programs produce motivation and dysfunctions. People who contribute at later stages frequently feel like second-class citizens. Also, any program that discriminates will create perceptions of unfair treatment and possible fallout in the operating organization. If the benefits are judged to be worth the effort, however, care should be taken to manage the fallout.

Rewards for Sponsors

The case history also demonstrates that sponsors need incentives, too. In the example, because they were being beaten in the market, the salespeople had an incentive to adopt a new product. The point is that sponsors will sponsor ideas, but these may not be innovating ideas unless there's something in it for them. The orchestrator's task is to create and communicate those incentives.

Sponsor incentives take many forms. At 3M, division managers have a bonus goal that is reached if 25 percent of their revenue comes from products introduced within the previous five years. When the percentage falls below the goal, and the bonus is threatened, these sponsors become amazingly receptive to new product ideas. The transfer process becomes much easier as a result. Sales growth, revenue increase, numbers of new products, and so on, may be the bases for incentives that motivate sponsors.

Another controversy can arise if the idea generators receive phantom stock. Should the sponsors who supervise these idea people receive phantom stock, too? Some banks have created subsidiaries so that sponsors can receive stock in the new venture. To the degree that sponsors contribute to idea development, they will need to be given such stock options, too.

Thus, the innovating organization needs reward systems for both idea generators and sponsors. It should start with a simple reward system and move to more motivating, more complex, and possibly more upsetting types of rewards only if and when attraction and motivation problems call for them.

People

The final policy area to be considered involves people practices. The assumption is that some people who are better at innovating are not necessarily good at operating. Therefore, the ability of the innovating organization to generate new business ideas can be increased by systematically developing and selecting those people who are better at innovating than others. But first the desirable attributes must be identified. These characteristics that identify likely idea generators and sponsors are spelled out in the following sections.

Attributes of Idea Generators

The field engineer in our case history is the stereotype of the inventor. He is not mainstream. He's hard to get along with, and he wasn't afraid to break company policy to perfect his idea. Such people have strong egos that allow them to persist and swim upstream. They generally are not the type of people who get along well in an organization. However, if an organization has reservations, innovating funds, and dual ladders, these people can be attracted and retained.

The psychological attributes of successful entrepreneurs include great need to achieve and to take risks. But, to translate that need into innovation, several other attributes are needed. First, prospective innovators have an irreverence for the status quo. They often come from outcast groups or are newcomers to the company; they are less satisfied with the way things are and have less to lose if there's a change. Successful innovators also need "previous programming in the industry"—that is, an in-depth knowledge of the industry gained through either experience or formal education. Hence, the innovator need industry knowledge, but not the religion.

Previous start-up experience is also associated with successful business ventures, as are people who come from incubator firms (for example high-technology companies) and areas (such as Boston and the Silicon Valley) that are noted for creativity.

The amount of organizational effort needed to select these people varies with the ability to attract them to the organization in the first place. If idea people are attracted through reputation, then by funding reservations and employing idea-getting processes, idea people will, in effect, select themselves—they will want to work with the organization—and over time their presence will reinforce the organization's reputation for idea generation. If the firm has no reputation for innovation, then idea people must be sought out or external reservations established to encourage initial idea generation. One firm made extensive use of outside recruiting to accomplish such a goal. A sponsor would develop an idea and then attend annual conferences of key specialists to determine who was most skilled in the area of interest; he or she would then interview appropriate candidates and offer the opportunity to develop the venture to those with entrepreneurial interests.

Another key attribute of successful business innovators is varied experience, which creates the coupling of a knowledge of means and of use in a single individual's mind. It is the generalist, not the specialist, who creates an idea that differs from the firm's current business line. Specialists are inventors; generalists are innovators. These people can be selected or developed. One ceramics engineering firm selects the best and the brightest graduates from the ceramics engineering schools and places them in central engineering to learn the firm's overall system. They are then assigned to field engineering where they spend three to five years with customers and their problems and then they return to central engineering product design. Only then do they design products for those customers. This type of internal coupling can be created by role rotation. Some aerospace firms rotate engineers through manufacturing liaison.

People who have the characteristics that make them successful innovators can be retained, however, only if there are reservations for them and sponsors to guide them.

Attributes of Sponsors and Reservation Managers

The innovating organization must also attract, develop, train, and retain people to manage the idea development process. Because certain types of people and management skills are better suited to managing ideas than others, likely prospects for such positions should have a management style that enables them to handle idea people, as well as early experience in innovating, the capability to generate ideas of their own, the skills to put deals together, and generalist business skills.

One of the key skills necessary for operating an innovating organization is the skill to manage and supervise the kind of person who is likely to be an idea generator and champion—that is, people who, among other characteristics, do not take very well to being supervised. Idea generators and champions have a great deal of ownership in their ideas. They gain their satisfaction by having "done it their way." The intrinsic satisfaction comes from the ownership and autonomy. However, idea people also need help, advice, and sounding boards. The successful sponsor learns how to manage these people in the same way that a producer or publisher learns to handle the egos of their stars and writers. This style was best described by a successful sponsor.

> It's a lot like teaching your kids to ride a bike. You're there. You walk along behind. If the kid takes off, he or she never knows that they could have been helped. If they stagger a little, you lend a helping hand, undetected preferably. If they fall, you catch them. If they do something stupid, you take the bike away until they're ready.

This style is quite different from the hands-on, directive style of managers in an operating organization. Of course, the best way to learn this style is to have been managed by it and seen it practiced in an innovating organization. Therefore, experience in an innovating organization is essential.

More than the idea generators, the sponsors need to understand the logic of innovation and to have experienced the management of innovation. Its managers need to have an intuitive feel for the task and its nuances. Managers whose only experience is in operations will not have developed the managerial style, understanding, and intuitive feel that is necessary to manage innovations because the logic of operations is counterintuitive in comparison with the logic of innovations. This means that some idea generators and champions who have experienced innovation should become managers as well as individual contributors. For example, the president in our case history was the inventor of the first-generation product and therefore understood the long, agonizing process of developing a business idea. It is also rare to find an R&D manager who hasn't come through the R&D ranks.

The best idea sponsors and idea reservation managers, therefore, are people who have experienced innovation early in their careers and are comfortable with it. They will have been exposed to risk, uncertainty, parallel experiments, repeated failures that led to learning, coupling rather than assembly-line thinking, long time frames, and personal control systems based on people and ideas, not numbers and budget variances. Sponsors and reservation managers can be developed or recruited from the outside.

Sponsors and reservation managers need to be idea generators themselves. Ideas tend to come from two sources. The first is at low levels of the organization where the problem gap is experienced. The idea generator who offers a solution is the one who experienced the problem and goes to a sponsor for testing and development. One problem with these ideas is that they may offer only partial solutions because they come from specialists whose views can be parochial and local. But sponsors are at the crossroads of many ideas. They may get a broader vision of the emerging situation as a result. These idea sponsors can themselves generate an idea that is suitable for the organization's business, or they can blend several partial ideas into a business-adaptable idea. Sponsors and reservation managers who are at the crossroads of idea flow are an important secondary source of new ideas. Therefore, they should be selected and trained for their ability to generate new ideas.

Another skill that sponsors and especially reservation managers need is the ability to make deals and broker ideas. Once an idea has emerged, a reservation manager may have to argue for the release of key people, space, resources, charters, for production time, or a customer contact. These deals all require someone who is adept at persuasion. In that sense, handling them is no different than project or product management roles. People do vary in their ability to make deals and to bargain, and those who are particularly adept should be selected for these roles. However, those who have other idea management skills may well be able to be trained in negotiating and bargaining.

And, finally, sponsors and reservation managers should be generalists with general business skills. Again, the ability to recognize a business idea and to shape

---

Exhibit 7
An Innovating Organization's Design Components

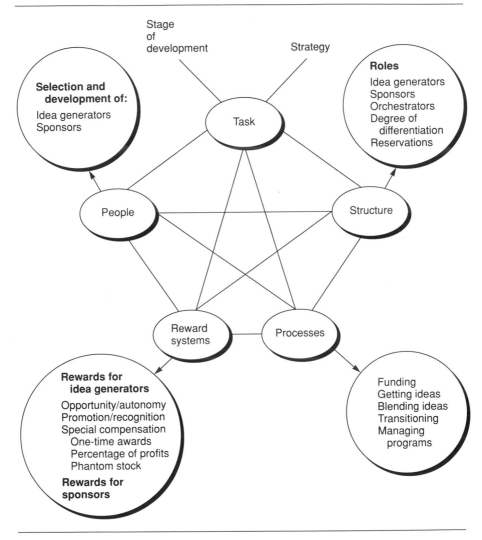

partial ideas into business ideas is needed. Sponsors and reservation managers must coach idea generators in specialties in which the idea generator is not schooled. Most successful research managers are those with business skills who can see the business significance in the good ideas that come from scientists.

In summary, the sponsors and reservation managers who manage the idea development process must be recruited, selected, and developed. The skills that these people need relate to their style, experience, idea-generating ability, deal-making ability, and generalist business acumen. People with these skills can either be selected or developed.

Thus some of the attributes of successful idea generators and idea sponsors can be identified. In creating the innovating organization, people with these attributes can be recruited, selected, and/or developed. In so doing, the organization improves its odds at generating and developing new business ideas.

Summary

The innovating organization described is one that recognizes and formalizes the roles, processes, rewards, and people practices that naturally lead to innovations. The point we have emphasized throughout this article is that the organization that purposely designs these roles and processes is more likely to generate innovations than in an organization that doesn't plan for this function. Such a purposely designed organization is needed to overcome the obstacles to innovation. Because innovation is destructive to many established groups, it will be resisted. Innovation is contrary to operations and will be ignored. These and other obstacles are more likely to be overcome if the organization is designed specifically to innovate.

Managers have tried to overcome these obstacles by creating venture groups, by hiring some entrepreneurs, by creating "breakthrough funds," or by offering special incentives. These are good policies but by themselves will not accomplish the goal. Exhibit 1 conveyed the message that a consistent set of policies concerning structure, process, rewards, and people are needed. The innovating organization is illustrated in Exhibit 7. It is the combination of ideal people, reservations in which they can operate, sponsors to supervise them, funding for their ideas, and rewards for their success that increase the odds in favor of innovation. Simply implementing one or two of these practices will result in failure and will only give people the impression that such practices do not work. A consistent combination of such practices will create an innovating organization that will work.

Selected Bibliography

The basic ideas of organization design and of blending structure, processes, rewards, and people practices are described in my earlier book, *Organization Design* (Addison-Wesley Publishing, 1978). The idea of differentiation comes from Paul Lawrence and Jay Lorsch's *Organization and Environment* (Harvard Business School, 1967). One can also find there the basic ideas of contingency theory.

The structure of the innovative organization and the three roles involved are similar to those identified in the investment idea and capital-budgeting process. These have been identified by Joseph Bower in *The Resource Allocation Process* (Division of Research at Harvard University, 1968).

Innovation itself has been treated in various ways by many people. Some good ideas about technological innovation can be found in Lowell Steele's *Innovation in Big Business* (Elsevier, 1975).

PART TWO

This part of the book expands our domain of analysis from the specialized subunit to the single-business company that consists of two or more specialized subunits. These organizations may be independent corporations or divisions of larger organizations.

Managers of single-business companies, as the cases illustrate, face many organizational issues that are most often associated with coordinating and controlling their interdependent subunits. The text suggests an analytical framework for thinking about those and other single-business issues. The cases provide a range of situations, from simple subunit interdependence (People Express), to complex interdependence (Au Bon Pain's Partner Manager Program). Ways to design organizations with a culture of high commitment are also discussed. Finally, the readings provide an in-depth description of numerous design tools used by single-business unit managers to deal with subunit interdependence.

C h a p t e r   4

Organizing Human Resources in a Single-Business Company

Designing the organization of human resources for a company operating in a single-business area requires answers to three basic questions:

1 Where do we draw the boundaries that define the company's major and minor specialized subunits? Exactly what tasks should be assigned to each subunit? For example, should the company be divided into three major parts, with one part focused on marketing activities, another part focused on manufacturing, and another part focused on administration? Or, should it be divided into two major parts, with one focusing on all activities associated with Product X, and the second part focusing on all activities associated with Product Y? Or, would another alternative be better? How should each major part be subdivided, if at all? If there is a manufacturing department, for example, should it be subdivided into two plants—one that produces Product X and one that produces Product Y? Or, should it be subdivided into an East Coast plant and a West Coast plant, each manufacturing X and Y? Or, is there a better alternative?

2. How do we organize each of the major and minor specialized subunits that we have created? How do we structure each of these units, and what types of measurement, reward, selection, and development systems are appropriate? For example, suppose that a company is divided into three major parts—the Product X group, the Product Y group, and administration. Also suppose that the two product groups are composed of a manufacturing department and a marketing department, and that the administrative unit comprises a finance group, an EDP group, and personnel. This second design question addresses the internal organization of each group. That is, should the two engineering departments be organized in the same way? If not, how should they differ? Should a single performance-appraisal system be used companywide, or should different systems be used by each of the three major subunits? How should jobs be designed in the finance group and in the personnel group? What type of training is needed in the two marketing departments?

3. How do we integrate these specialized subunits so that their individual contributions combine to achieve the company's overall objectives? How do we avoid a situation where each part performs its role adequately yet the whole doesn't accomplish its goals? For example, how should a company organize itself to ensure that its manufacturing and sales departments collaborate in a manner that achieves adequate levels of sales and profits? Would some type of companywide bonus system based on overall profits encourage the managers in manufacturing and sales to collaborate? Or, should the company just develop a set of clearly understood ground rules concerning what each department is expected to do under different circumstances so that their contributions integrate into a whole? Or, is another method needed?

The second of these three questions was discussed in Chapter 3. In this chapter, we address the other two questions. After gaining a basic understanding of the factors involved in these questions, it is easier to discuss the fundamental choices in the first question.

Interdependence: The Factor Creating a Need for Integration

All organizations are composed of specialized parts that are to some degree interdependent. It is because of this interdependence that organizations must design ways to integrate their parts. If their parts were totally independent, this would not be necessary. Furthermore, if the nature of the interdependence among parts or organizations was always the same or almost the same, then achieving integration would be simple from a design point of view; there would be a standard solution that could always be used. In reality, however, the nature of subunit interdependence varies significantly within and among organizations because of three important factors: (1) a company's external environment, (2) a company's technologies, and (3) a company's strategies and objectives. See Figure 4–1.

Consider, for example, Company A—a small company that makes and sells a standard product in a limited geographical area. The company's external environment has a stable and loyal customer base and little direct competition. The company develops no new products and relies on a simple manufacturing technology. It is a family-owned business with a primary objective of generating a stable income.

This company's sales and manufacturing activities are interdependent in a simple way. The manufacturing people depend on the salespeople to give them orders in an accurate and timely manner. Without those orders, the manufacturing people cannot accomplish their tasks effectively and efficiently. The salespeople, however, have no similar dependence on manufacturing. They can do their job for weeks at a time without thinking about the plant. Only if something catastrophic happens at

Figure 4–1
Factors Affecting the Nature of the Interdependence among a
Company's Parts

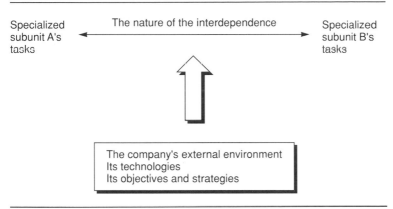

the plant—for example, something that stops shipments to customers—would sales-people be affected.

Company B, which operates in the same geographic area as Company A, is in a different situation. Company B operates in a competitive environment and sells a nonstandard set of products that are almost always custom-made. Although also a family business, the family's business objectives are focused on profitable growth.

Sales and manufacturing in Company B are interdependent in different ways than in Company A due to differences in environments, technologies, and business objectives. Sales at B depend on manufacturing for timely and accurate cost and delivery estimates because B's products, unlike A's, do not have standard cost and delivery times. If the plant doesn't respond quickly, or if it responds with cost and delivery times that are high, the salespeople will have great difficulty accomplishing their sales objectives. The salespeople (who deliver and install) also depend on the plant for supplying them with completed orders that are on time and of the quality promised. Again, if the plant does not cooperate, sales will have difficulty doing its job. At the same time, manufacturing depends on sales for orders, as was the case in Company A, as well as for other types of customer data. Because the plant does not make standard products, it needs to know both what types of products customers want and what customers think about the products it makes. Without this information from sales, manufacturing cannot effectively accomplish its task.

The differences between the sales/manufacturing interdependence at Company A and Company B are summarized in Figure 4–2. These differences place dissimilar demands on the mechanisms needed to integrate sales and manufacturing. The key implication for organizational design is obvious: one would not use the same mechanisms in these two companies to integrate manufacturing and sales. One would

Figure 4–2
Sales/Manufacturing Interdependence in Two Different Companies

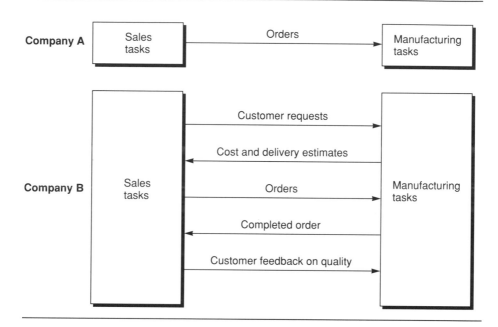

use a different set of tools in each case—tools that are designed to fit the particular nature of the interdependence involved.[1]

To design mechanisms that can most appropriately integrate the parts of an organization requires understanding of how those parts are interdependent. But that alone, or even in conjunction with an understanding of the organization design tools available to create integration, is not enough. One also needs an appreciation of factors that make achieving integration economically difficult.

Factors that Make It Difficult to Cope with Interdependence

In organizing an entire corporation, often the largest problem is related to the successful integration of its subunits. In talking to company presidents, they often report problems such as these:

- Our line and staff departments just won't cooperate with each other, and it's costing us a lot of money.

---

[1]For a further discussion of interdependence see James Thompson, *Organizations in Action* (New York: McGraw-Hill, 1967), chap. 5; and Pradip Khandwalla, *The Design of Organizations* (New York: Harcourt Brace Jovanovich, 1977), chap. 13.

- The manufacturing-sales interface is a constant source of problems, and this is giving us a bad reputation among our customers.
- We just can't seem to get the interdepartmental coordination we need to introduce new products quickly.

Complexity

Several factors typically contribute to these kinds of integration problems, one of which concerns the complexity and intensity of the interdependence.

Sometimes, because of the nature of a business's environment, technology, or strategy, its subunits are interdependent in simple ways. Such is the case for Company A in Figure 4–2. Other times, subunit interdependence can be moderate to complex because of:

1. The volume of information (per unit of time) that must go from one unit to another.
2. The multidirectionality of that information (e.g., it is not just A → B, but A ⇆ B).
3. The nonstandard nature of the information.

Consider, for example, a large, technologically complex manufacturer whose strategy is to achieve high profit margins by developing new products before any of its competitors. It has four major functional units: engineering, manufacturing, marketing, and administration (accounting, personnel, and so forth). Introducing complex new products that are successful in the marketplace requires hundreds of daily decisions, and often these decisions require expertise from many people in more than one functional unit. Consequently, a great deal of information must be transmitted among the functional units each day, and it would be difficult to predict, even a few days in advance, exactly what that information would be in a specific case. In situations like this, where the interdependence is intense and complex, achieving successful integration economically is more difficult than in situations where the interdependence is less complex.[2]

Differentiation

A second factor that contributes to integration problems is differentiation, that is, systematic differences in the values, attitudes, and behaviors of employees in different subunits. Social scientists have long established that communication and understanding usually are easiest to achieve among people who are similar.[3] With

---

[2]For further discussion of how organizations cope with varying amounts and types of information processing among functional units, see Jay Galbraith, *Designing Complex Organizations* (Reading, Mass.: Addison-Wesley Publishing, 1973), chap. 2.

[3]See Carl R. Rogers and F. J. Roethlisberger, "Barriers and Gateways to Communication," *Harvard Business Review*, July–August 1952, pp. 46–52.

similar goals, values, expectations, and world views, the potential for conflict or for simple misunderstandings is minimized. Through specialization, organizations purposely create differences among their subunits so that they can most effectively accomplish different kinds of tasks. But once created, these differences in objectives, personalities, education, time frames, and so on can make coordination of subunits even more difficult.[4]

The following scene, for example, is repeated, with slight variations, thousands of times.[5]

Factory supervisor: I'd like to get this work done as quickly as possible.

Laboratory group leader: Well, it will take us some time to understand the factors involved, and I also have to free up a person to work on it.

Factory supervisor: I understand that, but this work is critical to my operation. We've got a high spoilage rate now.

Laboratory group leader: [To himself—Hell, this isn't a challenging problem, none of my people will want to work on it.] I suspect we might make some progress in a month's time.

Factory supervisor: A month? You've got to be kidding! That's a month of bad products and reduced output. [To himself—My boss will eat me alive if we don't get this solved before then.] I was hoping you could do it this week.

Laboratory group leader: No way.

In analyzing this type of situation, people often assume the problem is a function of the specific individuals involved—without realizing that the organization has systematically created the conflict. To do a good job at the research task, the company in the example staffed the laboratory with managers who enjoyed working on unstructured tasks and gave them great autonomy. They measured and rewarded these managers on their long-term effect on innovation and knowledge building. At the same time, however, to achieve its production goals, the company organized the factory so that its managers thought in terms of costs, quality, and productivity in the short run. They liked a "no surprises," orderly operation. Under these circumstances, it is hardly surprising that a factory manager and a lab manager might find themselves arguing.

Poor Informal Relationships

A third factor that leads to integration problems is poor informal relationships among subunits. For example, if an organization's history has created informal norms that encourage subunit independence and if informal relationships among people in subunits have been characterized by suspicion and distrust, then the potential for conflict and problems will exist if the subunits become interdependent.

[4]See Paul Lawrence and Jay Lorsch, *Organization and Environment* (Boston: Harvard Business School, 1967).

[5]From Jay Lorsch, "Organization Design" (Boston: Intercollegiate Case Clearing House) 9–476–094, pp. 10–11.

When the type of conflict characterized by the factory manager and the laboratory manager continues over a period, it is easy for the subunits involved to grow resentful of each other. Once distrust has developed, it can perpetuate itself without much direct group-to-group contact. For example, a new factory manager may seldom, if ever, interact with anyone from the lab but may distrust those "long-haired crazies" simply because that attitude is pervasive in the factory.[6]

A common type of integration problem found in organizations, line-staff conflict, is created by a combination of the three factors discussed so far. Line and staff organizations are usually designed so that they are highly interdependent. The staff acts in an advisory capacity to the line people who are responsible for the good or service that the organization produces. Specifically, the staff often depends on the line managers to take their advice, act on it, and give them proper recognition for their achievements. The line depends on the staff to give them helpful advice that does not interfere with their efforts either to achieve their job objectives or to relate to their superiors. In addition, staff and line units tend to be comprised of different types of people who are measured and rewarded differently. The staff are more specialized. The results of their work are neither always directly measurable nor always tied to bottom-line results. Line executives' work is usually objectively measurable, and they can have considerable bottom-line responsibility. While these differences can produce a healthy degree of tension, they may produce conflict which, over time, may lead to a deterioration in the relations between line and staff people. The complex interdependence, the different orientations, and the bad relationships then produce more conflict. Under these circumstances, it is hardly surprising that line managers often accuse the staff of being too specialized, of making unrealistic recommendations, of taking credit when things go well and hiding when they don't succeed, and of acting as a spy for top management. Staff managers often complain that line people resist change and are unwilling to provide the staff with proper recognition or adequate authority.[7]

Poor informal relationships among subunits can sometimes be traced to personality incompatibility. Although this factor is less important than historical circumstances (historical conflict may have started with personal incompatibility), occasionally one finds integration problems that are created by two subunit heads or two key people in different subunits who would have difficulty relating to each other under any circumstance.

Size and Physical Distance

A fourth factor that can make integration difficult is size. As the number of employees in a firm increases, the number of potentially interdependent relationships among individuals in different subunits also increases. To take a simple example, in a firm with one sales employee and one production employee, there is just one

---

[6]Edgar Schein, *Organizational Psychology* (Englewood Cliffs, N.J.: Prentice-Hall, 1965), chap. 5.

[7]For an interesting description of line-staff conflict, see Melville Dalton, *Men Who Manage* (New York: John Wiley & Sons, 1969), chap. 4.

interdependent human relationship between the sales unit and the production unit. In a firm with 100 sales employees and 100 production employees, each salesperson or sales manager easily might have an interdependent relationship with half a dozen production people—that is, people that he or she needs to communicate with regularly. Overall, there could be hundreds of relevant interdependent relationships between the sales and production units. As the number of relationships grows, the potential for creating integration problems also increases.[8]

A final factor that can contribute to integration problems is physical distance. It is easier for people to manage their interdependence when they work in proximity to one another. In large corporations, offices may be separated by as much as 10,000 miles. Although technological advances in communications and transportation make it easier to integrate distant operations, physical separation can still create problems.[9]

A sensitivity to all factors that can contribute to integration problems is important. If several items are involved in a specific situation, then achieving effective integration will require considerable effort. See Figure 4–3. Moreover, in designing solutions, it is important to know the factors that are involved; just as with different types of interdependence, different complicating factors require different types of organizational design solutions.

Commonly Used Integrating Devices

Virtually all organizational design tools can be used to solve certain types of integration problems. The key to using them efficiently and effectively is knowing what each one can accomplish at what cost.

Management Hierarchy

Perhaps the most common solution to solving an integration problem among two or more subunits has been having them report to the same supervisor, who then sees that their activities are properly integrated by facilitating communications, resolving conflicts, and the like.[10] Furthermore, by having a continuous chain of command or a set of management positions that link the organization's major and minor subunits, one has a built-in mechanism for resolving conflict and coordinating activities throughout the organization. For example, if the head of the eastern sales office and the supervisor for an assembly line cannot settle a conflict regarding delivery delays, the problem would be communicated up the chain from both

---

[8]William G. Ouchi and Reuben T. Harris, "The Dynamic Organization: Structure, Technology, and Environment," in *Organizational Behavior—Issues and Research,* ed. George Strauss et al. (Madison, Wis.: Industrial Relations Research Association, 1974).

[9]Harold J. Leavitt, *Managerial Psychology* (Chicago: University of Chicago Press, 1964), p. 236.

[10]For example, "the most ancient, as well as the most important, device for achieving coordination is the supervisor." Harold Koontz and Cyril O'Donnell, *Principles of Management* (New York: McGraw-Hill, 1955), p. 38.

Figure 4–3
Factors that Make Achieving Effective Integration Difficult

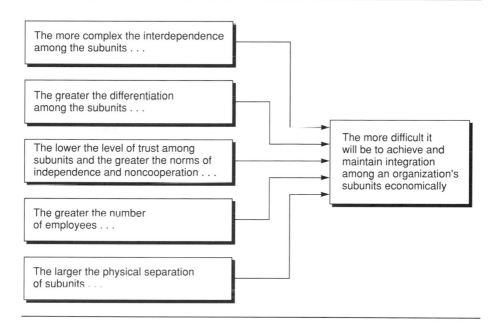

departments until both messages came to the same person (perhaps the division manager) who resolves the problem.

If staffed with appropriate individuals, a management hierarchy can effectively foster subunit integration. By itself, however, the hierarchy can become overloaded with conflicts to resolve, information to pass on, and so forth. In such cases, executives work long hours trying to coordinate activities personally while the backlog of conflicts and decisions to be made grows. One could reduce the overload by adding more positions in the hierarchy, which reduces the span of control. To a point, this solution can help; but, it can also become expensive and create a large number of levels in the hierarchy that can ultimately distort communication.[11]

Some organizations recently have attempted to minimize the hierarchy. These organizations found that as they grew, so did the hierarchical levels of the organization. As a result, more managers spent their time making decisions that could have been made more appropriately at lower levels of the organization. When compounded with the costs of maintaining a large hierarchical organization, the organizations became inefficient. These companies have "delayered" and cut their

---

[11]Jay Galbraith, *Organization Design* (Reading, Mass.: Addison-Wesley Publishing, 1977), pp. 48–49; and Richard H. Hall, *Organizations: Structure & Process* (Englewood Cliffs, N.J.: Prentice-Hall, 1972, chap. 9).

levels of hierarchy to cut costs, decrease the time needed to make decisions, and to drive employees toward taking initiative in their work.[12]

Staff

The problem of hierarchy overload can also be alleviated through the use of staff. By giving a line manager assistants or functional specialists, one increases the amount of information that position in the hierarchy can process, the number of decisions it can make, and the amount of conflict it can resolve. However, there are two drawbacks to using staff as an integrating device. The first is cost; it is not surprising that the smaller the company, the less staff available to managers. The second drawback, as already mentioned, is that a staff group can create integration problems as well as solve them—especially between themselves and line managers in the subunits.

Rules and Procedures

Rules and procedures are another mechanism that can keep the management hierarchy from becoming overloaded. When decision situations routinely arise that affect two or more parts of an organization, it is sometimes possible to establish rules or procedures regarding how they should be handled. For example: "Whenever a salesperson receives an order over $5,000, he or she should inform the plant's production scheduler, by phone or in person, within four hours."

This mechanism's biggest advantage is that it is an economical way to achieve integration. Compare, for example, the one-time cost of developing and implementing a set of procedures with the ongoing cost of using an entire management hierarchy or a large staff. The problem with these integration devices, however, is that they only work when intelligent rules can be established and when the situation is stable enough that the company does not have to constantly change the rules. Furthermore, when organizations rely heavily on rules for integration or other purposes, there are various dysfunctional consequences. For example, since rules have to be policed, they create stress between managers (policers) and workers. And since rules and procedures inevitably specify minimum acceptable behavior, they often cause behavior to settle at that minimum level.[13] Moreover, excessive reliance on rules and procedures can lead to "goal displacement," where the pursuance of rules and procedures becomes an end in itself rather than a means toward achieving the organization's goals. That, in turn, can produce rigid behavior and an inability to respond to changing circumstances.[14] For example, a customer service person may be unwilling to make a rule change or take initiative on changing a policy that could help make a purchasing procedure easier for a large-volume customer. The customer becomes angry and takes her order elsewhere. The customer service person obeyed the rule at considerable organizational cost.

---

[12]See Noel Tichy and Ram Charan's Interview with Jack Welch, "Speed, Simplicity, and Self-Confidence," *Harvard Business Review,* Spring, 1989.

[13]A. W. Gouldner, *Patterns of Industrial Bureaucracy* (New York: Free Press, 1954).

[14]R. K. Merton, "Bureaucratic Structure and Personality," *Social Forces* 18 (1970), pp. 560–68.

Goals and Plans

Goals and plans can serve a function similar to rules and procedures, but for a limited time. Once established, they allow two or more parts of an organization to operate independently yet have their outputs integrated. For example, by setting exact specifications for modifying a product and by determining timetables for its production and introduction dates, the engineering, marketing, and manufacturing departments of a company can work independently on their part of the new-product development task and at the same time be assured that it will still fit with the other parts; coordination is achieved.

Except in circumstances where planning and goal setting are not feasible, perhaps because events are too unpredictable, these devices are useful in facilitating integration. The major drawback to using goals and plans is their cost in time and resources. It takes time and energy to create realistic and intelligent goals and plans. In some circumstances, this cost precludes using these devices, particularly when compared with other devices such as rules and procedures.[15] Because of uncertainty about the exact nature of goals and plans (nothing can be exactly specified at the beginning), use of goals and plans alone can lead to mistakes in development and cost more in the long run than using other integrating devices.

Committees and Task Forces

Another set of structural devices used to facilitate integration consists of meetings, committees, task forces, and the like. To help coordinate sales and production, for example, the heads of the two units and some of their staff might meet for a few hours each week.

Committees, task forces, and meetings are attractive in that they can solve integration problems that some devices cannot. Unlike rules or plans, they can deal with nonroutine, spur-of-the-moment issues. Unlike a management hierarchy, they can process a lot of information and make many decisions in a short period. The primary drawback of this device is cost. One committee of eight middle-level managers that meets once a week for two hours can easily cost an organization (in salary, benefits, and support services) over $15,000 a year. A second drawback is related to the need for small-group decision-making skills by persons participating in committees or task forces. Without these skills, the groups become inefficient and ineffective, and employees become frustrated and angry.[16]

Integrating Roles

Under certain circumstances where coordination is particularly difficult to achieve and yet is particularly important, organizations can create special permanent integrating roles or departments. A product manager position, for example, might be created to integrate the sales, marketing, and production subunits for a specific

---

[15]Jay Galbraith, *Designing Complex Organizations* (Reading, Mass.: Addison-Wesley Publishing, 1973), pp. 12–14.

[16]For a good description of the types of skills that are needed and why, see Edgar Schein, *Process Consultation* (Reading, Mass.: Addison-Wesley Publishing, 1969), chaps. 3–7.

product or product line. Or, a project manager position might be created to help integrate personnel from different subunits—such as engineering, sales, marketing, and manufacturing—working on a new product development project.

Typically, the integrator does not have direct formal authority over the personnel he or she coordinates. This prevents the integrator from "railroading" decisions against the better judgment of the specialists being coordinated. It also means the integrator cannot require certain behaviors. This lack of authority can be frustrating because the coordinator is forced to rely on considerable initiative and personal influence skills (enthusiasm, energy, tact, and judgment) to coax the necessary integration and appropriate behaviors from those persons over whom s/he has no direct control. Accordingly, the selection of people with the appropriate background and skills for the integration roles becomes crucial. To be effective, an integrator must be a good leader and have a generalist orientation—one that differs from the specialized subunits yet allows understanding of each one. Similarly, integrating departments work best when they are structured in a way that is not identical to any of the subunits that they must integrate but is in between them on important dimensions.[17]

Full-time integrators can be an expensive addition to an organization. The cost of eight product managers can easily approach half a million dollars a year for salary and fringe benefits alone. A small company would have difficulty justifying or affording such an expense; however, they may be able to structure themselves in other ways to avoid such problems.

Formal Authority

Still another element of structure that can help or hinder effective integration is the distribution of formal authority in the organization, i.e., whether it is centralized or decentralized and whether subunits such as manufacturing and sales have equal power. To facilitate integration, authority should be distributed so that people or groups who have information relevant to making integrating decisions also have the power to make the decisions. For example, if a company depends on teams, meetings, and task forces to achieve integration, then power should be decentralized. If a company relies almost exclusively on rules and a management hierarchy, then power should be centralized.

The major problem with relying on formal authority to help achieve subunit integration is that it can be difficult to change when necessary. People seldom give up formal power without a fight.[18] In addition, formal authority alone does not mandate behavior.[19]

---

[17]For further discussion of integrating roles, see Paul R. Lawrence and Jay W. Lorsch, "New Management Job: The Integrator," *Harvard Business Review,* November–December 1967.

[18]Gene Dalton, Louis Barnes, and Abraham Zaleznik, *The Distribution of Authority in Formal Organizations* (Boston: Harvard Business School, 1968), chap. 3.

[19]John Kotter, "Power, Dependence, and Effective Management," *Harvard Business Review,* July–August 1977.

Measurement and Reward Systems

Measurement and reward systems are often used as integrating devices. In such cases, systems are formed to measure the variables related to the successful integration of certain subunits. This information is then sent to decision makers who have the most control over the successful integration of these subunits, and their rewards are partially contingent on their success.[20] For example, it is common for companies that utilize product managers to establish accounting systems that measure profitability, sales, and costs by individual product line. This information can be used by the product manager and is often tied to his or her compensation.

While well-designed measurement and reward systems can motivate behavior that focuses on effective integration, they also have drawbacks. The first, again, is the direct cost of establishing and maintaining these systems. Other drawbacks relate to the indirect costs associated with dysfunctional behavior that these systems sometimes produce. To obtain desired rewards promised by these systems, people sometimes ignore important but unrewarded behaviors. Supervisors will, for example, stop helping others or investing time in employee development unless their actions produce measured results. They sometimes focus on finding ways to fool the system into reporting invalid data that appear favorable. In other cases, they stop working as hard or cooperating as much because of resentment toward the "carrot and stick" system.[21]

Selection and Development Systems

Selection and development systems can serve as integration devices in two different ways. First, they can provide an organization with individuals who are capable of effectively playing key integrating roles. Second, by providing formal training programs, they can help build better relationships between individuals or groups with subunits requiring integration.

By seeking and hiring people who have the characteristics of good integrators, selection systems provide organizations with people who can serve integrating roles. Development systems can achieve similar results with existing personnel, through either formal training programs or job rotation in specialist departments, by developing them into effective integrators.

Selection systems can help improve relations between individuals or groups through occasional hiring and promotion decisions. For example, to maintain good relations between sales and manufacturing personnel, some organizations periodically promote a few people across departmental lines.

Development systems also help provide integration among representatives of an

---

[20]J. Leslie Livingstone, "Managerial Accounting and Organizational Coordination," in *The Accountant in a Changing Business Environment,* ed. Willard E. Stone (University of Florida Press, 1973), pp. 42–45.

[21]E. E. Lawler and J. G. Rhode, *Information and Control in Organizations* (Santa Monica, Calif.: Goodyear Publishing, 1976), chap. 6.

organization's subparts through team development and intergroup development activities. Team development activities usually focus on task forces, committees, or other groups that perform an integrating function. The objective of team development is to help these groups perform better. The method usually involves meeting in a nonwork setting for one to four days with an agenda that focuses on group process and group problems. An expert in small-group process usually meets with the team to help members identify and solve any communication, interpersonal, or leadership problems that impede effectiveness.[22] Intergroup development activities focus on improving relationships among the people in two or more subunits. They also usually involve an offsite meeting for one or two days with an expert facilitator. The activities typically focus on eliminating distorted beliefs on both sides, on helping each side understand the other better, and on building relationships and communication channels across the groups.[23] Both team and intergroup development activities also are used to encourage members to share norms in a company's culture that facilitate effective integration. For example, there is considerable evidence that successful companies have norms that favor confronting conflicts and dealing with them through problem solving rather than smoothing over or avoiding conflict or solving it by forcing one person's solution on another.[24] Team and intergroup development activities usually try to foster the development and maintenance of confronting and problem-solving norms.

Physical Setting

Another element of organizational design that is sometimes used to facilitate integration is architecture. Because physical proximity makes communication easier, some organizations design their offices, conference areas, and open space with an eye toward meeting critical integration needs. For example, one money-management firm felt that its 45-minute daily morning meeting was such an important device for facilitating coordination between the research and portfolio management departments that it spent over $100,000 to build a room specially designed for that meeting.[25] At times, even an unintentional architectural change can encourage integration. In a large health maintenance organization, senior medical staff housed on one floor were constantly at odds with administrative people located on a lower floor. Other than formal, conflict-loaded meetings, the two groups had little interaction. When space requirements necessitated widening a landing, a common coffee area was created, and the conflict between the two groups decreased as they interacted at the coffee stand.

---

[22]For more information on team development, see Shel Davis, "Building More Effective Teams," *Innovation* 15 (1970), pp. 32–41.

[23]For more information on intergroup development, see Robert Blake and Jane Mouton, *Managing Intergroup Conflict for Industry* (Houston: Gulf Publishing, 1964).

[24]See, for example, Lawrence and Lorsch, *Organization and Environment*.

[25]For an in-depth look at physical settings as an integrating device, see Fritz Steele, *Physical Settings and Organizational Development* (Reading, Mass.: Addison-Wesley Publishing, 1973).

Architecture has the same drawbacks as some other integrating devices. It can be expensive, and it can inadvertently reduce a company's needed specialization. For example, putting all specialists associated with Product X in the same office area and providing them with team-building activities will help integration efforts concerning Product X, but it might lead to an erosion of the specialists' particular expertise. This can be threatening to specialists who view their career development as contingent on continued specialization.

Departmentalization

A final way that managers can solve integration problems is to redesign subunit boundaries to include the required interdependence within the new subunit boundaries, where it can be more easily managed.

A common example of using departmentalization as an integrating device is an organization that switches from a functional structure to a product, market, or geographical structure. Small manufacturing firms typically use a functional structure; however, many of them switch to a product division structure after achieving a certain size. One of the key reasons they make this change is that integration across functions becomes increasingly difficult and expensive as the number of people and projects within functions increases. Increased size usually means a greater volume of information must flow between functions, thus increasing the complexity of interdependence. A larger size means additional people and more interdependent relationships to be managed across functions. Specialization also tends to increase with size, and with it the differences among specialists in different functions are multiplied. With increases in size, the physical proximity of people in different functions tends to decrease along with the possibility for easy face-to-face interaction. By shifting to product divisions, a company reduces the size of functional units being integrated around each product, the amount of information flowing between small functional units, and (sometimes) the physical distance between people in various functional units. These changes make functional integration around the designated products or product line easier.

Nevertheless, the switch from a functional to a product (or market or geographic) structure has some drawbacks. Achieving integration across the products can be more difficult. Often, some functional specialization and/or economies of scale are sacrificed.[26]

Organizations that need both strong functional specialization and a high degree of integration across functions sometimes use a matrix structure. In bipolar matrix structures (the most common),[27] all jobs and minor departments are grouped into

---

[26]For further discussion of the trade-off between product and functional structures, see Jay Lorsch and Art Walker, "Organizational Choice: Product versus Function," *Harvard Business Review,* November–December, 1968.

[27]Matrix structures can contain more than two dimensions. For an example of how a three-dimensional matrix is designed, see William C. Goggin, "How the Multidimensional Structure Works at Dow Corning," *Harvard Business Review,* January–February 1974.

two major departments: usually one is associated with some function and the other is associated with some product or market. Thus, everyone has two bosses.

A matrix is an attempt to gain the benefits of both functional and product/market structures. It can do so, but not without costs. Because a matrix calls for two hierarchies and because it requires time and effort to manage the ambiguity and tension that result from having multiple bosses for each person and subunit, a matrix can be expensive and difficult to maintain. In a matrix organization, conflicts are common, and it is easy for unresolved conflicts between the two dimensions to slow information flow and decisions. It is also possible for one side of the matrix to overpower the other, thus turning it back into a functional or a product/market organization if the managers on one arm are more capable of dealing with conflict and ambiguity than others.[28]

Most organizations use some combination of functional, product, market, geographical, and matrix structures. For example, a manufacturing company might have five major subunits, including four functional departments (manufacturing, marketing, engineering, and administration) and one geographical department (international—all non-U.S. sales, manufacturing, and so forth). The marketing department might be divided further into market-oriented subunits. Manufacturing might be divided geographically, with plants in different regions of the country. Engineering might be structured as a matrix, where one side represents engineering functions (electrical, mechanical, and so on) while the other side represents new-product development projects. The key ingredient is to organize in the most appropriate way to meet the needs of the firm's external environment, technologies, strategies, and to achieve the organization's goals.

Selecting a Set of Integrating Mechanisms

In selecting a set of integrating mechanisms, an awareness of their individual strengths and weaknesses (Figure 4–4) is required. In addition, two generalizations may be made:

1. The more factors that make achievement of integration difficult, the more costly the needed integration devices. In an organization where there is little interdependence among the parts, where the parts are not highly specialized, and where informal relations among the parts are good, effective integration can be achieved through a management hierarchy and some rules and procedures. In a large and geographically dispersed organization where there is intense interdependence among the parts, where the parts are highly specialized, and where informal relations among the parts are poor, effective integration might require a

---

[28]For more on matrix organizations, see Leonard Sayles, "Matrix Management," *Organizational Dynamics,* Autumn 1976, pp. 2–17; and Paul Lawrence, Harvey Kolodny, and Stanley Davis, "The Human Side of the Matrix," *Organizational Dynamics,* Summer 1977, pp. 43–61.

Figure 4–4
Costs and Benefits of Alternative Integration Methods

Integrating methods	Advantages	Drawbacks
The management hierarchy/ span of control	Provides a network that links together all of an organization's major and minor functional units.	Can become overloaded and break down. A narrow span can be expensive and cumbersome.
Staff	Can supplement the management hierarchy and help it perform a larger integration function.	Cost. Also can create its own integration problems (between staff and line).
Rules and procedures	Economical way to achieve integration around routine issues.	Limited to routine issues. Heavy use can create dysfunctional consequences.
Plans and goals	Can handle many nonroutine issues that rules and procedures cannot.	Cost, in time and effort.
Meetings, committees, task forces, and so forth.	Can deal with a large number of unpredictable problems and decisions.	Cost. People involved need skills at group decision making.
Integrating roles	Can deal with a large number of unpredictable problems and decisions.	Cost. Can be difficult to find people with the right characteristics to fill the role.
Formal authority	No direct cost.	Can be abused; difficult to shift when shifts are needed.
Measurement and reward systems	Can motivate behavior directed at integration.	Cost. Activities or outcomes not measured and rewarded can be ignored or undermined. Can produce dysfunctional behavior.
Selection and development systems	Can solve certain types of problems more efficiently than other devices.	Can be expensive. Can erode specialized expertise.
Architecture	Under some circumstances, can be an inexpensive solution.	Can be expensive. Can erode specialized expertise.
Departmentalization: Functional structure	Facilitates integration within functions.	Does not facilitate integration across functions.
Product/market/ geographic structure	Promotes integration within and among functions associated with each product/market/ geographical area.	Does not promote integration between product/market/geographic area
Matrix structure	Promotes integration between each side.	Expensive. Generates conflict and tension.

Figure 4-5
The Relationship of Integrating Needs to Integrating Devices Used*

	Industry		
	Container	**Foods**	**Plastics**
Integration needs	Low	Moderate	High
Structural integration devices used	Hierarchy Procedures Some plans	Integrators Plans Hierarchy Procedures	Cross-functional teams Integrators Departments of integrators Hierarchy, plans, and procedures

*Adapted from Paul R. Lawrence and Jay W. Lorsch, *Organization and Environment* (Boston: Harvard Business School, 1967).

hierarchy, rules, plans and goals, teams or task forces, integrating personnel, special measurement and reward systems, team building, and maybe more techniques.

Lawrence and Lorsch, for example, in a study of companies in three different industries, found this type of correlation between integration needs and integrating devices used.[29] See Figure 4–5.

2. The effective solution to any integration problem is the one that costs the least and that does not undermine the effectiveness of specialized subunits. A common problem that managers encounter when trying to solve integration problems is related to cost.

Managers who make integration decisions based on cost alone often generate unanticipated problems that result in higher future costs. For example, an organization recognized that a geographically widespread product team needed to communicate regularly. The organization would pay for phone calls, but air travel for meetings was deemed too expensive. Because the team never met together more than once, they had difficulty establishing relationships, and as a result, phone calls were not returned with the urgency they required. The team had difficulty introducing the new product and lost market share as a result.

A second common problem is related to unanticipated side effects. A good solution to any problem is one that does not create more serious problems of a different kind. In solving integration problems, managers sometimes undermine the type of organization needed at the subunit level. More than one well-intentioned company president has managed to "get employees to start pulling together," but in the process, made them less effective at their respective specialized tasks.

---

[29]Lawrence and Lorsch, *Organization and Environment.*

Drawing Subunit Boundaries

In designing organizations, managers must make fundamental choices regarding how to organize subunits, how to integrate them, and where to draw subunit boundaries. Addressing this issue involves making trade-off judgments between:

1. The benefits to be gained from developing specialized expertise and/or the economies of scale that are possible within subunit boundaries.

2. The cost of establishing, maintaining, and achieving effective integration across subunit boundaries.

An example will help clarify this issue. A manufacturing company with 400 employees sold one product line to customers in three different industries. The firm was organized functionally with marketing, engineering, manufacturing, and administrative departments reporting to the president (Figure 4–6A). In 1985, in response to an increasing number of recurring problems, the president decided to analyze the company's organization. A summary of his analysis follows:

> a. While we are currently serving customers in three industries, only eight years ago we were much smaller and were selling to customers in one industry only. This change is important because the demands that the customers in the three industries place on us are very different. The amount and type of special engineering that has to be done, the nature of selling and customer relations, and the way we can manufacture our products vary considerably between customers in different industries, but are very similar between customers in the same industry.
>
> b. Our organization, which has grown in size but has not changed its structure in the past eight years, is just not able to effectively handle all three industries. We still do the best job and are most profitable in our original industry. That, I believe, is due to the fact that our engineering, sales, and manufacturing are still basically geared to that industry. I'm convinced that the key to increased sales and profitability is to better serve the different needs of customers in our two newer industries while retaining our ability to serve our older customers.
>
> c. A number of people have suggested to me that we should organize into three industry-oriented groups (Figure 4–6B). I think that such a redefinition of our departmental boundaries would solve some problems but would create others. The industry-oriented structure would clearly allow us to develop expertise in serving customers in each of the three industries. But I think it is an impractical solution for a company of our size. It would require a number of additional managers. It would sacrifice a number of economies of scale that we now have. It would be difficult to switch some slack engineering availability from one division to another, for example, which we can easily do with our current structure. And, I'm not sure how we could keep from reinventing the wheel within the three sales groups, the three engineering groups, and so forth, unless we had a lot of time-consuming meetings.
>
> d. So, I have tentatively decided on a modification of our current structure (Figure 4–6C), which essentially leaves the main department boundaries as they are but creates a new set of groups within each department and adds three "industry coordinators" within marketing. This solution is economically feasible, and it will allow us to gain the expertise we need to serve all three industries.

Figure 4–6

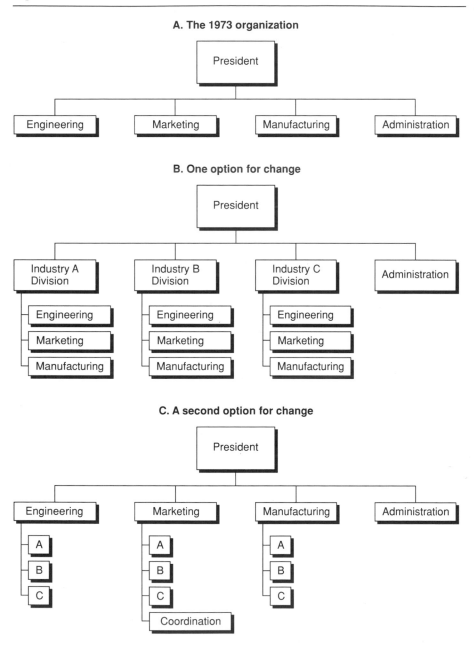

A. The 1973 organization

B. One option for change

C. A second option for change

This solution was implemented during 1986, and after a period of adjustment, the company experienced large increases in sales and profits in 1987 and 1988.

Deciding where to draw major and minor subunit boundaries always involves an analytical and judgmental process similar to the one just described. The decision cannot be made according to any formula, and it must be made while considering the implications for organizing as well as integrating the subunits thus defined. The key to making this judgment, as well as to answering the other two major organizational questions raised at the beginning of this chapter, is a thorough analysis of the specific situation.

Summary

The framework presented in Chapter 2 can be used as a guide to the design of an organization. Designing an organization or trying to solve an organizational problem from the point of view of an entire company requires a form of analysis that can be summarized in the following steps:

1. First, identify the company's key activities, their diversity, and their interdependence. This business analysis can be accomplished only by thoroughly examining the company's key success factors, its external environment, its technology, and its strategy or goals. It is important to be specific regarding exactly what the important characteristics of the activities are, how they differ, what the nature of the interdependence among them is, and what is critical for success. If any of these factors have changed in the past five years or so, it is important to identify them as well as the reasons for changes.

The biggest mistake that managers and consultants make in dealing with organizational issues is to begin defining problems and considering solutions without having completed a thorough examination of the business involved. Subunit boundary structure, integrating devices, and subunit organizational designs cannot be evaluated in the abstract. Rules, matrixes, and profit centers are not "good" or "bad" by themselves. They are only appropriate or inappropriate in light of how well they fit a specific situation. It is only through a thorough analysis that one can determine existing problem areas and potential solutions.

2. One must identify the company's current human resources in terms of staff characteristics, formal arrangements, and informal relationships. It is essential that one go beyond an analysis of the formal design. It is not the people one has "on paper," but the people who are organizational members. The two can differ, and a manager has to work with the actual human resource organization that has emerged in the situation. That organization is a function of the formal design and the emergent culture, informal relations, and employee characteristics. Again, if any of these factors have changed recently, it is important to recognize the changes and the forces creating change.

Figure 4–7

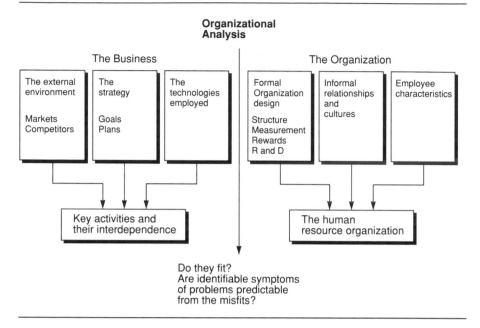

**Organizational
Analysis**

The Business | The Organization

| The external environment Markets Competitors | The strategy Goals Plans | The technologies employed | Formal Organization design Structure Measurement Rewards R and D | Informal relationships and cultures | Employee characteristics |

Key activities and their interdependence

The human resource organization

Do they fit?
Are identifiable symptoms
of problems predictable
from the misfits?

3. Next, make a judgment regarding how well the formal organization structure fits the company's business. See Figure 4–7.[30] These structures are the reward system, control system, selection and development system, and hierarchy. This judgment can be compared with one's knowledge of the existence or absence of any recurring problems. If the analysis is sound, the logical consequences of the misfits should exist as problems in the organization.

4. Finally, identify alternative organizational designs that might solve the problems. That is, as one develops different solutions to the three basic questions raised at the beginning of this chapter, one looks at the design in terms of the "fit" and congruence between the components. The answers and resultant designs can then be tested against the analysis, and design choices can be made.

This mode of analysis involves making difficult judgments and takes considerable time. No simple rule will dictate how a company should be organized. One uses the techniques outlined in this chapter to try and predict consequences of organizing in a particular way. The concepts and techniques outlined in this chapter provide analytical tools that can aid a manager in arriving at a decision that best fits the situation.

[30]For an example of this type of analysis as it pertains specifically to selecting management control systems, see Richard F. Vancil, "What Kind of Management Control Do You Need?" *Harvard Business Review,* March–April 1973.

Case 4–1

People Express

Debra Whitestone, Leonard A. Schlesinger

We're now the biggest air carrier in terms of departures at any New York airport. We've flown almost 3 million passengers and saved the flying public over one quarter of a billion dollars (not including the savings from fares reduced by other airlines trying to compete with us). We expect to see a $3 million profit this year. . . . We have a concept that works and is unique.

But with no growth horizon, people have been disempowered. We've started slowing down, getting sleepy. So, we've decided to set a new growth objective. Instead of adding 4 to 6 aircraft as we planned for this year, we are now thinking in terms of 12 or more new aircraft a year for the next few years.

With this announcement, Don Burr, founder, president, and CEO of People Express airline, concluded the business portion of the company's third quarterly financial meeting of 1982, graciously received rousing applause from several hundred of his stockholder-managers there to hear about and celebrate the success of their young company, and signaled for the music to begin.

Origins and Brief History

People Express had been incorporated on April 7, 1980. In July of that year it had applied to the Civil Aeronautics Board (CAB) for permission to form a new airline to be based in the New York-Newark metropolitan area and dedicated to providing low-cost service in the eastern United States. Organized specifically to take advantage of provisions of the 1978 Airline Deregulation Act, People Express was the first airline to apply for certification since its passage. (The act, which was

This case was prepared by Debra Whitestone and Leonard A. Schlesinger.
Copyright © 1983 by the President and Fellows of Harvard College. Harvard Business School case 483–103.

designed to stimulate competition, allowed greater flexibility in scheduling and pricing and lowered the barriers to new entrants.)

In applying to the CAB for a "determination of fitness and certification of public convenience and necessity," People Express committed itself to:

1. Provide "a broad new choice of flights" with high-frequency service.
2. Keep costs low by "extremely productive use of assets."
3. Offer "unrestricted deep discount price savings" through productivity gains.
4. Focus on several high-density eastern U.S. markets which had yet to reap the pricing benefits of deregulation.
5. Center operations in the densely populated New York-Newark metropolitan area with service at the underutilized, uncongested, highly accessible Newark International Airport.

The Civil Aeronautics Board was sufficiently impressed with this stated intent that it approved the application in three months (compared to the usual year or more). On October 24, 1980, People Express had its certificate to offer air passenger service between the New York-New Jersey area and 27 major cities in the eastern United States.

Start-Up

People Express's managing officers proceeded to work round the clock for the next six months to turn their plans and ideas into a certificated operating airline. They raised money, leased a terminal, bought planes, recruited, trained, established routes and schedules, and prepared manuals to meet the FAA's fitness and safety standards. "We were here every night . . . from November until April when they (the Federal Aviation Administration) gave us our certificate. . . . It was hell" (Burr). People's operating certificate was granted April 24, 1981.

Operations Begin

Flight service began on April 30, with three planes flying between Newark and Buffalo, New York; Columbus, Ohio; and Norfolk, Virginia. By the following year, the company employed a work force of over 1,200, owned 17 airplanes, and had flown nearly 2 million passengers between the 13 cities it was servicing. People Express had grown faster than any other airline and most businesses. It had managed to survive a start-up year filled with environmental obstacles, a severe national economic recession, a strike of air traffic controllers, and bad winter weather—all of which had serious negative effects on air travel. By June 1982, though the airline industry in general was losing money, and though competition resulting from deregulation was intense, People had begun showing a profit. Exhibit 1 lists milestones in the growth of People Express.

In the spring and summer of 1982, People underwent an extensive review of its infrastructure, added resources to the recruitment function so as to fill a 200-person

---

Exhibit 1
Major Events

April 1980	Date of incorporation.
May 1980	First external financing—Citicorp venture.
October 1980	CAB certificate awarded.
November 1980	Initial public offering—$25.5 million common.
March 1981	First aircraft delivered.
April 1981	First scheduled flight.
August 1981	PATCO strike.
October 1981	Florida service emphasized.
January 1982	1 millionth passenger carried.
March 1982	17th aircraft delivered.
April 1982	Reported first quarterly operating profit.
July 1982	Filed 1.5 million shares of common stock.

---

staffing shortfall, and modified and attempted to implement more systematically a governance and communication system for which there had been little time during start-up. By the fall of 1982 three more planes were about to arrive, and three more cities were scheduled to be opened for service.

Background and Precursors

Donald Burr had been president of Texas International Airlines (TI) before he left it to found People Express with a group of his colleagues. The airline business was a "hobby business" for Burr; his love of airplanes went back to his childhood, and he began flying in college, where as president of the Stanford Flying Club he could get his flight instruction paid for. After receiving an M.B.A. from Harvard Business School in 1965 he went to work for National Aviation, a company specializing in airline investments, thus combining his affinity for aviation with his interest in finance. In 1971 he was elected president of National Aviation. While at National Aviation, Burr began a venture capital operation which involved him in the start-up of several companies, including one which aimed at taking advantage of the recently deregulated telecommunications industry.

Eighteen months later he decided he wanted to get into the "dirty fingernails" side of the airline business. He left Wall Street and joined Texas International Airlines as a director and chairman of the Executive Committee. In June 1973 he became executive vice president and in 1976 assumed the responsibilities of chief operations officer. Between 1973 and 1977, Texas International moved from a position close to bankruptcy to become a profitable business. In June 1979 he was made president of Texas International. Six months later, he resigned.

Looking for a new challenge, one option he considered at that time was starting a new airline. The day after Burr left TI, Gerald Gitner, his VP of planning and marketing, and Melrose Dawsey, his own and the CEO's executive secretary at TI, both submitted their resignations and joined Burr to incorporate People Express.

By the fall of 1980, 15 of Texas International's top managers and several more experienced staff from the ranks followed Burr to become part of the People Express management team and start-up crew. Some gave up their positions even before they knew where the new company would be based, how it would be financed, whether they would be able to acquire planes, or what their exact jobs would be. In spite of the personal and financial risks, the opportunity to start an airline from scratch, with people they liked and respected, was too good to pass up. It was an adventure, a chance to test themselves. Burr at 39 was the oldest of the officers. Even if People Express failed, they assumed that they could pick themselves up and start again.

According to Hap Paretti, former legal counsel and head of government relations at Texas International, who became the fifth managing officer at People Express:

> We weren't talking about my job description or what kind of a budget I would have. It was more, we're friends, we're starting a new airline, you're one of the people we'd like to have join us in starting the company. . . . What you do will be determined by what your interests are. The idea of getting involved and letting my personality and talents come through to determine my job appealed to me. I'm not happy doing just one thing.

Bob McAdoo, People's managing officer in charge of finance, had been corporate comptroller at Texas International. For McAdoo, joining People Express "was an easy decision, though I was having a good time at Texas International. . . . I happen to be a guy driven by things related to efficiency. This was a chance to build an airline that was the most efficient in the business."

Lori Dubose had become director of human resources at TI—the first female director there—within a year after being hired.

> When Burr called to offer me the "People" job he explained that we would all be working in different capacities. I'd get to learn operations, get stock—I didn't know anything about stock, never owned any. At 28 how could I pass it up?

She came even though she was married and her husband decided not to move with her to Newark.

Financing and Airplane Acquisition

To finance this adventure, Burr put up $355,000, Gitner put in $175,000, and the other managing officers came up with from $20,000 to $50,000 each. Burr secured an additional $200,000 from FNCB Capital Corp., a subsidiary of CitiCorp. The papers for the CitiCorp money, People Express's first outside funds, were signed on May 8, 1980, Burr's 40th birthday. Subsequently, the investment firm of Hambrecht & Quist agreed to help raise additional start-up funds. Impressed with Burr's record and the quality of his management team, and aware of the opportunities created by airline deregulation. William Hambrecht agreed to Burr's suggestion of taking People Express public. (No other airline had ever gone public to raise start-up money.)

As soon as the CAB application was approved in October 1980 all eight managing officers went on the road explaining their business plan and concepts to potential investors throughout the country. They were able to sell over $24 million worth of stock—3 million shares at $8.50 per share.

The official plan stated in the CAB application had called for raising $4–5 million, buying or leasing one to three planes, and hiring 200 or so people the first year. According to Hap Paretti, "We thought we'd start by leasing three little DC–9s, and flying them for a few years until we made enough money to buy a plane of our own." According to Burr, however, that plan reflected Gitner's more cautious approach and what most investors would tolerate at the beginning. Even with the additional money raised, Gitner thought they should buy at most 11 planes, but Burr's ideas were more expansive. From the beginning he wanted to start with a large number of planes so as to establish a presence in the industry quickly and support the company's overhead.

With cash in hand they were able to make a very attractive purchase from Lufthansa of an entire fleet of 17 Boeing 737s, all of which would be delivered totally remodeled and redecorated to People's specifications. While other managing officers recalled being a bit stunned, Burr viewed the transaction as being "right on plan."

Burr's Personal Motivation and People's Philosophy

Government deregulation appears to provide a "unique moment in history," and was one of several factors which motivated Burr to risk his personal earnings on starting a new airline. At least as important was his strong conviction that people were basically good and trustworthy, that they could be more effectively organized, and if properly trained, were likely to be creative and productive.

> *I guess the single predominant reason that I cared about starting a new company was to try and develop a better way for people to work together. . . . That's where the name People Express came from* [as well as] *the whole people focus and thrust. . . . It drives everything else that we do.*
>
> *Most organizations believe that humans are generally bad and you have to control them and watch them and make sure they work. At People Express, people are trusted to do a good job until they prove they definitely won't.*

From its inception, therefore, People Express was seen as a chance for Burr and his management team to experiment with and demonstrate a "better" way of managing not just an airline but any business.

While Burr recognized that his stance was contrary to the majority of organized structures in the United States, he rejected any insinuation that he was optimistic or soft.

> *I'm not a "goody two-shoes" person. I don't view myself as a social scientist, as a minister, as a do-gooder. I perceive myself as a hard-nosed businessman, whose ambitions and aspirations have to do with providing goods and services to other people for a return.*

In addition, however, he wanted PE to serve as a role model for other organizations, a concept which carried with it the desire to have an external impact and to contribute to the world's debate about "how the hell to do things well, with good purpose, good intent, and good results for everybody. To me, that's good business, a good way to live. It makes sense, it's logical, it's hopeful, so why not do (it)?"

Prior to starting service, Burr and the other managing officers spent a lot of time discussing their ideas about the "right" way to run an airline. Early on, they retained an outside management consultant to help them work together effectively as a management team and begin to articulate the principles to which they could commit themselves and their company. Over time, the principles evolved into a list of six "precepts," which were written down in December of 1981 and referred to continually from then on in devising and explaining company policies, hiring and training new recruits, structuring and assigning tasks. These precepts were: (1) service, commitment to growth of people; (2) best provider of air transportation; (3) highest quality of management; (4) role model for other airlines and other businesses; (5) simplicity; (6) maximization of profits.

From Burr's philosophy as well as these precepts and a myriad of how-to-do-it-right ideas, a set of strategies began to evolve. According to People's management consultant, the "path" theory was the modus operandi—management would see what route people took to get somewhere, then pave the paths that had been worn naturally to make them more visible.

Thus, by 1982, one could articulate fairly clearly a set of strategies that had become "the concept," the way things were done at People Express.

The People Express Concept: The Philosophy Operationalized

The People Express business concept was broken down and operationalized into three sets of strategies: marketing, cost, and people. (Over Burr's objections, the presentation prepared by investment company Morgan Stanley for PE investors began with the marketing and cost strategies rather than the people strategies.)

Marketing Strategy

Fundamental to People's initial marketing strategy was its view of air travel as a commodity product for which consumers had little or no brand loyalty. (See Exhibit 2 for a representative advertisement.) People Express defined its own version of that product as a basic, cut-rate, no-nonsense, air trip. A People Express ticket entitled a passenger to an airplane seat on a safe trip between two airports, period. The marketing strategy was to build and maintain passenger volume by offering extremely low fares and frequent, dependable service on previously overpriced, underserviced routes. In keeping with this strategy, the following tactics were adopted:

Exhibit 2

SHOULD AN EXPERIENCED TRAVELER LIKE YOU FLY A NEW AIRLINE LIKE US?

Particularly a new airline, with the audacity to consistently charge two-thirds less than you're accustomed to paying.

For example, before we flew to Columbus, the standard air fare was $146. People Express charges $40 off peak and $65 peak. What's more, our price to Florida is just $75 off peak and $89 peak.

In short, People Express offers low prices every seat. Every flight. Every day.

And we always will.

But even if paying much less takes a little getting used to, you'll appreciate our other attributes. In no time flat.

OUR SCHEDULES ARE GEARED TO YOUR SCHEDULE.

Because we know how hectic your life can be, instead of the usual frequent excuses, we give you frequent flights — 98 non-stops each business day.

And, unlike any other major airline, People Express doesn't accept freight or mail. So you don't sit on a plane cooling your heels while mail bags and freight cartons are loaded and unloaded.

ALL OUR PEOPLE TREAT YOU AS ATTENTIVELY AS IF THEY OWNED THE AIRLINE. BECAUSE THEY DO.

At People Express, we don't offer jobs. We offer careers. From the person who welcomes you on the plane to the person who pilots the plane, each and every full time member of our staff owns an average of — amazing as it sounds — $13,000 of our stock. (And the stock of the company founders was not averaged in.)

The result quite simply, is the first airline where attitude is as important as altitude.

NON-STOP CHECK IN.

And to save a little more time and hassle, we've done away with another nemesis: the ticket counter. Purchase your ticket through your travel agent.

Or phone in your reservation in advance with us and purchase your ticket right on the plane.

YOU AND YOUR LUGGAGE NEED NEVER BE SEPARATED.

Someone whose time is as valuable as yours has no intention of wasting it waiting for luggage. So instead of hassling you about carry-on luggage, we actually encourage you — by providing unusually spacious overhead and underseat areas. But if you have luggage you want us to handle, we're happy to do it for $3 a bag.

TASTEFUL BOEING 737's. WITHOUT THE INDIGESTION OF AIRLINE FOOD.

People Express flies the finest equipment in the air: Boeing 737's. Easy on your eyes ... thanks to our clean, tasteful appointments. Easy on your weary bones ... thanks to our comfortable seats. And easy on your stomach ... because we don't serve airline food. Of course, if you're willing to spend a little of all that money you're saving, you can get a first rate beverage or snack on board.

THE FASTEST MOVING AIRLINE IN THE WORLD.

People Express offers more flights out of convenient Newark Airport than any other airline.

And we've already flown over a million passengers.

After only ten months of operation.

Perhaps it was our attitude. Or our prices. Or our frequency to all ten cities.

But no other airline has come this far this fast. Which proves we've offered the public something it's been waiting for a long time ... a better way to fly.

And nobody will appreciate us more than someone who has been around as much as you.

PEOPLExpress
FLY SMART

NEW YORK/NEWARK, BOSTON, WASHINGTON/BALTIMORE, SYRACUSE, BUFFALO, NORFOLK, COLUMBUS, JACKSONVILLE, SARASOTA, WEST PALM BEACH

(continued)

Exhibit 2 *(concluded)*

1. Very Low Fares.   On any given route, People's fares were substantially below the standard fares prevailing prior to PE's announcement of service on that route. For instance, People entered the Newark-to-Pittsburgh market with a $19 fare in April 1982, when U.S. Air was charging $123 on that route. Typically, peak fares ran from 40 percent to 55 percent below the competition's standard fares and 65 percent to 75 percent below during off-peak hours (after 6 P.M. and weekends).

2. Convenient Flight Schedules.   For any route that its planes flew, People tried to offer the most frequent flight schedule. With low fares and frequent flights, People could broaden its market segment beyond those of established airlines to include passengers who would ordinarily have used other forms of transportation. In an effort to expand the size of the air travel market, People's ads announcing service in new cities were pitched to automobile drivers, bus riders, and even those who tended not to travel at all. People hoped to capture most of the increase as well as some share of the preexisting market for each route.

3. Regionwide Identity.   People set out to establish a formidable image in its first year as a major airline servicing the entire eastern United States. Large, established airlines could easily wage price wars and successfully compete with a new airline in any one city, but they would probably have to absorb some losses and would be hard pressed to mount such a campaign on several fronts at once.

4. Pitch to "Smart" Air Travelers.   In keeping with its product definition, People's ads sought to identify People Express not as exotic or delicious or entertaining, but as the smart travel choice for smart, thrifty, busy travelers. The ads were filled with consumer information, as well as information about PE's smart people and policies. Unlike most airlines, for instance, every People Express plane had roomy overhead compartments for passengers' baggage, thereby saving them money, time, and the potential inconvenience of loss.

5. Memorable Positive Atmosphere.   Burr's long-term marketing strategy, once the airline was off the ground financially, was to make flying with People Express the most pleasant and memorable travel experience possible. The goal was for passengers to arrive at their destination feeling very well served. Thus, People Express's ultimate marketing strategy was to staff every position with competent, sensitive, respectful, up-beat, high-energy people who would create a contagious positive atmosphere. The message to staff and customers alike was: "At People Express, attitude is as important as altitude."

Cost Structure

People's cost structure was not based on a clear-cut formula so much as on an attitude that encouraged the constant, critical examination of every aspect of the business. According to Bob McAdoo, the management team "literally looked for every possible way to do things more simply and efficiently." McAdoo could point to at least 15 or 20 factors he felt were important in keeping costs down while preserving safety and quality. "If you look for one or two key factors, you miss the point." Cost savings measures affecting every aspect of the business included the following:

1. Aircraft.   Since fuel was the biggest single cost for an airline, People chose, redesigned, and deployed its aircraft with fuel efficiency in mind. Its twin engine Boeing 737–100 planes were thought to be the most fuel-efficient planes for their mission in the industry. By eliminating first-class and gallery sections, interior redesign increased the number of all coach-class seats from 90 to 118 per plane. Overhead racks were expanded to accommodate more carry-on baggage. The planes were redecorated to convey a modern image and reassure potential passengers that low fares did not mean sacrificing quality or safety.

PE scheduled these planes to squeeze the most possible flying time out of them: 10.36 hours per plane per day, compared with the industry average of 7.08 hours. Finally, plane maintenance work was done by other airlines on a contract basis, a practice seen as less expensive than hiring a maintenance staff.

2. Low Labor Costs.   Labor is an airline's second biggest expense. Though salaries were generally competitive, and in some cases above industry norms, People's labor costs were relatively small. The belief was that if every employee was intelligent, well trained, flexible, and motivated to work hard, fewer people (as much as one-third fewer) would be needed than most airlines employed.

People kept its work force deliberately lean, and expected it to work hard. Each employee, carefully selected after an extensive screening process, received training in multiple functions (ticketing, reservations, ground operations, and so on) and was extensively cross-utilized, depending on where the company's needs were at any given time. If a bag needed to be carried to a plane, whoever was heading towards the plane would carry the bag. Thus, peaks and valleys could be handled efficiently. This was in sharp contrast with other airlines which hired people into one of a variety of distinct "classes in craft" (such as flight attendants, reservations, baggage), each of which had a fairly rigid job description, was represented by a different union, and therefore was precluded from being cross-utilized.

3. In-House Expertise and Problem Solving.   In addition to keeping the work force small and challenged, cross-utilization and rotation were expected to add the benefits of a de facto ongoing quality and efficiency review. Problems could be identified and solutions and new efficiency measures could be continually invented if people were familiar with all aspects of the business and motivated to take managementlike responsibility for improving their company.

The Paxtrac ticketing computer was commonly cited as a successful example of how PE tapped its reservoir of internal brain power rather than calling in outside consultants to solve a company problem. Many of PE's longer routes were combinations of short-haul flights into and out of Newark. The existing ticketing system required a separate ticket for each leg of the trip, resulting in higher fares than PE wanted. Burr spotted the problem when he was flying one day (he tried to spend some time each month on board the planes or in the ground operations area). An ad hoc team of managers was sent off to a hotel in Florida for a week to solve the problem. They came up with a specially designed microprocessor ticketing machine with the flexibility to accommodate the company's marketing plans and fast enough (7 seconds per ticket versus 20 seconds) to enable on-board ticketing of large passenger loads.

4. Facilities.   Like its aircraft, People Express's work space was low cost and strictly functional. The main Newark terminal was located in the old North Terminal building, significantly cheaper to rent than space at the West and South terminals a mile away. People had no ticket counters. All ticketing was done either by travel agents in advance or by customer service managers on board the planes once they were airbound. Corporate headquarters, located upstairs over the main terminal, had none of the luxurious trappings associated with a major airline. Offices were shared, few had carpeting, and decoration consisted primarily of People Express ads, sometimes blown up poster size, and an occasional framed print of an airplane.

5. Reservations. The reservations system was kept extremely simple, fast, and therefore inexpensive. There were no interline arrangements with other airlines for ticketing or baggage transfer; no assistance was offered with hotel or auto reservations in spite of the potential revenue leverage to be derived from such customer service. Thus, calls could be handled quickly by hundreds of easily trained temporary workers in several of the cities People served, using local lines (a WATS line would cost $8,000 per month) and simple equipment ($900 versus the standard $3,000 computer terminals).

6. No "Freebies." Costs of convenience services were unbundled from basic transportation costs. People Express offered none of the usual airline "freebies." Neither snacks nor baggage handling, for example, were included in the price of a ticket, though such extras were available and could be purchased for an additional fee.

People

Burr told his managers repeatedly that it was People's people and its people policies that made the company unique and successful. "The people dimension is the value added to the commodity. Many investors still don't fully appreciate this point, but high commitment and participation, and maximum flexibility and massive creative productivity are the most important strategies in People Express."

Structure and Policies

As People moved from a set of ideas to an operating business, People's managers took pains to design structures and develop policies consistent with the company's stated precepts and strategies. This resulted in an organization characterized by minimal hierarchy, rotation and cross-utilization, work teams, ownership, self-management, participation, compensation, selective hiring and recruitment, multipurpose training, and team building.

1. Minimal Hierarchy. People's initial organizational structure consisted of only three formal levels of authority. At the top of the organization was the president/CEO and six managing officers, each of whom provided line as well as staff leadership for more than 1 of the 13 functional areas (see Exhibit 3 for a listing of functions).

Reporting to and working closely with the managing officers were eight general managers, each of whom provided day-to-day implementation and leadership in at least one functional area, as well as planning for and coordinating with other areas. People's managing officers and general managers worked hard at exemplifying the company's philosophy. They worked in teams, rotated out of their specialties as much as possible to take on line work, filling in at a gate or on a flight. Several had gone through the full "in-flight" training required of customer service managers. They shared office furniture and phones. Burr's office doubled as the all-purpose

Exhibit 3
Organizational Structure: November 1982—Author's Rendition (CEO, president*—chairman of the board, Don Burr)

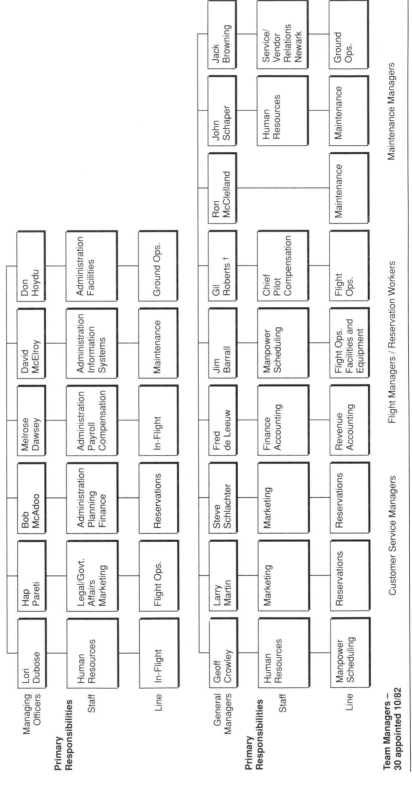

*Original president, Gerald Gitner, resigned in March 1982 and Burr assumed the presidency. †Gil Roberts appointed chief pilot in November 1982.

executive meeting room; if others were using it when he had an appointment, he would move down the hall and borrow someone else's empty space.

There were no executive assistants, secretaries, or support staff of any kind. The managers themselves assumed the activities that such staff would ordinarily perform. Individuals, teams, and committees did their own typing, which kept written communications to a minimum. Everyone answered his or her own phone. (Both practices were seen as promoting direct communication as well as saving money.)

Beyond the top 15 officers, all remaining full-time employees were either flight managers, maintenance managers, or customer service managers. The titles indicated distinctions in qualifications and functional emphasis rather than organizational authority. *Flight managers* were pilots. Their primary responsibility was flying, but they also performed various other tasks, such as dispatching, scheduling, and safety checks, on a rotating basis, or as needed. *Maintenance managers* were technicians who oversaw and facilitated maintenance of PE's airplanes, equipment, and facilities by contract with other airlines' maintenance crews. In addition to monitoring and assuring the quality of the contracted work, maintenance managers were utilized to perform various staff jobs.

The vast majority of People's managers were *customer service managers,* generalists trained to perform all passenger-related tasks, such as security clearance, boarding, flight attending, ticketing, and food service, as well as some staff function activities (see Exhibit 3).

By and large, what few authority distinctions did exist were obscure and informal. Managing officers, general managers, and others with seniority (over one year) had more responsibility for giving direction, motivating, teaching, and perhaps coordinating, but *not* for supervising or managing in the traditional sense.

2. Ownership, Lifelong Job Security. Everyone in a permanent position at PE was a shareholder, required as a condition of employment to buy, at a greatly discounted price, a number of shares of common stock, determined on the basis of his or her salary level. It was expected that each employee, in keeping with being a manager-owner, would demonstrate a positive attitude towards work, and participate in the governance of the company. As Managing Officer Lori Dubose pointed out, "We'll fire someone only if it is (absolutely) necessary. . . . For instance, we won't tolerate dishonesty or willful disregard for the company's policies, but we don't punish people for making mistakes." In exchange, People Express promised the security of lifetime employment and opportunities for personal and professional growth through continuing education, cross-utilization, promotion from within the company, and compensation higher than other companies paid for similar skills and experience.

3. Cross-Utilization and Rotation. No one, regardless of work history, qualifications, or responsibility, was assigned to do the same job all the time. Everyone, including managing officers, was expected to be "cross-utilized" as needed and to rotate monthly between in-flight and ground operations and/or between line and staff functions. (The terms *line* and *staff* in PE differentiated tasks which were directly flight related from those related to the business of operating the company.)

Seen by some as unnecessarily complicated and troublesome, cross-utilization and rotation was justified by PE in several ways. According to Burr, they were conceived primarily as methods of continuing education, aimed at keeping everyone interested, challenged, and growing. Bob McAdoo appreciated the flexible staff utilization capability which eventually would result from everyone having broad exposure to the company's functions. Rotation did create some difficulties:

It takes people a while to master each job. It might seem better to have an expert doing a given job. Cross-utilization also means you need high-quality people who are capable of doing several jobs. This in turn limits how fast you can recruit and how fast you can grow.

These were seen, even by McAdoo, the efficiency expert, as short-term inconveniences well worth the long-term payoff.

When you rotate people often, they don't develop procedures that are too complicated for newcomers to learn and master fast. This forces the work to be broken down into short, simple packets, easily taught and easily learned.

4. Self-Management.   People were expected to manage themselves and their own work in collaboration with their teams and co-workers. According to Jim Miller, coordinator of training:

We don't want to teach behaviors—we want to teach what the end result should look like and allow each individual to arrive at those results his or her own way. . . . When desired results aren't achieved, we try to guide people and assist them in improving the outcome of their efforts.

The written, though never formalized, guidelines regarding "self-management" read as follows:

Within the context of our precepts and corporate objectives, and with leadership direction but no supervision, individuals and/or teams have the opportunity (and the obligation) to self-manage, which encompasses the following:

Setting specific, challenging, but realistic objectives within the organizational context.

Monitoring and assessing the quantity/quality/timeliness of one's own performance ("How am I doing?") by gathering data and seeking input from other people.

Inventing and executing activities to remedy performance problems that appear and exploiting opportunities for improved performance.

Actively seeking the information, resources, and/or assistance needed to achieve the performance objectives.

When it came time for performance reviews, each individual distributed forms to those six co-workers from whom feedback would be useful. Again, growth rather than policing was the objective.

5. Work Teams. Dubose observed that "even with smart, self-managed people, one person can't have all the components to be the answer to every situation." People Express therefore had decided to organize its work force into small (3–4 person) work groups as an alternative to larger groups with supervisors. "If you don't have a hierarchical structure with 40 levels, you have to have some way to manage the numbers of people we were anticipating." Teams were seen as promoting better problem solving and decision making as well as personal growth and learning.

Every customer service manager belonged to a self-chosen, ongoing team with which he or she was assigned work by a lottery system on a monthly basis. Though monthly staff assignments were made individually according to interests, skills, and needs, staff work was expected to be performed in teams. This applied to flight managers and maintenance managers as well as customer service managers. Each team was to elect a liaison to communicate with other teams. Each staff function was managed by a team of coordinators, most of whom were members of the start-up team recruited from Texas International. Managing officers also worked in teams and rotated certain responsibilities to share the burden and the growth benefits of primary leadership.

6. Governance, Broad-Based Participation. People's governance structure was designed with several objectives: policy development, problem solving, participation, and communication.

While Burr was the ultimate decision maker, top management decisions, including plans and policies, were to be made by management teams with the assistance of advisory councils. Each of the eight managing officers and eight general managers was responsible for at least 1 of the 13 functional areas (see Exhibit 3) and served on a management team for at least 1 other function. The 13 function-specific management teams were grouped into 4 umbrella staff committees: operations, people, marketing, and finance and administration. For each staff committee, composed of managing officers and general managers from the relevant functional areas, there was an advisory council made up of selected customer service managers, flight managers, and maintenance managers serving on relevant line and staff teams. The councils were intended to generate and review policy recommendations, but until August 1982 they followed no written guidelines. A study done by Yale University students under the direction of Professor Richard Hackman, showed considerable confusion as to their purposes (influencing, learning, solving, communicating issues) and role (advising versus making decisions).

To minimize duplication and maximize communication, each advisory council elected a member to sit on an overarching "coordinating council" which was to meet regularly with Don Burr (to transmit information to and from him and among the councils). These ongoing teams and councils were supplemented periodically by ad hoc committees and task forces which could be created at anyone's suggestion to solve a particular problem, conduct a study, and/or develop proposals.

In addition to maximizing productivity, all of the above practices, teams, and committees were seen essentially to promote personal growth and keep people interested in and challenged by their work.

7. Compensation—High   Reward   for   Expected   High   Performance.   People's four-part compensation package was aimed at reinforcing its human resource strategy. Base salaries were determined strictly by job category on a relatively flat scale, ranging in 1981 from $17,000 for customer service managers to $48,000 for the managing officers and CEO. (Competitor airlines averaged only $17,600 for flight attendants after several years of service, but paid nearly double for managing officers and more than four times as much for their chief executives).

Whereas most companies shared medical expenses with employees, People paid 100 percent of all medical and dental expenses. Life insurance, rather than being pegged to salary level, was $50,000 for everyone.

After one year with PE all managers' base salary and benefits were augmented by three forms of potential earnings tied to the company's fortunes. There were two profit-sharing plans: (1) a dollar-for-dollar plan, based on quarterly profits and paid quarterly to full-time employees who had been with PE over one year; and (2) a plan based on annual profitability. The former was allocated proportionally according to salary level and distributed incrementally. If profits were large, those at higher salary levels stood to receive larger bonuses, but only after all eligible managers had received some reward. The sustained profits were distributed annually and in equal amounts to people in all categories. Together, earnings from these plans could total up to 50 percent or more of base salary. The aggregate amount of PE's profit-sharing contributions after the second quarter of 1982 was $311,000.

Finally, PE awarded several stock option bonuses, one nearly every quarter, making it possible for managers who had worked at least half a year to purchase limited quantities of common stock at discounts ranging from 25 percent to 40 percent of market value. The company offered five-year, interest-free promissory notes for the full amount of the stock purchase required of new employees, and for two thirds the amount of any optional purchase. As of July 1982, 651 employees, including the managing officers, held an aggregate 513,000 shares of common stock under a restricted stock purchase plan. Approximately 85 percent were held by employees other than managing officers and general managers. The total number of shares reserved under this plan was, at that time, 900,000.

8. Selective Hiring of the People Express "Type."   Given the extent and diversity of responsibilities People required of its people, Lori Dubose, managing officer in charge of the company's "people" as well as in-flight functions, believed firmly that it took a certain type of person to do well at People Express. Her recruiters, experienced CSMs themselves, looked for people who were bright, educated, well groomed, mature, articulate, assertive, creative, energetic, conscientious, and hard working. While they had to be capable of functioning independently and taking initiative, and it was desirable for them to be ambitious in terms of personal development, achievements, and wealth, it was also essential that they be flexible, collaborative rather than competitive with co-workers, excellent team players, and comfortable with PE's horizontal structure. "If someone needed to be a vice president in order to be happy, we'd be concerned and might not hire them" (Miller).

Exhibit 4

TEAMWORK TAKES ON A WHOLE NEW MEANING AT PEOPLExpress!

TOTAL PROFESSIONALISM

Customer Service Managers

PEOPLExpress has a whole new approach to running an airline! As a Customer Service Manager, you'll be a vital part of our management team, working in all areas from In-Flight Service, Ground Operations, and Reservations to staff support functions such as Marketing, Scheduling, Training, Recruiting, Accounting, and more.

This cross-utilization takes a lot of hard creative work but it's the best way we know to achieve greater professionalism and productivity! Instead of doing just one limited job, you'll be involved in both line and staff activities—so you can learn the airline business fully. Faced with our variety of challenge, you'll develop and *use* all your decision-making skills. That's how bright people grow at PEOPLExpress . . . by finding simple creative solutions to complex problems . . . solutions that contribute to our productivity and growth . . . and *yours*.

Even better, your productivity can show a direct return. As a Customer Service Manager, you'll have the opportunity to participate in our unique STOCK PURCHASE PROGRAM (subject to legal requirements) and our profit-sharing plan.

If challenge stimulates you, if you really want to pursue management and growth, . . and are willing to invest the time it takes to achieve TOTAL PROFESSIONALISM, joining PEOPLExpress could be the turning-point in your career (we're already one of the phenomenal success stories in the history of American business).

Our basic requirements are that, preferably, you've had previous business management experience—and that you be poised, personable, have some college education—and be between 5'2" and 6'4" with weight proportional.

If you would like to learn more about the opportunities available to you . . .

THE GRAND HYATT NEW YORK
Park Ave. at Grand Central Station, NYC

NO PHONE CALLS ACCEPTED
SATURDAY, APRIL 23, 1983
11 A.M. to 4 P.M.

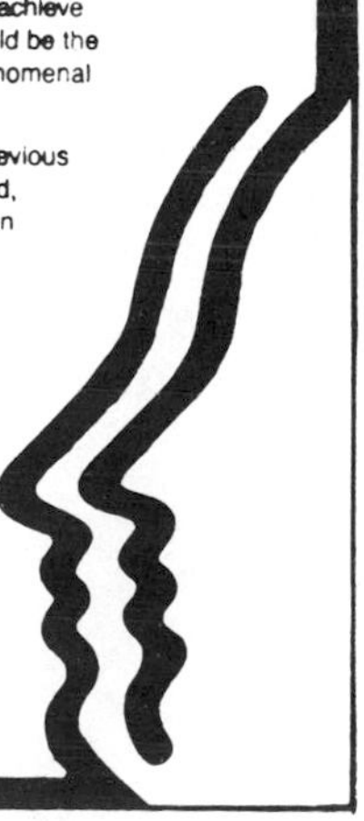

PEOPLExpress

We are an Equal Opportunity Employer M/F

Recruiting efforts for customer service managers were pitched deliberately to service professionals—nurses, social workers, teachers—with an interest in innovative management. No attempt was made to attract those with airline experience or interest per se (see Exhibit 4). Applicants who came from traditional airlines where "everyone memorized the union contract and knew you were only supposed to work x number of minutes and hours," were often ill-suited to People's style. They were not comfortable with its loose structure and broadly defined, constantly changing job assignments. They were not as flexible as People Express types.

The flight manager positions were somewhat easier to fill. Many pilots had been laid off by other airlines due to economic problems, and People Express had an abundant pool of applicants. All licensed pilots had already met certain intelligence and technical skill criteria, but not every qualified pilot was suited or even willing to be a People Express flight manager. Though flying time was strictly limited to the FAA's standard 30 hours per week (100/month, 1,000/year), and rules regarding pilot rest before flying were carefully followed, additional staff and management responsibilities could bring a flight manager's work week to anywhere from 50 to 70 hours.

Furthermore, FMs were expected to collaborate and share status with others, even nonpilots. In return for being flexible and egalitarian—traits which were typically somewhat in conflict with their previous training, and job demands—pilots at PE were offered the opportunity to learn the business, diversify their skills and interests, and benefit from profit sharing and stock ownership, if and when the company succeeded.

9. Recruitment Process.   As many as 1,600 would-be CSMs had shown up in response to a recruitment ad. To cull out "good PE types" from such masses, Dubose and her start-up team, eight CSMs whom she recruited directly from TI, designed a multistep screening process.

Applicants who qualified after two levels of tests and interviews with recruiters were granted a "broad interview" with at least one general manager and two other senior people who reviewed psychological profiles and character data. In a final review after a day-long orientation, selected candidates were invited to become trainees. One out of 100 CSM applicants was hired (see Exhibit 5 for a CSM profile).

In screening pilots, "the interview process was very stringent. Many people who were highly qualified were eliminated." Only one out of three flight manager applicants was hired.

10. Training and Team Building.   The training program for CSMs lasted for five weeks, six days a week, without pay. At the end, candidates went through an in-flight emergency evacuation role-play and took exams for oral competency as well as written procedures. Those who tested at 90 or above were offered a position.

The training was designed to enable CSMs, many without airline experience, to perform multiple tasks and be knowledgeable about all aspects of an airline. Three full days were devoted to team building, aimed at developing trainees' self-aware-

---

Exhibit 5
Profile of a Customer Service Manager

Look for candidates who:
1. Appear to pay special attention to personal grooming.
2. Are composed and free of tension.
3. Show self-confidence and self-assurance.
4. Express logically developed thoughts.
5. Ask intelligent questions; show good judgment.
6. Have goals; want to succeed and grow.
7. Have strong educational backgrounds; have substantial work experience, preferably in public contact.
8. Are very mature, self-starters with outgoing personality.
9. Appear to have self-discipline, good planners.
10. Are warm but assertive personalities, enthusiastic, good listeners.

Appearance guidelines:*
Well-groomed, attractive appearance.
Clean, tastefully worn, appropriate clothing.
Manicured, clean nails.
Reasonably clear complexion.
Hair neatly styled and clean.
Weight strictly in proportion to height.
No offensive body odor.
Good posture.
For women, make up should be applied attractively and neatly.
Good teeth.

---

*Above listed guidelines apply to everyone regardless of ethnic background, race, religion, sex, or age.

---

ness, communication skills, and sense of community. "We try to teach people to respect differences, to work effectively with others, to build synergy" (Miller).

On the last team-building day, everybody chose two or three others to start work with. These groups became work teams, People's basic organizational unit. Initially, according to Miller, these decisions tended to be based on personalities, and many trainees were reluctant to choose their own work teams. They were afraid of hurting people's feelings or being hurt. Trainers would remind them that People Express gave them more freedom than they would get in most companies, more than they were used to, and that "freedom has its price. . . . It means you've got to be direct and you've got to take responsibility" (Kramer).

Over time, trainers learned to emphasize skills over personalities as the basis of team composition and to distinguish work teams from friendship groups. Choosing a work team was a business decision.

Bottom Lines: Business Indicators

As of the second quarter of 1982, People was showing a $3 million net profit, one of only five airlines in the industry to show any profit at that time. In addition to short-term profitability, Burr and his people enjoyed pointing out that by several other concrete indicators typically used to judge the health and competitive strength of an airline, their strategies were paying off and their innovative company was succeeding.

Marketing Payoff.   Over 3 million passengers had chosen to fly with People Express. The size of air passenger markets in cities serviced by People had increased since People's entrance. In some instances the increase had been immediate and dramatic, over 100 percent. Annual revenue rates were approaching $200 million.

Cost Containment.   Total costs per available seat-mile were the lowest of any major airline (5.2 cents compared to a 9.4 cents industry average). Fuel costs were .5–.75 cents per seat-mile lower than other airlines.

Productivity.   Aircraft productivity surpassed the industry average by 50 percent (10.36 hours/day/plane compared to 7.06). Employee productivity was 145 percent above the 1981 industry average (1.52 compared to .62 revenue passenger miles per employee) for a 600-mile average trip. Return on revenue was 15.3 percent, second only to, and a mere .9 percent below, Southwest—the country's most successful airline. (Exhibit 6 shows operating statements through June 1982, and Exhibit 7 presents industry comparative data on costs and productivity.)

Explanations of Success

How could a new little airline with a funny name like People Express become such a formidable force so fast in such difficult times? Burr was fond of posing this question with a semipuzzled expression on his face and answering with a twinkle in his eye! The precepts and policies represented by that "funny" name—People— had made the difference. To back up this assertion, Burr and the other managing officers gave examples of how the people factor was impacting directly on the company's bottom line.

Consumer research showed that, notwithstanding heavy investments in award-winning advertisements, the biggest source of People's success was word of mouth; average customer ratings of passenger courtesy and personal treatment on ground and on board were 4.7 out of 5.

Several journalists had passed on to readers their favorable impressions of People's service: "I have never flown on an airline whose help is so cheerful and interested in their work. This is an airline with verve and an upbeat spirit which rubs off on passengers." Others credited the commitment, creativity, and flexibility of People's people with the company's very survival through its several start-up hurdles and first-year crises.

Perhaps the biggest crisis was the PATCO strike which occurred just months after PE began flying. While the air traffic controllers were on strike, the number of landing slots at major airports, including Newark, were drastically reduced. This made People's original hub-and-spoke, short-haul route design unworkable. To overfly Newark and have planes land less frequently without reducing aircraft utilization, People Express took a chance on establishing some new, previously

Exhibit 6
People Express

Statement of Operations
(in thousands, except per share data)

	April 7, 1980, to March 31, 1981	Nine Months Ended December 31, 1981	Six Months Ended June 30, 1982 (unaudited)
Operating revenues:			
Passenger	—	$37,046	$59,998
Baggage and other revenue, net	—	1,337	2,302
Total operating revenues . . .	—	38,383	62,300
Operating expenses:			
Flying operations	—	3,464	4,240
Fuel and oil	—	16,410	22,238
Maintenance	21	2,131	3,693
Passenger service	—	1,785	2,676
Aircraft and traffic servicing . . .	—	7,833	10,097
Promotion and sales	146	8,076	7,569
General and administrative . . .	1,685	3,508	2,498
Depreciation and amortization of property and equipment	6	1,898	3,087
Amortization—restricted stock purchase plan	—	470	131
Total operating expenses . . .	1,858	45,584	56,532
Income (loss) from operations . . .	(1,858)	(7,201)	5,768
Interest:			
Interest income	1,420	1,909	763
Interest expense	14	3,913	5,510
Interest expense (income), net	(1,406)	2,004	4,747
Income (loss) before income taxes and extraordinary item	(452)	(9,205)	1,021
Less: Provision for income taxes	—	—	(470)
Income (loss) before extraordinary item	(452)	(9,205)	551
Extraordinary item—utilization of net operating loss carryforward	—	—	470
Net income (loss)	$ (452)	$(9,205)	$ 1,021
Net income (loss) per common share:			
Income (loss) before extraordinary item	$ (.20)	$ (1.92)	$ .11
Extraordinary item	—	—	.09
Net income (loss per common share	(.20)	$ (1.92)	.20
Weighted average number of common shares outstanding . .	$2,299	$ 4,805	$ 5,046

Exhibit 7

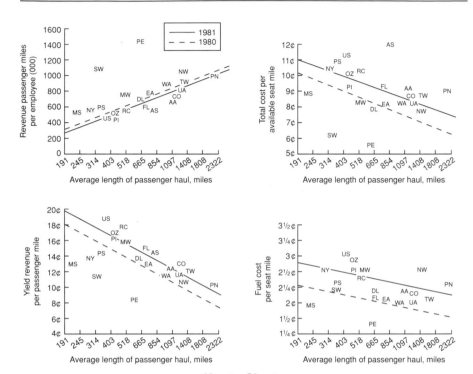

Key to Charts

Symbol	Airline	Symbol	Airline
AA	American	PN	Pan American
AS	Alaska	PS	Pacific Southwest
CO	Continental	PE	People Express
DL	Delta	PI	Piedmont
EA	Eastern	RC	Republic
FL	Frontier	SW	Southwest
MW	Midway	TW	Trans World
MS	Muse	WA	Western
NY	New York Air	UA	United
NW	Northwest Orient	US	USAir
OZ	Ozark		

*All data has been drawn from calendar 1981 results, except People Express and Muse, for which the first quarter of 1982 is used in order to offer comparisons not influenced by the start-up of operations.

†Total cost is operating cost plus interest expense net of capitalized interest and interest income.

‡Yield represents passenger revenues divided by revenue passenger miles (RPM).

§Average length of passenger haul is plotted on a logarithmic scale.

⁄The average line in each graph is a least-squared linear regression curve, based on 16 carriers which evolved in the regulated environment. Southwest, People Express, New York Air, Muse, and Alaska were not used in the calculations to determine the average. The 16 carriers were assigned equal weightings in the average.

Source: Hambrecht and Quist, June 1982.

unserviced, longer routes between smaller, uncontrolled airports—such as Buffalo, New York, to Jacksonville, Florida. This solution was tantamount to starting a new airline, with several new Florida stations, new advertising, and new route scheduling arrangements. The costs were enormous. According to Hap Paretti:

> *We could have run out of $25 million very quickly, and there wouldn't be any People Express. The effort people made was astronomical, and it was certainly in their best interest to make that effort. Everybody recognized truly and sincerely that the air traffic controller strike was a threat to their very existence. They rearranged their own schedules, worked extra days, really put the extra flying hours in, came in on their off days to do the staff functions, all things of that nature; people just really chipped in and did it and did a damned good job. So when we went into these markets from Buffalo to Florida, we could go in at $69. If we went in at $199 like everybody else, we wouldn't have attracted one person. We could go in very low like that because we had a cost structure that allowed us to do that. That's where the people strategy, from a cost standpoint, resulted in our survival. If it wasn't there, we'd be in the same situation many other carriers are today, hanging on by a toenail.*

By way of comparison, New York Air, a nonunion airline started by others from Texas International around the same time as People Express with plenty of financial backing, economical planes, and a similar concept of low-cost, high-frequency service, but different people policies, was losing money.

The Human Dimensions: Positive Climate and Personal Growth

In addition to becoming a financially viable business, People Express had shown positive results in the sphere of personal growth, the number one objective of its "people strategy." High levels of employee satisfaction showed up in the first-year surveys done by the University of Michigan. Less tangible but nevertheless striking were the nonverbal and anecdotal data. A cheerful, friendly, energetic atmosphere permeated the planes and passenger terminals as well as the private crew lounge and hallways of corporate headquarters. Questions about the company were almost invariably answered articulately, confidently, and enthusiastically. Stories of personal change, profit, and learning were common:

Ted E., customer service manager:

> *I was a special education teacher making $12,000 a year, receiving little recognition, getting tired, looking for something else. I started here at $17,000, already have received $600 in profit sharing, and will soon own about 800 shares of stock worth $12 on the open market, all bought at very reduced rates.* [Two months after this statement the stock was worth $25 a share.]

Glenn G., customer service manager:

> *I was running a hotline and crisis program, then was assistant manager of a health food store before seeing the People Express recruitment ad in the newspaper and coming to check it out. I'm about to sell my car in order to take advantage of the current stock offer to employees.*

Both Glenn and Ted had worked primarily in training but had also done "in-flight" and "ground operations" jobs. They wanted more responsibilities, hoped to get them, but even if they didn't get promoted soon they expected to continue learning from and enjoying their work.

Michael F., a flight captain:

> *I'm making $36,000. With my profit-sharing checks so far I've got $43,000 and on top of that I'll get sustained profit-sharing deals. . . . I'm doing OK. . . . Granted, at* [another company] *a captain might be making $110,000 working 10 days a month* [but] *they're not really worth it.* [In other companies] *the top people might make over $100,000, but they throw on 200 guys at the bottom so they can continue to make their salary. Is that fair?* [Also, the seniority system would have kept Michael from being a captain at most other airlines.] *We're radically different and I believe radically better.*
>
> *Most pilots know very little about what's going on in their company. In a People flight manager position, the knowledge people gain in this ratty old building is incredible. It's a phenomenal opportunity. It's very stimulating and exciting, I never thought I would have this much fun.*

The stories of People's start-up team members and officers were even more dramatic. Each had profited and diversified substantially in their two years with People.

Melrose Dawsey, Burr's secretary at Texas International, was a managing officer at People with primary responsibility for administration. She owned 40,000 shares of stock, purchased at $.50 a share and worth, as of November 1982, over $20 per share. For her own career development, she had also begun to assume some line management, responsibilities in the in-flight area. In her spare time, she had earned her in-flight certification and run the New York marathon (as had Burr).

Lori Dubose, the youngest officer, had come to People to head the personnel function. In addition, she had taken on primary responsibility for the "in-flight" function as well as assuming the de facto role of key translator and guide vis-à-vis the company's precepts. As others came to see the value and purpose of People's precepts and human resource policies, Dubose's status among the officers had also risen.

Jim Miller had been a flight attendant for a year and base manager of in-flight services for four years at Texas International. As part of Dubose's start-up team, he had been coordinator of training, played a key role in recruitment, and then took on added responsibility for management and organizational development as well.

Hap Paretti, who began as legal counsel and head of government relations, quickly became involved in all aspects of the marketing function, and then went on to head flight operations, a move he acknowledged was "a little out of the ordinary" since he didn't have a technical background as a pilot. He spoke for all of the officers in saying, "As a managing officer you're expected to think about virtually every major decision that comes up for review."

Many spoke of the more subtle aspects of their personal development. Hap Paretti enjoyed the challenge of motivating other people and "managing by example" so as to enhance the growth of others.

Geoff Crowley, general manager in charge of ground operations and manpower scheduling, talked of becoming "less competitive" and "less uptight about winning alone" and more interested in working together with others to accomplish group and company goals.

The Downside of People's Growth and Strategies

People Express's growth rate and strategies were not without significant organizational, financial, and human costs. By Burr's own observation,

> *I would say at best, we're operating at 50 percent of what we'd like to be operating at in terms of the environment for people to do the best in. So we're nowhere near accomplishing what we would really like to accomplish in that regard. [But] I think we're better off today than we ever have been. And I think we're gaining on the problem.*

Chronic Understaffing

Lori Dubose saw the hiring rate as the most difficult aspect of the company's growth process, causing many other problems:

> *If we could get enough people to staff adequately in all three areas of the company so that people got some staff and some line responsibility and would have some time for management development. . . . I think things would be a lot different. [There's been] constant pressure to hire, hire, hire, and we just haven't gotten enough.*

She was adamant, however, about not relaxing People's requirements.

When Dubose came to PE she expected to have to staff a company flying three planes, which would have required rapid hiring of perhaps 200–300 people. The purchase of the Lufthansa fleet meant five or six times as many staff were needed. Given the time consumed by the selective recruiting process, and the low percentage of hires, the staffing demands for supporting and launching 17 planes stretched People's people to the limit. The result was chronic understaffing even by People's own lean staffing standards.

As of November 1982 the 800 permanent "managers" were supplemented with over 400 temporaries, hired to handle telephone reservations, a function trained CSMs were originally expected to cover. Some of these "res" workers had been there a year or more, but still were not considered full-fledged People people, though many would have liked to be. They received little training, did not work in teams, own stock, receive profit-sharing bonuses, or participate in advisory councils. They were just starting to be invited to social activities. For a while those wishing to be considered for permanent CSM positions were required to leave their temporary jobs first on the theory that any bad feelings from being rejected could be contagious and have a bad effect on morale. That policy was eventually seen as unfair, and dropped. Indeed, some managers saw the res area as a training ground for CSM applicants.

In August 1982 several MOs estimated that aside from reservation workers, they were short by about 200 people, though the recruiting staff was working 10 to 12 hours daily, often six days a week, as they had since January 1981. This under-staffing in turn created other difficulties, limiting profits, policy implementation, and development of the organization's infrastructure.

If we had another 100 to 150 CSMs without adding an additional airplane we could just go out and add probably another half a million to a million dollars a month to the bottom line of the company. . . . There is additional flying out there that we could do with these airplanes. . . . We could generate a lot more money . . . almost double the profits of the company. [McAdoo]

The policy of job rotation, critical to keeping everyone challenged and motivated, had been only partially implemented. Initial plans called for universal monthly rotations, with 50 percent of almost everyone's time spent flying, 25 percent on ground line work and another 25 percent in "staff functions." Due to staffing shortages, however, many people had been frozen in either line jobs without staff functions or vice versa. Some had become almost full-time coordinators or staff to a given function like recruiting and training, while others had done mostly line work and had little or no opportunity to do what they expected when they were hired as "managers." Since neither performance appraisal nor governance plans had been fully carried out, many felt inadequately recognized, guided, or involved.

There were also certain inherent human costs of People's people strategies. Rotating generalists were less knowledgeable and sometimes performed less effi-ciently than specialists on specific tasks. High commitment to the company plus expectations of flexibility in work hours could be costly in terms of individuals' personal and family lives. For many who were single and had moved to Newark to join People Express, there "was no outside life." As one customer service manager described it, "People Express is it. . . . You kind of become socially re-tarded . . . and when you do find yourself in another social atmosphere it's kind of awkward."

For those who were married, the intense involvement and closeness with co-workers and with the company was sometimes threatening to family members who felt left out. Of the initial 15 officers, three had been divorced within a year and a half. The very fact of People's difference, in spite of the benefits, was seen by some as a source of stress; keeping the hierarchy to a minimum meant few titles and few promotions in the conventional sense.

You might know personally that you're growing more than you would ever have an opportunity to grow anywhere else, but your title doesn't change, [which] *doesn't mean that much to you but how does your family react?* [Magel]

Even People's biggest strengths, the upbeat culture, the high-caliber perfor-mance, and positive attitude of the work force could be stressful. "It's not a com-petitive environment, it's highly challenging. Everybody's a star. . . . But, you know," said one customer service manager, "maintaining high positive attitude is enough to give you a heart attack."

High commitment and high ambition, together with rapid growth and under-staffing, meant that most of People's managers were working long, hard hours and were under considerable stress. Said one CSM, "Nobody is ever scheduled for over 40 hours (a week), but I don't know anybody who works just 40 hours."

Dubose recognized that the situation had taken a toll on everybody's health:

I was never sick a day in my life until I worked for People Express and in the last two years I've been sick constantly. [Other managing officers, including Burr, had also been sick a lot, as had general managers.] And start-up team members—oh my God, they've got ulcers, high blood pressure, allergies, a divorce. . . . It's one thing after another . . . We've all been physically run down.

She adds, however, "It's not required that we kill ourselves," asserting that personality traits and an emotionally rewarding workplace accounted for the long hours many worked.

Burr's stance on this issue was that there were no emotional or human costs of hard work. "Work is a very misunderstood, underrated idea. In fact human beings are prepared and can operate at levels far in excess of what they think they can do. If you let them think they're tired and ought to go on vacation for two years or so, they will."

By the fall of 1982, though people were still generally satisfied with their jobs and motivated by their stock ownership to make the company work, many of People's managers below the top level were not as satisfied or optimistic as they once were. A University of Michigan 18-month climate survey taken in September 1982 showed signs of declining morale since December 1981.

People are feeling frustrated in their work (and feel they can't raise questions), cross-utilization is not being well received, management is viewed as less supportive and consultative, the total compensation package (including pay) is viewed less favorably. Clearly there is work to be done in several areas. [Exhibit 8 contains excerpts from the 1982 survey.]

The report found significant differences in the perceptions of FMs and CSMs: flight managers were more skeptical of cross-utilization and more uncertain of what self-management meant; they felt most strongly that management was nonconsultative.

When questioned about such problems, those in leadership positions were adamant that both business and personal difficulties were short term, and the costs were well worth the long-term benefits. They felt that virtually every problem was soluble over time with better self-management skills—including time management and stress management, which everyone was being helped to develop—and with evolving improvements in organizational structure. Even those responsible for recruitment insisted, "The challenge is that it seems impossible and there's a way to do it" [Robinson].

I don't think the long-term effects on the individual are going to be disastrous because we are learning how to cope with it. And I think the short-term effects on the organization will not be real bad because I think we're trying to put in place all the structure modifications at the same time that we're continuing the growth.

Exhibit 8
Excerpts from the 1982 Survey

Changes since the December 1981 Climate Survey

In comparing the responses from the December 1981 and September 1982 surveys, the following significant changes have apparently taken place:*

— Getting help or advice about a work-related problem is not as easy.

— What is expected of people is not as clear.

— People are not being kept as well informed about the performance and plans of the airline.

— Satisfaction with work schedules has decreased.

— The number of perceived opportunities to exercise self-management is lower.

— The process used to create initial work teams is viewed less favorably.

— The work is generally perceived to be less challenging and involving.

— The overall quality of upper management is being questioned more.

— Fewer opportunities for personal growth and career development are apparent.

— People are not very comfortable about using the "open door" policy at People Express.

— People feel that their efforts have less of an influence on the price of People Express stock.

— The buying of discounted company stock is being perceived as less of a part of the pay program.

— The compensation package is thought to be less equitable considering the work people do.

— People feel they have to work too hard to accomplish what is expected of them.

— The team concept at People Express is being questioned more.

— Officers and general managers are thought to be nonconsultative on important decisions.

— People Express is thought to be growing and expanding too fast.

— There is a stronger perception that asking questions about how the airline is managed may lead to trouble.

All of these changes are in a negative direction. Clearly, people are frustrated with the "climate" at People Express: morale and satisfaction are on the decline.

On the positive side, people's expectations of profiting financially were somewhat greater.

---

*Responses on many of these items were still quite positive in an absolute sense, though showing statistically significant decline from earlier studies.

That makes it take longer to get the structure modifications on the road. Which isn't real good. But they'll get there. Long term I think they will have a positive effect. I think. I wish I knew for sure. [Dubose]

Within two months of the climate survey report, Dubose and others from the People advisory council made a video presentation to address many of the items raised in the report. For almost every major item a solution had been formulated.

In spite of all the new initiatives, each of which would entail considerable time and energy to implement, People's officers did not believe they should slow down the company's rate of growth while attending to internal problems. Their standard explanations were as follows:

If you don't keep growing then the individual growth won't happen. People here have a very high level of expectation anyway, I mean unrealistic, I mean there's no way it's going to happen. They're not going to be general managers tomorrow, they're not going to learn each area of the airline by next month. But they all want to. And even a reasonable rate of growth isn't going to be attainable for the individual if we don't continue to grow as a company. And the momentum is with us now we're on a roll. If we lose the momentum now we might never be able to pick it up again. [Dubose]

Burr put it even more strongly:

Now there are a lot of people who argue that you ought to slow down and take stock and that everything would be a whole lot nicer and easier and all that; I don't believe that. People get more fatigued and stressed when they don't have a lot to do. I really believe that, and I think I have tested it. I think it's obvious as hell, and I feel pretty strongly about it.

He was convinced that the decrease in energy and decline in morale evident even among the officers were not reason to slow down but to speed up. For himself, he had taken a lot of time to think about things in his early years and had only really begun to know what was important to him between his 35th and 40th years. Then he had entered what he hoped would be an enormous growth period, accelerating "between now and when I get senile. It's sensational what direction does. The beauty of the human condition is the magic people are capable of when there's direction. When there's no direction, you're not capable of much."

Approaching 1983, the big issue ahead for People Express, as Burr saw it, was not the speed or costs of growth. Rather, it was how he and People's other leaders would "keep in touch with what's important" and "not lose sight of their humanity."

C a s e   4–2

F International (A)

Diane Franklin, Janice McCormick

In mid-1984, top managers and board members of the F International Group (FI), a British consultancy and software house, met to discuss a serious problem confronting the company. In a curious way, the company's problem was to some extent engendered by its considerable success. Rapid growth between 1982 and 1984 had strained FI's managerial resources and anticipated further growth, desired by all, was viewed as likely to strain them still further. In addition, changes in the computer industry were calling into question practices which had served the company well until that point. Now, faced with the need for continued growth and with a changing industry that required new skills and centralized planning which would be difficult to achieve under the company's current decentralized structure (Exhibit 1), FI's management realized it would have to make some changes in the company's organizational structure and bring in some outside managerial talent in areas which had formerly been the province of internally grown managers.

In themselves these changes were important and necessary for the company's survival, but underlying the concerns about organizational structure and managerial resources and talent was another more fundamental issue having to do with F International's essential character. Like other computer consulting companies in a changing market, FI had to struggle with the problem of continuing to achieve rapid growth under increasingly competitive conditions, but in addition it had to figure out how to do so in a way that would not destroy the very things that distinguished it from its competitors. These included its innovative work system wherein the majority of its work force worked from home on a self-employed basis, its virtually all-female management and staff, and the charismatic leadership of its founder

This case was prepared by Associate for Case Development Dr. Diane Franklin under the supervision of Assistant Professor Janice McCormick, as the basis for class discussion rather than to illustrate either effective or ineffective handling of an administrative situation.

Exhibit 1
F INTERNATIONAL (A)
                    Organizational Structure, Pre-November 1984

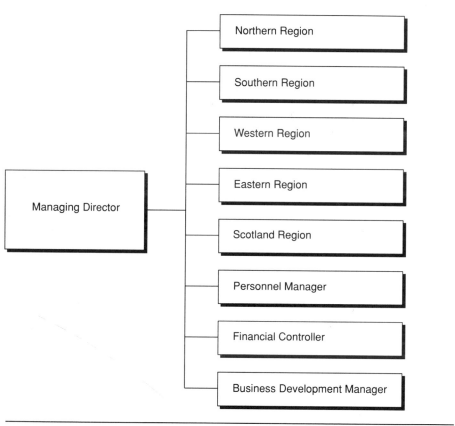

Sources: Company records.

whose ideas still permeated the company's culture. Though they knew they had to change some things for the company's survival, at the same time, in doing so, FI's board wanted to minimize the risks of undermining the company's uniqueness.

The Computer Industry in Britain

At the industry level, the situation which confronted F International in 1984 was very different from the way things had been at the company's inception. In the '60s when FI was started, the demand for computer expertise far exceeded the supply. Clients were so hungry for assistance that, throughout most of the '70s, they were willing to accept unconventional work forces and work arrangements.

During its infancy, the computer industry did not have rigid hiring requirements. Anyone with an analytical mind who was willing to learn was welcome in many companies as a trainee programmer, and it was very common, upon leaving school, for people to enter the computer field with degrees in history or literature. This situation continued for some time. A number of FI managers who had been with the company since its early days commented that because of the skill shortages in the industry, it was more open to women than might otherwise have been the case and noted that, as more men began to work with computers, some of the advancement opportunities formerly available to women began to decrease.

By the late '70s and early '80s, the supply of trained computer personnel began to catch up with the demand. A degree in computer sciences increasingly became a requirement for entry into the field.

The software market had also became more competitive during this time. A lot of the small software houses started during the boom period were squeezed out, and the medium-sized companies were forced to grow at a faster rate than previously and to diversify both the services they offered and the market niches in which they operated in order to survive. Some companies entered into alliances and mergers as an alternative to dissolution.

Company Background

History

F International was started by Steve Shirley in 1962 and was originally based in one room in her home. Its beginnings coincided with the boom period of the burgeoning computer industry. Mrs. Shirley's impetus for founding F International was her desire to continue working after the birth of her child in an era when, according to one FI manager, "pregnancy was equivalent to resignation," as a result of British employment practices in effect at that point. At the time of her pregnancy, Shirley was a highly skilled software developer and a junior manager at ICL (Britain's largest computer manufacturing company), and she realized that the kinds of skills she possessed were very valuable but also had to be utilized on an ongoing basis if they were to be kept up-to-date. Aware that once her child was born she could not keep her present job or find part-time employment in another company at the level of her capabilities, Shirley decided to go freelance and to gather around herself a team of people with whom she could work from home. In 1964, she formalized this group of 12 self-employed people as Freelance Programmers Limited. The concept of working at home, mainly on a contract basis, became the foundation of its work system even as it grew into a much larger company, renamed F International.

From these humble beginnings, FI developed into the 20th largest computer consultancy and software house in Britain, with annual sales in 1985 of £7.5 million. At first, FI's growth was slow, but during the '60s the company built up its work

Exhibit 2
F INTERNATIONAL (A)
        F International Group: Organizational Structure, 1985

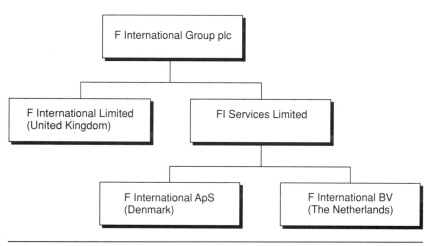

Source: Company records.

force and client base so that by 1970 it was able to utilize the skills of about 100 people. Hard hit by the 1972–73 recession in the computer industry during which many of its client companies were liquidated, FI retrenched and drastically cut back its work force, but by the late 70s it again experienced rapid growth.

In the 1970s the company set up its first overseas subsidiaries in the Netherlands and Denmark. In 1983, FI tried to enter the U.S. market by acquiring the issued share capital of Heights Information Technology Service, Inc., a New York-based company set up under license to FI in 1978, which concentrated on software development in the field of computer-aided education. In late 1985, the Dutch and Danish subsidiaries were rapidly growing, but the American operations, which had suffered substantial losses, were suspended. (Exhibit 2 shows the group's structure as of 1985.)

Structure and Management Style

In the beginning, F International was a centralized company with a highly person-alized management style. Steve Shirley, as the founder of the company, was its inspirational leader, and along with her small staff she played a major role in the company's day-to-day operations. Loosely structured and operating on an intuitive basis, the company allowed its highly skilled work force to carry out their tasks in a flexible and improvised manner. The fact that they were "special" people enjoying a unique working arrangement and a close relationship with their company's founder engendered great enthusiasm in those who worked for the company, enthusiasm that helped fuel its growth and success.

With growth came the pressure to regionalize into manageable business units, and over time an increasing number of decisions were made on a decentralized basis by a growing staff of managers. Some of the flexibility and informality that had characterized the company in its early days was lost. A woman who had been with FI for some years remarked on the changes that accompanied this more "managed environment": "There seems to be a deepening sense of hierarchy and power structure within FI. I suppose this is inevitable in a growing company."

Regionalization itself was a mixed blessing. On the one hand it made it possible for the company to broaden its potential client base thereby aiding further growth. But on the negative side, it changed the character and tone of the company and, from a business perspective, made it more difficult to accommodate centralized planning and a concentration of managerial talent at the corporate level. As the computer industry grew more competitive, centralized planning, sales, and marketing became increasingly necessary for FI's growth. Yet the regions had neither the resources nor the broad industry overview that would enable them to market and sell FI's services most effectively.

Despite decentralization and the fact that Steve Shirley no longer ran the company on a day-to-day basis, her ideas and others' respect for her abilities still influenced top management's thinking. Though somewhat plain in appearance, Shirley exuded a charm and energy which animated and transformed her entire being. In talking with her, it was almost impossible not to be embraced by the force of her personality and swept into an impassioned discussion of her ideas. As a German refugee to England in the late '30s, Shirley brought with her memories and values which imbued her thinking and helped shape her beliefs about the importance of providing services to others in addition to thinking about oneself. Putting her beliefs into practice, Shirley has served on many boards and government committees, a number of which have focused on youth and handicapped employment. In 1980 she received a civic award, the Order of the British Empire, for her services to the computing industry. Because of her strong personality and her subsequent celebrity, Shirley was often treated as an awesome figure by her subordinates; while this troubled and puzzled her, she also understood it as a tribute to the strength of her character and abilities which had so deeply influenced F International's culture and its ways of organizing work.

Company Strategy

Because F International had originated from its founder's personal needs and views about the way work should be carried out, these views permeated the company's entire culture and organizational forms. Freelance and flexibility, symbolized by the F in the company's name, have been hallmarks of the company's philosophy

---

Exhibit 3
F INTERNATIONAL (A)

F International Charter

F International is a group of companies which have sprung from seeing an opportunity in a problem: one woman's inability to work in an office has turned into hundreds of people's opportunity to work in a non-office environment. Because of its unusual origin, F International has a clear sense of its mission, its strategy and its values.

MISSION

F International's mission is to stay a leader in the rapidly growing and highly profitable, knowledge intensive software industry. It aims to achieve this by developing, through modern telecommunications, the unutilised intellectual energy of individuals and groups unable to work in a conventional environment.

STRATEGY

F International's strategy is to maximise the value of its unusual asset base by establishing a competitive advantage over conventionally organised firms, and imitators of its approach, through cost and quality competitiveness. This occurs by the development of a methodology which ensures quality and by establishing a company ethos which binds people who work largely independently and often alone.

VALUES

People are vital to any knowledge intensive industry. The skills and loyalty of our workforce are our main asset. Equally important is the knowledge which comes from the exchange of ideas with our clients and their personnel. It follows that human and ethical values play a pivotal role in the way in which an organisation like F International conducts itself. This is even more true in a structure as open and free as F International. To maintain a high level of creativity, productivity and coherence in such an environment requires a set of high ethical values and professional standards that any member of the organisation can identify with and see realised, and reinforced, in the organisation's behaviour. F International has defined for itself such a charter of values.

1. Professional Excellence

Our long term aim is to improve our professional abilities so as to maintain a quality product for our clients. It is also our aim to develop fully our professional potential as people and to develop our organisation in a way which reflects our own individuality and special approach.

2. Growth

We aim to grow our organisation to its full potential, nationally and internationally. We aim to grow at least as rapidly as the software industry as a whole in order to maintain our own position as an attractive employer and a competitive supplier.

(continued)

Exhibit 3
(concluded)

3. Economic and Psychological Reward
We also aim to realise and enjoy fully the economic and psychological rewards of
our efforts resulting from the development of the unique competitive advantage
of our structure and capabilities. We aim to achieve profits, reward our workforce, maintain the Employee Trust and provide an attractive return to our
shareholders.

4. Integrated Diversity
We have a commitment to consistent procedures worldwide as a means of
lowering cost, but aim to conduct ourselves as a national of each country in which
we operate.

5. Universal Ethics
We respect local customs and laws, but see ourselves as members of a world
society with respect for human dignity and ethical conduct beyond the profit
motive and local circumstances.

6. Goodwill
An extension of our ethical view is a belief in the goodwill of others: colleagues,
clients and vendors. We also believe that goodwill results in positive, long term
relationships.

7. Enthusiasm
Finally we believe that enthusiasm for our people and our product, and the ability
to engender that enthusiasm in others, is the most essential quality of leadership within the organisation. Enthusiasm promotes creativity, cooperation and
profit.

Steve Shirley

since its inception. The 1985 F International prospectus stated very clearly that the
company's mission is, through technology, to make use of the intellectual energy
of individuals and groups unable to work in a conventional environment. This theme
was more fully developed in F International's charter (Exhibit 3).

At no time, however, was this mission seen as an end in itself. Rather, the
company has always clearly recognized that allowing its work force to operate in
a nonconventional way is a strategy which benefits both panel members and the
entire computer industry by utilizing skills that would otherwise be wasted and also

benefits clients by offering them more flexibility, slightly lower prices, and greater worker productivity than would be obtainable in a traditional work environment.

An element of FI's strategy is a series of values having to do with professional excellence, the production of a quality product, and appreciation of the people who produce the product. While no dividends have ever been paid, profit and capital growth have never been disdained by the company and are indeed emphasized as extremely important, though they are not the sole criteria against which the company has measured its success.

FI's Business

In 1984, the total software and computer services market in the United Kingdom was estimated as between £1 and £2 billion with an annual growth rate of over 20%. Within this sector, the consulting and custom software market was valued at £500 million. In the fiscal year ending in April 1985, F International's share of this market was 1.5%, with significant growth expected in the future. Because the computer services market was an extremely fragmented one, no single company had a market share of more than 4%. Annual sales in 1985 for the largest software house were £70 million, with a market mix including hardware, compared to FI's £7.5 million in software.

F International's core businesses were (1) the development of custom software applications for clients and (2) consulting and project assignments related to the application or use of computer systems in specific business situations. Custom software development encompassed all aspects of building a software application, from the analysis of a client's requirements to the testing of the system that was ultimately developed. Approximately 86% of FI's business came from the development of custom software, 11% from consultancy and project management, and 3% from the provision of miscellaneous services.

In 1984, having recognized the importance of the ready-made software market for micros and personal computers, the company developed some applications that could be used on an "as is" rather than a bespoke basis. One such application was their treasury management system, an accounting package designed to be used by corporate treasurers. Also, having developed an expertise in and reputation for good project management as a consequence of supervising its own work force, the company began to market this expertise by developing training courses in project management for interested clients.

FI's clients have been located in a number of different industries. Though the company did not initially decide to focus on certain kinds of industries or businesses, in fact the majority of its clients have come from local government or from companies involved in insurance, financial services, technological development, or food and beverage manufacturing and distribution. (Exhibit 4 shows the percentage of revenues derived from each of the company's major markets.) Within each of these industries, FI has had many different kinds of clients (Exhibit 5). Among these have been a high percentage of *The Times* Top 500 Companies.

Exhibit 4
F INTERNATIONAL (A)
Percentage of Revenues Derived From
Various Industries, 1984–85

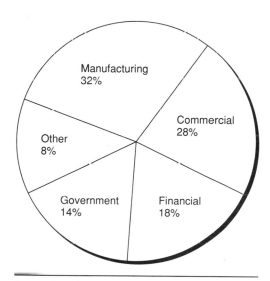

Source: Annual report, April 30, 1985.

Because it has worked with such varied clients, the company has not been allied with any single computer manufacturer, and in its work force it has retained people experienced with many different kinds of hardware and computer languages.

Over the years F International has worked with clients in differing ways. Although in the beginning the company accepted short-term programming jobs, it began in 1984 to turn away this kind of business unless it saw the potential for obtaining larger-scale projects in the immediate future as a result of providing piecemeal services on a short-term basis. Increasingly, it has sought to obtain long-term, totally managed projects with several components rather than to provide temporary help.

The kinds of projects undertaken by the company have varied tremendously in their content and scope. In 1985, for example, FI designed a stock control system and modified an existing invoicing system for a large automobile manufacturing company. During the same period, it collaborated with the Department of Transportation in Bristol to build a computerized highway accident-prevention system that utilized feedback from sensors built into the road. The ultimate goal of the project was the prevention of accidents in a dangerous fog-bound area by means of a computerized system that would automatically detect and warn motorists of unusual traffic build-ups on the road ahead.

Exhibit 5
F INTERNATIONAL (A)
Sample of F International Clients, 1984–85

Industry and Commerce	Public Sector	Finance	Overseas
Allied Breweries Management Services Limited	AERE Harwell	Forward Trust Group Limited	Esselte Dymo A/S
Avis Management Services Limited	City of Birmingham District Council	Norman Frizzell Motor & General	F L Smidt & Company A/S
Birds Eye Wall's Limited	London Borough of Lambeth	The Royal Bank of Scotland PLC	Fokker BV
British Aerospace PLC (civil aircraft division)	Warwickshire County Council	Sun Alliance Insurance Group	Hoogovens IJmuiden
H Samuel PLC		Thomas Cook Financial Services Limited	Oce-Nederland NV
Unilever UK Central Resources Limited		UK Provident	Quaker Oats BV
Van den Berghs & Jurgens Limited			

Source: Company documents.

FI has accepted both fixed-price and time-spent contracts, though the latter have been the norm. For example, during the fiscal year ending in April 1985, time-spent contracts accounted for 87.5% of FI's U.K. sales. Project fees have ranged from £1,000 to £750,000, with a typical contract price of around £50,000.

Financial Data

Exhibit 6 shows FI's sales and profit growth between 1981 and 1985. For the period between 1984 and 1985, sales increased by 30%, compared to an industry average of 19%. Exhibit 7 summarizes the group's financial data in greater detail.

In 1985, after much planning and effort, F International became a public limited company. On October 1, 1985, 217,600 new shares, equal to 11.21% of issued plus new share capital, were put on offer to FI's employees and panel members. Twenty-four percent of the work force purchased shares under the offer; at the same time two institutional investors bought shares from Steve Shirley.

FI's Work Force

Consistent with its origins, FI has always been run according to the principle that high-quality work is best achieved by people who have both technical competence and personal commitment. The company's employee selection and control processes have ensured the first criterion, while its work system and values have contributed

Exhibit 6
F INTERNATIONAL (A)
Sales and Profit Growth, 1981–85

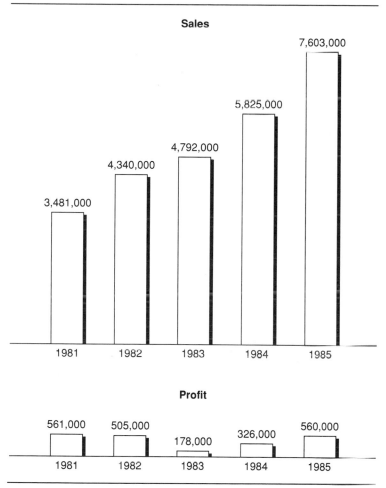

Sales

7,603,000

5,825,000

4,792,000

4,340,000

3,481,000

| 1981 | 1982 | 1983 | 1984 | 1985 |

Profit

561,000   505,000   178,000   326,000   560,000

| 1981 | 1982 | 1983 | 1984 | 1985 |

Source: Company slide presentation.

to the second. In addition, the fact that FI was a "company of women" has subtly pervaded many aspects of the company's style, values, and ways of working.

FI's work force (Exhibit 8) consisted of two groups: freelance panel members and salaried employees. F International used the term "panel members" to describe freelancers who contracted to work with the company. Panel members, all of whom were highly skilled, could hold either technical or managerial positions. In 1985, out of 1078 people, 261 were salaried while 817 were freelancers. Only about half of the salaried employees and virtually none of the panel members worked full

Exhibit 7
F INTERNATIONAL (A)

F International Group Limited:
Consolidated Balance Sheet, April 1985

		1985		1984
		£		£
Fixed assets				
Tangible assets:				
Land and buildings		255,719		260,711
Equipment		234,474		137,561
Fixtures and fittings		65,114		58,822
Motor vehicles		265,001		136,445
		820,308		593,539
Current assets				
Debtors	2,077,642		1,594,865	
Cash at bank and in hand	13,025		12,326	
	2,090,667		1,607,191	
Less: Creditors				
amounts falling due within one year				
Bank overdraft	203,928		14,184	
Trade creditors	773,092		587,030	
Corporation tax	216,994		168,494	
Other taxes and social security costs	244,381		205,750	
Other creditors	111,628		62,167	
Accruals	258,615		274,500	
	1,808,638		1,312,125	
Net current assets		282,029		295,066
Total assets less current liabilities		1,102,337		888,605
Creditors:				
amounts falling due after more than one year				
Hire purchase liabilities		(127,119)		(53,543)
		975,218		835,062
Provision for liabilities and charges				
Deferred taxation		(94,000)		(87,000)
		£881,218		£748,062
Capital and reserves				
Called up share capital		23,936		23,936
Profit and loss account		857,282		724,126
		£881,218		£748,062

Exchange rate as of April 30, 1985, £1 = $1.24.
Source: *Annual Report,* April 30, 1985.

Exhibit 8
F INTERNATIONAL (A)
Description of Work Force

	Full-Time	Part Time	
Panel Members	81	736	817
Salaried Employees	123	138	261
	204	874	

Source: Company records.

time. The majority of both salaried employees and panel members worked from home rather than in a conventional office setting.

Britain's tax laws are quite strict in distinguishing between employed and self-employed workers. As a result, the company has been very careful to emphasize the freelance status of panel members, and it does not refer to these people as employees nor offer them the state-mandated employment benefits that salaried employees receive.

Because the majority of FI's work force were freelancers, the company was able to retain an extraordinary degree of flexibility to respond to business fluctuations. By having access to a large pool of talent, it could quickly staff new projects; on the other hand, because it did not have a large number of employees on its payroll, it did not have to lay off people during a business downturn. In addition, because FI did not maintain a large central office out of which all its employees and panel members worked, its fixed overhead costs were lower than those of other consulting firms. While the company did incur other kinds of overhead costs as a result of its structure, especially the project control and communications costs necessary for managing a remote work force, it was still able to keep its fixed costs down, and it thus retained the ability to adapt quickly to changes in the market.

Similarly, panel members also benefited from the flexibility of the system. Except in times of deep recession or in regions hard hit by economic difficulties, as long as the company was doing well they could, subject to minimal requirements, work as little or as much as they liked and could feel free not to work for periods of time in order to pursue other responsibilities or interests. If they did this, they did not have to worry about jeopardizing their careers or undermining their promotion prospects within F International.

Panel Members

In any given week or year, panel members worked varying amounts of time for F International. The majority averaged 20 to 30 hours of work per week and less than 29 weeks per year, though 23% worked 46 or more weeks annually. Panel members were not guaranteed work by the company, and the amount of work available to them was negotiated on an individual basis. Since it was not an employment agency, F International received no placement fees either from its freelancers or its clients for assigning panel members to projects and instead derived its income solely from its consulting fees. It also did not prohibit panel members from working for other clients except in cases of obvious conflict of interest.

Because of their self-employed status, panel members received full fees and expenses. No health insurance or tax deductions were withheld from their fees, and they were responsible for paying their own income tax and social security contributions.

Ninety-six percent of the panel members were women, and over 90% of them had children. The majority of them worked as programmers but others were systems designers or analysts, and a few worked as business or strategy consultants on a freelance basis. Because of their child-rearing commitments, many panel members were unable or unwilling to hold conventional jobs. Some chose to return to regular employment once their children were able to look after themselves, while others continued to remain on the panel, preferring FI's flexibility to conventional work hours. FI itself was somewhat surprised by its high retention rate in an industry notorious for frequent job-hopping.

To be eligible to join F International, panel members had to have had at least four years' technical experience in the computer industry. In fact, many joined with much greater experience, and the average number of years' experience for panel members, including those who had worked for FI for some time, was 13.5. Panel members had to be available for work at least 20 hours per week, be able to make two or more weekly client visits, have a telephone, and own or have access to transport.

The typical panel member in 1985 was a middle-class woman who had received a good technical or science education from a moderately rated university or who had had a number of years of experience in a computer-related job without having graduated from a university. She lived in a pleasantly furnished, semi-detached house in a relatively new suburban district, drove a well-kept-up car which she did not share with her husband, dressed neatly if blandly, and had good relationships with neighbors, friends, and family. Nothing in her outward demeanor or appearance readily distinguished her from millions of other middle-class British women engaged in other kinds of paid employment or occupied with the rearing of children.

Salaried Employees

Salaried employees of F International, employed on a full- or part-time basis, worked either in key managerial, sales, or clerical positions. Most had begun their careers as panel members while a few had been recruited from outside the company to perform specific functions or tasks. The responsibilities of this group ranged from providing secretarial or administrative support services to overseeing the company's accounting and control procedures or managing its personnel functions at the corporate level.

Most senior managers at FI were salaried employees, and most worked on a full-time basis. Except at the most senior level, salaried staff, like panel members, frequently worked part time. They were paid on a time-spent basis and received overtime for hours worked beyond those to which they had originally committed.

Managers

Until 1984, most managers in the company had come up through the ranks. But whether recruited internally or from the outside, F International managers were expected to fit into the company culture and to "project an F image." Commitment, self-discipline, strong administrative skills, and highly developed interpersonal abilities were managerial qualities that the company greatly valued.

As panel members assumed managerial roles, they frequently began to differentiate themselves from other panel members in subtle ways. One manager commented that outside observers could always recognize the "F type" in a crowd of women, and the truth of this observation became apparent in the course of interviewing FI managers. Though these women varied widely in their appearances, personalities, and styles of dress, overall they presented a consistent image. Most managed to be both smart and feminine at the same time as they appeared competent and self-confident. In general, the higher in the company a manager was placed, the more she had developed a sense of personal style in her overall demeanor. This contrasted with the less differentiated image of panel members and lower level managers.

Project Managers

Within the company managers played a variety of roles. At one level were project managers. After a contract had been negotiated with a client and the details of it worked out, a project manager, herself often a panel member, was assigned to head the project team. Kay Vickery, a typical project manager, exemplified this group. A quiet and unassuming woman, Vickery projected an image of technical competence and strength.

Sometimes supervised by more experienced senior project managers, project managers had complete responsibility for the project's day-to-day operations, for writing month-end reports to the regional office detailing the financial and completion status of each project and summarizing the contributions made by each panel member, and for preparing financial reports and invoices for clients.

Either alone or with an accounts manager, project managers held frequent client meetings. Vickery, for example, along with her immediate supervisor, met with a client to discuss a recently completed inventory control system that her project team had just designed. At that meeting, she mainly took a back-seat role and let others do the talking, only entering the discussion when she had specific points to make. Despite her self-confidence and obvious ability, Vickery seemed "unseasoned." One sensed that she had leadership potential but that it would take time and training for this potential to develop.

Sales and Accounts Managers

Above project managers were sales and accounts managers, positions that were complementary. Sales managers were in charge of the sales teams which marketed the company's services and generated business with new clients.

Once a sales team obtained a client contract, the account was turned over to an accounts manager who took primary responsibility for servicing and maintaining that account and for generating new business within it. If, for example, the contract was with one department of a client company, the accounts manager attempted to learn about other departments within the client's business that might have need of FI's services and to obtain introductions to managers in those departments. Barbara Mitchell, an accounts manager who had risen quickly in the company, demonstrated her ability to seek new business by skillfully and subtly raising the subject of additional business at a client meeting held immediately after the completion of a successful new project. Comfortable both with herself and her clients, Mitchell was aware that good client and staff relationships involved a combination of technical competence and strong interpersonal skills, and she cultivated her abilities in both areas.

Accounts managers also had to develop financial skills since they were responsible for billing clients and for meeting agreed-upon revenue targets for each account.

Estimating Managers

Estimating managers, on the same level with sales and accounting managers, performed a more technical function. Before an account was obtained, either with a new or existing client, the estimating manager became part of the FI team. Accurate estimating has been one of the key ingredients of FI's success, and the details of how estimating is done remain a closely guarded secret within the company. Essentially, estimating managers looked at a project's specifications and broke the work into a series of "chunks," each with a fixed time and value allotted to it. The work was then allocated to panel members who contracted to complete a certain number of chunks within a specified time period.

In the past, when fixed-price rather than time-spent contracts were more typical in the company, the role of the estimating manager was a particularly crucial one. The costs incurred as a result of any mistakes made at the estimating phase had to be subtracted from the company's profits. Even on time-spent contracts, managers were held accountable for staying within estimates, and any slippages had to be documented and explained. Decisions about how to handle cost overruns resulting from estimating mistakes were made at the upper management level.

Regional Managers

The most senior managers below the corporate level were the regional managers. They were responsible for the overall functioning of their geographical areas, each of which was treated as a profit center, and they had to ensure that ongoing projects were run profitably and well.

Jenny Williams served as the regional manager for the Western region. An elegant woman with a strikingly individualistic style, Williams seemed to combine both an incisive, analytical mind with a great deal of personal warmth. Equally at home discussing the changing markets in her region or lunching with her subordinates in a relaxed manner, Williams embodied the three qualities that in combination symbolized F International's uniqueness: business acumen, technical competence, and a high degree of caring for the personal lives and career development of the people who worked for the company.

As a regional manager, Williams had to meet sales targets for generating new business and attempt to utilize panel members in her region to the maximum extent. With a series of staff members to assist her in her duties, she did not get involved in the day-to-day operations of projects under her jurisdiction. Instead, she engaged in overall planning at a regional level, made major decisions, solved problems and coped with crises as they arose, and met once or twice a year with all current clients.

The Company's Attitudes and Beliefs about Its Work Force

FI's emphasis on "growing" almost all of its managers internally had been one of the company's hallmarks, and it reflected Steve Shirley's attitudes about the people who worked for her. Shirley believed that FI's employees, panel members or salaried, managerial or clerical, were the company's most important asset and that, as in all service companies, what FI had to offer was only as good as the people who offered it. She also felt that by treating people in a caring manner and by providing opportunities for them to grow and develop, she could maximize creativity and loyalty as well as enhance productivity. From the beginning the company had developed a participative management style characterized by team work, openness, and smooth administration. In the company's vision of itself, these attitudes and practices engendered loyalty even in times of economic retrenchment and made it possible for panel members to remain committed to F International during economic downturns.

Though obviously aware of FI as a "company of women," surprisingly few people within the company made an explicit connection between it being a caring company and one that was largely female. When asked specifically to comment on whether F International was different from other companies because of this female aspect, Steve Shirley linked the company's femininity with its managers' ability both to delegate control and to listen, two things she thought less likely to happen had most managers been men. She also suggested that an aspect of the company's femininity was its recognition of more than the profit motive:

> I wrote "profit" into the company's charter; it's one of the first words and it's literally the last word, but it's not everything. In between, there are a lot of other things that are important, like recognizing the whole person. Maybe that's the feminine part.[1]

Another manager felt that because the company was largely female, there was a greater diversity of aspirations than would have been true in a company comprised primarily of men. She pointed out that those who worked for FI did so for a variety of reasons. While some women in the company wanted a career and saw FI as a good place in which to receive exposure to a variety of clients and roles, others saw it as a company that offered them maximum flexibility, an absence of total commitment rituals, and reasonably good money at a time in their lives when other demands were equally as important as their career demands. Because enough managerial positions were generally available for those who wanted them and because not all panel members wanted the managerial positions that did become available, little energy was wasted on jostling for these positions. Instead people were able to focus their attention on the task at hand rather than on internal politics.

Linked to this diversity of aspirations were the economic realities of the British labor market. In Britain in the mid-80s, labor force participation rates for women were lower than in the United States (42% as opposed to 54%). Life-styles were therefore not built around the presumption of two full-time wage earners, and many women perceived themselves as having some choice about the degree of their labor market involvement. This fact influenced the relationship of panel members to F International. The prevailing opinion of FI managers was that the majority of panel members worked because they wanted to, not because they had to for financial reasons. To the extent that panel members had such financial flexibility, they could be selective about the projects they undertook. Many felt this ability to be selective increased overall satisfaction with the company and with the specific jobs undertaken.

Project Control

Formal Mechanisms

Because F International's panel members worked without direct supervision at least part of the time, the company had to develop effective methods of project control. Some degree of project control was built into the selection process for new panel members. Because the company utilized only mature people with several years of

---

[1]Quoted from Steve Shirley, interviewed by Eliza G. C. Collins, "A Company Without Offices," *Harvard Business Review,* January–February 1986.

work experience, they did not have to contend with training an entry-level work force. In addition, some self-selection occurred in the recruitment process. FI and its work methods were well-known within the computer industry, and for the most part those who tended to apply for the panel already viewed themselves as disciplined and self-motivated workers. Management felt that most panel members, aware that they had only a finite time to accomplish their tasks and having built into their lives time for accomplishing nonwork-related tasks and for fulfilling social and personal goals, exhibited little nonproductive behavior and were generally willing to work hard during their chosen work time.

Despite these favorable a priori conditions, the company had carefully developed a series of formal project control mechanisms. Since the key to FI's survival and growth was its ability to offer a quality product at a competitive price, panel members' work had to be strictly monitored both for quality and for delivery within a stipulated time period. Steve Shirley had quite explicitly stated that F International was interested in controlling "products, productivity, and quality—not time spent." Thus the company's project control mechanisms mainly focused on the accuracy of work and on increased productivity rather than on when and where panel members worked.

When a panel member contracted to undertake a project for F International, she received a project assignment sheet (Exhibit 9) which spelled out in detail the work she agreed to do and the deadline by which it would have to be completed. During her work on the project, she was required to complete a weekly time sheet documenting the use of her time in 15-minute intervals. This was turned in to the project manager who could audit its veracity by comparing the tasks done on the current project both with tasks performed on previous projects of a similar kind and with the estimates earlier made for the current project. Work was audited at fixed points during the project in order to obtain, as soon as possible, an estimate of how complex the complete task would be. Potential overruns were immediately discussed with the client in order to obtain advance approval for going over estimated costs.

Senior programmers also technically audited programmers' work throughout the project by looking at the code sheets, screens, or listings as they were completed. Questions that arose during this phase were discussed with the panel member involved so that any necessary corrections could be made prior to the testing phase.

Because FI's panel members were experienced when they signed on with the company, they were expected to be able to provide a quality product without a great deal of technical support. If they did not perform up to expectations, however, project managers, sometimes with the aid of the regional personnel and training manager, attempted to ascertain and then resolve the problem. In some cases, a panel member may have contracted for work that was too unstructured or was outside of her area of expertise. If this occurred, the project manager tried to provide any extra help or project-related training that was needed and to ensure that on the next project the panel member was not stretched too far beyond her limits. Occasionally panel members were disciplined for nonperformance or noncompliance with company policies, and very rarely someone was struck off the roster of panel members.

Exhibit 9
F INTERNATIONAL (A)

Project Assignment Sheet

Project Number:
Client's Name & Address

Client Contact:
Name:
Job Title for Project:
Responsible to:

Project & Personal Brief:

Hardware & Software:
Standards:
Fee Structure:

Useful time £   per hour
Travel time £   per hour
Telephone, postage & travel expense at cost
(£0.   per mile if travelling by car)

Month-end claims:

Timetable:

Progress Reports:

Conditions:

F International reserves the right to reduce or withhold payment for work not of the required standard. One month's notice of termination of this contract should be given.

Copyright:

If Copyright subsists in any product of a panel member's services rendered pursuant to these terms, then, to the extent (if any) that such Copyright would have vested in the panel member such Copyright shall forthwith vest upon its coming into existence in F International to the intent that these Terms of Service shall operate as an assignment of future Copyright therein.

Signed: _____
For and on behalf of F International Limited

Date: _____

Signed: _____

Date: _____

Source: Company document.

Part of the project control process involved weekly client meetings which kept the client up-to-date about the project's status and allowed a discussion of any problems that had recently surfaced and the steps that should be taken to correct them. These were usually between the project manager and a client representative, although in some instances the FI accounts manager and other client staff were also present. Often characterized by joking and desultory conversation in addition to formal reports, client meetings were generally relaxed. The rapport which developed at these meetings and during the course of the project itself added to clients' satisfaction with the technical output and with the company itself.

At the end of every project, an audit was done by a team consisting of an accounts manager whose primary responsibility was quality assurance and several panel members (not part of the project team) assigned to the audit. The auditors' job was to provide feedback both to the project team about the quality of their work and to the regional senior, estimating, and personnel managers about the project's financial control, overall management, accuracy of estimation, and quality of staffing and teamwork. (Exhibits 10 and 11 show the forms used for technical and project management audits.) Like the estimating process, auditing is another of FI's strengths, and the cumulative wisdom garnered from many years of estimating and auditing experience has given the company some of its competitive advantage.

Informal Mechanisms: Communication and Personal Relationships

Although highly detailed formal project control mechanisms were important to FI's project management, many people within the company felt that the real strength of FI's project management lay in the personal relationships and good communication that project managers developed with panel members on their teams. This was in keeping with the overall ethos of caring and personal relationships that characterized the company at all levels.

Pam Elderkin, a senior accounts manager who formerly held many other positions in the company including that of project manager, emphasized the importance of personal communication in the project control process. She talked about the way that telephone conversations, made partly to check work progress, also substituted for the social interactions that were a normal part of everyday office life:

> Just as in an office, at your coffee break, you might talk about what you watched on television last night, how the children are, or what's going on in your social life . . . really you have to try and create that atmosphere over the phone. You want them to see you as somebody they can talk to. . . . You have to see, through words, how these people tick.

Elderkin noted that because most interactions between project managers and panel members were by telephone, rather than face-to-face, project managers needed to develop their sensitivity to nuances in the conversation that might alert them to potential problems.

Barbara Mitchell elaborated on this theme and linked it to motivation. She stressed that retaining motivation was particularly crucial in the case of new panel

Exhibit 10
F INTERNATIONAL (A)
End-of-Project Report—Panel Assessment (Technical)

Project No: Date:

Client:

Name:

Machine: **Language:**

Work Type: Consultancy/Systems/Specification/Programming/Other

Project Type: Time spent/Fixed Price/Time spent (max.)

Project Manager:

Type of Work:

Panel Grade:

Hours Worked: **Earnings:**

Rate per Hour: Useful Work

                    Travel

Technical Competence: (Use Grades—Excellent, Very Good, Average, Poor)

  Quality: _____   Meets Schedules: _____

  Flexibility: _____   Communications: _____

  Speed: _____   Comprehension: _____

Strengths:

Weaknesses:

New Skills:

Project Manager   **Panel Member**
Comments:

Signed—Project Manager: _____

Signed—Panel Member: _____

Source: Company documents.

Exhibit 11
F INTERNATIONAL (A)
   End-of-Project Report—Panel Assessment (Project Management)

Project No: Date:

Client:

Name:

Machine: **Language:**

Work Type:

Project Type:

Team Size:

Hours Worked: **Earnings:**

Rate per Hour: Useful Work

              Travel

Project Mgmt Competence: (Use Grades—Excellent, Very Good, Average, Poor)

   Quality: _____   Meets Schedules: _____

   Flexibility: _____   Communications: _____

   Speed: _____   Comprehension: _____

Strengths:

Weaknesses:

New Skills:

Project Manager   **Panel Member**
Comments:

Signed—Project Manager: _____

Signed—Panel Member: _____

Source: Company documents.

members who had been accepted into the company and then put on the "pending list" where they might wait for up to six months until the right job came along. In such instances, the initial "high" from being accepted onto the panel quickly dissipated, and the company had to figure out ways to maintain the commitment that would be necessary once an assignment was made. Mitchell also spoke about the importance of project managers being able to get along with and meet the needs of different groups of people. New panel members, "old-timers," and other subgroups each had to be treated differently:

> You have to try and get under the skin of people and work out what makes them tick and therefore what you need to do to get them to do the right job for you.

She also saw communication and leadership skills as the most important managerial qualities and emphasized that "managers have to be very aware that not only are they managing and worrying about getting a particular task done, but that they also have very strong personnel functions." Like Elderkin, Mitchell also mentioned the importance of attending to nuances in the voice and of being willing to discuss personal matters as well as work-related issues just as one would in a conventional office.

Training and Promotion Opportunities

Training

FI made training opportunities available both to its panel members and to its salaried employees. Panel members could be offered technical training only on a project-related basis since any other kind of training would have violated British laws pertaining to freelancers. Depending on its objective, the company either developed internal training courses, using trainers or self-study video modules, or it sent staff out to external courses. Though the company tried to recruit panel members who already possessed the up-to-date skills it needed to attract new clients, it also recognized that the technical market was swiftly changing. Thus already technically competent personnel also had to be brought "up-to-speed" in important new developments.

In addition to offering technical training, FI provided management training courses for employees at different levels. Panel members who were identified in the course of a post-project audit as having managerial potential and who had themselves expressed interest in becoming managers were periodically invited to a "leadership day." At that time they participated in group exercises and role-playing sequences that helped sort out those who should go on for further training. Once a panel member was selected to become a project manager, she was given both self-study modules and a tutor with whom she could discuss her progress and questions.

Within regions, project managers met for group workshops run by a senior project manager, and twice a year cross-regional project management workshops were held. Above the project manager level, senior executives held an annual retreat with representatives of a local business school to develop their team-building and leadership skills. Other training courses for upper management, focusing on particular issues, were developed as needed.

Promotion

Promotion opportunities resulted from the confluence of a position opening up and an individual expressing interest in being considered for that position. One manager described the speed with which this process could occur and reported how, during her last performance appraisal, she had expressed interest in moving to a different kind of position over the next couple of years. Six months later as result of growth within the company she found herself in the very job she had coveted for the future.

At the lower levels of the company, regional staffing coordinators and project managers attempted to assign panel members to projects that "stretched" them somewhat and developed their technical and managerial skills. This process resulted in an internally grown pool of managerial talent that was available to move into managerial positions as they became available.

F International also recognized that many technically competent people did not want to move out of their technical specialties into managerial roles and yet did not want to remain as panel members forever. For these people, the company provided some growth opportunities such as crucial and highly technical positions on the estimating team and, for those so inclined, positions on the sales and marketing teams. These opportunities, however, were viewed as only partly satisfactory solutions to the problem of providing technical career ladders, and the issue was continually being discussed within the company. On the administrative level also, career progression was possible for those who desired it; secretaries, for example, could become administrative managers in a regional or head office.

Whether on a full- or part-time basis, once a person became salaried at F International, she participated in an annual performance appraisal. As part of this assessment she received feedback about her performance and an evaluation of her short-term promotion prospects; in addition, she could also give input about where she herself would like to move next.

Because it valued flexibility and believed that people could grow into new roles, F International was willing to give its employees trial periods as managers, to allow them to move from one kind of managerial position to another, and, to some extent, give them opportunities to learn new responsibilities on the job. Pam Elderkin, Barbara Mitchell, and a number of managers at the corporate level had all once been panel members, and each described her meteoric rise with relish and with a sense that stories such as hers were quite typical within the company.

Assessment of the System

From the outside and to those in positions of power within the company, FI's work system seemed to be an effective one. It was commonly accepted by FI managers that the company provided career paths where "you could go as far as you wanted to if you had the ability." Further, in analyzing FI's work system, many mid-level managers saw a connection between the company's project control process and the promotion and training opportunities that it provided. Some felt that panel members were easier to manage and more committed to the company because they perceived numerous opportunities for their own personal and professional development, opportunities not provided by contract agencies[2] that placed computer personnel in temporary assignments.

Although contract agencies offered higher fees than F International, they did not provide ongoing technical support during the course of projects nor did they develop new skills rather than just match existing ones to the client's requirements. Many managers viewed these growth opportunities, career ladders, and the flexibility of work hours that FI offered to panel members as a fair trade-off for fees which, though not exploitative, were a little lower than the industry average for full-time computer personnel and considerably lower than the fees which contract agencies paid to freelancers who worked conventionally on clients' premises.

But despite this positive assessment of the company by its mid-level managers, some top managers had begun to wonder if the managerial perspective was shared by panel members. Already there had been some rumblings that all was not well at the panel level, particularly among those who had been with the company for a long time and had seen it develop an increasingly formalized structure. Some resented the strains on the system which accompanied FI's rapid growth. They missed the shared camaraderie and sense of struggling together in a fledgling enterprise that had characterized the company in its beginnings, and they wondered if FI would remain a caring environment as it grew larger. Other panel members were beginning to believe that the option of working from home was diminishing as it became more necessary to test programs on the client's equipment, and a few were having difficulty seeing how FI differed from its competitors on this dimension. When a number of these concerns were described and commented upon in a book[3] politically critical of home work in general and hence implicitly of F International by example, top management knew they had to address these problems directly.

The 1984 Reorganization

By mid-1984, faced with both the company's changing market position and internal strains on its human resources and functional capabilities, FI's board realized that it had to act and to do so quickly. But at the same time board members felt caught in a seemingly insoluble dilemma. On the one hand, their present structure was untenable from a business perspective, since further growth would certainly require increased centralization. On the other, they realized that they had already moved far afield from the company FI had once been. They knew that the current structure,

---

[2]F International was a consulting firm rather than a contract agency and, as such, even its freelance panel members were directly connected to the company. FI saw itself as providing project teams, some of whose members worked on a freelance basis, rather than temporary help.
[3]Ursula Huws, *The New Homeworkers*, London, 1984.

already far more formalized than it had been at the company's inception, and the increasing distance of the bulk of the work force from Steve Shirley had contributed to some dissatisfaction and resentment among FI's work force, particularly those panel members who had been with the company for some time.

Could the company, the board wondered, continue to grow and still retain its distinctiveness? What kind of new structure would be most beneficial both to growth and to staff morale? What new systems and management positions would be needed? Once a new structure was agreed upon, how should it be presented and then put into place?

Confronted with these difficult problems, the board struggled with ways to resolve them.

Case 4–3

The Partner/Manager Program
at Au Bon Pain

Lucy N. Lytle, W. Earl Sasser, Jr.

*Au Bon Pain has tried every progressive human-resource strategy or policy avail-
able—we've had them all. Quite honestly, I don't believe that any incremental
strategies work long term in the multi-site service business, particularly in a labor
market—like Boston—that is characterized by low unemployment levels. I'm convinced that developing* new *solutions for human-resource management at the unit
level is the basis of competitive advantage. Instituting our Partner/Manager Program throughout the company now could give us an important edge. This is our
chance to blow the company out, or to blow ourselves up.*

This is how Len Schlesinger, executive vice president and treasurer of the Au
Bon Pain (ABP) Company, described the situation he and company president Ron
Shaich faced in January 1987. Six months earlier, in July 1986, 2 of the 24 company-
owned stores had embarked on an experiment that could lead to a revolutionary
change in the company's store-manager compensation system. The Partner/Manager
Program Experiment ran for six periods of four weeks each (the first period of the
experiment, period 8, ran from July 13 through August 9). The experiment concluded on December 20, 1986. Now, Schlesinger and Shaich had to decide whether
to roll out the program in all of the company's stores, run it on a trial basis involving

This case was prepared by Research Assistant Lucy N. Lytle, under the supervision of Professor W.
Earl Sasser Jr., as the basis for class discussion rather than to illustrate either effective or ineffective
handling of an administrative situation.

only some of the stores, withdraw it to make needed improvements, or abandon it.

History

Au Bon Pain, a chain of upscale French bakeries/sandwich cafes, opened its first store in Boston's Faneuil Hall in 1977. This store was originally developed as a marketing vehicle for Pavallier, a French manufacturer of ovens and other bakery equipment. In 1978, Louis Kane, an experienced venture capitalist, bought the store and the rights to the concept. Two years later, Kane teamed up with Ron Shaich, a Harvard MBA who had worked as the director of operations for the Original Cookie Company, a national chain of over 80 retail cookie stores, and who had just opened The Cookie Jar, a cookie store in a high-traffic location in downtown Boston. The two agreed to merge their businesses, enabling Kane to utilize his extensive real estate skills while Shaich handled the operational end of the business.

ABP quickly became known both for the high quality of its croissants and baguettes and for its prime locations. Although the company was based in Boston, Massachusetts, the chain expanded rapidly during the next six years to include stores in New York, New Jersey, Maine, Pennsylvania, Connecticut, and New Hampshire. By 1986, there were 24 company-owned units in the ABP chain. (For a complete list of ABP store locations and sizes, see Exhibit 1.)

Originally, each of the ABP units operated as a self-contained production bakery in the back, with a retail store and seating area in the front. A bakery chef was assigned to each store to handle the demanding process of rolling out croissants and baking breads in the classic French style. In addition to croissants and breads, sandwiches, coffee, and beverages were also sold. Some test stores offered soups, salads, omelettes, cookies, and sorbets as well. Generally, 65% of a unit's business was take-out.

In 1980, Shaich and Kane decided to centralize production, and they fired 15 of the company's 18 bakers. They transferred the remaining three to the Prudential Center store, where the dough was prepared, frozen, and then shipped to the other units. This change eliminated the need for a highly trained chef in each unit, improved inventory control, increased product consistency, and reduced the size of each unit's production area. Three years later, production was moved to ABP headquarters in South Boston. Frozen dough, which had a shelf life of eight weeks, continued to be shipped to all the units on a weekly, or semi-weekly basis.

Len Schlesinger, formerly an associate professor in organizational behavior at the Harvard Business School, joined the company as its executive vice president and treasurer in early 1985. He was charged with the task of systematizing efforts to increase sales and improve quality throughout ABP by increasing employee ownership—both financial and psychological—in the organization.

ABP's major competitors included Vie de France, PepsiCo's La Petite Boulangerie, and Sara Lee's Michelle's Baguette and French Bakery. By 1986, however, all three were suffering from a combination of low profitability and decreased sales.

Exhibit 1
Au Bon Pain, The Partner/Manager Program
Company-Owned Stores

Location	City	State	Year Opened	Square Footage	Number of Managers
Faneuil Hall Marketplace	Boston	MA	1977	1,400	4
Burlington Mall	Burlington	MA	1978	1,400	2
Logan Airport	Boston	MA	1981	800	4
Cherry Hill Mall	Cherry Hill	NJ	1984	1,000	2
Harvard Square	Cambridge	MA	1983	2,500	4
Park Plaza	Boston	MA	1984	1,000	4
Arsenal Mall	Watertown	MA	1984	2,300	3
CityPlace	Hartford	CT	1984	2,400	2
2 Penn Center	Philadelphia	PA	1985	2,700	2
Riverside Square	Hackensack	NJ	1984	1,800	3
Crossgates Mall	Albany	NY	1984	1,400	1
Cape Cod Mall	Hyannis	MA	1985	1,000	3
Crystal Mall	Waterford	CT	1984	600	2
Rockefeller Center	New York	NY	1985	2,500	5
Prudential Center	Boston	MA	1985	3,000	4
Filene's	Boston	MA	1984	800	3
Filene's (Franklin St.)	Boston	MA	1985	150 }	4
Filene's (Basement)	Boston	MA	1984	600 }	
Copley Place	Boston	MA	1984	2,500	4
Copley Place (Stuart St.)	Boston	MA	1985	1,000	2
Maine Mall	South Portland	ME	1983	500	1
Cookie Jar	Boston	MA	1980	700	2
Newington	Newington	NH	1984	800	2
Kendall Square	Cambridge	MA	1986	2,600	3
Dewey Square	Boston	MA	1986	2,400	2

"The Cycle of Failure"

According to Schlesinger and Shaich, in 1985 ABP's retail operations confronted for the first time a set of human resource problems endemic to the fast-food industry. These problems included a continuing crew labor shortage, a chronic shortage of associate managers, an inability to attract and select high-quality management candidates, an inadequately trained management staff, and what Schlesinger referred to as the tendency of many district managers to play "super GM" (general manager)—meaning that they focused obsessively on following up day-to-day activities (a GM's responsibility) at the expense of defining clearly the district manager's role. Labeled by Shaich as "the cycle of failure," the problems interrelated systematically to induce a pattern of poor performance at the store level. Shaich noted:

> Our lack of attention to these issues had created problems at the crew level that remained unsolved. These, in turn, magnified managerial problems, and vice-versa.

It created a vicious cycle—the cycle of failure—and led to a significant degradation of the customer experience. Len and I concluded that if Au Bon Pain was to achieve its objectives of delivering a high-quality customer experience which resulted in sales and profitability, we had to break out of this cycle once and for all.

Schlesinger added:

It was clear, especially in the Boston market, that the labor crisis had engendered a serious decline in the quality of the crew candidates we attracted and ultimately hired. In the past, we had focused on simply staffing our stores rather than on attracting desirable candidates. All of our energies were devoted to the short-term operational needs of the business in this area.

At the same time, training for the crew was practically nonexistent and, where it did exist, poorly executed. Development, too, tended to follow a Darwinian "survival of the fittest" approach. The problem was compounded by the fact that we were committed to a promote-from-within policy which precluded the opportunity to acquire skilled talent from outside.

Beyond that, considerable work remained to be done to develop our reward system into a long-term compensation system which more directly tied the managers into the success of their stores.

Existing Compensation System in 1986

Our existing compensation system, which we devised in 1985, goes a long way toward addressing the problems contributing to the cycle of failure. It's a simple system under which managers are paid according to their level of responsibility and the sales activity of their stores.

Shaich made this observation as he outlined the two basic components of ABP's existing compensation system (i.e., the system in place prior to the development of the Partner/Manager Program): base pay and a volume adjustment. Under the plan, general managers earned a base salary of $375 a week. Salaries rose as weekly sales volumes increased, up to $633.75 a week at the highest-volume store.

Base Pay. A manager's base pay was determined by his or her level in the organization: general manager, senior associate manager, first associate manager, or second associate manager (which included manager trainees). In July 1985, the base pay levels were as follows:

Level	Weekly Pay	Annual Pay
General Manager	$375.00	$19,500
Senior Associate Manager	350.00	18,200
First Associate Manager	341.54	17,760
Second Associate Manager	336.54	17,500

Volume Adjustment.   In addition to base pay, a volume adjustment was calculated each week for first associate, senior associate, and general managers. (Second associate managers were not eligible for a volume adjustment). Because ABP had a wide range of store volumes with varying managerial responsibilities and workloads, it established three categories of stores:

Store Volume	Weekly Sales
Low	$ 4,000–10,000
Medium	$10,000–20,000
High	over $20,000

The formulae for determining salaries for general, senior associate, and first associate managers (i.e., base pay plus volume adjustment) are presented in Exhibit 2.

The Development of the Partner/Manager Program

In the spring of 1986, Schlesinger and Shaich developed a draft of a new compensation/incentive system—the Partner/Manager Program—for the managers of ABP's stores. Shaich explained:

> Len and I had identified the problems inherent in the cycle of failure. The next step was to figure out how to pay people more. Since 1985, under our existing compensation system, we had tried to develop a pay system which allowed the managers to make more money than they had before while still tying them to the success of their stores and the company.

In brief, the Partner/Manager Program would reclassify general managers as "partner/managers" and provide them with a base salary of $500 per week. Each partner/manager could choose an associate manager, who would be paid $400 per week. The partner/manager would be entitled to a 35% share of the unit's incremental profits under the new system; the associate manager would receive 15%; and ABP would receive the remaining 50%.

A store-lease payment would be deducted monthly from the store controllable profits to cover unit-level fixed expenses, corporate overhead, and reasonable profit expectations. The amount of the store-lease payment would be guaranteed for 13 periods (i.e., one year), with the following exceptions, which would require an adjustment. First, the addition of fixed assets would trigger an increase in the store-lease payment of 25% of the total fixed asset cost divided across 13 periods. Second, additional sales, which triggered a percentage rent clause in the real estate lease, would increase the store-lease payment by the percentage specified in the real estate lease.

Incremental profits would be equal to a unit's net controllable profits minus its store-lease payment. These profits would be distributed to the managers at the close of each period (i.e., every four weeks). ABP would hold in reserve $7,500 for the

---

Exhibit 2
Au Bon Pain, The Partner/Manager Program
  Weekly Manager Salaries for Given Weekly Sales Volumes
  (compensation system prior to the Partner/Manager Program)

Volume/ Week	General Manager (Base = $375)		Senior Associate Manager (Base = $350)		First Associate Manager (Base = $341.54)	
	Volume Adjustment	*Weekly Total*	*Volume Adjustment*	*Weekly total*	*Volume Adjustment*	*Weekly Total*
$1–4,000	$ 0.00	$375.00	$ 0.00	$350.00	$ 0.00	$341.54
5,000	13.12	388.12	5.25	355.25	2.53	344.07
10,000	78.75	453.75	31.50	381.50	15.21	356.75
15,000	118.00	493.00	47.25	397.25	22.81	364.35
20,000	157.50	532.50	63.00	413.00	30.42	371.96
25,000	174.38	549.38	69.75	419.75	33.67	375.21
30,000	191.25	566.25	76.50	426.50	36.93	378.47
35,000	208.13	583.13	83.25	433.25	40.19	381.73
40,000	225.00	600.00	90.00	440.00	43.46	385.00
45,000	241.88	616.88	96.75	446.75	46.71	388.25
50,000	258.75	633.75	103.50	453.50	49.97	391.51

To compute the weekly salary for general managers, the following formulae were used:
  low volume store: base pay + .013125 (volume − $4,000)
  medium volume store: base pay + $78.75 + .00785 (volume − $10,000)
  high volume store: base pay + $157.50 + .003375 (volume − $20,000)

For senior associate managers, the formulae were:
  low volume store: base pay + .00525 (volume − $4,000)
  medium volume store: base pay + $31.50 + .00315 (volume − $10,000)
  high volume store: base pay + $63.00 + .00135 (volume − $20,000)

For first associate managers, the formulae were:
  low volume store: base pay + .002535 (volume − $4,000)
  medium volume store: base pay + $15.21 + .001521 (volume − $10,000)
  high volume store: base pay + $30.42 + .000625 (volume − $20,000)

---

partner/manager and $2,500 for the associate manager until the end of their contracts, which could last one, two, or three years.[1]

The managers would be required to work a minimum of 50 hours per week, and the partner/manager and/or the associate manager would have to be on duty in the store during 90% of its operating hours. The quality of each store would be monitored

---

[1] During The Partner/Manager Program Experiment, which is described in detail later in this case, Schlesinger and Shaich opted to distribute the managers' share of the incremental profits in a lump sum at the end of the six-month trial period.

through "mystery-shopping" reports, "white-glove" inspections, and 100% customer satisfaction "moment-of-truth" indicators. A violation of any of the listed rules could result in the dismissal of either or both of the managers if the problem was not corrected within a specified amount of time. (See Appendix A for a working draft of the Partner/Manager Program.)

Goals of the Partner/Manager Program

Product of Research.   The Partner/Manager Program was the result of research and careful thought, according to Schlesinger:

> It's not something that we developed overnight. We looked into the compensation systems of a number of fast-food chains, including Sambo's, Chick-Fil-A, Golden Corral, and Kentucky Fried Chicken. The Partner/Manager Program is a customized imitation of the processes we studied. In some ways, it is revolutionary—but it is not without precedent in this industry.
>
> Under this system, we would manage our partner/managers with loose controls and less overhead, hold them tightly accountable to outputs (i.e., customer satisfaction as determined by mystery shopping) rather than inputs, and require them to invest themselves in their stores. Hopefully, through their efforts, the good managers would earn considerably more than they do now.

Shaich added:

> We want to hire people who really care . . . the kind of person you'd want on your side when you go into a street fight. A person who does a good job for the people beneath him, not to impress somebody higher up. This is an organization that has rewarded trying for years. Now it's time to reward results.
>
> One of the aims of this program would be to employ fewer managers, who would work harder, and make more money than their predecessors. We want people willing to pay the price to earn big bucks.
>
> Personally, I believe that people earning less than $30,000 per year should be managed through individually based incentive/compensation plans.[2] People higher up in an organization, with a longer time horizon and broader responsibilities, should have a low salary and stock options, like at People Express. The problem at People was that while stock ownership is meaningful, it's money that gets results.[3]

The Role of the District Manager.   Not only would the Partner/Manager Program change ABP's compensation system, but it also would alter the ways in which the individual units were supervised. Schlesinger explained:

> Under this program, the district managers would function as coaches, rather than as policemen—and they would supervise 8 to 10 stores rather than the traditional 3 or 4. The district managers would serve as consultants by generating ideas for

---

[2]For an example of such a company, see Harvard Business School case #9-376-028, *The Lincoln Electric Company*.

[3]For further information, see Harvard Business School case #9-483-103, *People Express (A)*.

sales building and cost reduction, and as support people by helping out during busy seasons and assisting with the training of new associate managers. They would earn perhaps 5% of the incremental profits generated by each of the units they supervise. Of course, we haven't worked out all the details yet.

One of the factors necessitating the change in the district managers' role was what Shaich termed the "Stockholm effect" (psychological phenomenon that occurs when, over time, hostage victims develop sympathetic feelings toward their captors). He noted:

> In the past, the district managers, like the general managers, became excuse-givers. Instead of holding the general managers accountable to Au Bon Pain's standards— as customers do—the district managers began to sympathize with the managers' excuses. They became agents of the status quo rather than agents of change.
>
> Now it's clear that the partner/managers would be primarily responsible for handling any problems that arise. I expect that 90% of the problems we used to deal with at headquarters, the managers would now figure out on their own.

Increased Stability.   One of the goals of the Partner/Manager Program would be to increase stability at the unit level by reducing turnover and by encouraging managers to commit themselves to working at a specific unit for at least one year. Shaich discussed this idea:

> The program would require each manager to have a real financial commitment to his or her store in the form of his or her share of the incremental profits—some of which would be held back by Au Bon Pain until the end of the contract. We expect that after working in the same unit for at least a year, a manager would have the chance to become very familiar with the store's cycle—what its sales volume is like, when its peak periods are, and so on. In the long run, this knowledge would increase the quality of each store's operations.
>
> At the same time, the managers would get to know their customers and crew on a personal basis. Significantly, consulting psychologists have found that the most important single variable that keeps a customer coming back to a store is whether or not someone in the store knows that customer's name. There are employees at Golden Corral, for example, who know the names of 2,700 customers. This "retention quotient" has major implications for a company like Au Bon Pain as our research indicates that some of our customers—the ones we refer to as the "Au Bon Pain Club"—visit our stores up to 108 times per year.

Quality Control.   Although the Partner/Manager Program would reduce the degree of corporate supervision of the individual stores, a number of quality control measures were written into the system. One of these measures was a provision requiring that the units be mystery shopped at least once a week. Mystery shopping involved having a professional shopper hired from outside ABP evaluate the store from a customer's perspective, based on such criteria as service speed, quality of food, store cleanliness, and friendliness of store employees. In addition, white-glove inspections, using a 140-item checklist covering all phases of store operations, would be conducted by an Au Bon Pain auditor every period. The inspections would last eight hours, and the days when they would occur would not be announced in advance. Finally, the managers would be expected to comply with 12 moment-of-truth indicators (based on criteria generated in customer focus groups), which were aimed at achieving 100% customer satisfaction.

Decreased Recruiting Budget.   Schlesinger expected a dramatic decrease in ABP's recruiting budget as a result of the publicity surrounding the news that it would be changing its compensation system. He predicted:

> If we go public with this program, the resulting newspaper and trade journal articles would help us to attract and stockpile a new group of managerial candidates. We could cut our annual recruiting budget from $230,000 to $60,000 by substituting press for want ads.

Potential Problems

Burning Out.   Shaich and Schlesinger both raised the issue of managers burning out during the program. They agreed that being a partner/manager or an associate manager under the new program would be a potentially stressful experience— sufficiently stressful that it could cause some managers to drop out before their contract ended. Schlesinger, however, was philosophic about it:

> Burning out managers would be one concern. But the way I see it, we're all adults entering into a business contract. We understand the benefits and the risks.

Physical Limitations.   At least three physical factors limited productivity and sales: 1) each unit's proofing capacity (i.e., the capacity of the machines in which the dough rose for approximately two hours), 2) each unit's freezer capacity, and 3) the limitations of Au Bon Pain's product line. Schlesinger predicted:

> If Au Bon Pain adopts the Partner/Manager Program, people will claim that we have come up with a new way to con people—but that wouldn't be true. The program would establish a clear, tangible link between the results the managers achieved and the money they would make.
>
> We wouldn't hold up goals that aren't attainable, because we would need to create a base of heroes. Under the Partner/Manager Program most people would make about $40,000 a year. The heroes would make between $60,000 and $100,000, and they would set an example for which everyone would strive.

The Partner/Manager Program Experiment

Eager to discover if the program would be successful in a real-life situation, Schlesinger and Shaich invited the general and associate managers of two stores to participate in a six-month trial run of the Partner/Manager Program. Gary Aronson, the general manager of ABP's Burlington Mall store (30 miles west of Boston), and Frank Ciampa, his associate manager, agreed to give it a try. So did Brian McEvoy, the general manager of the CityPlace store in Hartford, Connecticut (100 miles south of Boston), and his associate manager, Stephen Dunn.

The managers did not feel that they were coerced into participating in the experiment. "We were able to choose whether or not we wanted to participate," McEvoy said. Before the experiment began, both Aronson and McEvoy met with Schlesinger and Shaich to discuss a rough draft of the program. "We gave them our input, and they incorporated our suggestions into a revised version," Aronson explained. Later, all four managers met with Schlesinger and Shaich to review the changes and discuss any questions about the program.

Aronson explained why he agreed to participate in the experiment:

> Frank and I decided that our number one priority was to show that a program like this could work. We wanted to convince people that this was something revolutionary, and that it would not only turn around this company, but that it has the potential to change the whole industry. The way I see it, this program is going to turn us all into a bunch of professionals.

McEvoy was motivated both by the "financial incentives of the program" and by his perception that it was an alternative to following the traditional career path—which would have involved moving to Boston and trying to get promoted to the position of district manager. He noted, "First of all, my wife and I didn't really want to relocate because it would have upset her career. At the same time, even if we did move, there wouldn't have been any guarantees that I would have been able to move up in the company."

Managers' Backgrounds.   "What initially attracted me to Au Bon Pain was that they allowed their managers more mobility and more access to upper-level management than most fast-food chains. They also let their managers have an input into the decision process. I believe that the only way you can grow as a manager is to work in a less structured environment. At Au Bon Pain, you can't run on buzzers and bells like you can at McDonald's or Burger King; you have to be able to think."

This is how Stephen Dunn, associate manager of the CityPlace store in Hartford, recalled his first impression of ABP. Dunn graduated from the University of Massachusetts in 1981 with a business degree in hotel/restaurant/travel administration, and he had experience working in full-service, fast-food, catering, and banquet situations. In 1985, he was recruited by a headhunter retained by ABP and accepted a position as the associate manager of the CityPlace store.

Ironically, Brian McEvoy, Dunn's partner and the general manager of the CityPlace store, never intended to work for ABP. After graduating from the University of Massachusetts in 1980 with a degree in history, followed by two years of teaching experience and a brief stint in the Navy, he viewed his original meeting with Shaich as a "practice interview." Later, impressed with the company, he took an entry-level job as an associate manager. At the start of the Partner/Manager Program Experiment, he had been with the company for three years.

Gary Aronson, the general manager of the Burlington Mall store, dropped out of college after one semester, and worked for Kentucky Fried Chicken for eight years before joining ABP in 1983 as an associate manager. He explained, "I switched jobs because I saw a lot of opportunity for me at a place like this. I didn't feel that the management team I was training with was that experienced, and I knew I'd find a way to shine real quickly."

Aronson's associate manager, Frank Ciampa, graduated from Bentley College in 1984 with a bachelor's degree in marketing management and an associate's degree in accounting. He joined ABP in 1985 as a manager trainee—in the hope that he could use this position as a stepping stone to a job in the corporate side of the business. He admitted:

> If you'd asked me a year ago what I wanted to be after working here for several months, it sure wasn't to be a partner/manager. But since I've been working with Gary under the Partner/Manager Program, my whole mentality has changed. Now, I'm in no hurry to work in the office—I enjoy being a manager.

Managers' Activities During the Experiment.   "Len tells people that I run the place like a family deli, and I suppose that could be true," Aronson admitted. Both his wife and Ciampa's mother worked in the store, and Ciampa's father, a manufacturing equipment mechanic, helped with maintenance.

Originally, Aronson employed two associate managers. When the experiment began, however, he took the opportunity to have one of the two transferred to another unit. He explained that, according to the program, he didn't need three managers to run the store. "It means that Frank and I have to work longer hours," he conceded, "but it's worth it." The Burlington Mall store was open from 9:00 A.M. until 10:00 P.M. Monday through Saturday, and 11:00 A.M. through 6:00 P.M. on Sunday.

During the experiment, Aronson took on a number of wholesale accounts, noting:

> The store doesn't open until 9:00 A.M., but Frank and I get here by 4:30 or 5:00 most mornings to prepare our wholesale products. We've even begun to do a little catering. If we can keep the four or five accounts we've got right now, I bet we could make about $40,000 worth of sales next year just on the wholesale line.

Aronson and Ciampa also took advantage of the increased managerial responsibility called for in the program and initiated some money-saving repairs. Ciampa recalled:

> During the first week of the experiment, we decided to knock out a platform built against one wall in order to make room for eight more seats in the cafe area. Of course, making this change wasn't high on the list of priorities for the company's construction department, so Au Bon Pain estimated it would cost $10,000. We found a guy who'd do it for only $3,000, and we did it right away.
>
> Similarly, when it was time to repaint the store, headquarters estimated it would cost $1,200 to paint one wall. We had the whole store painted ourselves for about $800.

At the same time, Aronson began calculating food cost on a monthly, rather than daily, basis. "It drives the people at headquarters crazy," he grinned, "but I'm running the best food cost of any of the stores. As long as I'm alert, and trust the people I'm working with, I've never had a problem with stealing or cheating." He added that the turnover rate in his store was close to 0%.

The CityPlace store was open from 6:30 A.M. until 6:00 P.M. Monday through Friday. It was closed on the weekends. McEvoy admitted, "I don't want to work 80 hours a week the way Gary does now. I'm starting to like having my weekends off." He alternated shifts among himself, Dunn, and Barbara Jones, his shift supervisor. Dunn observed:

> Au Bon Pain provides us with a labor grid to guide us in making decisions about how many people to schedule to work at different times during the day. We generally employ more people than the grid specifies. For example, they say that in the morning we should be able to run the store with four people. We always try to schedule six in an attempt to decrease the amount of time it takes to fill a customer's order.

McEvoy added:

> In order to schedule extra crew members to work during peak hours, we had to pay them more because they were only working a two-hour-long shift. However, having the extra workers allowed us to improve our service and decrease the time customers had to wait for their order, so it paid off in increased sales.

Approximately three months into the experiment, McEvoy and Dunn began a telephone express service. Under the new system, office workers called in orders of $25 or more, which they picked up a little while later. "It's a lot quicker than having to stand in line and wait while the order is filled, and it helps us to serve all our customers more efficiently," McEvoy explained. The telephone express service was currently available to only the office workers in the CityPlace building, but McEvoy was considering expanding it to other areas.

Managers' Evaluation of the Partner/Manager Program.   All four managers agreed that one of the program's benefits was less corporate supervision of the units. This change was most apparent in the new role assumed by the district managers. Schlesinger acted as the district manager for both stores, and Ciampa noted that he had visited the Burlington Mall store no more than three or four times in as many months, although he kept in contact over the telephone.

McEvoy predicted, "The district managers will become less like policemen, and more like advisors and coaches. Instead of being told 'You must do this,' managers will hear comments like 'How can we build sales?' and 'How can we improve the store?'"

Aronson added:

> Some managers love to have the district manager come around so that he or she can admire how clean the floor is. Frank and I don't need that. We know exactly what to do. Having someone else around actually brought down the quality of our work because we were busy explaining everything.

Aronson and Ciampa believed that the program had the potential to reduce the tendency of many managers in the fast-food industry to move from one job to another, starting at the ground level each time and slowly working their way up. Aronson explained:

> In most professions, if you're good at what you do, when you change jobs you start out making more money than you did before. The fast-food industry's mentality is different. For example, when I left International Food Services, I was the highest-paid manager there and I was working in the highest-volume store. But when I decided to join Au Bon Pain, I had to start at the ground floor again and work my way up. It's the same story everywhere. I had to take a $135/week cut in pay in addition to going through the emotional upheaval of moving from one job to another. The prevailing attitude seemed to be "Well, maybe you're a whiz with fried chicken, but you don't know anything about croissants."
>
> Now, Ron and Len have realized that they can't operate the way the Wendy's and the Burger Kings deal with people. To be successful in the future, this company will have to bring in established people who've shown that they can do the job. A manager with five or six years' experience in the fast-food industry has to be worth a lot more than someone just out of school. If we start paying people what they're worth, I believe we can pick up some prime-time players and make this a really interesting company.

Aronson felt that, in the past, some of the instability generated by managers moving from store to store was the result of decisions made at the company head-quarters. He asserted:

> Once a manager had a store running smoothly, BINGO! They suddenly wanted to transfer you to a problem store. The better a manager you were, the more problems you had to take care of. After a while you began to ask, "What am I? A clean-up crew?"

Dunn believed that holding back part of the managers' share of the incremental profits until the end of their contract would reduce the desire to store-hop. He said, "Now, I'm a lot less company-oriented, and a lot more store-oriented. I'm less willing to leave the unit where I'm working and move to another store." McEvoy pointed out, however, that "the way for an ambitious person to make even more money would be to move to a higher-volume store. Personally, I'm not interested in relocating right now, but the temptation is always there."

Despite the decreased corporate supervision of the units under the program, the managers still perceived a continuing corporate overemphasis on details and pa-perwork. Aronson complained:

> There's too much emphasis on the detail end, not enough on the meat-and-potatoes end. The majority of my customers want good food, quality service, and they want it fast. But every time we've been mystery shopped during the experiment, we've received the same basic criticism. Although our overall score is quite high, the mystery shopper generally objects that the floor hasn't been swept. Frankly, during

lunchtime this place is a zoo. If we tried to sweep then, we'd get complaints from the customers about the dust flying in their food.

McEvoy generally agreed with Aronson's point, but admitted that he was more concerned that he was close to reaching maximum output on much of his equipment. Dunn brought up another issue:

> Under this new program, an associate manager's greatest fear will be that everything that he or she can make or lose hinges on the partner/manager they're working with. The partner/manager calls the shots, that's the bottom line, even though you've got your money tied into this thing too.

The managers also discussed the length of their workweek. Aronson reported that he and Ciampa were each working an average of 80 hours per week—25 hours more per week than they had been working before. Aronson recalled:

> I knew that during the experiment I wouldn't have much time left over for anything else, and that was a real consideration. I finally told my family to put up with it for six months, and in the end I would make it worth their while. In the first 16 weeks, we had two days off. I've worked some days from 4:30 in the morning until 11:00 at night.

McEvoy and Dunn each worked 50 to 55 hours a week. McEvoy explained, "The amount of hours we're working hasn't really changed that much." Dunn added: "We work as long as it takes to get the job done. Whenever we've worked extra hours, it has been because we were understaffed, not because we decided to work long hours because of the experiment." Dunn summarized his evaluation of the experiment:

> To be blunt, parts of the program are good, and parts are bad. Burnout, particularly in this industry, is high. If someone is going to be locked into this thing, and they're going to have the added pressure of knowing that their money—a large part of their share of the bonus—is tied up in whether or not they can last out their contract, well, in my opinion, that kind of stress could actually cause a person not to perform as well as they could. I'm not trying to be negative, but they've got to be careful who they choose to be managers and how they monitor them.
>
> There are also the shift supervisors to deal with. A lot of them act like managers in every degree but in the paperwork, including sales building. In fact, when we began this experiment, Brian decided to pay our shift supervisor 2% of our half of the incremental profits. When other shift supervisors hear about the phenomenal amounts of money being made by the managers, how will that affect their motivation?
>
> Finally, even if this program dramatically improves the quality of our applicants for managerial positions, what are we going to do about the turnover rate for lower-level employees? It's close to 400% a year in this store. High turnover is an industry norm. How does that affect the quality of the customer experience?

Exhibit 3A
Au Bon Pain: The Partner/Manager Program

Store Operating Statement, Burlington Mall
(pre-experiment)
Percentage of Net Sales (numbers have been disguised)

	Periods						
	1	2	3	4	5	6	7
Regular Sales	100.0	98.5	98.9	100.0	100.0	100.0	100.0
Wholesale	0.0	0.0	0.0	0.0	0.0	0.0	0.0
Promotions	0.0	1.5	1.1	0.0	0.0	0.0	0.0
Net Sales	100.0	100.0	100.0	100.0	100.0	100.0	100.0
Discounts	0.4	0.4	0.6	0.7	1.0	0.9	0.5
Net Net Sales	99.6	99.6	99.4	99.3	99.0	99.1	99.5
Management	9.1	9.8	11.7	11.4	7.8	9.0	8.9
Shift Supervisor	0.0	0.0	0.0	0.0	0.0	1.2	1.1
Crew	15.1	14.3	14.9	13.8	14.1	13.2	13.9
Benefits	2.6	3.0	2.9	4.1	3.1	1.6	3.1
Total Labor	26.8	27.1	29.5	29.3	25.0	25.0	27.0
Food Cost	29.4	30.1	31.1	30.0	30.5	30.2	32.0
Paper Cost	1.8	1.2	1.4	1.2	2.0	1.4	1.8
Controllables	1.5	1.4	1.1	2.0	2.1	1.8	2.3
Utilities	1.9	2.8	2.3	2.3	1.8	2.1	2.2
Controllable Profit	38.2	37.0	34.0	34.5	37.6	38.6	34.2
Fixed Expenses	3.4	3.6	3.5	3.4	3.0	3.1	3.3
Occupancy	9.3	9.5	9.6	9.5	12.3	10.3	10.4
Store Profit	25.5	23.9	20.9	21.6	22.3	25.2	20.5

Results.   During the experiment, sales in the Burlington Mall and CityPlace stores increased dramatically. The operating statements for both units during periods 1–7 and during the experiment (periods 8–13) are shown in Exhibit 3. Exhibit 4 summarizes the stores' performance against the company's plan and compares it to their 1985 performance. While both McEvoy's and Aronson's base salaries remained at $500 per week, their actual, annual earnings were closer to $50,000 and $70,000, respectively.[4] A memo outlining the final distribution of profits is presented in Exhibit 5.

---

[4]Art Veves, Burger King's regional director of Human Resources in Boston, reported in a telephone conversation that the average Burger King manager earned between $24,000 and $30,000 annually, plus a bonus of approximately $2,500. The salary expectations for a McDonald's manager were roughly equivalent to these figures.

Exhibit 3B
Au Bon Pain: The Partner/Manager Program

Store Operating Statement, Burlington Mall
(experiment)
Percentage of Net Sales (numbers have been disguised)

	Periods					
	8	9	10	11	12	13
Regular Sales	97.0	97.1	96.0	95.2	93.9	95.8
Wholesale	3.0	2.9	4.0	4.8	6.1	4.2
Promotions	0.0	0.0	0.0	0.0	0.0	0.0
Net Sales	100.0	100.0	100.0	100.0	100.0	100.0
Discounts	0.4	0.3	0.2	0.2	0.2	0.2
Net Net Sales	99.6	99.7	99.8	99.8	99.8	99.8
Management	6.4	5.6	5.7	5.4	4.9	3.7
Shift Supervisor	1.8	0.8	0.1	1.3	2.4	2.3
Crew	13.0	12.9	12.9	12.5	11.9	11.3
Benefits	2.0	1.7	1.7	1.6	1.6	1.0
Total Labor	23.2	21.0	20.4	20.8	20.8	18.3
Food Cost	28.7	29.1	29.7	29.4	29.4	28.6
Paper Cost	1.7	1.5	2.0	1.6	1.9	1.7
Controllables	1.3	0.8	1.1	0.0	1.1	1.5
Utilities	3.4	2.7	2.8	2.2	1.3	0.4
Controllable Profit	41.3	44.6	43.8	44.9	45.3	49.3
Fixed Expenses	3.0	2.9	2.8	2.8	2.4	2.0
Occupancy	11.8	9.2	9.5	9.5	11.2	9.2
Store Profit	26.5	32.5	31.5	32.6	31.7	38.1

The Decision

Shaich considered the experiment a resounding success, and suggested that:

> The problems don't lie in the concept, which I'm convinced is basically sound. The challenges will be in its execution. There are a lot of implementation issues we still have to deal with—that's one of the costs of being in the vanguard on an issue like this—but I think the potential gain is worth the risks.
>
> The key to success will be for us to get out of the way once this thing starts. We've developed the concept, and now we have to stand back and let the managers operate it. In time, I believe we'll witness startling results. In my opinion, at least 25% more sales can be made. Len puts the figure closer to 50%, and Louis Kane thinks it's even higher. I'd love to flip the switch tomorrow and set the program in motion.

Exhibit 3C
Au Bon Pain: The Partner/Manager Program

Store Operating Statement, CityPlace
(pre-experiment)
Percentage of Net Sales (numbers have been disguised)

	Periods						
	1	2	3	4	5	6	7
Regular Sales	100.0	96.5	97.8	100.0	100.0	100.0	100.0
Wholesale	0.0	0.0	0.0	0.0	0.0	0.0	0.0
Promotions	0.0	3.5	2.2	0.0	0.0	0.0	0.0
Net Sales	100.0	100.0	100.0	100.0	100.0	100.0	100.0
Discounts	0.3	0.3	0.4	0.4	0.3	0.3	0.4
Net Net Sales	99.7	99.7	99.6	99.6	99.7	99.7	99.6
Management	7.0	6.8	7.3	6.5	7.1	7.1	6.8
Shift Supervisor	1.8	2.0	1.9	2.1	2.3	2.0	1.5
Crew	12.1	13.1	13.6	13.2	12.4	13.2	14.6
Benefits	2.3	2.9	2.1	2.9	2.3	2.3	2.8
Total Labor	23.3	24.8	24.9	24.7	24.1	24.6	25.7
Food Cost	28.0	29.1	29.9	31.2	27.5	29.1	30.9
Paper Cost	2.4	2.7	2.8	2.8	3.1	3.2	3.2
Controllables	1.3	1.5	1.9	3.8	2.0	4.7	1.8
Utilities	1.6	1.5	2.1	1.6	1.8	1.7	1.7
Controllable Profit	43.1	40.1	38.0	35.5	41.2	36.4	36.3
Fixed Expenses	8.5	8.9	9.9	8.3	8.8	9.1	7.8
Occupancy	12.4	12.9	12.4	12.2	12.1	12.1	11.7
Store Profit	22.2	18.3	15.7	15.0	20.3	15.2	16.8

Schlesinger added, "In time, this plan will be broadly applicable to any multi-unit service concept on the face of the earth." Aronson was more guarded, asserting:

> With the right people, this program can work. But to suddenly turn it over to all the stores—personally, I think that would be a big mistake. There are some people who would try and squeeze it dry. In the short term they could show fantastic results, food and labor costs down, etc., but in the long term you wind up with underportioning and dirty stores.

McEvoy agreed:

> I don't think they should roll out this program to every store right away, especially if they're hiring a lot of new managers. It takes a while for a person to settle in. The strict deadlines for solving problems set out in the Partner/Manager document would put too much pressure on new managers who aren't used to handling every-

Exhibit 3D
Au Bon Pain: The Partner/Manager Program

Store Operating Statement, CityPlace
(experiment)
Percentage of Net Sales (numbers have been disguised)

	Periods					
	8	*9*	*10*	*11*	*12*	*13*
Regular Sales	100.0	100.0	100.0	100.0	98.6	98.1
Wholesale	0.0	0.0	0.0	0.0	1.4	1.9
Promotions	0.0	0.0	0.0	0.0	0.0	0.0
Net Sales	100.0	100.0	100.0	100.0	100.0	100.0
Discounts	0.3	0.3	0.3	0.4	0.5	0.3
Net Net Sales	99.7	99.7	99.7	99.6	99.5	99.7
Management	6.0	5.8	6.2	5.0	5.7	5.7
Shift Supervisor	1.9	2.0	2.0	1.7	1.9	1.8
Crew	14.6	14.6	13.4	15.0	13.9	14.3
Benefits	2.2	3.0	2.1	3.0	2.1	2.0
Total Labor	24.7	25.4	23.7	24.7	23.6	23.8
Food Cost	27.6	29.6	29.6	29.9	31.0	30.6
Paper Cost	2.8	3.1	2.9	2.9	3.0	3.1
Controllables	2.6	2.3	1.6	2.1	1.7	1.6
Utilities	1.2	1.7	9.6	0.6	9.7	3.8
Controllable Profit	40.8	37.6	32.3	39.4	30.5	36.8
Fixed Expenses	6.9	7.6	11.3	7.2	5.9	7.4
Occupancy	9.6	10.3	9.7	9.2	13.0	8.9
Store Profit	24.3	19.7	11.3	23.0	11.6	20.5

thing by themselves. Holding them accountable could blow them right out of the water.

Ciampa added:

> Even under the best of circumstances, the company will be lucky if 50% of the people working for them now make it under the new program. People are used to getting a lot of supervision. It used to be that the louder you cried, the more attention you got.

Dunn added a final caution:

> During the experiment, we've had phenomenal sales growth. But, and I've said this to Len and Ron, 85% of that growth would have occurred in any case because of the type of individuals Brian and I are. It just happened that the experiment began when we were starting to get things together. Specifically, at that point, Brian and I had been working together for nine months. We were comfortable with

Exhibit 4
Au Bon Pain: The Partner/Manager Program

Performance Against Plan and Prior Year
(current dollars)

		Periods 1–7	Periods 8–13
Sales vs. Plan	Burlington	(11,695)	56,719
	CityPlace	12,903	69,311
	Total	1,208	126,030
		Periods 1–7	Periods 8–13
Sales vs. Last Year	Burlington	(1,600)	70,478
	CityPlace	33,512	93,558
	Total	31,912	164,036
		Periods 1–7	Periods 8–13
Controllable Profits vs. Plan	Burlington	(3,844)	53,562
	CityPlace	4,613	18,580
	Total	769	72,142
		Periods 1–7	Periods 8–13
Controllable Profits vs. Last Year	Burlington	(2)	57,449
	CityPlace	2,706	29,741
	Total	2,704	87,190

each other and we knew our customers. It was the middle of the summer and we were fully staffed because a lot of high school kids wanted summer jobs. Our equipment was functioning correctly for the first time in a long time, and we had just converted from an inefficient cafeteria-style system to one in which the person working the cash register automatically keyed in the sandwich order to the kitchen.

When asked if they planned to sign up for the long-term deal, Aronson, Ciampa, and McEvoy indicated they would if certain conditions were met (e.g., Aronson would sign up for only a one-year deal). Dunn replied, "No comment."

After a meeting in early January, during which he reviewed both his own and Shaich's comments and the reactions of the managers involved in the experiment, Schlesinger concluded:

From an MBA viewpoint, it's an interesting situation. We've got two hand-picked managers and six months of data on which to base a decision whether or not to shake up this whole company. Are we foolish if we grab at this opportunity?

Exhibit 5
Au Bon Pain: The Partner/Manager Program

Partner/Manager Profit Distributions

MEMORANDUM

TO: Gary Aronson, Frank Ciampa, Steve Dunn, Brian McEvoy
FROM: Len Schlesinger
DATE: January 15, 1987
RE: Partner/Manager Profit Distributions
cc: Ron Shaich
            Louis Kane

	Burlington	*CityPlace*
Store Lease Payment	$127,526.25	$103,619.50
Fixed Asset Additions	110.62	45.49
Percentage Rent	3,556.48	0.00
TOTAL DUE ABP	131,193.35	103,664.99
CREDITS		
Period 8	23,225.00	23,680.65
Period 9	28,740.00	20,218.65
Period 10	27,705.00	23,444.46
Period 11	29,445.00	23,809.65
Period 12	33,172.00	24,071.65
Period 13	45,122.00	23,024.65
TOTAL CREDITS	187,409.00	138,249.71
LESS TOTAL DUE ABP	131,193.35	103,664.99
PROFIT POOL	56,215.65	34,584.72
ABP Share	28,107.82	17,292.36
P/M Share	19,675.48	12,104.65
Assoc. P/M Share	8,432.35	5,187.71
P/M Weekly Wage		
Salary	500.00	500.00
Share	819.81	504.36
TOTAL	1,319.81	1,004.36
ANNUALIZED	68,630.12	52,226.72
Assoc. P/M Weekly Wage		
Salary	400.00	400.00
Share	351.35	216.15
TOTAL	751.35	616.15
ANNUALIZED	39,070.20	32,039.80

A p p e n d i x   A

Au Bon Pain: The Partner/ Manager Program An Introduction to the Partner/ Manager Program

I. Company Objectives

As Au Bon Pain moves into the future, we must develop for our bakery/cafe managers a compensation/incentive system that is second to none in our industry segment. The foundation of ABP's success is talented people who achieve results and, in turn, share in the financial rewards of their efforts. The Partner/Manager Program provides the opportunity for a select group of managers to be in business for themselves, but not by themselves. The company provides support by monitoring the quality standards, which will be vigorously enforced, and by refining and expanding our retail concept and system. Our ability to attract talented and enthusiastic people who thrive in our environment is nothing less than the prime ingredient necessary to achieve all the goals that we have set.

Au Bon Pain believes fundamentally that the individual bakery/cafe units' sales and profitability are strongly influenced by their retail operations' quality. Furthermore, we believe that the retail operations' quality is directly affected by the presence of:

- A management team that truly cares about the quality of the customer experience

Drafted: Spring 1986 by Len Schlesinger and Ron Shaich.
Abridged by Research Assistant Lucy N. Lytle, under the supervision of Professor W. Earl Sasser, January 1987.

- A management team that has experience and is committed to working at a specific unit for an extended period of time
- A management team that is committed to the Au Bon Pain operating system but that is flexible enough to make some of its own decisions and adaptations to build sales in its market
- A crew with strong interrelationships and a commitment to the management team, and thus to the customer
- An explicit focus on managing outputs (service, sales, food costs, controllable costs, labor costs) vs. inputs
- A store-manager/company "you win-we win" approach

Developing these traits has been very difficult, however, due to Au Bon Pain's internal structure and to the following dynamics of the fast-food labor market, specifically:

- A managerial labor pool that forces us to take more "chances" in hiring entry-level talent, in addition to significant turnover at the associate manager level
- A centralized, system-wide orientation toward the operations and marketing functions in our bakery/cafes which currently stifles our ability to exercise initiative at the store level
- Excessive crew turnover and sloppy hiring, which severely degrade the quality of the customer experience and exacerbate the day-to-day problems of the management team

To address these problems and to move toward reaching an idealized version of our retail operations, we are proposing a radically reconceptualized framework for managing human resources in Au Bon Pain bakery/cafe units. It is titled the Partner/Manager Program.

II. Objectives of the Partner/Manager Program

- To develop a management compensation system that enhances dramatically our ability to attract and retain the finest managers in the industry
- To shift our organizational focus from being promoted to district manager as the desired career path to achieving partner/manager status (a terminal general manager's position)
- To increase dramatically a store management team's tenure and thus its feelings of "local ownership"
- To lessen our top-down management approach to retail operations by:
  1. increasing local unit responsibilities for decision making and execution, with an accompanying reward system that increases management commitment to unit results
  2. encouraging partner/managers to "push" the corporate office to respond to local needs

- To reduce dramatically district manager supervision of retail stores and to shift the district manager's role from a policeman/checker to a business/sales consultant
- To provide a human-resource mechanism that frees ABP to grow at an accelerated rate without great pain ("hyperphased growth")
- To maximize simultaneously store-level profits, ABP return on investment, and management salaries
- To provide the opportunity for our partner/managers to build financial "nest eggs"
- To provide job security to those people who perform for ABP and for themselves

III. Management of the Partner/Manager Experiment

The experiment will run for six periods, from July 13 until December 20, 1986. Len Schlesinger will assume direct responsibility as the district manager for the two stores selected to participate.

Experimentation at the Burlington Mall store will test our abilities to revive a mature shopping mall location and to tap into area offices as a growth vehicle in the face of increased competition. The CityPlace experiment will provide us with considerable data on how best to leverage an office building location to its fullest potential.

IV. The Economics of the Partner/Manager Program

A. Each store's general manager will be reclassified as a partner/manager at a base salary of $500 per week. Each will be authorized to hire/retain one associate manager at a base salary of $400 per week. Any additional management support can be added at the partner/manager's discretion. All managers must, however, take their bonus (i.e., their 50% share of the store's incremental profits) from a fixed pool.

B. Au Bon Pain will determine a "store-lease" payment required to support a unit's fixed expenses, corporate overhead, and reasonable profit expectations. During the experiment, this payment will be $127,526 for the Burlington Mall unit, and $103,619 for the CityPlace unit.

C. The store-lease payment will be guaranteed for the period of the experiment, with the following exceptions, which will require adjustments:

   1. The addition of fixed assets will trigger an increase in the store-lease payment of: .25 × total fixed asset cost.

      EXAMPLE: A new counter is added to Hartford at a cost of $10,000. On an annual basis, this addition would increase the store-lease payment by $2,500.

2. Additional sales, which trigger a percentage rent clause in the real estate lease, will increase the store-lease payment by the percentage specified in the real estate lease.

   EXAMPLE: The rent for the Burlington unit assumes that the store will achieve the 1986 plan. All sales over this plan will increase the store-lease payment to Au Bon Pain by 8% of the incremental sales dollars.

D. Profits will be distributed to the partner/manager and associate manager as follows: actual store controllable profits − store-lease payment = incremental profits or losses.

   incremental profits × .50 = ABP share

   incremental profits × .35 = partner/manager share

   incremental profits × .15 = associate manager share

E. The partner/manager's and associate manager's share of the incremental profits will be distributed at the close of each period. Au Bon Pain will hold in reserve $7,500 for the partner/manager and $2,500 for the associate manager until the end of their contracts.

F. For the Partner/Manager Program Experiment, profit distributions will occur after the final review of the experiment is completed (approximately February 1, 1987).

V. Supervising and Managing the Partner/Manager Experiment

A. The two stores will be "mystery shopped" at least once a week, and the mystery-shopping reports will serve as critical indicators of store-level quality standards.

B. The two stores will be subjected to three "white-glove" inspections. These will be conducted by an independent ABP auditor who is not connected with the experiment. The inspections will cover all phases of store operations and will be a major input to the overall evaluation of the experiment.

C. The two stores will be expected to comply with the 100% customer satisfaction "moment-of-truth" indicators and will be evaluated against them.

D. The partner/manager, associate manager, or a certified ABP shift supervisor must be on duty in the store during all store hours. The partner/manager and associate manager must each work in the store a minimum of 50 hours a week, and the partner/manager and/or the associate manager must be on duty in the store during 90% of the operating hours.

E. Au Bon Pain reserves the right to discharge, remove, or replace the partner/manager or associate manager at any time. All store managers, crew, and shift supervisors will remain employees of Au Bon Pain.

VI. "The Rules"

Violation of the following conditions will engender a default and/or the termination of the partner/manager's and/or associate manager's experiment.

A. The partner/manager shall use the Au Bon Pain bakery/cafe premises solely for the operation of the business, keep the business open and in normal operation for such minimum hours and days as ABP may from time to time prescribe, and refrain from using or suffering the use of the premises for any other purpose or activity at any time.

B. The partner/manager shall maintain the bakery/cafe in the highest degree of sanitation, repair, and condition. In connection therewith, he or she shall make such additions, alterations, repairs, and replacements thereto as ABP may require, including without limitation, periodically repainting the premises; repairing impaired equipment, furniture, and fixtures; and replacing obsolete signs.

C. The partner/manager further understands, acknowledges, and agrees that—to ensure that all products produced and sold by the bakery/cafe meet ABP's high standards of taste, texture, appearance, and freshness, and to protect ABP's goodwill and proprietary marks—all products shall be prepared by only properly trained personnel in strict accordance with the Retail Baker's Training Program.

D. The partner/manager shall meet and maintain the highest health standards and ratings applicable to the bakery/cafe operation.

E. The partner/manager shall operate the bakery/cafe in conformity with such uniform methods, standards, and specifications as ABP may from time to time prescribe to ensure that the highest degree of quality and service is uniformly maintained.

F. Unless transferred at Au Bon Pain's request, the partner/manager and/or associate manager will not be eligible for the profit-sharing disbursements unless he or she completes the full time-period of the experiment. If transferred, the affected manager will receive a pro-rated share based on the percentage of total controllable profit contributed while he or she was employed in the store.

The partner/manager agrees:

1. To maintain in sufficient supply, and use at all times, only such products, materials, ingredients, supplies, and paper goods as conform with ABP's standards and specifications. The partner/manager shall not deviate from these standards by using nonconforming items.

2. To employ a sufficient number of employees to meet the standards of service and quality that ABP may prescribe.

3. To comply with all applicable federal, state, and local laws, rules, and regulations with respect to ABP employees.

4. To permit ABP or its agents or representatives to enter the premises at any time for the purposes of conducting inspections; to cooperate fully with ABP's agents or representatives in such inspections by rendering such assistance as they may reasonably request; and, upon notice from ABP or its agents or representatives, to take such steps as may be necessary to correct immediately any deficiencies detected during such inspections.

The partner/manager agrees further that failure to comply with the requirements of this paragraph will cause ABP irreparable injury and will result in the subject termination of his or her employment and the loss of any incremental profit funds held in reserve.

In addition, the partner/manager shall be deemed to be in default and ABP may, at its option, terminate this agreement without affording him or her any opportunity to cure the default, upon the occurrence of any of the following events:

A. The operation of the bakery/cafe results in a threat or danger to public health or safety that is not corrected by the partner/manager within one week of notice.

B. The partner/manager is convicted of a felony or any other crime or offense that is reasonably likely, in the sole opinion of ABP, to affect adversely the ABP system or goodwill associated therewith.

C. The partner/manager fails to comply with the covenants in A–E above provided, however, that for any correctable failure he or she has 30 days after notice from ABP to correct the failure.

D. The partner/manager, after correcting any default, engages in the same activity, giving rise to the same default, whether or not the deficiency is corrected after notice.

E. The partner/manager repeatedly is in default of or fails to comply substantially with any of the requirements imposed by this agreement, whether or not the deficiencies are corrected after notice.

Reading 4–1

Fit, Failure and the Hall of Fame

Raymond E. Miles, Charles C. Snow

There is currently a convergence of attention and concern among managers and management scholars across basic issues of organizational success and failure. Whether attention is focused on the very survival of organizations in aging industries, the pursuit of excellence in mature industries, or the preparation of organizations for the rapidly approaching challenges of the 21st century, the concern is real and highly motivated. U.S. managers and organizations have been indicted for low productivity, and management scholars have recognized the fragmentation of their literature and called for a new synthesis.

Clearly, neither organizational success nor failure has an easy explanation. Nevertheless, it is becoming increasingly evident that a simple though profound core concept is at the heart of many organization and management research findings as well as many of the proposed remedies for industrial and organizational renewal. The concept is that of *fit* among an organization's strategy, structure, and management processes.

Successful organizations achieve strategic fit with their market environment and support their strategies with appropriately designed structures and management processes. Less successful organizations typically exhibit poor fit externally and/or internally. A conceptual framework can be built upon the process of fit that will prove valuable to both managers and management scholars as they sift through current theories, perspectives, and prescriptions in search of an operational consensus. The main features of such a framework are structured around four main points:

- *Minimal* fit among strategy, structure, and process is essential to all organizations operating in competitive environments. If a misfit occurs for a prolonged period, the result usually is failure.

- *Tight fit,* both internally and externally, is associated with excellence. Tight fit is the underlying causal dynamic producing sustained, excellent performance and a strong corporate culture.

- *Early fit*—the discovery and articulation of a new pattern of strategy, structure, and process—frequently results in performance records which in sporting circles would merit Hall of Fame status. The invention or early application of a new organization form may provide a more powerful competitive advantage than a market or technological breakthrough.

- *Fragile* fit involves vulnerability to both shifting external conditions and to inadvertent internal unraveling. Even Hall of Fame organizations may become victims of deteriorating fit.

Minimal Fit, Misfit, and Failure

The concept of fit plays an undeniably important role in managerial behavior and organizational analysis. Fit is a process as well as a state—a dynamic search that seeks to *align* the organization with its environment and to *arrange* resources internally in support of that alignment. In practical terms, the basic alignment mechanism is *strategy,* and the internal arrangements are *organization structure* and *management processes.* Because in a changing environment it is very difficult to keep these major organizational components tightly integrated, perfect fit is most often a condition to be strived for rather than accomplished.

Although fit is seldom referred to explicitly, it has appeared as the hallmark of successful organizations in a variety of settings and circumstances. For example, in our own studies of organizational behavior in many widely different industries, we have regularly found that organizations of different types can be successful provided that their particular configuration of strategy, structure, and process is internally and externally consistent.[1] In his landmark historical analysis, Alfred Chandler found that the companies now recognized as the pioneers of the divisional organization structure were among the first to identify emerging markets, to develop diversification strategies to meet these market needs, and to revamp their organization structures to fit the new strategies.[2] In their study of the management of innovation in electronics firms, Tom Burns and G. M. Stalker found that organizations pursuing innovation strategies had to use flexible, organic structures and management processes; rigid, mechanistic approaches did not fit with such strategies.[3] Finally, in another highly acclaimed study, Paul Lawrence and Jay Lorsch found that successful organizations in three quite different industries were those that were sufficiently differentiated to deal with the complexities of their industrial environments while simultaneously being tightly integrated internally.[4]

These and other studies conducted by organization theorists have essentially if not directly reaffirmed the importance of fit. In addition, recent research in sociology and economics has supported the idea that achieving at least minimal fit is closely associated with organizational success. Industrial economists have identified a set of generic strategies that generally fit most industries, as well as some of the organizational and managerial characteristics associated with these strategies.[5] Sociologists, borrowing concepts and theories from biology, have examined, within different populations of organizations, certain features that fit (or do not fit) particular environments.[6] In sum, the concept of fit may at first glance appear to be obvious, but many studies from several disciplines indicate that while fit is fundamental to organizational success, it is enormously difficult to achieve and/or maintain.

Fit and Survival

It is appropriate to distinguish between degree of fit as well as the nature of fit, specifically that *minimal fit is required for organizational survival*. Under some circumstances, organizations that are "misfits" in their industries may survive, but sooner or later they must adjust their behavior or fail. For example, in one of our studies, the objective was to determine if certain strategies were both feasible and effective in different industries.[7] The industries selected for study were air transportation, autos, plastics, and semiconductors. We found that in general some strategies were effective and others were not. Organizations that we called "defenders," "prospectors," and "analyzers" were all effective; i.e., they met the test of minimal fit in each industry. On the other hand, organizations identified as "reactors" were generally ineffective, except in the air transportation industry, which was highly regulated at the time (1975). Reactors are organizations that have either a poorly articulated strategy, a strategy inappropriate for the industrial environment, or an organization structure and management system that does not fit the strategy. The findings from this study suggest that in competitive industries, there is a set of feasible strategies (e.g., defender, prospector, analyzer) each of which can be effective. Moreover, misfits—organizations whose behavior lies outside of the feasible set—tend to perform poorly unless they are in a "protected" environment such as that provided by government regulation.

Fit and Misfit

The line of demarcation between minimal fit and misfit, however, is not obvious No whistles blow warning an organization that its internal or external fit is coming undone. The process is more likely to be marked by a general deterioration whose speed is affected by competitive circumstances. For example, an in-depth study of the major firms in the tobacco industry during the years 1950–1975 illustrates the point.[8] Few American industries have experienced the degree of negative pressure that was exerted on the tobacco industry during these years, and the experiences of four companies (Philip Morris, R. J. Reynolds, American Brands, Liggett & Myers) pointedly show how organizations struggle to maintain an alignment with their shifting environments over time.

Each of the companies responded differently to severe, uncontrollable jolts such as the Sloan-Kettering report linking smoking to cancer (1953), the Surgeon General's report reaffirming this conclusion (1964), and events leading to and concluding with a ban on broadcast advertising of cigarettes (1970). Philip Morris, relying on a prospector strategy, engaged in a series of product and market innovations that propelled the company from last among the major firms in 1950 market share to first today. R. J. Reynolds largely pursued an analyzer strategy—rarely the first-mover in product market innovations but always an early adopter of the successful innovations of its competitors—and today it ranks a close second to Philip Morris. Both of these companies currently exhibit a minimal if not strong fit with environmental conditions in the tobacco industry.

American Brands followed a defender strategy in which it tried to maintain its traditional approach in the face of these environmental changes. This strategy essentially amounted to continued reliance on nonfiltered cigarettes even though the filtered cigarette market segment was growing steadily. American Brands, probably not wanting to cannibalize its sales of nonfiltered cigarettes, was at least 10 years behind Philip Morris and R. J. Reynolds in entering the filtered cigarette market, and during this period, the company fell from first to fourth place in overall market share. The company's internal fit among strategy, structure, and process was a good one throughout the mid-1950s to mid-1960s, but its strategic fit with the market underwent a gradual decline. Certainly, in retrospect, one could argue that American Brands was a misfit during this time, and the firm paid for it in declining performance.

Lastly, Liggett & Myers behaved almost as a classic reactor throughout this quarter-century period. It demonstrated substantially less internal consistency than its competitors, fared poorly in its product/market strategy, and doggedly hung on to its approach despite unfavorable performance. Described by one source as "always too late with too little," Liggett & Myers in the late 1970s was searching for someone to purchase its tobacco business. Here was a misfit bordering on failure.

In the case of the tobacco industry, major environmental changes resulted in declining fit and performance for one company and near-failure for another. Organizational misfit does not, however, have to come from external changes; it can result from internal shifts generated by the organization itself. To illustrate internally generated misfit, consider the well-known case of organizational disintegration and resurrection, the Chrysler Corp.[9]

From a strong position as the country's second largest automobile manufacturer in the 1930s, Chrysler arguably began to decline in the post-World War II period when it changed its strategy without significantly altering its organization structure or management processes. Prior to the 1950s, Chrysler kept its capital base as small as possible, subcontracted out a substantial part of its production, and rode its suppliers hard to keep costs down. But then Chrysler decided to emulate both General Motors and Ford, even to the point of matching their product lines model for model. From the early 1960s until its federal bailout in the 1970s, Chrysler seemed determined to be a full-line, worldwide, direct competitor of Ford and GM.

To support this product/market strategy, however, Chrysler was late in forming a subsidiary to monitor its distributors, late in making the necessary foreign acquisitions, and often late in designing its greatly broadened product line which was done mostly by a single, centralized engineering group. In fact, Chrysler largely remained a functionally departmentalized and centralized organization long after it adopted a strategy of diversification. Managerial problems in the areas of cost control, inventory, and production merely added to the misfit between Chrysler's strategy and its structure and management system. Despite its recent public attention and economic rebound, the company has not yet achieved stable performance.

In sum, the consequence of misfit is declining performance if not complete failure. Organizational misfits can be protected by a benign environment, sometimes for lengthy periods of time, but minimal fit is required for survival in competitive environments. However, minimal fit, as the term implies, does not guarantee excellent performance.

Tight Fit: The Foundation for Excellence

Corporate excellence requires more than minimal fit. Truly outstanding performance, achieved by many companies, is associated with tight fit—both externally with the environment and internally among strategy, structure, and management process. In fact, *tight fit is the causal force* at work when organizational excellence is said to be caused by various managerial and organizational characteristics.

In the late 1940s and early 1950s, Peter Drucker studied a number of top U.S. corporations, including General Motors, General Electric, IBM, and Sears, Roebuck.[10] Based on his observations, Drucker associated the widely acclaimed achievements of these organizations with such managerial characteristics as delegation and joint goal setting (MBO) and with organizational characteristics emphasizing the decentralization of operating decisions. He saw overstaffing as a threat to corporate responsiveness and argued that the best performance comes when jobs are enriched rather than narrowed. Finally, he felt that the overall key to the success of these companies was that they knew what business they were in, what their competences were, and how to keep their efforts focused on their goals.

Some 30 years later, Thomas Peters and Robert Waterman studied 62 U.S. companies and produced their own checklist of characteristics associated with corporate excellence.[11] As had Drucker before them, they noted that organizations with records of sustained high performance tended to have a clear business focus, a bias for action, and lean structures and staffs that facilitated the pursuit of strategy.

Drucker clearly acknowledged the importance of organization structure and was convinced at the time that the federally decentralized (i.e., multidivisional) organization structure was the design of the future. He did not, however, probe the relationship between alternative strategies and their appropriate structures and management processes. Similarly, while Peters and Waterman stressed structural leanness and responsiveness as universally valuable characteristics, they also noted the requirement of achieving a close fit among the seven "S's" of strategy, structure, skills, systems, style, shared values, and staff (people). Again, however, Peters and Waterman did not discuss the possible alternative organization forms appropriate for different strategies. In our view, the observations of Drucker, Peters, and

Waterman are accurate and extremely valuable. The discovery 30 years apart of the association of similar characteristics with organizational excellence is a powerful argument for the validity of that association—but it is not an explanation of why that association exists nor of the causal force that may be involved.

Both the managerial and organizational characteristics described by these observers, and the outstanding performance achieved by the organizations that they have examined, are the result of the achievement—by discovery or by design—of tight fit. That is, such characteristics as convergence on a set of core business values—doing what one does best, a lean, action-oriented structure that provides opportunities for the full use of people's capabilities at all levels, etc.—essentially flow from the achievement of tight fit with the environment and among strategy, structure, and process. In short, the causal dynamic of tight fit tends to operate in four stages:

- First, the discovery of the basic structure and management processes necessary to support a chosen strategy create a *gestalt* that becomes so obvious and compelling that complex organizational and managerial demands appear to be simple.

- Second, *simplicity* leads to widespread understanding which reinforces and sustains fit. Organization structure and key management processes such as reward and control systems "teach" managers and employees the appropriate attitudes and behaviors for maintaining focus on strategic requirements.

- Third, simplicity *reduces the need for elaborate coordinating mechanisms,* thereby creating slack resources that can be reallocated elsewhere in the system.

- Fourth, as outstanding performance is achieved and sustained, its *association* with the process by which it is attained is reinforced, and this serves to further simplify the basic fit among strategy, structure, and process.

It should be emphasized that we do not specify "finding the right strategy" as an important element of this causal linkage. In fact, finding strategy-structure-process fit is usually far more important and problematic. It may be that there is less to strategy than meets the eye. At any moment, in any given industry, it is likely that several organizations are considering the same strategic moves: to diversify, retrench, acquire other firms, etc. For example, in the 1920s, the top executives of Sears, Roebuck did not have a secret crystal ball that forecast the effects of the automobile on retail trade. Indeed most organizations—including Sears' major competitor, Montgomery Ward—saw similar trends. It was the case, however, that well ahead of competitors Sears developed a structure that would allow it to operate as a high-quality, low-cost nationwide retailing organization.

It is valuable, of course, that the chosen strategy be articulated—for example, Sears pursued the image of "a hometown store with nationwide purchasing power." Nevertheless, it is when the blueprint of how to achieve such strategic goals is drawn that real understanding begins to emerge throughout the system. As clarity involving means emerges, that which was enormously complex and apparently beyond accomplishment now seems straightforward and easy to achieve.

The process of searching for, discovering, and achieving tight fit is pervasive. At the individual level, for instance, learning to drive a car, fly an airplane, or serve a tennis ball are all activities that at first appear complex and difficult to learn but once mastered seem to be relatively simple. Mastery occurs, however, only when the gestalt is apprehended, felt, and understood. The same learning process occurs within organizations. The Baltimore Orioles, for example, believe they know how and why they won the recent World Series and have enjoyed success over the years. Strategy, structure, and process fit and are well understood by members at all levels of the organization. From the front office to the manager, coaches, and players (including those in the farm system), it seems clear how one goes about building a world-champion team. Much of the same could be said for Procter & Gamble, Johnson & Johnson, Minnesota Mining & Manufacturing, McDonald's, Schlumberger, and other excellent companies.

In sum, what we are suggesting is that focus, leanness, action, involvement, identification, etc., are likely *products* of tight fit. Fit simplifies complex organizational and managerial arrangements, and simple systems facilitate leanness, action, and many other observed manifestations of excellence. As one understands the system, one feels more a part of it, and as one's role becomes clear to self and others, participation is facilitated, almost demanded. Closeness and understanding provide a common culture, and stories and myths emerge that perpetuate key aspects of culture.

Early Fit: A Key to the Hall of Fame?

To this point we have argued that minimal fit is necessary for an organization's survival and that tight fit is associated with excellent performance. We now suggest that *early fit—the discovery and articulation of a new organization form—can lead to sustained excellence* over considerable periods of time and thus a place in some mythical Hall of Fame.

Picking a Hall of Fame company is difficult. In sports, Hall of Fame performers are individuals who have been selected only after their careers are over, and sometimes selection is preceded by an interval of several years so that the decision is relatively objective, based on complete information, and final. Organizations, on the other hand, are ongoing systems; therefore, any given Hall of Fame nominee might immediately have one or more "off" years. Nevertheless, some organizations would be likely to appear on every pundit's Hall of Fame list, and we believe that most of these organizations would share the characteristic of an early organizational breakthrough that was not quickly or easily matched by their competitors at the time.

There are, of course, many ways that companies can achieve a competitive advantage. For example, obtaining a patent on a particular product or technology gives a firm an edge on its competitors. Cornering the supply of a key raw material through location or judicious buying may permit a company to dominate a particular business. An innovative product design or the development of a new distribution channel can provide an organization with a competitive lead that is difficult to overcome. Yet all of these competitive advantages are more or less temporary—sooner or later, competitors will imitate and improve upon the innovation, and the advantage will disappear. Such abilities, therefore, do not guarantee induction into the Hall of Fame.

Sustained corporate excellence seems to have at least one necessary condition: the invention or early application of—and rapid tight fit around—a new organization form. Achieving early fit succeeds over the proprietary advantages mentioned above, because a new organization form cannot be completely copied in the short or even intermediate run. In this century, certain firms would appear to merit Hall of Fame nomination based on broad criteria such as product excellence, management performance, market share and responsiveness, and the like. We will discuss five of our own nominees, all of which meet these criteria but also share the characteristic of early fit through invention or application of a new organization form: Carnegie Steel; General Motors; Sears, Roebuck; Hewlett-Packard; and IBM.

Carnegie Steel

Carnegie Steel was one of the first companies to employ the fully integrated functional organization form complete with centralized management and technical specialization.[12] In his early 30s, Andrew Carnegie left a position with the railroad to concentrate on manufacturing steel rails. Convinced that the management methods he and others had pioneered on the railroad could also be applied to the manufacturing sector, Carnegie essentially started the modern steel business in the United States, and he played a major role in forging the world's first billion-dollar corporation, U.S. Steel.

At the heart of Carnegie Steel's success was its reliance on centralized management (particularly cost accounting and control) and full vertical integration. Carnegie recognized early the benefits of vertical integration in the fragmented, geographically dispersed steel industry in the latter half of the 19th century, and his company integrated backward into the purchase of ore deposits and the production of coke as well as forward into manufacture of finished steel products. Vertical integration permitted a new external alignment in the steel industry: substantially larger market areas could now be served much more quickly, efficiently, and profitably. Carnegie Steel supplemented its functional organization structure with careful plant design and transportation logistics, continuous technological improvements, successful (though limited) product diversification, and innovative human resources management practices and labor relations. Thus, internally, there was rapid development of a tight fit between management processes and the company's pioneering strategy and structure.

Carnegie Steel, of course, did not invent the vertically integrated, functional organization form; elements of this model were already available. However, the company's early and complete use of this form dramatically altered the steel business in a way that was not matched by competitors for decades. (See Table 1 for the evolution of major organization forms and our prediction of the next new form.)

**Table 1
Evolution of Organization Forms**

	Product/Market Strategy	Organization Structure	Inventory or Early User	Core Activating and Control Mechanisms
1800	Single product or service. Local/regional markets.	Agency.	Numerous small, owner-managed firms.	Personal direction and control.
1850	Limited, standardized product or service line. Regional/national markets.	Functional.	Carnegie Steel.	Central plan and budgets.
1900	Diversified, changing product or service line. National/international markets.	Divisional.	General Motors, Sears, Roebuck, Hewlett-Packard.	Corporate policies and division profit centers.
1950	Standard and innovative products or services. Stable and changing markets.	Matrix.	Several aerospace and electronics firms (e.g., NASA, TRW, IBM, Texas Instruments).	Temporary teams and lateral resource allocation devices such as internal markets, joint planning systems, etc.
2000	Product or service design. Global, changing markets.	Dynamic network.	International/construction firms; global consumer goods companies; selected electronic and computer firms (e.g., IBM).	Broker-assembled temporary structures with shared information systems as basis for trust and coordination.

General Motors

General Motors has the strongest claim as the inventory of the "federally decentralized" or divisional organization structure. Among the early automobile makers, William C. Durant was one of the strongest believers in the enormous potential market for the moderate-priced car.[13] Acting on his beliefs, Durant put together a group of companies engaged in the making and selling of automobiles, parts, and accessories. In 1919, the total combined assets of Durant's General Motors made it the fifth largest company in the United States. But although Durant had spotted a potentially large opportunity, and had moved rapidly to create an industrial empire to take advantage of it, he had little interest in developing an organization structure and management system for the enterprise he had created.

Indeed, in combining individual firms into General Motors Durant relied on the same organizational approach of volume production and vertical integration that he had used in his previous managerial positions and that was popular at the time. However, this approach led to little more than an expanding agglomeration of different companies making automobiles, parts, accessories, trucks, tractors, and even refrigerators. An unforeseen collapse in the demand for automobiles in 1920 precipitated a financial crisis at General Motors, which was quickly followed by Durant's retirement as president. Pierre du Pont, who had been in semiretirement from the chemical company, agreed to take the presidency of GM. One of du Pont's first actions was to approve a plan devised by Alfred P. Sloan, a high-level GM executive whose family firm had been purchased by Durant, that defined an organization structure for General Motors.

Sloan's plan, which went into effect in early 1921, called for a general office to coordinate, appraise, and set broad goals and policies for the numerous, loosely controlled operating divisions of GM. The general officers individually were to supervise and coordinate different groups of divisions and collectively were to help make policy for the corporation as a whole. Staff specialists were to advise and serve both the division managers and the general officers and to provide business and financial information necessary for appraising the performance of the individual units and for formulating overall policy. Although most of Sloan's proposals had been carried out by the end of 1921, it was not until 1925 that the original plan resulted in a smooth-running organization. The multidivisional decentralized structure allowed GM to diversify a standard product, the automobile, to meet a variety of consumer needs and tastes while maintaining overall corporate financial synergy.

From 1924–1927, General Motors' market share rose from 19 to 43 percent. Unlike its major competitor, Ford, which was devastated by the Depression, GM's profits grew steadily throughout the Depression and World War II. It has been the leading automobile manufacturer in the world since its implementation of the divisional structure and for years was the corporate model for similar structural changes in other large American industrial enterprises.

Sears, Roebuck

Just as General Motors can make a strong claim to the invention of the divisional structure for product diversification, Sears, Roebuck can claim to have been one of the earliest users of this structure outside of manufacturing. Sears has long enjoyed its reputation as the world's most successful retailer.[14] Since its inception in 1895, Sears has undergone two periods where it achieved an "early fit" among its competitors. The first phase of the Sears story began in 1895 when Julius Rosenwald, a consummate administrator, joined Richard Sears, a brilliant merchandiser, and together they built a company catering to the American farmer. Sears, Roebuck's Chicago mail-order plant was a major innovation in the retailing business. Designed by Otto Doering in 1903, this modern mass-production plant preceded by five years Henry Ford's acclaimed automobile assembly line, and it ushered in the "distribution revolution" that was so vital a factor in early 20th century America's economic growth.

The second phase of the Sears story begin in 1924 when Robert E. Wood left Montgomery Ward to join the company. Since farmers could now travel to cities in their automobiles and the urban population was more affluent, retail selling through local stores appeared to be more promising than mail-order sales. Promoted to president in 1928, Wood, with his new handpicked management team, moved ahead rapidly to create a nationwide retail organization. Montgomery Ward and other retail chains of the period (e.g., J. C. Penney, Eaton's, Woolworth's, Grant's, Kresge's) have not been able to this day to match Sears' performance.

The organization form developed at Sears bore many similarities to GM's multidivisional structure, but it was geared toward retailing rather than manufacturing. Whereas GM diversified by product, Sears diversified by geographic territory. Each of the territorial units became full-fledged autonomous divisions with their managers responsible for overall operating results, and the Chicago headquarters remained a central office with staff specialists and general executives. Sears' ultimate tight internal and external fit was not accomplished nearly as rapidly as those of Carnegie Steel or General Motors, but it was achieved first among Sears' competitors and gave the company a competitive advantage that has not, until recently, been seriously threatened.

Hewlett-Packard

The decentralized, divisional structure developed by General Motors and Sears (along with a few other outstanding companies such as Du Pont and Standard Oil of New Jersey) flourished in the 1950s under the spotlight of publicity from management consulting firms and from academics like Peter Drucker. For most companies, however, the divisional structure did not serve as a proprietary advantage but merely as a necessary means of maintaining alignment with a market demanding diversity. Nevertheless, one outstanding company, a Hall of Fame nominee on many early ballots, has taken this organization structure to new heights in its pursuit of leading-edge technological developments in an emerging industry. The company is Hewlett-Packard, and the industry, of course, is electronics. Founded in 1939 by William Hewlett and David Packard, this company is the world's largest manufacturer of test and measurement instruments as well as a major producer of small computers. The company is noted for its strong corporate culture and nearly continuous high performance in a very demanding industrial environment.

From the beginning, Hewlett-Packard has pursued a strategy that brings the products of scientific research into industrial application while maintaining the collegial atmosphere of a university laboratory. This means that the firm concentrates on advanced technology and offers mostly state-of-the-art products to a variety of industrial and consumer markets. A given product line and market are actively pursued as long as the company has a distinctive technological or design advantage. When products reach the stage where successful competition depends primarily on low costs and prices, Hewlett-Packard often moves out of the arena and turns its attention to a new design or an entirely new product. As a company that achieved early fit, its technological diversification rivals General Motors' product diversification and Sears' territorial diversification.

Hewlett-Packard's strategy of technological innovation is supported by an organization structure and management system that may be unparalleled in flexibility.

The fundamental business unit is the product division, an integrated, self-sustaining organization with a great deal of independence. New divisions arise when a particular product line becomes large enough to support its continued growth out of the profit it generates. Also, new divisions tend to emerge when a single division gets so large that the people involved start to lose their identification with the product line. Most human resources management practices—especially those concerning hiring, placement, and rewards—are appropriately matched with the company's structural and strategic decentralization.

International Business Machines

Any Hall of Fame list must include IBM.[15] One of the largest producers of calculating, computing, and office machinery, IBM is arguably the best-managed company in the United States, perhaps the world. Paradoxically, IBM's nomination to the Hall of Fame cannot be based on the invention of a particular organization form—nor, for that matter, a management innovation or technological breakthrough. The company is simply good at everything it does; it is a polydextrous organization that is consistently quick to adopt and refine any approach that it can use to its advantage.

The company was born when Thomas Watson, Sr. joined the Computing-Recording Corporation in 1914 and renamed it International Business Machines in 1924. However, the modern IBM dates to the stewardship of Thomas Watson, Jr., who was chief executive officer from 1956 to 1971 Today IBM is the most profitable U.S. industrial company, and its form of organization is a combination of time-honored and advanced approaches.

IBM takes advantage of two key characteristics of the functional organization, vertical integration and production efficiency. For example, IBM is the world's largest manufacturer of memory chips and installs its entire output in its own machines. And beginning in the late 1970s, a series of huge capital improvements has made IBM one of the most automated and lowest-cost producers in the industry.

IBM has also relied to a limited extent on acquisitions, a characteristic most often associated with the divisional organization. Unlike many large conglomerates, the company is very selective about its acquisitions, the most recent of which is intended to help IBM create the futuristic electronic office.

Finally, IBM uses a variety of the most advanced approaches to organization and management. First, the company has created at least 15 internal new ventures groups in the last few years to explore new business opportunities. The new units are independently run, but they can draw on IBM resources. Second, the company has increased its use of subcontracting. In its most recent product venture, the personal computer, IBM relied largely on parts obtained from outside suppliers and is selling the machine through retail outlets like Sears and ComputerLand as well as its own sales network. Software for the machine was developed by inviting numerous software firms to supply ideas and materials. Third, besides being a vigorous competitor, IBM has formed many successful cooperative agreements with other companies, especially in Japan and Europe. It is generally acknowledged that substantially more cooperative arrangements involving business firms, as well as governments and universities, will be needed in coming years to supplement traditional competitive practices. And, lastly, IBM is international in scope. It is the leading computer firm in virtually every one of the approximately 130 countries where it does business.

In sum, a close, current look at the Hall of Fame companies just described would probably not uncover the maintenance of perfect fit. As suggested earlier, even these organizations are vulnerable to external and internal slippage, perhaps even distortion. Therefore, it is important to explore the processes by which tight fit may be eroded.

The Fragility of Fit

As noted earlier, fit is a process as well as a state. Environmental factors outside an organization's control are constantly changing and may require incremental or major strategic adjustment. Strategic change, in turn, is likely to require changes in organization structure and/or management processes. When environmental jolts are extreme, some organizations may be unwilling or unable to adjust—recall the earlier examples from the tobacco industry and witness the recent plight of several airline companies under deregulation.

However, environmental change is not the only cause of alignment deterioration. For example, misfit may occur when organizations voluntarily change their strategies but fail to follow through with appropriate structural and managerial adjustments, as illustrated by the case of Chrysler. An even more intriguing alignment-threatening process is also demonstrable, one which may well account for more deterioration of fit than either environmental jolts or unsupported strategic changes. This process involves voluntary internal structure and process changes that are made without concern for their longer-run consequences for strategy and market responsiveness. Although usually subtle and long term in its development, this process of internal unraveling underscores the point that an organization's fit at any given time may be quite fragile.

Recall the earlier description of how the discovery of tight fit results in system simplicity: When strategy, structure, and process are completely aligned, both goals and means are visible, and task requirements are obvious and compelling. Resources previously required for coordination or troubleshooting can be redeployed in the primary system, and even tighter fit may result. However, as the spotlight of tight fit illuminates the overall system for everyone to see and understand, its bright glare may also begin to highlight the organization's inherent deficiencies. That is, each pattern of fit has its own distinct contribution to make. For example, the functional organization form is ideal for efficient production of standard goods or services, and the divisional form is most appropriate for diversification. Each form not only has its own strengths but also its own built-in limitations. The form best suited for efficiency is vulnerable to market change, and the form suited to diversification is sometimes clearly redundant.

As the pattern of fit becomes increasingly clear to managers and employees of excellent (tight fit) companies, they can easily describe why the organization prospers. But at least some members of these same companies can also point to the system's shortcomings. For example, in a vertically integrated, centralized, functional organization, perceptive managers will advocate the creation of task forces, project groups, or even separate divisions to facilitate quick development of new products or services. Conversely, one can anticipate in a decentralized, divisional structure that cost-conscious managers will suggest standardizing certain components or services across divisions in order to reduce redundancy and achieve scale economies. Most organizations regularly make minor adjustments in their structures and processes to accommodate demands for which their systems were not designed. In some organizations, however, what begins as a limiting adjustment may over time grow into a crippling, step-by-step unraveling of the entire system. Moreover, this may occur without conscious long-term planning or even awareness. Two brief examples, both associated with companies on our Hall of Fame list, serve as illustrations.

At General Motors, once Sloan's federally decentralized structure was fully in place, managers began to recommend standardization of various product components and production processes. Some aspects of engineering and production had been coordinated across divisions from the beginning, but the advocates of full-scale standardization finally began to override the divisional structure in the 1950s. Many readers may recall the "scandal" that occurred when buyers discovered that the General Motors' engine in their cars had not been made by that division and, in some cases, even by a division of lower status. In fact, those engines had been manufactured according to policies that reflected increasing interdivisional coordination and centralization of decision making. During the 1950s and 1960s when General Motors appeared invulnerable to competition—foreign or domestic—the cost of increased centralization and coordination was probably not visible. It almost appeared that the company could have its diversity and its cost savings, too. One wonders how much more rapidly General Motors might have responded to the challenge of foreign competition if it had been able to do so by simply aiming the operation of one autonomous division toward Japan and another toward Europe. In general, the more attention that is devoted to the known shortcomings of a particular organization form, the more likely is the possibility of unraveling a successful fit.

Could a similar process occur at Hewlett-Packard in the 1980s? In recent months, the company has been beset with problems caused by its decentralized management system and entrepreneurial culture, including overlapping products, lagging development of new technology, and a piecemeal approach to key markets.[16] The response to these problems was the launching of several programs to improve planning, coordinate marketing, and strengthen the firm's computer-related research and development efforts.

Hewlett-Packard's current CEO, John Young, recognizes that these organizational changes involve trade-offs; the benefits obtained from cross-divisional coordination have to be weighed against the threats to the entrepreneurial spirit of the various divisions. That is, the use of program managers and strategic coordinators to align product designs, to force the divisions to share components, and to coordinate pricing and marketing strategies has generated a number of successful cross-divisional development projects. However, these successes have been offset by a wave of manager and engineer defections to other companies. Thus, only time will tell if this reorganization improves the company's internal fit or begins to unravel the core threads among strategy, structure, and process that have produced Hewlett-Packard's success.

The moral of these examples is not that managers of excellent companies should not try to improve performance. Rather, it is that rearranging organization structure and management systems may in some cases preclude an organization from pursuing its desired strategy. Managers of truly outstanding companies recognize the strengths and limitations of alternate organization forms, and they will not undo a crucial link among strategy, structure, or process in order to "solve" predictable problems.

Future Fit: A New Organization Form

Our argument concerning the effects of minimal, tight, and early fit on organizational performance is based on the belief that the search for fit has been visible in organizations for at least the past 100 years. But will this search continue in the future? We believe it will. In fact, many managers are now considering a new organization form and are experimenting with its major components and processes in their organizations. The reality of this new form, therefore, simply awaits articulation and understanding.

In this century, there have been three major breakthroughs in the way organizations have been designed and managed (see again Table 1). The first breakthrough occurred at the turn of the century in the form of the functional organization. Prior to that time, small firms had relied on an informal structure in which the owner-manager's immediate subordinates acted as all-purpose "agents" of the chief executive, solving whatever problems arose. There was very little of the technical specialization found in today's organizations. The functional form allowed those companies that adopted it to become very large and to specialize in a limited set of products and markets. Next came the divisional form, which facilitated even more organizational growth, but, more importantly, it facilitated diversification in both products and markets. The third breakthrough was the matrix structure in which elements of the functional and divisional forms were combined into a single system able to accommodate both standard and innovative products or projects.

Now a promising new organization form is emerging, one that appears to fit the fast-approaching conditions of the 21st century. As was true of previous forms, elements of this new form are sprouting in several companies and industries simultaneously.

Large Construction Firms.   The construction industry has long been known for its use of subcontracting to accomplish large, complex tasks. Today, the size and complexity of a construction project can be immense, as evidenced by the multinational consortium of companies now building an entire city in Saudi Arabia. Under such circumstances, companies must be able to form a network of reliable subcontractors, many of them large firms which have not worked together before. Some companies, therefore, have found it advantageous to focus only on the overall design and management of a project, leaving the actual construction to their affiliates.

Global Consumer Goods Companies. Standardized products such as clothes, cameras, and watches can be designed, manufactured, and marketed throughout the world. Companies engaged in this type of business are prime examples of the "world enterprise": buying raw materials wherever they are cheapest, manufacturing wherever costs are lowest, and selling wherever the products will bring the highest price. To do so, however, requires many different brokers—individuals and groups who bring together complementary resources. All of the participants in the process— designers, suppliers, manufacturers, distributors, etc.—must be coupled into a smooth-running operation even though they are continents apart.

Electronics and Computer Firms. Certain firms in these industries already are dealing with conditions that in the future will be widespread: rapid change, de-massification, high technology, information abundance, and so on.[17] In these companies, product life cycles are often short, and all firms live under the constant threat of technological innovations that can change the structure of the industry. Individual firms must constantly redesign their processes around new products. Across the industry, spin-off firms are continually emerging. Thus, a common development model includes venture capitalists working with high-technology entrepreneurs in the development, manufacture, and distribution of innovative products or services.

Across these three examples, some key characteristics of the new organization form are clearly visible. Organizations of the future are likely to be *vertically disaggregated:* functions typically encompassed within a single organization will instead be performed in independent organizations. That is, the functions of product design and development, manufacturing, and distribution, ordinarily integrated by a plan and controlled directly by managers, will instead be brought together by *brokers* and held in temporary alignment by a variety of *market mechanisms*.

For example, one form of a vertically disaggregated organization held together by a market mechanism is the franchise system, symbolized by McDonald's or H & R Block. In a franchise system, both the product or service and its basic recipe are provided by the parent corporation to a local management group. Such a model, however, seems appropriate only for a limited set of standard goods or services. In our view, a more flexible and comprehensive approach—and hence a better analogue of the organization of the future—is the "designer" system associated with companies such as Yves St. Laurent or Gucci. In these companies, design skills can be applied in a variety of arenas, from electronics to household goods to personal products or services. Similarly, production expertise can be contracted for and applied to a wide array of products or services, as can skills in marketing and distribution. Thus, we expect the 21st century firm to be a temporary organization, brought together by an entrepreneur with the aid of brokers and maintained by a network of contractual ties. In some instances, a single entrepreneur will play a lead role and subcontract for various services. This same individual may also serve as a consultant to others attempting to form their own organizational networks. In other cases, linkages among equals may be created by request through various brokers specializing in a particular service.

Given these characteristics, we have found it useful to refer to this emerging form as the *dynamic network* organization. However, the full realization of this new type of organization awaits the development of a core activating and control mechanism comparable to those that energized the previous organization forms (e.g., the profit center in the divisional form). Our prediction is that this mechanism essentially will be a broad-access computerized information system. Note that most of today's temporary organizations (e.g., a general contractor) have been put together on the basis of lengthy experience among the key participants. Under future conditions of high complexity and rapid change, however, participants in the network organization will first have to be identified, trust between the parties will be a major issue, and fixed-fee contracts specified in advance will usually not be feasible. Therefore, as a substitute for lengthy trust-building processes, participants will have to agree on a general structure of payment for value added and then hook themselves together in a full-disclosure information system so that contributions can be mutually and instantaneously verified. Properly constructed, the dynamic network organization will display the technical expertise of the functional form, the market focus of the divisional form, and the efficient use of resources characteristic of the matrix. And, especially important, it will be able to quickly reshape itself whenever necessary.

Conclusion

The United States is in a period of economic challenge and organizational upheaval. There are myriad prescriptions for industrial and organizational renewal, and many of the factors linked to organizational success are being rediscovered today after a 30-day hiatus. Our own analysis, however, indicates that these characteristics, while important, are merely manifestations of a more fundamental, dynamic process called fit—the search for an organization form that is both internally and externally consistent. We have argued that minimal fit is necessary for survival, tight fit is associated with corporate excellence, and early fit provides a competitive advantage that can lead to the organization Hall of Fame. Tomorrow's Hall of Fame companies are working on new organization forms today.

References

1. Raymond E. Miles and Charles C. Snow. *Organizational Strategy, Structure, and Process* (New York: McGraw-Hill, 1978).
2. Alfred D. Chandler, Jr. *Strategy and Structure* (Garden City, N.Y.: Doubleday Publishing, 1962).
3. Tom Burns and G. M. Stalker, *The Management of Innovation* (London: Tavistock, 1961).
4. Paul R. Lawrence and Jay W. Lorsch, *Organization and Environment* (Boston: Harvard Graduate School of Business Administration, 1967).

5. Michael E. Porter, *Competitive Strategy* (New York: Free Press, 1980).

6. Michael T. Hannan and John H. Freeman, "The Population Ecology of Organizations," *American Journal of Sociology* 82 (March 1977), pp. 929–64; and Howard E. Aldrich, *Organizations and Environments* (Englewood Cliffs, N.J.: Prentice-Hall, 1979).

7. Charles C. Snow and Lawrence G. Hrebiniak, "Strategy, Distinctive Competence, and Organizational Performance," *Administrative Science Quarterly* 25 (June 1980), pp. 317–36.

8. Robert H. Miles, *Coffin Nails and Corporate Strategies* (Englewood Cliffs, N.J.: Prentice-Hall, 1980).

9. The description of Chrysler Corp. was adapted from James Brian Quinn, *Chrysler Corporation,* copyrighted case, the Amos Tuck School of Business Administration, Dartmouth College, 1977.

10. Peter F. Drucker, *The Practice of Management* (New York: Harper & Row, 1954).

11. Thomas J. Peters and Robert H. Waterman, *In Search of Excellence: Lessons from America's Best Run Companies* (New York: Free Press, 1983), chap. 3.

12. The description of Carnegie Steel was adapted from Paul R. Lawrence and Davis Dyer, *Renewing American Industry* (New York: Free Press, 1983). chap. 3.

13. The description of General Motors was adapted from Chandler, *Strategy,* chap. 3.

14. The description of Sears, Roebuck was adapted from Chandler, *Strategy,* chap. 5; and from Drucker, *Practice,* chap. 4.

15. The description of IBM was adapted from "The Colossus that Works," *Time,* July 11, 1983, pp. 44–54.

16. "Can John Young Redesign Hewlett-Packard?" *Business Week,* December 6, 1982, pp. 72–78.

17. For a complete discussion of these conditions, see Alvin Toffler, *The Third Wave* (New York: Bantam Books, 1981); and John Naisbitt, *Megatrends* (New York: Warner Books, 1982).

Reading 4–2

A Vision–Led Approach to Management Restructuring

Richard E. Walton

A recent development in business that has been gaining momentum since the late 1970s is "management restructuring." Consider the following example (from R. Walton, "From Control to Commitment in the Workplace," *Harvard Business Review*, March–April 1985.)

> After evidence of increased self-management and problem-solving capabilities of the work force, and with the stimulus of the division manager, a plant task force developed a phased plan to be implemented over three years. The plan was to remove two levels of the plant hierarchy, increase substantially supervisory spans of control, integrate the quality, development, and production activities at a lower level of the organization, structurally combine the production and maintenance organizations (except for some specialized maintenance functions), and open up new career path possibilities for managers and professionals. The plan was implemented on schedule. These changes achieved increased responsiveness, improved effectiveness, and better management development. Although decreased salaried personnel costs were not the primary motivation, they were a welcome benefit.

This pattern of restructuring is not confined to manufacturing organizations. Sales organizations and staff departments such as purchasing, materials management, and engineering have also eliminated managerial layers, layers that have been relaying information without adding value. To be as specific as possible, the ideas in this article are illustrated by referring to a manufacturing management organization. They could just as easily have been applied to a division organization composed of marketing, engineering, manufacturing and other support units.

This article does not cover all types of management restructuring, such as efforts motivated simply by a desire to cut out "deadwood" or get rid of surplus managers. Most managements already know how to do this, because in many companies they do it with every downturn in the business cycle. Management restructuring is designed to increase not only the efficiency but also the effectiveness of the management organization. There should be a more rapid response to problems, better integration of functional specialties, more coherence and consistency in priorities pursued throughout the organization, better utilization and development of human talent, and more satisfying careers. It is possible to achieve gains in organizational effectiveness while reducing head count, but only when the driving force is effectiveness.

This article outlines an approach to planning the management organization. It builds on (and also overlaps) planning for change on the shop or office floor. It involves management's departure from a strategy based on securing compliance toward one based on eliciting employee commitment, where management has set demanding business objectives for planning and where management has articulated a commitment-type philosophy requiring long-term change throughout the organization.

During the 1970s management began restructuring work at the operator level to increase both productivity and the quality of work life. There is now considerable experience and literature relevant to the design of worker jobs and job environments. Only in recent years has management begun to seriously rethink the total management organization; at present there is limited literature to guide this redesign activity. This article is an attempt to help fill the gap.

Vision-Led Versus Problem-Driven Planning

The approach to planning set forth here can be characterized as "vision-led" rather than "problem-driven." Management generally makes a specific change in its organization in response to a specific problem. It decides to centralize some support services in order to achieve economies of scale, disperse other activities to increase its accountability to the line organization it supports, or modify the reward system to overcome a tendency for some performance aspect to be ignored. This "problem-driven" approach is appropriate whenever the present organizational model is judged to be basically sound and satisfactory for the future.

In recent years, many conditions have caused American executives to question the soundness of their organizations. Invariably the central condition prompting this review is an escalation of performance standards. A tire company faced with more demanding customers and more competition concludes that the level of performance that gave the company leadership yesterday is inadequate today. An airline that could hold its own in a regulated environment concludes it will not be able to survive in today's environment without a more effective use of human resources. An aerospace supplier that forecasts a continued upward trend in the cost and quality standards of its customers concludes it will need a more effective management organization to keep winning business. A research and development organization serving a dramatically restructured telecommunications industry formulates a new strategic approach to the markets for its services and redesigns its organization. In the examples just cited, management is advised to pursue an approach to organizational planning that I characterize as vision-led. The vision of the future organization usually begins as a general concept and eventually becomes a more detailed model.

The vision-led process has many distinguishing characteristics. It usually is guided by a philosophy to which management is committed but which is not yet obvious in the organization's daily life. It contemplates heightened levels of performance that are not yet realizable but that can be inspiring. It covers interrelated aspects of the organization, not just one or a few elements. The importance of those and other characteristics of vision-led planning will be discussed as I describe the process.

Inputs into the Planning Process

Organization, as used here, means much more than can be conveyed on an organization chart. It includes the management structure, systems, personnel, and style.

- Management Structure
    Basis of organization
    Levels of hierarchy and spans of responsibility
    Roles and positions
    Integrative mechanisms
    Consultative and problem-solving mechanisms
- Management Systems
    Decision-support systems
    Measurements
    Rewards
    Communication systems
- Management Personnel
    Selection criteria and procedures
    Development
    Career paths and planning
- Management Style
    Facilitative versus directive
    Goal- versus rule-oriented
    Team versus individualistic
    Status symbols

A fundamental criterion for good organizational design is that each policy area be consistent with the others. In powerful organizations, all the design elements send similar messages and reinforce each other. Thus, for example, when one is

Exhibit 1
Framework for Planning Management Organization

Inputs into the Design Process	Design Elements	Strategic Aspects of the Functioning Organization	Valued Outcomes
Management philosophy	*Structure:* Alignments	Quality of integration	Delivery
Business strategy	Layers/spans	Response time	Quality
Evolving technology	Integrative	Clarity of	Cost superiority
Contextual	mechanisms	priorities	Innovation
conditions		Utilization of	Flexibility
	Systems:	available skills	Good place to
───────	Rewards	Development of	work
Assumptions about	Measures	skills	Development
worker skills and	Computer	Upward influence	
attitudes	*Personnel:*	Downward	
	Selection	communication	
	Training		
	Style:		
	Facilitation		
	status		

designing a role, one must be certain the selection process will yield people able to perform the role. In addition, when one is designing measurements and rewards, one must ensure that they are consistent with the preferred management style.

The major factors to be assessed in order to develop a model for the future management organization are summarized in Exhibit 1 and discussed in the following pages.

Two general factors influence the spirit and purpose of the organization: management philosophy and business strategy. A management philosophy sets forth the values and principles that should be reflected in the way management performs its job. It should have a life expectancy longer than the planning horizon. A business strategy sets forth the business goals and plans of the future organization. They may be a continuation of the present, or they may reflect a predictable shift in present goals and strategies. For example, how focused will a particular factory be in terms of products and processes? What role will the plant play in the division? What will be its performance priorities—cost, quality, delivery, innovation? In brief, what will be the key success factors?

Two other general factors determine the major problems and opportunities to be taken into account in planning the future management organization: contextual factors and computer-based work technology. Some of the effects of one contextual factor, future competition, will already have been taken into account in the formulation of business goals and strategies. Competition may have other effects, such as constraining what type of employment security can be offered. One may forecast other organizational constraints or opportunities: supply and demand for future talent; corporate policies regarding compensation, college hiring, capital resource allocation, and plant location; and government regulations.

Changes in production and office technologies (new closed-loop process controls, automated materials handling, word processing, automated filing, etc.) not only directly affect the nature of workers' jobs and job environments, but also indirectly change management roles and careers. If, for example, the technology transforms the work of skilled craftsmen into button pushers, this will require a change in supervisory style and content. On the other hand, if the technology replaces unskilled labor with a smaller number of skilled technicians, a different supervisory change will be required.

New professional tools have an even more direct effect on the management organization. For example, in a consumer products organization computer-aided design (CAD) was applied to the design of the bottles that are an integral part of the products. This tool had the effect of integrating product and process design and quality engineering. It reduced the time required to assess and modify the bottle configuration to meet criteria for market, product, manufacturing feasibility, and efficiency as well as product-quality testing requirements. It also merged some of the disciplines that had previously performed separate sequential functions.

The tools utilized by managers to perform their work will also change, with effects on the nature of planning, decision making, communication, monitoring, and reporting. New computer-based technologies for production, office, professional, and managerial work *will* impact the management organization. But because there are options in the way these technologies' applications are designed, management can make choices that influence their impact on the organization.

Indeed, management can sometimes choose whether the application will:

- Centralize control or decentralize and delegate control.
- Routinize the performance of a function or leave discretion to individuals.
- Limit access to a few personnel or make it highly accessible.
- Encourage narrow specialization of roles or broaden roles.

As stated above, this article assumes that some planning has already occurred regarding changes in the production process (automation, for example), in policies affecting the nonexempt workforce (job design and involvement, for example), and in workforce attitudes and skills that result from the new technologies and policies.

Let us be more specific about how planning the management organization is dependent upon the output of this earlier planning. One cannot design supervisory roles and propose selection criteria until one makes certain assumptions about what will be accomplished in the following terms:

Employee commitment. How much dedication to organization goals will exist?

Employee competence. How much task expertise, participative problem-solving skill, and capacity for further development will exist in the workforce?

Employee capabilities for self-supervision. How much individual autonomy and work-team responsibility for self-supervision will the workforce be able to handle?

Union/management cooperation. How much will legalism and power bargaining give way to problem-solving?

The four attitudes and capabilities listed above will not occur without specific changes in the way work is managed. The changes may include broader and more flexible operator jobs, mechanisms for employee involvement and consultation, a new pay and advancement system favorable to growth, more facilitating supervision, new employment assurances, and joint union/management endorsement of many of the above changes. Thus, those making the assumptions underlying the design of the future management organization must realize that changes like these will probably be initiated and will succeed in promoting greater employee commitment and competence.

Design Choices

The management-organization design processes involve both top-down logic and bottom-up logic. A top-down design process first considers whether the basic structural alignment will be appropriate for strategic integrative tasks the organization will perform. A plant organization, for example, can range from a purely functional structure (in which many support functions report to the plant manager) to a highly divisionalized structure (in which support functions report to the "general managers" of several suborganizations within the plant). The suborganization can be aligned by products or by processes. Furthermore, a matrix structure can be used to focus on both the functional specialty and the product (or process) dimensions of the organization.

Structural alignment influences who feels accountable for what and what information is most readily available for different types of decisions. The general advantages and disadvantages of functional specialization are well understood. Its advantages usually include standardization, better exchange of information within functional specialties, flexibility and efficiency in utilizing limited specialists, and advancement opportunities within the specialty. The disadvantages include more concern with the specialty than with the broader organizational purpose, lack of communication with interdependent activities, slower decision making, and lack of development of general managers. An alternative to the functional organization, namely decentralization of responsibility for integrating functional specialties, may have the following advantages: broader jobs for lower-level managers, greater motivation, less precise coordination systems, and greater organizational flexibility and adaptability.

A given structural alignment can only emphasize a few of the many interdependencies among activities. Therefore, appropriate structures must ensure that the most important types of coordination occur. Other types of coordination can be promoted by a number of alternative integrative mechanisms, including the following: hierarchy, integrating roles/groups/meetings, rules/procedures, plans/goals, measurements/rewards, and selection/development. Therefore, what is not assigned to be integrated structurally within an organizational unit must be integrated across units by one of the above means.

In summary, the following questions lead to choices regarding basic structural alignment:

- What will be the important integrative tasks?
- Will they be effectively performed by the current structural alignment and integrative mechanisms?
- What alternative structural forms and different integrative mechanisms promise most advantage?

Whereas key success factors and their integration tasks are the starting point for a top-down design process, actual physical work flow analysis starts a bottom-up process. The production technology, the physical transformation of materials, and the operating requirements impose their own requirements first on the organization of operators' work and then on the supervisory and support organization.

The task technology, the attitudes and skills of the work force, and the techniques used for managing this work will influence such factors as the supervisory span of responsibility and the skills required. In turn, the definition of the role of first-line supervisor will influence the span of responsibility and skills required of the next level of management, and so on up the line.

The top-down design logic and the bottom-up logic are complementary; both are required. These logics and the plans they produce are influenced by the management philosophy. In commitment-oriented companies I have observed that design principles such as the following were used to guide the management restructuring:

1. Influence should be based on a person's information, expertise, and other capabilities, rather than on positional authority. Decisions should be delegated to the lowest level that has the requisite capabilities.
2. Management should rely as much as possible on results-oriented role definitions and performance expectations, rather than on input-oriented or means-oriented requirements.
3. The organization should rely largely on shared values and common information to achieve coordination, rather than on hierarchical controls.
4. The organization should try to achieve equity by applying common principles to varying situations rather than by seeking uniformity in practice.
5. Individuals influenced by decisions should, whenever possible, have an opportunity to participate in the decision-making process.
6. The organization's goals should reflect the interests of all stakeholders including shareowners, management employees, and other employee groups.

The advantages these companies expected to derive from these organizational principles included the following:

Greater goal clarity.

Wider commitment to goals.

Better integration of functions.

Faster decision making.

More adaptiveness to changing requirements.

Better utilization of talent.

Better development of human resources.

More meaningful/satisfying managerial and professional roles.

Better leadership and management of the unionized work force in a commitment mode.

Significantly superior performance: cost, quality, delivery, innovation.

In addition to formulating and applying organizational principles such as those outlined above, management often observed the actual practices adopted by other commitment-oriented companies in order to generate design possibilities. It is not absolutely essential to review the trends in other commitment companies in order to develop the future organization, but it can be helpful. While every situation has its unique circumstances, there are still similarities in the many problems requiring solution.

The section below (See Exhibit 2) presents some of the actual design trends I have observed in industry. It is organized by columns, with the left column indicating the design element in question and the right reporting patterns typical of management restructuring.

Once a picture of the organization of the future is formulated, some interim stages can be described. They are not merely interpolated from the starting picture of the future. They take into account issues that affect timing and rate of change. For example, when can the training and organizational development work required to support a change of roles be completed? When can one make the personnel moves into as well as out of key roles? How much change can the organization handle in a given time frame? What additional information is required to confirm the appropriateness of the move to a second or third stage? When will the information be available?

In developing snapshots of the future organization at several stages, transitions will not always follow a straight line. Consider, for example, the transition to an organization in which the first-line supervisors' span of responsibility could move from 15 to 25 employees in five years. If the broader span is to be made possible by developing operators' technical expertise, their commitment to the task, and their development into largely self-supervising work teams, it may be advisable to first decrease the span from 15 to 10 employees to allow for the intensive work required to develop the necessary employee capabilities.

Planning Process

I have outlined a comprehensive rethinking of the management organization. The level of effort required is substantial; it cannot be accomplished by a few people in a matter of weeks. The review of the relevant design inputs and the exploration of available alternatives in a number of design areas require involvement by representatives of the entire organization.

Exhibit 2
Design Trends in Industry

Elements	Observed Patterns
Management Structure	
Basis of organizational alignment	If the organization is in manufacturing, its alignment can be organized by product, part, process or area. If practicable, managements tend to adopt an autonomous product organization. Subunits tend to become more self-contained in terms of support activities.
Levels of hierarchy and their implications	Invariably management finds it can operate better with fewer levels. This involves broader spans of control. Often plant organizations already have broad spans at the top and bottom but narrow spans in between.
	Influence is based on a person's information and expertise, rather than on positional authority. Decisions are made at the lowest level that has the requisite information and expertise.
Integrative mechanisms	Some support functions, such as quality inspection, may be assumed by line organization. Some support functions are combined organizationally, sometimes with cross training of the professional staffs.
	More use is made of direct lateral coordinative mechanisms, with less involvement by the hierarchy.
	More use is made of task forces composed of professionals drawn from different units and different levels.
Consultative and problem-solving mechanisms	A variety of mechanisms are developed for consultation and involvement. Sometimes these consultative mechanisms constitute a "parallel structure."
Roles and positions	One specific type of role change involves support staff: the relative size of staff support organizations is decreased and the roles of staff groups charged from performing the support activities to imparting their knowledge and skills to those they have supported.
	Role responsibilities are not static as they tend to be captured in job descriptions; rather, they are contingent on the circumstances.
	Role responsibilities are defined more in terms of results expected than in terms of input required.
	Role responsibilities at levels of the hierarchy are not uniform or constant over time; rather, one level is expected to delegate responsibilities as the developed capability of a subordinate warrants. This is true in most organizations. It is more pronounced in the commitment organization and is explicitly recognized as desirable.
Management Systems	
Measurements	The role of measurements tends to change as the organization moves from a control to a commitment orientation. More measurements are used to aid those whose performance is measured rather than to inform higher levels of management. There is more self-design of measurements. The fewer measures used by upper levels of the hierarchy are focused on *results*. More measures have a temporary life as they are introduced to heighten awareness and diagnose problem areas and then dropped when these purposes have been achieved.
	With new computer-based work technology it is feasible and inexpensive to give management an increasing number of performance measures. Managements decide that they must be very selective and careful to consult those whose activities would be measured.

**Exhibit 2
(continued)**

Elements	Observed Patterns
Rewards	The organization usually does not change its overall compensation policy relative to industry. The decrease in the number of hierarchical levels often requires broader classification and salary ranges for each of the new levels. In cases where professional staff positions are broadened to include multiple specialties, they are reevaluated upward.
	Different types of performance are rewarded. The differences relate to the different role structures discussed above.
	Overall, the commitment organization tries to emphasize the intrinsic rewards for managers more than pay. However, this is more complicated in the managers' case. Many managers are ambivalent about changes that decrease the number of levels, deemphasize status symbols, and require them to consult workers. Thus, it is doubly important in planning the management organization to consider how one can improve the satisfaction and career optimism of managers. For example, if managers consult their subordinates but are not themselves consulted by their superiors, they often experience a loss rather than a gain. This is one of several areas in which practice has fallen short of ideals in commitment organizations to date.
	An important gain in intrinsic satisfaction comes from the professional and personal development promoted by new organizations. The development process itself can be satisfying, provided the change involves appropriate training, support, and involvement.
Communication	The management organization is characterized by a much freer flow of information both formally and informally. There is not necessarily more or less use of computer-based information systems to support decision making. However, the systems' development usually involves much more dialogue between the users and developers, especially during the *design* phase. The potential effects of these systems for the control/commitment aspects of the management organization should be anticipated during this phase. Unfortunately this does not always occur, even in the dedicated commitment companies.

Management Personnel	
Selection	Selection criteria change in obvious ways to ensure the individuals selected for particular positions can handle the broader responsibilities, more ambiguous definition of roles and authority, greater premium on leadership, etc.
	Often in the leaner organization more careful thought is given to how to achieve both breadth and depth, both analytical skill and operations experience. One technique is to select so that one alternates in the hierarchy between a person with breadth and analytical skills and a person with depth of task skills and experiences.
	In developing selection procedures, one must give even more consideration than is historically given to ensuring the process is (and is perceived as being) fair.

**Exhibit 2
(concluded)**

Elements	Observed Patterns
Training, coaching, and organization development	Training emphasized the same qualities as selection.
	There is a much greater commitment to professional and managerial training and education and to organization development. Groups which receive training are given more opportunity to influence the nature of training.
	The pedagogy used in training is consistent with the new management style, e.g. emphasizing more active learning formats.
Career paths and planning	The traditional paths by which people have moved through the professional and managerial organizations need to be reviewed for suitability for the new roles.
	A greater commitment is made to discussions about alternative career opportunities than most organizations have made in the past.
Management Style	
Facilitative versus directive	Managers rely more on facilitating and less on directing. Management and professionals rely more on imparting skills and knowledge and less on direct performances of required activities.
	In order to manage the multitude of dependencies, management relies upon building a cooperative climate among peers; it relies less on the superior personally orchestrating subordinates' performances.
Goals versus rules	This style element is closely related to the discussion of roles above. Management devotes maximum effort to clarifying goals and priorities and ensuring that they are understood and accepted by subordinates. If this leadership task is accomplished, the manager does not worry about rules as a way to channel behavior.
Status symbols	Status differences are minimized and deemphasized.

This planning effort must be mandated by a group of the organization's leaders who can make a commitment to a philosophy and business strategy and who have the authority to make changes in structures, roles, and rewards. Much of the analysis (for example, of current organizational strengths and weaknesses and of future work technology) must be performed by other members of the organization—members who can devote much of their time to these activities over many months.

A typical organizational planning structure involves a steering committee headed by one of the organization's top executives and a number of working groups focused on areas of the planning. As it would be unwieldy to include everyone with relevant input in the process, other devices must be developed to get their input. The working group may use interviews or questionnaires tailored to the data outlined in Exhibit 1. For example, a worksheet could elicit assessments of the quality of coordination, the rapidity of response, and other aspects of the current organization listed in Column 3 of Exhibit 1. Another worksheet could help identify the new management and professional tools planned for future implementation and project their organizational implications.

Another device for getting relevant reactions, especially where organizational options are being developed and tested, is to hold "hearings." After draft proposals are made available for review by individuals outside the planning committees, working group and/or steering committee representatives may meet with interest groups to outline the rationale of proposed options and to hear the views of interested parties.

Throughout the planning process, design consultants can help design the process, offer an objective critique of the organization's self-assessment, and identify organizational options. If there are no internal resources to perform these functions, an outside consultant may be needed. Another, more viable alternative may be a program for visiting other companies that have engaged in similar efforts. This pattern of company-to-company education is now well developed in relation to work redesign at the shop floor level, greatly reducing the need for outside consultants. Less outside consultation will be needed as more companies have direct experience in this type of planning.

It is not necessary for all aspects of the future organization to be clarified before some aspects can be decided and even implemented. For example, if the directional thrust of the future structure has been clarified, specific changes can be made in response to personnel changes that occur for other reasons. Structural changes can be decided first, and the implications for certain systems and staffing policies can be sorted out later. The determination of matters of sequence—what must be decided when and what can be left open for how long—is itself an important aspect of the planning process.

Conclusions

This article presents an approach to management restructuring. It envisions a movement toward a commitment-oriented organization, and many of the specific recommendations follow naturally from this assumption. One recommendation is that the goal of the restructuring be increased effectiveness rater than greater efficiency. Another is that the process allow for wide involvement. Still another is that a coherent philosophy of creating high commitment be a cornerstone of the planning process.

Equally important is the formulation of more ambitious performance expectations. In one organization the process may be driven by a new commitment to "cost superiority"; in another by a concept of new industry standards of "service excellence"; and in another by the goal to dramatically reduce "the cost of poor quality." These increased performance expectations can induce the creative thinking required to successfully modify the existing organization.

Selected Bibliography

There is an extensive literature on the design of management organizations. The book most directly related to the type of management organization treated in this paper is *Managing Creation: The Challenge of Building a New Organization* by Dennis Perkins, Veronica Nieva, and Edward Lawler III (Wiley, 1983).

An article analyzing the implications of advanced technology for the management organization of the future is Calvin Pava's "Managing New Information Technology" in *HRM: Trends and Challenges,* edited by Richard Walton and Paul Lawrence (Harvard Business School Press, 1985).

The basic shift in workforce management strategy referred to as "commitment strategy" in the paper is outlined in a paper I authored entitled "From Control to Commitment in the Workplace" (*Harvard Business Review,* March–April 1985).

Reading 4–3

Substitutes for Hierarchy

Edward E. Lawler III

The terms "hierarchy" and "organization" have become virtually inseparable. Most people cannot even imagine what an organization would look like without layers of management and support staff to provide counsel and, at times, direction to that hierarchy. Few, if any, business organizations in the United States lack a substantial amount of hierarchy. However, the idea of extensive and expensive hierarchies is currently under attack as never before, particularly in organizations that face intense cost competition.

More and more organizations are concluding that they simply cannot afford the salary and other costs of maintaining an extensive hierarchy. In many instances, that expense is escalated by such practices as pay systems that base pay levels on level of hierarchy and the tendency for each level to justify its existence by asking for reports and data from lower levels. Compounding the problem, managers at each level tend to request that they be given their own staff groups to provide support for their activities.

In a real sense, all members of the organizational hierarchy above the people who produce the organization's products or services produce nothing of value. Their only purpose is facilitating the performance of those involved in making the organization's products or delivering the organization's services. Thus they constitute an overhead expense whether they are in line or staff positions. They are worth having only if they add significant value to what is done by the people who actually produce the organization's products or services.

A considerable amount of experimentation already underway at some manufacturing organizations indicates that the potential cost savings through reducing hierarchy are substantial. Some organizations have found that they can operate with

Reprinted by permission of the publisher, from *Organizational Dynamics,* Summer 1988 © 1988, American Management Association, New York. All rights reserved.

at least one less level of supervision and with spans of control at the first level of organization that approach 100 to 1. Of course, simply eliminating hierarchy is not a guarantee of improved performance. Costs in other areas must not increase as a consequence, and critical activities must continue to be done. Even more important, the productive behavior of the organization's performers must remain the same or increase as a result of the change.

To help answer the question of how hierarchy can be reduced effectively, we need to look at the functions of hierarchy and ask what substitutes are available for them. Clearly, the more that substitutes can be found for particular features of the hierarchy, the more that the hierarchy can be reduced. After reviewing the substitutes, we can consider what an organization that adopts all or most of them would look like.

Functions of Hierarchy

Supervisors at all hierarchical levels are expected to perform a number of activities, of which the major ones are listed below:

- *Motivating.* Supervisors are expected to motivate employees to perform effectively. They can accomplish this task through interpersonal skills, and rewards such as pay and promotions. Sometimes they may be able to restructure work to make it more interesting and challenging. Also, they can set goals that motivate individuals.

- *Recordkeeping.* For supervisors, and indeed for the entire hierarchy of the organization, recordkeeping is a major task. In fact, supervisors often complain that they spend an inordinate amount of time filling out records concerning personnel, quality, productivity, and financial matters. These records, in turn, are analyzed by staff groups, which seem to request increasing amounts of data.

- *Coordinating.* A major responsibility of both supervisors and staff groups is the coordination of the activities of people doing different pieces and kinds of work. Lower-level supervisors work on intragroup as well as intergroup issues. At higher levels, coordination involves getting different functions, different product lines, and different staff groups to work together.

- *Assigning work.* Supervisors are expected to monitor workflow and to assign people to particular tasks. In the event of work overloads, they are expected to schedule overtime, bring in temporary workers, or do whatever it takes to get the work done.

- *Making personnel decisions.* Supervisors, often aided by the personnel department, are expected to make many personnel decisions. They hire and fire, discipline, pay, and promote within their area of responsibility.

- *Providing expertise.* Most supervisors act as a source of expertise in their work areas. If they do not have the expertise, they are expected to find it (often through a staff group) and provide it to their work group. Staff groups are expected to provide expertise to the entire organization.

- *Setting goals.* In many cases, supervisors set productivity goals, quality goals, and other goals for their work unit. This function, of course, is related to the functions of motivation, coordination, and planning. Staff groups play a role here as well. They often develop measures, suggest goals, and measure accomplishments.

- *Planning.* Supervisors and planning specialists are expected to plan the activities of work groups. They determine the sequence in which work should be done, create production schedules, and make a whole host of decisions concerning work methods and procedures. Senior staff groups also do longer-range planning involving market changes, new products, financing, and other strategic issues.

- *Linking communications.* Supervisors are key communication links in an organization. In particular, they are charged with downward communication, relaying orders, performance feedback, and other messages from the higher levels of the hierarchy to the performers. They also communicate upward so that higher levels in the hierarchy are aware of performance levels, productivity levels, and human resources conditions in the work group. Finally, they are expected to provide a horizontal communications link in the organization.

- *Training/coaching.* On the job training is expected of supervisors. If supervisors cannot do the training themselves, they are expected to find other people, typically staff people, to provide the training. Supervisors also coach employees in new skills.

- *Leading.* One of the most nebulous, yet most important, functions of a supervisor is leadership. Supervisors are expected to do more than control, plan, and direct. Other, more intangible qualities are required to inspire work groups with a sense of vision, empowerment, and common goals and direction.

- *Controlling.* One rarely mentioned function of hierarchy involves meeting the control needs of people at higher levels. An extensive control system involving many levels of management and expert staff groups provides a face-valid sense of control. Who can argue with the view that an organization is under control when it has the experts designing all key functions and supervisors tightly controlling the activities of everyone in the organization?

Organizational Policies and Practices

A number of specific organizational design features and practices can substitute for hierarchy. These include work design, information systems technology, financial data, reward system practices, supplier/customer contact, training, vision/values, and emergent leadership. No one feature alone is considered to be a solution, but taken together they often can reduce the need for supervisors and staff groups.

Work Design

Research on work design clearly shows that it is one of the most important elements in determining the amount and kind of hierarchy needed in an organization. The need for extensive hierarchy has its foundations in the scientific management approach to designing work. When jobs are designed to be simple, standardized, and specialized, the need for coordination, control, and hierarchically driven motivation is greatly increased. In essence, when jobs are highly specialized, it is difficult for people performing a job to coordinate their work with that of others. They often do not know what others are doing, and they lack the links and power to influence it. Motivation becomes a problem because the work itself typically is not intrinsically interesting. It lacks the elements of variety, control, wholeness, and meaning that produce motivation. Thus some other source of motivation such as a supervisor is needed.

Research on job enrichment and work teams clearly demonstrates that when work is designed around whole products or services, much of the need for a supervisor to coordinate work and motivate workers disappears. The work becomes intrinsically interesting and challenging. Coordination problems are dramatically reduced because key interdependencies are contained within the work unit. The need to relate on a close, ongoing basis with other work units or individuals is minimized.

As work teams mature and become more self-managing, they can take on some of the other functions normally performed by a supervisor. For example, with the help of a personnel staff group, they can make many personnel decisions, schedule their own work assignments, and do limited training on a peer basis. Finally, individual team members can be assigned to take care of recordkeeping and communicating both horizontally and vertically within the organization. In practice, communication responsibilities often are assigned by teams to individuals on a rotating basis, as are such duties as production, scheduling, planning, and training.

In one sense, work teams generally can take on more self-management responsibility than individuals performing enriched work since work teams can do more in the areas of making personnel decisions, assigning work, and planning. However, one significant disadvantage of work teams is the considerable amount of skill building and team building required to make them effective. Enriching individual work designs does not require those kinds of development efforts (which create a significant expense). In addition, work teams require meeting time for making decisions, which may curtail production.

Information Systems Technology

Personal computers, computer terminals, and computer networks can be powerful substitutes for hierarchy. Of course, they create their own need for staff support; but if they are used in a way that allows workers to be more self-managing, the reduced costs of hierarchy can more than offset the cost of the support personnel required and the cost of the technology.

In some new computer-integrated manufacturing (CIM) environments, recordkeeping is done directly by operators and job performers. They enter their own data into a terminal or personal computer, and it is centrally stored. Productivity data, quality data, and personnel data such as hours of work, overtime, and attitudinal responses can be recorded in this manner. In effect, much of the record-keeping is done by the individual performers instead of by staff and overhead personnel. In addition, much of the coordination traditionally done by supervisors can be done by the computer network. When individual workers have access to operating data, they can plan, schedule, and adjust their own work to fit what others are doing.

In some cases, the computer can also be an excellent training resource. Directions for certain tasks can be entered into the information system. More interactive systems can even detect errors, set goals, and support decision making. For example, at some companies networking allows employees to ask employees at other locations to help them solve technical problems and allows them to compare production rates at different locations.

Moreover, networked computer systems can partly deal with the control needs of senior management because they allow senior managers to access information on production and cost measures throughout the organization. As a result, senior management no longer needs to ask staff groups to gather and report this information.

Financial Data

The distribution of financial data to work teams can enhance their awareness of the economic priorities and results of the organization. When cost, sales, profitability, and investment data are given to performers and they are trained in interpreting and using those data, motivation, coordination, and goal setting can be enhanced. Individual performers get a sense of how the organization is measured and can begin to measure themselves in the same way. They can also set priorities and plan on the basis of financial decision-making models rather than on simple production-optimization models. Providing people with this kind of feedback can have a dramatic impact on motivation. For an even more powerful impact, data on the competitive situation of the organization can be included to help focus attention on external business competitors rather than on internal competitions and grievances.

Reward System Practices

At least three reward system practices can directly reduce the need for hierarchy: gain-sharing, profit sharing, and skill-based pay. Gainsharing and profit sharing can enhance motivation, coordination, and communication. They provide a tangible extrinsic reward for effective performance and directly answer the motivational issue. Gainsharing in particular also provides a reason to coordinate work within a group and between different groups because it pays off on organizational results; thus it encourages teamwork and cooperation. Both gainsharing and profit sharing can improve communication of financial results and provide feedback about how well the organization is performing.

Skill-based pay is an increasingly popular approach for determining base pay. Since workers are paid for the number of skills that they have, they are strongly motivated to learn how to do a number of different tasks. By rewarding workers for learning scheduling, financial analysis, and other supervisory and staff-support skills, skill-based pay can create a workforce that understands the whole operation and can coordinate itself. It enables work groups to do more planning because they have the expertise to deal with many parts of the organization. It also encourages peers to train each other so that each one of them can get an increase in pay. Skill-based pay is a key reward system change if a work team or self-managing work group is to operate effectively in a self-directing sense.

Supplier/Customer Contact

To be effective in managing itself, a work team must control its inputs and outputs. Control of inputs entails dealing with suppliers and being allowed to influence their behavior. This holds true whether the suppliers are inside or outside the organization.

Closely related to supplier contact is customer contact. Customer contact provides workers with feedback on how well they have performed their task. Feedback is a critical element of intrinsic motivation and contributes to self-regulation, coordination, and goal setting. Getting performance results from the people who purchase the products and services of an organization or a work group thus is critical in allowing and motivating workers to take responsibility for controlling their own work activities.

When work groups have control over both their inputs and outputs, they can do their own scheduling and handle much of their own planning. The need for staff support personnel who deal with suppliers and customers is reduced, thereby decreasing the organization's overhead costs.

Training

Nothing can substitute for extensive formal training if the activities typically performed by higher levels of the hierarchy are to be pushed downward. The scope of training needs to range from financial education to interpersonal skills and problem-solving skills. The type of training needed is determined by the type of work design chosen. If self-managing work teams are chosen, training needs are extensive and clear-cut. The teams need to learn to plan, solve problems, make group decisions, and gather feedback. Individual team members need to develop interpersonal skills. Training is also needed in recordkeeping, dealing with customers and suppliers, quality, performance evaluation, and setting goals. Because of the extensive training demanded by self-managing work groups, one part of the hierarchy cannot be reduced, at least initially: Extensive training resources and staff specialists are still needed.

If job enrichment for individual workers is chosen, less training is needed in interpersonal skills and group decision making. Regardless of which work design approach is chosen, however, training in the economics of the organization and its business is needed. For workers to behave effectively, they need to know how their actions will affect the organization's financial results and they need to be able to interpret the financial results the organization achieves. This takes training.

If an organization is to operate with a minimum of hierarchy, peer training must support and complement the extensive formal training that is required. If all the needed training is done by special staff groups, there is a danger that the elimination of supervisors will only lead to the comparable addition of training specialists. The only way to avoid this situation is to encourage extensive on-the-job peer training by providing skill-based pay and by making work teams responsible for their own training. In many cases, training can be done on the job and thus in a cost-effective manner.

Vision/Values

Without an extensive bureaucracy that specifies tasks and develops extensive measures to ensure that those tasks are carried out in an effective and timely manner, something is needed to provide an overall sense of direction for the organization and to guide each employee's behavior. A vision/values statement, or set of cultural core beliefs, can serve this purpose.

When a common set of values can be defined, self-managing units can focus on goals and performance results that are consistent with those values. No one needs to be there to specify how workers should act. They can be guided by the larger vision and can focus on what needs to be done rather than on what is the prescribed thing to do. A positive set of core values can also enhance motivation, attraction, and retention by giving meaning to work activities. Thus it can be both a guide to action and a motivator of action.

Emergent Leadership

Leadership is always needed in an organization even though substitutes for it can be developed. In reality, leaders are constantly appearing in organizations, and they are not always the formally appointed managers. In a traditional hierarchy, this phenomenon can be disturbing and dysfunctional because it causes conflicting directions and competing agendas. When reducing the hierarchy, however, it is desirable to have leaders emerge in work groups. If those leaders are committed to seeing the organization perform well, they can motivate and provide a sense of direction to a work group. If they are put in charge of communicating with the outside world, working on group-process issues, and leading the group in problem solving, they can fulfill many of the functions performed by a traditional supervisor.

The key to the emergence of the right kind of leader rests in many of the practices that have already been discussed as possible substitutes for leadership. If they are in place, work groups probably will accept and seek leadership that is oriented toward organizational goals and that has a positive impact on performance.

Integrated Impact

The substitutes for hierarchy that have been suggested so far clearly require a substantial alteration in the way most organizations are managed if they are to be installed and if they are to be effective. In essence, they require a move from a control type of organization to a commitment type of organization. However, if they are instituted in combination, they can go a long way toward making organizational hierarchy unnecessary. To be successful in reducing the need for hierarchy, most or all of the substitute approaches need to be introduced. They are not stand-alone practices in the sense that installing one of them or a few of them can make a difference. As the many "fit" models of organization design stress, when changes are made in one important feature of an organization, changes are needed in a number of others if the organization is to be effective.

As shown in Exhibit 1, each of the typical functions of hierarchy is handled by several of the substitute approaches. However, no one approach effectively substitutes for all or perhaps even any of the functions of a hierarchy. Indeed, installing just one or a few of the approaches may cause more problems than gains. For example, increased training alone may lead to just more costs. Installing skill-based pay without training simply sets up a conflict situation and creates the risk that all control will be lost in the resulting chaos.

Even if all the practices that have been suggested are implemented, some functions of hierarchy will probably still be necessary, including long-range planning, certain types of customer contact, setting a strategic vision and values, investment and financing decisions, and certain types of expertise and training. My point is not that all hierarchy can be made unnecessary but rather that it can be reduced and the remaining part of it freed from its traditional control activities in order to allow senior management to do more strategic-level work, which after all is what it is supposed to be doing.

Situational Fit

It is important to point out that work situations vary in the degree to which they can be managed with a reduction in hierarchy. Technology, work interdependence, work complexity, and required knowledge clearly influence the opportunities for adopting an organizational approach that is based on minimal hierarchy and high involvement.

Perhaps the overriding determinant of how an organization should approach hierarchy is the kind of work it does and the technology it uses. Managers' values and attitudes can be changed over time, and older, control-oriented organizations can evolve their practices from a hierarchical approach to an involvement approach. However, organizations cannot necessarily change the kind of technology they use or the kind of jobs that the technology dictates.

Technology is only partly driven by the products and services the organization offers. As many advocates of the sociotechnical approach have pointed out, organizations have some flexibility in the technology they choose to use. In addition, technology does not completely dictate the nature of the jobs an organization has.

Exhibit 1
Substitutes for Hierarchy

Supervisory Functions	Work Design	Information Systems Technology	Financial Data	Reward System Practices	Supplier/ Customer Contact	Training	Vision/ Values	Emergent Leadership
Motivating	X		X	X	X	X	X	
Recordkeeping	X	X						
Coordinating	X	X	X	X	X	X	X	X
Assigning Work	X							X
Making Personnel Decisions	X						X	X
Providing Expertise		X				X		X
Setting Goals	X	X	X	X	X	X	X	
Planning	X	X	X					
Linking Communications	X	X	X	X			X	
Training/Coaching	X	X			X			X
Leading	X							X
Controlling		X	X	X				

Some technologies can be modified to produce the types of jobs that are congruent with minimal hierarchy. In many cases, however, an organization's control over technology is limited. There is, for example, little flexibility when it comes to refining oil and generating electricity. Thus, in some situations, the production technology may not be amenable to large reductions in hierarchy.

Two aspects of technology strongly influence an organization's ability to reduce hierarchy: degree of interdependence and degree of complexity. Degree of interdependence is determined by how much workers need to coordinate, cooperate, and relate to others in order to produce the products or services the organization offers. Organizations vary on this dimension from very high interdependence to low interdependence. For example, university professors, check encoders, and insurance salespersons are typically in a low-interdependence situation, while chemical plant operators, basketball players, and computer-design engineers are in a high-interdependence situation.

With high interdependence, the choice is between work teams and individual approaches to work design with extensive hierarchy. In most cases, work teams are the best alternative because they are more cost-effective. Low interdependence favors maximizing individual performance through job enrichment or well-structured individual tasks with large amounts of incentive pay and an extensive hierarchy. A crucial issue in determining which way to go with low-interdependence jobs is the complexity of the work involved.

Technology, to a substantial degree, tends to influence the complexity of the work. Complexity can vary all the way from the highly repetitive jobs associated with assembly lines to the highly complex knowledge work represented by professional jobs and state-of-the-art manufacturing. If the work is simple and repetitive by necessity, it is hard to put in place an involvement approach unless the technology can be changed. These situations are often best run in a traditional hierarchical manner. With complex knowledge work, the clear choice is involvement and minimal hierarchy because people who do this kind of work have the ability to participate in a wide range of decisions and to coordinate their own work. They also often expect and want to have an approach to management that has a minimal hierarchy.

Values and Beliefs

The values and beliefs of the key participants need to fit the involvement approach for a reduction in hierarchy to be successful. The involvement approach requires that managers believe in the capabilities, sense of responsibility, and commitment of workers throughout the organization. In short, they need to believe not only that people are a key resource of the organization but also that people can and will behave responsibly if given the opportunity. They need to be willing to develop and live by a management philosophy that states their commitment to pushing decision making and information to the lowest levels of the organization. If managers do not have the right values, they are unlikely to make the changes needed; and even if the changes are made, they are likely to be reversed in the face of problems that may be solved by creating more hierarchy.

Employees' values are also important. For any form of self-management to work, most employees have to want to learn, grow, develop, contribute, and take on new responsibilities. Researchers have argued that most American workers want to be involved in their work, but no one argues that this is universally true. Particularly in situations in which autocratic management has a long history, workers may not want to operate without an extensive hierarchy. They may have become conditioned to the control-oriented approach that comes with a hierarchy and appreciate the fact that they can just put in their eight hours and not have to take the job home with them. In addition, self-selection may have taken place so that those who most valued involvement quit long ago, leaving behind those who prefer to be told what to do and when and how to do it.

Societal values also can influence an organization's approach to involvement. Democratic societies provide much more supportive environments for reducing hierarchy than do traditional, autocratic societies. The United States, with its long democratic tradition and commitment to individual rights, appears to provide the ideal setting for involvement-oriented management. Historically, however, U.S. society has exempted the workplace from the societal commitment to democracy and individual rights. Yet there are many signs that this is changing, particularly in the area of individual rights. Thus it seems inevitable that Americans will increasingly demand greater participation and involvement in the workplace.

A Manufactured Need

Organizations can operate with much less hierarchy if a number of important features of the organization are changed. The changes are not minor; they are major and, to an important degree, mutually reinforcing. To reduce hierarchy substantially, most of the changes probably need to be made.

Typically, organizations have reduced layers of management and staff groups in order to reduce costs—only to find that in a few years the level of management and the staff groups have reappeared. The reason for their reappearance is obvious; nothing was done to substitute other organizational features for the functions traditionally performed by the parts of the organization that were eliminated. Many of those functions can be done by other workers and can be made completely unnecessary if changes are made in the way work is organized and designed.

Without a thorough redesign of the organization, however, it is unlikely that a significant part of the hierarchy can be made unnecessary. Hierarchies perform some very important organizational functions that must be done in some way if coordinated, organized behavior is to take place. On the other hand, if an organization design is adopted that includes work teams, new reward systems, extensive training, and the various other practices considered here, organizations can operate effectively with substantially less hierarchy.

In short, hierarchy is not inevitable; it is a manufactured need. As such, the need for it can be substantially reduced.

Selected Bibliography

For a discussion of what is being done in the area of participative management, see my book *High Involvement Management* (Jossey-Bass, 1986), *Working Smarter* edited by *Fortune* (Viking, 1982), *Thriving on Chaos* by Thomas Peters (Knopf, 1987), "From Control to Commitment in the Workplace" by Richard E. Walton (*Harvard Business Review,* April 1985), and *Corporate Transformation* by Ralph H. Kilman, Teresa J. Coven, and Associates (Jossey-Bass, 1987).

For a range of views on work design, see *Work Redesign* by J. Richard Hackman and Greg R. Oldham (Addison-Wesley, 1980), *Organizations in Action* by James Thompson (McGraw-Hill, 1967), *Organization and Environment: Managing Differentiation and Integration* by Paul R. Lawrence and Jay W. Lorsch (Division of Research, Harvard Business School, 1967), *The Human Side of Factory Automation* by Ann Majcharzak (Jossey-Bass, 1988), and *Designing Effective Organizations* by William Pasmore (Jossey-Bass, 1988).

Some helpful references on pay systems include my book *Pay and Organization Development* (Addison-Wesley, 1981) and my article with Gerald E. Ledford, Jr., "Skill-Based Pay: A Concept That's Catching On" (*Personnel,* September 1985).

The role of leadership is considered in *Leaders* by Warren Bennis and Bert Nanus (Harper and Row, 1985), "Substitutes for Leadership: Their Meaning and Measurement" by Steven Kerr and John Jermier (*Organizational Behavior and Human Performance,* December 1978), and "Self-Management as a Substitute for Leadership: A Social Learning Theory Perspective" by Charles C. Manz and Henry P. Sims (*Academy of Management Review,* July 1980).

Marshall Sashkin's article "Participative Management Is an Ethical Imperative" (*Organizational Dynamics,* Spring 1984) presents an interesting discussion of the ethical issues involved in participation.

Reading 4–4

The Coming of the New Organization

Peter F. Drucker

The typical large business 20 years hence will have fewer than half the levels of management of its counterpart today, and no more than a third the managers. In its structure, and in its management problems and concerns, it will bear little resemblance to the typical manufacturing company, circa 1950, which our textbooks still consider the norm. Instead it is far more likely to resemble organizations that neither the practicing manager or the management scholar pays much attention to today: the hospital, the university, the symphony orchestra. For like them, the typical business will be knowledge-based, an organization composed largely of specialists who direct and discipline their own performance through organized feedback from colleagues, customers, and headquarters. For this reason, it will be what I call an information-based organization.

Businesses, especially large ones, have little choice but to become information-based. Demographics, for one, demands the shift. The center of gravity in employment is moving fast from manual and clerical workers to knowledge workers who resist the command-and-control model that business took from the military 100 years ago. Economics also dictates change, especially the need for large businesses to innovate and to be entrepreneurs. But above all, information technology demands the shift.

Advanced data-processing technology isn't necessary to create an information-

Peter F. Drucker is Marie Rankin Clarke Professor of Social Sciences and Management at Claremont Graduate School, which recently named its management center after him. Widely known for his work on management practice and thought, he is the author of numerous articles and books, the most recent of which is *The Frontiers of Management* (F.P. Dutton/Truman Talley Books, 1986). This is Mr. Drucker's twenty-fourth contribution to *Harvard Business Review*.

based organization, of course. As we shall see, the British built just such an organization in India when "information technology" meant the quill pen, and barefoot runners were the "telecommunications" systems. But as advanced technology becomes more and more prevalent, we have to engage in analysis and diagnosis   that is, in "information"—even more intensively or risk being swamped by the data we generate.

So far most computer users still use the new technology only to do faster what they have always done before, crunch conventional numbers. But as soon as a company takes the first tentative steps from data to information, its decision processes, management structure, and even the way its work gets done begin to be transformed. In fact, this is already happening, quite fast, in a number of companies throughout the world.

We can readily see the first step in this transformation process when we consider the impact of computer technology on capital-investment decisions. We have known for a long time that there is no one right way to analyze a proposed capital investment. To understand it we need at least six analyses: the expected rate of return; the payout period and the investment's expected productive life; the discounted present value of all returns through the productive lifetime of the investment; the risk in not making the investment or deferring it; the cost and risk in case of failure; and finally, the opportunity cost. Every accounting student is taught these concepts. But before the advent of data-processing capacity, the actual analyses would have taken years of clerical toil to complete. Now anyone with a spreadsheet should be able to do them in a few hours.

The availability of this information transforms the capital-investment analysis from opinion into diagnosis, that is, into the rational weighing of alternative assumptions. Then the information transforms the capital-investment decision from an opportunistic, financial decision governed by the numbers into a business decision based on the probability of alternative strategic assumptions. So the decision both presupposes a business strategy and challenges that strategy and its assumptions. What was once a budget exercise becomes an analysis of policy.

The second area that is affected when a company focuses its data-processing capacity on producing information is its organization structure. Almost immediately, it becomes clear that both the number of management levels and the number of managers can be sharply cut. The reason is straightforward: it turns out that whole layers of management neither make decisions nor lead. Instead, their main, if not their only, function is to serve as "relays"—human boosters for the faint, unfocused signals that pass for communication in the traditional pre-information organization.

One of America's largest defense contractors made this discovery when it asked what information its top corporate and operating managers needed to do their jobs. Where did it come from? What form was it in? How did it flow? The search for answers soon revealed that whole layers of management—perhaps as many as 6 out of a total of 14—existed only because these questions had not been asked before. The company had had data galore. But it had always used its copious data for control rather than for information.

Information is data endowed with relevance and purpose. Converting data into information thus requires knowledge. And knowledge, by definition, is specialized. (In fact, truly knowledgeable people tend toward overspecialization, whatever their field, precisely because there is always so much more to know.)

The information-based organization requires far more specialists overall than the command-and-control companies we are accustomed to. Moreover, the specialists are found in operations, not at corporate headquarters. Indeed, the operating organization tends to become an organization of specialists of all kinds.

Information-based organizations need central operating work such as legal counsel, public relations, and labor relations as much as ever. But the need for service staffs—that is, for people without operating responsibilities who only advise, counsel, or coordinate—shrinks drastically. In its *central* management, the information-based organization needs few, if any, specialists.

Because of its flatter structure, the large, information-based organization will more closely resemble the businesses of a century ago than today's big companies. Back then, however, all the knowledge, such as it was, lay with the very top people. The rest were helpers or hands, who mostly did the same work and did as they were told. In the information-based organization, the knowledge will be primarily at the bottom, in the minds of the specialists who do different work and direct themselves. So today's typical organization in which knowledge tends to be concentrated in service staffs, perched rather insecurely between top management and the operating people, will likely be labeled a phase, an attempt to infuse knowledge from the top rather than obtain information from below.

Finally, a good deal of work will be done differently in the information-based organization. Traditional departments will serve as guardians of standards, as centers for training and the assessment of specialists; they won't be where the work gets done. That will happen largely in task-focused teams.

This change is already under way in what used to be the most clearly defined of all departments—research. In pharmaceuticals, in telecommunications, in paper-making, the traditional *sequence* of research, development, manufacturing, and marketing is being replaced by *synchrony:* specialists from all these functions work together as a team, from the inception of research to a product's establishment in the market.

How task forces will develop to tackle other business opportunities and problems remains to be seen. I suspect, however, that the need for a task force, its assignment, its composition, and its leadership will have to be decided on case by case. So the organization that will be developed will go beyond the matrix and may indeed be quite different from it. One thing is clear, though: it will require greater self-discipline and even greater emphasis on individual responsibility for relationships and for communications.

To say that information technology is transforming business enterprises is simple. What this transformation will require of companies and top managements is much harder to decipher. That is why I find it helpful to look for clues in other kinds of information-based organizations, such as the hospital, the symphony orchestra, and the British administration in India.

A fair-sized hospital of about 400 beds will have a staff of several hundred physicians and 1,200 to 1,500 paramedics divided among some 60 medical and paramedical specialties. Each specialty has its own knowledge, its own training, its own language. In each specialty, especially the paramedical ones like the clinical lab and physical therapy, there is a head person who is a working specialist rather than a full-time manager. The head of each specialty reports directly to the top, and there is little middle management. A good deal of the work is done in ad hoc teams as required by an individual patient's diagnosis and condition.

A large symphony orchestra is even more instructive, since for some works there may be a few hundred musicians on stage playing together. According to organization theory then, there should be several group vice president conductors and perhaps a half-dozen division VP conductors. But that's not how it works. There is only the conductor-CEO—and every one of the musicians plays directly to that person without an intermediary. And each is a high-grade specialist, indeed an artist.

But the best example of a large and successful information-based organization, and one without any middle management at all, is the British civil administration in India.[1]

The British ran the Indian subcontinent for 200 years, from the middle of the eighteenth century through World War II, without making any fundamental changes in the organization structure or administrative policy. The Indian civil service never had more than 1,000 members to administer the vast and densely populated sub-continent—a tiny fraction (at most 1%) of the legions of Confucian Mandarins and palace eunuchs employed next door to administer a not-much-more populous China. Most of the Britishers were quite young; a 30-year-old was a survivor, especially in the early years. Most lived alone in isolated outposts with the nearest countryman a day or two of travel away. And for the first hundred years there was no telegraph or railroad.

The organization structure was totally flat. Each district officer reported directly to the "Coo," the provincial political secretary. And since there were nine provinces, each political secretary had at least 100 people reporting directly to him, many times what the doctrine of the span of control would allow. Nevertheless, the system worked remarkably well, in large part because it was designed to ensure that each of its members had the information he needed to do his job.

Each month the district officer spent a whole day writing a full report to the political secretary in the provincial capital. He discussed each of his principal tasks—there were only four, each clearly delineated. He put down in detail what he had expected would happen with respect to each of them, what actually did happen, and why, if there was a discrepancy, the two differed. Then he wrote down what he expected would happen in the ensuing month with respect to each key task and what he was going to do about it, asked questions about policy, and commented

---

[1]The standard account is Philip Woodruff, *The Men Who Ruled India,* especially the first volume, *The Founders of Modern India* (New York: St. Martin's, 1954). How the system worked day by day is charmingly told in *Sowing* (New York: Harcourt Brace Jovanovich, 1962), volume one of the autobiography of Leonard Woolf (Virginia Woolf's husband).

on long-term opportunities, threats, and needs. In turn, the political secretary "min-uted" every one of those reports—that is, he wrote back a full comment.

On the basis of these examples, what can we say about the requirements of the information-based organization? And what are its management problems likely to be? Let's look first at the requirements. Several hundred musicians and their CEO, the conductor, can play together because they all have the same score. It tells both flutist and timpanist what to play and when. And it tells the conductor what to expect from each and when. Similarly, all the specialists in the hospital share a common mission: the care and cure of the sick. The diagnosis is their "score"; it dictates specific action for the X-ray lab, the dietician, the physical therapist, and the rest of the medical team.

Information-based organizations, in other words, require clear, simple, common objectives that translate into particular actions. At the same time, however, as these examples indicate, information-based organizations also need concentration on one objective or, at most, on a few.

Because the "players" in an information-based organization are specialists, they cannot be told how to do their work. There are probably few orchestra conductors who could coax even one note out of a French horn, let alone show the horn player how to do it. But the conductor can focus the horn player's skill and knowledge on the musicians' joint performance. And this focus is what the leaders of an information-based business must be able to achieve.

Yet a business has no "score" to play by except the score it writes as it plays. And whereas neither a first-rate performance of a symphony nor a miserable one will change what the composer wrote, the performance of a business continually creates new and different scores against which its performance is assessed. So an information-based business must be structured around goals that clearly state man-agement's performance expectations for the enterprise and for each part and spe-cialist and around organized feedback that compares results with these performance expectations so that every member can exercise self-control.

The other requirement of an information-based organization is that everyone take information responsibility. The bassoonist in the orchestra does so every time she plays a note. Doctors and paramedics work with an elaborate system of reports and an information center, the nurse's station on the patient's floor. The district officer in India acted on this responsibility every time he filed a report.

The key to such a system is that everyone asks: Who in this organization depends on me for what information? And on whom, in turn, do I depend? Each person's list will always include superiors and subordinates. But the most important names on it will be those of colleagues, people with whom one's primary relationship is coordination. The relationship of the internist, the surgeon, and the anesthesiologist is one example. But the relationship of a biochemist, a pharmacologist, the medical director in charge of clinical testing, and a marketing specialist in a pharmaceutical company is no different. It, too, requires each party to take the fullest information responsibility.

Information responsibility to others is increasingly understood, especially in middle-sized companies. But information responsibility to oneself is still largely neglected. That is, everyone in an organization should constantly be thinking through what information he or she needs to do the job and to make a contribution.

This may well be the most radical break with the way even the most highly computerized businesses are still being run today. There, people either assume the more data, the more information—which was a perfectly valid assumption yesterday when data were scarce, but leads to data overload and information blackout now that they are plentiful. Or they believe that information specialists know what data executives and professionals need in order to have information. But information specialists are tool makers. They can tell us what tool to use to hammer upholstery nails into a chair. We need to decide whether we should be upholstering a chair at all.

Executives and professional specialists need to think through what information is for them, what data they need: first, to know what they are doing, then, to be able to decide what they should be doing; and finally, to appraise how well they are doing. Until this happens MIS departments are likely to remain cost centers rather than become the result centers they could be.

Most large businesses have little in common with the examples we have been looking at. Yet to remain competitive—maybe even to survive—they will have to convert themselves into information-based organizations, and fairly quickly. They will have to change old habits and acquire new ones. And the more successful a company has been, the more difficult and painful this process is apt to be. It will threaten the jobs, status, and opportunities of a good many people in the organization, especially the long-serving, middle-aged people in middle management who tend to be the least mobile and to feel most secure in their work, their positions, their relationships, and their behavior.

The information-based organization will also pose its own special management problems. I see as particularly critical:

1. Developing rewards, recognition, and career opportunities for specialists.

2. Creating unified vision in an organization of specialists.

3. Devising the management structure for an organization of task forces.

4. Ensuring the supply, preparation, and testing of top management people.

Bassoonists presumably neither want nor expect to be anything but bassoonists. Their career opportunities of moving from second bassoon to first bassoon and perhaps of moving from a second-rank orchestra to a better, more prestigious one. Similarly, many medical technologists neither expect nor want to be anything but medical technologists. Their career opportunities consist of a fairly good chance of moving up to senior technician, and a very slim chance of becoming lab director. For those who make it to lab director, about 1 out of every 25 or 30 technicians, there is also the opportunity to move to a bigger, richer hospital. The district officer in India had practically no chance for professional growth except possibly to be relocated, after a three-year stint, to a bigger district.

Opportunities for specialists in an information-based business organization should be more plentiful than they are in an orchestra or hospital, let alone in the Indian civil service. But as in these organizations, they will primarily be opportunities for advancement within the specialty, and for limited advancement at that. Advancement into "management" will be the exception, for the simple reason that there will be far fewer middle-management positions to move into. This contrasts sharply with the traditional organization where, except in the research lab, the main line of advancement in rank is out of the specialty and into general management.

More than 30 years ago General Electric tackled this problem by creating "parallel opportunities" for "individual professional contributors." Many companies have followed this example. But professional specialists themselves have largely rejected it as a solution. To them—and to their management colleagues—the only meaningful opportunities are promotions into management. And the prevailing compensation structure in practically all businesses reinforces this attitude because it is heavily biased towards managerial positions and titles.

There are no easy answers to this problem. Some help may come from looking at large law and consulting firms, where even the most senior partners tend to be specialists, and associates who will not make partner are outplaced fairly early on. But whatever scheme is eventually developed will work only if the values and compensation structure of business are drastically changed.

The second challenge that management faces is giving its organization of specialists a common vision, a view of the whole.

In the Indian civil service, the district officer was expected to see the "whole" of his district. But to enable him to concentrate on it, the government services that arose one after the other in the nineteenth century (forestry, irrigation, the archaeological survey, public health and sanitation, roads) were organized outside the administrative structure, and had virtually no contact with the district officer. This meant that the district officer became increasingly isolated from the activities that often had the greatest impact on—and the greatest importance for—his district. In the end, only the provincial government or the central government in Delhi had a view of the "whole," and it was an increasingly abstract one at that.

A business simply cannot function this way. It needs a view of the whole and a focus on the whole to be shared among a great many of its professional specialists, certainly among the senior ones. And yet it will have to accept, indeed will have to foster, the pride and professionalism of its specialists—if only because, in the absence and opportunities to move into middle management, their motivation must come from that pride and professionalism.

One way to foster professionalism, of course, is through assignments to task forces. And the information-based business will use more and more smaller self-governing units, assigning them tasks tidy enough for "a good man to get his arms around," as the old phrase has it. But to what extent should information-based businesses rotate performing specialists out of their specialties and into new ones? And to what extent will top management have to accept as its top priority making and maintaining a common vision across professional specialties?

Heavy reliance on task-force teams assuages one problem. But it aggravates another: the management structure of the information-based organization. Who will the business's managers be? Will they be task-force leaders? Or will there be a two-headed monster—a specialist structure, comparable, perhaps, to the way attending physicians function in a hospital, and an administrative structure of task-force leaders?

The decisions we face on the role and function of the task-force leaders are risky and controversial. Is theirs a permanent assignment, analogous to the job of the supervisory nurse in the hospital? Or is it a function of the task that changes as the task does? Is it an assignment or a position? Does it carry any rank at all? And if it does, will the task-force leaders become in time what the product managers have been at Procter & Gamble: the basic units of management and the company's field officers? Might the task-force leaders eventually replace department heads and vice presidents?

Signs of every one of these developments exist, but there is neither a clear trend nor much understanding as to what each entails. Yet each would give rise to a different organizational structure from any we are familiar with.

Finally, the toughest problem will probably be to ensure the supply, preparation, and testing of top management people. This is, of course, an old and central dilemma as well as a major reason for the general acceptance of decentralization in large businesses in the last 40 years. But the existing business organization has a great many middle-management positions that are supposed to prepare and test a person. As a result, there are usually a good many people to choose from when filling a senior management slot. With the number of middle-management positions sharply cut, where will the information based organization's top executives come from? What will be their preparation? How will they have been tested?

Decentralization into autonomous units will surely be even more critical than it is now. Perhaps we will even copy the German *Gruppe* in which the decentralized units are set up as separate companies with their own top managements. The Germans use this model precisely because of their tradition of promoting people in their specialties, especially in research and engineering; if they did not have available commands in near-independent subsidiaries to put people in, they would have little opportunity to train and test their most promising professionals. These subsidiaries are thus somewhat like the farm teams of a major-league baseball club.

We may also find that more and more top management jobs in big companies are filled by hiring people away from smaller companies. This is the way that major orchestras get their conductors—a young conductor earns his or her spurs in a small orchestra or opera house, only to be hired away by a larger one. And the heads of a good many large hospitals have had similar careers.

Can business follow the example of the orchestra and hospital where top management has become a separate career? Conductors and hospital administrators come out of courses in conducting or schools of hospital administration respectively. We see something of this sort in France, where large companies are often run by men who have spent their entire previous careers in government service. But in most countries this would be unacceptable to the organization (only France has the *mystique* of the *grandes écoles*). And even in France, businesses, especially larger ones, are becoming too demanding to be run by people without firsthand experience and a proven success record.

Thus the entire top management process—preparation, testing, succession—will become even more problematic than it already is. There will be a growing need for experienced businesspeople to go back to school. And business schools will surely need to work out what successful professional specialists must know to prepare themselves for high-level positions as *business* executives and *business* leaders.

Since modern business enterprise first arose, after the Civil War in the United States and the Franco-Prussian War in Europe, there have been two major evolutions in the concept and structure of organizations. The first took place in the ten years between 1895 and 1905. It distinguished management from ownership and established management as work and task in its own right. This happened first in Germany, when Georg Siemens, the founder and head of Germany's premier bank, *Deutsche Bank,* saved the electrical apparatus company his cousin Werner had founded after Werner's sons and heirs had mismanaged it into near collapse. By threatening to cut off the bank's loans, he forced his cousins to turn the company's management over to professionals. A little later, J.P. Morgan, Andrew Carnegie, and John D. Rockefeller, Sr. followed suit in their massive restructurings of U.S. railroads and industries.

The second evolutionary change took place 20 years later. The development of what we still see as the modern corporation began with Pierre S. du Pont's restructuring of his family company in the early twenties and continued with Alfred P. Sloan's redesign of General Motors a few years later. This introduced the command-and-control organization of today, with its emphasis on decentralization, central service staffs, personnel management, the whole apparatus of budgets and controls, and the important distinction between policy and operations. This stage culminated in the massive reorganization of General Electric in the early 1950s, an action that perfected the model most big businesses around the world (including Japanese organizations) still follow.[2]

Now we are entering a third period of change: the shift from the command-and-control organization, the organization of departments and divisions, to the information-based organization, the organization of knowledge specialists. We can perceive, though perhaps only dimly, what this organization will look like. We can identify some of its main characteristics and requirements. We can point to central problems of values, structure, and behavior. But the job of actually building the information-based organization is still ahead of us—it is the managerial challenge of the future.

---

[2]Alfred D. Chandler, Jr. has masterfully chronicled the process in his two books *Strategy and Structure* (Cambridge: MIT Press, 1962) and *The Visible Hand* (Cambridge: Harvard University Press, 1977)— surely the best studies of the administrative history of any major institution. The process itself and its results were presented and analyzed in two of my books: *The Concept of the Corporation* (New York: John Day, 1946) and *The Practice of Management* (New York: Harper Brothers, 1954).

PART THREE

In Part Three, our scope of attention expands to multibusiness and multinational corporations.

As the cases illustrate, the size, product/market diversity, and geographical dispersion of multibusiness and multinational companies all contribute to presenting managers with organizational issues that can differ from, and often be more complex than concerns addressed in earlier parts. However, as the text demonstrates, the basic conceptual framework introduced in Parts One and Two also applies to multibusiness and multinational companies.

Chapter 5

Organizing Human Resources for Multibusiness and Multinational Companies

Because of their greater size, greater diversity of products and markets, and greater geographical dispersion, multibusiness and multinational companies face organizational problems that are different and often more complex than issues facing single businesses. For example, many companies included in the Fortune 500 list of largest industrial corporations operate in dozens of different countries, making and selling hundreds of different products through an organization staffed by thousands of people. In doing so, these companies must deal with questions such as:

- How can we coordinate and control our divisions and subsidiaries when no one has the necessary breadth of experience and knowledge to fully understand our diverse businesses?

- How can we simultaneously cope with the need to adapt our major product lines to the unique cultural and marketing characteristics of each country that we operate in, and the need to achieve economies of scale worldwide and to coordinate all of our new-product development efforts?

- How can we ensure that our dispersed employees do not misuse our significant economic power?

This chapter discusses these questions and others related to organizational issues in multibusiness and multinational companies. Initially, however, we show that despite differences in size, product/market diversity, and geographical spread, the basic approach of organization design in single businesses also apply for multibusiness and multinational companies.[1]

---

[1]We talk about three types of companies in this chapter: domestic multibusiness, single-product multinational, and multiproduct multinational. Although one could devote a chapter to each company, as with domestic single-product companies, that is beyond the scope of this book.

The Three Design Questions

Question 1: Drawing Subunit Boundaries

Just as in single businesses, in drawing subunit boundaries for multibusiness and multinational firms, one must consider the diversity and interdependence of activities engaged in by the corporation; the tradeoff between the gains of specialization and economies of scale that can occur within subunit boundaries; and the costs of establishing subunits and integrating across their boundaries.

For example, in one large multinational company, the president's staff reviewed its organization in 1985 in response to numerous complaints and problems within its European operations. Specifically, after an initial period of success in Europe, the company was having difficulty penetrating new and larger markets. The staff report concluded that its functional organization in Europe should be changed to a national organization—that is, its major subunit boundaries should include all activities within a country and not all European activities associated with particular functions such as manufacturing marketing. Their rationale, in summary, was the following:

> When we originally established the European organization, our sales were $10 million. Today they are $300 million. Back then we had to organize Europe by functions because we couldn't afford any other option—our sales just would not support separate manufacturing facilities and sales forces in each country. But today we can afford a country-by-country organization, and we desperately need one. The cultural, economic, and legal conditions in each European country are different. Our current organization serves none of these differences very well. We need an organization that can sell a French variation of our product with a French sales force, for example. If we organize our European operation by countries, we can achieve this.

In another moderate-sized ($700 million in sales) American multibusiness company, a second type of boundary choice problem arose in 1980 regarding long-range planning activities. The chairman of the board believed that the company had grown to the point where it managed a large amount of assets for its stockholders and that it had a duty to do some long-range thinking (10–20 years) to protect those assets. This raised the question of where long-range planning activity should occur. While one executive suggested that long-range planning should be included in all management jobs—that is, that a special function or set of functions should not be created—the suggestion was disregarded quickly. Almost everyone agreed that because the long-range planning task was sufficiently different from most tasks that managers did that it would not be carried out well, if at all, by line managers. Two options emerged. In the first one, a special long-range planning function would reside at the divisional level. Operationally, that meant a staff person would report to each of the company's six division managers. Their efforts would be coordinated by a planner who reported to the president. In the second option, a corporate long-range planning subunit would be created and staffed with seven planners reporting to the president. This latter arrangement was chosen because "the advantages to be

Figure 5–1

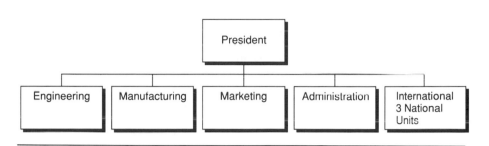

gained by having long-range planning better integrated into operating divisions were more than offset, we felt, by the need for a group of a certain minimum size—that is, a group that could include a Ph.D. economist, a political scientist, a professional planner, and so on."

Because the situations are sometimes more complex than in single-business contexts, judgments about where to draw subunit boundaries can be more difficult in multibusiness and multinational firms. Nevertheless, the process is the same.

Question 2: Organizing within Subunits

The major subunits of multibusiness organizations are usually single-product companies or groups of such companies. (Recall that a number of the cases in Part Two concerned divisions of multibusiness companies.) The major subunits of multinational companies are sometimes single-business companies and sometimes functional units or geographical organizations. We have already dealt with the question of internally organizing these units in Part One (subunits specialized by function, area, or product) and Part Two (single-business companies).

An example will help demonstrate the applicability of these approaches to an international setting. Consider a company that makes and sells about $20 million a year in specialized electrical equipment. In 1975, it was organized functionally. See Figure 5–1.

When establishing a fourth geographical subunit in the international department, the sales manager had to deal with the following types of decisions:

■ *Should I have local nationals as salespeople and train them as best I can? Or, should I introduce some of our experienced salespeople from other countries?* (The manager decided the sales task required salespeople to be from the same culture as the buyer, so the manager hired local nationals and trained them.)

■ *Should I compensate the sales force at the local wage rate and risk upsetting them when they learn how much more their colleagues in other areas receive? Or, should I hire them at a higher rate and accept the direct economic consequences?*

(The manager decided to set the base salaries above local wages but below salaries for salespeople in other areas.)

■ *How can I best deal with the culturally based reluctance of most nationals to be away from their homes on sales trips?* (The manager decided to draw small sales territories for six salespersons in the six most densely populated areas, which contained about 85 percent of all potential buyers. Then, the manager hired six people, each of whom lived within one of the six territories. Thus, overnight travel was unnecessary.)

Regardless of the setting, the key to organizing effectively within subunits is a thorough knowledge of the tasks (or the business), the employees (or the organization) involved, and the organizational design tools that can be used. In multibusiness settings, this means understanding a diverse set of businesses. And, in multinational settings, this usually means understanding a diverse group of people and cultures.[2]

Question 3: Integrating the Subunits

Essentially the same integrating devices used by single-business companies are also used by multibusiness and multinational companies. For example, to integrate its 12 product/market divisions, one multibusiness company relies on:

1. Three key positions in the management hierarchy called group vice presidents. These managers, who are stationed at corporate headquarters, each have four divisions reporting to them.
2. Goals and plans jointly agreed on each year by corporate headquarters and each of the divisions.
3. A corporate staff that helps the company's president and group vice presidents examine division plans and establish reasonable goals.
4. A monthly meeting of division managers, group vice presidents, the president, and some corporate staff to review results to date.
5. A financial measurement system that focuses on each division separately and the company as a whole.
6. A compensation system that rewards division managers for both corporate and divisional results.

Just as in the case of a single-business company, the problem of integration is probably the organizational issue that most plagues multibusiness and multinational

---

[2]For a discussion of the importance of understanding multicultural work forces and some common problems that managers face in doing so, see "The Symposium on Human Resource Management in the Multinational Corporation," *Human Resource Management* 27, no. 1 (Spring 1988); and Susan Schneider, "National vs. Corporate Culture: Implications for Human Resource Management," *Human Resource Management* 27, no. 1 (Summer 1988).

managers, despite the fact that subunits in multiproduct and multinational firms are often less interdependent than subunits in a typical domestic single-product company. The large volumes of complex information that must move among subunits can sometimes make the nature of interdependencies complex. But more important, the high degree of subunit differentiation caused by the diverse products, markets, and cultures that these organizations deal with, in addition to the large number of employees involved and their geographical dispersion, all make achieving effective integration difficult.

Organizational Problems Caused by High Diversity, Large Size, and Geographical Dispersion

In a typical multibusiness organization, the problem of achieving effective integration among the subparts operationally means motivating thousands of people—most of whom are thousands of miles apart, have never met each other, and none of whom really understand all of the businesses that the others are involved in—to behave in ways that facilitate achievement of corporate goals.[3]

This becomes particularly complicated in situations where mergers and acquisitions of companies occur; organizations must be reconstructed. At its best, this occurs with minimal pain and maximum effectiveness; at its worst, two organizations struggle hopelessly with the new, often other-imposed diversity.

Consider, for example, the case of a diversified American corporation that acquired its first consumer-goods manufacturing business. The acquisition came into the company as a division reporting to a group vice president, but since no one at corporate headquarters knew much about the new business, it operated with a high degree of autonomy (a fact that some other division managers quickly spotted and resented). The new division was required to report financial results monthly, and for the first 12 months, it met sales and profit objectives each month. In the 13th month, however, sales fell 20 percent, and profits declined 35 percent.

The group vice president in charge of the new division requested an immediate report from the division manager outlining reasons for the declining sales and profits as well as corrective actions being taken. The report arrived three weeks later and satisfied neither the group vice president nor persons on the corporate staff. The group vice president asked for a more detailed report. Before this report arrived, the next month's financial figures reported that sales were off 25 percent and profits were wiped out completely. The corporation's president became very concerned because he felt the division's performance could cause the company to miss its overall profit goals for the year. He urged the group vice president to take more aggressive action, so the group vice president and five other corporate staff people immediately visited the division. The division manager and his staff resented the "interference" and indicated that they were doing the best they could to deal with

---

[3]See R. N. Anthony and J. Dearden, *Management Control Systems*, 3rd ed. (Homewood, Ill.: Richard D. Irwin, 1976), chap. 8.

an unusual situation; they were reluctant to talk with the corporate staff. Division and corporate staff negotiated a new budget and a set of specific actions for the division manager to take. The next financial report showed that the division almost broke even; yet, the following month it again lost a large amount of money. The corporate president thereupon fired the division manager.

The new division manager encountered a variety of unexpected problems. He quickly discovered that his background with the company's other manufacturing divisions had not adequately prepared him to understand this division's business; he had to go through a learning period. Also, he found a company culture that differed from his experience. Meanwhile, the division continued to lose money. The losses increased when another company division pulled out of a joint venture, which left the troubled division with excess capacity in a partially built facility. Despite pressure from the corporation's president, the other division refused to have anything to do with what they referred to as a "snake pit."

After 16 months, the corporation controlled the situation. But, the cost was high—even in corporate terms. Although this example illustrates problems resulting from an acquisition, they typify the type of control and collaboration issues that business diversity can cause in multibusiness organizations.

Multinational organizations can sometimes operate in even more diverse environments than the one just illustrated. They often have considerable product diversity and must cope with cultural and legal diversity.[4] The economic changes occurring across Europe with the emergence of the European Economic Community present a major challenge to multinational corporations. Successful integration with and among products and cultures can, as the following example illustrates, be difficult.[5]

> To hear officials of some multinational companies talk, there is a surefire success formula for any large corporation with global facilities. First of all, they say the multinational should unify its product lines around the world to obtain mass-production efficiency. Second, it should make its parts wherever such manufacturing is most economical. Third, it should focus its sales efforts on countries where markets are growing fastest. The result, say the formula's proponents, is a maximization of profits.
>
> If all this sounds reasonable, not to say obvious, one might consider the fact that Ford Motor Co. has been following just that formula in recent years and is finding that the scheme isn't as surefire as it seems. This by no means implies that the giant automaker is thinking of abandoning its integrated approach; however, it does mean that Ford is finding some major flaws in the approach—a finding that is emphasized by talking to Gerd Maletz, an owner of one of the biggest Ford dealerships in Germany.

---

[4]For example, many European countries have laws regarding worker participation on management boards (so-called codetermination), while most other countries do not. But even in Europe, each country has slightly different laws regarding worker participation. See, for example, Robert Kuhne, "Co-Determination: A Strategy Restructuring of the Organization," *Columbia Journal of World Business,* Summer 1976, pp. 17–25.

[5]From William Carley, "A Giant Multinational Finds Unified Activities Aren't Easy to Set Up." Reprinted with permission of *The Wall Street Journal,* © Dow Jones & Company, Inc. 1974. All rights reserved.

"Take spare parts," Mr. Maletz says. "An engine for one Ford model now must come from Britain, and we may wait months for it. And if the British workers are on strike—and they're always on strike—we wait and wait and wait. We could get a German engine in a couple days."

Ford decided on integration in 1967. At the time, the company's rationale for so doing seemed sound indeed: integration would avoid unnecessarily duplicating the amount—some $100 million—that it costs to engineer and produce a new auto model.

So Ford decided to produce just one European line in place of the completely different cars that used to be turned out by its British and German plants. And the single line began to reduce costs in another way, since the company began to buy parts in bigger volumes—meaning lower prices—from its suppliers.

To achieve integration, Ford began to weave a complex manufacturing web that stretched from its big plants in Britain and Germany to its smaller units in Belgium, France, Ireland, the Netherlands, and Portugal. It was planned that some units would make parts, some would assemble finished autos, and some would do both, with the entire operation being directed from Ford of Europe's headquarters in Warley, outside of London.

But even in the very early stages, there were problems. One Ford executive, an American who moved from Detroit to Britain to help set up Ford of Europe, says he quickly ran into nationality differences. "It was easy to get our British people to agree (to a plan), but five minutes later they were always back questioning it," the American recalls. "It seemed almost impossible to get the German Ford people to agree to anything; but once they did, they just kept marching even if they were marching right off the end of the earth."

The first all-new auto launched by Ford of Europe was a medium-sized Caucasian American that was called the Cortina Mark III in Britain and the Taurus in Germany. The launch, which began in 1970, was a disaster, and the aftereffects are still plaguing Ford. "There's no question we screwed that one up," one official concedes.

The fiasco stemmed partly from British inexperience with the metric system. Ford's British workers had just converted to that system, long used by Germany and other Continental countries; but, says one of the British workers, "we were still thinking in inches." As a result, the British and German parts often didn't mesh. "The doors didn't fit, the bonnet (hood) didn't fit, nothing fit," says Arthur Naylor, a metal finisher in Ford's Dagenham, England, body plant.

It has also been argued by British workers that some of the German-designed parts were too precise. "Our men often work with a one-16th inch tolerance, but on the German engine suspension system, we had to work down to two or three 1000ths of a bloody inch," contends Jock Macraw, a union shop steward at Dagenham. "The Germans wanted an engineering job done on the production line, and that's impossible."

Because of all the snafus, the Cortina-Taurus assembly line in Dagenham barely moved along. By January 1971, when some kinks had been ironed out, the line was speeded up—much to the displeasure of some workers, Mr. Macraw says. Coincidentally, Ford's wage contract was expiring at the time; and on January 20, 1971, unions struck Ford in Britain, halting production for nine weeks. It wasn't until September, nearly a year after initial production of the new car had begun, that Degenham hit peak production. Ford says the peak should have been reached in two months.

Significant geographic dispersion, beyond that found in this example from Ford in Europe, can intensify organizational problems faced by multinational and multibusiness companies. An important message in such companies may pass through dozens of people before reaching its appropriate destination. Because the potential for distortion and miscommunication increases with each person involved, it is easy for information to be lost or distorted.

A more troubling consequence of large size and geographical dispersion relates to the potential for power misuse. The substantial resources of large companies can lead to an inherently dangerous situation. Because a great deal is at stake, because managers have considerable power to protect those stakes, and because there are many geographically separated managers who can be difficult to control, some managers have involved corporations in unethical and illegal activities.[6] The result for large corporations in general, and large multinational enterprises in particular, has been the development of a cadre of vocal critics.[7]

Finally, a problem common to all organizations is that what is best for the whole is not necessarily best for each of its parts. The inevitable conflict, and the problems it can cause, is exacerbated in multibusiness and multinational organizations for two reasons. First, the conflict is often more visible because the performance measures for the whole and the parts are clearer. For example, one parts plant, instead of separate ones in each European country, might increase a corporation's net income through economies of scale, but it might reduce the net income of a subsidiary that lost sales while waiting for spare parts. Second, getting the subparts to do what is in the best interest of the corporation is often more difficult for the reasons previously mentioned (e.g., a corporate president might desperately want to enforce a rule that no bribes be paid by her company's employees but not be able to do it).

Coping with Extreme Diversity, Size, and Geographical Dispersion

Multibusiness and multinational organizational companies rely on a variety of mechanisms to help them cope with difficult integration problems, the most common being modern communication and transportation facilities. The airplane, telephone, telex, or Fax machine that we take for granted today play an important role in tying together distant parts of large enterprises. Likewise, future technological advances in transportation and communication could significantly help multinational enterprises.

Other integrating mechanisms used more selectively include group structures, corporate staffs, elaborate measurement and reward systems, selective transfers, area structures, and presidential "offices."

---

[6]"The Pressures to Compromise Personal Ethics," *Business Week*, January 31, 1977, p. 107. See also Steven N. Bresner and Earl A. Molander, "Is the Ethics of Business Changing?" *Harvard Business Review*, January–February 1977, pp. 57–71.

[7]See Richard Barnet and Ronald E. Muller, *Global Reach: The Power of The Multinational Corporation* (New York: Simon & Schuster, 1974).

Group Structures with Corporate Staff

Multibusiness firms often rely heavily on group structures as integrating devices. In a typical case, product divisions that are related because of technology or markets are grouped together under a group vice president. The group vice president becomes a specialist in that product/market group and attempts to identify and manage any interdependence among divisions in the group. He also helps the president, with the aid of corporate staff, to make decisions regarding funding requests, financial objectives, and business plans from his divisions. And, he works with the president and the staff to monitor division performance on the measurement systems they have developed (which often involve a monthly or quarterly reporting requirement). When designed to fit the business situation, these arrangements can significantly increase a corporation's ability to process relevant information and make effective integrating decisions, as well as to take speedy action when problems develop.

The size of a corporate staff group, the complexity of the reporting systems, and the number of decisions made or reviewed at corporate headquarters can vary among companies that use this set of integrating devices. Companies that have little diversity among their businesses and high interdependence among them tend to rely on a large corporate staff and a centralized decision-making system; with more business diversity and less interdependence, corporations often use a smaller corporate staff and decentralized management. At the extreme, some multibusiness companies with diverse and independent businesses do not use this device but instead rely on other mechanisms such as the careful selection and transfer of division managers.[8] In such cases, the diversity among businesses makes it impractical to actively manage them from corporate headquarters.

Companies that have varying degrees of diversity and interdependence among their divisions often treat different divisions in different ways. As a rule, the lower a division's interdependence with other parts of the company, the higher the chances that it will be allowed to operate autonomously, that it will be treated as a profit center, and that the division manager will be offered the opportunity for significant bonuses based on divisional profits.[9]

Selection and Transfer of Managers

Careful selection and transfer of people into subunit manager slots can be a key integrating device. To facilitate the integration of a subunit into the corporation, for example, the president might select someone with whom he or she has a good relationship, who can be trusted to pass on accurate and timely information, and someone who has a background in a business area that is the subunit's focus. Similarly, to facilitate integration of two divisions that are highly interdependent,

[8]Harold Stieglitz, "On Concepts of Corporate Structure," *The Conference Board Record,* February 1974, pp. 7–13; see also Jay Lorsch and Stephen Allen, *Managing Diversity and Interdependence* (Boston: Harvard Business School, 1973).

[9]Richard F. Vancil, *Decentralization* (New York: Financial Executive Research Foundation, 1978).

a company might rotate division managers.[10] The major reason that this solution is not used frequently is that companies often do not have the type of people needed to make it work. They do not always have someone the president knows and trusts who has a background in a certain product or area and who is available to be moved. Some companies systematically try to develop a pool of people who might be used to support such a selection, promotion, and transfer policy.[11] They might, for example, hire some Europeans graduating from a U.S. business school, initially give them assignments at corporate headquarters, and then give them a series of assignments in different European subsidiaries, all to prepare them for positions as European division managers. Even then, career and skill issues should be assessed and managed before the assignment, during the assignment, and after repatriation.[12] Time frames for length of service should be set, support systems should be established, and training needs should be tracked. Toward the end of a manager's stint overseas, they should be counseled on their repatriation. This approach can be quite expensive.

Product/Area Structure

Multinational organizations also rely heavily on a variety of product/area structures to help with integration problems. In cases where they feel an area focus is more important than a product focus, companies depend on a geographic structure combined with some type of product management; companies with a product focus rely on a product division structure aided by some type of area coordination.[13] Companies that feel they need to focus equally on products and markets (and sometimes on functions, too) may rely on a product/area matrix. All except the smallest multinational organizations use one of these three structures or move toward using one of them.[14]

The trend toward global product/area structures is new; yet, because of its advantages, that structure will become more important in the future.[15] The slowness

---

[10] For an interesting discussion of how corporations use management transfer to aid coordination and control, see Jay Galbraith and Anders Edstrom, "International Transfer of Managers: Some Important Policy Considerations," *Columbia Journal of World Business,* Summer 1976, pp. 100–112.

[11] Robert A. Pitts, "Unshackle Your 'Comers'," *Harvard Business Review,* May–June 1977, pp. 127–36.

[12] Mark Mendenhall, Edward Dunbar, and Gary Oddou, "Expatriate Selection, Training, and Career-Pathing," *Human Resource Management* 26, no. 3 (Fall 1987).

[13] Stanley Davis, "Trends in the Organization of Multinational Corporations," *Columbia Journal of World Business,* Summer 1976, p. 70.

[14] A typical multinational company evolves in the following way. When it starts selling internationally, it sets up foreign subsidiaries. When sales from these subsidiaries become significant or after its investment abroad becomes significant, the company establishes an "international division." Later, it shifts to either a global product division or a global area division. Finally, it reorganizes using some form of product/area matrix.

[15] For a good discussion of a complex matrix's advantages for a multibusiness and multinational company, see William Goggin, "How the Multidimensional Structure Works at Dow Corning," *Harvard Business Review,* January–February 1974, pp. 54–65.

with which companies have adopted this structure is a function of the problems it can cause, which are similar to matrix structures in single businesses. As a result, one writer has warned that multinational/multibusiness companies should not implement a matrix unless:

1. There is diversification of both products and markets requiring balanced and simultaneous attention.

2. The opportunities lost and difficulties experienced by favoring either a product or geographic unity of command cannot be ignored.

3. Environmental pressure to secure international economies of scale require the shared use of scarce human resources.

4. There is a need for enriched information-processing capacity because of uncertain, complex, and interdependent tasks.

5. Information, planning, and control systems operate along the different dimensions of the structure simultaneously.

6. As much attention is paid to managerial behavior as to the structure. The corporate culture and ethos must actively support and believe in negotiated management.[16]

Office of the President

Some multibusiness and multinational organizations have recently developed another mechanism to promote integration. Usually called "the office," this device is commonly used at the presidential level. Instead of having one person act as president, under an "office" arrangement, three or four people work together in that role. When it is successful, this device fosters faster and more competent information processing.[17] One significant requirement for this arrangement's success is that excellent relationships exist among people in the office.

Corporate Culture

Another integrative device used by multibusiness and multinational organizations is a corporate "culture" developed and maintained by top management. Through their words and deeds, top managers attempt to clearly set norms and values.[18] For example, if a corporate president can establish the norm that "we do not engage in illegal activities even if the countries we operate in expect it," that norm can have an effect more powerful than the most expensive control systems or the most elaborate hierarchies.

---

[16]Stanley Davis, "Trends in the Organization of Multinational Corporations," *Columbia Journal of World Business,* Summer 1976, p. 70.

[17]For an example of how an "office" was developed and how it works, see Gilbert Burck, "Union Carbide's Patient Schemers," *Fortune,* December 1965.

[18]Roger Harrison, "Understanding Your Organization's Character," *Harvard Business Review,* May–June 1972.

Figure 5–2
Multinational Business Integrating Devices: Pros and Cons

Integrating Device	Advantages	Drawbacks
Modern communication and transportation facilities	To some degree available to everyone.	Cost—especially in time and energy for traveling managers.
Group structures with corporate staff and elaborate measurement/ reward systems	Can significantly increase a corporation's ability to make optimizing decisions and spot problems quickly.	Absorbs subunit manager's time. If businesses are extremely diverse, this option may not work.
Selection and transfer of subunit managers	Can be less expensive and cumbersome than structural solutions.	It is sometimes impossible to find the types of individuals needed. Extensive transfers are expensive.
Product/area structure: Area subunits with product managers	Best when area focus is most important.	Does not provide best product focus.
Product subunits with area coordination	Best when product focus is most important.	Does not provide best area focus.
Matrix	Can achieve integration within and across products, areas, and other dimensions (e.g., functions).	Can be difficult to maintain the balance in the system and to manage the tensions and conflicts.
Office of the president	Allows a key "office" to process information faster and more competently than if it were staffed with a single individual.	Requires the development and maintenance of excellent working relationships among the people involved.
Corporate culture	Once established, can be more powerful and less expensive than other solutions.	Difficult and slow to develop.

The more companies that do not try to create and maintain an integrating culture attests to its difficulty. Establishing certain norms and values in a global organization is a slow and time-consuming process that may not be practical in many circumstances.

Summary

The approach outlined for dealing with organizational questions in single-business companies is equally applicable to multibusiness and multinational companies. Nevertheless, because of their greater product/market diversity, their greater size, and their geographical dispersion, the latter type of company often faces more difficult integration problems. To cope with these problems, they tend to use the integration devices used by single-business companies plus additional ones that are appropriate for their specific problems. See Figure 5–2.

In designing a solution to an organizational problem in a multibusiness or multinational corporation, one must consider, as in single-business contexts, the diversity and interdependence of activities that the corporation engages in and the current organization (formal, informal, and people). One must make judgments about what fits and what does not. Also, one must avoid the temptation to solve troublesome integration problems by ignoring important aspects of the corporation's product/market diversity and by reducing needed differentiation in the organization.

A common mistake that managers in multinational and multibusiness organizations make is to ignore important aspects of their product/market diversity—often because they are unhappy with the implications of organizationally accounting for diversity. Corporate staff managers, for example, often try to implement uniform compensation and performance-appraisal systems throughout a worldwide corporation, regardless of important differences among divisions and countries.[19] After acquiring a new division in a different business or in a different country, corporate managers often try to treat it like the rest of the corporation, regardless of important differences. This behavior eventually leads to serious organizational problems.

---

[19]See, for example, Howard Perlmutter and David Heenan, "How Multinational Should Your Managers Be?" *Harvard Business Review,* November–December 1974, p. 129.

Texana Petroleum Corporation

Jay W. Lorsch, Paul R. Lawrence,
and James A. Garrison

During the summer of 1966, George Prentice, the newly designated executive vice president for domestic operations of the Texana Petroleum Corporation, was devoting much of his time to thinking about improving the combined performance of the five product divisions reporting to him (see Exhibit 1). His main concern was that corporate profits were not reflecting the full, potential contribution that could result from the close technological interdependence of the raw materials utilized and produced by these divisions. As Prentice saw it, the principal difficulty was that the division general managers reporting to him were not working well together:

> As far as I see it, the issue is where do we make the money for the corporation? Not how do we beat the other person. Nobody is communicating with anybody else at the general manager level. In fact they are telling a bunch of secrets around here.

Recent Corporate History

The Texana Petroleum Corporation was one of the early major producers and marketers of petroleum products in the southwest United States. Up until the early 1950s, Texana had been almost exclusively in the business of processing and refining crude oil; it was also involved in selling petroleum products through a chain of company-operated service stations in the southwestern states and in Central and South America. By 1950 company sales had risen to approximately $500 million, with accompanying growth in profits. About 1950, however, Texana faced increas-

This case was prepared by Jay W. Lorsch, Paul R. Lawrence, and James A. Garrison, and made possible by the cooperation of a firm which remains anonymous.

Exhibit 1
Partial Organization Chart, 1966

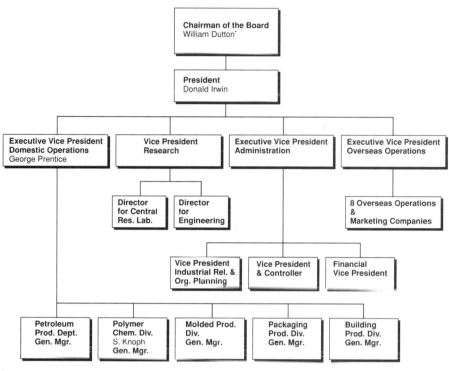

* Names are included for those mentioned in the case.

ingly stiff competition at the retail service station level from several larger, national petroleum companies. As a result sales volume declined sharply during the early 1950s. By 1955 sales had fallen to only $300 million, and the company was operating at just above the break-even point.

At that time, Roger Holmes, who had been a dominant force in the company since its founding, retired as president and chief executive officer because of his age. He was replaced by Donald Irwin, 49, who had been a senior executive with a major chemical company. William Dutton, 55, who had spent his entire career with Texana, was appointed chairman of the board to replace the retiring board chairman. Prior to his appointment as chairman, he had been senior vice president for petroleum products, reporting to Holmes.

Irwin and Dutton, along with other senior executives, moved quickly to solve the problems facing Texana. They gradually divested the company of its retail outlets and abandoned the domestic consumer petroleum markets. Through both internal development and acquisition they expanded rapidly, increasing the company's involvement in the business of processing petroleum for chemical and plastics products. By moving in this direction, they were further expanding on initial moves made by Texana in 1949, when the company built its first chemical processing plant and began marketing these products. To speed the company's growth in these areas, Irwin and Dutton selected aggressive general managers for each division and gave them a wide degree of freedom in decision making. Top management's major requirement was that each division general manager create a growing division with a satisfactory return on investment capital. By 1966 top management had reshaped the company so that it was an integrated producer of chemicals and plastic materials in both domestic and foreign markets. In foreign operations the company continued to operate service stations in Latin America and in Europe. This change in direction was successful; by 1966 company sales had risen to $750 million, along with a healthy rise in profits.

In spite of this success, management believed that there was a need for an increase in return on invested capital. The financial and trade press, which had been generous in its praise of the company's recovery, was still critical of the present return on investment, and top management shared this concern. Dutton, Irwin, and Prentice were in agreement that one important method of increasing profits was to take further advantage of the potential cost savings that could come from increased coordination among the domestic operating divisions as they developed new products, processes, and markets.

Domestic Organization 1966

The product divisions reporting to Prentice represented a continuum of producing and marketing activities, from the production and refining of crude oil to the marketing of several types of plastics products to industrial consumers. Each division was headed by a general manager. While there was some variation in the internal organizational structure of the several divisions, they were generally set up along functional lines (manufacturing, sales, research, and development). Each division also had its own controller and engineering activities, although these were supported and augmented by the corporate staff. While divisions had their own research efforts, there was also a central research laboratory at the corporate level that carried out longer range research of a more fundamental nature, thus outside the scope of any of the product divisions's activities.

The Petroleum Products Division was the remaining nucleus of the company's original producing and refining activities. It supplied raw materials to the Polymer and Chemicals Division and also sold refining products under long-term contracts to other petroleum companies. In the early and mid-1950s this division's management had generated much of the company's revenue and profits through its skill in negotiating these agreements. In 1966 top corporate management felt that this division's management had accepted its role as a supplier to the rest of the corporation, and they also felt that there were harmonious relations between it and its sister divisions.

The Polymer and Chemicals Division was developed internally during the late 1940s and early 1950s as management saw its share of the consumer petroleum market declining. Under the leadership of Seymour Knoph (who had been general manager for several years) and his predecessor (who was executive vice president—administration in 1966), the division had rapidly developed a line of chemical and polymer compounds derived from petroleum raw materials. Most of the products of this division were manufactured under licensing agreements, or they were materials with well understood formulations. Nevertheless, technical personnel in the division had developed an industrywide reputation for their ability to develop new and improved processes. Top management of the division took particular pride in this ability. From the beginning the decisions of what products to manufacture were based, to a large extent, upon the requirements of the Molded and Packaging Products Divisions. Moreover, Polymer and Chemicals Division executives had always attempted to market these same products to external customers, and at this they had been highly successful. These external sales were extremely important to Texana, for they assured the company a large enough volume of operation to process a broad product line of polymer chemicals profitably. As the other divisions had grown, however, they required a larger proportion of the division's capacity, which meant that Polymer and Chemical Division managers had to reduce their commitment to external customers.

The Molded Products Division was also an internally developed division, which had been formed in 1951. It produced a variety of molded plastic products, ranging from toys and household items to automotive and electronic parts. This division's major strengths were its knowledge of molding technology and in particular, its marketing ability. While it depended on the Polymer and Chemicals Division for its raw materials, its operations were largely independent of those of the Packaging Products and Building Products Divisions.

The Packaging Products Division was acquired in 1952. Its products were plastic packaging materials, including films, cartons, bottles, and so forth. All of these products were marketed to industrial customers. Like the products division, the packaging division depended on the Polymer and Chemical Division as a source of raw materials, but it was largely independent of other end-product divisions.

The Building Product Division was acquired in 1963 to give Texana a position in the construction materials market. The division produced and marketed a variety of insulation roofing materials and similar products to the building trade. It was a particularly attractive acquisition for Texana, since it had achieved some success with plastic products for insulation and roofing materials prior to the acquisition. Although the plastic products accounted for less than 20% of total division sales in 1965, plans called for these products to account for over 50% of division sales in the next five years. Its affiliation with Texana gave this division a stronger position in plastic raw materials through the Polymer and Chemicals Division.

Selection and Recruitment of Management Personnel

The rapid expansion of the corporation into these new areas had created the need for much additional management talent, and top management had not hesitated in bringing new people in from outside the corporation, as well as advancing promising younger people inside Texana. In both the internally developed and acquired divisions, most managers had spent their careers inside the division, although some top division managers were moved between divisions or into corporate positions.

In speaking about the type of people he had sought for management positions, Donald Irwin described his criterion in a financial publication: "We don't want people around who are afraid to move. The attraction of Texana is that it gives the individual responsibilities which aren't diluted. It attracts the person who wants a challenge."

Another corporate executive described Texana managers: "It's a group of very tough-minded, but considerate individuals with an enormous drive to get things done."

Another manager, who had been with Texana for his entire career and considered himself to be different from most Texana managers, described the typical Texana manager as follows:

> Texana attracts a particular type of person. Most of these characteristics are personal characteristics rather than professional ones. I would use terms such as cold, unfeeling, aggressive, and extremely competitive, but not particularly loyal to the organization. He is loyal to dollars, his own personal dollars. I think this is part of the communication problem. I think this is done on purpose. The selection procedures lead in this direction. I think this is so because of contrast with the way the company operated ten years ago. Of course I was at the plant level at that time. But today the attitude I have described is also in the plants. Ten years ago the organization was composed of people who worked together for the good of the organization, because they wanted to. I don't think this is so today.

Location of Division Facilities

The Petroleum Products, Chemical and Polymer, and Packaging Products Divisions had their executive offices on separate floors of the Texana headquarters building in downtown Chicago. The plants and research and development facilities of these divisions were spread out across Oklahoma, Texas, and Louisiana. The Molded Products Division had its headquarters, R&D facilities, and a major plant in an industrial suburb of Chicago. This division's other plants were at several locations in the Middle West and East Coast. The Building Product Division's headquarters and major production and technical facilities were located in Fort Worth, Texas. All five divisions shared sales offices in major cities from coast to coast.

Evaluation and Control of Division Performance

The principal methods of controlling and evaluating the operations of these divisions were the semiannual review of division plans and the approval of major capital expenditures by the executive committee.[1] In reviewing performance against plans, members of the executive committee placed almost sole emphasis on the division's

---

[1]The executive committee consisted of Messrs. Dutton, Irwin, and Prentice, as well as the vice president of research, executive vice president—administration, and the executive vice president of foreign operations.

actual return on investment against budget. Corporate executives felt that this practice, together with the technological interdependence of the divisions, created many disputes about transfer pricing.

In addition to these regular reviews, corporate executives had frequent discussions with division executives about their strategies, plans, and operations. It had been difficult for corporate management to strike the proper balance in guiding the operations for the divisions. This problem was particularly acute with regard to the Polymer and Chemicals Division, because of its central place in the corporation's product line. One corporate staff member explained his view of the problem:

> This whole matter of communications between the corporate staff and the Polymer and Chemical Division has been a fairly difficult problem. Corporate management used to contribute immensely to this by trying to get into the nuts and bolts area within the Chemical and Polymer organization, and this created serious criticisms; however, I think they have backed off in this manner.

A second corporate executive in discussing the matter for a trade publication report put the problem this way: "We're trying to find the middle ground. We don't want to be a holding company, and with our diversity we can't be a highly centralized corporation."

Executive Vice President—Domestic Operations

In an effort to find this middle ground, the position of executive vice president— domestic operations, was created in early 1966 and George Prentice was its first occupant. Prior to this change, there had been two senior domestic vice presidents— one in charge of the Petroleum and Polymer and Chemicals Divisions and the other in charge of the end-use divisions. Prentice had been senior vice president in charge of the end-use divisions before the new position was created. He had held that position for only two years, having come to it from a highly successful marketing career with a competitor.

At the time of his appointment one press account described Prentice as "hard-driving, aggressive, and ambitious—an archetype of the self-actuated dynamo Irwin has sought out."

Shortly after taking his new position, Prentice described the task before him:

> I think the corporation wants to integrate its parts better and I am here because I reflect this feeling. We can't be a bunch of entrepreneurs around here. We have got to balance discipline with entrepreneurial motivation. This is what we were in the past, just a bunch of entrepreneurs, and if they came in with ideas we would get the money. But now our dollars are limited, and especially the Polymer and Chemical people haven't been able to discipline themselves to select from within ten good projects. They just don't seem to be able to do this, and so they come running in here with all ten good projects which they say we have to buy, and they get upset when we can't buy them all.
>
> This was the tone of my predecessors [senior vice presidents]. All of them were very strong on being entrepreneurs. I am going to run it different. I am going to take a marketing and capital orientation. As far as I can see, there is a time to

compete and a time to collaborate, and I think right now there has been a lack of recognition in the Polymer and Chemicals executive suite that this thing has changed.

Other Views of Domestic Interdivisional Relations

Executives within the Polymer and Chemicals Divisions, the end-use divisions, and at the corporate level shared Prentice's view that the major breakdown in interdivisional relations was between the Polymer and Chemicals Division and the end-use divisions. Executives in the end-use divisions made these typical comments about the problem:

> I think the thing we have got to realize is that we are wedded to the Polymer and Chemicals Division whether we like it or not. We are really tied up with them. And just as we would with any outside supplier or with any of our customers, we will do things to maintain their business. But because they feel they have our business wrapped up, they do not reciprocate in turn. Now let me emphasize that they have not arbitrarily refused to do the things that we are requiring, but there is a pressure on them for investment projects and we are low man on the pole. And I think this could heavily jeopardize our chances for growth. . . .
>
> I would say our relationships are sticky, and I think this is primarily because we think our reason for being is to make money, so we try to keep Polymer and Chemicals as an arm's length supplier. For example, I cannot see, just because it is a Polymer and Chemicals' product, accepting millions of pounds of very questionable material. It takes dollars out of our pocket, and we are very profit centered. . . .
>
> The big frustration, I guess, and one of our major problems, is that you can't get help from them [Polymer and Chemicals]. You feel they are not interested in what you are doing, particularly if it doesn't have a large return for them. But as far as I am concerned this has to become a joint venture relationship, and this is getting to be real sweat with us. We are the guys down below yelling for help. And they have got to give us some relief. . . .
>
> My experience with the Polymer and Chemicals Division is that you cannot trust what they say at all, and even when they put it in writing you can't be absolutely sure that they are going to live up to it.

Managers within the Polymer and Chemicals Division expressed similar sentiments:

> Personally, right now I have the feeling that the divisions' interests are growing further apart. It seems that the divisions are going their own way. For example, we are a polymer producer but the molding division wants to be in a special area, so that means they are going to be less of a customer to us, and there is a whole family of plastics being left out that nobody's touching, and this is bearing on our program. . . . We don't mess with the Building Products Division at all, either. They deal in small volumes. Those that we are already making we sell to them, those that we don't make we can't justify making because of the kinds of things we are working with. What I am saying is that I don't think the corporation is integrating, but I think we ought to be, and this is one of the problems of delegated divisions. What happens is that an executive heads this up and goes for the place that makes the most money for the division, *but* this is not necessarily the best place from a corporate standpoint. . . .

We don't have as much contact with sister divisions as I think we should. I have been trying to get a liaison with people in my function but it has been a complete flop. One of the problems is that I don't know who to call on in these other divisions. There is no table of organization, nor is there any encouragement to try and get anything going. My experience has been that all of these operating divisions are very closed organizations. I know people up the line will say that I am nuts about this. They say to just call over and I will get an answer. But this always has to be a big deal, and it doesn't happen automatically, and it hurts us.

The comments of corporate staff members describe these relationships and the factors they saw as contributing to the problem:

Right now I would say there is an iron curtain between the Polymer and Chemicals Division and the rest of the corporation. You know, we tell our divisions they are responsible, autonomous groups, and the Polymer and Chemicals Division took it very seriously. However, when you are a three-quarter billion dollar company, you've got to be coordinated, or the whole thing is going to fall apart—it can be no other way. The domestic executive vice president thing has been a big step forward to improve this, but I would say it hasn't worked out yet. . . .

The big thing that is really bothering [the Polymer and Chemicals Division] is that they think they have to go develop all new markets on their own. They are going to do it alone independently, and this is the problem they are faced with. They have got this big thing, that they want to prove that they are a company all by themselves and not rely upon packaging or anybody else.

Polymer and Chemicals Division executives talked about the effect of this drive for independence of the divisional operating heads on their own planning efforts:

The Polymer and Chemical Division doesn't like to communicate with the corporate staff. This seems hard for us, and I think the [a recent major proposal] was a classic example of this. That plan, as it was whipped up by the Polymer and Chemicals Division, had massive implications for the corporation both in expertise and in capital. In fact, I think we did this to be competitive and one-up on the rest of our sister divisions. We wanted to be the best-looking division in the system, but we carried it to an extreme. In this effort, we wanted to show that we had developed this concept completely on our own. . . . Now I think a lot of our problems with it stemmed from this intense desire we have to be the best in this organization. . . .

Boy, a big doldrum around here was shortly after Christmas [1965] when they dropped out a new plant, right out of our central plan, without any appreciation of the importance of this plant to the whole Polymer and Chemicals Division's growth. . . . Now we have a windfall and we are back in business on this new plant. But for a while things were very black and everything we had planned and everything we had built our patterns on were out. In fact, when we put this plan together, it never really occurred to us that we were going to get it turned down, and I'll bet we didn't even put the plans together in such a way as to really reflect the importance of this plant to the rest of the corporation.

A number of executives in the end-use divisions attributed the interdivisional problems to different management practices and assumptions within the Polymer and Chemicals Division. An executive in the packaging division made this point:

We make decisions quickly and at the lowest possible level, and this is tremendously different from the rest of Texana. I don't know another division like this in the rest of the corporation. . . .

Look at what Sy Knoph has superfluous to his operation compared to ours. These are the reasons for our success. You've got to turn your people loose and not breathe down their necks all the time. We don't slow our people down with staff. Sure, you may work with a staff, the wheels may grind, but they sure grind slow. . . .

Also, we don't work on detail like the other divisions do. Our management doesn't feel they need the detail stuff. Therefore, they're [Polymer and Chemicals] always asking us for detail which we can't supply; our process doesn't generate it and their process requires it, and this always creates problems with the Polymer and Chemicals Division. But I'll be damned if I am going to have a group of people running between me and the plant, and I'll be goddamned if I am going to clutter up my organization with all the people that Knoph has got working for him. I don't want this staff, but they are sure pushing it on me.

This comment from a molding division manager is typical of many made about the technical concerns of the Polymer and Chemicals Division management:

Historically, even up to the not too distant past, the Polymer and Chemicals Division was considered a snake pit as far as the corporate people were concerned. This was because the corporate people were market-oriented and Polymer and Chemicals Division was technically run and very much a manufacturing effort. These two factors created a communication barrier and to really understand the Polymer and Chemicals Division problems, they felt that you have to have a basic appreciation of the technology and all the interrelationships. . . .

Building on this strong belief, the Polymer and Chemicals Division executives in the past have tried to communicate in technical terms, and this just further hurt the relationship, and it just did not work. Now they are coming up with a little bit more business or commercial orientation, and they are beginning to appreciate that they have got to justify the things they want to do in a business or commercial orientation rather than just a technical sense. This also helps the problem of maintaining their relationships with the corporation as most of the staff is nontechnical; however, this has changed a little bit in that more and more technical people have been coming on and this has helped from the other side. . . .

They work on the assumption in the Polymer and Chemicals Division that you have to know the territory before you can be an effective manager. You have got to be an operating person to contribute meaningfully to their problems. However, their biggest problem is this concentration on technical solutions to their problems. This is a thing that has boxed them in the most trouble with corporate and the other sister divisions.

These and other executives also pointed to another source of conflict between the Polymer and Chemicals Division and other divisions. This was the question of whether the Polymer and Chemicals Division should develop into a more independent marketer, or whether it should rely more heavily on the end-use divisions to "push" its products to the market.

The following comments by end-use division executives are typical views of this conflict:

The big question I have about Polymer and Chemicals is what is their strategy going to be? I can understand them completely from a technical standpoint, this is no problem. I wonder what is the role of this company? How is it going to fit into what we and others are doing? Right now, judging from the behavior I've seen, Polymer and Chemicals could care less about what we are doing in terms of integration of our markets or a joint approach to them. . . .

I think it is debatable whether the Polymer and Chemicals Division should be a new product company or not. Right now we have an almost inexhaustible appetite for what they do and do well. As I see it, the present charter is fine. However, that group is very impatient, aggressive, and they want to grow, but you have got to grow within guidelines. Possibly the Polymer and Chemicals Division is just going to have to learn to hang on the coattails of the other divisions, and do just what they are doing now, only better. . . .

I think the future role of the Polymer and Chemicals Division is going to be, at any one point in time for the corporation, that if it looks like a product is needed, they will make it. . . . They are going to be suppliers because I will guarantee you that if the moment comes and we can't buy it elsewhere, for example, then I darn well know they are going to make it for us regardless of what their other commitments are. They are just going to have to supply us. If you were to put the Polymer and Chemicals Division off from the corporation, I don't think they would last a year. Without their huge captive requirements, they would not be able to compete economically in the commercial areas they are in.

A number of other executives indicated that the primary emphasis within the corporation on return on investment by divisions tended to induce, among other things, a narrow, competitive concern on the part of the various divisional managements. The comment of this division executive was typical:

As far as I can see it, we [his division and Polymer and Chemicals] are 180 degrees off on our respective charters. Therefore, when Sy Knoph talks about this big project we listen nicely and then we say, "God bless you, lots of luck," but I am sure we are not going to get involved in it. I don't see any money in it for us. It may be a gold mine for Sy but it is not for our company; and as long as we are held to the high profit standards we are, we just cannot afford to get involved. I can certainly see it might make good corporate sense for us to get it, but it doesn't make any sense in terms of our particular company. We have got to be able to show the returns in order to get continuing capital and I just can't on that kind of project. I guess what I am saying is that under the right conditions we could certainly go in but not under the present framework; we would just be dead in terms of dealing with the corporate financial structure. We just cannot get the kinds of returns on our capital that the corporation has set to get new capital. In terms of the long run, I'd like very much to see what the corporation has envisioned in terms of a hookup between us, but right now I don't see any sense in going on. You know my career is at stake here, too.

Another divisional executive made this point more succinctly:

Personally, I think that a lot more could be done from a corporate point of view and this is frustrating. Right now all these various divisions seem to be viewed strictly as an investment by the corporate people. They only look at us as a banker might look at us. This hurts us in terms of evolving some of these programs because we have relationships which are beyond financial relationships.

The remarks of a corporate executive seemed to support this concern:

One of the things I worry about is where is the end of the rope on this interdivisional thing. I'm wondering if action really has to come from just the division. You know in this organization when they decide to do something new it always has been a divisional proposal—they were coming to us for review and approval. The executive committee ends up a review board; not us, working downward. With this kind of pattern, the talent of the corporate people is pretty well seduced into asking questions and determining whether a thing needs guidelines. But I think we ought to be the idea people, as well, thinking about where we are gong in the future, and if we think we ought to be getting into some new area, then we tell the divisions to do it. The stream has got to work both ways. Now it is not.

Case 5–2

Jacobs Suchard: Reorganizing for 1992

Philip Holland, Robert G. Eccles

Klaus J. Jacobs, chairman and chief executive officer of Jacobs Suchard, has presided over much change in the past year. Now it was May 1989, and more change was still to come.

The main impetus to change had come from the European Economic Community's (EEC) plan to "bring down the frontiers" by 1992, freeing the flow of goods, people and capital across the borders of the 12-member countries. It meant for Jacob Suchard, the Swiss-based producer of coffee, chocolate and sugar confectionery (or, confectionery, for short), that no longer would it face an EEC of twelve unique and independent markets, each serviced by autonomous business units, producing and selling for their own local markets; now the EEC would be unified, and the company could take advantage of the larger scale, eliminating some factories and marketing its brands more globally.

Since confectionery was already more "global" across Europe in taste than was coffee, Jacobs had been able to move faster in its confectionery operations to change the organization and eliminate factories. People in different countries preferred different coffee blends, so there was less immediate opportunity to produce and sell one brand for all countries. Nevertheless, the coffee business, under Charles Gebhard, was preparing to launch a few global brands, one, for example, called NIGHT & DAY.

This case was prepared by Philip Holland (under the direction of Professor Robert G. Eccles).

Copyright © 1989 by the President and Fellows of Harvard College. Harvard Business School case 489-106.

Gerhard Zinser managed the confectionery business. In preparing for the coming common market, Jacobs and the chief executive office had already appointed "global brand sponsors" within Zinser's organization, to begin struggling with how to market the five basic brands across Europe, rather than independently in each country. Jacobs had also moved the manufacturing functions from Zinser to Hermann Pohl, the new corporate manufacturing and logistics manager, reporting to Jacobs. Thus, much had already been done.

Yet there was still more to do in organizing and setting new measurements and procedures. One proposal, made by a team formed to look again at the organization, called for breaking up the independent business units even further. But the proposal was very controversial and few supported it. So the question remained: What more had to be done?

Jacobs Suchard

Jacobs Suchard was a Swiss-based producer and marketer of coffee and confectionery products. Klaus Jacobs, chairman and CEO, was the majority shareholder. He had joined the company at the age of 18, and in the next 16 years took assignments not only in Switzerland, but also in Austria, Germany and Central America. In 1970, aged 34, he succeeded his uncle and became chairman and CEO.

The company's 1988 revenues of 6.4B SFr were divided between its three businesses: coffee (2.7B SFr), confectionery (2.9B SFr), and trading, industrial and finance (0.8B SFr). (See Exhibit 1 for the company's financial performance.) In 1971, Suchard purchased the chocolate manufacturer Tobler, to form the Interfood company, and in 1982 Jacobs, the coffee manufacturer, purchased Interfood to combine the two popular products. To further expand its markets, the company in 1986 purchased the Van Houten Group, a German-based confectionery manufacturer, and in 1987 E. J. Brach, the confectionery manufacturer based in Chicago, and Cote d'Or, the Belgian chocolate manufacturer. Jacobs Suchard employed roughly 16,800 worldwide, 76% of whom were in the confectionery business.

Its basic confectionery brands featured the famous MILKA line, with the recent additions, LILA PAUSE and NUSSINI (bars), I LOVE MILKA (filled chocolates), MILKA DREAM (sponge cake), LILA STARS (small foods, such as nuts, covered with chocolate) and MILKA DRINK (chocolate powder and liquid). The other main brands were TOBLERONE, popular worldwide, COTE D'OR and the SUCHARD assortments. Jacobs Suchard was first in market share of confectionery products across the EEC, though not in all individual markets, its largest competitors being Nestlé, Mars, and Lindt. The company had offices in Switzerland, Germany, Austria, France, Italy, Denmark, Belgium, the Netherlands, Great Britain, Spain, Greece, North and South America, Japan, and Australia, as well as principal licensees in Portugal, Africa, Asia, and Latin America.

Exhibit 1
Jacobs Suchard: Reorganizing for 1992
Consolidated Financial Statements of the Group
Important corporate data (five-year summary)
(million francs, except per share data)

	1988	1987	1986	1985	1984
Sales	6,382	6,104	5,236	5,382	5,111
Operating profit	476	471	338	265	244
Income on ordinary activities	307[a]	265	191	150	120
Cash flow (net income and depreciation of buildings and plant)	441[a]	394	294	243	205
Income as percentage of average shareholder's equity (%)	19.7[a]	20.5	13.6	14.1	16.6
Income as percentage of sales (%)	4.8[a]	4.3	3.6	2.8	2.4
Current assets	3,556	2,206	2,920	2,008	1,390
Fixed assets	1,024	886	832	674	666
Shareholders' equity	1,980	1,143	1,450	1,352	776
Total assets	4,580	3,092	3,753	2,682	2,056
Capital expenditure	211	158	85	100	153
Employees	16,799	16,053	10,063	9,260	10,632
Income per bearer share[b]	503.-[a]	503.-	414.-	353.-	351.-
Dividend per bearer share	166.-[c]	165.-	160.-	155.-	150.-
Dividend as percentage of net income (%)	33[c]	31	35	39	34

[a]Excluding the extraordinary income of 36.4 million Fr.
[b]Adjusted figures
[c]Board of directors' proposal before considering the extraordinary income of 36.4 million Fr. and the proposed bonus of 50 Fr.

Corporate Principles

In 1982, after acquiring Interfood, the company set down four corporate principles to guide all decisions.

- SWISS: Jacobs Suchard is a Swiss public company. The character of the firm is fostered and practiced by the management through its entrepreneurial orientation, its spirit of personal relationship and its value for historical cultures.

- LEADING: The Jacobs Suchard Group is an international leader in the manufacturing and marketing of confectionery and beverage products. Its leading position is achieved by the high image of the various products as supported by the quality, the low manufacturing cost orientation and company know-how.

- INNOVATIVE: The Jacobs Suchard Group is an innovation-oriented corporation. This is true for the products, the technology applied, the people and the relationships with the client and consumer.
- GROWTH-ORIENTED: The Jacobs Suchard Group is growth-oriented and prefers long-term performance to short-term profit thinking. Growth will be concentrated in markets with products such as confectionery and beverages or in markets where potential business opportunities can be identified.

A Company of Entrepreneurs

"Jacobs Suchard is an enterprise of entrepreneurs." So read the opening statement of the company's 1987 annual report. It had been the company's basic philosophy since its three founders began their respective ventures: Philippe Suchard in 1825, and Johann Jakob Tobler in 1867, with their confectionery shops; and Johann Jacobs, in 1895, with his coffee shop.

Decentralization.   The principle of entrepreneurship meant for the modern Jacobs Suchard corporation a great degree of decentralization, both in decision-making authority and Klaus Jacobs's determination to keep a small corporate staff. Based on this principle, Jacobs in 1986 approved a new organization structure. One person would manage each core business (coffee and confectionery) and would supervise general managers, who each had clear profit responsibility for an independent business unit. For confectionery, the manager was Gerhard Zinser, to whom 13 general managers reported. (See Exhibit 2 for his organization chart). This restructuring cut two levels of management between Jacobs and the general managers. In a letter sent to his top executives, Jacobs said of the new structure:

> We want to have as flat an organization as possible; personal relationships are what make this organization work and not hierarchical reporting relationships.
>
> Our type of business succeeds—or fails—at the front line; our money is made or lost at the business unit level depending on how effectively we run the business and at the very top-management level where we set global strategies, allocate resources and plan and execute strategic alliances.
>
> Any organization layers between these two levels must be justified on the basis of their value to the business units; most of our headquarters units are the servants, not the masters of the business units.
>
> No cost centers, but we should be striving for profit centers in all areas, including administrative activities.

"Entrepreneurial," said Zinser, "means that people make their own decisions. It's a 6 billion SFr company with only 60 people in the corporate office." To Jacobs, it was unfortunate that they even had 60: he wanted less. Said Rudy Fischer, manager of corporate management development, "Here we have fast decision making. Often major decisions are made in 10 minutes! The worst thing in this company is if you

Exhibit 2   Jacobs Suchard: *1988 Organization Chart*

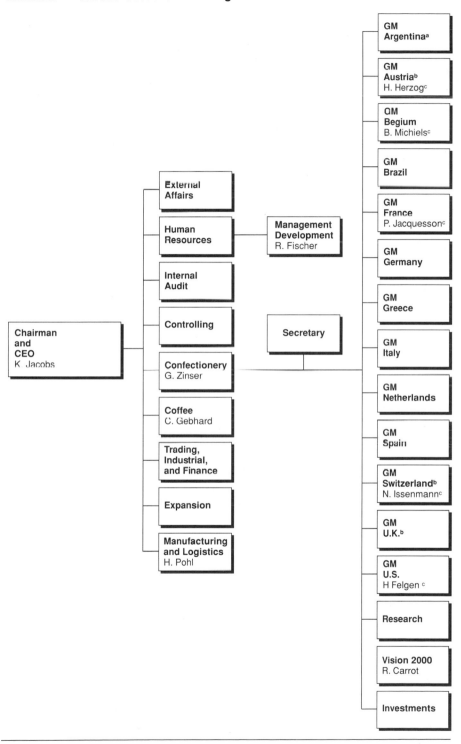

[a]"GM" indicates general manager
[b]Group manager, both Coffee and Confectionery
[c]Also a global brand sponsor

don't do anything." People were expected to learn by doing. They could make mistakes, so long as they didn't try to hide them. Decentralization also meant that management typically used task forces to make the highest level decisions. They appointed managers from across countries and functions to achieve a bottom-up solution to problems.

The Role of the CEO and Chief Executive Office.   Jacobs saw himself not as a traditional CEO but as the "major coach" or "cheerleader" or "friend." In his memos to others in the company he often opened with, "Friends." To make decisions or review policy, he worked with the chief executive office, which he had formed about four years earlier. Making up the chief executive office were Jacobs, Zinser, Gebhard, Pohl, Gunter Bolte (manager of the trading, industrial and financial business), and Robert Jaunich (manager of expansion). Jacobs did not want to be, nor have the others in the office to be, decision makers, "controllers" or "supervisors." Instead, he wanted the general managers to make most of the decisions. He had chosen the name of the chief executive office with this role in mind; he could not, for example, have called it the "executive committee," because that name would have implied that it "executes."

Jacob's own style was informal. Sometimes he would give others complete autonomy; sometimes he would make decisions at the business unit level, particularly around issues of marketing. Other top managers described him as supportive, while still being very much involved with the business. His aggressiveness, many said, his willingness to take risks and commit resources to new opportunities, was uncommon in Europe.

Job Rotation.   Another key practice related to the aggressive committing of resources, was to rotate people frequently—usually within three years—to avoid letting them fall into routines and "sit too long." Jacobs feared that otherwise managers would associate themselves too strongly with one role and would not build the informal links, beyond the formal structure, that he wanted to rely on. As he put it, "Culture equals relationships." The idea was that people who had a wide exposure to different parts of the business and different problems would work together and cooperate more effectively. Jacobs wanted them to be "round"—that is, to have a broad view of the company and its products—and to have a world view. He wanted them, in the spirit of the corporate principle that the company was Swiss, to have, culturally, an open mind.

As a result of this practice, "there was no clear separation of jobs," as one chief executive office member put it. Managers often recommended actions to others. "If you're strong enough," he said, "if others will listen to you, you can get your way."

The practice of job rotation also fit with Jacobs's view of how to organize. "I don't believe in structure," he said. "I believe in people. The people are the structure." Managers typically were assigned additional responsibilities more because they were capable of them or could handle the workload than because the assignments matched their current position in the organization. "All assignments are temporary, anyway," Jacobs would say.

The Ideal Manager

The company thought a great deal about the type of leader it wanted to encourage and develop. At a seminar, five teams of 20 top managers had worked to define the ideal Jacobs Suchard leader. The following is a consolidation of what they listed:

1. Daring entrepreneur
2. Motivating leader
3. Pertinent product know-how
4. Seasoned professional with international experience
5. Able to attract good people

The General Manager

The key position in the decentralized structure of Jacobs Suchard was the general manager of a business unit. Typically, the general manager was responsible for a core business in one country, such as confectionery in France or coffee in Germany. In a few cases, such as with Switzerland, the general manager managed both the coffee and confectionery businesses.

The general managers had total profit responsibility for their businesses. They had Trade Marketing (sales), Consumer Marketing (marketing) and Manufacturing functions reporting directly to them. They sold to their own local markets, and they produced what those markets demanded. (See Exhibit 3 for the organization chart for a typical general manager of a business unit, prior to any changes for the Common Market.) They made almost every decision pertaining to their businesses. Zinser described the position as "a man in his own market acting as an entrepreneur, making share and profit in his own business."

A general manager could receive a bonus of up to 100% of base salary; the average bonus was 50%, and nearly all fell within the range of 20% to 80%. The bonus was calculated by weighing the general manager's performance in three areas: corporate profit after tax (PAT) and return on total assets (ROTA); business unit PAT and ROTA; and personal MBO objectives. The weight given to corporate performance was 20% (10% each for PAT and ROTA), business unit performance, 40% (20% each for PAT and ROTA), and personal objectives (40%). Within each area, the general manager was measured on a nine-point scale versus budget, "1" being the lowest score, "5" being "on target," and "9" being "outstanding." The scale was calibrated as follows:

Score	% of Target	Bonus
1	<90%	0%
3	90–100%	30%
5	100–105%	50%
7	105–120%	70%
9	>120%	100%

Exhibit 3
Jacobs Suchard: Reorganizing for 1992
Typical General Manager
Organization Prior to Changes for Globalization

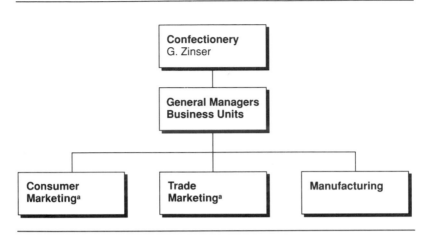

Performance
■ General manager: Profit (profit after tax [PAT], return on total assets [ROTA])
[a]The equivalent of what might normally be referred to as "marketing"
[b]The equivalent of "sales"

For example, a general manager could earn a "5" in corporate PAT (bonus = 50%) and a "7" in corporate ROTA (bonus = 70%), a "1" in business unit PAT (bonus = 0%) and a "5" in business unit ROTA (bonus = 50%), and finally a "5" in personal objectives (bonus = 50%). Thus, the general manager's annual bonus would be:

$$(10\% \text{ WEIGHT})(50\% \text{ BONUS}) + (10\%)(70\%) + (20\%)(0\%)$$
$$+ (20\%)(50\%) + (40\%)(50\%)$$
$$= 42\% \text{ OF SALARY.}$$

Those who reported directly to the general managers and sometimes those one more level down, depending on the size of the business unit, could also receive bonuses, though without the tie to corporate performance. For these managers, half the bonus came from business unit performance (PAT and ROTA) and half from performance against personal objectives.

To be a general manager was the career goal of many within the business units—they would move up the hierarchy of a particular function—and many general managers did not want to move any higher in the organization. To many, it was THE position. One general manager, Pierre Jacquesson (France, confectionery), when asked why he thought general managers stayed in their positions, said: "They are the position. They think, 'It's my results, my people, my company.' They feel they are the owners."

European Economic Community: 1992

On March 25, 1957, representatives of six European countries—Belgium, France, the Federal Republic of Germany, Italy, Luxembourg, and the Netherlands—signed the famous "Treaty of Rome," establishing the European Economic Community. In 1973, three more countries joined: Denmark, Ireland, and the United Kingdom; Greece joined in 1981; and with the addition of Spain and Portugal in 1986, the total in the community became 12.

Then, in February 1986, the 12 governments took their greatest step toward creating a common market: they signed the "Single European Act," which aimed "for the citizens of the European community to wake up on the morning of 1 January 1993 in a frontierless Europe." The commission set out more than 300 measures for removing the border obstacles, about a quarter of which had already been implemented by May 1989. Lord Cockfield, the program's architect, in discussing the EEC's lagging economic performance, commented:

> The fragmentation of the European markets into 12 penny packets is not the only reason for this indifferent performance but it is one of the major reasons. It means that we impose on ourselves quite unnecessary costs in complying with frontiers and frontier controls; we deny ourselves the economies of scale that would flow from being able to manufacture and market on the basis of a market of 320 million consumers.

Three types of barriers existed between borders: physical, technical and fiscal. Physical barriers were the customs, frontier controls, and restrictions on the importation of certain products. Transport vehicles commonly spent days trying to cross certain borders. Technical barriers were the different standards and regulations that producers had to comply with in each country. For example, most countries had differing limits on the amount of vegetable fat permitted in chocolate and ice cream. By 1992, these would all be eliminated. Finally, fiscal barriers were the value-added and excise taxes levied on products crossing borders. In 1989, they varied greatly from country to country. By 1992, though not eliminated, they would be harmonized.

Most likely the slowest to become common would be the differing tastes of each country's consumers. But as people began to travel more freely across Europe and to live and work where they chose, even these were likely to become more uniform.

For countries not in the EEC, such as the EFTA (European Free Trade Association) countries—Switzerland, Sweden, Norway, Iceland, Finland, and Austria—what was happening in the EEC was still a call to action. Some, like Austria, might try to join the EEC; others, like Switzerland, that wished to remain politically independent, might try to negotiate for reduced external barriers to the EEC.

The Globalization of Jacobs Suchard

Because of tariffs, duties and difficulties with transportation between countries, the original Suchard company, rather than expand by exporting, decided to set up independent offices and factories in the countries it entered outside Switzerland. It placed many of its new factories just across the Swiss border. Tobler had pursued a similar strategy, though on a smaller scale. This strategy, along with Suchard's— and later, Jacobs Suchard's—acquisitions strategy, left the company with 19 different confectionery manufacturing plants across Europe, some of which, because of what was happening in the EEC, were redundant.

No longer were 19 small, low-volume factories needed; now Zinser could take advantage of greater economies of scale by producing in fewer, larger factories, and then shipping the products more easily across Europe. And no longer would he have to produce the same brand with different recipes and packaging for each country, but could reduce the variation in the products. Even advertising and pricing could become more global.

Jacobs and his managers began to move on these opportunities. Now there would be "global brands"; and someone would have to coordinate this work. Now, too, instead of having a factory in every country, reporting to a general manager, the company could have fewer factories, servicing many general managers; someone would need to coordinate this work, as well. Globalization became the top issue for the company. It was featured in the 1988 annual report and was the chosen theme for the first year of the Marbach Center of Communication, Jacobs Suchard's brand-new management development center.

The company took a number of steps to make itself more global. The chief executive office had begun a task force, "Vision 2000," that addressed how to reduce the number of factories. It appointed "global brand sponsors." It ran another task force and sent one team to the Harvard Business School to look at how to reorganize for the changing responsibilities. And it appointed a manager of manufacturing and logistics, after eliminating some factories and pulling the responsibility away from the general managers.

Vision 2000: Creating the International Manufacturing Centers

Even before the EEC had voted to create a frontierless Europe, Jacobs had seen the need to eliminate some factories and improve the economies of scale. He hired consultants from McKinsey to study which plants to eliminate. The name of the study became Vision 2000; its goal was to make manufacturing a low-cost producer.

Each factory had become part of an autonomous business unit that reported directly to a general manager and produced everything it needed to serve its local market. Every factory produced all brands and all combinations of forms: fillings (hard, crunchy and layered); baked (wafers, cookies and crusts); molded (chocolate poured into a mold); and enrobed (chocolate dripped over a solid filling). Furthermore, each country produced its own cocoa liquor (from roasting and grinding the cocoa beans) and chocolate mass (from adding cocoa butter and sugar to the liquid), as well as handled all packaging, including flowpacks (vacuum sealed), folded (wrapped flat around a chocolate bar), and twisted (sealed in a wrapper by twisting one or two ends). Thus, the countries handled many products, each of limited volume—a loading that hurt productivity.

Not only were there 19 factories all producing a similar set of products, but each also used different processes to produce the same product, in order to satisfy local laws that required different processing temperatures or durations. For example, one factory might roast the cocoa beans, or "conch" the chocolate (the final mixing), differently from another.

Jacobs reviewed the Vision 2000 recommendations in December 1987, then appointed Robert Carrot, manager of the Strasbourg factory, to coordinate the implementation. The main recommendation was to cut the number of primary factories to six (not including two or four smaller factories and third-party manufacturers which would remain for flexibility and new product start-ups. These factories would then be expanded, retooled for automation and loaded with certain brands or forms to be shipped throughout Europe. Two of the factories would be new. Each would produce from between 80,000 to 100,000 tons of chocolate a year, whereas some of the old plants produced only 5,000 tons a year. The six factories would be:

Berlin, Germany (new)	Countlines and MILKA LILA PAUSE
Bern, Switzerland	TOBLERONE
Halle, Belgium	COTE D'OR
Herentals, Belgium	Wafer products (e.g., NUSSINI)
Lorrach, Germany	MILKA tablets and bars
Strasbourg, France	Pralines (boxed chocolates)

The six factories would be called International Manufacturing Centers (IMCs). Given the company's entrepreneurial philosophy and decentralized decision making, the more centralized IMCs presented a challenge. How would they fit into the organization? And how could they be made acceptable to the general managers, who had been responsible for manufacturing?

Global Brand Sponsors

The next major step in making the confectionery business more global, came in early 1987 when the chief executive office began appointing "global brand sponsors" for the five major confectionery brands. Each sponsor was also a general manager of a business unit, who now would be responsible both for the local business and for coordinating the strategy and implementation of one global brand. The following were the five sponsors in May 1989, the countries of the business units they already managed and the global brands they were assigned.

Hans Herzog (Austria) . . . . SUCHARD
Nico Issenmann (Switzerland) . . . . TOBLERONE
Pierre Jacquesson (France) . . . . MILKA
Baudoin Michiels (Belgium) . . . . COTE D'OR
Frank Schiesser (Hong Kong) . . . . BRACH/SUGUS[1]

Neither the chief executive office nor Zinser specified what the job would involve. Essentially, the managers were told that they were responsible for the global brand. Each manager got a separate budget to cover this new activity, but no additional people.

The Issenmann Task Force

The plant closings begun after Vision 2000 had raised questions about pricing and delivery procedures, so Jacobs kicked off a task force in March 1988, chaired by Nico Issenmann, the business unit manager, responsible for both the confectionery and coffee businesses in Switzerland. The goal of the task force was to define the roles of the international manufacturing centers, the general managers, and the global brand sponsors, and the rules by which the three should interact. Six other managers joined Issenmann on the task force: one came from headquarters in Zurich, the others were general managers, factory managers and finance managers from Switzerland, Germany, and France. The task force focused on the confectionery business, but suggested that its recommendations could apply to the coffee business, as well. The team published its recommendations in August 1988.

Organizationally, the group recommended the appointment of one "manufacturing center sponsor" to manage the six new manufacturing centers. They suggested the following responsibilities for the different managers:

- General Manager Business Unit: Brand penetration and business development in countries, i.e., business units;

- Global Brand Sponsor: Brand, product, pricing harmonization, standardization, and inspiring new product and sub-brand development in all countries/business units and thus on a global basis;

- Manufacturing Center Sponsor: Optimization of manufacturing economies of scale by concentrating on standardized "global product" production in few large-scale manufacturing centers allowing for competition and entrepreneurial production of new/test products at the same time.

Under this organization, the general managers would keep Trade Marketing and Consumer Marketing, but lose Manufacturing. Five of the general managers would become global brand sponsors, as well. The manufacturing center sponsor would be an independent manager, reporting to Zinser, manager of the confectionery

---

[1]Frank Schiesser was the only sponsor who did not work for Zinser (he worked for Robert Jaunich). This appointment exemplifies how assignments were handed out less to be consistent with any structure and more to match capability and workload.

Exhibit 4
Jacobs Suchard: Reorganizing for 1992
        Organization Structure Proposed by Issenmann Task Force

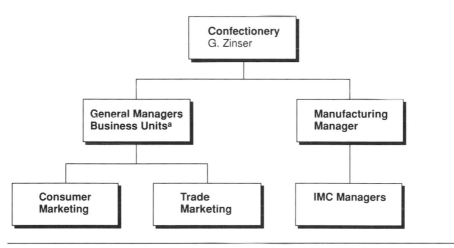

Measurements

- General manager: Profit (revenue minus cost of goods bought from IMCs)
                ROTA (current assets)
- Manufacturing manager: COGS, productivity, ROTA

[a]Five of whom are also global brand sponsors

Source: Company records.

division. (See Exhibit 4 for the proposed structure.) In addition to its organization recommendations, the task force also proposed how each manager should be measured, and on how the transfer pricing—or, the "intercompany business regulations"—between the IMCs and general managers should take place.

General Managers.   As before, the general managers would be measured on PAT and ROTA. (Profits were calculated by subtracting total costs from revenues for the business unit, net of taxes). However, "costs" now would be the cost of goods sold incurred at the IMCs and charged to the general managers, and ROTA now would be based on current assets, such as inventory and accounts receivable, rather than the previous total assets, since the fixed assets now belonged to the IMCs.

Regarding the general managers' role, the task force said: The "focus lies on consumer marketing, trade marketing (sales) and economic affairs (finance), based on agreed strategies with relevant global brand sponsor and core business manager." In other words, the general managers would still be responsible for Consumer Marketing and Trade Marketing, though now under the coordination of the global brand sponsors.

Global Brand Sponsors.   Since they were also general managers, the global brand sponsors had a lot to do. As the task force put it: They "have responsibility for a rather vast area of activities they cannot handle all by themselves. The individual sponsor is therefore encouraged to form a team of people from his own and other sister units."

The global brand sponsors would have to "develop and safeguard the financial well-being and share growth of (their brands) on a global basis." They would develop and get agreement from the general managers regarding the following:

actions to be taken to increase the importance and share of the global brand in terms of tons or sales units and return on sales

international advertising strategies for the global brands, helping the general managers with the implementation

standardized sales units packaging for international usage

activities together with the general managers and corporate R&D to introduce new products for the global brands

activities together with the manufacturing center sponsor to use existing capacities to a maximum and to facilitate and make less complex intercompany relations and logistics

The task force did not specify how the global brand sponsors should be measured, beyond their measurements as general managers of business units.

Manufacturing Center Sponsor.   The manufacturing center sponsor, who was to report to Zinser, and to whom the six IMC managers would report, had the responsibility to ensure that all manufacturing sites were state-of-the-art, and that capacity was shared between the global brands based on the demand statements from the general managers. The global manufacturing sponsor was to allocate where each brand or form was to be manufactured and for which business units, taking into account capacity, productivity, logistics and duties (if any).

The task force recommended that the appropriate performance measurements should be productivity (both in terms of sales units per man-hour and tons per man-hour), maximization of raw materials usage, and ROTA for the total corporation.

IMC Managers.   In the past, the managers of the manufacturing plants had reported directly to the general managers and for the most part served only them. Now, however, the IMC managers would report to the global manufacturing sponsor and "provide the business units only with products prior agreed to by the manufacturing sponsor and the responsible global brand sponsor." Based on the sales plans prepared by the local business units, each IMC would consolidate its orders and in turn provide delivery plans for each business unit.

One of the most difficult steps for manufacturing in terms of the variability of the product line was packaging. In the past, the business units in each country had used different labels, largely because of language difference, and packages of different sizes; for example, three versus six bars to a package. Now the IMCs would get their packaging instructions from the global brand sponsors, who would try to standardize the products. The IMC managers would be measured on productivity and maximization of raw materials usage, and would add to the prices they set a ROTA charge of four to five percent, to ensure that they were generating enough capital for reinvestment.

Harvard and Managing Change

In August 1988, just after the Issenmann task force had published its recommendations, Fischer, Carrot, and Christian Bridoux went to Harvard to attend the Managing Change program. The team's mission was to take another look at how to organize marketing and manufacturing for Europe 1992. Carrot had been a member of the Issenmann task force.

They recommended the following for the confectionery division, which might later be followed by the coffee division:

1. Establish each global brand as a clear-cut profit center. The five profit centers' executives report directly to the executive vice president (EVP) of the Confectionery Division.

2. Change the current business units to sales units, reporting directly to one European sales executive who reports to the EVP Confectionery Division. The performance of the sales units are measured on total volume and on volume per brand. In this structure the global brand executive and the sales unit General Manager will be two different people.

3. Establish independent core factories reporting directly to one Manufacturing executive. This Manufacturing executive will report to the EVP, Confectionery Division. There is no organizational link between the core Factory Managers and the Sales Unit. The cost of goods sold of the core factories are to be charged to the Global Brands.

(See Exhibit 5 for the proposed organization structure). The team believed that the global brand managers should get profit responsibility; otherwise, "the gap between the authority and responsibility will be too wide." In addition, unlike what the Issenmann task force had proposed, they thought that the global brand managers and the sales unit manager had to be different people: a single person doing both jobs, they felt, could get into conflicts between global strategy and local sales unit profits.

The old business units would be called sales units, because consumer marketing would be moved from them to the global brand managers. The business units would also lose manufacturing, which would be independent of both the global brands and the sales units. The team also recommended having regular meetings between the global brand managers, the manufacturing and sales managers, and the confectionery EVP. Summing up their proposal, the members wrote:

> The above sketched model allows us to stay as close as possible to the competitive attitude which characterizes Jacobs Suchard. Many sources of conflict are reduced since there are always direct line responsibilities to only one superior. For example,

Exhibit 5
Jacobs Suchard: Reorganizing for 1992
Organization Structure Proposed by Harvard
Managing Change Team

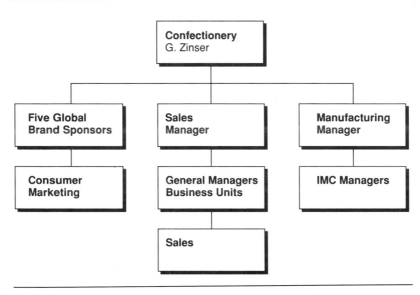

Measurements

- Global brand sponsors: Profit (based on revenues and costs from all functions)
- Sales manager: Total volume and volume/brand
- Manufacturing manager: Cost of goods sold

Note: In actual organization announced February 1989, H. Pohl named manager of IMCs reporting directly to K. Jacobs, not G. Zinser.

Source: Company records.

consumer marketing reports directly and only to the global brand executive and the sales unit, General Managers directly to the sales executive, etc. However, the level of potential conflicts will still be substantially higher than in the present organization, for intensive negotiations between the centralized manufacturing, centralized consumer marketing and the local sales units have to take place.

The Announcement of Hermann Pohl, IMC Manager, and Follow-on Task Forces

In February 1989, Jacobs announced that he was appointing Hermann Pohl head of corporate manufacturing and logistics. Pohl reported directly to Jacobs, and the six IMCs reported to Pohl. Thus, Zinser no longer had responsibility for manufacturing, even though both the Issenmann task force and the Harvard team recommended that the global manufacturing sponsor remain under the core business unit manager. Pohl, who had previously reported to Jacobs as manager of corporate economic affairs, had been working to implement Vision 2000 and clarify issues of structure, pricing and complexity reduction. Pohl had been the most available of the chief executive office members and the most knowledgeable on these issues. He felt also that it would take someone at his level to get the position established, though perhaps it could be moved into Zinser's organization in a few years.

The Issenmann task force had dealt with the broad issues of roles and responsibilities, so many specifics still had to be worked out before anything could be implemented. In March 1989, therefore, five new task forces began meeting to address the following: transfer pricing, ordering and delivery procedures, reporting procedures between the IMCs and the business units, information services support, and a new cost accounting system. Each task force had from four to eight members, representing different countries and areas of responsibility. Pohl oversaw the task forces.

May 1989: Status of the Changes

By May 1989, many of the 19 old factories had been closed. The organization had been changed as far as it would be for now; what remained was to work out the implementation of the follow-on task force items and to further reduce the product and packaging variability so that the brands became truly global. Whether the organization at the general manager level should be further changed was also still in debate, although most people believed that they should not go as far as Bridoux, Carrot, and Fischer had recommended; that is, to separate the role of global brand sponsor from the role of the general manager and give them Consumer Marketing, leaving the general managers with only Trade Marketing. Some thought that such an organization might be possible in the future; others disagreed, believing the general managers had to remain the key position in the company.

Global Brand Sponsors

With no clear direction as to how they should carry out their new assignments, the global brand sponsors began experimenting with how to work with the general managers on global brand strategies. Themselves general managers, the global brand sponsors understood the strong incentives their peers had to maximize profits for the business units, incentives that would make the general managers balk at standardization if it hurt local sales. Since the global brand sponsors had no consumer marketing or trade marketing support of their own—all the consumer marketing and trade marketing managers reported to the local business unit general managers—the challenge for the global brand sponsors was to get the general managers, as Issenmann put it, to "think globally and act locally."

Zinser saw the relationship working this way. The global brand sponsors should make strategy in cooperation with the general managers, who then would try to develop that strategy in the local market. "For example," he said:

Italy is developing a MILKA sponge product and Belgium is developing a marsh-
mallow MILKA. Both will be tested in the local markets for global possibilities.
Who will pay for this development? The local managers. Why would they? One,
because they benefit; and two, it's fun to contribute to the global business. A
general manager knows that success with a product will get global attention.

The same idea applied to research and development, which resided both in the
business units and at the corporate level. To promote entrepreneurship and decentralization and to keep the bottom-up decision-making process, Zinser expected the
business units to come up with new product ideas and develop them locally for
ultimate distribution in the global market.

The global brand sponsors and general managers worked together informally,
and whether the relationship worked or failed depended on how much both parties
respected and trusted each other. According to one top manager, those global
sponsors who tried to be "tough" failed, and those who worked "nicely" succeeded.
Many of the rules that would govern the relationship were still being worked out
in the task forces, and the global brand sponsors were still searching for how to
unify the different business units' objectives. Jacquesson, general manager of French
confectionery and global brand sponsor for MILKA, began by holding formal
meetings with the consumer marketing managers from the different business units,
to discuss global consumer marketing strategy, but stopped the meetings after six
months. The business unit consumer marketing managers couldn't make decisions,
because the general managers to whom they reported often changed those decisions
later. Then he tried holding regular meetings with 15 general managers, but couldn't
get agreement on anything. Finally, he set up a steering committee of four of the
general managers with the largest markets—Germany, Belgium, England, and
France—and asked them to meet every two months. This system, at least, produced
some recommendations that the others felt some pressure to accept. Jacquesson
characterized his role as "nearly an impossible mission." What did he think were
the conditions for success? "The ability to fight, to be fair, to be open—to be
young!"

Inevitably, there were conflicts—every day, according to Zinser. What the global
brand sponsors wanted often clashed with what the local general managers wanted.
There were conflicts over packaging sizes, what language to put on packages, how
to advertise, who would pay for international media, which factory to source from
(there were still options, and some general managers preferred certain factories),
who would pay for investments—and many others. Sometimes a global brand
sponsor and the general managers would agree on a European advertising strategy,
but when it came time to share the costs, some general managers would refuse. In
such cases, the global brand sponsor would be stuck with the cost in his own local
budget, thereby hurting his own profits, and would have to go to Zinser to get the
general managers to pay. Sometimes general managers refused to go along with a
global advertising strategy because of cultural differences, such as the hair color
of the people in the advertisement.

Jacquesson explained how he handled such conflicts. If a general manager refused to implement the global strategy, "I listen to the facts," he said, "if he makes a strong enough case, maybe I'll let him do what he wants. If he just says he doesn't feel the strategy will work, I won't accept that. Much of the conflict has to do with personalities. I try to be fair and take into account what they're concerned about."

When a global brand sponsor and a general manager reached an impasse, then the global brand sponsor could go to Zinser for resolution. This was a last resort, however, because Zinser had such a large span of control and so couldn't get involved in every difference of opinion. Some believed that Zinser would most often support the local business unit management, fearing that otherwise he would hurt profits.

Despite these conflicts, Issenmann and Jacquesson all believed that, contrary to what Bridoux, Carrot, and Fischer had proposed, the global brand sponsors had also to be general managers. They contended that a separate global brand sponsor would have no credibility with the general managers—the general managers would not want to take orders from someone who did not also have to take the same risks with a local business—but also that setting up a separate global brand sponsor might threaten the independence of the general managers, who still had THE position. Said Issenmann, "A purely global manager would become like a staff member and would just get frustrated, trying to deal with the line managers." Jacquesson gave an example of when he had needed that credibility. He had had to launch a new product globally, LILA PAUSE, and so had to decide on a package size. He insisted on six-packs, which was different from the traditional three-packs. When he tried the six-packs in his own country, he got 2.4 times the expected sales, which then made it possible for him to convince Germany to use the six-packs. Otherwise, he thought, Germany never would have gone along.

Yet if they agreed that a global brand sponsor also had to be a general manager, they also agreed that the workload was excessive. "We can't do it all," said Issenmann, "but it's the best way to do it." Said Jacquesson, simply: "The workload is too much."

The global brand sponsors were measured for bonuses as general managers, with the personal objectives part of the bonus formula reflecting the additional duties. Typically, the global brand sponsors were expected to complete projects associated with globalization, such as launching advertising campaigns, and were measured according to the number and effectiveness of those projects. Those general managers who were not global sponsors were not measured on how much they contributed to the globalization projects.

The International Manufacturing Centers

By May 1989, the confectionery business had moved about 80% toward concentrated production in the six IMCs. By the end of the year, all the extra factories would be closed.

Like the relationship between the general managers and the global brand sponsors, the relationship between the general managers and IMC managers was also fraught with conflict. Where the IMCs sought standardization of a product line to maximize volumes and reduce costs, the general managers sought distinctive packaging and other requirements to serve their local markets.

Having Pohl as their manager, with direct access to the chief executive office and Jacobs, gave the IMC managers a new independence. When they were still reporting to the general managers, the IMC managers had had to follow what the general manager wanted. They could not act against the general manager's profit goals, even if they thought it was best for globalization. Now, however, they reported only indirectly to the general managers.

The general managers had not liked losing manufacturing, but, according to Pohl, most now saw the benefits. The key was how the change was handled. "People realize," he said "that when the top guys get involved with change, it's serious. Plus, they know they'll be involved. We have to involve them in how we do it." Pohl always sought agreement from the general managers on what he was trying to do. On some issues, getting this agreement took a long time; on the issue of standardized pricing, for example, it took four months.

The general managers still were responsible for profit in their business units, and so when the IMCs wanted to do something that would affect their bottom line, the general managers fought it. For example, the first fully international brand, I LOVE MILKA—which had one recipe and one box—would soon be produced solely in Strasbourg, France, to be sold across Europe. Currently, it was sold mainly in Germany. Nevertheless, before the Strasbourg line was even completed for I LOVE MILKA, Germany was already developing four new recipes, which would greatly expand the need for space and capacity at the IMC. Whether or not Strasbourg would respond to what Germany wanted, depended on the agreed-upon global strategy. Said Carrot, now IMC manager of Strasbourg, "We are awaiting a decision from the global brand sponsor on this. What's holding them up? Consumer marketing is still independent and local." Consumer marketing managers still reported to the general managers, and did not always have the incentives to follow what the global sponsors wanted. Pohl described another standard conflict:

> We wanted to have one MILKA language wrapper for all of Europe, but people screamed, because we couldn't fit all the languages on the package. So, to compromise, we decided on three different packaging versions: one for the Mediterranean countries, one for the German-speaking countries, and one for the others. I agreed to this for now, because I needed the full commitment of all the general managers. It's the only way to get movement.

Jacquesson thought that many of the problems would not exist if there was a clear financial structure, outlining who had to pay for what. "The IMCs have good ideas, but they don't care where the profit is," he explained.

> The unwritten rule is, "Help yourself." There's no formal decision structure. It's conflict management by design—which is very tough! For example, I wanted Germany to pay for the start-up of a product made in France for Germany, but they originally said no. Case by case, issue by issue, we are trying to establish a philosophy for dealing with these cases, to build rules.

For Pohl, the most important issue to be dealt with was product complexity. Before standardization had begun, there were about 1500 stock-keeping units (SKUs) for confectionery, considering all the variations of flavors, sizes and languages. Pohl didn't want to begin centralizing manufacturing with this "chaos." So he began task forces with the consumer marketing managers to try to reduce the SKUs. Others had tried the same thing before Pohl, and twice had gotten nowhere, because no one would compromise and no one could get beyond the issue of package design. The third time, Pohl took package design off the discussion table and simply asked the teams for a big reduction, wanting to let them recommend what was to be done. When they were finished, it looked as though they could cut the number from 1500 down to 750.

Another open issue was how the IMCs should be measured and compensated, and how the IMCs should charge the general managers. Should the IMCs charge by standard costs, and if so, who would cover the risk of the volatile swings in the commodity prices of cocoa beans and cocoa butter, as well as fluctuations in currencies? A number of these related issues still needed to be worked out in the task forces. Once the task forces were done, they would have to present their recommendations to all the general managers for acceptance, and then to Jacobs.

How Far to Go?

Was the present organization sufficient to create the incentives and priorities for a successful launch of the global brands, or did the company need to separate the role of global brand sponsor from general manager? Jacobs hadn't said no to the idea, but neither did he think the organization was ready. And, could the company maintain its decentralized structure and entrepreneurial spirit, while trying to deal with products and markets that seemed to require more centralization? As Fischer put it, "We are trying to both centralize and keep a small staff." Finally, what was the future of the general manager? Many were already upset at losing functions; most would resign without profit responsibility. In a truly global business, it wasn't clear precisely what the role of the general managers might be. What further complicated the problem was the fact that there would always be local brands. These were some of the questions facing Jacobs as he looked ahead to EEC 1992, which was fast approaching.

MNCs: Get Off
the Reorganization
Merry-Go-Round*

Christopher A. Bartlett

For many companies, international expansion has been the major strategic thrust of the postwar era. Yet even successful, well-established organizations face difficult problems in managing global operations. Heady years of overseas expansion have been followed by a persistent organizational hangover, unresponsive to traditional remedies.

In the 1960s, the answer to the international challenge seemed clear: managers simply needed to identify key strategic goals and restructure the corporation around them. But after two decades of experimentation, an "ideal international structure" remains elusive. Many companies still reorganize in the hope of finding it—but with only isolated cases of success.

With so many companies searching for this structural solution, why have results been so poor? Could it be that managers, obsessed with structure, were focusing on the wrong variable? A study I have made of 10 diverse and successful MNCs indicates that companies that persistently reorganize may be misdirecting their efforts. The companies I studied have *not* continually reorganized their operations. Each has retained for years a simple structure built around an international division— a form of organization that many management theorists regard as embryonic, appropriate only for companies in the earliest stages of worldwide growth.

These companies see the international challenge as one of building and maintaining a complex decision-making process rather than of finding the right formal structure. The critical task is to develop new management perspectives, attitudes, and processes that reflect and respond to the complex demands companies with international strategies face. Such a process might sound too time consuming, too subtle, or too difficult to imitate. But companies that want to better meet the challenge can use as a guide the patterns established by these successful companies.

Broken Promise

To understand why these companies have succeeded, we first should look at the reasons others have failed. As companies began to feel the strain of controlling fast-growing foreign operations, managements intuitively looked for structural solutions. This generation of top managers was on the front line when the wave of postwar product diversification led to the widespread shift from functional to multidivisional organization structures. They saw, firsthand, the powerful linkage between strategy and structure. The conventional wisdom was that if the divisional organization structure had helped managers implement the corporate strategy of diversification, surely an equivalent structure would facilitate their new international strategic thrust.

Managers had other reasons to reorganize. For one, changing the formal structure was recognized as a powerful tool through which management could redefine responsibilities and relationships. Top managers could make clear choices, have immediate impact, and send strong signals of change to all hierarchical levels. Furthermore, companies were encouraged to pursue such international reorganization because it seemed many others were doing likewise. In fact, the pattern of reorganization became so familiar that management theorists had documented and classified it.

Frustration came when managers discovered that no one structure provided a long-term solution. To many executives, it seemed they had no sooner developed a new set of systems, relationships, and decision-making processes than the international operations again needed to be reorganized. For example, Westinghouse disbanded its separate international division in 1971 when the 125 domestic-product division managers were given worldwide responsibilities. By early 1979, however, concern about the lack of coordination among divisions and the insensitivity to certain nations had mounted. A task force recommended a global matrix, and by midyear the new structure was in place. It was the third reorganization of international operations in one decade.

Like the executives at Westinghouse, many managers turned to a global matrix because they were frustrated by the one-dimensional biases built into a global-product or area-based structure. It was supposed to allow a company to respond to national and regional differences while simultaneously maintaining coordination and integration of worldwide business. But the record of companies that adopted this structure is disappointing. The promised land of the global matrix quickly turned into an organizational quagmire, forcing a large number of companies to retreat from it. Some of these cases were widely publicized, such as that of Dow Chemical.

Dow, which served as the textbook case study of the global matrix, eventually returned to a more conventional structure in which the emphasis is on geographically based managers. Citibank became the new case illustration in one important book on matrix organization.[1] Yet within a few years, Citibank was reportedly retreating from its global matrix structure.

The same problems with the global matrix kept coming up: tension and uncertainty built into dual reporting channels sometimes escalated to open conflict, complex issues were forced into a rigid two-dimensional decision framework, and minor issues became the subject of committee debates. More important, the design of matrix organization implied that managers with conflicting views or overlapping responsibilities communicate problems and confront and resolve differences. Yet barriers of distance, language, and culture impeded this vital process.

Managing the Process

The 10 companies that escaped the organizational merry-go-round had a number of things in common, but the most fundamental was their adaptability to complex demands without restructuring. Underlying the approach to global operations of managers of these companies was the way they thought about the strategic demands and the appropriate organizational response.

Two major forces exerted opposite pressures on international strategies during the 1970s. First, as global competitors emerged in many industries, skirmishes for single-country markets gave way to battles for worldwide market position and global-scale efficiencies. Second, host country governments raised their demands, and competition for market access tilted the bargaining power more in the government's favor. MNCs had to increase local equity participation, transfer technology, built local manufacturing and research facilities, and meet export quotas.

With one set of pressures suggesting global integration and the other demanding local responsiveness, it is easy to see why executives of many companies thought in either-or terms and argued whether to centralize or decentralize control and whether to let the product or the geographic managers dominate corporate structure.

While managers in the 10 companies remained sensitive to those conflicting demands, they resisted the temptation to view their tasks in such simple either-or terms. The managers understood that such clear-cut answers would not work since *both* forces are present to some degree in all businesses. Moreover, thinking of strategy in "global" or "local" terms ignored the complexity, diversity, and changeability of the demands facing them.

---

[1]See Stanley M. Davis and Paul R. Lawrence, *Matrix* (Reading, Mass.: Addison-Wesley Publishing, 1977). Citibank CEO Walter Wriston acknowledged in his foreword to this book the difficulty of managing in a global matrix.

For example, a growing threat of Japanese competitors forced Timken, the leading bearings manufacturer, to become more globally competitive in the 1970s. Unlike the Japanese, Timken chose not to compete solely as the low-cost producer of standard bearings. Rather, the company opted to reinforce its position as the technological leader in the industry. While this strategy required the strengthening and integrating of a worldwide research function, Timken's management thought such global integration was unnecessary in manufacturing. It trimmed and standardized product lines to gain efficiencies, but plants still specialized on a regional—not a worldwide—basis. Moreover, because customer service and response time were at the core of Timken's strategy, sales forces and engineering services retained their strict local focus.

Savvy managers realize that it is often difficult to know how to focus responsibility even within a single function. For example, Corning Glass Works's TV tube marketing strategy required global decision making for pricing and local decision making for service and delivery.

The Challenge of Subtlety

It is not surprising that with this subtle perception of the nature of strategy, the managers in the 10 corporations set objectives, adopted a focus, and used tools that were different from those in most other MNCs. They realized that if the pressures in the international operating environment were intrinsically complex, diverse, and changeable, they had to create an internal management environment that could respond to these external demands and opportunities.

With this perception, managers viewed the organizational challenge not as one of finding and installing the right structure but as one of building an appropriate management process. As a result, they focused attention on the individual decision and the way it was reached rather than on the overall corporate structure. Questions changed from "Do we need worldwide product divisions or an area structure?" to "How can the company take the regional product group's perspective more into account in capacity expansion decisions?"

Finally, they looked for management tools with a finer edge than the blunt instrument of formal structural reorganization. Managers in other companies seemed so captivated by architectural problems that they forgot that the boxes they sketched on the back of an envelope represented not just positions but also people; the lines they casually erased and redrew stood not only for lines of authority but also for personal relationships. It was not unusual then to announce major reorganization very suddenly and install the structure in a few weeks or months. The result was often traumatic readjustment, followed by a long recovery. At Westinghouse, for example, the decision to reorganize into a global matrix structure was made by a senior management task force after a 90-day study of the problems and was put in place over the following 90 days.

Managers in the companies studied used tools that influenced individuals' behavior and attitudes or group norms and values in a more discrete and flexible manner.

A Multidimensional Decision Process

The experience of the companies studied suggests that development of the diverse and flexible organizational process follows three closely related stages. First, because an organization must take into account the richness of the environment it faces rather than view the world through a single, dominant management perspective, the companies developed internal groups that allowed the organization to sense, analyze, and respond to a full range of strategic opportunities and demands.

In most companies, a necessarily formal organizational structure limits interaction between such diverse interests. Therefore, during the second stage, the company builds additional channels of communication and forums for decision making to allow greater flexibility.

Finally, in the third stage, the company develops norms and values within the organization to support shared decisions and corporate perspectives. Value is placed on corporate goals and collaborative effort rather than on parochial interests and adversary relationships.

Developing Multiple Management Perspectives

In this environment of changeable demands and pressures, managers must sense and analyze complex strategic issues from all perspectives. Top management's job is to eliminate the one-dimensional bias built into most organizations.

The traditional bias in companies with international divisions, for example, allowed country and regional managers to dominate decision making from their line positions, with product and functional staff groups relegated to support and advisory roles. As a result, the companies underestimated or even ignored strategic opportunities that might have been realized by global coordination and integration of operations.

Similarly, organization by product divisions fostered decisions favoring worldwide standardization and integration. The power of headquarters product managers over their geographic and functional counterparts was usually reinforced within the structure in formal as well as informal ways. For instance, the companies constructed information systems around products that allowed headquarters-based product management to collect and analyze data more easily than their functional or geographic counterparts. Furthermore, the strongest managers were appointed to product management positions, which reinforced their influence over the decision process.

Top management can begin to gradually eliminate these biases in the decision process by:

1. *Upgrading Personnel.*   Assigning capable people to the right positions not only allows skills to be brought to bear in important areas but also sends strong signals that top management is serious about its objectives and priorities. For example, top managers of the hospital supply company Baxter Travenol decided to counterbalance the strength of country managers in the international division with a strong global business perspective. First, they replaced existing product

managers with M.B.A.s who, while lacking the product expertise of their predecessors (ex-sales representatives), brought a more analytical and strategic perspective to the role. While this interim step upgraded the role, it was only with the appointment of more experienced managers from the domestic product divisions and foreign subsidiaries that the company achieved a strong global business perspective in its international strategy decisions.

2. *Broadening Responsibilities.* Aggressive, ambitious, and able managers will naturally resist transfer to positions viewed as less powerful and having fewer responsibilities and lower status. So companies must redefine the role of the positions at the same time they upgrade the personnel. In the example of Baxter Travenol, when top management appointed M.B.A.s to product manager positions, it enlarged the role from primarily a support responsibility to one that focused on monitoring and analyzing global product performance. When experienced product and country managers superseded the M.B.A.s, the company allowed them to get involved in the budgeting and strategic planning processes, making recommendations about the management of their lines of business worldwide.

Such progression of roles is fairly typical when a company is trying to develop groups previously underrepresented in the decision process. The company first broadens advisory and support roles to encompass responsibility for monitoring and control. Exposure to the information necessary to undertake these new tasks then helps develop the ability to make analyses and recommendations of key issues, and finally to implement strategy.

3. *Changing Managerial Systems.* The biggest impediment to these changes is often the existing line management group; as happened at Baxter Travenol, country subsidiary managers may greatly resent the increased "interference" of product and functional staff. So top management needs to back up the desired changes.

If the newly upgraded managers are to succeed, they need information tailored to their responsibilities. Management systems usually parallel the formal organization structure and give line managers a tremendous information advantage. Top executives must be sure managers representing other perspectives also have the information needed to support their proposals and arguments.

Originally, Corning consolidated data only by geographic entity. When the company decided to upgrade the role of product and functional managers, however, it found that consolidating data along these dimensions was both difficult and expensive. Inconsistent product-line definitions, different expense allocation practices, and numerous tangled cases of double counting were impediments to system restructuring. By the time management sorted out these problems (with the help of a consultant and a couple of high-powered software packages), the new systems had cost well over $1 million.

Through these three steps, the company elevates previously underrepresented management groups. The organization recognizes the need to monitor the environment from their perspective, acknowledges their competence to analyze the strategic implications of key issues, and accepts the legitimacy of representing such views in the decision process. Happily, many old distinctions between line and staff blur, and organization clichés about the locus of power become less relevant. As the president of Bristol-Myers' International Division told me: "The traditional distinctions between line and staff roles are increasingly unclear here. . . . But by motivating managers and giving them latitude rather than writing restrictive job descriptions, we believe we can achieve much more."

Creating Supplementary Information Channels

It is not enough for a company simply to develop an organization that can sense and analyze issues from various perspectives. Managers representing diverse points of view need access to the decision-making processes.

As I mentioned earlier, in most companies formal communication channels parallel formal organization structures. The focus is one-dimensional, and the decision-making process hierarchical and formal. The structure reinforces the power of dominant line managers while limiting the influence of managers representing other perspectives.

Top management must create forums for decision making that take many perspectives into account and are flexible. While the formal reporting lines and management systems provide one way to channel communications, management can use an equally strong set of informal channels.

Influencing Informality.   Informal relationships among people, of course, naturally develop in any organization, and to date, many corporate executives have regarded them as an uncontrollable by-product of the formal organization. Increasingly, however, they recognize that they can, and indeed should, influence the organization's informal systems if the environment is to allow people representing diverse and frequently conflicting interests to influence decisions. In any MNC, managers are separated by barriers of distance, time, and culture; the extent to which top management works to overcome these barriers, the way in which it builds bridges, and the groups among which it develops contacts and relationships all have an important influence on the organization's informal network and processes.

A variety of tools is available. By bringing certain individuals together to work on common problems, for example, or by assigning a specific manager to a position that requires frequent contact with colleagues, management can influence the development of social relationships. Such personal bonds break down the defensiveness and misunderstanding that often build when line managers feel their power is threatened.

Senior management of Eli Lilly's International Division was conscious of this dynamic. As a normal part of career development, it transferred managers from line to staff positions, from one product line to another, and from headquarters to country subsidiaries. Although the original idea was to develop a broad perspective, an equally important benefit has been the development of an informal network of friends and contacts throughout the organization. In the words of one manager,

"Those who moved about had far better information sources than computer reports, and more important, they developed the influence that comes with being known, understood, and respected."

Baxter Travenol's top management used frequent, well-planned meetings to help develop informal relationships. The company had long held annual general-manager's meetings in which country and regional line managers listened to formal presentations of the year's financial results, of the latest corporate plans, and of one or two new products. Recognizing that staff-line relationships were becoming very strained, the division president changed the traditional meeting into a senior management conference to which product managers and functional managers were also invited. He replaced most formal presentations with discussions, during which senior managers jointly identified and tried to resolve strategic and organizational issues.[2] The team formed bonds that endured far beyond the meetings.

Avoiding Strategic Anarchy.   Of course a company cannot resolve complex issues by simply allowing different interests to clash in a trading-room-floor atmosphere. The formal hierarchy will still constrain and limit the influence of nonline managers as key issues are actually decided. There are, however, ways to ensure the representation of appropriate interests and at the same time allow headquarters to retain control.

Most managers are familiar with such things as task forces, interdepartmental teams, and special committees. These devices are often used ad hoc, after the formal decision process has failed, for example, or in response to a crisis. But managers can also use them in a more routine manner to pull certain issues out of the mainstream and to tailor the analysis and decision making.

Bristol-Myers' international organization, for instance, feared that the company was dissipating scarce research resources. Each project typically had the backing of a country subsidiary manager who claimed that the project was absolutely essential to his or her national strategy. By creating a "pharmaceutical council" comprised of senior geographic line managers and division-level business development staff managers, the division president forced these managers to make compromises and to combine these separate proposals into a single cohesive program. By appointing the business development director as the council's chairman, he increased this manager's influence and leverage and ensured that the deliberations would have a global perspective.

In Warner Lambert, country managers had for years influenced decisions on manufacturing capacity toward constructing local plants. Believing that such decisions compromised efficiency, the division president set up a task force of geographic and functional managers to conduct an 18-month review of global capacity needs. Recognizing the sensitivity of country managers to any loss of autonomy, he appointed regional managers to represent the line organization. The task force's

---

[2]For a description of the process used, see my article, written with David W. DeLong, "Operating Cases to Help Solve Corporate Problems," *Harvard Business Review,* March–April 1982, p. 68.

manufacturing, finance, and marketing managers convinced regional managers of the need for greater coordination of manufacturing operations and rationalization of facilities to gain scale economies. With regional managers behind the idea, country managers were forced to recognize the program's considerable savings.

One note of caution: the purpose of such temporary task groups is to supplement rather than replace the mainstream decision process. The company must consider carefully which decisions cannot be resolved by the regular managerial process. It should clearly define and limit the number of issues taken "off-line" and keep them out of the mainstream only as long as necessary.

Building a Supportive Culture

There is no guarantee that decisions will reflect the mix of interests and views represented in the process. Simply putting people together does not mean they will interact positively and productively. It is necessary to build an organizational culture that supports multidimensional, flexible decision making.

In many companies, a culture that stresses internal competition has proven the major barrier to the development of a flexible decision process. In one of the companies studied, a well-known motto was that "only your final result counts." The company's formal structure and reward systems reinforced the value.

When internal competition is overemphasized, managers with different perspectives easily become entrenched adversaries and the decision-making process deteriorates, as protecting territory and even subversion become the norms. In fact, many companies discovered that upgrading nonline management groups and supplementing the hierarchical decision process triggered such adverse reactions.

To make the organization flexible, top management of the companies studied made certain that managers understood how their particular points of view fit with corporate strategies; it reinforced this understanding with a culture supportive of cooperation and compromise. The organizational norms and values creating such an environment obviously could not be established by management fiat. Rather, they were carefully developed through a variety of small actions and decisions.

Articulate Goals and Values.   Elementary and simplistic as it may seem, one of the most powerful tools for top management is the precise formulation and communication of specific strategic objectives and behavioral norms. In a surprising number of companies, however, middle managers have only the vaguest notion of overall corporate objectives and of the boundaries of acceptable behavior.

Eli Lilly places great importance on mutual trust, openness, and honesty in all interpersonal dealings. In an orientation brochure for new employees, the late Eli Lilly, grandson of the founder, was quoted as saying: "Values are, quite simply, the core of both men and institutions. . . . By combining our thoughts and by helping one another, we are able to merge the parts [of this organization] into a rational, workable management system." It is clear that adversary relationships and parochial behavior do not fit in the culture he envisioned.

At Baxter Travenol, senior management conferences provided an ideal communication forum for the International Division president. In addition to articulating overall objectives and priorities, he acknowledged the conflicts implicit in particular important issues and encouraged managers to discuss how they might subjugate individual interests to the overall strategy. The participation of managers ensured not only their understanding of the issues but also their involvement in, and commitment to, corporate goals.

Modify Reward Systems. It is clear that a company cannot ask managers to compromise parochial interests for a broader good if it continues to evaluate and reward them on the basis of indicators tied tightly to a small area of responsibility. Successful international companies in the sample made sure managers understood they did not compromise career opportunities or expose themselves to other organizational risks by adopting a cooperative and flexible attitude. Many companies altered management evaluation criteria and modified formal reward systems.

As the decision-making processes became increasingly complex at Corning Glass Works, top managers changed the criteria for promotion. One top manager said to me:

> In addition to the analytic and entrepreneurial capabilities we have always required, managers must now have strong interpersonal skills to succeed in key positions. To contribute to our decision making process, they must be good communicators, negotiators, and team players. We had to move aside some individuals who simply could not work in the new environment.

Eli Lilly's formal evaluation and reward systems are tied even more directly to the need for cooperation and flexibility. Rather than being evaluated only by a direct superior, each manager's performance is also appraised by others with whom he or she deals. This multiple review process not only encourages cooperative behavior but also serves as a control to identify those who are unwilling or unable to develop positive work relationships.

Provide Role Models. Top managers know that their words and actions are models that strongly influence values and behavioral norms in the organization. Yet few top managers routinely use these powerful tools. With a little thought and planning, they can send signals that encourage behavior conducive to achieving the organization's goals.

After one restructuring failed, Corning's president and vice chairman recognized that the role model they were providing as top management was one of the fundamental problems. They were simply not communicating and cooperating on efforts to integrate the international and domestic operations, and this lessened the willingness of domestic division managers to share information and cooperate with their overseas counterparts. Later, as these top managers made a strong effort to work closely on issues and to let the organization see their joint commitment to decisions, they saw their cooperative behavior reflected throughout the organization.

The Key Is Flexibility

Clearly, the approach outlined is vastly different from one in which a company installs a new structure to "force the product managers to interact with geographic specialists."[3] Building a multidimensional and flexible decision process means the company will sense and respond to the complex, diverse, and changeable demands most MNCs face.

Several benefits flow from this approach. First, matching decision processes with the task keeps managers' attention focused on the business issues. By contrast, in an organization going through a major restructuring, management's attention tends to be riveted on changes in formal roles and responsibilities, as people debate the implications of the new structure and jockey for position and turf.

Second, by working to achieve a gradual organizational evolution rather than a more rapid structural change, a company can avoid much of the trauma associated with reorganization. Changes in roles and relationships are best achieved incrementally.

Finally, by thinking in terms of changing behavior rather than changing structural design, managers free themselves from the limitations of representing organizations diagrammatically. They are not restricted by the number of dimensions that can be represented on a chart; they are not tempted to view the organization symmetrically; and they are not limited by the innately static nature of an organization diagram.

---

[3]This was the objective of the Westinghouse reorganization study, according to the report in "Westinghouse Takes Aim at the World," *Fortune*, January 14, 1980, p. 52.

R e a d i n g   5–2

The Human Side of the Matrix*

Paul R. Lawrence, Harvey F. Kolodny, Stanley M. Davis

Matrix management and organization have become increasingly common in recent years. If we were pressed to pick one word that characterizes the potential of the matrix organization, it would have to be *flexibility*. The matrix structure offers the potential of achieving the flexibility that is so often missing in conventional, single-line-of-command organizations and of reconciling this flexibility with the coordination and economies of scale that are the historic strengths of large organizations. (See box for the basic elements of matrix design.)

Essential Characteristics of Matrix Organizations

- The identifying feature of a matrix organization is that some managers report to two bosses rather than to the traditional single boss—there is a dual rather than a single chain of command.
- Firms tend to adopt matrix forms when it is absolutely essential that they be highly responsive to two sectors, such as markets and technology; when they face uncertainties that generate very high information-processing requirements; and when they must deal with strong constraints on financial and/or human resources. The matrix form can help provide flexibility and balanced decision making, but at the price of complexity.
- Matrix organization is more than matrix structure. It must also be reinforced by matrix systems such as dual control and evaluation systems, by matrix leadership behavior that operates comfortably with lateral decision making, and by a matrix culture that fosters open conflict management and a balance of power.

- Most matrix organizations assign dual command responsibilities to functional departments (marketing, production, engineering, and so on) and to product/market departments. The former are oriented to specialized resources while the latter focus on outputs. Other matrix organizations are area-based departments for either products or functions.
- Every matrix organization contains three unique and critical roles: the top manager who heads up and balances the dual chains of command; the matrix bosses (functional, product, or area) who share subordinates; and the 2-boss managers who report to two different matrix bosses. Each of these roles has its own unique requirements.
- The matrix organization started in aerospace companies, but now firms in many industries (chemical, banking, insurance, package goods, electronics, computer, and so on) and in different fields (hospitals, government agencies, professional organizations) are turning to different forms of the matrix structure.

Now that the use of the matrix structure is so widespread, it has become apparent that it calls for different kinds of managerial behavior than are typical in conventional line organizations. This article will identify the key management roles in a matrix organization and describe the essential aspects called for in each of them.

Envision the matrix structure as a diamond [Exhibit 1]. The general executive, who heads up the matrix, is at the top of the diamond. The matrix bosses, or matrix managers, who share common subordinate(s), are on the sides of the diamond. The person at the bottom is the 2-boss manager.

Top Leadership

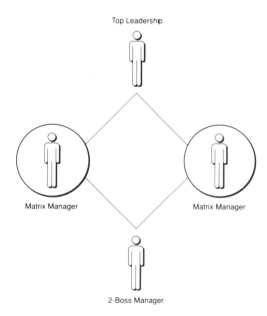

Top Leadership

Matrix Manager   Matrix Manager

2-Boss Manager

Exhibit 1

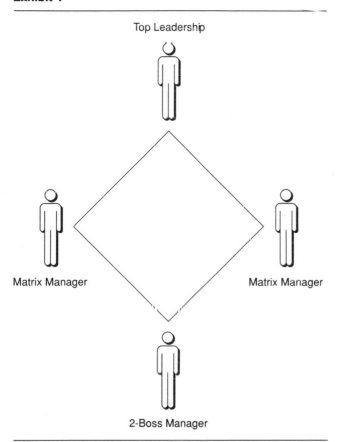

Top Leadership

Matrix Manager

Matrix Manager

2-Boss Manager

The top leadership is literally atop, or outside of, the matrix organization. This is not generally appreciated. Even in totally matrix organizations, the top executives are not *in* the matrix. Despite this, however, they are *of* it: It is the top leaders who oversee and sustain the balance of power.

In a corporationwide matrix, the top leaders are the chief executive and a few other key individuals; in a product group or a division matrix, the top leader is the senior manager. The individual does not share power with others, and there is no unequal separation of authority and responsibility. Formally, the role itself is the same as in any traditional organization. What distinguishes it from the traditional top slot is the leadership process as it is applied to the people in the next levels down.

The top leader is the one who must "buy" the matrix approach. He must be convinced of its merits to the point that he believes it is the best (although not necessarily the ideal) of all alternative designs. He must also "sell" it; he must be very vocal and articulate in developing the concept and arousing enthusiasm for it among the ranks.

One of the several paradoxes of the matrix approach, then, is that it requires a strong, unified command at the top, to ensure a balance of power at the next level down. In some senses, this is the benevolent dictator: "You will enjoy democracy (shared power), and I will enjoy autocracy (ultimate power)"; or "I'm OK, you're OK; but I'm still the boss."

Balancing power as a top leader therefore calls for a blend of autocratic and participative leadership styles. A clear example of this comes from Bastien Hello, head of the B–1 bomber division at Rockwell International. The *New York Times* called his project the most costly and complex plane project in history. In an interview he said:

> Today I have some formidable people working for me. When you have a group like that, you have two choices, running a Captain Bligh operation, or a Mr. Roberts operation. I would call one autocratic, the other group therapy.
>
> If I have to lean in one direction, I would shave a little closer to group therapy. It's not because I, and the fellows who work for me, don't have autocratic tendencies: We do. But if you're going to keep everybody working in the same direction, you've got to have group participation in the decisions.
>
> So I like to get my team of managers together and thrash out problems with them, and I like to hear all sides. It's not that I'm a goody-goody about it; there *is* malice aforethought to it.
>
> Once they have participated in and agreed to the decision, you can hold their noses right to it. It's not that I like group sessions—I don't, they're painful—but they do bring the team along. And once you get them signed up, then you become autocratic about it.

The general executive of a matrix organization has the unique role of heading up both of its dual command structures, administrative and technical. As we understand this role, it involves three unique aspects: *power balancing, managing the decision context,* and *standard setting.* These three processes, while of concern to any top executive, take on a very special importance in a mature matrix organization. The reason for this importance is not hard to find. It stems directly from three basic reasons as to why a matrix can be a desirable organizational form.

1. The existence of dual pressures calls for balanced decision making that considers both aspects simultaneously. The general executive's critical role in achieving such decision making is to establish and sustain a reasonable balance of power between the two arms of the matrix.

2. The second necessary condition for a matrix organization to be effective is that a very high volume of information be processed and focused for use in making key decisions. If the organization is to cope with such an information-processing load, the top leader must be only one among several key decision makers—he must delegate. However, he cannot delegate to other decision makers the job of setting the stage; he must himself manage the decision context.

3. Last, the top executive must set the standards of expected performance. Others contribute to this process, but unless the top individual has high expectations for the organization, it is unlikely that the matrix organization will respond adequately to the environmental pressure for resource redeployment, which we have identified as a third necessary condition for a matrix organization. Let us look at each of these three special aspects of the top leader's role in the matrix organization in more detail.

Power Balancing

The power-balancing element of the general executive's role is, in our experience, vital to mature matrix organization performance. Any general manager must of course pay attention to this process, but it is uniquely critical in matrix organizations. If we contrast the pyramid diagram of a conventional hierarchy and the matrix diamond diagram, we have a clue as to why this is true. The diamond diagram, unlike the pyramid, is inherently unstable. For the structure to remain in place despite environmental pushing and pulling that lead to changed administrative and technical requirements, its emphasis and activities must be constantly rebalanced by hands-on top leadership. The analogy is crude but relevant. Managers in a leadership role are usually quite explicit about this requirement of their job. The "tuning" of a matrix organization needs continuing attention.

The basic methods that general executives use to establish a power balance are both obvious and important. The two arms of a matrix organization are, first of all, usually described in the formal documents that establish the structure as being of equal power and importance. The top executive uses every possible occasion to reinforce this message, and one way that is often used is by establishing dual budgeting systems and dual evaluation systems.

Most mature matrix organizations adopt dual budgeting systems, in which a complete budget is generated within each arm of the matrix. As with a double-entry accounting system, the dual budgets count everything twice—each time in a different way and for a different purpose. Functional budgets are primarily cost budgets—unless the functions sell their services outside. The budgets begin with product- and business-area estimates of work required from each functional area, usually expressed in man-hours and materials requirements. Functional groups then add indirect and overhead costs to these direct hours and come up with an hourly rate for services to the product or business managers.

Product or business units accept these rates or challenge them, sometimes by threatening to buy from the outside. This is the time when the difference in outlook is most striking. Business units, for example, have little sympathy for functional desires to hold people in an overhead category for contingencies or for the development of long-term competence. A business unit is hard pressed to see the need to develop competence that may be required three years hence, or for another business, when its own central concern is with short-term profit and loss. When the rates are approved for all the different functions, the product or business units develop their own profit and loss budgets for each of their product lines.

The parallel accounting systems provide independent controls that are consistent with the characteristic of the work in each type of unit and that recognize the partial autonomy of each organizational subunit. Each unit has the means to evaluate its own performance and to be evaluated independent of others. The CEO of one organization described the dual control systems in his organization as follows:

> The accounting system matches the organization precisely; so that's an aspect the product manager and I don't have to talk about. He can see how he's doing himself. When resources seem to be a problem, then I must get involved.
>
> Both product managers and functional managers get accounting evaluations. The functional shops have budgets but little spending money. They have a cost budget, but in theory it's all released into the projects. From the functional side, the accounting system locates and isolates unused capacity. As soon as the task requirement disappears the excess capacity turns up. The functional shop then has a "social" problem. The key thing is that the excess turns up immediately. There is no place to hide. Matrix is a free organization, but it's a tough organization.

With dual budgets, some interesting possibilities arise in achieving flexibility of organizational response. In the aforementioned organization, the CEO resolved an internal dispute: A product group was lobbying for control of repair and overhaul contracts on products in the field that it had developed and sold, over the protests of a functional group that had always managed the organization's field repair and overhaul activity. In the resolution of the dispute, the function remained in charge of the activity, but the product group was credited with the profits from all repair and overhaul contracts on its products. Both sides were satisfied.

Dual personnel evaluation systems go hand in hand with dual budgeting to help sustain a power balance. If a person's work is to be directed by two superiors, in all logic both should take part in that person's evaluation. Occasionally, the duality is nothing more than a product or business group sign-off of an evaluation form prepared by the functional boss. At other times, the initiative comes from the other side, primarily because the individual involved may have been physically situated within the product or business unit and had limited contact with the functional unit during the period covered by the evaluation.

Regardless of the particular system design, the person with 2-bosses must know that both have been a part of the evaluation if that person is to feel committed to consider both orientations in his activities. For this reason many matrix organizations insist that both superiors sit in on the evaluation feedback with the employee and that both advise the employee of salary changes so that rewards will not be construed as having been secured from only one side of the matrix.

These basic formal arrangements for setting up a reasonable balance of power are essential in a mature matrix, but they are seldom sufficient. Too many events can upset the balance, and a loss of balance needs to be caught by the general manager or it can degenerate into a major power struggle and even an ill-advised move away from the matrix organization. The matrix can be thrown off balance in many ways, but a common cause of a loss of balance is a temporary crisis on one side of the matrix structure that is used as an excuse for mobilizing resources in that direction. Up to a point such a reaction to a true crisis is certainly appropriate, but it can be the start of a lasting imbalance unless it is corrected by the general manager.

A more lasting source of instability arises from the fact that product- and business-area managers manage a whole business and thereby have that special mystique associated with bottom-line responsibility. This is a source of power. They are seen as the sources of revenue—the people who make the cash register ring. The general manager needs to be alert to this one-sided source of power to avoid its unbalancing potential. The profit center manager is often tempted to argue that he must have complete control over all needed resources, but this argument has no place in a matrix organization.

Given the inherent power instability of the matrix, the general managers of mature matrix organizations use a wide variety of supplemental ways to maintain the balance of the matrix. These methods are not new, but they are worth remembering as especially relevant for use in a matrix. Here are five such means:

1. Pay levels, as an important symbol of power, can be marginally higher on one side of the matrix, thus acting as a countervailing force.

2. Job titles can be adjusted between the two sides as a balancing item.

3. Access to the general manager at meetings and informal occasions is a source of power that can be controlled as a balancing factor.

4. Situation of offices is a related factor that carries a status or power message.

5. Reporting level is a frequently used power-balancing method. For instance, product managers can report up through a second in command while functional managers report directly to the general manager.

We have talked about the unbalancing potential possessed by profit center managers. But this imbalance of potential fluctuates from situation to situation. In many cases, the organization traditionally gave top priority to the functional side. Here the general manager employs his stratagems to shore up the prestige and position of the business-area or product managers and to make them, in fact as well as in name, the equals of the functional managers.

Managing the Decision Context

There is no substitute in a matrix organization for the sensitive management of the decision context by the top leadership. The existence of a matrix structure is an acknowledgment that the executive leaders cannot make all the key decisions in a timely way. There is too much relevant information to be digested, and too many points of view must be taken into account. But the general manager must set the stage for this decision making by others. He must see that it happens.

We have already seen that dual environmental pressures and complexity make conflict inevitable. To cope with this situation, the top manager must sponsor and act as a model of a three-stage decision process:

1. The conflicts must be brought into the open. This is fostered in the matrix structure, with its dual arms; but beyond this, the given manager must reward those who bring the tough topics to the surface for open discussion.

2. The conflicting positions must be debated in a spirited and reasoned manner. Relevant lines of argument and appropriate evidence must be presented. The executive manager's personal behavior has to encourage this in others.

3. The issue must be resolved and a commitment made in a timely fashion. The leader cannot tolerate stalling by others or passing the buck up the line.

All these decision processes call for a high order of interpersonal skills and a willingness to take risks. They also call for a minimum of status differentials from the top to the bottom ranks. Top leaders can favorably influence these factors by their own openness to dissent and willingness to listen and debate. One of the noticeable features of most leaders of matrix organizations is the simplicity of their offices and the relative informality of their manner and dress. The key point here is that this behavior must start at the top as part of setting the decision context.

Standard Setting

The leadership of matrix organizations is where high performance standards start. We earlier identified environmental pressures for high performance as a necessary condition for matrix organizations. But it is all too easy for organizational members to insulate themselves from these outside pressures. The general executive in a mature matrix organization internalizes the outside pressures and articulates them in the form of performance standards. Each subsystem on both sides of the matrix structure will of course be making its own projections and setting specific targets for higher review. But the overall level of aspiration in the organization begins with the general executive. This is a duty, as we said before, that he cannot afford to delegate.

The Matrix Boss

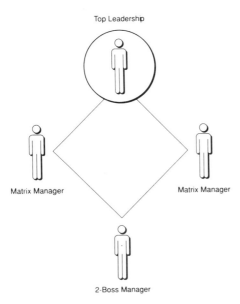

Top Leadership

Matrix Manager

Matrix Manager

2-Boss Manager

The matrix organization boss shares subordinates in common with another boss. As matrixes evolve, this means that the matrix structure boss will find himself positioned on one of the dimensions in the power balance. Whether the dimension is the one that is given or the one that is grown can make a significant difference for the perspective that evolves. Since one of the most typical evolutions is from a functional structure through a project overlay to a business function balance, let us examine the matrix boss role for each of these two dimensions in detail. The same lessons, however, apply to matrix structure bosses who are in charge of areas, markets, services, or clients.

The Functional Manager

One of the greatest surprises of the matrix organization form comes in the changing role of functional managers. In a functional organization, managers have authority over the objectives of their function, the selection of individuals, the priorities assigned to different tasks, the assignment of subordinates to different tasks and projects, the evaluation of progress on projects, the evaluation of subordinates' performance, and decisions on subordinate pay and promotions. They consult or take direction only from their boss in these matters, but much of the function is self-contained.

In a matrix organization, by contrast, one of these responsibilities is the sole responsibility of the functional manager. He must share many of the decisions with program or business managers or other functional managers at his level. Many matrix structures require dual sign-offs on performance evaluations and on pay and promotion decisions. Even when this is not so, consultation on these matters with others is essential for the effective functioning of the matrix and the power balance discussed previously. Tasks, assignments, and priority decisions have to be shared with business managers and indeed often come about as the result of decisions made by project or business teams. Even a function's objectives are partially determined by the resource demands of projects and businesses. The functional manager in his matrix role is responding in areas in which he has traditionally been the initiator. A manufacturing manager, for example, struggled against and for several years resisted the notion that many of the plant managers who reported to him had to set their goals in response to a business team's needs and that review of goal accomplishment, from a time point of view, was the business manager's and team's responsibility. He had difficulty in understanding that his responsibility was to review goal accomplishment from the point of view of a functional specialty.

Thus, for the functional manager, a matrix organization is often experienced as involving a loss of status, authority, and control. He becomes less central and less powerful as parts of his previous role as initiator move from the function to the business manager. The ultimate example of this is the increased confrontation of functional managers by their functional subordinates, who are now also members of a business team that provides the legitimate need and social support for such upward initiation and confrontation. For managers who have been in relative control of their domain, this is a rude awakening that can create initial hostility and a quite predictable resistance to a matrix form of management.

As a matrix organization matures, however, functional managers adapt to these changes, and they find the role not only tolerable but highly challenging. Even though in matrix organizations it is the business managers who tend to control the money that buys human resources, functional managers must engage in very complex people planning.

They must balance the needs of the different product lines and/or businesses in the organization, they must anticipate training needs, and they must handle union negotiations if layoffs or promotions are involved. They must also administer support staff (supervisors, managers, secretaries, clerks) and accompanying resources (equipment, facilities, space, maintenance), many of which must be shared with the business units.

To accomplish this with any degree of efficiency, functional managers must balance workloads to avoid excessive peaks and valleys in resources. They must do this in any organization, but in a matrix, business managers act with relative autonomy, and functional managers cannot be effective by holding to some central plan prepared primarily for budget purposes. It is imperative that they know the product- and business-workload projections and changes well in advance; that they negotiate constantly with these managers to speed up, slow down, schedule, plan, and replan the pace and amount of their activities. In other words, they must go to the business unit managers and be *proactive* if they are to manage their functions effectively.

Some comments from managers in 2 matrix organizations serve to underscore this need for proactive behavior:

> Functional managers have to learn that they're losing some of their authority to product units, and they will have to take direction from the product bosses. They have to segment their work along product lines, not functional lines, and they must be willing to establish communication channels with product lines.
>
> Functional managers have to learn to become more aware of the impact of their decisions on our productmarket success and become more responsive to the product organization needs that reflect the market. They have to remove their blinders and look around them while they turn the crank.

One functional manager concurred heartily:

> We have to learn to serve as well as dictate; become more customer oriented— where the customer is the product line. We must realize that the function's mission is to perform the function and prove that the function is the best available. There is a burden of proof in matrix that did not exist in functional organization.

The Business Manager

As we have pointed out, in a matrix organization various functional specialists are brought together in temporary (project) or permanent (business or product) groupings. These groups are led by product or business managers who have the responsibility for ensuring that the efforts of functional members of the team are integrated in the interest of the project or business. In this regard they have the same responsibilities as a general executive; their objective is project accomplishment or the long-term profitability of a business.

However, in a matrix organization these business managers do not have the same undivided authority as does the general executive. People on the team do not report to them exclusively since many also report to a functional manager. Thus, as many such managers have complained, "We have all the responsibility and little of the required authority."

Top leaders in traditional organizations have the benefit of instant legitimacy because people understand that reporting to them means being responsive to their needs. This is because their boss not only has formal title and status, but influences their performance evaluation, their pay, their advancement, and, in the long run, their careers. In a matrix organization these sources of authority are shared with functional managers, thus lessening, in the eyes of team members, the power of the project or business manager. He does not unilaterally decide. He manages the decision process so that differences are aired and trade-offs made in the interest of the whole. Thus he is left with the arduous task of influencing with limited formal authority. He must use his knowledge, competence, relationships, force of personality, and skills in group management to get people to do what is necessary to the success of the project or business.

This role of the matrix organization (business) boss creates both real and imagined demands for new behaviors that can be particularly anxiety producing for individuals who face the job for the first time. The matrix (business) manager must rely more heavily on his personal qualities, on his ability to persuade through knowledge about a program, business, or function. He must use communication and relationships to influence and move things along. His skills in managing meetings, in bringing out divergent points of view and, it is to be hoped, working through to a consensus are taxed more than the skills of general managers in conventional organizations.

Thus, for individuals who face these demands for the first time, the world is quite different. They can easily experience frustration, doubt, and loss of confidence as they begin to rely on new behaviors to get their job done. They begin to question their competence as they experience what in their eyes is a discrepancy between final and complete responsibility for a program and less certain means of gaining compliance from others. Some individuals learn the required new behaviors; others never do.

Not only does the actual and required change in behavior create a problem for new matrix organization business managers, but so does their own attitude toward the change. In our experience, individuals assigned to this role must first break through their perception of the job as impossible. Individuals who have spent all their time in traditional organizations have firmly implanted in their minds the notion of hierarchy and formal authority as the source of influence and power. They are convinced that the job cannot be done because they have never had to think through how power and influence, in reality, are wielded in the traditional organization. They cling to the myth that the formal power a boss has is what gives him influence.

This myth remains even after they themselves have developed and used other means of gaining influence. The myth about power and influence is often the first barrier that must be broken before the individual can be motivated to address the real demands for new behavior.

In his relations with his peers in both arms of the matrix organization, a business manager needs to assume a posture that blends reason and advocacy; bluster and threats are out. It is through these relations that he obtains the human resources needed to accomplish his goals. He has to expect that a number of these resources will be in short supply and that competing claims will have to be resolved.

In these dialogues the business manager must stand up for his requirements without developing a fatal reputation for overstating them. He must search with his peers for imaginative ways to share scarce resources. He must reveal any developing problems quickly while there is still time for remedial action. These actions do not come easily to managers conditioned in more traditional structures.

Last, in his relations with the various functional specialists represented on his team, the matrix organization business manager must establish a balanced or intermediate orientation. He cannot be seen as biased toward one function. He cannot have an overly long or short time horizon. His capacity to obtain a high-quality decision is dependent on an approach that seeks to integrate the views and orientations of all the various functions. If he shows a bias, team members will begin to distrust his objectivity and his capacity to be a fair arbiter of differences. This distrust can be the seed of a team's destruction.

For many individuals, this is a difficult task. A career spent in one side of the matrix structure creates a bias imperceptible to the individual but quite obvious to others. The need to wear multiple hats believably and equally well creates heavy attitudinal and behavioral demands.

It requires of an individual the capacity to have empathy with people in a number of functional areas and to identify with them while at the same time maintaining a strong personal concept and orientation that guides his own behavior and role performance.

Since the heir to the chief executive office is likely to come from this rank, there is generally a great, though diplomatic, battle going on for supremacy among the shared-subordinate bosses. The statesman's posture is an ingredient essential to success. The appearance of being threatened by sharing subordinates is fatal: This brands the individual as not being top management material.

Top leadership often uses the matrix structure to let the candidates for the top spar with each other in a constructive arena. The matrix structure is a better form than the pyramid for testing managers' ability to make things happen because of the strength of their personalities, their ability to lead, and the validity of their perceptions rather than because of their superior position in the hierarchy.

The perceptive matrix organization manager is aware that subordinates have other voices to attend to, other masters to please. Orders that seem irrational or unfair can more easily be circumvented under the protection of the other boss, than they can in a single chain of command. More care is therefore given to making clear the logic and importance of a directive.

For senior managers who must share their people with other senior managers, the matrix organization is both a training ground for how to assume the institutional reins and an incentive to go beyond having to share those reins equally with anyone else.

The rule for success in this role is to accept that while it can place contradictory demands on people, it is the best solution to accommodate simultaneous competing demands. Assume that there is no best way to organize; each alternative has equally important claims, and the correct choice is both—in varying proportions.

2-Boss Managers

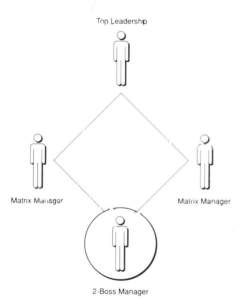

Top Leadership

Matrix Manager

Matrix Manager

2-Boss Manager

The most obvious challenge built into this matrix organization role is the sometimes conflicting demands of two bosses. For example, a representative from a manufacturing plant on a business team may know that his plant is having profitability problems and that the last thing the plant manager wants is to disrupt ongoing production activities with developmental work such as making samples or experimenting with a new process. Yet, as a business team member, the plant's representative may see the importance of doing these things immediately to achieve project success.

In this situation the individual in a 2-boss position experiences a great deal of anxiety and stress. These come from the difficulties of weighing the conflicting interests of his function and his project team. Both have legitimate viewpoints. But which is the more important viewpoint from the perspective of the whole organization? This is not an easy question to answer or an easy conflict to resolve. But added to this are the questions of identification and loyalty to the individual's function or business team and the consequences of rejection or even punishment from the side of the matrix organization that perceives it has lost in a given conflict. To compound the problem, even if the plant representative on a project team decides that he needs to go against what he knows is in the interest of his plant, how does he communicate this back to his organization members and convince them of the merits of his views? The same problem would exist if he were to favor his functional orientation and have to persuade the team that sample runs will have to be delayed.

We can see from this description and the earlier discussion that there are problems of dual group membership—new demands for communication, uncertainty about the kinds of commitment that can be made, uncertainties about how to influence other people in the function or team, and uncertainties created by a more generalist orientation not demanded in a conventional functional organization. There are of course differences in the capacity of individuals to deal with ambiguity, but all individuals new to matrix management lack some of the knowledge and the skills needed to navigate through the ambiguities and conflicts generated by a matrix organization.

Remember that this manager is also at the apex of his or her own pyramid—subordinates to this role need not be shared. It is the multiple demands from above and beyond the immediate command that must be managed. But his approach, to be successful, must be no different from that of the top role: Both must pay heed to competing demands, make trade-offs, and manage the conflicts that cannot be resolved. Any skillful politician knows that alternative sources of power increase one's flexibility. It is the unimaginative 2-boss manager who would trade extra degrees of freedom for finite and singular sources of action.

One operating manual for this role, developed after about a year's experience in a matrix organization, included the following points in a section titled "Practices for Managing Matrix Relationships":

- Lobby actively with relevant 2-boss counterparts and with your matrix bosses to win support before the event.

- Understand the other side's position in order to determine where trade-offs can be negotiated; understand where your objectives overlap.

- Avoid absolutes.

- Negotiate to win support on key issues that are critical to accomplishing your goals; try to yield only to the less critical points.

- Maintain frequent contact with top leadership to avoid surprises.

- Assume an active leadership role in all committees and use this to educate other matrix players; share information/help interpret.

- Prepare more thoroughly before entering any key negotiation than you would in nonmatrix situations; and use third-party experts more than normally.

- Strike bilateral agreements prior to meetings to disarm potential opponents.

- Emphasize and play on the supportive role that each of your matrix bosses can provide for the other.

- If all else fails:
  a. You can consider escalation (going up another level to the boss-in-common).
  b. You can threaten escalation.
  c. You can escalate.
- Before traveling this road, however, consider your timing. How much testing and negotiating should be done before calling for senior support? Does the top leadership want to be involved? When will they support and encourage your approach? Does escalation represent failure?

This kind of advice relies on managerial behavior, not on organization structure, for success. It sees personal style and influence as more important than power derived from either position or specialized knowledge. Success flows from facilitating decisions more than it does from making them. To remain flexible in this managerial role, it suggests, the manager must minimize the formal elements, move from fixture to actor, from bureaucracy to process.

The role problems of the 2-boss manager can of course become manageable in a mature matrix organization. This happens primarily because for the most part the functional and business managers learn to avoid making irreconcilable demands of their shared subordinates. This will still happen on occasion, however, even in a smoothly functioning matrix organization. In a familiar instance, the 2-boss manager may be directed to be in two places at the same time.

In addition to a balanced structure and shared roles, a matrix organization should have mechanisms for processing information along overlapping dimensions simultaneously. In a product-area matrix organization, a way of dealing with such situations is to establish the norm that the 2-boss individual is expected, and even directed, to convene a meeting between his two bosses to resolve any such conflict. The 2-boss manager is reprimanded only if he suffers such a conflict in silence.

Beyond handling such occasional problems, the 2-boss manager learns in a mature matrix organization that his role gives him a degree of influence not usually experienced at his level in a conventional organization. He not infrequently finds himself striking a balance in a discussion with his two bosses over some point of conflict. If he knows his facts and expresses his judgment on the merits of the particular issue, he often finds it is taken very seriously. This is the heart of training for general management.

This is exactly how the matrix organization is intended to work—with decisions being made at a level where the relevant information is concentrated and where time is available for a thorough airing of the options. In such a framework a higher percentage of decisions will, in fact, be given careful attention and decided on for their unique merits rather than in terms of a single orientation.

In reviewing the general characteristics of the mature matrix organization, we have emphasized the quality of flexibility. By looking in some detail at the four roles unique to the matrix, we have discovered where that flexibility comes from—from the individuals in key roles who have been challenged by the matrix structure to respond to each new situation in a fresh and flexible fashion. This constant pressure for fresh thinking and for learning in the mature matrix organization has, in fact, seemed to greatly increase the organization's productivity, especially at middle management levels. This may be fine for the organization, but how about the individuals as they initially face new and demanding role expectations? Is this a problem or an opportunity? In most cases it is probably both.

The Future of the Mature Matrix

A matrix organization includes matrix behavior, matrix systems, and a matrix culture, as well as a matrix structure. After years of working with a matrix, some organizations find that they no longer need the contradictory architecture of the matrix structure to accomplish their goals. Instead, they revert to the simpler pyramid for their structural form, while at the same time retaining the dual or multiple perspective in their managerial behavior, in their information processing, and in the culture of their firms.

This interpretation suggests that the matrix organization is not likely to become the dominant feature in the *structure* of American organizations. Its utility is more likely to be in helping organizations become more flexible in their responses to environmental pressures. Structures are intended to channel people's behavior in desired ways. Like laws, they are strongest when they are not invoked or tested. To the extent that managers behave effectively, they have little need to bump up against formal structures and reporting walls. In traditional pyramids, managers were always bumping against something—either the structure was centralized, and there wasn't enough freedom, or it was decentralized, and there wasn't enough control.

Organizations with mature matrix structures therefore appear to follow one of two paths, and the extent to which the structural framework survives depends on the path an organization takes. One is to maintain dual command, shared use of human resources, and an enriched information-processing capacity. The other is to maintain matrix behavior, matrix systems, and a matrix style or culture, but without using the matrix's structural form. Some organizations tear down the matrix entirely and revert to the traditional forms, practices, and managerial behavior of the pyramid.

The distinction between a pathological breakdown and an evolutionary rotation, where the matrix is a transitional form, is a matter of interpretation. As we observe the change in these organizations we may ask, was the matrix thrown out or did the firm grow beyond it? The distinction is more than academic. As long as the environmental pressures that initially propelled an organization into a matrix structure remain, the original inadequacies of the pyramid form will reappear if the matrix structure is actually abandoned. Our observations suggest that this would be fairly evident in three to six months and painfully obvious within one to one and a half years.

Because the structural element of the matrix is so fiendishly difficult to many, we observe organizations trying to shed the form while maintaining the substance. Our diagnosis is that it can be done successfully only where appropriate matrix behavior is so internalized by all significant members that no one notices the structural shift. Even then, however, we anticipate that through the years the structural imbalances will increase.

Where We Stand on the Learning Curve

Not too many years ago few managers in our classrooms had heard of matrix organization, and today nearly half of them raise their hands when asked whether they work in a matrix organization. Objectively, this self-reporting is inaccurate. What is relevant, however, is the perception itself. Like Molière's gentleman who was surprised to learn that he had been speaking prose all his life, many managers find that they have been "matrixing" all along. The word is jargon, but the grammar connotes people's behavior more than the form of their organization. The unrealistically high self-reporting also demonstrates an increasing comfort and familiarity with the idea among a very large body of executives.

Our major purposes have been to broaden traditional treatments of the matrix structure by demonstrating its applicability in diverse settings and by suggesting ways to change a seemingly radical conception into a familiar and legitimate design. The matrix structure seems to have spread despite itself. It is complex and difficult; it requires human flexibility in order to provide organizational flexibility. But the reverse is also true. For these reasons, we believe, many managers shied away. The academic literature, until now, has limited the utility of the matrix structure to high-technology project organizations. We have shown how both in organization theory and in application, the matrix structure has a much broader applicability. Behavioral descriptions were replete with words like "tension," "conflict," and "confusion." For many it was not pleasant, but it seemed to improve performance. Success gave it legitimacy, and as the concept spread, familiarity seemed to reduce the resistance.

Matrix structure gained acceptance in the space age of the late 1960s. In fact, for a while in the early 1970s it almost seemed to be a fad. Organizations that should never have used it experimented with the form. It was in danger of becoming another hot item from the behavioral science grab bag for business. When this occurred, the results were usually disastrous, thus fueling the sense that if an organization played with the matrix structure it might easily get burned. Despite many misadventures, however, the matrix structure gained respectability. What was necessary was made desirable.

More organizations are feeling the pressure to respond to two or more critical aspects of their businesses simultaneously—that is, to consider and organize by function *and* by product, by service *and* by market area at the same time. There is also increasing pressure to improve information-processing capacity, and recent technological advances make multiple matrix systems feasible. Last, it is clear that there is an increased sense of the scarcity of all resources and hence pressures for achieving economies of scale. As we described, these were the necessary and sufficient conditions for the emergence of matrix organizations in the first place. Because these conditions are increasingly prevalent, we feel that more organizations will be forced to consider the matrix organizational form.

Each organization that turns to the matrix structure has a larger and more varied number of predecessors that have charted the way. Despite our belief that matrix structures must be grown from within, the examples of wider applicability must nevertheless suggest that we are dealing less and less with an experiment and more and more with a mature formulation in organization design. Familiarity, here, reduces fear. As more organizations travel up the matrix structure learning curve, the curve itself becomes an easier one to climb. Similarly, as more managers gain experience operating in matrix organizations they are bound to spread this experience as some of them move into other organizations on their career journeys.

When pioneers experiment with new forms of organization, the costs are high and there are usually many casualties. In the case of the matrix structure, this has been true for both organizations and individuals. As the matrix has become a more familiar alternative, however, the costs and pressures have been reduced. Today, we believe that the concept is no longer a radical one; the understanding of the design is widespread, and the economic and social benefits have increased.

People in the Middle Ages had a very clear view of the world order. Galileo changed that. Newton changed the view of universal order once more, and Einstein did too in a later age. In each period there was certainty of the logic and correctness of the structure of the universe. And each period lasted until a new formulation posed a previously unthinkable question. After varying periods of resistance or adjustment, people become comfortable with the new formulation and in each instance assume it to be the final word.

The organization of large numbers of people to accomplish uncertain, complex, and interdependent tasks is currently nowhere as susceptible to the same exactness in calculation as the physical world. And there are those who would say that to compare the world of physics and the world of organizations is to compare the sacred with the profane. But the process of acceptability and then increased applicability of new formulations is similar, even if rather more humble. We believe, therefore, that in the future, matrix organizations will become almost commonplace and that managers will speak less of the difficulties of the matrix structure and will take more of its advantages almost for granted.

Selected Bibliography

Chris Argyris's "Today's Problems with Tomorrow's Organizations" (*Journal of Management Studies*, February 1967, p. 31–55) is an empirical study of nine British matrix organizations. The study is positive about the structure, but demonstrates how implementation has been unsuccessful because of traditional management behavioral styles. Arthur G. Butler's "Project Management: A Study in Organizational Conflict" (*Academy of Management Journal*, March 1973, pp. 8–101) contains an excellent review of the project management literature and deals extensively with the conflict faced by professionals involved in project work. David I. Cleland and William R. King's *Systems Analysis and Project Management* (McGraw-Hill, 1968) is one of the best and most thorough books available that explains project management and locates it in the larger setting of systems and organization theory. And Stanley M. Davis's "Two Models of Organization: Unity of Command versus Balance of Power" (*Sloan Management Review*, Fall 1974, pp. 29–40) spells out the basic theories and how they evolved in both domestic and international organizations.

Jay R. Galbraith's "Matrix Organization Design" (*Business Horizons*, February 1971, pp. 29–40) contains a fictitious case through which the author describes the decisions involved in adding a product orientation to a functional organization until an appropriate balance is reached. The article delimits the boundaries of matrix organization. William C. Goggin's "How the Multidimensional Structure Works at Dow-Corning" (*Harvard Business Review*, January–February 1974, pp. 54–65) is a case description of how Dow-Corning expanded a matrix form of organization into one that added an area dimension to the product and function areas plus a fourth dimension to consider organizational evolution. And Sherman K. Grinnell and Howard P. Apple's "When Two Bosses Are Better than One" (*Machine Design*, January 9, 1975, pp. 84–87) includes brief but practical guidelines on when to use a matrix organization and how to make it work.

Leonard R. Sayles's recent article in *Organizational Dynamics*, "Matrix Management: The Structure with a Future" (Autumn 1976, pp. 2–18), expresses a viewpoint similar to our own and has developed a suggestive typology that encompasses five different types of matrix structures.

Chapter 6

Managing Organizational Change

Even an appropriate organizational design has a limited lifetime. Inevitable changes in a company's environment—whether cultural, economic, or technological—create misfits and their associated problems. Consequently, an important aspect of managerial work involves the *process* of managing changes in organizational design. The remainder of this book focuses on such processes.

Organizational Change Strategies and Tactics

Just as there are different types of job designs, compensation systems, and training programs, there are also different approaches to planning and implementing changes in those systems.

Strategically, managers sometimes try to introduce organizational change quickly—in a matter of days or weeks, perhaps even before people realize what has happened. At other times, they proceed slowly; change efforts have taken years before they are successfully completed. Managers sometimes involve no one but themselves in the planning and execution of a change; at other times, they involve many people—perhaps everyone affected by the change.

In dealing with specific individuals or groups of individuals, managers can employ many tactics to implement an organizational change. These tactics include:

- Persuading people about the change's merits.
- Forcing or coercing people to accept the change without resistance.
- Offering people some compensation in lieu of what they will lose due to the change.
- Supporting people emotionally or with education to help them accept the change.
- Scaring people into accepting the change.

- Asking people to participate and help in designing or implementing the change.
- Co-opting people—making them feel as if they are participating.

The appropriateness of these tactics varies in different change efforts.

Problem-Solving Change versus Developmental Change

Organizational change efforts exist on a continuum where at one extreme a company attempts to solve some current organizational problem and at the other extreme attempts to prevent problems from emerging in the future. Most change efforts are somewhere between the extremes. Distinguishing between problem-solving and developmental change is also important because managers tend to approach these two kinds of change efforts using different strategies and tactics.

Choices

In managing organizational change, managers are confronted with many choices. They must decide:

1. How much change to try to accomplish.
2. How much effort will be directed at problem-solving versus developmental change.
3. What specific strategy and tactics to use.

The difficulties inherent in making these choices are increased by the number of options possible in any instance. The remainder of this book is designed to help develop decision-making abilities in these areas. Part Four focuses mostly on problem-solving change while Part Five focuses on developmental change.

PART FOUR

Part Four shifts from questions of organizational design to issues associated with implementing changes in design tools to solve organizational problems regardless of the type of organization involved.

Managers who attempt to introduce major organizational changes often run into problems of human resistance. The text in this part provides a framework for analyzing such resistance and for selecting appropriate change strategies and tactics. The cases present examples of different change strategies and tactics. The readings provide specific discussions of two different approaches to change: strategies aimed at minimizing any resistance and strategies aimed at overcoming resistance.

Chapter 7

Organizational Change Strategies and Tactics

Solving and avoiding organizational problems inevitably involves the introduction of organizational change. When the required changes are small and isolated, they usually can be accomplished without major problems. However, when they are large and involve many people and subunits, they often can cause significant problems.

Managing the change process is a critical skill for any manager. Very few organizations exist in a static state; the world is constantly changing. Outside the organization, in the space of a fiscal year, product development cycles go from two years to six months, because customers demand new products, better, and faster. Governments impose new regulations, and/or remove others. The financial environment becomes difficult to predict. Communications across organizations is intense and rapid, as the business environment becomes more global.

This kind of change in the competitive environment has an effect on organizations as well. They must seek and adopt more effective ways to set strategies, to market and manufacture products, to work effectively in an ever changing environment. Most organizations have to make major changes in their management style, beliefs, systems, and perhaps even culture in order to meet this challenge. Whereas some companies make changes in their design factors and their management styles very easily, most do it with great difficulty. They become accustomed to their proven ways of managing, even if those ways are no longer as effective as they once were.

A Model for Assessing the Need for Change

Several factors need to be examined before one begins a change process. Managers can use the concepts of "fit" presented in the first parts of this text to analyze the organization's design problems. The ideas presented in this chapter will address ways to assess the need for organizational change, develop the "vision" for change, design implementation plans for change, and manage the change process. The ideas presented here can apply equally to managers at any organizational level.

Most organizations have a difficult time in preparing the organization for change. Once the organization is ready to change, it is often difficult to implement and sustain the process. Managers who are supporters of the change often meet resistance from many fronts. One president of a hotel company, for example, believes that the managers should be more attentive to the levels of service in their units. He exhorts them to change in a speech at the annual meeting; they all leave convinced that their unit will offer the best service imaginable. Once they return to their units, however, the speeches and new ideas fade in the day to day processes of the organization. Clearly, the change effort was not effective. If we look at the above example in terms of the model presented below, we can understand why.

There are many ways to conceptualize the change process.[1] We have found that change is more likely to be effective when the costs of making the change are outweighed by factors which create the motivation to change. The relationship can be explained as follows:[2]

$$\text{Change} = D \times M \times P > C$$

where D = the levels of dissatisfaction with the status quo, M = the new model for managing implicit in the change, P = the planned implementation process for making the change, and C = the cost of the change to the relevant stakeholders, the individuals, and groups in the organization.

Change can occur only when sufficient dissatisfaction (D) with the status quo is present in key individuals or groups, such as the Hotel President in our example. These individuals have to articulate the new way of managing (M) which is necessary to make the changes. In our previous example, it was to pay more attention to customer service as a management tool. While most companies have articulated some kind of vision statement, the model for management is the way that managers have to put the vision into managerial practice. Finally, the organization has to have a process (P) for managing the change that is sufficiently well-planned, anticipates that resistance to the change will occur, understands where that resistance will come from, and outlines effective intervention methods for dealing with these changes. Unfortunately for our Hotel President, this is the piece he missed. Exhortation through speeches will not suffice. All of these variables combined must be greater than the cost (C) of the change economically and emotionally to the organization in question.

---

[1]See Michael Beer, *Organization Change and Development,* Scott, Foresman and Company, 1980; Richard Beckhard and Reuben T. Harris, *Organizational Transitions,* Addison-Wesley Publishing Company, 1987; and Rosabeth Kanter, *The Change Masters,* Simon and Schuster, 1983 for three examples.

[2]Michael Beer, *Organizational Change and Development,* Scott, Foresman and Co., 1980.

Creating Dissatisfaction

Most dissatisfaction comes when key organizational members recognize a crisis. A major customer suddenly shifts to another supplier. The bottom falls out of the market and managers are forced to make layoffs. Examples of organizational crises are as numerous as examples of the often traumatic change that results. However, a prescient manager is always looking for ways for the organization to improve continuously. S/he is constantly on the lookout for ways to make the organization more effective, and looks to communicate these ideas as a way to generate dissatisfaction with the status quo.

Often these ideas come from many sources. One source is from the competitive environment. Perhaps the hotel staff does not see the effects of poor service on customers—what difference can one angry customer make? Another source is the employees within the organization itself; the annual employee attitude surveys can be a powerful tool for diagnosing the culture and style of the organization. If the employees seem to be demoralized, dissatisfaction is present. In order to spread the word about the dissatisfaction present, to make it more known around the organization so as to arouse people to change, managers must communicate this concern through their letters, memos, actions, and expectations.

Developing a New Model for Managing

A vision of the future state, the structures and systems of the organization as well as the behaviors and attitudes of the employees, is essential for a change to occur. The vision a manager has of his/her unit or company's future can energize change, by uniting the people in a common goal. It also serves as a road map for change; establishing this model across the organization can be a planning exercise on just what the organizational problems are, and the solutions for them. Managers arrive at this vision through discussion, analysis, and observation. It should specify the "fit" of all the organization's elements, and be viable and adaptable over the long term.

At times the vision originates in a small part of the organization which itself serves as the role model for change. For example, one manufacturing company had a group of employees who focussed on improving the cross-functional processes involved while they worked on developing a new product. Their results were so successful that they not only cut the introduction time from two years to one, but they also improved cross functional communication at the same time. Senior managers were so impressed by their efforts that they developed a "vision" of the organization as one which focussed on process as well as on product, and developed a detailed model and plan for implementing process and product teams across the organization.

Managing the Process for Change

Having a vision of what ought to be does not translate directly into organizational life, however. Managers must work to develop a process for the implementation of the model they hold. This process is the sequence of events, meetings, speeches, communiques, celebrations, and design factor changes (personnel decisions, reward system changes, structural changes) directed at helping the model become a reality.

The readings at the end of this chapter describe particular methods managers can use to implement the process of change. These include[3] building a coalition of backers and supporters, articulating and communicating the shared vision through symbols, signals, and rewards, assigning responsibility and accountability, ensuring communication, education, and training, and constantly monitoring the process as it goes forward. The particular strategies one uses to implement the desired change depends on many factors, most notably the amount and kind of resistance encountered, the position of the change initiator relative to the resistors, the sources of data and the energy of the change initiators for managing the implementation, and the stakes involved. These can be partially understood by looking at the costs of the change to those affected by it.

Costs of the Change

Change does not occur without costs to some parts of the organization. For example, the employee who has been used to performing one job the same way for years, who has developed a routine for work, may be terrified at the prospect of becoming a member of a self-managing work team where s/he is required to perform many tasks. The costs can be expressed in terms of the losses those with a stake in the change feel will occur. For some it is power, or a sense of competence, or a key relationship, or a sense of identity, or perhaps a key intrinsic or extrinsic reward. For whatever reason, understanding the costs to key individuals is crucial to planning the process of change.

It is useful for the change initiator to perform an assessment of each stakeholder affected by a change. What is that person's "stake" in the status quo? What do they believe they will lose? How can the cost of the change be decreased for that stakeholder? What techniques can one use to deflect the resistance that stakeholder will present? These data should be used in the planning of the change process itself.

Taken together, this model becomes a powerful tool for making sure a manager has considered all of the aspects of a change before embarking on one. Most managers can see the places where misfits or mismatches occur, and most have a particular view of where they would like to see the organization (or division or unit) be in the future. By understanding the nature and source of the resistance to the new model, the manager can plan the process to deal with that resistance.

---

[3]Rosabeth Kanter, *The Change Masters,* Simon and Schuster, 1983.

Human Resistance to Change

Human resistance to change takes many forms—from open rebellion to subtle, passive resistance. It emerges for many reasons—rational and irrational. Some reasons are primarily self-centered; others are selfless.

Politics and Power Struggles

One major reason that people resist organizational change is that they see they will lose something of personal value due to the change. Resistance in these cases is often called "politics" or "political behavior" because people focus on their own interests and not the total organization.[4]

After years of rapid growth, for example, the president of one organization decided that its size demanded the creation of a new staff function—new-product planning and development—to be headed by a vice president. Operationally, this change eliminated most of the decision-making power that the vice presidents of marketing, engineering, and production had over new products. Inasmuch as new products were important in this organization, the change also reduced the status of marketing, engineering, and production VPs. Yet, status was important to those three vice presidents. During the two months after the president announced his idea for a new-product vice president, the existing vice presidents each came up with six or seven reasons why the new arrangement might not work. Their objections grew louder and louder until the president shelved the new job idea.

In another example, a manufacturing company traditionally employed a large group of personnel people as counselors to production employees. This group of counselors exhibited high morale because of the professional satisfaction they received from the helping relationships they had with employees. When a new performance-appraisal system was installed, the personnel people were required to provide each employee's supervisor with a written evaluation of the employee's emotional maturity, promotion potential, and so on, every six months. As some personnel people immediately recognized, the change would alter their relationship with most employees—from a peer helper to more of a boss/evaluator. Predictably, they resisted the new system. While publicly arguing that the new system was not as good for the company as the old one, they privately put as much pressure as possible on the personnel vice president until he significantly altered the new system.

Political behavior emerges in organizations because what is in the best interests of one individual or group is sometimes not in the best interests of the total organization or of other individuals and groups. The consequences of organizational change efforts often are good for some people and bad for others. As a result, politics and power struggles often emerge through change efforts.

---

[4]For a discussion of power and politics in corporations, see Abraham Zaleznik and Manfred F. R. Kets De Vries, *Power and the Corporate Mind* (Boston: Houghton Mifflin, 1975), chap. 6; and Robert H. Miles, *Macro Organizational Behavior* (Santa Monica, Calif.: Goodyear Publishing, 1978), chap 4.

While this political behavior sometimes takes the form of two or more armed camps publicly fighting it out, it usually is subtle. In many cases, it occurs completely under the surface of public dialogue. In a similar way, although power struggles are sometimes initiated by scheming and ruthless individuals, they are fostered more often by those who view their potential loss as an unfair violation of their implicit, or psychological, contract with the organization.[5]

Misunderstanding and a Lack of Trust

People also resist change when they incorrectly perceive that it might cost them considerably more than they will gain. Such situations often occur when people are unable to understand the full implications of a change or when trust is lacking in the change initiator-employee relationship.[6]

For example, when the president of a small midwestern company announced to his managers that the company would implement a flexible work schedule for all employees, it never occurred to him that he might run into resistance. He had been introduced to the concept at a management seminar and decided to use it to make working conditions at his company more attractive, particularly to clerical and plant personnel. Shortly after the announcement to his managers, numerous rumors began to circulate among plant employees—none of whom really knew what flexible working hours meant and many of whom were distrustful of the manufacturing vice president. One rumor suggested that flexible hours meant that most people would have to work whenever their supervisors asked them to—including weekends and evenings. The employee association, a local union, held a quick meeting and then presented the management with a nonnegotiable demand that the flexible hours concept be dropped. The president, caught completely by surprise, decided to drop the issue.

Few organizations can be characterized as having a high level of trust between employees and managers; consequently, it is easy for misunderstandings to develop when change is introduced. Unless misunderstandings are surfaced and clarified quickly, they can lead to resistance.

Different Assessments of the Situation

Another common reason people resist organizational change is that their analysis of the situation differs from that of persons initiating the change. In such cases, their analysis typically sees more costs than benefits resulting from the change, for themselves and for their company.

For example, the president of one moderate-sized bank was shocked by his

---

[5]Edgar Schein, *Organizational Psychology* (Englewood Cliffs, N.J.: Prentice-Hall, 1965), p. 44.

[6]See Chris Argyris, *Intervention Theory and Method* (Reading, Mass.: Addison-Wesley Publishing, 1970), p. 70.

staff's analysis of their real estate investment trust (REIT) loans. Their complex analysis suggested that the bank could easily lose up to $10 million and that possible losses were increasing each month by 20 percent. Within a week, the president drew up a plan to reorganize the bank division that managed REITs. However, because of his concern for the bank's stock price, he chose not to release the staff report to anyone except the new REIT section manager. The reorganization immediately ran into massive resistance from the people involved. The group sentiment, as articulated by one person, was "Has he gone mad? Why is he tearing apart this section of the bank? His actions have already cost us three very good people [who quit] and have crippled a new program we were implementing [which the president was unaware of] to reduce our loan losses."

Persons who initiate change sometimes incorrectly assume that they have all relevant information required to conduct an adequate organizational analysis. They often assume that persons affected by the change have the same basic facts, when they do not. In either case, the difference in information that groups work with often leads to differences in analysis, which can lead to resistance. Moreover, insofar as the resistance is based on a more accurate analysis of the situation than that held by persons initiating the change, that resistance is good for the organization, a fact that is not obvious to some managers who assume resistance is always bad.[7]

Fear

People sometimes resist change because they know or fear they will not be able to develop the new skills and behaviors required. All human beings are limited in their ability to change their behavior, with some people more limited than others.[8] Organizational change can inadvertently require people to change too much, too quickly. When such a situation occurs, people typically resist the change—sometimes consciously but often unconsciously.

Peter Drucker has argued that the major obstacle to organization growth is managers' inability to change their attitudes and behaviors.[9] In many cases, he points out, corporations grow to a certain point and then slow down or stop growing because key managers are unable to change as rapidly as their organizations. Even if they intellectually understand the need for changes in how they operate, they sometimes cannot make the transition.

All people who are affected by change experience some emotional turmoil because change involves loss and uncertainty—even changes that appear positive or

[7]See Paul R. Lawrence, "How to Deal with Resistance to Change," *Harvard Business Review*, May–June 1954.

[8]For a discussion of resistance that is personality based, see Goodwin Watson, "Resistance to Change," in *The Planning of Change*, ed. Warren Bennis, Kenneth Benne, and Robert Chin (New York: Holt, Rinehart & Winston, 1969), pp. 489–93.

[9]*The Practice of Management* (New York: Harper & Row, 1954).

"rational."[10] For example, a person who receives a more important job as a result of an organizational change will probably be happy. But, it is possible that such a person feels uneasy. A new and different job will require new and different behavior, new and different relationships, and the loss of some current activities and relationships that provide satisfaction. It is common under such circumstances for a person to emotionally resist giving up certain aspects of the current situation.

Still Other Reasons

People also sometimes resist organizational change to save face; to go along with the change would be an admission that some of their previous decisions or beliefs were wrong. They may resist because of peer pressure or because of a supervisor's resistant attitude. Indeed, there are many reasons why people resist change.[11]

Because of all the reasons for resistance to organizational change, it is hardly surprising that organizations do not automatically and easily adapt to environmental, technological, or strategic changes. Indeed, organizations usually adapt only because managers successfully employ strategies and tactics for dealing with potential resistance.

Tactics for Dealing with Resistance

Managers may use a number of tactics to deal with resistance to change. These include education/communication, participation, facilitation and support, negotiation, co-optation, coercion, and manipulation.[12]

Education/Communication

One of the most common ways to deal with resistance to change is education and communication. This tactic is aimed at helping people see the need for and logic of a change. It can involve one-on-one discussions, presentations to groups, or memos and reports. For example, as a part of an effort to make changes in a division's structure, measurement system, and reward system, the division manager put together a one-hour audiovisual presentation that explained changes and their reasons for changes. Over a four-month period, he made this presentation a dozen times to groups of 20 or 30 corporate and divisional managers.

Education/communication is ideal when resistance is based on inadequate or inaccurate information and analysis, especially if the initiators need the resister's

---

[10]See Robert Luke, "A Structural Approach to Organizational Change," *Journal of Applied Behavioral Science,* 1973.

[11]For a general discussion of resistance and reasons for it, see Gerald Zaltman and Robert Duncan, *Strategies for Planned Change* (New York: John Wiley & Sons, 1977), chap. 3.

[12]There are many ways to label change tactics. This list of seven tactics is one useful approach. Other writers use variations of this list.

help in implementing the change. But, this tactic requires at least a good relationship between the initiators and the others, or the resisters may not believe what they hear. It also requires time and effort, particularly if many people are involved.

Participation

Participation as a change tactic implies that the initiators involve the resisters or potential resisters in some aspect of the design and implementation of the change. For example, the head of a small financial services company once created a task force to help design and implement changes in the company's reward system. The task force was composed of eight second- and third-level managers from different parts of the company. The president's specific request was that they recommend changes in the company's benefits package. They were given six months and were asked to file a brief progress report with the president once a month. After making their recommendations, which the president largely accepted, they were asked to help the firm's personnel director implement them.

Participation is a rational choice of tactics when change initiators believe they do not have all the information they need to design and implement a change or when they need the wholehearted commitment of others in implementing a change. Considerable research has demonstrated that participation generally leads to commitment, not just compliance.[13] But participation has drawbacks. It can lead to a poor solution if the process is not carefully managed, and it can be time consuming.

Facilitation and Support

Another way for managers to deal with potential resistance to change is through facilitation and support. As a tactic, it might include providing training in new skills, giving employees time off after a demanding period, or simply listening and providing emotional support.

For example, one rapidly growing electronics company did the following to help people adjust to frequent organizational changes. First, it staffed its human resource department with four counselors who spent most of their time talking to people who were feeling "burned out" or who were having difficulty adjusting to new jobs. Second, on a selective basis, it offered people "minisabbaticals," which were four weeks in duration and involved some reflective or educational activity away from work. Finally, it spent money on in-house education and training programs.

Facilitation and support are best suited for resistance due to adjustment problems. The basic drawback of this approach is that it can be time consuming and expensive and still fail.[14]

---

[13]See, for example, Alfred Marrow, David Bowers, and Stanley Seashore, *Management by Participation* (New York: Harper & Row, 1967).

[14]Zaltman and Duncan, *Strategies for Planned Change,* chap. 4.

Negotiation

Negotiation as a change tactic involves buying out active or potential resisters. This could mean, for example, giving a union a higher wage rate in return for a work rule change, or it could involve increasing an individual's pension benefits in return for early retirement.

Effective use of negotiation as a change tactic can be seen in the activities of a division manager in a large manufacturing company. The divisions in this company were highly interdependent. One division manager wanted to make some major changes in the division's organization. Yet, because of interdependencies, she recognized that she would be forcing some inconvenience and change on other divisions. To prevent top managers in other divisions from undermining her efforts, she negotiated with each division a written agreement that promised certain positive outcomes (for them) within certain time periods as a result of her changes and, in return, specified certain types of cooperation expected from the divisions during the change process. Later, whenever other divisions began to complain about changes or the process, she pulled out the negotiated agreements.

Negotiation is particularly appropriate when it is clear that someone will lose out as a result of a change and yet has significant power to resist. As a result, it can be an easy way to avoid major resistance in some instances. Like the other tactics, negotiation may become expensive—and a manager who once makes it clear that he or she will negotiate to avoid resistance opens up the possibility of being blackmailed by others.[15]

Co-optation

A fifth tactic managers use to deal with potential or actual resistance to change is co-optation. Co-opting an individual usually involves giving him or her a desirable role in the design or implementation of the change. Co-opting a group involves giving one of its leaders, or someone it respects, a key role in the design or implementation of a change. A change initiator could, for example, try to co-opt the sales force by allowing the sales manager to be privy to the design of the changes and by seeing that the most popular salesperson gets a raise as part of the change.

To reduce the possibility of corporate resistance to an organizational change, one division manager in a large multibusiness corporation successfully used co-optation in the following way. He invited the corporate human relations vice president, a close friend of the president's, to help him and key staff analyze some division problems. Because of his busy schedule, the corporate VP was not able to do much information gathering or analysis, thus limiting his influence on the diagnoses. But, his presence at key meetings helped commit him to the diagnosis and the solution designed by the group. The commitment was subsequently im-

---

[15]For an excellent discussion of negotiation, see Gerald Nierenberg, *The Art of Negotiating* (New York: Cornerstone, 1974).

portant because the president, at least initially, did not like some of the proposed changes. Nevertheless, after discussion with his human resource VP, he did not try to block them.

Co-optation can, under certain circumstances, be an inexpensive and easy way to gain an individual's or a group's support (less expensive, for example, than negotiation and quicker than participation). Nevertheless, it has drawbacks. If people feel they are being tricked into not resisting, they may respond negatively. And, if they use their ability to influence the design and implementation of changes in ways that are not in the best interests of the organization, they can create serious problems.

Manipulation

Manipulation, in this context, refers to covert influence attempts. Co-optation is a form of manipulation. Other forms do not have specific names but involve, for instance, the selective use of information and the conscious structuring of events so as to have some desired (but covert) impact on participants.

Manipulation suffers from the same drawbacks as co-optation, but to a greater degree. When people feel they are not being treated openly or that they are being lied to, they often react negatively. Nevertheless, manipulation can be used successfully—particularly when all other tactics are not feasible or have failed.[16] With one's back to the wall, with inadequate time to use education, participation, or facilitation, and without the power or other resources to use negotiation, coercion, or co-optation, a manager might resort to manipulating information channels to scare people into thinking there is a crisis coming that they can avoid only by change.

Coercion

The seventh tactic managers use to deal with resistance is coercion. They essentially force people to accept a change, explicitly or implicitly threatening them with the loss of jobs, promotion possibilities, raises, or whatever else they control. Like manipulation, coercion is a risky tactic because people resent forced change. Yet, coercion has the advantage of overcoming resistance quickly. And, in situations where speed is essential, this tactic may be the only alternative.

For example, when assigned to "turn around" a failing division in a large conglomerate, the chosen manager relied mostly on coercion to achieve the organizational changes she desired. She did so because she felt, "I did not have enough time to use other methods and I needed to make changes that were pretty unpopular among many of the people."

---

[16]See John P. Kotter, "Power, Dependence, and Effective Management," *Harvard Business Review,* July–August 1977, pp. 133–35.

Figure 7–1
Tactics for Dealing with Resistance to Change

Tactic	Best for:	Advantages	Drawbacks
Education/communication	Resistance based on lack of information or inaccurate information and analysis.	Once persuaded, people will often help with implementing the change.	Can be very time consuming if large numbers of people are involved.
Participation	Situations in which initiators do not have all the information needed to design the change and where others have considerable power to resist.	People who participate will be committed to implementing change. Any relevant information they have will be integrated into the change plan.	Can be time consuming. Participators could design an inappropriate change.
Facilitation and support	Dealing with people who are resisting because of adjustment problems.	No other tactic works as well with adjustment problems.	Can be time consuming, expensive, and still fail.
Negotiation	Situations where someone or some group will lose in a change and where they have considerable power to resist.	Sometimes it is an easy way to avoid major resistance.	Can be too expensive in many cases. Can alert others to negotiate for compliance.
Co-optation	Specific situations where the other tactics are too expensive or are not feasible.	Can help generate support for implementing a change (but less than participation).	Can create problems if people recognize the co-optation.
Manipulation	Situations where other tactics will not work or are too expensive.	Can be a quick and inexpensive solution to resistance problems.	Costs initiators some credibility. Can lead to future problems.
Coercion	When speed is essential and the change initiators possess considerable power.	Speed. Can overcome any kind of resistance.	Risky. Can leave people angry with the initiators.

Figure 7–2
Strategic Options for the Management of Change

Rapid changes	Slow changes
Clearly planned	Not clearly planned initially
Little involvement of others	Lots of involvement of others
Attempt to overcome any resistance	Attempt to minimize any resistance

Key Situational Variables
- The amount and type of resistance that is anticipated.
- The position of the initiators vis-à-vis the resisters (in terms of power, trust, etc.).
- The locus of relevant data for designing the change and of needed energy for implementing it.
- The stakes involved (e.g., the presence or absence of a crisis, the consequences of resistance and lack of change).

Using Change Tactics

Effective organizational change efforts are almost always characterized by the skillful use of a number of these change tactics. Conversely, less effective change efforts usually involve the misuse of one or more of these tactics.

Managers sometimes misuse change tactics simply because they are unaware of the strengths and limitations of each tactic (see Figure 7–1). Sometimes they run into difficulties because they rely only on the same limited number of tactics regardless of the situation (e.g., they always use participation and persuasion or coercion and manipulation).[17] Sometimes they misuse the tactics simply because they are not chosen and implemented as a part of a clearly considered change strategy.

Change Strategies

In approaching an organizational change situation, managers explicitly or implicitly make strategic choices regarding the speed of the effort, the amount of preplanning, the involvement of others, and the relative emphasis of different change tactics. Successful change efforts are those in which choices are both internally consistent and fit some key situation variables.

The strategic options available to managers exist on a continuum.[18] See Figure 7–2. At one end of the continuum, the strategy calls for a rapid implementation of changes, with a clear plan of action and little involvement of others. This type of

---

[17]Ibid., pp. 135–36.

[18]See Larry E. Greiner, "Patterns of Organizational Change," *Harvard Business Review,* May–June 1967; and Larry E. Greiner and Louis B. Barnes, "Organization Change and Development," in *Organization Change and Development,* ed. Gene Dalton and Paul Lawrence (Homewood, Ill.: Richard D. Irwin, 1970), p. 3–5.

strategy mows over any resistance and, at the extreme, would involve a fait ac-
compli. At the other end of the continuum, the strategy would call for a slower
change process that is less clearly planned from the start and that involves many
people in addition to the change initiators. This type of strategy is designed to
reduce resistance to a minimum.[19]

With respect to tactics, the farther to the left one operates on the continuum in
Figure 7–2, the more one uses coercion and the less one uses other tactics—
especially participation. The opposite is true the more one operates to the right on
the continuum—less coercion is used and other tactics are used more.

Exactly where a change effort should be strategically positioned on the continuum
in Figure 7–2 is a function of four key variables:

1. *The amount and type of resistance anticipated.* The greater the anticipated
resistance, other factors being equal, the more appropriate it is to move toward the
right on the continuum.[20] The greater the anticipated resistance, the more difficult
to simply overwhelm it and the more one needs to find ways to reduce it.

2. *The position of the initiator vis-à-vis the resisters, especially regarding power.*
The greater the initiator's power, the better the initiator's relationships with the
others; and the more the others expect that the initiator might move unilaterally,
the more one can move to the left on the continuum.[21] On the other hand, the
weaker the initiator's position, the more he or she is forced to operate to the right.

3. *The locus of relevant data for designing the change and of needed energy
for implementing it.* The more the initiators anticipate they will need information
from others to help design the change and commitment from them to help implement
it, the more they must move to the right.[22] Gaining useful information and commitment requires time and the involvement of others.

4. *The stakes involved.* The greater the short-run potential for risks to organizational performance and survival, the more one must move to the left.

Organizational change efforts that are based on an inconsistent strategy, or ones
that do not fit the situation, run into predictable problems. For example, an effort
that is not clearly planned but quickly implemented will almost always have unanticipated problems. Efforts that attempt to involve large numbers of people and
at the same time try to move quickly will always sacrifice either speed or involvement. Efforts in which the change initiators do not have all the information that
they need to correctly design a change but which nevertheless move quickly and
involve few others sometimes encounter enormous problems.

---

[19]For a good discussion of an approach that attempts to minimize resistance, see Renato Tagiuri, "Notes
on the Management of Change," Working Paper, Harvard Business School.

[20]Jay Lorsch, "Managing Change," pp. 676–78.

[21]Ibid.

[22]Ibid.

Implications for Managing Organizational Change

Organizational change efforts are aided by an analysis and planning process composed of the following three phases:

1. Conducting a thorough organizational analysis—one that identifies the current situation, any problems, and the forces that are possible causes of problems. The analysis must clearly specify:

    a. The actual significance of the problems.

    b. The speed with which the problems must be addressed if additional problems will be avoided.

    c. The types of changes needed.

2. Conducting a thorough analysis of factors relevant to implementing the necessary changes. This analysis focuses on questions of:

    a. Who might resist the changes, why, and to what extent.

    b. Who has information that is needed to design the change and whose cooperation is essential in implementing it.

    c. The position of the change initiator vis-à-vis other relevant parties in terms of power, trust, normal modes of interaction, and so forth.

3. Selecting a change strategy based on the analysis in Phases 1 and 2, a set of change tactics, and then designing an action plan that specifies:

    a. What must be done.

    b. By whom.

    c. In what sequence.

    d. Within what time frame.

When initiating and managing an organizational change, it is conceivable that some or all of these steps will need to be repeated if unforeseen events occur or if new and relevant information surfaces. At the extreme, in a highly participative change, the process might be repeated a dozen times over a period of months or years. The key to successful organizational change is not whether these steps are repeated once or many times but whether they are done competently and thoroughly.

Case 7–1

First National City Bank Operating Group (A)

John A. Seeger, Jay W. Lorsch, Cyrus F. Gibson

John Reed paced along the vast glass walls of his midtown Manhattan office, hardly noticing the panorama of rooftops spread out below him. One of 41 senior vice presidents of the First National City Bank, Reed, at 31, was the youngest man in the bank's history to reach this management level. He headed the bank's Operating Group (OPG)—the back office, which performed the physical work of processing Citibank's business transactions and designing its computer systems, as well as managing the bank's real estate and internal building services. Today, musing about the forthcoming 1971 operating year and his plans for the next five years, John Reed was both concerned and angry.

He was concerned that his recent reorganization of the Operating Group, though widely recognized as a success, was not sufficient. His area still followed the traditional working procedures of the banking business, and OPG was still seen by the rest of the bank as a necessary evil which, tolerated by its more intelligent brethren, should muddle along as it always had. After a year with OPG and five months as its head, he still had few concrete measures of its performance. But most of all, John Reed was concerned that his initial concept of what OPG needed—massive new computerized systems for coping with a growing mountain of paper-based transactions—might be both impractical and irrelevant. Reed's new staff assistant, Bob White, had been pushing hard for a change in management approach, to emphasize budgets, costs, and production efficiency instead of system development.

This case was prepared by John A. Seeger, Jay W. Lorsch, and Cyrus F. Gibson.
Copyright © 1974 by the President and Fellows of Harvard College. Harvard Business School case 474–165.

And, uncharacteristically, John Reed was angry. He looked again at the management report he had received the day before. Only now, in September, had he learned that his manpower had grown by 400 people in July and August. Maybe Bob White really had something in his stress on control and management.

First National City Bank

The Operating Group was one of the six major divisions established in a reorganization of Citibank at the end of 1968. The five market-oriented divisions, shown in the organization chart in Exhibit 1, generated varying demands for OPG services; all of them were looking forward to continued growth in 1971, and all were pressing for improved performance by the Operating Group.

Citibank's Personal Banking Group (PBG), with 181 branches and 6,000 employees, provided a full range of services to consumers and small businesses in the metropolitan New York area. As the area's leading retail bank, PBG projected a 3 percent annual growth in checking account balances and a 2 percent annual growth in savings accounts over the next several years; in addition to an increase in number of accounts, PBG anticipated continuation of the recent trend toward more activity per account.

The Investment Management Group, with 1,700 employees, managed assets for personal and institutional investors, and provided full banking services to wealthy individuals. In the latter category, the group currently carried some 7,000 accounts, and it hoped to increase this figure by 25 percent in the next four years.

The Corporate Banking Group (CBG), itself subdivided into six industry specialist divisions, served big business (generally, companies with more than $20 million in annual sales), financial institutions, and government accounts within the United States. CBG aimed at an annual growth rate over 5 percent, but qualified its ambitions: In order to gain market share in the increasingly competitive world of the major corporations, the bank would have to improve both its pricing structures and the quality of its services. Operating Group errors, CBG said, had irritated many major accounts, and OPG's reputation for slow, inaccurate service made expansion of market share very difficult.

The Commercial Banking Group operated 16 regional centers in the New York area to serve medium-sized companies, most of which did not employ their own professional finance executives and thus relied upon the bank for money advice as well as banking services. The fastest-growing group of the bank, Commercial Banking projected an annual growth rate of about 10 percent.

The International Banking Group (IBG) operated some 300 overseas branches, in addition to managing several First National City Corporation subsidiary units concerned with foreign investments, services, and leasing. Although IBG conducted its own transaction processing at its overseas centers, still its rapid growth would nevertheless present new demands on the Operating Group in Manhattan. All business originating in New York was handled by Reed's people, and the IBG complement of 160 New York-based staff officers was expected to double in five years.

Worldwide, First National City Corporation had shown assets of $23 billion in

Exhibit 1
Institutional Organization, 1970

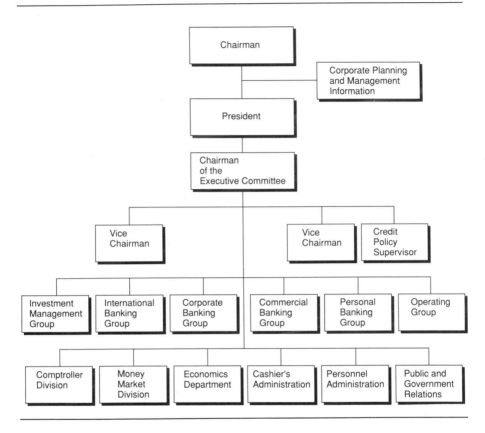

its financial statement of December 31, 1969. Earnings had been $131 million after taxes (but before losses on securities traded). The corporation employed 34,000 people, having doubled its staff in the previous 10 years, while tripling its assets. Citibank's published goals for financial performance presented another source of pressure for improvement in OPG: Board Chairman Walter B. Wriston had recently committed the bank to an annual growth rate of 15 percent in earnings per share of common stock. President William Spencer had made it clear to Reed that OPG was expected to contribute to this gain in earnings.

The Operating Group's Functions

As the bank had grown, so had its back office. Increases in services offered, in customers, in volume per customer, and in staff all meant added transactions to be processed by OPG. As the volume of paper flowing through the bank increased, so did the staff and budget of the back office. In 1970, John Reed had some 8,000 people on his group payroll, and he would spend $105 million on the direct production of the bank's paperwork. For several years, transaction volume had increased at an annual rate of 5 percent; OPG's total expenditures had grown faster, however, at an average of 17.9 percent per year since 1962.

OPG headquarters was a 25-story building at 111 Wall Street, several miles south of the bank's head offices at 399 Park Avenue. The volume and variety of work flowing through this building were impressive; in a typical day, OPG would:

- Transfer $5 billion between domestic and foreign customers and banks.
- Process $2 billion worth of checks—between 1.5 million and 2 million individual items.
- Start and complete 900 jobs in the data processing center, printing 5 million lines of statements, checks, and other reports.
- Process $100 million worth of bill and tax payments for major corporations and government agencies. (During the 16 weeks between February 1 and May 30, the group also processed 50,000 income tax returns per day for the City of New York.)
- Handle 102,000 incoming and outgoing telephone calls and 7,000 telegrams and cables.
- Mail out 30,000 checking account statements and 25,000 other items, requiring postage expenditures of $10,000 a day.

Operating Group Organization

In 1969, John Reed transferred into OPG from the International Banking Group to become a vice president of the bank and to set up a task force pointed toward reorganization of the group. He had assembled a team of young, technically oriented managers (most of them relatively new to OPG) to analyze and rearrange the basic functions of the group. Systematically, this task force had examined the structure and function of each OPG subdepartment, working with the line managers to question where the subgroups fit in the organization; to whom their managers reported and why; what processes and technologies they shared with other groups; and how the physical output of each group affected the operation of the next sequential processing step. The result of this study was a complete realignment of reporting responsibilities, pulling together all those groups doing similar work, and placing them under unified management.

A leading member of OPG's systems management team during this reorganization effort was Larry Small, who had followed Reed from the planning staff at the IBG in 1969. Small, a 1964 graduate of Brown University (with a degree in Spanish literature), set the keynote for the task force approach with his concept of basic management principles:

> Managing simply means understanding, in detail—in *meticulous* detail—where you are now, where you have to go, and how you will get there. To know where they are now, managers must measure the important features of their systems. To know where they are going, managers must agree on their objectives, and on the specific

Exhibit 2
Basic Organization: Operating Group

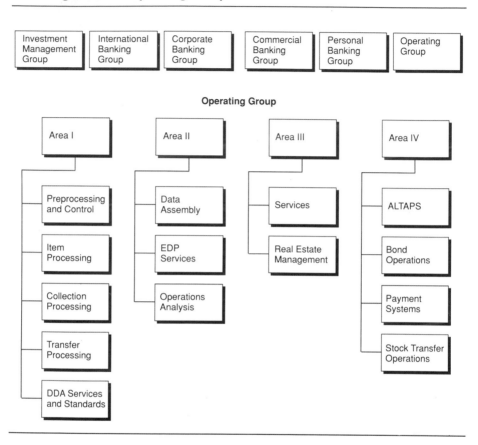

Exhibit 2
Basic Organization: Operating Group

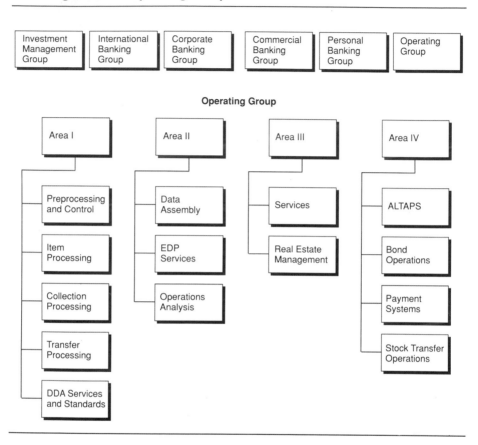

desired values of all those measured factors. And to know how to get there, managers must understand the processes which produce their results. Significant change demands the participation of the people involved, in order to gain the widespread understanding required for success. Management is essentially binary; all change efforts will be seen as either successes or failures. Success follows from understanding.

Few major changes in equipment or physical space were required by the new organization, and the approach characterized by Small's statement made the transition an easy one. By late 1969, OPG was running smoothly under a four-area structure as shown in Exhibit 2.

Area I was the operating part of the Operating Group; it included the people who processed the transactions that constituted the bank's business. Area I operated the computer systems, processed checks for collection from other banks, posted the accounts for Citibank's customers, transferred funds from one customer to another, and prepared customers' bank statements.

Area II encompassed system design and software for computer operations; it was the intellectual side of OPG, developing new computer systems for the use of Area I. The subgroups in charge of operations analysis, management information systems, and data control also belonged to Area II, as did the programming group in charge of ALTAPS, a new automated loan and time payment processing system.

Area III, quite removed from OPG's paper-oriented processing groups, was a freestanding organization in charge of Citibank's real estate, physical facilities, and building services. (When he was not concerned about processing transactions in the back office, Reed could worry about the quality of cafeteria food and the cleanliness of the bathrooms.)

Area IV was composed of the relatively low-volume, high-value transaction-processing departments—stock transfer, corporate bonds, corporate cash management, mutual funds, and government services.

In addition to the routine of day-to-day operations, Reed was responsible for the long-range development of both hardware and software systems. For several years, a subsidiary of the bank—with operations in Cambridge, Massachusetts, and California—had been working on the kind of on-line systems and terminals that would be required to support the checkless society which the financial community expected would some day replace paper-based record processing. Reed had decided to maintain the separation of this advanced research and development activity from OPG. "Let's face it," he said, "the computer systems we have now will never evolve into the systems needed for point-of-sale transaction processing. When those new systems come, they'll come as a revolution—a total replacement of existing technology. We should develop the new systems, sure. But we shouldn't let them screw up the systems we need today and tomorrow in the meantime."

In September 1970, John Reed, feeling comfortable with the overall structure of OPG but impatient with its lack of measured progress, had assigned Small to head Area IV. Small's demonstrated skills in management of change held out the promise that this highly sensitive area, where any errors could cause major problems for the bank's most important customers, would soon be under more effective control. Now Reed was considering the future course of Area I, where even more people and dollars were involved.

Area I: The Demand Deposit Account System

The largest single job performed by OPG was demand deposit accounting (DDA), the complex process of handling the physical flow of paper and communications, posting transactions, distributing processed items, and producing the bank's daily statement of operating condition. Some 2,000 employees in Area I performed this work. The process was composed of three parts: the "front end," which received, encoded, and read transactions into magnetic computer tapes; the data center, which sorted the data and printed statements; and the "back end," which microfilmed and filed the checks of Citibank's own customers, prepared and mailed their statements, and handled accounting exceptions.

Around the clock, mail sacks containing checks, deposit slips, travelers' checks, transfer vouchers, credit memos, and other paper transaction records arrived in the eighth-floor receiving room at 111 Wall Street to enter the front end of the demand deposit accounting system. The first step of that process was to weigh the bags, gauging the volume of work coming in: one pound of mail equaled about 300 items to be processed.

Each incoming mailbag contained a control sheet, listing the various bundles of checks and the aggregate total of the bundles. Contents were checked against control sheets to ensure that all bundles listed were actually received. From this point onward in the DDA system, each batch of material was signed for whenever it moved from one area of responsibility to another. The records of these transfers, together with any changes in batch totals as discrepancies were discovered or generated, were accumulated by a proof clerk on each operating shift. The following morning, these proof worksheets were consolidated into the bank's daily report of its operating condition, as required by the Federal Reserve System.

Materials arriving from other banks and check clearinghouses were already partly processed, but items from domestic Citibank branches, the head office, mail deposits, and lockboxes had to be encoded with machine-readable information. These papers were distributed to one of the 150 magnetic-ink encoding machines, where operators would key the dollar amounts into a keyboard. The machines would print these amounts on the checks, accumulating batch totals for each 300 checks processed. Some machines had several pockets, and sorted the work into different pockets for different kinds of media, adding up separate control totals for each pocket. As the pockets filled up, the paper was unloaded into conveyor trays, to be transported to the next operation, where the checks were read by machines and sorted by their destination, while the information from the checks was recorded on computer tape.

Encoder operators were generally women, who worked on an incentive pay arrangement and processed 800 to 1,100 items per hour. No direct record of keypunching accuracy was kept, and operators were not penalized for errors. About 600,000 checks each day entered the back end of Citibank's process, where they were microfilmed, screened for exceptions, and filed by customer for rendition and mailing of statements.

At the read/sort machines, on the floor above, the paper media were sorted into two major classifications. "On us" checks—those written against the accounts of Citibank's own customers—were directed to the back end of the DDA system; "transit" checks, written on other banks, were directed to the various check clearinghouses and exchanges. Firm deadlines held for these exchanges. For example, the major Manhattan banks met at 10 A.M. each morning to trade checks with each other, and to settle the differences between the checks paid and collected for other banks. This meeting had been a New York tradition for well over a hundred years; banks were not late for the exchange.

Overdrafts, stop payment orders, and "no-post" items were listed by the computer and referred to exception clerks, who searched through the incoming paper for the offending items, in order to route them to the proper offices for special handling. No-posts were especially troublesome; about 1,300 items per day, with an average value of $1,000 each, would flow into the back end, destined for accounts that had been closed, or were burdened by attachments, or had invalid numbers, or belonged to recently deceased owners, or were suspected of fraudulent activity. On a typical day, the exception clerks would fail to find between 50 and 100 of these checks, and the cases would be referred to the investigations unit.

In the filing and and signature-checking section, women worked at 158 large filing machines, where each operator was responsible for 5,000 to 7,000 accounts. In addition to simply filing the day's flow of checks, each operator handled telephoned check-cashing authorizations; reconciled "full sheets" (the first pages of multipage monthly statements); compiled the daily activity of medium-volume accounts (between 25 and 125 items per day) into so-called SMUT listings;[1] and ruled off the accounts scheduled for next-day statement rendition.

Nine clerks in the breakdown section received the checks for the next day's statements from the filing clerks, collated them with the statements arriving from the computer printer, and prepared the work for the rendition group for the following day. The 60 women in rendition confirmed the count of checks to go with each statement, observed special mailing instructions, and sorted the outgoing mail into heavy, medium, and light weight classifications.

Throughout the DDA process, errors could be generated in a variety of ways. If out of adjustment, any of the machines could eat a check. Multipocket encoders could add a check into the total for one pocket, but sort the paper into a different pocket, creating a shortage in one batch of material and a corresponding overage in another. Conveyor trays could be spilled, and loose paper could be stored in desk drawers, or shoved under furniture, or swept out in the trash. The bank's proofing system recorded variances in all the processing steps, and accumulated the errors in the "difference and fine" account—commonly called the D&F.[2]

The Operating Group Staff

By tradition, OPG was a service function to the customer-contact divisions of the bank. Citibank's top management attention was directed outward—toward the market. OPG was expected to respond to change as generated and interpreted by the customer-contact offices. As a consequence, tradition held that the career path to the top in banking led through line assignments in the market-oriented divisions. "The phrase 'back office' is commonly assumed to mean 'backwater,'" said Reed. "Operations is a secure haven for the people who have grown up in it; it's a place of exile for people in the other divisions."

---

[1]The Citibank executives interviewed for this background material were generally young men who had served with OPG for only two or three years. They did not know the antecedents of the acronym SMUT.

[2]The source of the name "D&F" for the variance account was obscure—one manager thought that a monetary fine once may have been levied against the bank that failed to balance its accounts perfectly.

In 1970, most of OPG's management was made up of career employees who had spent 15 to 25 years with the group, often beginning their service with several years of clerical-level work before advancing to supervisory jobs. Through years of contact with "their" outside divisions of the bank, managers had built up rich personal acquaintance with the people they served. Frequent telephone contacts reinforced these relationships. Dick Freund, OPG's vice president for administration and a veteran of 42 years' service with the group, commented on the close interaction between OPG people and the customer-contact offices:

> Problem solving here is typically done on a person-to-person basis. For example, an account officer in International Banking, faced with tracing some amendment to a letter of credit, would know that Jerry Cole, an assistant vice president on the 22nd floor, could find the answer. He'd call Jerry, and yes, Jerry would get him an answer. Whatever else Jerry was doing in the Letter of Credit Departments could wait; when a customer needs an answer, our men jump. They're proud of the service they can give.

Recruits for the managerial ranks of the bank typically came directly from the college campus. Freund described the process:

> We hire people straight out of college—most of them without business experience—and shuttle them around in a series of low-level jobs while they learn the bank. The Yale and Princeton and Harvard types eventually settle in the customer-contact offices; the Fordham and St. John's and NYU types come to Operating Group. We don't have the glamorous jobs that IBG and Corporate can offer, but even so there's a lot of prestige to working for First National City, and the security we offer means a lot to some of these people. I know one officer who bases his whole employment interview on security. "You come to work for us," he says, "and put in a good day's work, and you'll never have to worry about your job. Never."

Management Succession and the Changing Role of the Operating Group

Freund traced the recent succession of top managers at OPG:

> From 1964 to 1968, when he retired, we had a top man who convinced the Policy Committee that our operating capabilities were becoming more and more important—that we simply couldn't afford to take them for granted. There was a tidal wave of paperwork coming—the same wave that swamped so many brokerage houses in 1968—and we had to pay attention. Until 1968, nobody cared much.
>
> The first clear signals that management attitudes towards the Operating Group were changing came in 1968, when Bill Spencer was appointed executive vice president in charge of Operations. Mr. Spencer was generally regarded as a prime candidate for the bank's presidency. It was plain that his appointment wasn't some form of punishment. He had to be here for a reason, and the reason had to be that Operations was, after all, an important part of the corporation.

It was Spencer who recruited John Reed to move from the International Banking Group to Operations, and who promoted Reed to senior vice president, in 1969. "And that was another sign that things were changing," Reed said. "For one thing, nobody my age had ever made SVP before. But more important, I wasn't a 'banker' in the traditional sense. Most of Operations' management had been in the group for 15 to 30 years; I'd only been with Citibank for 5, and none of that was with OPG."

Reed's undergraduate training had been in American literature and physical metallurgy. After a brief job with Goodyear Tire and Rubber and a tour in the army, he had taken a master's degree in management at Massachusetts Institute of Technology, and then joined the IBG planning staff, where he applied systems concepts to the international banking field with impressive results. His rise in the organization was not at all the usual pattern of career development, as the experience of other bank officers suggests. For example, a gray-haired senior vice president from the Corporate Banking Group reported: "I've spent all my life in the bank. I was trained by assignment to different departments every two years; then, when I went into a line position, I had enough experience to correct something by doing it myself. At the very worst, I always knew people in the other departments who could straighten out any problem."

A PBG vice president said: "I started with Citibank as a night clerk in Personal Banking. It was 10 years before I reached supervisory ranks, and by then I'd had a lot of experience in Credit and in Operations as well."

A newly appointed assistant vice president in the Operating Group added: "I joined the bank as a naive liberal arts graduate, and spent three years in clerical work before making first-line supervision. After eight years as a supervisor, you get a pretty good feeling for what's happening around you."

In May 1970, to the surprise of no one, William Spencer was named president of First National City Corporation. Reed—youth, nonbanking background, and all—was selected to head the Operating Group.

Operating Group Costs

By tradition, the method of meeting increased workloads in banking was to increase staff. If an operation could be done at the rate of 800 transactions per day, and the load increased by 800 pieces per day, then the manager in charge of that operation would hire another person; it was taken for granted. Financial reports would follow, showing in the next month-end statement that expenses had risen, and explaining the rise through the increased volume of work processed.

But in the late 1960s, the workload began to rise faster than the hiring rate could keep up; moreover, operator productivity decreased. Backlogs of work to be done would pile up in one OPG department or another, and they could not be cleared away without overtime. Even with extensive reassignment of people and with major overtime efforts, some departments would periodically fall behind by two or even three weeks, generating substantial numbers of complaints from customers. Three or four times a year, special task forces would be recruited from other branches of the bank to break the bottlenecks of these problem departments. Trainees, secretaries, junior officers, and clerks would be drafted for evening and weekend work, at overtime pay rates. "The task force approach is inefficient, annoying, and expensive, but it gets us out of the hole," said Freund. "A lot of these people don't *want* to work these hours, but it has to be done." In 1970, OPG spent $1,983,000 on overtime pay.

There were other sources of expense in the Operating Group that did not show up on financial reports. Reed described a major area of hidden costs:

> If we have cashed a $1,000 check drawn on the Bank of America in California, we are going to be out $1,000 until we send them the check. If we miss sending the check out today, it will wait until tomorrow's dispatches to the West Coast, and we'll wait a day longer for that $1,000. There are rigid deadlines for each of the clearinghouses; even a relatively small number of checks missing these deadlines can cost us a great deal of money. If each day only 3 percent of the $2 billion we handle is held over, then we will lose the interest on $60 million for one day. That turns out to be something like $3 million a year in lost earnings. We call it "lost availability."
>
> That's a big number. Yet, until a few months ago we were making no effort to reduce it, or even to measure it. No one had thought of it as a cost. Check processing has always been treated as a straight-line operation, with bags of checks going through the line as they were received. Whatever wasn't processed at the end of the day was held over, and cleaned up the following day. It was just another clerical operation.

In 1970, lost availability amounted not to 3 percent of the value of checks processed, but to 4 percent.

Operating Group Quality

"Quality is something we really can't measure," said Freund. "But we can get perceptions that the level of service we're providing isn't acceptable. For all our outlay of expenses, it seems we are not improving, or even maintaining, our performance."

Indications of poor service came to OPG in the form of customer complaints, usually voiced through account officers from the market-contact divisions of the bank. Failures could take many forms, including loss of checks after they had been posted, late mailing of statements, miscoding of checks, payment of checks over stop orders, misposting of transfers, and, on occasion, loss of whole statements. Since any kind of error could cause inconvenience to the customer, the people in direct touch with the market were highly sensitive to quality. These account officers frequently assumed the role of problem solvers on the customer's behalf, traveling to the Wall Street office to work directly with OPG staff to remedy specific errors affecting their accounts. A separate section had been set up to analyze and correct errors in customer accounts; its backlog of unsolved inquiries was a major indicator to management of OPG's quality level. In the fall of 1970, this investigations department faced a backlog of 36,000 unsolved cases.

The importance of error-free operation to the customer-contact officers was pointed out by several officers from outside of OPG. A vice president from Corporate Banking Group said:

> Sure, I know the volume of paper has gone up. I know we have 750,000 accounts, and most of them are handled for years without a mistake. But Operations has to perform at 100 percent, not at 99 percent. Errors can be terribly embarrassing to the customer; repeated errors can lose customers for us. I have 600 checks missing from last month's statement for a major government account . . . and there were 400 missing from the previous month's statement. Now how can I sell additional services to that account, when we can't even produce a correct monthly statement for him?

An assistant vice president from Personal Banking added:

> We tell the customer that his canceled check is his legal receipt, and then we lose the check. What am I supposed to tell the man then? I can get him a microfilmed copy of the check, but that's not very useful as a legal document, is it?

An account officer in the International Banking Group said:

> Just getting a simple transfer through the books can generate a whole family of problems. Here's a typical case. A translator at 111 Wall Street miscodes the original transaction (it was written in Portuguese), and the transfer goes to the wrong account. When that customer inquires, we trace the error and reverse it. But before the correction goes through, a follow-up request comes in from Brazil; it's a duplicate of the first request, and our people don't catch the fact it's a follow-up, so they put through another transfer. Now the same item has gone through twice. Where does it all end? My customer is tired of writing letters about it.

And a CBG vice president sighed: "If our operations were perfect, we'd have a tremendous tool to go out and sell against the competition."

The Technological Fix

An important issue for OPG was the extent to which its problems could be remedied through technology. Reed explained:

> The customer-contact side of the bank, and to some extent the top management group, shows a natural tendency to press in the direction of great, massive, new, total computer systems—bringing the ultimate promise of technology into instant availability. It has been natural for all of us to blame mistakes and daily operating problems on inadequate systems; after all, if the systems were perfect, those mistakes would be impossible. But maybe we've all been brainwashed. Maybe we expect too much.

Fifteen years before, Citibank had acquired its first computer—a desk-sized Burroughs machine used to calculate interest on installment loans. Over the next four years, OPG had cooperated in an extensive research program on automated check processing, based on equipment developed by ITT to encode and sort mail in European post offices. This experimental system had progressed to the point of pilot use on the accounts of First National City's own employees when, in 1959, the American Banking Association adopted magnetic ink character recognition (MICR) as an industrywide standard approach to check processing. Citibank immediately dropped the ITT system and installed MICR equipment.

Although the computer facilities had grown immensely in the ensuring decade, the basic process performed by OPC remained the same. "For example," said Reed, "people used to verify names and addresses against account numbers by looking them up in paper records. Now they sit at cathode-ray tubes instead, but they're still doing the same operation."

Reed's computer people had reported to him that Citibank's use of machines was already highly efficient. The Operating Group was—and had been for several years—at the state-of-the-art level of computer use. A new survey by the American Bankers Association seemed to verify this conclusion: whereas the average large bank spent over 30 percent of its back-office budget on machine capacity, OPG spent less than 20 percent.

Reed paused beside his corner window and said:

> Think about this for a minute. We've been running this operation as if it were a computer center. We've been hoping for some Great Mother of a software system to come along and pull the family together. Well, she's slow. None of us children has heard one word from her. Maybe she's not coming. What if it's not a computer center we have here? What other point of view could we take that would result in running the Operating Group differently? Better? What if it's a factory we've got here?

The Factory Concept

Through much of August 1970, Reed had worked with Small and White to develop the implications of viewing OPG as a high-speed, continuous-process production operation. White, working without an official title, had just joined Reed's staff after six years with Ford Motor Co., most recently as manager of engineering financial analysis for Ford's product development group. At the age of 35, with an Ohio State bachelor of science degree and an M.B.A. from the University of Florida behind him, White brought a firm conviction to OPG that the McNamara philosophy of budgets, measurements, and controls was the only way to run a production operation.

Now, in early September, Reed was trying some of these ideas on Freund to get a sense of their impact on the traditional banker. Freund, with more than four decades in the organization, was serving as a sounding board; Reed had almost decided to carry a new program to the Policy Committee of the bank, and he wanted to anticipate their reactions:

> We know where we want the Operating Group to be in five years' time. For 1971 and 1972 we want to hold expenses flat; in spite of the rising transaction volumes, we'll keep the same $150 million expense level as this year, and after that we'll let costs rise by no more than 6 percent a year. By 1975, that will mean a $70

million annual saving compared to uncontrolled growth at 15 percent. At the same time, we want to improve service, and eliminate out bottlenecks and backlogs like the jam-up in investigations.

To accomplish those goals, though, we will have to put over a fundamental change in outlook. We must recognize the Operating Group for what it is—a factory—and we must continually apply the principles of production management to make that factory operate more efficiently.

It is not important for the people in the factory to understand banking. We'll take the institutional objectives and restate them in terms of management plans and tasks that are quite independent of banking. The plain fact is that the language and values we need for success are not derived from banking, and we couldn't achieve what we want in terms of systems development and operations if they were.

To control costs, we must think in terms of costs. That means bringing in management people trained in production management—tough-minded, experienced people who know what it is to manage by the numbers and to measure performance against a meaningful budget. We have to infuse our management with a new kind of production-oriented philosophy, and the process has to start with new, outside points of view. Good production people in here can provide a seed crystal, and the present management staff can grow around the seed. Some of them will make it; others won't. Our headhunters can find the top factory management people to start the reaction. From there on, it's up to us.

Our costs are out of control because we don't know what they are, let alone what they should be. Our quality is criticized when we don't have any idea what quality really is, or how to measure what we're already doing. Our processes run out of control and build up backlogs because our efforts are aimed at coping with transactions instead of understanding what made them pile up in the first place.

I'm not talking about turning the Operating Group into a factory. I'm talking about recognizing that it *is* a factory, and always has been. The function isn't going to change, but the way we look at it and manage it must.

Reed turned to Freund, who had been listening intently, and said: "What will they say to that, Dick?"

Freund smiled and his eyes sparkled:

They'll go for the stable budget idea, and in spite of skepticism they will hope you can do it. They'll love the idea of improved service, but they'll know you can't pull that one off if you're holding costs down. And the factory management idea?

There's one other bit of history you should know, John. The first engineer we ever hired came to work here in 1957, the year after we bought our first little computer. He was an eager guy, really impressed by the challenge of managing back-office operations. He poked around for a few days and then came back to the head office to declare that this wasn't a bank at all. It was a factory, he said. Nothing but a goddamn paperwork factory. That was after just two weeks on the job. It was his last day on the job, too.

Reed grinned broadly and turned to face White. "Are you ready to move out of the office, Bob? This concept is going to fly, and we're going to need someone down at Wall Street who can make it happen. Why don't you get yourself ready to take over Area I?"

Case 7–2

First National City Bank Operating Group (B)

John A. Seeger, Jay W. Lorsch, Cyrus F. Gibson

Picture a high-pressure pipeline, five feet in diameter, carrying money to dozens of different distribution pipelines. Your job is to make a lot of plumbing changes in the pipes, but you can't shut off the flow of money while you work. If anything goes wrong and the pipe breaks, all those dollars are going to spill out on the floor. In a week's time, you'll be wading around in $10 billion. You'll be up to your eyebrows in money. Other people's money.

John Reed, one of six executive vice presidents of Citibank and the officer in charge of the bank's Operating Group (OPG), was reflecting on the process of change in a continuous-process, high-volume production operation. It was January 1973, and Reed was reviewing the accomplishments of the past two and a half years. On the surface, it was easy to document progress; OPG had numbers to show for its efforts. But Reed was anticipating criticism, too, as he prepared for the policy committee meeting at the end of the month. After all, the group's performance hadn't been perfect; the money pipeline had broken down for the second time only four months ago. Several customer-contact divisions still complained that service and quality levels in OPG were going downhill, in spite of numeric measurements that showed substantial improvement. And Reed's fellow EVPs and division heads on the policy committee had tenacious memories.

Added to his other concerns was a new situation, highly visible to the bank as a whole. Organizers for the Office and Professional Workers Union (OPWU) were handing out thousands of leaflets to workers at 111 Wall Street, OPG's office building. Citibank's pay scales were competitive with other Manhattan employers' rates, but there were some indications of dissatisfaction in the work force. The previous year, for example, 125 women had walked off the job with a list of grievances; bringing the situation back to normal had required four months' full-time effort by one of OPG's most experienced assistant vice presidents. There was little feeling among top management that unionization was an immediate threat, but still the OPWU leaflets could not be ignored.

How, Reed wondered, could changes in the bank's office be evaluated in terms of their impact on the rest of the institution? How could the new nonbanking approach of the Operating Group be made meaningful to the traditional bankers from the market-oriented divisions? For that matter, how could Reed himself picture the full impact of his changes on OPG and on the bank?

He stood at the window of his Manhattan office, high above the early morning traffic on Park Avenue. Behind him on his huge desk lay the two documents he had studied the night before. One was a draft of a speech that Robert White, senior vice president in charge of the production areas of OPG, would soon deliver to the American Bankers Association (ABA). The speech outlined the management approaches Citibank had applied to its back-office operations over the previous two years. Citibank's success in gaining control of its paperwork had attracted industrywide attention; in 1971 and 1972, OPG had handled substantial increases in volume of work, while reducing its expenditures below the 1970 level. The chairman of the First National City Corporation had been widely quoted as crediting the Operating Group for a major share of the bank's increased earnings. Judging by the numbers, John Reed had few reasons for concern.

The second document on his desk, however, seemed to tell a different story. It was a consultant's report, which Reed had commissioned in order to hear an outside viewpoint on the effects of the changes he and his colleagues had engineered in the past two years. The report was based largely on interviews the consultants had conducted with some 70 officers of the bank, both inside OPG and in the market-contact divisions; it focused sharply on some undesirable side effects of OPG's changes. The imposition of tight control policies, the report suggested, could lead to anxiety and insecurity in middle management. These fears could lead, in turn, to the establishment of unrealistic goals (as an effort to please the new bosses), and to increased resistance to change (as middle management's effort to protect itself). The consequence of these two factors could be poor performance, seen as missed deadlines and crises, and as a sensed need by top management for still tighter controls. It was a classic vicious circle.

Placed side by side, the two documents made interesting reading. Reed wondered how OPG could learn from comparison—how it could avoid unanticipated consequences of change in the future.

Change in the Operating Group, 1970–1972

Soon after his promotion to head OPG in May 1970, Reed had faced the question of defining just what OPG was. Was it, as banking tradition dictated, simply a mechanical support group for the customer-contact offices of the bank? Or could it be seen as an independent, high-volume production operation—a factory—which designed and controlled its own processes and products in the style of a manufacturing organization?

Reed decided that OPG was a factory. As such, it badly needed managers who knew how to run factories—people skilled in planning and controlling mass-production processes. Dick Freund, OPG's vice president for administration and a veteran of 45 years' service with the bank, described the group's first effort to recruit professional production management:

What industries do you think of when you want examples of outstanding factory management? Well, automotives have to be close to the top of the heap. And what companies do you think of? The winners: General Motors and Ford. The first headhunter Reed turned loose on the job happened to have his foot in the door at Ford. You should have seen the first man who came to interview: we really went all the way to impress him. Reed had the fellow out to his home to talk, and so did Spencer (the bank's president). The guy was obviously impressed, and went back to Detroit to think it over. Then he told us "no." His family was well established in their present home, and he didn't want to bring them to New York. His kids had put on a very convincing flip-chart presentation, he told us. Can you imagine it? Reed and Spencer were just incredulous—couldn't believe it. Here's a really top guy, and he lets his kids decide what he's going to do! We were flabbergasted.

Succeeding efforts at recruiting production-oriented executives were more fruitful, and OPG began to fill its management ranks with young, aggressive talent. One of the early arrivals was Bob White, who left Ford Motor Co. to work as John Reed's assistant. For several months, the two men worked intensively to build a specific action framework around the 1971 goals of OPG. Then White, supported by other newly recruited executives—three of them from Ford—moved into the line organization to take charge of the transaction-processing responsibilities of OPG's Area I. (See Case 7–1.)

Top-Down Management

The draft of Bob White's speech for the ABA explained how the change process began with a fundamental look at the group's whole philosophy of management:

In general terms, we can say that "administering" connotes a passive mode, while "managing" bespeaks an active mode. An administrator is, in a sense, a bystander, keeping watch on a process, explaining it if it goes awry. But managing means understanding your present world, deciding what you would like it to be, and making your desired results happen. A manager is an agent of the future, of change.

The fact is that, traditionally, banking operations are not really managed at all. In a sense, the people in charge are running alongside the processing line, instead of being on top of it pressing the process levers. All you can do in such a situation is react. At Citicorp, we decided that this was unacceptable. We wanted to manage our back office, not administer it.

There are two critical prerequisites for this: conviction and orientation toward results. Each manager must be absolutely convinced that he can control all factors relevant to his operation. That conviction must be at the top, and must carry with it a willingness to spend for results. I am talking about spending in terms of change to the organization, its structure, its fabric—about the amount of top management time and energy expended, and about the type of people you are willing to accept in your culture.

To ensure an environment that will foster the kind of dedication and commitment we need, we use a pass/fail system as a management incentive. A manager passes or fails in terms of result objectives he himself has set within the top-down framework. He is rewarded or not rewarded accordingly. No excuses or rationalization of events "beyond one's control" are accepted.

I've been treated better in the past three years than in all of the previous nine years.[1]

Reed has been very fair with everybody who has produced, in a salary sense.

The feeling was we should do things, especially make or beat budget, and that if we didn't we should expect to be out.

The ABA speech continued:

The style of management we sought was top-down management. Each manager sets his own objectives for his own level in translating objectives set from above. Although people felt initially constrained by a top-down approach, I am fully convinced that it is the *only* approach. Each manager is not only free to exercise his vision—he is expected to do so. He is unfettered by what is traditional, by what is the norm. Nothing is sacred. The real problem is that the top-down system *strains* people, but it does not *constrain* them. Good people thrive in such an environment.

This job is exciting, like working for a glamour company, almost like having your own company. I really like being a "maverick."

I like the opportunity to work for change, and to have responsibility for it. What I don't like is the incompetence of those who resist.

I work 10 to 12 hours a day. I guess Reed works 24 hours.

OPG has lived in crisis for the past six years, but it's worse now, especially the hours and pressure that everyone is under. I spent the whole summer working six days a week and never saw the kids. Finally got up the courage to tell my wife I was working Labor Day week-end. She put it to me; well, I called and said I wasn't coming in. The guys I used to work with say to me now, "Congratulations," even though my new job isn't a promotion. They see me as being better off, just to be out of that place.

---

[1] Italicized quotations used throughout this case are are representative comments of other managers who were involved in or affected by the OPG reorganization, as reported to the consultants whom Reed had hired. These quotations, of course, did not appear in the ABA speech.

White's speech continued:

> If you start your management process with the first-line supervisors and accumulate upward, you are assuming that the smartest people and the strategic direction for the business come from the bottom of the management pyramid. If this is true, we need to reverse the present salary structure so that the first-line people are paid the most money. It is not a question of brightness or ability, it is rather that top management has a better view of the overall organization, its direction, goals, strengths, weaknesses, and so forth.

The speech went on to outline the basic management theories that OPG had formalized and applied to its functions in the past three years. "Management 101," it was called, and it was simply stated as "knowing *where we are, where we want to be, and how we plan to get there*." Responsible mangers were expected to know, in formal terms, the current state of their world and all the processes that were producing their current results; the *desired* state of their area and the processes that would produce *those* results; and finally the changes they would make in today's processes to turn them into tomorrow's processes. "It is not results we are managing, but processes that achieve the results." After defining the 1970 situation of the Operating Group and its three goals for 1971 (flat costs, improved service, and elimination of the investigations backlog), the speech proceeded:

> What was left was to design the action plan—the processes that would get us to the results we wanted. [See Figure A, which reproduces a slide shown to the audience at this point in the speech.]
> We planned to build a strong management team, to hire managers who had the conviction and motivation to control their own operations with management skills as opposed to administrative skills.
> We planned in 1971 to cut out all the fat accumulated during the prior 10 years of 18 percent annual cost rises—at that rate we knew there was some fat.
> We planned to develop and install a financial control system, emphasizing simplicity and the major cost elements: (1) people, (2) overtime, (3) process float, or lost availability, and (4) equipment and computers.
> We planned to define a process for cleaning up "rocks," such as the 36,000 backlogged investigations, so that we could come out from under the crisis environment and get control of our processing. This meant designing the techniques to separate rocks out from current work so that we could both dissolve the rock and do today's work today so that the rock would not grow.
> In fact, the real significance of the Phase I action plan was that it enabled us to get a handle on the operating environment. With this program, we started to get on top of the back office so as to control and manage it.

The whole management team was brought in cold, predominantly from Ford. So you had this whole new team applying industrial concepts to paper flow. It has worked. But people took affront that these bright young stars were coming along and changing the whole new world.

The number of people actually severed from the bank was actually very small for the organization—only 179—but the image is very negative.

Figure A
Phase I Action Plan, November 1970–June 1971

- Hire the right "top management" people to build up a new style of management team
- Squeeze out the "Fat"
- Implement major new computer systems
- Develop a Financial Control System that **forecasts**

    —People and annual salary rates
    —Overtime
    —Lost availability
    —Inventory

- Define the "rock" cleanup process

    —Separate backlog from current work
    —Do today's work today

The fear of a cut—a layoff—wasn't a very realistic one. In fact, there have been very few—but the perception of it was the important thing.

The key issue in the bank today is job security.

There was a language problem. The buzz words used by the new guys differed from the language the old managers used and understood.

Lots of people close to retirement retired early. People at the AVP level are running scared.

The bank no longer offers security to old-timers. My chance to become a VP is almost nil, regardless of performance; I just don't have the right background.

People have really put out in this place, some of them have really worked. But when some old-timers were pushed out, it hurt a lot of us. We said, "Is that what's in store for us if we keep going here?" Also, when the old-timers who knew other parts of the bank left, we lost a way to get a lot of contacts with the other groups.

To gain control of costs, it was necessary to forecast what our expenditures would be *before* we were committed. We developed a one-page expense summary report based on forecast, rather than on history. [See Exhibit 1.] The manager is in control of all his variables. We do not recognize any type of expense as controllable or institutional. Forecasts are updated monthly and are met.

Exhibit 1
1973 Expense Forecast ($000s)

AREA	DIVISION	DATE	EXHIBIT
Area I	DDA Recap		

	Month of January				Month of February			March–December			Full Year 1973			
	Actual	Actual (O)/U Budget	Actual (O)/U Forecast	Actual (O)/U 1972 Actual	Forecast	Forecast (O)/U Budget	Forecast (O)/U 1972 Actual	Forecast	Forecast (O)/U Budget	Forecast (O)/U 1972 Actual	Forecast	Forecast (O)/U Budget	Forecast (O)/U Prior Forecast	Forecast (O)/U 1972 Actual
Salaries														
Official and nonofficial														
Part time														
Fringe benefits														
Overtime														
Temporaries														
Severance														
Subtotal salaries														
Other operating (including 799s)														
Education and training														
Computer time—outside vendors														
Consultants														

Computers	
Furniture and equipment	
Insurance and legal	
Postage	
Stationery and supplies	
Telephone, telegrams, and cables	
Travel, memberships, and subscriptions	
Business, promotions and entertainment	
Food	
Operating losses and losses not insured	
Difference and fine	
Lost availability	
Rent	
Rental income	
OPC occupancy expense	
Real estate taxes	
Building depreciation	
Utilities	
Freight and cartage	
Other	
1972 related expense	
Provisions	
Subtotal other operating	
Total Expense	

We have a tendency now to try to meet due dates at all costs.

Due dates for changes are, in most cases, absurd. Time commitments are ridiculous, and the consequences of not meeting due dates aren't made known beforehand.

People try to be optimistic to please the boss. When they miss the milestones, they get screwed.

But when we set about implementing new computer-based systems, we learned a very important lesson: We hadn't gone back to basics enough. We found we did not really understand the present processes completely.

And so a second action plan, Phase II, was devised in June of 1971. We called it the performance criteria system, PCS. What we were aiming at was breaking up the operations into manageable, controllable, understandable pieces. These were the key approaches to defining the back-office dynamics.

1. Define the products/services as recognized by the customer.
2. Develop a customer-to-customer flowchart and procedures for processing each product/service.
3. Develop the organization to match and support the product definition and process flow on a customer-to-customer basis.
4. Develop our physical layout into a closed-room, one-floor layout that matched the flows, procedures, and organization so as to enhance control and minimize movement.
5. Decentralize all peripheral equipment.
6. Incorporate support functions into the responsible line organization.

Our processing had always been conceived of in functions, rather than in system processes. All the work flowed into one pipeline of processing functions; for example: preprocessing, encoding, read-to-tape, sorting, reconcilement, repair, and dispatch. You can visualize the functions along a vertical axis, and the people and time frame along a horizontal axis [see Exhibit 2], giving us a very wide pipe carrying 2–3 million transactions per day. If the one pipe breaks, all the work in the pipe before the break stops or spills out. That shouldn't happen often; but when it does, the whole operation stops.

We aimed to break down that pipeline into several smaller lines, each carrying a different product and each supervised by a single manager who controlled every aspect of his process, from the time a customer originates a transaction all the way through a straight line until we dispatch the results back to the customer. [For an example of this straight-line flow, see Exhibit 3.]

We began by breaking the operations out on the basis of six separate input streams: two flows from our domestic branches, separate domestic and international mail deposit flows, one flow from our head office department, and one from incoming exchanges. Each of these became a separate processing line [see Exhibit 4]. These flows are not mere theory; they exist in documented fact.

In came flowcharting and the product-line concept. We had a flowchart that stretched across the room and back. White had an incredible ability to understand the whole

Exhibit 2
Functional Organization Pipelines

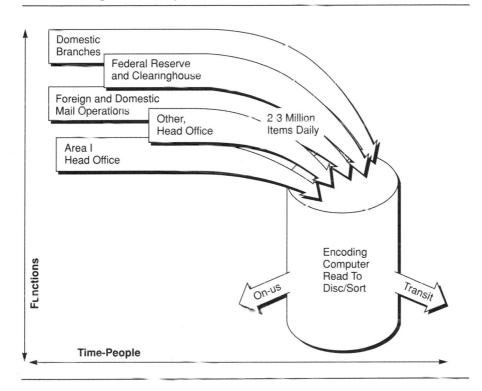

thing—to point to something and just ask the critical question about how something worked, or why it was part of our activity and not somewhere else. The result was a definition of 11 different products, and a full reorganization in one month. It's the only way to run a bank.

Changes were viewed differently by different people. People started flowcharting everything, and Bob White was going over everything, step by step. But lots of people got the feeling that they didn't know what to do. They didn't fit in this new environment.

The Blowup: September 1971

In August of 1971, White decided it was time to act on the new organization of Area I. "We had been talking a lot about reorganizing the flows," he said, "but nothing was actually happening. We had spent months with people, talking about implementation, and we thought they understood. It was time to move."

**Exhibit 3
Straight-Line Organization**

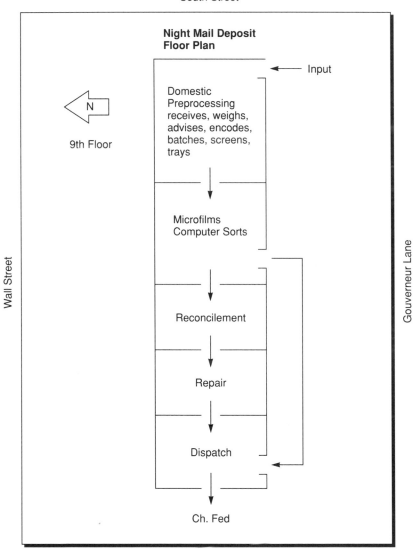

South Street

**Night Mail Deposit
Floor Plan**

Input

Domestic
Preprocessing
receives, weighs,
advises, encodes,
batches, screens,
trays

N

9th Floor

Microfilms
Computer Sorts

Reconcilement

Repair

Dispatch

Ch. Fed

Wall Street

Gouverneur Lane

Front Street

Exhibit 4
Product/Process Organization Pipelines

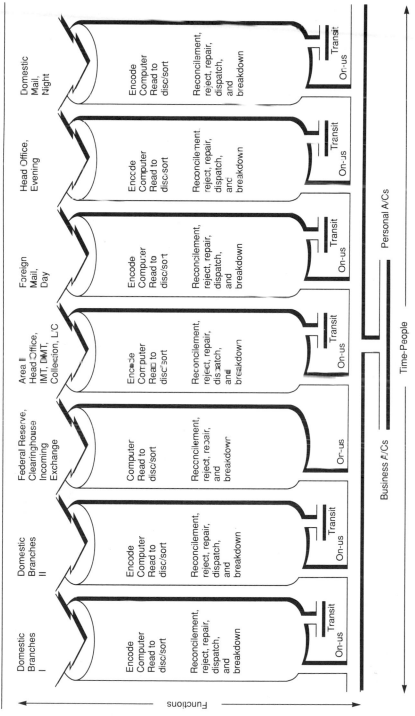

On a hot September Friday evening, when the regular work shift went home, equipment crews began the job of rearranging the facilities at 111 Wall Street. By Monday morning the physical layout was set up for six separate lines, each with its own full complement of peripheral equipment, ready to begin work. And soon after the work force reported on Monday, it became clear that the demand deposit accounting (DDA) system had problems. Equipment had been moved and connected, but technicians had not had time to check operations before it went back into service; some of the machines refused to operate at all. Machine operators, informed on Friday they would still have their same machines but in different locations on Monday, arrived at work with questions, and there were not enough supervisors to answer them. Leftover work from Friday's processing, tucked away in accustomed corners by machine operators, was nowhere to be found; the customary corners were gone.

The money pipeline creaked and groaned under the strain.

As the week wore on, new problems came to light. The three proofing clerks, who had handled three shifts of consolidated front-end operations, could not keep up with the load generated by decentralized work streams. With new people in charge of new areas, proof clerks did not know whom to call to resolve apparent discrepancies; the "Difference & Fine" (D&F) account of accumulated variances began to grow alarmingly. By the end of the week, it was apparent that Citibank's problems were greater than just debugging a new system. OPG's managers were inventing new systems on the spot, attempting to recover. By the second weekend of September, the disturbance had grown to tidal wave proportions. The D&F account hit $1.5 billion on each side of the ledger before heroic weekend work by the group's middle managers brought it back down to $130 million. First National City Bank failed to meet the other New York bankers at the 10 A.M. exchange, and it failed to file its Federal Reserve reports.

The money pipeline had burst.

Geoffrey MacAdams, the grey-haired head of the proofing operation, walked into the computer room, waving his hands in the air. "Stop the machines," he said haltingly to the computer operations head. "Stop the machines. It's out of control."

"I remember walking through the area and finding a pile of work, out on a desk top, with a note on the top saying, 'This is out by a million, and I'm just too sleepy to find it,' " said one manager. "There was maybe $20 or 30 million in the stack. At least the girl was good enough to put a note on it. We were learning, the hard way, not to put papers like that into desk drawers."

Larry Stoiber, operations head for four of the six processing lines, looked up slowly one morning when White greeted him, and he delayed several seconds before showing signs of recognition. Stoiber had been at work for 55 hours without a break. White sent him home in a Citibank car, with instructions not to let him back into the bank until he was coherent.

In two weeks' time the new production processes began to work. Within a month of the change, routine operations once more ran routinely (not the difference between White's memo of August 30 and the status report of October 8 on lost availability,

Exhibit 5
White's Memorandum of August 30, 1971

MEMORANDUM TO: J. Cavaiuolo, operations head
L. Stoiber, operations head
F. Whelan, operations head

Effective Tuesday, August 31, I would like a report (attached) from each of you showing lost availability and deferred debits and credits for each of your operations:

—Branch—Whelan.
—Domestic mail—Stoiber.
—Foreign mail—Stoiber.
—Head office—Stoiber.
—Lockbox—Stoiber.
—Exchanges—Cavaiuolo.

The first lost-availability report should cover the period from the first city–country deadline on Monday to the New York–New Jersey deadline on Tuesday. The deferred debits and credits report should be based on one DDA update to the next.

The report should be completed and on my desk by 1:45 P.M. daily. Initially the report will be in addition to the regular lost-availability daily report—I assume you will ensure the report will tie. You are now each *personally* responsible for ensuring that all lost availability is measured. I would rather not *ever* find any more "undiscovered" lost availability.

If you have any questions or any problems in meeting this deadline, see me today. If not, I will expect the first report at 1:45 P.M. on Tuesday.

Robert B. White
Vice President
August 30, 1971

---

included as Exhibits 5 and 6). But it was five months before the backlog of work and problems generated by the DDA blowup were resolved.

In early October, as the DDA system began to return to normal, and its managers turned their attention to the problems of cleaning up the side effects of the blowup, Reed visited the Wall Street building to talk to Small and White. "I wanted to be the first to tell you this news," he said. "The promotions committee met this morning. You have both been named senior vice presidents of the bank." He smiled broadly. "Congratulations."

The design change from the top just cannot anticipate all the problems that are going to arise at the first-line supervisor level; those people have to know more than just the before-and-after job description.

Exhibit 6
Excerpt from October 8, 1971, Internal Report on the Status of "Rocks" in the Demand Deposit Accounting System

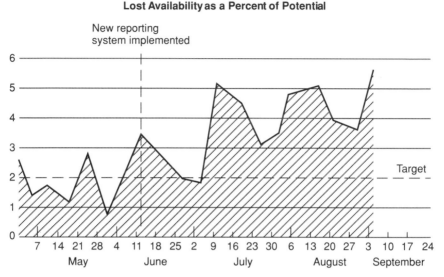

Lost Availability as a Percent of Potential

Float

Float statistics for the month of September were not available due to incomplete data as a result of procedural changes caused by the recent reorganization. A data-capturing network has now been developed and implemented; and reliable and complete data were reported on October 1 and thereafter, indicating an average 3.2 percent lost availability for the three-day period October 1–5.

I'll tell you why people didn't protest the change, or question their instructions. We were scared—afraid of losing our jobs if we didn't seem to understand automatically.

The changes were accompanied by a great fear that people would get fired. Most lower managers and clerical workers felt management—that's AVP level and above— was highly insensitive to people.

Reed and White and the new guys know what they're doing; they're good at setting up cost and quality measures and conceptualizing the system. But at the practical level, things haven't worked. In the past, new instructions would be questioned and worked through until they were either understood or the designer was convinced there was a problem. For example, if I go out there and tell Mary to start writing upside down and backwards on what she is doing, she'll look at me and say "Why?" because she knows me and to her it doesn't make sense. If one of the new guys

Exhibit 7
Expense Forecast Summary

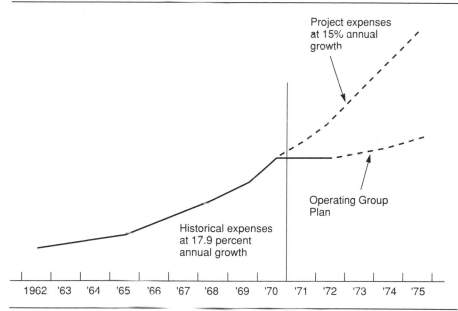

Source: Slide taken from ABA speech.

tells her to write upside down and backwards, she'll do it and not say a word. If anything a little unusual starts to happen, she won't know why it's important, and she won't say a word about it. When the "Ford kids" say do it, people do it. But they're scared.

It hurt us, credibilitywise, with the rest of the bank. The sharks smelled blood in the water and came at us from all directions. But things are better now—an order of magnitude better.

Just a year later, in September 1972, the demand deposit accounting system blew up again, this time centered in the back end of the process, where the filing and telephone authorization process was being changed to anticipate the installation of computer voice answer-back equipment. The changes altered the way accounts were ruled off in preparation for statement rendition, making it impossible for the file clerks to select the proper checks to match with the computer-printed last pages of customers' statements. Unlike the 1971 crisis, this blowup affected customers directly and immediately. "The problem looked critical to the branch people, who had customers standing in line at the tellers' windows waiting for answers that never came. And it seemed critical to account officers in corporate banking, who couldn't get statements for their customers. But it was actually much less serious than the 1971 episode, because it didn't involve the proofing system," said White.

**Exhibit 8
Results: 1970–73**

Year	Headcount		Overtime		Lost Availability	
	Number of Employees	Cumulative Percent Decrease From 1970	$ (000)	Cumulative Percent Decrease From 1970	$ (MMs)	Percent of Potential
1970	7,975	—	1,983	—	56.4	4.0%
1971	6,610	17%	1,272	35%	32.8	2.0%
1972	5,870	26%	845	57%	26.5	1.8%
1973	5,528	30%	564	71%	14.2	0.5%

Source: Slide taken from ABA speech.

"We were able to react much more quickly, and we were pretty much recovered from it within a month and a half."

Achievements in the Operating Group

The draft speech for the American Bankers Association summarized the results of Operating Group's improvement efforts in two charts reproduced as full-color slides (see Exhibits 7 and 8). By the end of 1973, according to the forecast, personnel in the group would be reduced by 30 percent from 1970 levels; overtime would be down by 71 percent; lost availability would be down by 75 percent; and the backlog of investigations would be shrunk from 36,000 to 500 cases—one day's load. The speech elaborated:

> The real achievement here, though, is that we forecasted what we would achieve and then made it happen. Moreover, we *did* put together the kind of management team we wanted, and we *did* get hold of the processes within our shop. At the same time, we developed a control system to measure the two facets of service to our customers: quality and timeliness. Quality measures error rate; it is the number of errors as a percentage of the total work processed on a daily basis.
>
> We currently measure 69 different quality indicators, and we are meeting the standards 87 percent of the time. When a given indicator is met or beaten consistently, we tighten the standard; we expect to continue this process indefinitely.
>
> Timeliness is the percentage of work processed in a given time period—generally a 24-hour time period. At the moment, we have defined 129 different standards for timeliness, and we expect that number to continue to grow. Today, we are meeting 85 percent of these standards. Moreover, we also continually tighten these standards as soon as we prove they can be consistently met. I think it is fair to

say that our service performance has improved greatly since we began to hold costs flat—if for no other reason than that we now *really* know what we are doing.

In order to make progress, we had to be firm with the other divisions of the bank. We used to interrupt anything in order to handle a special request. No more. We're consciously shutting them out, so we could work on the basic processes here. Now we have no people wandering in here to distract our clerks.

Changes were also evident from outside of OPG. Three officers from the customer-contact divisions commented as follows:

My frustration is I wish there were more old-time bankers in there and fewer systems and organization types. There is a huge loss of old guys I can turn to for help in getting things done, people who know banking. Maybe they should keep just a few. Some. A few cents a share might well be worth it.

People over here say that if those guys are so good, why do they keep screwing up? You'd think they'd learn something in two years.

In the old days, when the old guys were running things, you knew who to go to. Now we don't know. Even if we find somebody, he's faced with a process where he couldn't give special service even if he wanted to.

White's speech concluded:

> These, then, were the achievements of two years of fundamental change. They are, I think, substantial, and they provide us with the solid base we need to focus in on the future.

One of John Reed's magazine articles that came around said something about people being replaceable, like machines. That hurt. You lose solidarity.

Somebody asked me once if I liked it that we were working in what Reed called a factory. That really struck home. So, maybe it is like a factory. Why do they have to say it?

Case 7–3

Peter Browning and Continental White Cap (A)

Mary Gentile, Todd D. Jick

On April 1, 1984, Peter Browning assumed the position of vice president and operating officer of Continental White Cap, a Chicago-based division of the Continental Group, Inc. Having completed a successful five-year turnaround of Continental's troubled Bondware division, Browning found this new assignment at White Cap was a very different type of challenge. He was taking over the most successful of Continental's nine divisions, "the jewel in the Continental crown," as one Continental executive described it. White Cap was the market leader in the production and distribution of vacuum-sealed metal closures for glass jars.

Browning's charge, though, was to revitalize and reposition the division to remain preeminent in the face of threatened, but not yet fully realized, changes in the competitive environment. Sales were down and costs were up. Recent years had brought changes in the market: one competitor in particular was utilizing price cuts for the first time to build market share and the introduction of plastic packaging to many of White Cap's traditional customers threatened sales. White Cap had not yet developed a plastic closure or the ability to seal plastic containers. After more than 50 years of traditional management and close control by White Cap's founding family, corporate headquarters decided it was time to a bring in a proven, enthusiastic, young manager to push the business toward a leaner, more efficient, and

This case was prepared by Research Associate Mary Gentile (under the direction of Associate Professor Todd D. Jick), as the basis for class discussion rather than to illustrate either effective or ineffective handling of an administrative situation.

more flexible operation, an operation capable of responding to the evolving market conditions.

From the very start, Browning recognized two major obstacles that he would have to address. First, few managers or employees at White Cap acknowledged the need for change. Business results for more than 50 years had been quite impressive and when dips were experienced, they were perceived as cyclical and transient. And, second, White Cap had a family-style culture characterized by long-term loyalty from its employees, but also long-standing traditions of job security, liberal benefits, and paternalistic management. Attempts to alter these traditions would not be welcome.

Reflecting on his new assignment at White Cap, Browning recalled that at Bondware he had walked into a failing business where he "had nothing to lose." Now he was entering "a successful business with absolutely everything to lose." One White Cap manager observed: "White Cap will be the testing period for Peter Browning in the eyes of Continental." His success in reframing the business would be critical for his future in corporate leadership there. And Browning thought about the stern words of caution he had received from his boss, Dick Hofmann, executive vice president of the Continental Group: "White Cap needs changes, but just don't break it while you're trying to fix it. Continental can't afford to lose White Cap."

White Cap Background

In 1926, William P. White ("old W.P.") and his two brothers started the White Cap Company on Goose Island in the Chicago River, in an old box factory. From the beginning, the White Cap Company was active not only in closure production and distribution, but in new product development and in the design of cap-making and capping machinery. Thus, White Cap promoted itself as not only a source of quality closures but as providers of a "Total System" of engineering and R&D support and service to the food industry; the latest in closure technology (for example, in 1954 White Cap pioneered the "twist-off" style closure and in the late 1960s they developed the popular P.T. ("press-on/twist-off") style cap); capping equipment; and field operations service. Their customers were producers of ketchup, juices, baby foods, preserves, pickles, and other perishable foods.

In 1956, the Continental Can Company bought White Cap, and in 1984, the Continental Group, Inc. went from public to private as it was merged into KMI Continental, Inc., a subsidiary of Peter Kiewit and Sons, a private construction company. The White Cap Company became Continental White Cap, the most profitable of the parent firm's nine divisions, each of which produced different types of containers and packaging.

Despite the sale of White Cap in 1956, the White family continued to manage the organization and its traditional company culture persisted. As the manager of Human Resources at the Chicago plants expressed it: "I really think that many employees felt that White Cap bought Continental Can, instead of the other way around." W. P. White, the company founder, and later his son, Bob, inspired and encouraged a strong sense of family among their employees, many of whom lived in the Polish community immediately surrounding the main plant. Once hired, employees tended to remain and to bring in their friends and relatives as well. At the two Chicago plants, 51.2% of the employees were over 40 years old and 30% were over 50 in 1985.

The Whites themselves acted as patrons or father figures, and legends recounted their willingness to lend money to an hourly worker with unexpected medical bills, or their insistence, in a bad financial year, on borrowing the money for Christmas bonuses. In exchange for their hard work and commitment, employees received good salaries, job security and the feeling they were part of a "winner." In an area as heavily unionized as Chicago, these rewards were potent enough to keep White Cap nearly union-free. Only the lithographers, a small and relatively autonomous group, were unionized.

White Cap was rife with rituals, ceremonies, and traditions. In the early days of the company, Mrs. W. P. White would prepare and serve lunch every day for the company employees in the Goose Island facility. Over the years, White Cap continued to provide a free family-style hot lunch for all salaried employees and free soup, beverage, and ice cream for the hourly workers.

A Press Department manager, a White Capper for 28 years, explained:

> For work in a manufacturing setting, you couldn't do better than White Cap. White Cap isn't the real world; when the economy is hurting, White Cap isn't. White Cap always lived up to the ideal that "our people are important to us." They sponsored a huge family picnic every year for all White Cappers and friends. When they first instituted the second shift in the factory, they lined up cabs to take late workers home after their shift. They sponsored golf outings and an "old-timers' softball team." People generally felt that there's nothing going to happen to us as long as we've got a White there.

But in 1982, Bob White stepped down and turned the management over to Art Lawson, who became vice president and executive officer. Lawson, 63 years old, was an old-time White Capper and many saw him as simply proxy for the Whites; even Lawson would say that he saw himself as a caretaker manager, maintaining things as they had always been.

At about this time, price competition began to heat up in the closure industry. White Cap had been the market leader for over 50 years, but customers were beginning to take the Total System for granted. There were by then five significant manufacturers in the national marketplace and 70 worldwide who offered the twist-off cap. Competitors like National Can Company were beginning to slash prices, aware that the very advantage White Cap had maintained in the market—i.e., their R&D and full service—made it difficult for them to compete effectively with drastic price cutting.

Just at this time, plastic containers, requiring plastic closures, began to be available (see Exhibit 1). In 1982, the Food and Drug Administration had approved the use of a particular plastic substance as an appropriate oxygen-barrier for food containers. Subsequently, the American Can Company's Gamma™ bottle, a squeezable plastic container, was adopted by the Heinz Company for their ketchup and

---

Exhibit 1
Peter Browning and Continental White Cap (A): Changes in the Container Industry

Percentage of Rigid Containers Shipped in 1974 and 1984

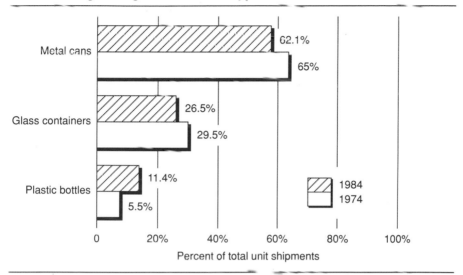

Percent of total unit shipments

Source: Bureau of the Census, Can Manufacturers' Institute, International Trade Association, and *U.S. Industrial Outlook 1985.*

Shipments of Plastic Bottles for Food

Market Year	1978	1982	1983	1984 (estimated)
Millions of Units	260	697	798	900

Source: Bureau of the Census, International Trade Administration, and *U.S. Industrial Outlook 1985.*

by Hunt for their barbecue sauce. (White Cap had held 100% of the ketchup business worldwide.) Welch's jams and jellies also adopted this new technology and the firm's reasons were typical:

> Welch's expects the new packaging to help revitalize a relatively flat product category, having conducted research indicating that their customers are willing to pay more for the convenience of the squeezable plastic bottle.[1]

Another major White Cap account had announced plans to introduce a new juice line in plastic containers for the spring of 1986, as well. Without a competitive plastic closure, White Cap would continue to lose customers.

---

[1]Melissa Horson, "Dispensing Closures Revitalize Flat Markets," *Packaging,* August 1985, p. 25.

In 1984, two years after Bob White had left, Peter Browning was named vice president and operating officer, reporting to Art Lawson. He took over a division with $175 million in gross sales; 1450 employees, of whom 480 were salaried; 12 sales offices; and four plants (two in Chicago, Illinois; one in Hayward, California; and one in Hazleton, Pennsylvania).

Peter Browning's Background

I'm Peter Browning and I'm 43 years of age. I have four children—three girls, twenty, sixteen, and twelve, and a seven-year-old son. My undergraduate degree is in history, and while at White Cap, I earned by M.B.A. through the Executive Program at the University of Chicago. I have been with Continental for 20 years.

This was Peter Browning's characteristic opening each time he presented himself and his ideas to a new audience. On first impression, Browning appeared youthful, charming, and intellectually and socially curious. Various employees and managers described him alternately as: "Mr. Energy," "ambitious," "direct," "the most powerful boss I've had," "the quintessential old-time politician, shaking hands and kissing babies." His speeches to management and staff were peppered with inspirational aphorisms and historical, often military, metaphors, repeated as refrains and rallying cries.

In spring 1985, the Continental Group arranged for each of the nine divisional managers to be interviewed by industrial psychologists. The psychologist's report on Browning stated:

His intellectual ability is in the very superior range. . . . He is a hard-driving individual for whom success in an organization is extremely important. . . . Further, he is completely open in communicating the strategy he has conceived, the goals he has chosen, and the ongoing success of the organization against these goals. He cares about people, is sensitive to them, and makes every effort to motivate them. . . . His own values and beliefs are so strong and well defined that his primary means of motivation is the instilling of enthusiasm and energy in others to think and believe as he does. By and large he is successful at this, but there are those who have to be motivated from their own values and beliefs which may be different but which may nonetheless lead to productive action. These people are apt to be confused, overwhelmed, and left behind by his style.[2]

Browning's career began with White Cap and Continental Can in 1964 when he took a position as sales representative in Detroit. He continued in marketing with White Cap for nine years and then in other Continental divisions until 1979. At that time, he returned to Chicago to become vice president and general manager of Continental's Bondware division. Once in the area again, Browning was able to touch base with old contacts from White Cap and to observe first hand the challenges they faced.

---

[2]Alexander B. Platt, Platt & Associates Inc., May 2, 1985.

At Bondware (producers of waxed paper cups for hot and cold beverages and food), Browning took over a business that had lost $24 million in five years (1975–79) and that Continental could not even sell. Browning adopted a drastic and accelerated change program, employing what he called "radical surgery" to reduce employees by half, from 1200 to 600; to eliminate an entire product line; to close four out of six manufacturing sites; and to turn the business around in five years.

Marching Orders

Then in early 1984, Browning received his new marching orders from the executive officers of the Continental Group (Stamford, Conn.). They wanted definite changes in the way the White Cap division did business, and they believed Browning, fresh from his success with Bondware and a veteran of White Cap himself, was surely the man to make those changes.

Continental had several major concerns about White Cap. First of all, they saw a competitive onslaught brewing that they believed White Cap managers did not recognize. They believed the business instincts of White Cap's management had been dulled by a tradition of uncontested market leadership. The majority of these managers had been with the firm for over 25 years, and most of them had little intention of moving beyond White Cap, or even beyond their current positions. They were accustomed to Bob White's multilayered, formal, and restrained management style, a style which inhibited cross-communication and which one manager dubbed "management without confrontation." Some of them were startled, even offended by the price-slashing tactics practiced by White Cap's most recent competitors, and they spoke wistfully of an earlier, more "gentlemanly" market style.

Continental was also concerned that White Cap's long-time success, coupled with the benevolent paternalism of the White family management, had led to a padded administrative staff. They instructed Browning to communicate a sense of impending crisis and urgency to the White Cap staff, even as he reduced the salary and administrative costs which Continental perceived as inflated. And he was to do all this without threatening White Cap's image in the marketplace or their tradition of employee loyalty.

Browning recognized that corporate attitudes toward White Cap were colored by a history of less than open and cooperative relations with Bob White:

> Bob White engendered and preserved the image of White Cap as an enigma, a mystery. He had an obsession with keeping Continental at arm's length, and he used the leverage of his stock and his years of experience to preserve his independence from corporate headquarters. After all, Bob never wanted to leave White Cap or go further.
>
> This kind of mystery, coupled with White Cap's continued success, engendered doubts and envy and misconceptions at the corporate level.

A former Continental Group manager elaborated:

> White Cap has always been seen as a prima donna by the Continental Group. I'm not convinced that there aren't some in Connecticut who might want to see White

Cap stumble. They have always looked at the salary and administrative costs at 13% of net sales, compared with a 3–4% ratio in other divisions, and concluded that White Cap was fat.

Perhaps the demand for cost cuts was fueled by the fact that the Continental Group was going through its own period of "radical surgery" at this time. Since 1984 when Peter Kiewit and Sons acquired the company, corporate headquarters had "sold off $1.6 billion worth of insurance, paper products businesses, gas pipelines and oil and gas reserves," and had cut corporate staff from 500 to 40.[3] The corporate climate was calling for swift, effective action.

Taking Charge

In the first month of his new position, Browning turned his attention to three issues. To begin with, he felt he had to make some gesture or take some stand with regard to Bob White. White was very much alive in the hearts and minds of White Cap's employees and although retired, he still lived in the Chicago area. Although White represented many of the values and the style that Browning hoped to change, he was also a key to the White Cap pride and morale that Browning had to preserve.

In addition, Bob White's successor, Art Lawson, was another link to White Cap's past and his strong presence in the marketplace represented continuity in White Cap's customer relations. Since corporate headquarters was determined to maintain an untroubled public image throughout White Cap's transition, they brought Browning in reporting to Lawson, the division's vice president and executive officer and a man Browning had known for over 20 years (see Exhibit 2). Browning knew he had to give some strong messages about new directions if he was to shake up the comfortable division, but he had to do this from below Lawson and in spite of White's heritage.

A second challenge facing Browning was White Cap's Marketing department. At a time when major, long-term customers in mature markets were faced with the attraction of an emerging plastic packaging technology and were beginning to take the White Cap Total System for granted, Browning found a Marketing and Sales organization that, according to him, "simply administered existing programs." They were not spending constructive time with the customers who had built the business, nor were they aggressively addressing new competitive issues.

Jim Stark had been the director of Marketing for the previous five years. He had a fine track record with White Cap customers and, as an individual, maintained many strong relationships in the field. Customers knew him well and relied on him. He had been with the company for 30 years and had been a regional sales manager before his transfer to marketing. In this prior position, Stark's strengths had clearly been his ability to deal with the customers as opposed to his people managing skills. Despite his strong presentation and selling ability, his internal relationships with his marketing staff and with the field sales force had apparently soured over the

---

[3]Allan Dodds Frank, "More Takeover Carnage?" *Forbes,* August 12, 1983, p. 40.

Exhibit 2
Peter Browning and Continental White Cap (A): Organization Chart, April 1984

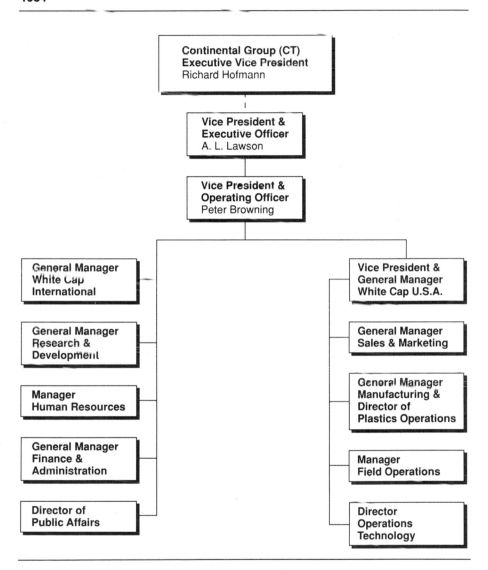

years. Team spirit was not in evidence. Stark complained that he didn't receive the support he needed to make changes in marketing.

Stark's boss, the GM for Sales and Marketing, urged Browning to avoid any sudden personnel changes and "to give Stark a chance." Moreover, relieving a manager of his responsibilities would be unprecedented at White Cap. Yet, for some, Stark was like "a baseball coach who has been with the team through some slow seasons and was no longer able to turn around his image."

Browning also inherited a manager of Human Resources, Tom Green, whose role and capabilities he began to question. Browning had always been a proponent of a strong Human Resources function. He met with Tom Green and asked him to help identify and evaluate key personnel throughout the divisions in terms of promotion and reassignment decisions. Green was a veteran White Capper with 20 years seniority and 5 years in his current position. Older managers were very comfortable with him and he was well liked. He offered few surprises to employees and helped maintain all the traditional and popular benefit policies and practices that they came to expect from White Cap.

Browning soon recognized a problem with Green:

> In reviewing the personnel files with Green, I found he had few constructive ideas to offer. He seemed to do a lot of delegating and to spend a lot of time reading *The Wall Street Journal*. And a lot of managers seemed to work around him. I found myself getting involved in decisions that he should have been taking care of, such as deciding whether a departing secretary in another department needed to be replaced or not.
>
> One possibility was to replace Green with the Human Resources manager from Bondware who had helped me with the changes I had made there. But Green was also a valuable information source and someone who could be a non-threatening conduit to and from White Cap employees.

Peter Browning pondered these initial choices and decisions carefully. He wanted to rejuvenate White Cap and yet not demoralize its loyal work force and management. Browning knew that Dick Hofmann, his boss, expected him to push for real, measurable change in the division's culture and performance. What was less clear was how far he should push, and how fast in order to succeed. Even Hofmann acknowledged that Browning's assignment put him "smack dab between a rock and a hard place."

Case 7–4

Peter Strassman

Roger Schwarz, Vijay Sathe

In May 1978, Peter Strassman was assessing his progress as general manager of Electechs, one of LEM Corporation's divisions. Since 1974 he had undertaken the task of creating a single divisional identity from the seven companies that LEM had acquired during the period 1972–78. Prime Motors was proving the hardest to fold into the division, although others were posing similar challenges. In addition to getting each acquired company to think in Electechs terms of planning and control, Strassman sought to ensure that the companies worked well together to offer better products and services to end users.

> When you acquire a company, you have to provide directions. It's like a lieutenant who is always out in front of his troops. "Why are you always out in front?" someone asked him. "Because you can't push a toy with a string," he answered. Each acquisition is a community unto itself, and they are very resistant to change. They are small, entrepreneurial, and used to flexibility. They built their business on enthusiasm and pride around their name. . . .
>
> Prime Motors has been the most difficult of all the acquisitions because of a couple of people at the top of the business. Their concept of how to run a business is dramatically opposed to mine. I could have let them run on their own, but that's not what I think we should do. I am trying to build an integrated business in motors and switches by using a unified strategy. I want to create crosspollination internally, and project this Electechs image outside.

By crosspollination, Strassman meant that each operation would work with the others toward meeting the customers' needs. For example, Strassman expected Prime Motors to tell customers about the other companies in the Electech Division.

If a customer needed a product that none of the Electech companies produced, Strassman expected that two or more of them would work together to design a product that met the customer's needs.

Strassman had some simple ways to judge whether and to what extent the Electechs identity was being created. One was whether the switchboard operators answered calls with "Electechs-Prime Motors" or just "Prime Motors." Another indication was whether the acquired company used business cards that carried the Electechs name and logo. Strassman had found that most of the operation's cards did not carry the Electechs name. He solved the problem by having the Pittsburgh headquarters print business cards. Name recognition surveys also gave Strassman an indication of Electechs' identity as it affected competitors' and customers' perception.

Electechs had acquired three companies prior to 1974. Prime Motors, acquired in 1975, had been Strassman's first acquisition as division manager. Three more companies were acquired between 1975 and 1978. Strassman believed that each acquired company had its own methods of control, market strategies, and attitudes toward its workers. One couldn't shove changes in these areas "down the throats" of managers. Change was a slow process that involved building loyalty and demonstrating that the changes benefited the acquired company. Strassman felt that once the managers of an acquired company saw the benefits of the suggested changes, resistance would diminish.

Strassman was aware that the managers of the acquired companies tended to see him as constraining their autonomy and, at times, exerting too much influence. Strassman realized that their view of him was not unlike his view of corporate LEM.

Career and Background

Peter Strassman began as project engineer with Aqua Motors in 1958. In 1963, he was named operations manager of Aqua. By 1970, when Aqua Motors was acquired by the LEM Corporation, he was senior vice president for marketing and engineering. His biographical sketch appears in Exhibit 1.

When Strassman took over as division general manager in 1974, the Electechs business was not very large—$22 million in sales. His operations managers were "pretty green" and Strassman spent considerable time developing them. This fit well with his active hands-on personal style. Strassman felt that his boss, Ted Landek, "nodded a lot" and took an essentially laissez-faire stance toward Strassman and Electechs. As long as Strassman kept Landek informed, Landek made few requests, unless the president or chairman wanted something done.

Strassman believed that his major accomplishments as general manager of Electechs had been to develop business through diversification and internal product development and to provide efficient solutions to customer problems. His subordinates and those outside the division viewed him as an entrepreneur who often felt constrained by corporate policy but who recognized the need for corporate control. Strassman earned his reputation, in part, by jointly developing proprietary products

---

Exhibit 1
Strassman's Background

Education	College—Rutgers University, B.S. Engineering 1962. Harvard Business School, Summer AMP program 1975–76.
Military Service	U.S. Air Force, June 1941–August 1944.
Professional Career	1945–1958: Employed by Atlantic Motors Corporation starting as technician and advancing to project engineer.
	1958–1970: Joined Aqua Motors, Inc. Held positions of chief engineer, manager of manufacturing, marketing and sales manager during this period. Became senior vice president responsible for both marketing and engineering in 1966 and served as member of the Board of Directors.
	1970–present: Became LEM Corporation employee in 1970 through the acquisition of Aqua Motors by LEM Corporation. Retained the position of senior vice president of Aqua Motors through 1972. Appointed Electechs' division general manager in 1974.

---

with other corporations and by purchasing new technologies for making products. Strassman's actions were noticed at the upper levels. At one board meeting, the chairman stated that LEM needed more entrepreneurs and cited Strassman and another general manager as examples.

Prime Motors

In 1975, Electechs was looking to acquire a motor business that was compatible with and complementary to its other operations. Strassman wanted to develop the motor and switch business so that Electechs could sell motor systems rather than isolated components. A corporate acquisition group brought Prime to Strassman's attention.

When Strassman first visited Prime's operations near Los Angeles, California, he had mixed reactions. Prime had been in business for 35 years. It was started by three principals who had a proprietary technology—motors that were very reliable under extreme conditions. To Strassman, the high-performance plant looked like a glorified machine shop, but to the Prime employees, it was a sophisticated organization. They told Strassman they were always looking for products that would sell in large quantities, but Strassman got the impression they were really a specialty house.

All those who were in authority at Prime had grown up in the organization. That wasn't necessarily bad in Strassman's view, but he felt that many of the managers were not capable of developing new ideas or providing direction. Prime management believed in participative management. When Strassman asked to see an organization chart, they didn't have one. The president drew one up on a piece of paper; he drew a number of boxes: one each for the chairman, president, two vice presidents, and the remainder represented committees.

From talking with Prime president Scott Morgan, Strassman realized that the whole organization was built on conflict rather than cooperation. Each function distrusted the other functions, and each had individuals assigned to handle complaints from the others. Morgan said he wanted this type of conflict. He saw it as a way of auditing functional operations, a way for each function to keep the others honest. In addition, functions second-guessed each other: When a customer inquired whether Prime could make a certain product, marketing would forward the inquiry to engineering without any discussion. After engineering drew up a design it believed met the customer's needs, manufacturing costed out the product. When marketing received the plans and costs, it decided the price was too high. It sent the plans to the potential customer but cut the cost, believing that manufacturing could make the product for less than it had quoted. Once the customer placed the order and engineering drew up detailed plans, manufacturing found it could not make the product at the price marketing had quoted.

When Prime made decisions on larger issues, such as capital investments, a committee was set up to consider the issues. Sometimes the committee reached a decision only to find that Prime's chairman, Dan Steadman, had independently arrived at another. Once a committee that Steadman had appointed to decide whether and how much the machine shop should be expanded recommended that Prime invest several hundred thousand dollars; at that point Steadman told the committee he was willing to spend only $100,000 and suggested the specific pieces of machinery to be purchased. Strassman believed that Steadman, who started the business, could have made these decisions alone; the committees seemed to be a form of pseudoparticipation.

Strassman learned that Steadman, who owned 45 percent of Prime, was a conservative but paternalistic individual. For instance, the top 15 to 20 people at Prime were given an annual bonus, and all of the 400 employees were invited to visit and stay at Steadman's ranch in Arizona and his lakeside property in northern California during most of the weeks of the year when Steadman was not using them. There was no charge; even meals and drinks were on the house when employees took advantage of the standing offer from Steadman. This paternalism extended to job security—there never had been a layoff at Prime, even during an occasional off year. As one old timer recalled: "Prime doesn't pay well, but we like the place and have a dedication to getting the job done. We bitch and moan about the low pay, but no one is leaving because we have a lot of fun here."

Prime Motors appeared to be an attractive acquisition because its extreme-condition, high-performance motor was the Cadillac of the industry. Strassman knew the company had a good reputation from his earlier years as a rocket propulsion engineer. Also, corporate LEM's analysis of the company revealed that it had good manufacturing facilities, a good location, and good growth potential. More important, the growth had been limited by the owner's desire to avoid debt. With corporate's approval, Electechs acquired Prime Motors for $18 million in the spring of 1975.

At that time Electechs bought out Prime Motors' president and chairman and offered them one-year consulting contracts. Scott Morgan, the president, was the marketing expert, and Dan Steadman, the chairman, had been responsible for the technical area. Steadman considered John Howell, the vice president of marketing, to be the heir apparent. Strassman learned that Steadman always looked after Howell, an engineering graduate from Stanford and that he had appointed Howell president just before selling Prime.

Strassman spent a day with Howell before the acquisition and was very impressed with his knowledge of the operation and the level of detail with which he spoke about it. A charismatic individual, who apparently had a strong following at Prime, Howell talked at length about manufacturing and spoke only briefly about marketing and engineering.

Management Differences

The first sign of differences between Strassman and Howell became evident when Electechs attempted to install its control system at Prime, as it did in all acquired companies. The control system required forecasts of sales and gross margins for the upcoming 30 and 60 days. Ideally, marketing and manufacturing worked with the controller to develop the forecasts. In acquisitions where marketing and manufacturing had not worked closely with the controller, the burden of preparing the forecasts usually fell on the controller. One and a half years before the acquisition, Prime's controller had left and had not been replaced, so Strassman placed Harvey Burke, an LEM controller, in Prime to install the new system and to remain as controller. But Howell had his own "push-through" method of control, which he continued to use and from which he questioned the numbers that Burke worked up.

The push-through method of control dispensed with a perpetual physical inventory. Instead, Howell would decide how much profit he wanted to make in a given period and adjust the value of the inventory accordingly by declaring certain inventoried products obsolete and "recomputing" the cost of goods sold. Strassman pressed Howell to drop the push-through method and adopt the Electechs system, but Howell would either not respond or would agree half-heartedly and fail to follow up. He continued to use the push-through method and continually questioned the validity of the numbers Burke generated using the LEM control system.

From the beginning, Howell felt he should be allowed to run Prime as an autonomous operation. Whenever Strassman or other Electechs managers gave him advice, Howell would say that he had his own ideas on the topics or would try to appease them by agreeing, but would never implement their ideas. In personnel matters, he emphasized that California was different and that LEM didn't understand the needs of his employees.

Howell never told Strassman how their needs differed from those of other employees, but Strassman did concede there were some differences in attitudes and behavior. Prime employees were reluctant to work on weekends and sometimes refused to do so even when tight deadlines had to be met. This was usually not a

Exhibit 2
Sales and Return on Sales (ROS) for Electechs and Prime Motors

Electechs

		FY 1975	FY 1976	FY 1977
Sales ($ millions)	Plan	34.6	51.3	66.7
	Actual	51.2	57.6	69.9
ROS (pretax percentage)	Plan	16.2	14.0	17.0
	Actual	5.4	13.5	17.0

Prime Motors

		FY 1975	FY 1976	FY 1977
Sales ($ millions)	Plan	14.5	17.5	19.1
	Actual	16.3	16.8	20.6
ROS (pretax percentage)	Plan	13.8	20.0	14.0
	Actual	18.5	13.5	16.5

problem for Electechs' operations outside California. Howell wanted to hire Californians to fill key positions at Prime, ostensibly because it took a Californian to understand and work with Californians.

Although Strassman thought Howell was technically well qualified, he became concerned that Howell was focusing too much on details. Howell did not seem to have enough understanding of the total business or to think about growth. While Howell believed the company would continue to grow, Strassman tried to convince him that Prime could grow even faster by melding with other Electechs operations, and through central distribution and advertising. Strassman's conception was that the combined products and efforts of the Electechs operations could provide comprehensive, unified systems and solutions that addressed customers' problems.

In October 1975, six months after the acquisition, Prime's performance was discussed at the annual Electechs Planning Meeting, which Strassman conducted. Prime had achieved good performance in fiscal year ending October 1975, its first year as part of LEM Corporation, with pretax ROS of 18.5 percent (Exhibit 2). Strassman attributed this largely to the accumulator of customer orders from the previous year, which remained unfilled while Prime's owners were busy negotiating Prime's sale. Strassman noted the delayed shipments had left plenty of Prime's customers unhappy, and their resentment would soon have to be addressed.

There were other areas in which Strassman believed Prime could substantially improve performance. He felt that Prime, like many small, owner-managed companies, had inefficient work methods and inadequate planning and control systems. Productivity would be dramatically increased by rearranging existing equipment, by automating certain production processes, and by reducing the work force. For instance, Prime's current approach to planning and budgeting was to project increases in all expense categories by the same percentage as the projected percentage increase in sales. Thus failure to seek gains in operating leverage would lead to an overburdened operating plan. Similarly, level loading of manufacturing facilities was not planned for—a disproportionately high percentage of monthly production shipments occurred in the last two weeks of the month. Direct labor was staffed at the level required for these peak periods, resulting in underutilizing labor during the first two weeks of each month. Based on his analyses of these factors, Strassman reasoned that Prime could easily effect a permanent 10 percent reduction in the 400-person work force through more efficient production planning and labor utilization.

Strassman also believed Prime was not realizing its full earnings potential—the earnings it could return given the value of its service to customers. Prime offered customized products to aerospace companies, as well as more standardized commodity products for industrial use. The aerospace business, involving made-to-order items, commanded 75 percent in gross margins; the industrial business yielded 30 percent gross margin with efficient distribution of these commodity products. By emphasizing selected segments of the aerospace business and by better managing distribution of the industrial products, Strassman believed Prime could achieve its earnings potential—45 percent gross margin and 20 percent pretax ROS.

The 20 percent figure was cast in concrete when Strassman sent it to corporate LEM as part of Electechs' financial forecast. When Strassman told Howell about the 20 percent ROS target, Howell said he could not do better than 9 percent based on his push-through calculations. Between October 1975 and June 1976, Strassman and Howell discussed whether Prime's earnings potential was 9 percent, 20 percent or something in between. Strassman could not get Howell to see that Prime's earnings potential should be 20 percent. To Strassman, Howell seemed unable to grasp the concept of earnings potential.

In early June 1976, Strassman flew out to California to review Prime's performance with Don Johnson, Electechs' manufacturing director. Johnson was Howell's other superior in the matrix (Exhibit 3). During the operations review, the issue of the company logo also arose. As part of his plan to build a division identity, Strassman insisted that each operation's letterhead and advertising carry LEM Electechs' logo with the operation's name underneath. Howell wanted to keep the Prime Motors' logo and told Strassman that Prime's customers would not recognize the product without the logo. He also told Strassman that after 35 years, all old timers and most of the rest of the employees were emotionally attached to the logo and proudly looked up to it as their symbol of quality. Strassman responded, "We're not going to take the logo away immediately. Put the logo on the product if you want."

Howell argued that the logo was a $480,000 asset, and they could not claim it

Exhibit 3
Electechs Division Structure—Prior to the June 1976 Reorganization

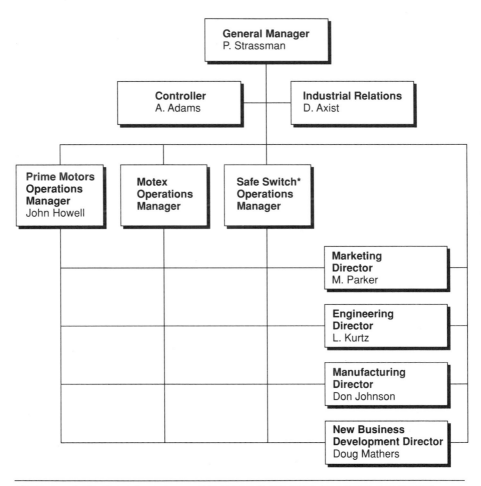

*Similar organizational reporting arrangement for Eastern Switch, Matel, Aqua Motors, and Allied Wire.

if they did not use it. Strassman told Howell that if they were really concerned about the $480,000, he would find a way around it. In the end, Howell agreed to use the Electechs logo. Strassman realized why Howell was so adamant about the logo. His entire career had been with Prime: He had grown up with the logo and could not part with that symbol from his past.

When the subject turned to productivity, Strassman told Howell that Prime should be able to reach at least 14 percent pretax ROS in fiscal year 1976, instead of the 9 percent Howell had quoted last October. In the 14 months since Electechs had acquired Prime, Strassman had learned much about Prime's business. With more knowledge of Prime's costs and information about its competition, Strassman could better estimate Prime's earnings potential. He realized the 20 percent ROS was slightly high, although it was appropriate for fiscal year 1976 because of Prime's order backlog. Acknowledging that it would take some time for Prime to increase volume and cut costs, Strassman told Howell he would accept 14 percent ROS for fiscal year 1977 but insisted on an 18 percent ROS for fiscal year 1978 (Exhibit 2).

Strassman suggested reducing the number of Prime's 400 employees as a way of increasing productivity. Strassman believed that 20 could be cut immediately, but Howell would not entertain the thought. "I have never laid off anyone in the history of Prime Motors, and I am not going to start now." "It's not your decision to make," Strassman snapped, and added, "I want a staff reduction plan on my desk by next Friday."

By the following Thursday, Strassman had not yet received the plan in Pittsburgh and called to see if it would be there the next day. Howell told Strassman he had not worked on the plan and was not going to. "Get on a plane Sunday night and be here first thing Monday morning," Strassman demanded.

When Howell arrived at Electech's headquarters on Monday morning, he was indignant at having to fly out "under orders." Strassman and Howell met with Don Johnson and together developed a plan to lay off Prime's staff and increase productivity. Even after the plan had been developed, Strassman doubted that Howell was convinced, and Howell never said he would implement the plan.

A couple of weeks later, Howell called Strassman and asked for a raise. Surprised, Strassman told Howell he had not done anything to deserve one. Howell maintained he was due for a higher salary because similar positions in the industry paid more. Howell mentioned that under the LEM contract he had signed at the time of the acquisition, he was to receive "equitable salary increases." Strassman had not heard of this contract and told Howell this. Howell thought he was very employable and said he wanted to look elsewhere as well as to seek professional placement advice. Strassman encouraged him to do so, recognizing that it was important for Howell to "clear his conscience."

Strassman later called his boss, group vice president Ted Landek, and asked about the contract. Landek explained that Howell signed the standard LEM contract. The contracted stated that, as an LEM employee, Howell was entitled to equitable salary increases, but it did not mention any specific timetable or amounts. As it turned out, Howell was earning more than anyone else in a comparable position in LEM.

Serious Doubts

By late June 1976, Strassman had serious doubts about Howell's ability to do the job in areas other than manufacturing. As Strassman saw it, he had three options. He could keep things as they were and expend what he felt was an inordinate amount of his time on Prime. He could replace Howell with Don Johnson, director of manufacturing and currently Howell's other immediate superior. Or he could effect a reorganization of the division to address the problem.

Exhibit 4
Electechs Division, after the June 1976 Reorganization

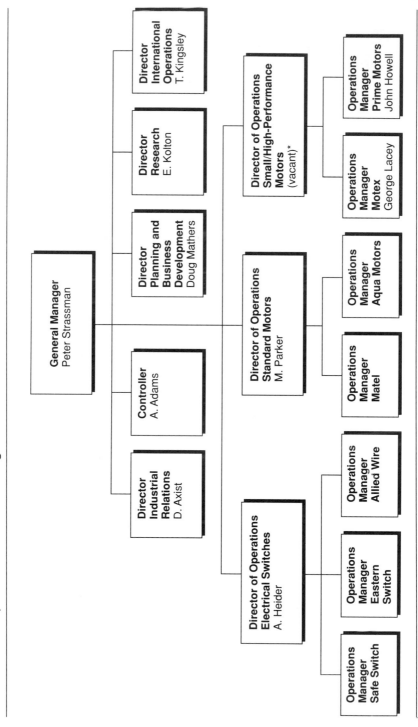

*Doug Mathers, effective September 1976.

Leaving things as they were was intolerable to Strassman because of the 2,000 miles separating him from Howell. If Strassman were at Prime, he could give Howell objectives and control him more closely. Replacing Howell with Don Johnson was an attractive option. Strassman considered Johnson a supersound manager, a type Prime needed badly. Strassman believed Johnson, unlike Howell, was a generalist who worked through the people and could bring the functions together. He was straightforward and loyal to those who worked for him. If anyone from outside California could be accepted in Prime, Strassman believed it was Johnson. Johnson had been with LEM for 41 years and would have gone to California if Strassman had asked. However Johnson was planning to retire in two years, and Strassman thought it was unreasonable to ask him to move.

Strassman's third option was to reorganize the division, which is what he did. In late June 1976, Strassman dismantled the matrix and established the structure shown in Exhibit 4. The matrix structure had been set up in 1973 by John Hansen, then general manager of Electechs, upon his return from Harvard Business School's AMP program. Strassman, then senior vice president for operations, had each of the operations managers reporting to him, and he in turn reported directly to Hansen. The matrix structure had not been easy to work in. The managers who ran the operating groups had persistent difficulties with those heading the marketing, manufacturing, and engineering functions. For example, engineering director Larry Kurtz attempted to apply statistical quality control to the operations. His group wrote many reports and made recommendations, but none of the operations adopted the method (see Exhibit 3). The matrix was unwieldy, and Strassman felt he needed to establish clearer lines of authority. An even greater impetus for the reorganization was to help solve the problems at Prime. Strassman thought restructuring the division would free up some of the time he was spending on Prime. Strassman grouped the seven operations into three areas: electrical switches under Arthur Heider; standard motors under Martin Parker; and small/high-performance motors, for which he was seeking an appropriate director (Exhibit 4).

Doug Mathers

In September 1976, Strassman made Doug Mathers director of the small/high-performance motor area. With the change, Howell reported directly to Mathers (see Exhibit 4). Mathers had sold his company, Motex, to Electechs in 1972 and through the sale became moderately wealthy. He served as Motex operations manager until May 1976, when Strassman gave him special acrospace projects to work on as director of Planning and Business Development.

Strassman described Mathers as a true entrepreneur, "the type that likes to work on the back of an envelope." As a business owner, Mathers had been a taskmaster. He had worked his employees long hours and often on holidays. He had been involved in the day-to-day workings of the company. When problems developed, he had been quick to get rid of the person responsible. Mathers had a solid grasp of engineering and marketing of aerospace products, which required working on a one-on-one basis with aerospace people.

Strassman knew Mathers' strong aerospace background could become his short suit as well. One of Prime's major problems, according to Strassman, was that it focused too much on the aerospace industry and not enough on industrial applications. Prime managers maintained that their strategy was to develop products for aerospace and then push them through the industry, a strategy that so far had succeeded with only one motor. Strassman believed the other push-through attempts failed because the motors were overdesigned and too expensive for industrial use. Since industrial sales accounted for 85 percent of Prime's volume, but only 55 percent of its earnings, Strassman wanted Prime to focus more on industry sales by raising prices slightly and by developing other products for industrial use. Strassman wondered whether Mathers would push the industrial side of the business, given his aerospace orientation, but decided to go ahead with his appointment as director of small/high-performance motors for lack of a better candidate.

The reorganization freed Strassman's time but absorbed Mathers. Mathers was responsible for two operations but was spending literally 99 percent of his time on Prime, primarily on marketing and engineering. Mathers established basic marketing strategies and dealt directly with customers, something Howell had never done. He helped engineering develop new aerospace products.

Mathers became directly involved in these activities, rather than getting Howell to do them. As a result, he spent little time building the general small/high-performance motors area, his main responsibility as director. In addition, Strassman felt that Mathers was beginning to side with Howell. On one trip back to Pittsburgh, Mathers told Strassman, "We have this problem with the logo, Peter." Strassman thought to himself, "He's starting to become one of them." Although not raised in California, Mathers' quick assimilation into the West Coast work style led Strassman to think of Mathers as having become "part of the granola bowl." Strassman believed Mathers' entrepreneurial instincts made him especially sensitive about being seen as a loser. He got defensive whenever Strassman pointed out problems or would rationalize that the problems were already present when he took over as director of small/high-performance motors.

Continuing Problems with Howell

Although Strassman continued to question Howell's attitude and ability, he was not ready to let him go. Howell was conscientious and personable, and Strassman had scored what he viewed as some victories with him. Howell had agreed to move advertising and promotion to the Electechs headquarters in Pittsburgh. Over the summer, Strassman had told Howell that he would not have complete autonomy in running Prime and would have to confirm to Electechs' objectives, plans, and controls. Strassman thought Howell had understood and accepted this.

Strassman was also reluctant to let Howell go so soon after appointing Doug Mathers as director of small/high-performance motors because of the possible disruption this might create. Besides, Strassman felt he owed Mathers an opportunity to develop Howell. Mathers was confident that Howell would work out if he worked more closely with him and moved his office to Prime's operations in Los Angeles in order to work with Howell on a day-to-day basis. As an outsider to Prime, Mathers' strategy was to develop loyalty slowly, rather than to move quickly and possibly risk resistance. It was conceivable to Mathers that others at Prime would resist him if they saw that Howell did.

In December 1976, three months after Mathers' appointment as Howell's boss, Strassman had a conversation with Howell that left him in greater doubt about Howell's ability and judgment. Prime's marketing manager had just quit, and Strassman suggested this would be a good opportunity for Howell to learn more about marketing; he wanted Howell to get a broader sense of the business. Howell admitted he did not know much about marketing, but showed no interest in Strassman's suggestion.

Other problems were also developing at Prime. Howell had decided to market a new motor (number 61) and had budgeted $500,000 of inventory. Howell built up $1 million in inventory instead, even though distributors showed little interest in the 61 motor. Prime was thus saddled with all the inventory. Essentially the same mistake had been made by Prime prior to the acquisition—distributors wanted to carry a full line of motors, rather than stand-alone items, such as the 61. Furthermore, Prime had bought specialized machinery to manufacture the 61, instead of the general-purpose machinery that Strassman had recommended. The specialized machinery was useless except to produce more 61 motors. At this point, Strassman's communication with Howell was principally through Mathers. He instructed Mathers to figure out a way to get rid of the 61 motor inventory. Mathers took on the responsibility himself, and soon Prime managers were bypassing Howell and going directly to Mathers instead.

About one year later, in December 1977, Strassman thought the attitudes at Prime had changed somewhat. Prime had accepted certain Electechs suggestions, and a few key managers were telling Strassman that his persistence was beginning to pay off. However, the personnel manager, Joanne Danbury, who had been secretary to Prime's chairman Dan Steadman, was creating more problems.

Joanne Danbury

Joanne Danbury was personnel manager when Electechs acquired Prime. Strassman dubbed her a "social worker type." Shortly before the acquisition, the union had attempted to organize Prime and had lost by one vote. Danbury believed that unions were necessary because management often did not give the workers what they deserved. Back in 1976, when Strassman was at Harvard Business School's Summer AMP program, Prime increased compensation for employees—something Strassman did not support. On a subsequent trip to Prime, Strassman had raised the subject with Danbury.

Danbury lectured Strassman on how workers at all levels were entitled to homes, food, and cars, and what was a minimum income to live on in California. Strassman said he understood, but that he didn't agree with her decision to raise compensation for Prime employees. Danbury then began to tell Strassman about Maslow's theory of hierarchy needs, and she started writing these on the board. Strassman interrupted,

"Joanne, erase the board and stop right there. I'm not listening." Strassman thought, "She is trying to maintain the old ways. She is just like a union rep." The next day Strassman told Mathers to "get Danbury out of there."

As a first step, Strassman required that Danbury report directly to him, and he questioned her about everything. For example, she was not willing to place an engineer from outside Prime above an engineer who had been at Prime a long time. Strassman also placed Danbury on a corporate responsibility committee, "to give her a chance to broaden her perspective." She felt like an outcast there, realized she had no power to change things, and gave up.

Soon afterwards Danbury approached Mathers and expressed her frustration with Strassman. Mathers suggested that she probably would not be able to make the changes she wanted and that this was probably a good time for her to earn her doctorate in psychology that she had hoped to get. Three months after Strassman had told him to get rid of Danbury, Mathers had gotten her to leave. He had done it by patiently, periodically suggesting to Danbury that she would be better off if she left Prime.

Herb Gardner

With Danbury gone, Strassman told Mathers to find someone in LEM in industrial relations (IR) who was not from California. When Mathers suggested Herb Gardner, Howell resisted, feeling that only someone from California could be the IR person in California because California was different. When Strassman heard this, he told Mathers to "get them to accept Gardner." When Gardner was scheduled to fly out to Prime to meet Howell and other key managers, Strassman warned Howell, "If I get any indication that Herb was discouraged, I will be very upset."

Mathers and Gardner liked each other from the start. They were of the same religion, and Mathers helped Gardner find a home and a good school system for his children. The other key managers also liked Gardner. At first Gardner sometimes got ensnarled in policies Danbury had previously established. For example, Danbury had planned a job fair when Gardner took over. Danbury had placed an ad in the local paper which stated that engineering and other professional jobs were available and invited interested individuals to tour the plant. The purpose of the fair was to allow employees' families to see where Mom or Dad worked and also to attract potential new employees in an extremely tight hiring market (local unemployment was only 4 percent). When Strassman heard about this, he told Howell to cancel the job fair because he was concerned that Prime's competition would tour the plant and obtain useful information. With the ad in the paper, it was too late to cancel. The fair was held. A month later, ostensibly under pressure from Howell, Gardner held a second job fair. When Strassman found out a second fair had been held, he was furious.

After a while, Gardner was able to make changes that were accepted, such as changing the performance review system. In the past, supervisors had written narratives that focused on the subordinates' traits, rather than objectives the subordinates were to accomplish. The narratives were usually extremely complimentary, and it was difficult to distinguish among subordinates' performances.

The problem came to a head when Prime needed a new materials manager. Materials accounted for 40 percent of product cost, and it was important that Prime find a highly competent manager for this position. Within the last year, several people who had come up from the hourly ranks had filled the position; when one could not do the job, another replaced him or her. Gardner set up an MBO performance review system. Based on Strassman's instructions, Gardner had each superior rank order his or her subordinates. Strassman believed that ranking personnel would, among other things, prevent the "musical chairs" phenomenon that had plagued the position of materials manager.

Escalating the Battle with Howell

Howell continued to ignore Mathers' suggestions to drop the push-through accounting method. Harvey Burke, the LEM controller whom Strassman placed in Prime, had already quit in frustration. Before Burke had left, he told Strassman that he was quitting for five reasons and three of them were Howell. Strassman warned Howell, "If you don't get rid of your bookkeeping system, I will have to consider some serious changes."

Production problems also continued. Larger variances in the cost of production caused Prime to raise its prices, and Strassman thought Prime was close to pricing itself out of the market. Part of the problem stemmed from inefficient use of labor. The plant would plan on 20,000 earned labor hours for the year and get only 12,000. When Strassman asked for specific costs, such as start-up costs, Howell would parry the question, stating he could dig up the information, but it would take a lot of time and probably would not be helpful.

Despite these problems, Prime's fiscal year 1977 ROS was 16.5 percent, better than the 14 percent goal Strassman had set. Later, Strassman found out that Prime reached the 16.5 percent figure by adjusting inventory profits. The unfavorable variance resulting from discrepancies between Prime's actual and standard costs had been capitalized and closed into finished inventory, effectively deferring the unfavorable flow-through to the income statement for the following year. This procedure, which was acceptable within the LEM accounting system, presumed fairly accurate standard costs, something Prime did not have.

Strassman, more and more frustrated with Howell, told Mathers to back off Howell. (Mathers had established Howell's previous set of objectives.) It was time for Howell to show he could set his own business objectives. Strassman added that if he had to tell Howell what the new opportunities were, then "someone is going to lose their situation." Mathers still had confidence in Howell, and Strassman respected Mathers' judgment. Yet Strassman wondered whether Mathers, after having sold his business to Electechs, had run out of gas in being demanding and just wanted to be a nice guy.

The Annual Planning Meeting

Strassman, those reporting directly to him, and each of the operations managers (Exhibit 4) met each year in March for the three-day Electechs Planning Meeting. The first two days were typically devoted to an informal but in-depth review of each of the divisions' businesses—objectives, strategies, products, markets, growth opportunities, critical issues, three-year plans, and annual budgets. From these preliminary discussions was to be synthesized a one-hour presentation on the third day for LEM's top brass. Those attending typically included Ted Landek, group vice president in charge of Electechs, Bob Delega, corporate vice president for planning, and Robert Schmidt, LEM's president. The three other divisions under Landek made similar presentations. Strassman traditionally elected to have his three directors of operations each make 20-minute presentations, limiting his own role to brief opening and closing remarks. Strassman participated much more actively in the informal but more critical give-and-take that typically followed the prepared presentations.

Strassman and other Electechs executives arrived in Palm Beach, Florida, for the annual planning meeting on Sunday, March 12, 1978. Since Doug Mathers was not going to attend because his wife was ill, Strassman suggested that either George Lacey or John Howell, the two operations managers reporting to Mathers (Exhibit 4), take on the additional responsibility of making the 20-minute presentation for small/high-performance motors before corporate senior management on Wednesday. It was decided that John Howell would undertake this task. Although Howell had been on a two-week vacation immediately preceding the planning meeting, he had attended the previous year's meeting and knew what was expected.

Strassman was disappointed with Howell's performance during the preliminary sessions on Monday and Tuesday, March 13 and 14. Howell did not appear to have done his homework and was unresponsive to questions from colleagues and superiors. Despite some reservations, Strassman decided he owed Howell the opportunity to make the 20-minute presentation to corporate senior management on Wednesday, March 15, as planned. Unfortunately, according to Strassman, Howell's presentation was long, poorly prepared, and overly detailed. Howell talked about the new machinery Prime had purchased and how well it operated. At one point, Howell began talking about how the new corporate bonus system was unfair, because it excluded several managers at Prime who were included in the previous corporate bonus system. Howell announced that, to rectify this inequity, he and Mathers would share their bonuses with these managers. Howell directed these last comments at Schmidt, the corporate president. Strassman thought Howell had made a fool of himself; he was embarrassed by Howell's performance.

When Doug Mathers reported to work, Strassman told him what had happened. "Doug, you have to come to grips with this. There is a problem in your organization, and John Howell is that problem." Strassman said he had spoken to some key managers at Prime and they were frustrated with the situation. Howell had begun to ask each of the key managers to develop reports; Strassman and the managers considered these reports unnecessary make-work projects. Strassman gave Mathers the option of either getting rid of Howell or quickly changing the situation.

Toward the end of April 1978, Strassman sent Electechs' controller Al Adams to Prime to assess what changes had been made since Strassman last spoke with Howell in March. While Adams was speaking with the Prime controller, the controller received a call from the shop foreman. The foreman wanted to know if 35 people, for whom he had no work, should be let go. Adams found it hard to believe that Howell had been resisting a layoff despite excess manpower.

During the week of May 8, 1978, Strassman planned to meet with Mathers at Prime to decide what to do about Howell. Howell was taking the remaining two weeks of his vacation. Mathers preferred that Strassman did not come to the Prime plant because if he did, there would be some tough questions for Strassman that Mathers felt would be difficult to dodge. For example, the managers were likely to ask Strassman if Howell would be replaced. Mathers said he did not want to put Strassman in the position where he would have to respond to that question. Instead, he suggested they meet for dinner in Los Angeles to decide what to do.

Reading 7–1

Organizational Change Techniques: Their Present, Their Future*

Stephen R. Michael

The French say that the more things change, the more they remain the same. George Odiorne's law says that things that do not change remain the same. These two views suggest that, change or no, life will go on. I would like to suggest another possibility: Things that do not change may not remain at all. Translated into a management context, lack of change may endanger the survival of organizational life itself.

It seems reasonably clear, for example, that the change from a Democratic to a Republican administration at the federal level is bringing about some drastic alterations in the political environment of business. Changes in government regulation, subsidies for business, and assistance to state governments are just a few changes that are occurring. The implications of these changes for business may be obvious because they are so well publicized. Ignorance as such may not impede organizational adaptation.

But other changes that occur in the environment are not so obvious, such as gradual shifts in population, in social and business conventions, and in attitudes. The implications of these changes are not only not obvious; they may be difficult to forecast even after serious study. Adaptation, therefore, may be difficult.

*Reprinted, by permission of the publisher, from *Organizational Dynamics,* Summer 1982. © 1982 AMACOM, a division of American Management Associations, New York. All rights reserved. The data reported in this study were obtained during a research project funded by the Graduate School of the University of Massachusetts/Amherst.

The Manager's Two-Front Job

This continuum of change in the environment—from the obvious to the unpredictable—is merely one way of emphasizing the developing responsibilities of managers. While the manager has historically had what can be referred to as an "inside job"—keeping operations going—that role is changing. Management is now a two-front job. There is an outside as well as an inside responsibility. The first front is the traditional one—guiding the organization to achievement of its goals by getting on with its tasks. The second front is a newer responsibility—maintaining a watch on the external environment for problems that will afflict and opportunities that can be exploited for the organization. These two responsibilities can be seen to merge in the new role of managers as change agents. Drastic changes in technology, the proliferation of new products and the obsolescence of old, tough international competition, as well as inflation and energy problems: All of these events, trends, and changes in the environment will require managers in the 1980s to spend more time than they did in the 1970s acting as agents of organizational change.

As they do, they will find that they have a variety of organizational change techniques from which to choose in carrying out their tasks. It will not be necessary—indeed it may be inadvisable—to proceed in a haphazard, trial-and-error approach to implementing change.

In what follows, the nature of organizational change will be discussed; the available organizational change techniques will be reviewed, compared, and contrasted; and data showing the relative use of the various techniques by a sample of *Fortune* 500 companies will be presented.

Organization-Environment Fit

Organizational change is the process of adjusting the organization to changes in the environment. It is carried out when there is reason to believe that there is a poor fit between the organization and the environment. The result, if done properly, should be a better organization-environment fit. Exhibit 1 illustrates the major factors and actions involved. In summary, the environment gives rise to problems that the organization has to face and opportunities that it can exploit. The organization's potential responses are a function of its strengths and weaknesses. Analysis of the organization's strengths and weaknesses in the light of environmental problems and opportunities suggests the nature of the organization-environment fit. A poor fit should give rise to a problem definition. The definition, in turn, should point the way toward developing alternative strategic solutions. The choice of a strategic solution is a function of the relative payoffs—money, morale, goodwill, time, productivity, and so forth—that the alternatives offer. Implementation of the chosen solution should bring about a better organization-environment fit.

Exhibit 1
Adjusting the Organization to its Environment

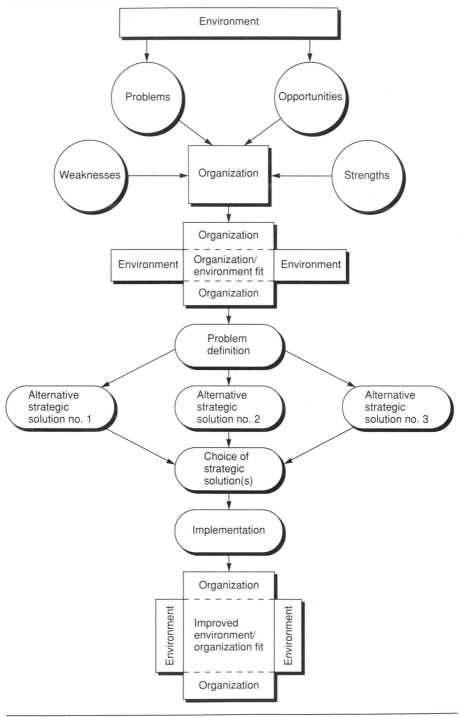

When making organizational change, bear these problem areas in mind:

1. Even under the best of circumstances, organizational change isn't easy.
2. Because of the intricate web of organizational interrelationships and dependencies and the large-scale financial and human investments in the existing order, organizational change cannot be implemented on a catch as-catch-can basis; it must be highly systematized.

The difficulty in bringing about organizational change is well documented in management literature and will be remembered by managers who have had to introduce changes in technology, launch a new product, or drastically change the division of labor under their jurisdictions—just to cite a few examples. What is involved here is the age-old conflict between bureaucratization and innovation.

Bureaucratization is the formalization of the organizational structure in terms of routine, standardized work. Its most obvious manifestations are a finer and more rigid division of labor and the proliferation of policies and procedures. These outcomes represent the learning derived from experience. The consequences should include lower costs. But the lessons learned become work habits and expectations, and therefore they become very resistant to change.

Innovation involves the substitution of a new idea for an old idea. New ideas require new work habits and different expectations. Hence the conflict between bureaucratization and innovation.

It is easier initially, of course, to take an unplanned, uncoordinated approach to organizational change. Like other people, managers are reluctant to spend time thinking and proceeding in a formal, orderly fashion so long as it appears unnecessary to do so. The consequence is a tendency to tinker. A slight change here, a slight change there; such small steps seem easy and safe. Small steps are also reversible. But the danger here is the inevitable losing sight of the forest because of the trees.

The solution is not to take one big step instead of several little ones. Rather, it is the taking of necessary steps in an orderly format of change. Such structured formats are provided by the organizational change techniques to be discussed below. They provide programmed approaches that enable managers to control the changes they wish to bring about. Not only do the techniques provide coordination; the procedures involved in the techniques make it possible to get meaningful participation from personnel who will be affected by changes. Such participation is likely to reduce the resistance to change and to facilitate successful implementation.

Techniques of Organizational Change

Exhibit 2 describes and compares the six commonly used techniques of organizational change: organizational behavior modification, management by objectives, management development, organization development, management auditing, and the control cycle of planning, implementing, and evaluating operations. Some of these are more familiar than others because managers react to fads and fashions

Exhibit 2
Comparison of Organizational Change Techniques

Types of Techniques

Characteristic	Organizational Behavior Modification	Management by Objectives	Management Development	Organization Development	Management Auditing	Control Cycle
Focal point	Individuals.	Individuals.	Individuals.	Entire organization or part.	Entire organization or part.	Entire organization or part.
Symptoms of problems requiring attention	Undesirable behaviors of workers resulting in substandard performance.	Different expectations and interpretations by superiors and subordinates of subordinates' performance.	Deficiencies in performance of tasks requiring mental or social skills to do present job and/or lack of skills to do future job.	Destructive conflict and lack of cooperation among individuals and groups.	Existing or anticipated problems or opportunities in product demand and supply, structure, functions, and processes.	Inability to adapt organization to changing environment using feedback control on product demand and supply, structure, functions, and processes.
Kinds of changes sought or achieved	Improved fit between individual and job, primarily at nonmanagerial levels.	Improved fit between individual and job at managerial and professional levels.	Improvement in mental and social skills at managerial and professional levels.	Improved interpersonal and intergroup behavior.	Improvements in product demand and supply, structure, functions, and processes.	Improvements in product demand and supply, structure, functions, and processes.

418

	Theoretical bases	Type of control	Continuity	Change agent
	Behavioral theory.	Feedback to resolve problems.	Intermittent.	Superiors and/or inside and outside consultants.
	Behavioral and management theories.	Feedforward/feedback to forestall problems or exploit opportunities.	Continuous.	Superiors; inside and outside consultants can assist.
	Behavioral theory.	Feedforward/feedback to forestall problems or exploit opportunities, or feedback to resolve problems.	Intermittent or continuous.	Superiors, with personnel or training department to coordinate.
	Behavioral theory.	Feedback to resolve problems.	Intermittent.	Outside and/or inside consultants with backing of higher management.
	Management theory.	Feedforward/feedback to forestall problems or exploit opportunities, or feedback to resolve problems.	Intermittent.	Outside and/or inside consultants with backing of higher management.
	Management theory.	Feedfoward/feedback to forestall problems and exploit opportunities.	Continuous.	All managers, with assistance of staff group and/or outside consultants.

Source: Stephen R. Michael et al., *Techniques of Organizational Change* (McGraw-Hill Book Company, © 1981). Reproduced by special permission.

just as other people react to new hemlines and hairdos. The current popularity of a particular technique may derive from publicity rather than its appropriateness for the tasks at hand. Their simultaneous presentation here is in accord with the contingency theory of management: The proper solution to a management problem depends on the situation. As we shall see, the techniques are not interchangeable, though they are complementary.

These techniques have not always been viewed as change processes, although they help bring change about. For example, management by objectives (MBO) is often viewed as a technique for improving communications between superiors and subordinates and for providing a basis for performance appraisals. But MBO is also a vehicle for change. The way in which each technique helps bring about change will be described. Then the techniques will be compared and contrasted.

Organizational Behavior Modification

Organizational behavior modification (OBMod) is based on B. F. Skinner's theory of learning. In brief, this theory holds that people as well as laboratory animals learn to change behavior through the feedback they get from the environment in response to overt behaviors. OBMod, therefore, is concerned with identifying desirable or undesirable behaviors and maintaining or changing such behavior by manipulating the environment and/or providing positive reinforcement.

This technique is implemented in a series of five steps. The first involves the identification of critical behaviors—those that have a significant impact on organizational performance and results. Only such overt, observable behaviors as absenteeism and tardiness in turning in reports are important here. Attitudes, motivations, and other inner states of individuals are not considered. To quote Fred Luthans, "(1) Can it be seen? and (2) Can it be measured?"

The latter question leads to the second step, measurement of the critical behaviors. The frequencies of specific behaviors will indicate whether there is a problem.

If the frequencies show a problem, the third step is to make a functional analysis of the behavior. This step is to determine the antecedent events and the consequences of the behavior. For example, the arrival of a mail clerk in an office (antecedent) could serve as a stimulant for the office employees to stop working and begin to socialize. The consequence would be a pleasant but unscheduled work break.

Once the analysis is completed, the fourth step requires an intervention in the situation. Basically, the intervention should involve positive reinforcement. For example, the supervisor could enter the work area at the same time as the mail clerk and make complimentary remarks to any personnel who do not interrupt their work. The others will get the message.

Step five, the last step, consists of evaluating the results of this process. Four factors are evaluated: the reaction to the use of OBMod, the extent to which supervisors have learned to use the techniques, the degree to which behaviors have changed, and the improvement in performance.

Management by Objectives

MBO achieves change by using superior-subordinate discussions to plan a subordinate's work. During such discussions, objectives, plans, and programs are established for changes in routine work, the resolution of problems, and the introduction of innovation.

The rationale behind MBO stems from observations that supervisors and subordinates usually fail to agree on the subordinate's expected level of output, on the subordinate's major problems, and on the ways in which the subordinate's job can be improved. Note that each of these areas of disagreement may involve change unless the superior agrees to the status quo—which is not likely.

Consequently, superior and subordinate look at the subordinate's tasks from the standpoints of routine work, unresolved problems, and opportunities for innovation. Task objectives and performance standards are set on the basis of mutual agreement in these three areas. Strategies and budgets, among other managerial considerations, are usually on the collaborative agenda.

The subordinate manager, therefore, has information about his or her job that permits and encourages self-control. This reduces the superior's control tasks. Nevertheless, superior and subordinates do meet periodically to review interim results. At the end of the MBO period, they also meet to look at final results to appraise subordinate performance, as a preliminary to the next cycle.

To underscore what may be an obvious point, management by objectives is a technique used primarily with managerial, professional, and technical personnel. The more routine the work, the lower the probability that MBO can help produce benefits that exceed its costs.

Management Development

Training and development lead to organizational change by altering the capabilities of managerial personnel. Such a process may be implemented to bring managers up to some set standard of performance or to prepare them for higher-level duty. Development of new or more highly developed skills provides the foundation for altered behavior.

The felt need for management development may arise from any aspect of managerial behaviors. A major source, however, is likely to be performance appraisals and other, less formal appraisals of management performance and potential. Any change in technology and tasks, as well as policies and strategies, could also trigger the need for management development.

Some firms routinely put all those who are hired for entry-level managerial jobs through a company training and development program. In such cases, the intent is to acculturate new employees to the organization's unique mode of operations—in effect, to domesticate them.

If a person survives that initial training program, other needs or opportunities for training will usually arise. Essentially, there will be a need for training to bring about a better fit between the individual and the current or future job. The former situation arises when the individual doesn't measure up to an existing job or when the job is enlarged or changed in some other way. On the other hand, the individual may be groomed to take on a higher-level job as vacancies occur. Management development does not merely fit a person to an existing role, however. More likely than not, the trained manager will find ways to change the job and the associated tasks. The usual sequence of change in the manager is the acquisition of new knowledge, the translation of the knowledge into new skills, and the transformation of new skills into new behaviors.

Training and development range from the casual to the formal; they range from on-the-job training to coaching and counseling by a superior, to special but short programs and seminars, and finally, to extended periods of residence at a business school or institute.

Organization Development

Collective behaviors of all or of some subset of organizational members are changed through the use of organization development (OD). The results are accomplished by improving interpersonal skills, the mutual resolution of common problems, and team building—among other methods.

As implied above, organization development relies upon knowledge of the behavioral science field. The intent is to improve organizational effectiveness by applying this knowledge to organizational members' behavior. This treatment includes six stages.

- OD begins with the *entry* stage in which a particular organization suffers the symptoms of poor interpersonal relationships among organizational members. An outside consultant or internal OD expert is then called in.
- The second stage involves some form of *contract* between the organization and the OD expert. The commercial form of contract is ideally supplemented by informal agreements that emphasize open communications and the exploration and classification of mutual expectations.
- At this point *data collection and diagnosis* signal the beginning of the actual study. Data are collected through observation, from documents and questionnaires, and from interviews. The data are collected, analyzed, and evaluated.
- *Feedback* to organizational members follows. The information is summarized according to the pattern of collection, then it is categorized conceptually, and finally, the OD consultant synthesizes the observations, impressions, and emotional reactions that characterize the data gathering.
- The change process itself is termed *intervention*. Typical interventions include structural change, team building, intergroup conflict resolution, role analysis, training, and the like.
- Finally, there is an *evaluation* stage to assess the results of organization development. The evaluation should be both quantitative and qualitative. The

former would include such things as turnover, grievances, and productivity. The latter would be subjective reactions of organizational members, especially top management.

Management Auditing

Management auditing is a survey technique that is used to anticipate or solve organizational problems having to do with product demand and supply, structure, functions, and processes. The audit results in recommendations for changes that are implemented at the appropriate management level.

The management audit resembles the financial audit; only the focal issues are different. The financial audit is concerned with organizational operations exclusively from the financial perspective. The management audit is concerned with questions of management efficiency and effectiveness. Of course, one may lead to the other. Financial audits sometimes point up the need to conduct a management audit. Some public accounting firms recommend management audits when the financial audit suggests difficulties that have financial consequences, but whose origins actually lie outside the financial realm.

Management audits may also be compared with a physical checkup. Indeed, management auditors typically conduct their investigations armed with a checklist of factors to be reviewed and evaluated. These usually include an array of specific topics to be checked in terms of general management and functional areas. In organizations with product divisions and subsidiaries, the checklist would be applied to each organizational unit as well as the total corporate entity. Included in the checklist are such factors as products, prices, production control, capital requirements, and a host of others.

The auditors must be well versed in management knowledge and practices. Eventually they prepare a report recommending ways in which the organization's operations can be improved. If it approves, top management may implement the recommendation itself or retain the auditors to help carry out the changes.

The Control Cycle

Finally, the control cycle provides for the planning, implementation, and evaluation of changes in operations and organizational arrangements to bring about or maintain an appropriate fit between the organization and its environment.

Overall, the control cycle is used to monitor on a continuous basis and to change the organization, focusing primarily on demand for the organization's products, programs, and services. Change is then brought about in the organization's supply capabilities to maximize efficiency and effectiveness. To achieve a new equilibrium between supply and demand may require adjusting output, adding to or deleting from the product line, changing organizational structure, making personnel changes, increasing long-term debt, opening new facilities or closing old plants, and so forth.

Although the technique of the control cycle includes planning, implementing plans, and evaluating results, most oral and written commentary emphasizes planning. Thus, for example, there is short-range (or tactical) planning that usually covers the next year, and long-range (or strategic) planning that generally covers five years, but possibly more or less. The short range tends to emphasize the consequences of the current organizational state while the long range emphasizes strategic or discretionary choices about the organization's future course.

Differences and Similarities in Techniques

These six techniques are used to achieve a better organization-environment fit in different ways. Organizational behavior modification focuses on individual behaviors. If successful, the result should be greater productivity at the work level by the individuals affected. Management by objectives focuses on managerial, professional, and technical personnel and is intended to achieve greater effectiveness (thus making a better organization-environment fit) by assuring that superiors and subordinates are in harmony about the subordinate's task objectives and performance standards. Such agreements should result in maximum goal-seeking behavior by both superior and subordinate. Management development makes a somewhat more indirect contribution to organization-environment fit. It does this by first changing the manager; then the manager is expected to change the organization as the need arises.

Like management by objectives, organization development focuses on increasing harmony among organizational members; but the focus is on larger numbers than MBO's two-by-two in the chain of command. Improved cooperation should result in increased ability to deal with the environment. Management auditing is a problem-solving, opportunity-exploiting technique that, as problems are solved and opportunities exploited, helps bring about a better organization-environment fit whenever it is used. Finally, the control cycle constitutes a constant watch on the environment to maintain a dynamic equilibrium between it and the organization.

As this review of organizational change techniques shows, there are considerable differences among them. There are more differences than mentioned thus far; there are also some similarities.

For example, some techniques focus on personnel as individuals. That is, the individual is the unit of change. Organizational behavior modification, management by objectives, and management development are in this category. The other techniques—organization development, management auditing, and the control cycle—focus on the whole organization or some major part.

In terms of timing of organizational change, the techniques also differ among themselves. Organizational behavior modification and organization development utilize feedback control and are typically used to correct or resolve organizational problems that already exist. The other techniques rely upon both feedback and feedforward control. Feedback control is remedial in nature, while feedforward is anticipatory; feedback is used to correct an existing problem, while feedforward is used to prevent or mitigate a potential problem. While feedback control can be used alone, feedforward cannot. This is because the feedforward actions taken to forestall a problem cannot fully anticipate all details; unanticipated details are left to be corrected through the use of feedback control.

As a common example of the above differences in control, consider the use of the control cycle of planning, implementing, and evaluating organizational change that utilizes both feedforward and feedback control. The control cycle is used for a variety of purposes, including the anticipation of changes in product demand and the concomitant need to change supply capabilities. In the course of planning next year's operation, demand is expected to increase by 10 percent. Therefore, the organization makes plans to increase operational levels to produce the additional goods. This is the feedforward aspect of control. The forecast of increased demand, however, is obviously only an estimate. Therefore, to more closely tailor supply to actual demand, feedback on product flow must be provided periodically, and further changes made in supply capabilities if actual demand is significantly different from the forecast. The typical result is that the difference between demand and supply is less when feedforward and feedback control are combined than when only feedback control is used.

The differences in the controls used in various techniques also have an impact upon continuity of use. The techniques that depend primarily on feedback control—organizational behavior modification, organization development, and management auditing—are used intermittently, as required when feedback shows a problem exists. The other techniques can, or of necessity must, be used continuously for maximum effectiveness. For example, management by objectives and the control cycle typically are incorporated into the organization's routine processes.

There are also differences and similarities in the identity of the change agents. Organization development and management auditing require, for example, the services of either internal or external experts and the active backing of higher management. Some other techniques must be applied by the manager whose operations are affected by the technique—for example, MBO, management development, and the control cycle; in organizational behavior modification, however, managers and/or consultants implement the process. These points are summarized in Exhibit 1.

The variations in the techniques reinforce a point made earlier in connection with the contingency approach to management; each is most appropriate for specific situations. They are also complementary; management by objectives and the control cycle, for example, are mutually supportive in anticipating and dealing with related aspects of organizational change.

Fortune 500 Use of Techniques

A survey conducted among *Fortune* 500 companies indicates that all of these organizational change techniques are currently used in the business world. The survey, sent to a randomly selected sample of 50 percent of this group, elicited a response rate of 28 percent (71 respondents). The organizations surveyed were asked the question that is spelled out in Exhibit 3.

Exhibit 4 summarizes the incidence of usage of these techniques among the responding companies. To state a summary fact, more than 10 times as many companies were currently using one or more of the techniques as had tried and given up on any one of them. Among the companies that had stopped using the techniques, the average usage was four companies per technique. Among the firms

---

Exhibit 3
**Question on Organizational Change Techniques Posed
to *Fortune* 500 Companies**

Have you in the past five years used, or are you now using, any of the following
organizational change techniques? (Check all applicable.)

Techniques	Used in Past Five Years, but Not Using Now	Using Now
Organizational behavior modification	( )	( )
Management by objectives	( )	( )
Management development	( )	( )
Organization development	( )	( )
Management auditing	( )	( )
Control cycle (planning, directing, and evaluating results)	( )	( )

Exhibit 4
Use of Organizational Change Techniques by *Fortune* 500 Companies*

Technique	Used in Past Five Years, Not Using Now		Using Now	
	Number	Percent	Number	Percent
Organizational behavior modification	5	7	8	11
Management by objectives	8	11	53	75
Management development	2	3	54	76
Organization development	1	1	33	46
Management auditing	4	6	38	53
Control cycle	0	0	71	100

*Number of responses—71; response rate—28 percent.

---

that are currently using one or more of the techniques, the average usage was 41 companies per technique. The greatest disillusionment was with management by objectives, tried and given up by eight companies. Users seemed least disillusioned with organization development and the control cycle. One company tried and gave up the former; none of the companies had given up the latter—and all of them are currently using this technique.

We do not have background facts to explain why various techniques were dropped after being tried. In some, perhaps most, instances, it may be that the particular problem or problems dealt with were resolved satisfactorily, and there was no further need for the technique. On the other hand, it is possible that the choice of a technique may have been dictated by selective exposure rather than a thorough evaluation of the situation—an evaluation that might have suggested the use of a different technique.

In terms of current usage, some interesting facts emerge. Organizational behavior modification is the least used technique and organization development the second least used. The fact that the incidence of being tried and dropped is higher for organizational behavior modification than for organization development may be because the former is newer than the latter, with less experience to guide its use. But both may be used less than the other techniques because they are the newest of the six. We can also speculate that the practically equal usage of management by objectives and management development is more than a coincidence. MBO may very likely be the technique that reveals the need for management development. Eighty-five percent of the companies using MBO also use management development. Finally, the sample's 100 percent use of the control cycle of planning, directing implementation, and evaluating results indicates that it is the organizational change technique of choice. The other, less popular techniques may very well be used to deal with problems and opportunities uncovered through the control cycle.

The success of the *Fortune* 500 companies is undoubtedly based on a great variety of factors: capable management, up-to-date technology, large domestic markets, a highly educated work force, and the like. But it is quite reasonable to assume that the resort to organizational change techniques—rather than uncoordinated trial-and-error approaches—may very well have contributed substantially to their success.

The simultaneous use of various techniques also attests to a level of sophistication in these firms that warrants comment. Management literature tends to reflect the fads and fashions of academic research, and management practice follows as well as leads these movements. Currently, organizational behavior modification and organization development are in the limelight more than the other techniques, if only because they are newer. They therefore may appear more seductive to managers seeking an approach to organizational change. The results of this survey suggest that the best criterion for choosing a technique is its suitability for dealing with a specific problem or situation, rather than its current popularity in the literature and at management seminars.

Summary and Conclusions

Previous comments have suggested that our ideas about organizational change are continually changing. In addition, our identification and understanding of what constitutes an organizational change technique also change.

Are the above-mentioned techniques here to stay? One tentative conclusion we can draw from the usage data is that there is an apparent inverse correlation between the "age" of a technique and its use by the *Fortune* 500 companies. The control cycle is the oldest and most widely used; organizational behavior modification is the newest and least used. Because the companies constitute a select sample of large, well-managed firms, it is also reasonable to assume that the data show a higher incidence of usage than would be the case for a purely random sample of companies, which would include smaller firms and a larger array of industries. From the foregoing (keeping in mind the expected increase of turbulence in the environment), we can sensibly predict that the use of the organizational change techniques will increase.

That does not mean that such techniques will not change in form and content, however. For example, one such change may occur in management by objectives. Some critics point out that MBO is a one-sided arrangement. It commits the subordinate to do certain things but does not call for a concomitant commitment by the superior to provide adequate resources and other forms of support. A possible change might be the transformation of MBO into management by contract to overcome this deficiency.

Furthermore, there may be more productive, incipient techniques lurking on the management horizon. As a matter of fact, over 20 years ago, Jay W. Forrester began to write about what he called "industrial dynamics." This is a mathematical and computer-based approach to simulating the firm, with the focus on informational and operational delays that result from business fluctuations. While industrial dynamics can be thought of as a particular form of planning and control covered in the control cycle, these two techniques differ from each other at least as much as organizational behavior modification and organization development.

Despite the fact that it has been around for some time, industrial dynamics does not appear to be particularly popular. But then, neither is organizational behavior modification, at least as compared with the other techniques. There may be a common reason for the slow adoption of each.

Management is a set of skills that are learned on the job, from management literature, and from training. The willingness and ability to learn the art of management depend in part on previous learning in the basic disciplines from which management derives its content. A manager deficient in knowledge about the social sciences is probably not likely to be attracted to organizational behavior modification and organization development. Similarly, a manager repelled by mathematics and the computer is unlikely to delve into industrial dynamics.

Ultimately, these more recently developed organizational change techniques may become more popular as a newer breed of lower-level managers works their way up the hierarchy in their organizations. This newer breed will be better versed in the social sciences, mathematics, and the computer. Therefore they will probably expand the use of existing techniques and perhaps even help spawn new ones.

Selected Bibliography

Organizational change has always been a concern for organizational managers. It predates the days when Moses gave up trying to adjudicate all disputes among his Hebrew followers and delegated authority to do so to levels of lesser officials. But organizational change increasingly became a concern and, for some, an obsession after World War II. The bulk of the literature, however, consists of articles and reports, and these have not been systematically compiled in book form. One such book, however, is Newton Margulies and John Wallace's *Organizational Change* (Scott, Foresman, 1973).

The organizational change techniques, on the other hand, have been much publicized, both in articles and books—but always one technique at a time. A discussion of all the techniques has finally been brought together by Stephen R. Michael, Fred Luthans, George S. Odiorne, W. Warner Burke, and Spencer Hayden in *Techniques of Organizational Change* (McGraw-Hill Book Company, 1981). This book includes comprehensive bibliographies for each technique. Many writings on Jay W. Forrester's industrial dynamics have been brought together in Edward B. Robert's (ed.) *Managerial Applications of System Dynamics* (MIT Press, 1978).

These techniques are options, and their effective use is governed by the contingency approach to management, a rather simple idea with enormous ramifications. An early collection of writings illustrating contingency is contained in Fremont D. Kast and James E. Rosenzweig's *Contingency Views of Organization and Management* (Science Research Associates, 1973). A brief introduction to the subject is given in Stephen R. Michael's "The Contingency Manager: Doing What Comes Naturally" (*Management Review*, November 1976).

Reading 7–2

Managing Large-Scale Organizational Change

Gloria Barczak, Charles Smith, David Wilemon

Today's business organizations face an era of turbulent change, the sources of which are varied, often unpredictable, and difficult to understand. In the last decade, companies have had to deal with such traumas as dramatic technological shifts (for example, the explosion in electronic capabilities); deregulation in such industries as banking, telecommunications, the airlines, and energy; economic uncertainty; fast growth; increased global competition; and major shifts in demography and values. In his article "Lear's Fool: Coping with Change Beyond Future Shock" (*New Management,* Vol. 2, No. 2, 1984), D. Verne Morland summarizes the impact of rapid change on organizations:

> With some effort we could learn to cope with very high-speed change that flowed along a reasonably predictable course. We'd have to work faster, probably harder, and definitely smarter, but we could handle it. The greater challenge, by far, is to cope with high-speed change that is subject to frequent alterations in direction. More difficult still is to cope with change that follows an apparently random course where the linkages between cause and effect are obscure. Those are the kinds of unsettling changes we all face more frequently with each passing day. In such a world, behavior that has been reinforced by yesterday's success can become a liability tomorrow, when the environment shifts.

The rapidity with which organizations must respond to change is becoming legend. For example, International Business Machines Corporation, a late entrant into the personal computer market, needed to develop its PC in record time. Using a large task force, IBM was able to achieve this development in little over a year, and its product soon became the industry standard.

A portrait in contrast is provided by Osborne Computer, which was founded in January 1981 for the purpose of manufacturing and marketing the first commercial portable computer. In only two years' time, Osborne's sales reached nearly $100 million. Soon after reaching this peak, however, the company, having accumulated some $45 million in debts, declared bankruptcy. Osborne's technological success was not matched by sustained marketing muscle, a reliable service network, or a sense of strategic timing. Further, Osborne Computer was not able to manage its rapid growth and complex change. The IBM and Osborne examples illustrate the speed with which company fortunes are made and lost in today's rapidly changing environment.

During the past five years, companies such as Xerox Corporation, Texas Instruments Incorporated, American Motors Corporation, Eastman Kodak, and the Intel Corporation have also faced important changes. While each company had its own reasons for encountering change, one thread common to all of them has been their difficulty in dealing with rapidly changing technological, competitive, and market realities.

Unless large corporations can learn to manage dramatic change, they will not survive in today's competitive business environment. However, their death need not be a foregone conclusion. We propose that large firms can better deal with large-scale change by viewing it in terms of a systems framework requiring certain key elements for effective functioning.

Focus

In the face of complex conditions and organizational turbulence, many of our ways of managing change are no longer appropriate. How can we possibly plan, organize, and control our organizations when our products, markets, and technologies change in such unpredictable ways? We clearly need to use specific management methods to create order and balance within our organizations. We need not discard the classic management functions for achieving these stabilizing conditions; however, every manager knows that the traditional tools are not always helpful. During these times, any attempt to restore order and balance may be not only fruitless, but actually damaging. It can magnify problems and increase complexity, thereby heightening disorder and moving the organization further toward chaos.

In his book *Patterns of Technological Innovation* (Addison-Wesley, 1981), Devandra Sahal has called a situation that only seems to result in disorder an "untidiness phenomenon." He uses examples in the development of electronics technology to illustrate what happens in such cases and why it happens. Sahal states that when the semiconductor was first being developed, the component became so complex that any change—even a change that would have made it more efficient or better adapted to shifting technology—actually increased the chances that the entire component would malfunction. The many relationships among parts created a system so complex that the only way it could be improved upon was through a complete recreation of the components—hence, the development of the integrated circuit.

As every manager knows, this stimulus to recreate is an organizational reality. The attempt to adapt by changing a few products, procedures, or staff members, or by initiating a new department or training program, often creates more problems

---

Exhibit 1
Large-Scale Change in Systems: Some General Concepts and Processes

When examining large-scale change in systems, researchers find parallels in how the processes of change take place. It is helpful to summarize these similarities and to identify the potential key success elements of large-scale change.

Large-scale change is differentiated from adaptive, incremental change, which occurs over a long period of time. Adaptive responses ensure continuity in the system, at least for a while, but will not ensure effectiveness. Over time, changing bit by bit will increase inefficiency. Large-scale change counters the movement toward inefficiency and involves an overall reorganization of parts into a harmonious or symmetrical relationship.

When change takes place in a highly turbulent or chaotic environment, a "self-organizing process" can occur. In a turbulent situation, the environment is not the primary reference point or organizing faculty that the system utilizes to provide order; in fact, the environment in such situations can act as an impediment to emerging order. Trying to continually "align" with the environment may involve creating more chaos; instead, there is a system ability to find or develop an order from within, to self-organize and become creative rather than adaptive.

A wealth of recent research has been devoted to the study of large-scale change in systems operating within turbulent and often chaotic environments. Under these conditions, certain key elements are necessary for survival and for successful large-scale change. The key elements involve the dissolution of existing patterns (structures or processes) and the creation and development of new ones.

These processes include:
1. *Pattern breaking:* freeing the system from structures, processes, or functions that are no longer effective or useful.
2. *Experimenting:* generating new patterns better suited to the present environment.
3. *Visioning:* choosing a new perspective around which a system can reorganize.
4. *Bonding and attunement:* harmonizing members to move the system toward new ways of doing, thinking, and learning.

---

than it solves. Companies recognize this problem and, though they may still need adaptive, incremental tools, they have begun to develop systems whereby large-scale, macro changes can take place.

Some recent examples of the use of large-scale systems to effect change include the Apollo Moon Program, within which reorganizations occurred faster than the National Aeronautics and Space Administration staff could track them; Chrysler Corporation's reorganization and redefinition of its mission; and the General Electric Company's current overall strategic change. The ability to effect large-scale change has often been cited as IBM's best reason for remaining fluid and flexible. Through the capacity to change, IBM has been able to compete with smaller, more innovative firms.

In this article, we will focus on understanding and managing the process by which an entire organizational system changes. The paradigm we will use is based on the premise that successful large-scale change requires the presence of certain key ingredients that exist in the proper mix. These key ingredients are briefly described in Exhibit 1 as general systems ideas and are explained in a more specific management context in the following sections. The final section provides insight into the issues of leadership, culture, and organizational learning that are directly related to successful large-scale change.

Key Ingredients of Large-Scale Change

Pattern Breaking

In order to undergo successful large-scale change, organizations must be open to environmental turbulence and willing to move beyond old operational patterns. Familiar but dysfunctional ways of doing things need to be "unlearned" so that new approaches may emerge. We call this releasing process "pattern breaking."

In their article "The Art of High-Technology Management" (*Sloan Management Review,* Winter 1984), Modesto Maidique and Robert Hayes emphasize the need for organizational systems to help break through and change dysfunctional patterns.

> Established organizations are, by their very nature, innovation-resisting. By defining jobs and responsibilities and arranging them in serial reporting relationships, organizations encourage the performance of a restricted set of tasks in a programmed, predictable way. Not only do formal organizations resist innovation, they often act in ways to stamp it out. Overcoming such behavior—which is analogous to the way the human body mobilizes antibodies to attack foreign cells— is therefore a core job of high-tech management.

The pattern-breaking process was used extensively within NASA's Apollo Program, where restructurings and questioning of existing systems were constantly encouraged. By contrast, the Challenger disaster investigations reveal a dramatic decline in NASA's testing and experimenting with technological options.

Since pattern breaking tends to disturb equilibrium, managers must be able to gauge when their organizations should be in a turbulent state and when they should be stable. Maidique and Hayes comment on the importance of managing firms "ambivalently"; this implies an ability to reap the benefits of both the balanced and the dynamic states of organizational life. They explain:

> Knowing when and where to change from one stance to the other, and having the power to make the shift, is the core of the art of high-technology management. James E. Webb, administrator of the National Aeronautics and Space Administration during the successful Apollo (Man on the Moon) Program, recalled that "we were required to fly our administrative machine in a turbulent environment, and . . . a certain level of organizational instability was essential if NASA was not to lose control."

We have recently seen many clear examples of pattern breaking in the American automobile industry. Industry forecasts in the mid-1970s indicated that U.S. auto manufacturers would no longer be able to compete with foreign companies if the U.S. companies continued to use their existing manufacturing and quality-control practices. In addition, the adversarial relationship that had developed between the auto companies and labor in the battle over wages was driving up the cost of American cars. Since the early 1980s, however, there have been massive changes within the industry, such as the creation of new ways of manufacturing through robotics, new agreements with labor unions, and significant change in the technological sophistication of automobiles through the use of computers.

Experimenting

Since pattern breaking moves the organization beyond its existing principles and practices, new perspectives must be generated. These new ideas, which can enhance the firm's effectiveness, often require changes in the strategies the firm will follow, the structures it will use, and the culture it will develop.

The importance of experimentation in groups and organizations has been emphasized in Michael J. Kirton's article "Adaptors and Innovators—Why New Initiatives Get Blocked" (*Long-Range Planning,* April 1984). Kirton notes that innovators are most often the individuals who are able to break established patterns, generate novel ideas, and engage in experimental behavior. By performing these activities, innovators can move the organization into new directions. In a similar fashion, some management theorists encourage "play" and "foolishness" in organizations to facilitate new behavioral and operational patterns. These new patterns increase the probability that the organization will survive and remain effective in uncertain and volatile environments. In their book *In Search of Excellence* (Harper & Row, 1982), Thomas Peters and Robert Waterman also note that "excellent" companies encourage experimentation and are willing to try things out:

> The experimenting process is almost revolutionary. It values action above planning, doing above thinking, the concrete above the abstract. It suggests, in a very Zen-like fashion, going with the flow: doable tasks, starting with the easiest and most ready targets, looking for malleable champions rather than recalcitrant naysayers.

Within experimentation, differences between adaptive, incremental change and large-scale change are easily distinguished. There are many organizations that do experiment incrementally—they try a new product, start a new venture, try a new structure. However, the type of experimentation in a large-scale change process involves the unfolding of an entirely new configuration for the system. Changes in context, products, personnel, and structures take place all at once, so that the company can more completely orchestrate the process of optimizing choices. We hypothesize that many companies would benefit from such thorough change processes; however, most firms attempt to control change by altering only a few aspects of their systems at a time.

It is important to note that experimentation in the large-scale change process does not imply random behavior. The system that is successful in large-scale change will experiment along the lines of its underlying purpose and vision; in other words this vision, translated into the thinking of organizational members, will help to determine the choices through which organizational experimentation takes place. This careful selection process helps to minimize the cost of experimentation. A similar process is mentioned in James Brian Quinn's *Strategies for Change* (Irwin, 1980), in which the author presents the idea of following an experimenting path that is not predetermined, but that emerges through a testing process guided by the firm's strategy and vision.

Visioning

The vision serves as an organizing principle or coalescing force around which an organization can re-form after it has broken its previous patterns. Several management theorists stress the importance of the vision as a force that gives form and direction to a changing organization. In their article "Strategic Management in an Enacted World" (*Academy of Management Review*, October 1985), Linda Smircich and Charles Stubbart note that organizations are ambiguous systems unless managers give meaning to them. Thus the manager's role is to create a code or language that manifests a vision within which events, activities, and goals may be understood. In this context, managers can catalyze change by helping participants envision and create the organization's values and norms.

In a similar way, Walter Bennis' article "The Artform of Leadership" (*The Executive Mind*, edited by Suresh Srivastva, Jossey-Bass, 1983) and Charles Kiefer's and Peter Senge's article "Metanoic Organizations: New Experiments in Organizational Design" (*Transforming Work*, edited by John Adams, Miles River Press, 1984) discuss the concept of visionary leadership. These theorists found that successful leaders in uncertain environments maintained an ongoing vision and commitment that gave an inherent strength to their organization.

Henry Brohms and Henrik Gamberg take a somewhat different perspective on creating and maintaining a vision in their article "Communication to Self in Organizations and Cultures" (*Administrative Science Quarterly*, September 1983). To them, a vision is reinforced and communicated through a strategic plan; thus the strategic plan is a vehicle for giving perspective and meaning to the organization. The authors note:

> Many plans act as mirrors held in front of the organization indicating, "This is what you should look like." . . . In almost any strategic plan, one can find the element of hope and belief. The important goal is that creating images and . . . beliefs . . . induces enthusiasm, which any organization needs. If there is no belief, there is no result.

Bonding and Attunement

In order to develop and manifest a vision without dependence on rigid structures, an organization undergoing large-scale change must have a high degree of alignment among its members. An organization's members achieve this alignment when they transcend traditional role requirements and cultivate a greater sense of community, trust, respect, and shared values. The terms "organizational bonding" and "attunement" are used here to identify such a state. For bonding and attunement to evolve in the large-scale change process, organization members need to develop a high level of interpersonal skills. Through development of these skills, members are empowered to care, to trust, to share, and ultimately to take risks.

One organization that has successfully used the bonding process is W. L. Gore and Associates. It uses a "lattice organization" that deemphasizes titles and authoritarian relationships. Gore's philosophy of human resources development is to help new employees extend self-responsibility, take initiative, and optimally contribute to the organization's goals. The company attributes its success to the close-knit, familial relationship that both provides the basis for and emerges from this philosophy.

Another example of the powerful effect of bonding and attunement is found in Tracy Kidder's *The Soul of a New Machine* (Avon Books, 1981). This book describes the design of a new minicomputer by a Data General project team:

> The entire Eclipse Group, especially its managers, seemed to be operating on instinct. Only the simplest visible arrangements existed among them. They kept no charts and graphs or organizational tables that meant anything. But those webs of voluntary, mutual responsibility, the product of many signings-up, held them together. Of course, to a recruit it might look chaotic. Of course, someone who believed that a computer ought to be designed with long thought and a great deal of preliminary testing, and who favored rigid control, might have felt ill at the spectacle. Criticism of that sort flattered West. "Show me what I'm doing wrong," he'd say with a little smile.

Bonding and attunement assume even greater meaning when they are viewed as ways of maximizing communication and response capabilities in highly complex, quickly changing environments. One organization that has recognized the significance of this greater meaning is the Intel Corporation. Realizing that its newly hired engineers have state-of-the-art knowledge, the company stresses the development of open and frequent contacts between the new hires and senior staff; in order to accomplish this, it deemphasizes status relationships. Intel's strategy is supported by a recent study, which found that informal contacts between superiors and employees were the most important source of relevant information for high-technology project engineers.

Balancing the Four Critical Elements of Large-Scale Change

The same elements that account for success in large-scale organizational change can also be damaging if misused. Exhibit 2 summarizes the positive and negative aspects of each of the four major change elements. The negative effects can be avoided by insuring that all the key elements are present in the organization in adequate proportions. When all the elements are present, it is more probable that none of them will be used to an extreme—a situation that would produce an undesirable outcome.

The NASA Challenger disaster illustrates the cost of an imbalance among the four key elements. Many members of the NASA organization held to an "all systems go" view in their excitement over mastering space technology. This strong vision, while critical to NASA's previous successes, had to be tempered by an awareness of serious problems. However, some engineers' concern over the condition of the solid rocket boosters was seen as antithetical to the NASA vision. If employees had objected more forcefully or transcended formal communication and authority

Exhibit 2
Positive and Negative Uses of the Elements of Large-Scale Change

	Positive Effects	*Negative Effects*
Pattern Breaking	Eliminates dysfunctional patterns and modes of behavior Allows for new learning to occur. Opens system up to new options.	Requires too much unlearning. Requires abandonment of behaviors and values still appropriate to new organizational conditions.
Experimenting	Yields options. Provides flexibility. Encourages openness. Enhances choice.	Too often results in lack of focus. Yields experimentation that is too random. Often requires collusion on accepting lower standards. Leads to lack of creativity. Creates pressure toward conformity. Results in paralysis—too many options, which overwhelm decision makers.
Visioning	Provides direction. Generates commitment. Strengthens bonding. Cultivates support.	Sometimes causes change agents to be blinded by the vision. Leads to inflexibility—refusal to alter the vision. Can be inappropriate—doesn't reflect what the organization really wants.
Bonding and Attunement	Generates alignment. Cultivates mutual respect and trust. Encourages people to become committed to each other and to the task.	Results in groupthink, i.e., lack of conflict, confrontation, and questioning. Leads to rebellion against authority. Creates illusion of invulnerability.

lines, or if NASA had gone against its usual stance of discounting pessimistic information, this knowledge could have provided a means for better fulfilling the vision.

Exhibit 3 provides questions that aid in assessing the presence or absence of the four large-scale change elements. These same questions can help the manager determine if any element of the change process is overutilized or underutilized. In a large organization, these questions can also be asked about small business units, divisions, or other subunits that could independently undergo the large-scale type of change.

The Roles of Leadership, Culture, and Learning

In large-scale change, leadership plays a vital role. Leaders guide the change process by insuring the presence of visioning, experimenting, pattern breaking, and bonding, and by keeping these four elements in balance.

Leadership in large-scale change can be individual or emergent (that is, shared).

Exhibit 3
Assessing an Organization's Propensity to Change

Key Variable	Indicators
Pattern Breaking	Is the organization willing and able to "let go" of approaches that no longer yield desired results?
	Are managers and departments rewarded for weeding out unproductive operations, products, and practices?
	Does the organization try to improve performance by challenging long-held traditions—e.g., large staff groups and layers of middle managers?
Experimenting	Does the organization encourage creativity and the implementation of new ideas and approaches? Are organizational mechanisms in place that facilitate experimentation and implementation, such as venture and project teams, basic research groups, and organizational simulation and modeling groups?
	What is the organization's track record in terms of innovation in products, manufacturing processes, and managerial approaches?
Visioning	Is there a shared meaning throughout the organization that guides positive and purposeful action?
	Are concerted efforts made to periodically assess, update, and extend the organization's mission?
	Are departments, work units, managers, and personnel encouraged to suggest new strategic options for organizations? Are there methods of evaluating and acting on these options?
Bonding and Attunement	What is the quality of interpersonal relationships? Does the organization's culture promote diverse integration of members around important tasks?
	Do members share a "sense of inclusion"?
	What is the extent of "sandbox tending" by functional and staff managers? How permeable are organizational boundaries?
	Do informal organizations function in a positive, purposeful way?
	Does needed information flow via informed networks of experts or via the formal hierarchy?

The individual who takes full charge of a large-scale change is necessarily strong, determined, and masterful at mobilizing people around a vision. There may be times when large-scale change will require such a leader, one who is aided by others but who essentially orchestrates and manages events single-handedly. Lee Iacocca, chairman of the Chrysler Corporation, might be seen as the archetype of this approach. In three years, he was able to complete a massive change within Chrysler; this was accomplished by several dramatic steps, including major concessions from labor, new styling programs, new products, joint ventures, extensive plant modernization, and downsizing the entire workforce.

While the single-leader approach to large-scale change can work, it requires a rare individual and, even then, it is a potentially dangerous course. When one leader has a vision and directs the course of change, creativity may be lost. In addition, organization members are not as committed to the vision as they might be if shared leadership were utilized. Further, the commitment and involvement needed for bonding are harder to muster when the power to initiate and direct change is controlled by one individual.

Emergent leadership involves sharing power in the midst of the change process. This leadership mode seems to better fulfill the need to balance the four critical elements of success. When leadership is emergent, every individual can potentially exert influence on the change process. At certain times, individuals who are skilled at experimenting and who are creative and innovative can take on a prominent role. At other times, those with vision can help to make order out of the fruits of experimentation and to inspire individuals to transform ideas into realities. The use of shared leadership results in more creativity and a greater sense of satisfaction among those involved in change; it also greatly reduces individuals' natural resistance when they perceive that change is being imposed upon them.

The organization's culture also plays an important role in successful large-scale change. The culture must support change; however, such support is not immediately forthcoming. This is one reason why large-scale change originates and develops momentum in smaller subsystems; such a phenomenon is frequently noted in innovative organizations. Only when an innovation has gained momentum will the wisest innovators interact with the larger system and seek support for their projects. This organizational dynamic was evident in the innovation teams that developed the IBM PC and Data General's Eclipse minicomputer.

Unfortunately, there are drawbacks to isolating teams and small business units from the overall organization's culture and activities. One such drawback is that information sharing is shut off, a condition that can result in a segmented and blocked organizational system. Further, separating subunits from other operations and insulating them from corporate rules and procedures can generate internal jealousy and great resentment, as Apple found when it was developing its Macintosh computer.

Instead of assuming that one culture must dominate and another must be isolated, a new approach fosters a supra-culture that maintains a norm of appreciating differences. If differences among units were more openly accepted, these units might operate in synergistic ways—complementing each other rather than remaining isolated.

The development of an overall culture that encourages conflicting perspectives and purposes is a tremendous challenge. As more change ensues in organizations, and especially as corporate mergers and takeovers bring different organizational cultures together, the art of living with different subcultures will take on even greater importance.

Accepting and applauding differences seems to be another trait that American managers can learn from the Japanese, a people who understand the value of multiple perspectives. As Masakazy Yamazaki writes in his article "The Impact of Japanese

Culture on Management" (*The Management Challenge,* edited by Lester Thurow, Massachusetts Institute of Technology, 1985):

> The Japanese are reluctant to believe any unitary view of the world thoroughly . . . (they) take an ironical attitude toward any sort of dogma or truth. It is the attitude of believing in something and yet not believing it completely. It is the conviction that all truths harbor their opposite truths inside them.

This bipolar orientation may account for the conflicting and paradoxical reports we hear about Japanese companies. They support teamwork, but are authoritative; they try to instill individual responsibility, but are harsh and sometimes even punitive when expectations are not met; they are careful to inform workers of change and gain support, but rarely use the bottom-up consensus methods that are popularly viewed as theirs; they encourage the pursuit of ideals and quality, but avoid ideologies and nonpragmatic, theoretical approaches to things.

The issues of leadership and culture require a capacity for change and new learning. This type of learning is not merely the rote accumulation of data and facts; rather, it is the ability to remain open to new ways of seeing, to question appearances, to reflect on and reframe situations, and to find previously ignored patterns and meaning. The ideal in learning is the integration of external reality with an internal vision—a match between what is seen and what is known. Whether it be called "intuition" or "talent," there is an evolutionary quality to learning that captures the essence of experience and imparts the organizational vision.

Conclusion

Perhaps the most important question to ask about large organizations that failed is not what caused them to fail but what might have saved them. Though there may be many possible answers, the basic one seems to be the firm's ability to quickly and efficiently restructure itself amidst the complexity of a changing environment. To do this, large-scale changes must apparently first take place in the settings in which they are most likely to succeed—in senior management teams, departments, small business units, and highly innovative product groups. Thus large-scale organizational change might best be seen as a modular concept, one that originates in subsystems that ultimately create a restructured organization from its example.

International Business Machines Corporation is essentially an example of such an organization. It has recently demonstrated that the key to dealing successfully with complex change is to remain in a constant state of readiness. Such fluidity allows the company both to change the relationships among its small business units and to remain open to active organizational learning.

The IBM organization is in constant flux, adjusting and reorganizing itself whenever it needs to do so. To the systems scientist, it is a living example of the "law of requisite variety," which states that variety in an environment (for example, changing competitors and technologies) can be met successfully when there is sufficient variety within the overall system. When the environment changes and

IBM initiates a new strategy, it often utilizes a different combination of basic units and divisions.

The changes made within IBM come from the vision of the overall organization. They require greater communication among certain units and a great deal of experimenting; the whole process, as might be expected, is far from tranquil. Conflict and competition are evident within the company, and the effects of change, intraorganizational strife, and reshuffling are felt strongly within the units. Yet the overall organization is saved from the greater chaos that would result if it only made piecemeal adaptations to the changing environment. IBM has chosen to live with reshuffling, and this strategy is apparently the key factor in its ability to respond quickly and to maintain its competitive edge in volatile markets.

IBM is not the only organization that has learned to live with complex change. More and more companies are recognizing that current management practices are no longer sufficient to handle large-scale shifts in the current business environment. Managers in these companies are inventing new approaches to the management of change, approaches that give individuals the freedom to utilize their fullest potentialities. We believe that these managerial "inventors," whom Rosabeth Moss Kanter has called "the change masters," will make increasing use of the concepts, ideas, and processes presented here.

Acknowledgment

The authors are grateful to Gary Gemmill for sharing his thoughts on bonding and attunement with us for this article.

Selected Bibliography

The systems perspective used in this article was developed by Erich Jantsch in *The Evolutionary Vision* (Westview Press, 1982) and *The Self-Organizing Universe* (Pergamon Press, 1980).

For each of the critical elements of change process identified, a number of management works could be cited. The following is a representative selection:

For pattern breaking: Michael J. Kirton's study "Adaptors and Innovators—Why New Initiatives Get Blocked" in *Long-Range Planning* (April 1984); Paul Nystrom and William Starbuck's article "To Avoid Organizational Crises, Unlearn" in *Organizational Dynamics* (Spring 1984); and Modesto Maidique and Robert Hayes, "The Art of High-Technology Management," *Sloan Management Review* (Winter 1984).

For experimenting: the ideas on "play and foolishness" found in James March's "Footnotes to Organizational Change," *Administrative Science Quarterly* (December 1981) and in Karl Weick's "Organizational Design: Organizations as Self-Designing Systems," *Organizational Dynamics* (Autumn 1977); Thomas Peters and Robert Waterman, *In Search of Excellence* (Harper & Row, 1982); and James Brian Quinn, *Strategies for Change* (Irwin, 1980).

For visioning: the ideas on culture and meaning of Linda Smircich and Charles Stubbart, found in "Strategic Management in an Enacted World," *Academy of Management Review* (October 1985); of Warren Bennis in "The Artform of Leadership" in *The Executive*

Mind, edited by Suresh Srivastva (Jossey-Bass, 1983); of Bernard Bass in "Leadership: Good, Better, Best," *Organizational Dynamics* (Winter 1985); of Henri Brohms and Henrik Gamberg in "Communication to Self in Organizations and Cultures," *Administrative Science Quarterly* (September 1983); and of Milan Zeleny and Norbert Pierre, "Simulation of Self-Reviewing Systems" in *Evolution and Consciousness,* edited by Erich Jantsch and Conrad Waddington (Addison-Wesley, 1976).

Insights into bonding and attunement may be found in Charles Kiefer and Peter Senge's "Metanoic Organizations: New Experiments in Organizational Design," in *Transforming Work,* edited by John Adams (Miles River Press, 1984), and in Roger Harrison's article "Strategies for a New Age," *Human Resource Management* (Fall 1983).

Some interesting supplementary works are "The Impact of Japanese Culture on Management" by Masakazy Yamazaki, a study on the way that Japanese culture accommodates plurality, found in Lester Thurow's *The Management Challenge* (MIT, 1985). An excellent summary of how the dynamics of the IBM organization exemplify many of the system ideas and dynamics described here in their present modular type of organization structure may be found in Brian Jeffery's article "IBM's Protean Ways" in *Datamation* (January 1986). Other works include D. Verne Morland, "Lear's Fool: Coping with Change Beyond Future Shock," *New Management* 2, no. 2 (1984); Tracy Kidder's account of the Eclipse team within Data General, *The Soul of a New Machine* (Avon Books, 1981); and Rosabeth Moss Kanter's acclaimed work *The Change Masters* (Simon & Schuster, 1983).

Reading 7-3

Why Change Programs Don't Produce Change*

Michael Beer, Russell A. Eisenstat, Bert Spector

In the mid-1980s, the new CEO of a major international bank—call it U.S. Financial—announced a companywide change effort. Deregulation was posing serious competitive challenges—challenges to which the bank's traditional hierarchical organization was ill-suited to respond. The only solution was to change fundamentally how the company operated. And the place to begin was at the top.

The CEO held a retreat with his top 15 executives where they painstakingly reviewed the bank's purpose and culture. He published a mission statement and hired a new vice president for human resources from a company well-known for its excellence in managing people. And in a quick succession of moves, he established companywide programs to push change down through the organization: a new organizational structure, a performance appraisal system, a pay-for-performance compensation plan, training programs to turn managers into "change agents," and quarterly attitude surveys to chart the progress of the change effort.

As much as these steps sound like a textbook case in organizational transformation, there was one big problem: two years after the CEO launched the change program, virtually nothing in the way of actual changes in organizational behavior had occurred. What had gone wrong?

The answer is "everything." Every one of the assumptions the CEO made—

about who should lead the change effort, what needed changing, and how to go about doing it—was wrong.

U.S. Financial's story reflects a common problem. Faced with changing markets and increased competition, more and more companies are struggling to reestablish their dominance, regain market share, and in some cases, ensure their survival. Many have come to understand that the key to competitive success is to transform the way they function. They are reducing reliance on managerial authority, formal rules and procedures, and narrow divisions of work. And they are creating teams, sharing information, and delegating responsibility and accountability far down the hierarchy. In effect, companies are moving from the hierarchical and bureaucratic model of organization that has characterized corporations since World War II to what we call the task-driven organization where what has to be done governs who works with whom and who leads.

But while senior managers understand the necessity of change to cope with new competitive realities, they often misunderstand what it takes to bring it about. They tend to share two assumptions with the CEO of U.S. Financial: that promulgating companywide programs—mission statements, "corporate culture" programs, training courses, quality circles, and new pay-for-performance systems—will transform organizations, and that employee behavior is changed by altering a company's formal structure and systems.

In a four-year study of organizational change at six large corporations (see the insert, "Tracking Corporate Change"; the names are fictitious), we found that exactly the opposite is true: the greatest obstacle to revitalization is the idea that it comes about through companywide change programs, particularly when a corporate staff group such as human resources sponsors them. We call this "the fallacy of programmatic change." Just as important, formal organization structure and systems cannot lead a corporate renewal process.

While in some companies, wave after wave of programs rolled across the landscape with little positive impact, in others, more successful transformations did take place. They usually started at the periphery of the corporation in a few plants and divisions far from corporate headquarters. And they were led by the general managers of those units, not by the CEO or corporate staff people.

The general managers did not focus on formal structures and systems; they created ad hoc organizational arrangements to solve concrete business problems. By aligning employee roles, responsibilities, and relationships to address the organization's most important competitive task—a process we call "task alignment"—they focused energy for change on the work itself, not on abstractions such as "participation" or "culture." Unlike the CEO at U.S. Financial, they didn't employ massive training programs or rely on speeches and mission statements. Instead, we saw that general managers carefully developed the change process through a sequence of six basic managerial interventions.

Once general managers understand the logic of this sequence, they don't have to wait for senior management to start a process of organizational revitalization. There is a lot they can do even without support from the top. Of course, having a CEO or other senior managers who are committed to change does make a difference—and when it comes to changing an entire organization, such support is essential. But top management's role in the change process is very different from that which the CEO played at U.S. Financial.

Grass-roots change presents senior managers with a paradox: directing a "nondirective" change process. The most effective senior managers in our study recognized their limited power to mandate corporate renewal from the top. Instead, they defined their roles as creating a climate for change, then spreading the lessons of both successes and failures. Put another way, they specified the general direction in which the company should move without insisting on specific solutions.

In the early phases of a companywide change process, any senior manager can play this role. Once grass-roots change reaches a critical mass, however, the CEO has to be ready to transform his or her own work unit as well—the top team composed of key business heads and corporate staff heads. At this point, the company's structure and systems must be put into alignment with the new management practices that have developed at the periphery. Otherwise, the tension between dynamic units and static top management will cause the change process to break down.

We believe that an approach to change based on task alignment, starting at the periphery and moving steadily toward the corporate core, is the most effective way to achieve enduring organizational change. This is not to say that change can *never* start at the top, but it is uncommon and too risky as a deliberate strategy. Change is about learning. It is a rare CEO who knows in advance the fine-grained details of organizational change that the many diverse units of a large corporation demand. Moreover, most of today's senior executives developed in an era in which top-down hierarchy was the primary means for organizing and managing. They must learn from innovative approaches coming from younger unit managers closer to the action.

The Fallacy of Programmatic Change

Most change programs don't work because they are guided by a theory of change that is fundamentally flawed. The common belief is that the place to begin is with the knowledge and attitudes of individuals. Changes in attitudes, the theory goes, lead to changes in individual behavior. And changes in individual behavior, repeated by many people, will result in organizational change. According to this model, change is like a conversion experience. Once people "get religion," changes in their behavior will surely follow.

This theory gets the change process exactly backward. In fact, individual behavior is powerfully shaped by the organizational roles that people play. The most effective way to change behavior, therefore, is to put people into a new organizational context, which imposes new roles, responsibilities, and relationships on them. This creates a situation that, in a sense, "forces" new attitudes and behaviors on people. [See the box, "Contrasting Assumptions About Change."]

Tracking Corporate Change

Which strategies for corporate change work, and which do not? We sought the answers in a comprehensive study of 12 large companies where top management was attempting to revitalize the corporation. Based on preliminary research, we identified 6 for in-depth analysis: 5 manufacturing companies and 1 large international bank. All had revenues between $4 billion and $10 billion. We studied 26 plants and divisions in these 6 companies and conducted hundreds of interviews with human resource managers; line managers engaged in change efforts at plants, branches, or business units; workers and union leaders; and, finally, top management.

Based on this material, we ranked the 6 companies according to the success with which they had managed the revitalization effort. Were there significant improvements in interfunctional coordination, decision making, work organization, and concern for people? Research has shown that in the long term, the quality of these 4 factors will influence performance. We did not define success in terms of improved financial performance because, in the short run, corporate financial performance is influenced by many situational factors unrelated to the change process.

Researchers and Employees—Similar Conclusions

	Extent of Revitalization		
	Ranked by	Rated by Employees	
Company	Researchers	Average	Standard Deviation
General Products	1	4.04	.35
Fairweather	2	3.58	.45
Livingston Electronics	3	3.61	.76
Scranton Steel	4	3.30	.65
Continental Glass	5	2.96	.83
U.S. Financial	6	2.78	1.07

To corroborate our rankings of the companies, we also administered a standardized questionnaire in each company to understand how employees viewed the unfolding change process. Respondents rated their companies on a scale of 1 to 5. A score of 3 meant that no change had taken place; a score below 3 meant that, in the employee's judgment, the organization had actually gotten worse. As the table suggests, with one exception—the company we call Livingston Electronics—employees' perceptions of how much their companies had changed were identical to ours. And Livingston's relatively high standard of deviation (which measures the degree of consensus among employees about the outcome of the change effort) indicates that within the company there was considerable disagreement as to just how successful revitalization had been.

One way to think about this challenge is in terms of three interrelated factors required for corporate revitalization. *Coordination* or teamwork is especially important if an organization is to discover and act on cost, quality, and product development opportunities. The production and sale of innovative, high-quality, low-cost products (or services) depend on close coordination among marketing, product design, and manufacturing departments, as well as between labor and management. High levels of *commitment* are essential for the effort, initiative, and cooperation that coordinated action demands. New *competencies* such as knowledge of the business as a whole, analytical skills, and interpersonal skills are necessary if people are to identify and solve problems as a team. If any of these elements are missing, the change process will break down.

The problem with most companywide change programs is that they address only one or, at best, two of these factors. Just because a company issues a philosophy statement about teamwork doesn't mean its employees necessarily know what teams to form or how to function within them to improve coordination. A corporate reorganization may change the boxes on a formal organization chart but not provide the necessary attitudes and skills to make the new structure work. A pay-for-performance system may force managers to differentiate better performers from poorer ones, but it doesn't help them internalize new standards by which to judge subordinates' performances. Nor does it teach them how to deal effectively with performance problems. Such programs cannot provide the cultural context (role models from whom to learn) that people need to develop new competencies, so ultimately they fail to create organizational change.

Similarly, training programs may target competence, but rarely do they change a company's patterns of coordination. Indeed, the excitement engendered in a good corporate training program frequently leads to increased frustration when employees get back on the job only to see their new skills go unused in an organization in which nothing else has changed. People end up seeing training as a waste of time, which undermines whatever commitment to change a program may have roused in the first place.

When one program doesn't work, senior managers, like the CEO at U.S. Financial, often try another, instituting a rapid progression of programs. But this only exacerbates the problem. Because they are designed to cover everyone and everything, programs end up covering nobody and nothing particularly well. They are so general and standardized that they don't speak to the day-to-day realities of particular units. Buzzwords like "quality," "participation," "excellence," "empowerment," and "leadership" become a substitute for a detailed understanding of the business.

And all these change programs also undermine the credibility of the change effort. Even when managers accept the potential value of a particular program for others—quality circles, for example, to solve a manufacturing problem—they may be confronted with another, more pressing business problem such as new product development. One-size-fits-all change programs take energy *away* from efforts to solve key business problems—which explains why so many general managers don't

Contrasting Assumptions About Change	
Programmatic Change	**Task Alignment**
Problems in behavior are a function of individual knowledge, attitudes, and beliefs.	Individual knowledge, attitudes, and beliefs are shaped by recurring patterns of behavioral interactions.
The primary target of renewal should be the content of attitudes and ideas; actual behavior should be secondary.	The primary target of renewal should be behavior; attitudes and ideas should be secondary.
Behavior can be isolated and changed individually.	Problems in behavior come from a circular pattern, but the effects of the organizational system on the individual are greater than those of the individual on the system.
The target for renewal should be at the individual level.	The target for renewal should be at the level of roles, responsibilities, and relationships.

support programs, even when they acknowledge that their underlying principles may be useful.

This is not to state that training, changes in pay systems or organizational structure, or a new corporate philosophy are always inappropriate. All can play valuable roles in supporting an integrated change effort. The problems come when such programs are used in isolation as a kind of "magic bullet" to spread organizational change rapidly through the entire corporation. At their best, change programs of this sort are irrelevant. At their worst, they actually inhibit change. By promoting skepticism and cynicism, programmatic change can inoculate companies against the real thing.

Six Steps to Effective Change

Companies avoid the shortcomings of programmatic change by concentrating on "task alignment"—reorganizing employee roles, responsibilities, and relationships to solve specific business problems. Task alignment is easiest in small units—a plant, department, or business unit—where goals and tasks are clearly defined. Thus the chief problem for corporate change is how to promote task-aligned change across many diverse units.

We saw that general managers at the business unit or plant level can achieve task alignment through a sequence of six overlapping but distinctive steps, which we call the *critical path*. This path develops a self-reinforcing cycle of commitment, coordination, and competence. The sequence of steps is important because activities appropriate at one time are often counterproductive if started too early. Timing is everything in the management of change.

1. *Mobilize commitment to change through joint diagnosis of business problems.* As the term task alignment suggests, the starting point of any effective change effort is a clearly defined business problem. By helping people develop a shared diagnosis of what is wrong in an organization and what can and must be improved, a general manager mobilizes the initial commitment that is necessary to begin the change process.

Consider the case of a division we call Navigation Devices, a business unit of about 600 people set up by a large corporation to commercialize a product originally designed for the military market. When the new general manager took over, the division had been in operation for several years without ever making a profit. It had never been able to design and produce a high-quality, cost-competitive product. This was due largely to an organization in which decisions were made at the top, without proper involvement of or coordination with other functions.

The first step the new general manager took was to initiate a broad review of the business. Where the previous general manager had set strategy with the unit's marketing director alone, the new general manager included his entire management team. He also brought in outside consultants to help him and his managers function more effectively as a group.

Next, he formed a 20-person task force representing all the stakeholders in the organization—managers, engineers, production workers, and union officials. The group visited a number of successful manufacturing organizations in an attempt to identify what Navigation Devices might do to organize more effectively. One high-performance manufacturing plant in the task force's own company made a particularly strong impression. Not only did it highlight the problems at Navigation Devices but it also offered an alternative organizational model, based on teams, that captured the group's imagination. Seeing a different way of working helped strengthen the group's commitment to change.

The Navigation Devices task force didn't learn new facts from this process of joint diagnosis; everyone already knew the unit was losing money. But the group came to see clearly the organizational roots of the unit's inability to compete and, even more important, came to share a common understanding of the problem. The group also identified a potential organizational solution: to redesign the way it worked, using ad hoc teams to integrate the organization around the competitive task.

2. *Develop a shared vision of how to organize and manage for competitiveness.* Once a core group of people is committed to a particular analysis of the problem the general manager can lead employees toward a task-aligned vision of the organization that defines new roles and responsibilities. These new arrangements will coordinate the flow of information and work across interdependent functions at all levels of the organization. But since they do not change formal structures and systems like titles or compensation, they encounter less resistance.

At Navigation Devices, the 20-person task force became the vehicle for this second stage. The group came up with a model of the organization in which cross-functional teams would accomplish all work, particularly new product development. A business-management team composed of the general manager and his staff would set the unit's strategic direction and review the work of lower level teams. Business-area teams would develop plans for specific markets. Product-development teams would manage new products from initial design to production. Production-process teams composed of engineers and production workers would identify and solve quality and cost problems in the plant. Finally, engineering-process teams would examine engineering methods and equipment. The teams got to the root of the unit's problems—functional and hierarchical barriers to sharing information and solving problems.

To create a consensus around the new vision, the general manager commissioned a still larger task force of about 90 employees from different levels and functions, including union and management, to refine the vision and obtain everyone's commitment to it. On a retreat away from the workplace, the group further refined the new organizational model and drafted a values statement, which it presented later to the entire Navigation Devices work force. The vision and the values statements made sense to Navigation Devices employees in a way many corporate mission statements never do—because it grew out of the organization's own analysis of real business problems. And it was built on a model for solving those problems that key stakeholders believed would work.

3. *Foster consensus for the new vision, competence to enact it, and cohesion to move it along.* Simply letting employees help develop a new vision is not enough to overcome resistance to change—or to foster the skills needed to make the new organization work. Not everyone can help in the design, and even those who do participate often do not fully appreciate what renewal will require until the new organization is actually in place. This is when strong leadership from the general manager is crucial. Commitment to change is always uneven. Some managers are enthusiastic; others are neutral or even antagonistic. At Navigation Devices, the general manager used what his subordinates termed the "velvet glove." He made it clear that the division was going to encourage employee involvement and the team approach. To managers who wanted to help him, he offered support. To those who did not, he offered outplacement and counseling.

Once an organization has defined new roles and responsibilities, people need to develop the competencies to make the new setup work. Actually, the very existence of the teams with their new goals and accountabilities will force learning. The changes in roles, responsibilities, and relationships foster new skills and attitudes. Changed patterns of coordination will also increase employee participation, collaboration, and information sharing.

But management also has to provide the right supports. At Navigation Devices, six resource people—three from the unit's human resource department and three from corporate headquarters—worked on the change project. Each team was assigned one internal consultant, who attended every meeting, to help people be effective team members. Once employees could see exactly what kinds of new skills they needed, they asked for formal training programs to develop those skills further. Since these courses grew directly out of the employees' own experiences, they were far more focused and useful than traditional training programs.

Some people, of course, just cannot or will not change, despite all the direction and support in the world. Step three is the appropriate time to replace those managers who cannot function in the new organization—after they have had a chance to prove themselves. Such decisions are rarely easy, and sometimes those people who have difficulty working in a participatory organization have extremely valuable specialized skills. Replacing them early in the change process, before they have worked in the new organization, is not only unfair to individuals; it can be demoralizing to the entire organization and can disrupt the change process. People's understanding of what kind of manager and worker the new organization demands grows slowly and only from the experience of seeing some individuals succeed and others fail.

Once employees have bought into a vision of what's necessary and have some understanding of what the new organization requires, they can accept the necessity of replacing or moving people who don't make the transition to the new way of working. Sometimes people are transferred to other parts of the company where technical expertise rather than the new competencies is the main requirement. When no alternatives exist, sometimes they leave the company through early retirement programs, for example. The act of replacing people can actually reinforce the organization's commitment to change by visibly demonstrating the general manager's commitment to the new way.

Some of the managers replaced at Navigation Devices were high up in the organization—for example, the vice president of operations, who oversaw the engineering and manufacturing departments. The new head of manufacturing was far more committed to change and skilled in leading a critical path change process. The result was speedier change throughout the manufacturing function.

4. *Spread revitalization to all departments without pushing it from the top.* With the new ad hoc organization for the unit in place, it is time to turn to the functional and staff departments that must interact with it. Members of teams cannot be effective unless the department from which they come is organized and managed in a way that supports their roles as full-fledged participants in team decisions. What this often means is that these departments will have to rethink their roles and authority in the organization.

At Navigation Devices, this process was seen most clearly in the engineering department. Production department managers were the most enthusiastic about the change effort; engineering managers were more hesitant. Engineering had always been king at Navigation Devices; engineers designed products to the military's specifications without much concern about whether manufacturing could easily build them or not. Once the new team structure was in place, however, engineers had to participate on product-development teams with production workers. This required them to reexamine their roles and rethink their approaches to organizing and managing their own department.

The impulse of many general managers faced with such a situation would be to force the issue—to announce, for example, that now all parts of the organization must manage by teams. The temptation to force newfound insights on the rest of the organization can be great, particularly when rapid change is needed, but it would be the same mistake that senior managers make when they try to push programmatic change throughout a company. It short-circuits the change process.

It's better to let each department "reinvent the wheel"—that is, to find its own way to the new organization. At Navigation Devices, each department was allowed to take the general concepts of coordination and teamwork and apply then to its particular situation. Engineering spent nearly a year agonizing over how to implement the team concept. The department conducted two surveys, held off-site meetings, and proposed, rejected, then accepted a matrix management structure before it finally got on board. Engineering's decision to move to matrix management was not surprising, but because it was its own choice, people committed themselves to learning the necessary new skills and attitudes.

5. *Institutionalize revitalization through formal policies, systems, and structures.* There comes a point where general managers have to consider how to institutionalize change so that the process continues even after they've moved on to other responsibilities. Step five is the time: the new approach has become entrenched, the right people are in place, and the team organization is up and running. Enacting changes in structures and systems any earlier tends to backfire. Take information systems. Creating a team structure means new information requirements. Why not have the MIS department create new systems that cut across traditional functional and departmental lines early in the change process? The problem is that without a well-developed understanding of information requirements, which can best be obtained by placing people on task-aligned teams, managers are likely to resist new systems as an imposition by the MIS department. Newly formed teams can often pull together enough information to get their work done without fancy new systems. It's better to hold off until everyone understands what the team's information needs are.

What's true for information systems is even more true for other formal structures and systems. Any formal system is going to have some disadvantages; none is perfect. These imperfections can be minimized, however, once people have worked in an ad hoc team structure and learned what interdependencies are necessary. Then employees will commit to them too.

Again, Navigation Devices is a good example. The revitalization of the unit was highly successful. Employees changed how they saw their roles and responsibilities and became convinced that change could actually make a difference. As a result, there were dramatic improvements in value added per employee, scrap reduction, quality, customer service, gross inventory per employee, and profits. And all this happened with almost no formal changes in reporting relationships, information systems, evaluation procedures, compensation, or control systems.

When the opportunity arose, the general manager eventually did make some changes in the formal organization. For example, when he moved the vice president of operations out of the organization, he eliminated the position altogether. Engineering and manufacturing reported directly to him from that point on. For the most part, however, the changes in performance at Navigation Devices were sustained by the general manager's expectations and the new norms for behavior.

6. *Monitor and adjust strategies in response to problems in the revitalization process.* The purpose of change is to create an asset that did not exist before—a learning organization capable of adapting to a changing competitive environment. The organization has to know how to continually monitor its behavior—in effect, to learn how to learn.

Some might say that this is the general manager's responsibility. But monitoring the change process needs to be shared, just as analyzing the organization's key business problem does.

At Navigation Devices, the general manager introduced several mechanisms to allow key constituents to help monitor the revitalization. An oversight team— composed of some crucial managers, a union leader, a secretary, an engineer, and an analyst from finance—kept continual watch over the process. Regular employee attitude surveys monitored behavior patterns. Planning teams were formed and reformed in response to new challenges. All these mechanisms created a long-term capacity for continual adaptation and learning.

The six-step process provides a way to elicit renewal without imposing it. When stakeholders become committed to a vision, they are willing to accept a new pattern of management—here the ad hoc team structure—that demands changes in their behavior. And as the employees discover that the new approach is more effective (which will happen only if the vision aligns with the core task), they have to grapple with personal and organizational changes they might otherwise resist. Finally, as improved coordination helps solve relevant problems, it will reinforce team behavior and produce a desire to learn new skills. This learning enhances effectiveness even further and results in an even stronger commitment to change. This mutually reinforcing cycle of improvements in commitment, coordination, and competence creates a growing sense of efficacy. It can continue as long as the ad hoc team structure is allowed to expand its role in running the business.

The Role of Top Management

To change an entire corporation, the change process we have described must be applied over and over again in many plants, branches, departments, and divisions. Orchestrating this companywide change process is the first responsibility of senior management. Doing so successfully requires a delicate balance. Without explicit efforts by top management to promote conditions for change in individual units, only a few plants or divisions will attempt change, and those that do will remain isolated. The best senior manager leaders we studied held their subordinates responsible for starting a change process without specifying a particular approach.

Create a Market for Change.   The most effective approach is to set demanding standards for all operations and then hold managers accountable to them. At our best-practice company, which we call General Products, senior managers developed ambitious product and operating standards. General managers unable to meet these product standards by a certain date had to scrap their products and take a sharp hit to their bottom lines. As long as managers understand that high standards are not arbitrary but are dictated by competitive forces, standards can generate enormous pressure for better performance, a key ingredient in mobilizing energy for change.

But merely increasing demands is not enough. Under pressure, most managers will seek to improve business performance by doing more of what they have always done—overmanage—rather than alter the fundamental way they organize. So, while senior managers increase demands, they should also hold managers accountable for fundamental changes in the way they use human resources.

For example, when plant managers at General Products complained about the impossibility of meeting new business standards, senior managers pointed them to the corporate organization-development department within human resources and emphasized that the plant managers would be held accountable for moving revitalization along. Thus top management had created a demand system for help with the new way of managing, and the human resource staff could support change without appearing to push a program.

Use Successfully Revitalized Units as Organizational Models for the Entire Company.   Another important strategy is to focus the company's attention on plants and divisions that have already begun experimenting with management innovations. These units become developmental laboratories for further innovation.

There are two ground rules for identifying such models. First, innovative units need support. They need the best managers to lead them, and they need adequate resources—for instance, skilled human resource people and external consultants. In the most successful companies that we studied, senior managers saw it as their responsibility to make resources available to leading-edge units. They did not leave it to the human resource function.

Second, because resources are always limited and the costs of failure high, it is crucial to identify those units with the likeliest chance of success. Successful management innovations can appear to be failures when the bottom line is devastated by environmental factors beyond the unit's control. The best models are in healthy markets.

Obviously, organizational models can serve as catalysts for change only if others are aware of their existence and are encouraged to learn from them. Many of our worst-practice companies had plants and divisions that were making substantial changes. The problem was, nobody knew about them. Corporate management had never bothered to highlight them as examples to follow. In the leading companies, visits, conferences, and educational programs facilitated learning from model units.

Develop Career Paths that Encourage Leadership Development. Without strong leaders, units cannot make the necessary organizational changes, yet the scarcest resource available for revitalizing corporations is leadership. Corporate renewal depends as much on developing effective change leaders as it does on developing effective organizations. The personal learning associated with leadership development—or the realization by higher management that a manager does not have this capacity—cannot occur in the classroom. It only happens in an organization where the teamwork, high commitment, and new competencies we have discussed are already the norm.

The only way to develop the kind of leaders a changing organization needs is to make leadership an important criterion for promotion, and then manage people's careers to develop it. At our best-practice companies, managers were moved from job to job and from organization to organization based on their learning needs, not on their position in the hierarchy. Successful leaders were assigned to units that had been targeted for change. People who needed to sharpen their leadership skills were moved into the company's model units where those skills would be demanded and therefore learned. In effect, top management used leading-edge units as hothouses to develop revitalization leaders.

But what about the top management team itself? How important is it for the CEO and his or her direct reports to practice what they preach? It is not surprising—indeed, it's predictable—that in the early years of a corporate change effort, top managers' actions are often not consistent with their words. Such inconsistencies don't pose a major barrier to corporate change in the beginning, though consistency is obviously desirable. Senior managers can create a climate for grass-roots change without paying much attention to how they themselves operate and manage. And unit managers will tolerate this inconsistency so long as they can freely make changes in their own units in order to compete more effectively.

There comes a point, however, when addressing the inconsistencies becomes crucial. As the change process spreads, general managers in the ever-growing circle of revitalized units eventually demand changes from corporate staff groups and top management. As they discover how to manage differently in their own units, they bump up against constraints of policies and practices that corporate staff and top management have created. They also begin to see opportunities for better coordination between themselves and other parts of the company over which they have little control. At this point, corporate organization must be aligned with corporate strategy, and coordination between related but hitherto independent businesses improved for the benefit of the whole corporation.

None of the companies we studied had reached this "moment of truth." Even when corporate leaders intellectually understood the direction of change, they were just beginning to struggle with how they would change themselves and the company as a whole for a total corporate revitalization.

This last step in the process of corporate renewal is probably the most important.

If the CEO and his or her management team do not ultimately apply to themselves what they have been encouraging their general managers to do, then the whole process can break down. The time to tackle the tough challenge of transforming companywide systems and structures comes finally at the end of the corporate change process.

At this point, senior managers must make an effort to adopt the team behavior, attitudes, and skills that they have demanded of others in earlier phases of change. Their struggle with behavior change will help sustain corporate renewal in three ways. It will promote the attitudes and behavior needed to coordinate diverse activities in the company; it will lend credibility to top management's continued espousal of change; and it will help the CEO identify and develop a successor who is capable of learning the new behaviors. Only such a manager can lead a corporation that can renew itself continually as competitive forces change.

Companies need a particular mind-set for managing change: one that emphasizes process over specific content, recognizes organization change as a unit-by-unit learning process rather than a series of programs, and acknowledges the payoffs that result from persistence over a long period of time as opposed to quick fixes. This mind-set is difficult to maintain in an environment that presses for quarterly earnings, but we believe it is the only approach that will bring about successful renewal.

PART FIVE

Part Five expands our scope from short periods (a few months to a few years), to longer periods. Like Part Four, it addresses change in all organizational units but it focuses on change directed at developing an organization capable of being effective in the long run.

Managing the development of organizations usually involves—as the text, cases, and readings illustrate—attempts to increase adaptability so that organizations can cope with future growth and/or environmental changes. The text in this part identifies the characteristics of highly adaptive and flexible organizations as well as tools and strategies available to managers for developing these characteristics. The cases describe managers whose primary interest is in ensuring long-term positive outcomes as an outgrowth of necessary immediate organizational decisions. The readings provide an overview of organization development—a long-term managerial and organizational effectiveness strategy—as well as frameworks for conceptualizing and managing the growth of organizations over the long run.

Chapter 8

Developing an Organization that Contributes to Long-Run Effectiveness

Effective management is more than the production of immediate results. For companies that want to continue operating in the future, effective management includes creating the potential for achieving good results over the long run. The manager who as president of a company produces spectacular results for a 3- to 10-year period is hardly effective if, at the same time, he or she allows plant equipment to deteriorate, creates an alienated and militant work force, gives the company a bad name in the marketplace, and ignores new-product development.

Our focus up to this point—dealing with current problems or potential problems of the immediate future—reflects a key reality of managerial behavior in almost all modern organizations. That is, coping with the complexities associated with today and the immediate future absorbs the majority of time and energy for most managers.[1] In this chapter, however, we shift to a long-run time frame: How do managers develop their human organizations to assure that they have the potential for facilitating organizational effectiveness in the long run?

The Long Run

Most managers admit that their ability to predict their company's future is limited. Indeed, with the possible exception of death and taxes, the only thing entirely predictable is that things will change. Even for the most bureaucratic company in the most mature and stable environment, change is inevitable.[2]

Over a period of 20 years, it is possible for a company, even one that is not

---

[1]See Henry Mintzberg, *The Nature of Managerial Work* (New York: Harper & Row, 1973), chap. 3.

[2]Warren Bennis, *Changing Organizations* (New York: McGraw-Hill, 1966), chap. 1.

growing, to experience numerous changes in its business, product markets, competition, government regulations, available technologies, labor markets, and strategy. These changes are the inevitable product of its interaction with a world that is not static.

Growing organizations tend to experience even more business-related changes over a long period. Studies have shown that they increase the volume of products or services provided and tend to increase the complexity of products or services, forward or backward integration, the rate of product innovation, the geographic scope of operations, the number and character of distribution channels, and the number and diversity of customer groups. While all of this growth-driven change occurs, competitive and other external pressures also increase.[3] Companies that grow rapidly experience even more and faster changes.[4]

From a manager's point of view, these types of business changes are important because they generally require organizational adjustments. For example, a company's labor markets might change over time, subsequently requiring it to alter its selection criteria and make other adjustments to fit the new type of employee. New competitors might emerge with new products, thus requiring renewed new-product development efforts and a new organizational design to support that effort. In a growing company, business changes tend to require major shifts periodically in all aspects of its organization. See Figures 8–1 and 8–2.

The inability of an organization to anticipate the need for change and to adjust effectively to changes in its business or in its organization causes problems, as seen in previous examples. Sometimes these problems take the form of poor collaboration and coordination. Sometimes they involve high turnover or low morale. Always, however, they affect the organization's performance, in that goals are not achieved and/or resources are wasted.

Because change is inevitable and because it can easily produce problems for companies, the key characteristic of an effective organization from a long-run point of view is that it can anticipate needed organizational changes and adapt as business conditions change. Anticipatory skills can help prevent the resource drain caused by organizational problems, while adaptability helps an organization avoid the problems that change can produce. Over long periods, this ability to avoid an important and recurring resource drain can mark the difference between success and failure for an organization.

A Case of Organizational Decline

To fully appreciate the importance of anticipatory skills and adaptability in the long run, consider this extreme case. The company involved was founded in the late 1920s primarily through acquisitions. It was created as the response of an entrepreneur to a variety of changing market conditions. Over a 5- to 10-year period,

---

[3]Donald K. Clifford, Jr., "Growth Pains of the Threshold Company," *Harvard Business Review*, September–October 1973, p. 146.

[4]George Strauss, "Adolescence in Organizational Growth: Problems, Pains and Possibilities," *Organizational Dynamics*, Spring 1974.

Figure 8–1
Greiner's Summary of Required Changes in Organization Practices during Evolution in the Five Phases of Growth

Category	Phase 1	Phase 2	Phase 3	Phase 4	Phase 5
Management focus	Make and sell	Efficiency of operations	Expansion of market	Consolidation of organization	Problem solving and innovation
Organization structure	Informal	Centralized and functional	Decentralized and geographical	Line-staff and product groups	Matrix of teams
Top management style	Individualistic and entre-preneurial	Directive	Delegative	Watchdog	Participative
Control system	Market results	Standards and cost centers	Reports and profit centers	Plans and investment centers	Mutual goal setting
Management reward emphasis	Ownership	Salary and merit increases	Individual bonus	Profit sharing and stock options	Team bonus

Source: Larry E. Greiner, "Evolution and Revolution as Organizations Grow," *Harvard Business Review,* July–August 1972, p. 45.

he established an enormously successful venture; in its market it became the largest and most profitable organization of its kind.

It is difficult to tell from historical records how much, if anything, the entrepreneur did to develop the company's long-run organizational adaptability. Two facts, however, are known. The ongoing operations were so profitable that he submitted to the demands of the national union just to avoid a disruption of operations. This resulted in the establishment of innumerable "work rules" and the entry of first-line supervisors into the union. Second, he did almost nothing to bring in or develop middle- and top-level managers. As an extremely talented person, capable of making many effective business decisions himself, he saw no need for assistance from others.

In the mid-1940s, the entrepreneur died. His brother took over as president and tried to maintain the company's existing policies and profitability. For the first few years of his tenure, everything seemed to work well.

Nevertheless, the company's industry, like many others, experienced significant changes after World War II. These changes occurred gradually but continuously over at least a 10-year period. During this time, the company made few organizational adjustments to adapt to these changes for several reasons. First, the few people who had real decision-making authority in the company did not see any need for many changes. They did not have the information that would have shown them what was happening in their industry and in their market area. Second, when

Figure 8–2
Summary of Changes during Three Stages of Organizational Development

Company Characteristics	Stage I	Stage II	Stage III
The business:			
1. Product	Single product or single line.	Single product line.	Multiple product lines.
2. Distribution	One channel or set of channels.	One set of channels.	Multiple channels.
3. R&D	Not institutionalized— oriented by owner-manager.	Increasingly institutionalized search for product or process improvements.	Institutionalized search for *new* products and for improvements.
4. Strategic choices	Needs of owner versus needs of firm.	Degree of integration. Market share objective. Breadth of product line.	Entry and exit from industries. Allocation of resources by industry. Rate of growth.
The organization:			
1. Organization structure	Little or no formal structure.	Specialization based on function.	Specialization based on product/ market relationship.
2. Product/service transactions	Not available	Integrated pattern of transactions: □→□→□⤵ Market	Not integrated: [A] [B] [C] ↓ ↓ ↓ Markets
3. Performance measurement	By personal contact and subjective criteria.	Increasingly impersonal, using technical and/or cost criteria.	Increasingly impersonal, using *market* criteria (return on investment and market share).
4. Rewards	Unsystematic and often paternalistic.	Increasingly systematic with emphasis on stability and service.	Increasingly systematic with variability related to performance.
5. Control system	Personal control of both strategic and operating decisions.	Personal control of strategic decisions with increasing delegation of operating decisions based on control by policies.	Delegation of product/market decisions within existing businesses with indirect control based on analysis of "results."

Source: Adapted from Bruce Scott, "Stages of Corporate Development" (Boston: Intercollegiate Case Clearing House, 1971).

they did have information on changes, they often had difficulty deciding how to adjust to them. They were, for example, completely unaware of the typical developmental sequences shown in Figures 8–1 and 8–2. The intuitively brilliant leadership once supplied by the original entrepreneur was gone, and nothing took its place. Finally, when they did identify a change and saw what response was needed, the managers generally could not implement it. For one thing, union rules prohibited large changes; for another, there was no middle management to help implement it. The firm was not flexible.

Some of the company's competitors were successful in identifying and reacting to the industry and market changes. As a result, the rate of increase of this company's sales and profits began to decrease. At the same time, problems with employees and the union surfaced.

The company's president initially focused his efforts on trying to stop the profit decline. In this endeavor, he was somewhat successful. Yet, in slowing the profit decline, he was forced to hold salaries and maintenance budgets down, thereby adding to problems with employees and the union. A climate of antagonism and distrust developed.

Between 1956 and 1965, the company's real (noninflated) annual growth in sales declined from 5 percent to 0 percent. Its profits leveled out and then fell to a net loss in 1965. By that time, the company's stock price was so low that a larger corporation successfully acquired a controlling interest. This corporation brought in its own top management group (which included a number of extremely successful managers) and predicted a quick turnaround.

The company resumed profitable operations in 1969 and, with the exception of 1973, has remained profitable. Nevertheless, its profitability levels remain below the industry average, and its 1975 sales were, in real dollars, about the same as in 1965. It has had two more presidents since 1965 and the current one has been quoted in the business press as saying that the job of organizational "renewal" ahead of them is still very large.

Characteristics of an Effective Organization—From a Long-Range Point of View

It is possible to infer the characteristics that contribute to long-run effectiveness by looking for what was missing in the previous example. If we consider our discussion of the difficulty of organizational change in the Citibank cases, we can deduce other characteristics. The picture that emerges is an organization where changes in its business are anticipated or quickly identified, where appropriate responses are designed quickly, and where responses are implemented at a minimum cost.[5] This behavior is possible because the company is staffed with talented managers skilled at organizational analysis, as well as with adaptable employees. Informal relations

---

[5]The many social scientists who have approached the topic of organizational adaptability from different perspectives agree, in general terms, with this conclusion. See, for example, Edgar Schein, *Organizational Psychology* (Englewood Cliffs, N.J.: Prentice-Hall, 1965), p. 99.

Figure 8–3
Characteristics of a Highly Effective Organization: A Long-Run Point of View

Employees:
1. The company is staffed with more than enough managerial talent.
2. Managers are skilled at organizational analysis and understand typical stages of organizational development.
3. Many employees are adaptive and have skills beyond a narrow specialty.
4. Employees have realistic expectations about what they will get from, and have to give to, the company in the foreseeable future.

Informal relations:
1. There is a high level of trust between employees and management.
2. Information flows freely with a minimum of distortion within and across groups.
3. People in all positions of responsibility are willing to listen to, and be influenced by, others who have relevant information.

Formal design:
1. The organizational structure includes more than enough effective integrating mechanisms for the current situation and relies minimally on rules and procedures.
2. Measurement systems thoroughly collect and distribute all relevant data on the organization's environment, its actions, its performance, and changes in any of these factors.
3. Reward systems encourage people to identify needed changes and help implement them.
4. Selection and development systems are designed to create highly skilled managerial and employee groups and to encourage the kinds of informal relations described above.

among these people are characterized by trust, open communications, and respect for others' opinions. The formal design includes effective integrating devices, sensitive and well-designed measurement systems, reward systems that encourage adaptability, and selection and development systems that help support all other characteristics. See Figure 8–3.

Unlike the declining company described earlier, an organization with the characteristics listed in Figure 8–3, as well as other characteristics that specifically fit its current business, can successfully respond to growth industry changes, top management turnover, and anything else that appears. Its adaptability allows it to continue changing its organization to fit its changing business, and it will both survive and prosper over long periods.

Bureaucratic Dry Rot

Few companies or nonprofit businesses have organizations with characteristics close to those described in Figure 8–3. This fact has been emphasized by social scientists who, in the past decade, have expressed serious concern over what they call "bureaucratic dry rot."[6] We all pay a heavy price, they note, for the large, bureaucratic,

---

[6]See Warren Bennis, *Beyond Bureaucracy* (New York: McGraw-Hill, 1966), chap. 1.

unadaptive organizations that are insensitive to employees' needs, ignore consumers' desires, and refuse to accept their social responsibilities.

Existing evidence suggests that although most contemporary organizations cannot be described as adaptive, many managers nevertheless appreciate the benefits of adaptability. When polled, managers often respond that "ideally" they would like to have the kind of organization suggested by Figure 8 3, but they also admit that their current organization does not have some or all of these characteristics.[7]

There are at least five reasons for the inflexibility and shortsightedness of most contemporary organizations. The first and most significant is related to resources. Creating a highly adaptive organization requires time, energy, and money. For example, in the case of the company that went into decline, creating an adaptive organization early in its history might have required:

- Hiring, assimilating, and training a management team, both at the top and in middle-level ranks.
- Careful selection and training of all other personnel.
- Concentrated effort from the managers to develop integrative devices, measurement systems, and the like.
- Steady effort from the managers to develop and maintain good, informal relationships among themselves and their employees.

Possibly the organization did not have the resources to invest in these systems. Had it tried, it might have been necessary to divert resources from some of its current operations; and if its competitors did not choose to follow its lead but continued to invest as heavily as possible in current operations, perhaps the company would have lost market share and income and even gone out of business long before it could enjoy the benefits of its long-term investment in adaptability.[8]

A second reason for the unadaptive and bureaucratic behavior of modern organizations is that their managers are not skilled at producing the characteristics of an effective organization in the long run. Because organizations generally invest resources in current operations and not in producing adaptive human systems, the on-the-job education of managers is usually focused on current operations, not on producing adaptability. Generating the characteristics shown in Figure 8–3 requires skills that have to be developed and nurtured.[9]

A third reason for the inflexibility of many contemporary organizations is that some people clearly benefit from a static situation. The entrepreneur who established the unadaptive organization described earlier thoroughly enjoyed the way he ran the company. It is doubtful that he would have invested resources in developing a

---

[7]Rensis Likert's "System 4" organization is similar to what we call a highly adaptive organization. He asked many managers, via a questionnaire, what type of organization they would like to have, and they usually answered "System 4." See Rensis Likert, *The Human Organization: Its Management and Value* (New York: McGraw-Hill, 1967), p. 28.

[8]See John P. Kotter, *Organizational Dynamics* (Reading, Mass.: Addison-Wesley Publishing, 1978).

[9]Chris Argyris, *Increasing Leadership Effectiveness* (New York: John Wiley & Sons, 1976).

management team, or developed one even if it cost him nothing. Furthermore, financial backers approved of how he ran the business, which included passing on a large share of the firm's earnings in dividends. Had he tried to cut the dividends to invest more in something as nontangible as adaptability, they undoubtedly would have protested.

A fourth reason for unadaptive behavior can also be seen from the case of decline. Once an organization reaches a certain size, if it has not developed a certain minimally adaptive human organization, it becomes difficult to turn things around without a gigantic infusion of resources. Considerable effort is required to overcome the "organizational entropy"[10] that makes the organization even more unadaptive and rigid.

A fifth reason why more companies do not have organizational characteristics like those in Figure 8–3 is that their management has decided they are unnecessary. Based on their projection of what the future has in store for their company, they estimate how much adaptability they will need and then invest resources that produce only that level of adaptability. If they are growing quickly or if they are in a volatile market, and if they expect that rapid changes will continue in their business, they invest considerable resources in creating an adaptive human organization. If they are not growing, if they are in a stable market, and if they feel the future will not demand many changes from them, they invest few resources.

In short, the forces that prevent organizations from developing a high level of adaptability are strong. The forces that can push successful organizations into decline also are numerous. As a result, one of the most difficult of all management tasks involves developing an organization that has *enough* adaptability to promote effectiveness in the long run.

Organizing for the Future

Developing an organization that is adaptive enough to ensure a company's continued success requires, most of all, a dedicated and skilled top manager or top management group—one both willing and able to make decisions that will balance the needs of the present and the needs of the future. Deciding whether to use an available resource to solve a current problem or to develop flexibility for the future is difficult.[11] Without serious dedication to success in the long run, short-run pressures often take precedence.

Deciding exactly how to develop future adaptability best, but at minimum cost, can also be difficult. Obviously the words and deeds of the people on top are important. If they stress learning, planning, adaptability, open communications, and the like, that behavior will help set norms for others. Training and development activities are also important, as are periodic reviews of the state of the human organization, which identify more adaptive and less adaptive components. In each

---

[10]Chris Argyris, *Intervention Theory and Method* (Reading, Mass.: Addison-Wesley Publishing, 1970), chap. 3.

[11]See Peter Drucker, *Management* (New York: Harper & Row, 1976), pp. 43–44.

of these cases, however, managers have many options regarding how to stress learning, to design training, or to review the organization.

Organizational Development (OD)

A new management specialty called organization development (OD) has emerged in the past 20 years. OD specialists focus mostly on methods for increasing the adaptability of human organizations.[12] Although the total number is small, more businesses have established OD functions usually within the personnel or human resources department.[13] People who work in these functions utilize a variety of techniques to help managers develop human organizations with the characteristics shown in Figure 8–3. The most commonly used techniques include:

1. Kepner-Trego clinics,[14] Phase One Managerial Grid sessions,[15] T-groups,[16] and other training seminars designed to improve a manager's ability to work with others, solve problems, and lead.

2. Methods of resolving conflict and improving relationships in organizations, such as team building,[17] intergroup labs,[18] confrontation meetings,[19] and third-party consultations.[20]

3. Methods for designing formal organizational structure,[21] spatial arrangements,[22] pay systems,[23] jobs,[24] and performance-appraisal systems.[25]

---

[12]People who call themselves OD specialists sometimes also help solve short-run organizational problems and involve themselves in other activities.

[13]Fred Luthans, "Merging Personnel and OD," *Personnel,* May 1977.

[14]Kepner-Trego Inc., Princeton, N.J. Problem-solving decision-making classes.

[15]R. R. Blake and J. S. Mouton, *Building a Dynamic Corporation through Grid Organization Development* (Reading, Mass.: Addison-Wesley Publishing, 1969).

[16]Chris Argyris, "T-Groups for Organizational Effectiveness," *Harvard Business Review,* March–April 1964, pp. 84–97.

[17]Shel Davis, "Building More Effective Teams," *Innovation* 15 (1970), pp. 32–41.

[18]R. R. Blake, H. A. Shepard, and J. S. Mouton, *Managing Intergroup Conflict in Industry* (Houston: Gulf Publishing, 1964).

[19]Richard Beckhard, "The Confrontation Meeting," *Harvard Business Review,* March–April 1967, p. 45.

[20]Richard Walton, *Interpersonal Peacemaking: Confrontations and Third-Party Consultations* (Reading, Mass.: Addison-Wesley Publishing, 1969).

[21]Paul R. Lawrence and Jay W. Lorsch, *Developing Organizations* (Reading, Mass.: Addison-Wesley Publishing, 1969).

[22]Fritz I. Steele, *Physical Settings and Organizational Development* (Reading, Mass.: Addison-Wesley Publishing, 1973).

[23]F. G. Lesieur, ed., *The Scanlon Plan: A Frontier in Labor-Management Cooperation* (MIT Industrial Relations Section, 1958).

[24]W. J. Paul, K. B. Robertson, and F. L. Hertzberg, "Job Enrichment Pays Off," *Harvard Business Review,* March–April 1969, pp. 61–78.

[25]H. H. Mayer, E. Kay, and J. R. P. French, "Split Roles in Performance Appraisal," *Harvard Business Review,* January–February 1966, pp. 123–29.

4. Methods for measuring the current state of employee attitudes,[26] small-group functioning,[27] organizational climate,[28] and organizational processes.[29]

5. Broad approaches to the whole development process such as process consultation[30] and survey feedback.[31]

Applied appropriately, all of these techniques can help develop more adaptive human organizations, although they are not a panacea for long-run effectiveness and can be misused like any other managerial tool.[32] Organizations that have been most successful in using these techniques usually have had a competent OD staff or a set of OD consultants as well as a talented top management group that guided their efforts.

OD Change Efforts

Efforts to change an organization for developmental purposes, using any of the techniques previously listed, tend to differ in two important ways from organizational change efforts aimed at solving a current problem.

First, developmental change efforts are of a more ongoing nature. Unlike problem-solving organizational change, they tend not to begin and end in a period of months.

Second, developmental change efforts generally use coercive tactics to a lesser degree than other change efforts. For a variety of reasons, coercion cannot be used constantly over long periods to create an effective organization.

Summary

Developing a human organization that contributes to long-run effectiveness means developing enough flexibility and anticipatory ability so that the organization can adapt to inevitable changes in its environment. Creating and maintaining such an organization requires that managers invest resources in its human organization beyond what is needed merely for current operations. It also requires skill in making decisions that affect the human organization's adaptability.

---

[26]M. E. Shaw and J. M. Wright, *Scales for the Measurement of Attitudes* (New York: McGraw-Hill, 1967).

[27]J. K. Hemphill, *Group Dimensions: A Manual for Their Measurement* (Columbus: Ohio State University, Bureau of Business Research Monograph 87, 1956).

[28]G. H. Litwin and R. A. Stringer, *Motivation and Organizational Climate* (Boston: Harvard Business School, Division of Research, 1968).

[29]Likert, *The Human Organization.*

[30]Edgar H. Schein, *Process Consultation: Its Role in Organization Development* (Reading, Mass.: Addison-Wesley Publishing, 1967).

[31]P. Chase, "A Survey Feedback Approach to Organization Development," *Proceedings of the Executive Study Conference* (Princeton: Educational Testing Service, November 1968).

[32]For a good general discussion of OD, see Raymond E. Miles, "Organization Development" in *Organizational Behavior: Research and Issues,* ed. George Strauss et al. (Industrial Relations Research Association, 1974).

A process that can help managers make effective developmental decisions requires periodic consideration of the following questions:

1. How much change will our organization experience in the next 5, 10, and 20 years? In what directions will these changes take us? How certain are our estimates of change? How much flexibility is needed to respond to these estimated changes?

2. How flexible is our human organization currently? That is, what is its current state on the dimensions shown in Figure 8–3? Is this adequate to cope with the change estimates?

3. If more flexibility is needed, how much is needed and how quickly? Where is additional flexibility needed: everywhere, in top management, or in just the formal systems?

With perceptive answers to those questions, managers can develop and implement over time a set of interventions that keeps a company's organization adaptive enough to cope with its probable future.

Case 8–1

Jeff Bradley (A)

C. Paul Dredge, Vijay Sathe

Jeff Bradley looked back with considerable pride at the way he had thrived on the supposed adversity of his initiation into Heartland Heavy Industries, the company he had joined upon graduation from HBS in 1975. Jeff had survived difficult situations, and he felt he had built an enduring team spirit in an organization where none existed before. Jeff had been able to apply much of what he had learned at HBS, but he also knew that his own personal resources had been instrumental in his success.

Now, in early 1977, Jeff faced a new set of challenges as head of a problem Heartland plant. Three weeks into his new assignment as plant manager, a position in line management that he had coveted, Jeff had to deal with a boss who was constantly looking over his shoulder, a "cowboy" work force whose indifference to danger had given the plant a poor safety record, and a machine called the "spinner" that both workers and supervisors believed could be tamed only by ritual and magic. Jeff knew his promising start at Heartland could come to a screeching halt if he could not bring these problems under control and turn the plant around.

Background

Jeff had grown up on a modest western Kansas farm, a life that he said had helped develop his ability to "sort the wheat from the chaff" quickly. After graduating as valedictorian in his engineering class at the University of Kansas, Jeff joined Rapid Air Lines in St. Louis, where he soon moved into a management track. The first few months of what was to become four years of experience in successively more

This case was prepared by C. Paul Dredge (under the direction of Vijay Sathe).
Copyright © 1984 by the President and Fellows of Harvard College.
Harvard Business School case 484–066.

responsible management positions at Rapid had confirmed Jeff's earlier suspicions that he would enjoy putting aside his drawing board and calculator for the satisfaction of managing and working effectively with other people. His next step in management would require additional training, and Jeff learned that Rapid would pay for at least part of his tuition for an MBA, with no obligation to return to Rapid, provided that he could get admitted to one of several top schools.

In his first year at HBS, Jeff studied hard and did well; his highly organized lifestyle gave him plenty of time for athletic activity, adequate rest, and correspondence with his fiancée, Carol, in Kansas City. During the summer after his first year, Jeff went to work for the Premium National Bank of Kansas, turning down an offer from Rapid in order to learn something in a new area of business and be with his fiancée. Jeff found that, for his own tastes, people at the bank were too interested in political games and the cut of their clothes and not enough in accomplishing something really concrete. As for Rapid Air Lines, Jeff felt that advancement in that large, rather bureaucratic organization would probably be safe and secure, but much too slow, and he was not looking for that kind of a career.

Job Luck

During his second year at HBS, Jeff started a systematic job search. His criteria limited his choices. One thing Jeff wanted to avoid was the East Coast. "No need to bang my head in New York with all the other MBAs, and Boston never interested me all that much." Jeff preferred to locate in the heartland, where he grew up, to be near his family and the family of his wife-to-be in Kansas City. More important than location, however, was his desire to find a position with a manufacturing company where he could use his engineering background. He also wanted to get a job that would guarantee line management experience within 18 months.

The beginning of April found Jeff with offers to return to Rapid Air Lines and the Premium National Bank, and a certain feeling of desperation. Three or four weeks before he had to decide on these offers, he received a call at 11 one night from Harold Maxfield, a corporate VP at Heartland Heavy Industries in Omaha, Nebraska. Maxfield indicated that he had noted the engineering degree and the four and a half years' work experience on Jeff's resume in the HBS Engineers' Club resume book, which the club had sent to 500 companies. He asked if Jeff would be interested in talking to him when he visited Cambridge the following Saturday. "Yes, I'm interested," was Jeff's happy reply.

Jeff went to the Sonesta Hotel room expecting the standard interview procedure— "Nobody really saying what they think." Maxfield told him to take off his coat and tie, sit down wherever he pleased, and without any of the usual polite preliminaries, started firing questions about everything imaginable. Maxfield was wearing a turtleneck shirt and lying on the bed in his stocking feet. "Why do you want to work for Heartland? What can you do for us? Why is a Harvard MBA such hot stuff, anyway? What is r^2?" Jeff sensed that Maxfield didn't want "the usual interview stuff" and responded with tough-minded answers and some jibes of his own. "The guy who came out of there before I went in looked awful, and I figured that the most important thing was not to buckle." On the phone and now in the interview, what Maxfield said about Heartland was appealing, even though he himself was a bit abrasive.

Maxfield explained that Heartland executives had decided they would have to tighten their management style in order to prosper in an increasingly competitive environment. In the past, the corporation had been run as a loosely knit group of operations, and management was becoming concerned that it had not developed sufficient numbers of young managers. Their proposed method was to hire some high-potential people, familiarize them with the company through an intensive on-the-job training program, and then use their new employees' knowledge of more modern management techniques to improve Heartland's operations. When they parted, Maxfield indicated that there was a good chance of an offer, that he would be back in touch within a week, and that he would send additional information on the company to help Jeff make a decision. Jeff indicated that he had three or four weeks before he'd have to decide on another offer.

Jeff did receive a fair bit of information on the company as Maxfield had promised, but he didn't hear from Maxfield. Jeff found out that Heartland, a billion dollar corporation, had average performance within its industry. On a Monday, nine days after the interview, Jeff called Maxfield. He was very cordial, apologized for not calling back, and said: "You're on the short list." Maxfield indicated that he would be leaving the office until Thursday, but would call Jeff then with the final word. Jeff thanked him, but after hanging up he started to worry about the timing of the possible offer and his limited knowledge of Heartland. How could he make a decision for or against Heartland on the basis of a short interview with Harold Maxfield and the information in the reports he had received? Since Jeff was inclined to go to Kansas City anyway to visit Carol and do some on-site job hunting, he decided by Wednesday to call Heartland to see if he could arrange a visit to company headquarters in Omaha.

As expected, Maxfield wasn't there, but his secretary asked if Jeff would like to speak with Clark White, the president of the corporation. Jeff said that would be fine. When Clark White came to the phone, Jeff introduced himself, acknowledged that no firm offer of a job had been made, and then expressed his reservations about responding favorably to an offer that might come. Jeff said that although he had been impressed with the company, he was reluctant to make a decision on the basis of an hour's interview. If Heartland was still interested, Jeff wanted to know if it would be possible for him to visit company headquarters and talk to a few more people about the position. White indicated that he had talked with Maxfield about a possible offer, that they were indeed still interested, and that he fully understood Jeff's reservations. White then arranged for Jeff's visit for the next day.

Jeff spent Thursday at a Heartland plant in Pittsburgh and Friday at company headquarters in Omaha taking a closer look. He soon found, with some relief, that Maxfield's brusque manner was the exception among the company officers he met. On the other hand, he was impressed, as he had been with Maxfield, with the hard-driving, no-nonsense style of several of the managers. Jeff was particularly interested in the very lean staff at headquarters—it was obvious to him they had good people and did a lot of delegating to division-level managers.

At the end of the day on Friday, Jeff had another interview with Maxfield and was offered the job. When asked about salary, Jeff told Maxfield that he would be happy with at least as much as the $23,500 Rapid Air Lines was offering him. (The median starting salary for the Class of 1975 was $18,600). Maxfield offered Jeff a $24,500 starting salary and added: "If you are not making $35,000 with us in a couple of years, you are not the man we want." Jeff had one other stipulation: Assuming that he did well in his initial assignments, he wanted to be sure he could move into a line management position after 18 months. Maxfield indicated that the company's timetable already called for that.

Before the interview ended, Maxfield told Jeff about what they had in mind for his training in the company. Maxfield indicated that it was of the utmost importance that Heartland managers be able to get along with "the dirty hands people" in the plants. Jeff would start out with nitty-gritty experience as a foreman in a foundry, Maxwell said, but he wasn't sure just where Jeff would be placed for this initial assignment:

> Just six months in purgatory and the new training program will take you somewhere more hospitable. For now we want you to start out in the dirtiest, hottest, noisiest job we can find.

As he deliberated his offers, Jeff knew that he could go back to Rapid—a known, comfortable situation in the location he preferred—and retire after 35 years with a gold watch, a good pension, and an easy life. With Heartland he would take the risk of working in a new and unknown industry, but would have the job in manufacturing he was seeking and also live closer to where he wanted to live. He sensed that, more than the other two places from which he had received offers, at Heartland he could learn from old hands in the company and simultaneously apply and test what he had learned at HBS. Moreover, there was a noticeable lack of young management talent at Heartland, which boded well for the rapid advancement Jeff hoped to achieve.

The Fiery Furnace

On June 7, 1975, Jeff graduated from HBS, with his mother and new bride on hand to celebrate. In Kansas City on June 9, Jeff went to Sears to buy a black metal lunch box, steel-toed shoes, and some green work outfits. "Is this the kind of job you get after a Harvard MBA? You should have stayed at Rapid!" his father said. Even Carol asked why she should have to make sandwiches every day for this supposed "executive." But Jeff felt confident about his job decision.

Jeff went to work as a foreman in a Heartland iron pipe plant in Gary, Indiana. His responsibility was to supervise 18 men in what seemed to be the dirtiest, least interesting job in the place: cleaning off the newly cast, angled fittings (e.g., elbows, reducers or "cones") that were used to connect the standard lengths of pipe.

> Dickens never described anything worse than our section of the plant. Soot, boiling ladles of molten iron, the incessant din of pneumatic chipping hammers, welding the wheelabrator machine, grinding, and banging. The steel toes saved my feet more than once.

Jeff knew that he was being tested and that his career with Heartland would not go well if he complained or faltered in the inferno. But the challenge was more than just enduring the environment. Headquarters had set Jeff the goal of a 30 percent increase in productivity for his department over the six months he was to be foreman.

For the first week or two, Jeff was like a detective, looking for clues to the problems in his fittings shop. Jeff learned that the foreman in the adjacent shop had for the past 10 months also supervised the group of workers Jeff was currently responsible for. The men in Jeff's shop were mostly emigrants from Italy, Portugal, and Greece. Jeff thought they were willing enough to work hard if he could give them some good reason to. He set about finding what was keeping production levels so low.

The first thing Jeff noticed was that the men were incessantly late, following the example of the foreman in the adjacent shop and of Mel Linton, Jeff's boss and the work floor supervisor who was near retirement. Jeff made sure he himself was on the floor 10 minutes early every morning, and he began to dock the pay of those who came in late.

Jeff's men spent a lot of time going to other parts of the plant in search of things like gloves, work aprons, and tools. Jeff had a large, new cabinet built and placed in his department, and he kept it well stocked with everything his men could possibly need. The men no longer had an excuse to wander.

The men in the cleaning shop were spending long periods of time with chisels, hammers, and pneumatic chipping tools, cleaning off by hand the imperfections that didn't get knocked off in the big wheelabrator machine that barraged the pipe castings with brass shot. Jeff ignored plant precedent and Linton's advice when, at the suggestion of one of the workers he had learned to respect (a fellow who in fact had complained that other foremen and supervisors never listened to any of the men's suggestions), he issued an order to triple the time spent for each fitting in the wheelabrator. The fittings came out much cleaner, and the time necessary for hand chipping was drastically reduced. After this change, Jeff's men began to keep up occasionally with their production schedules; Jeff also sensed that they now felt he might be okay, after all.

Jeff's subordinates, peers, and even his boss, Mel Linton, didn't know that Jeff would be there for only six months. But Jeff felt they suspected he would stay for a short period of time, perhaps a year or two. Jeff didn't confine himself to his shop, but would periodically visit other parts of the plant to make new acquaintances and observe other comparable shops. One worker in an adjacent shop that he observed frequently, got to know, and came to respect, was an immigrant who kept hinting he had a secret formula ("The key is molasses") for the wash coating used in the casting molds. Following the usual method Jeff had developed for dealing with his boss, Jeff got "permission" to try the new wash coat:

Jeff: Patrick, the Irishman, wants to use molasses in the wash.

Linton: That so?

Jeff: I think it's worth trying, so I'm willing to pay for the molasses out of my miscellaneous expense account.

Linton: Mmmmm.

Jeff: So we'll start working on it in the morning.

Linton: Mmmmm.

Jeff knew Linton was not going to take a stand, and Jeff decided to go ahead on his own. Almost magically, the castings came out shiny clean with the new wash coat, even in the deep grooves where the fittings would be joined to the regular pipe. Jeff now had the wheelabrator time cut back by half, for the castings that came out from the new wash coat needed considerably less scouring.

Jeff tried for over a month to get division purchasing to procure for his department a renewed supply of short sledge-hammer handles. When his supply completely ran out, he finally gave up on them, got some petty cash, jumped into his car, and was back at the plant within an hour with a week's supply of handles (for $40) from a local hardware store. Jeff's plant manager, Howard McCall, got wind of the story on the handles and was soon on the phone asking division purchasing why his foreman could find in an hour what purchasing couldn't get in a month. George Kondopoulos, one of the Greek workers who used the hammers almost constantly, smiled and slapped Jeff on the back, holding his hammer in the air and pointing to the new handle.

After three months, Jeff's shop had increased production by 25 percent. It was then that Howard McCall announced a rush order to be shipped to Venezuela, something that would require the utmost efficiency in day-to-day operations if they were to meet the very tight shipping schedule. Jeff went to his men with enthusiasm and confidence, noting that they would have all the overtime they could handle, and they responded by working even harder. Jeff designed a new reporting system that kept track of every fitting as it moved through casting and cleaning—he knew they couldn't afford to forget to recast even one fitting that got ruined the first time through. Previously, such lapses of memory and attention to detail had caused very costly and embarrassing delays in shipping out orders, but this time the fittings shop did not miss the boat.

After a full six months as foreman, Jeff was transferred out of the iron pipe plant. His department was operating with 40 percent higher productivity than when he began. There was also a backlog of worker applications to transfer into his fitting shop, which was formerly considered the "dog" of the plant.

Other Assignments

Jeff's next six-month assignment involved various products in different areas of the country. Commuting home on weekends at company expense, Jeff worked in Houston as an internal consultant in an oil rig repair operation that had been losing money since Heartland acquired it two and a half years previously. His final recommendation was to sell the operation off, even though acquiring it had been the brainchild of two Heartland corporate vice presidents. Jeff backed up his recommendation with a thorough quantitative analysis, which centered on the lack of competitive advantage for Heartland in the oil rig repair business. In the end, the vice presidents reluctantly sold their "baby" ($1/2 million sales) to a company ($2 million sales) that folded only four months later.

Jeff's next six-month assignment was as a heavy equipment salesman. He was surprised at how much he enjoyed sales, though he was also frustrated from time to time at not having enough control over the variables that affected the success of his sales. Jeff still felt more at home in manufacturing, where the people and decisions were largely internal to the organization, but he was glad for an opportunity to learn about another important aspect of Heartland's business.

Plant Manager

After 18 months with Heartland, Jeff was offered a line management position as a plant manager, right on schedule, as Harold Maxfield had promised. He had to choose between plants near Pittsburgh and Colorado Springs, Colorado. Carol's desire to continue her own professional development in the insurance industry happily coincided with Jeff's own preference for a move to Colorado.

Earlier in December 1976, a two-day visit to the Colorado Springs plant had given Jeff a feel for the task ahead. Jeff's new boss, Glen Morgan, the concrete pipe operations manager, and a new manager who was taking over a different plant under Morgan, had accompanied Jeff on this visit to learn from Morgan and get initiated as well. Actually located in Widefield, a small town 20 miles from the center of Colorado Springs, the almost-new plant was unionized, was the largest single employer in town, and had defeated two previous managers in less than two years since it had begun operating. While the start-up management team had been very enthusiastic, they had been unable to deal effectively with the rather happy-go-lucky attitudes of many of the hourly workers. Work force problems, especially the high rate of accidents in the plant, combined with difficulties in some of the manufacturing processes—most notably the "spinner" machine—had helped to keep the operation in the red.

When he visited Colorado in December, Jeff inquired about his immediate predecessor, who had already left the company. Evidently Stu Little had felt that his boss, Glen Morgan, was too difficult to deal with. The foremen at the plant later told Jeff that Stu used to hide out in obscure corners of the plant to avoid Glen's phone calls, or even hide away somewhere during his frequent visits. Eventually, Stu quit.

Now, under the temporary management of the plant superintendent, a 17-year-veteran of Heartland named Dick Hill, the Widefield plant was struggling along with frequent accidents, production and shipping delays, labor unrest, and of course still no black ink. Glen Morgan, the concrete pipe operations manager, would spend days and weeks at the plant running the show. As with the previous manager, Glen was out of his Omaha office and onto a plane to Colorado the minute anything went wrong. He called once or twice a day to see if he was needed.

Jeff was impressed with the level of experience and dedication of the foremen and the supervisors, however, and felt that they and the hourly staff (about 120 people in all) could be built into a good team with the right approach.

Moving In

On January 4, 1977, Jeff moved into the corner office at the Widefield plant. The plant interior held a Spartan office area, with spaces for 10 people in small offices and a large space at one end where the foremen took breaks and ate their lunches. To the office Jeff brought his steel-toed boots (his were hiking style), which were required by safety regulations when he was on the plant floor. He had a white hard hat, too, with a piece of plastic name tape stuck on the front that spelled out "Jeff Bradley." Jeff liked the hat better than his silk tie, though he did keep the tie on at the plant.

Assigned Objectives

Jeff had been assigned six objectives to work toward in this new position, and safety had first priority. During 1976, Widefield had had the worst record of all Heartland's plants for accidents that caused lost production time; 24 such accidents had occurred in the plant during the year. The accident rate was important to labor relations, productivity, and to the pipe division generally because the company's contributions for insurance were tied directly to the accident rate. More accidents meant higher expenses for corporate. Jeff's assignment was to reduce accidents to *six or fewer* during 1977.

The other five objectives involved improvements in labor productivity, indirect and direct materials cost, task force ratings on safety, efficiency and housekeeping, improved communications between various levels and areas of plant operations and management, and a positive performance appraisal for Jeff at the end of the year. Bill Ashton, the division general manager, and Glen Morgan, Jeff's immediate boss, made sure Jeff understood that the overriding objective was to manage a profitable operation. The ratings on most of Jeff's specific objectives would be determined in biannual on-site inspections and reviews, carried out by a pipe division task force which visited each of the 21 Heartland plants to provide comparative assessments.

Making Pipe

The production of reinforced concrete pipe, in 24-foot lengths and widths varying from 14 inches to 54 inches in diameter, involved machine welding of rolled sheet steel into cylinders (known in the plant as "cans"), testing for and spot repairing of leaks in the welded seam, coating the inside of the can with up to a 2-inch layer of concrete, wrapping the outer steel surface with reinforcing wire (the more closely the strands were wrapped and the thicker the original sheet steel, the higher the "grade" of the pipe), and finally brush coating the outside of the pipe with a 1/4- to 3/4-inch layer of concrete. After both stages of adding concrete, the pipe was fork-lifted into large drying kilns for quick curing. Cans could become scrap any-where along the assembly line, but it became progressively more expensive with added input of material and labor.

The operation that produced the most scrap was coating the inside of cans with concrete on the machine called the spinner. After loading onto the belts of the spinner, which was housed inside a steel mesh cage, cans were rotated at high speeds atop rolling belts while a long "spoon" full of concrete was hydraulically inserted into the center of the pipe. As the spoon slowly dumped its load of soupy concrete, the force of the gradually accelerated spinning motion distributed the concrete in an even layer inside the pipe.

A smaller space in the plant housed the quality control laboratory and the fittings shop. In the latter, all the odd-shaped and angled fittings, which attached to standard lengths of straight pipe, were made to order. Pipe orders were generated by a separate sales staff; the plant was solely a manufacturing concern.

Glen and Spinner Magic

Jeff soon learned that the spinner had an aura of mystery and intrigue and that it was dangerous and unpredictable, particularly when producing larger sizes of pipe. One hair-raising incident occurred during his first week at the plant with a relatively small 24-inch pipe on the spinner. The machine sent part of the can up through the roof into the tower where the concrete was mixed. The concrete-swathed can then plunged down the chute and crashed to the floor just a few feet from the man operating the wet concrete spoon. After that incident, Jeff supervised the rebuilding of the wire mesh cage, this time with two layers of a higher-strength mesh.

The mystique of the spinner stemmed from the fact that over 50 variables had to be set just right for the giant machine to function smoothly. Further, these settings had to be worked out separately for each size of the pipe by trial and error, because each machine was custom made. There was only one other spinner in another Heartland plant, and only six or seven other spinners with competitors in the United States.

Technicians and engineers who were calm and rational with other machines became masters of sorcery with regard to the spinner. Each of the five or six people involved in running the spinner had his own magical solution to getting it to work right. The complexity of the variables that affected how the spinning turned out made it very difficult to pinpoint just what the problem might be when a can flew off the spinner and was ruined.

Dick Hill, the plant superintendent, recalled for Jeff the famous "scrap of 48" incident, when Glen Morgan had established himself as the jinx of the spinner. It was in December 1976, a month before Jeff took over, and Dick had been supervising the running of an order of 48-inch pipe. The spinner threw one of the first cans, and Dick consulted with the operator, the foreman, and Guiermo Martinez, the quality control supervisor who had enjoyed some previous success at charming the spinner. Guiermo insisted that the problem was dry concrete. "You've gotta run soup," he said, so the mixture was watered down before loading the spoon, and they tried again. The can flew off and crumpled into a soupy concrete and steel pretzel.

"We forgot to adjust the height of the pulleys," said the operator, referring to one of the more logical steps needed to assure a good spin. The belts had to be tight enough that the can could sit on the belts alone, not on the pulleys that turned the belts. If the belts were *too* tight, the can could easily fly off. They adjusted the belts and pulleys, dumped the soup, and got another pretzel.

Guiermo made sure that water was poured on top of the belts. Putting water on the belts was one of the stranger rituals, one that had seemed to work the day Guiermo had first tried it a year earlier. Guiermo thought it kept the belts from overheating and thereby getting too loose. Since that first time they never neglected this step in the rites, but the machine operators really only added water to please Guiermo—they had other theories of their own. They sprinkled sand on the inside of the belts, their own part in what had become a canonized ritual sequence.

By now Glen Morgan had arrived and started calling the shots, and a number of the men had gathered around the spinner to see the spectacle of the white hats at work. As each can crumpled in turn, Glen barked more orders: "Slow it down!" "Adjust the torque!" "Speed it up!" "Lubricate the bearings!" During this episode, Glen was called to the front office to take a phone call. When he returned, the spinner was working, though no one, including Glen, knew why or how. From then on, whenever Glen was in the plant the men on the spinner tried to shut it down if they were ahead of schedule—they now knew that Glen was a jinx. "There are no demons in that machine," he would say, but the men had seen it all happen. In the following weeks, worker folklore around the lunch table often captured the spirit of the occasion in gleeful recollections of that day.

Getting Acquainted

Jeff's first, most obvious task was to dig out from under the paper work that had accumulated during the two months that Dick Hall had been both supervising production and managing the plant. Six feet tall, with a trim grey mustache and receding hairline, at 52 Dick Hill looked just right for his role as plant superintendent. Dick had first been an electrician, then maintenance foreman, and then plant superintendent for five years in one of Heartland's other concrete pipe facilities before coming to Widefield to help open the new plant. Jeff therefore felt Dick could be an invaluable member of his staff. But Dick knew little about calculating cost variances, indirect manufacturing expense (IME), or filling out other production reports; he was much more a floor man than an office man, and Jeff had lots of catching up to do.

Jeff learned that total plant manufacturing cost was about $30 million a year (roughly $120,000 in product cost per day), of which about $9 million a year (30 percent) were indirect manufacturing expenses. The modern, largely mechanized facility was highly capital-intensive, and direct labor accounted for only 6 percent of the product cost.

During his first week at the plant, Jeff had asked all 20 of the management and office staff employees to come in and visit with him, one at a time, so he could get to know them and find out what kind of support they needed. Dick Hill told Jeff that it was no problem to run the plant, but to do that *and* answer to Glen

Morgan was very difficult. Jeff responded: "Don't worry about Glen—I'll do that and you just worry about running the plant operations." They agreed on a slight overlap in their working schedules so as to provide supervision over a longer period of the working day. Dick would be in the plant at 6:45 to start up and would leave between 3:30 and 4; Jeff would arrive at 7:45 and leave between 5 and 5:30.

Jeff underscored some of his basic management policies. One was that all his employees should be given authority commensurate with their responsibilities. This meant that Dick Hill would deal with the foremen and that Jeff would uphold Dick's authority. For instance, Jeff stood by Dick's decision one day to shut down the brush coat machine early for preventive maintenance, even though Jeff felt that by doing so they would fail to meet the week's production schedule. "I always tried my best to back Dick's decisions," Jeff said, "but instruct him on my own view when we disagreed. That week we missed our quota, but Dick learned I would back him even if I thought he was wrong—up to a point, of course."

One afternoon during the second week after Jeff took over, Dick had already left when the late shift foreman came to tell Jeff that one of the machines was down; it would take two hours to fix. Dick Hill's assignment to the late shift had been to produce 20 pipes—that now meant they would be in the plant until at least 11 P.M. Jeff decided to have the maintenance crew fix the machine immediately, but to send the other workers home. Before he left, Jeff wrote a detailed note to Dick, explaining what he had done and why. "That way, when Dick came the next morning and saw only three pipes finished, he didn't have to call around and find out what happened from someone else." It was important to Jeff that Dick, and the entire management team, be protected from looking bad or uninformed. He felt that his own policy of open, quick communication would encourage people to cooperate and share information rather than just cover for themselves.

Jeff discovered that the 100 unionized plant workers could be divided into two somewhat distinct groups. About 70 percent of the workers seemed interested in stable jobs, whereas the other 30 percent appeared transient and less committed to either the town or their jobs. The former group, whom Jeff referred to as the "regular guys," were mostly married and over 25 years of age. The latter group, "the cowboys," were mostly single and under 25 years of age. About one third of the members of each group were relatively highly skilled. These workers, about 30 in all, held the following jobs, which were highly specialized and specific to concrete pipe manufacturing: welders (10), spinner machine operators (5), and lift truck operators (15). These workers were especially difficult to replace, but even the 70 others who held relatively unskilled jobs were hard to replace because of a tight local labor hiring market.

Accidents and Safety

During his first three weeks as plant manager, while Jeff was digging out from under the paperwork and getting acquainted with his staff, there were four lost-time accidents in the plant. Luckily, they involved only minor injuries—a cut hand, a bruised foot, a smashed finger, a sprained wrist. But they were enough to put a significant crimp in Jeff's production schedule and use up two thirds of his annual accident quota.

Jeff had noted that workers in the plant, especially the cowboys, routinely neglected to wear their safety glasses, and often their blue hard hats as well. Many of the regular guys, and even the foremen, also failed to adhere to the safety regulations. Jeff found, moreover, that the cowboys were fatalistic about accidents; like some World War II flyers, they figured they would only get hurt when their number was up. They expressed a certain thrill in living "close to the edge," and the plant seemed to be one arena for their lifestyle of brinksmanship. Jeff's impression was that most of these self-professed cowboys found their deepest contentment in a case of beer and a full tank of gas. Though Heartland needed them, their macho, devil-may-care ideal was less than ideal for profits.

Many of Jeff's transient cowboys in Colorado were, as Jeff said, "short-sighted sons of fairly well-to-do ranchers and businessmen." They didn't seem to have any commitment to careers and knew they could get other jobs easily in what had been a booming economy. They were physically robust, outdoor types—most of them cultivated a Marlboro man image that interfered with taking orders willingly or being particularly cooperative. Working at the plant was a way of financing their *real* lives—fast pickup trucks, motorcycles, a horseback ride on the range, wild game hunting, and a boom town night life. Many of these cowboys considered working five days a week to be "the pits" and usually managed to skip work (with loss of pay) for a day or two every other week or so in order to have a good time outside the plant. Still, Jeff hoped to get most of them to take the plant a little more seriously. Poor attendance and safety hurt productivity badly, especially because the plant had a lean staff to begin with. If a worker was unavailable to do his or her job, worker assignments had to be shuffled to get the necessary work done, which was disruptive and frequently resulted in a less-than-optimal allocation of worker skills. Despite his concerns about his cowboys, Jeff knew that when they wanted to work hard, they were as good as *any* group of workers, *anywhere*.

Glen Morgan

As expected, Glen Morgan did not sit quietly by. From Jeff's first day on the job, he called daily in the morning and again in the afternoon. Jeff wasn't much concerned about Glen as a spinner jinx, but he badly wanted to find a way to make him quit calling so he could get his own work done. Glen sometimes called to talk about interesting and somewhat useful details, such as the prices of sheet steel out of Gary and Pittsburgh, but he usually relayed items that were low on Jeff's list of priorities. At other times, Glen wanted to come down to the plant to do things that Jeff felt he should be free to handle in his own way. The accident problem was a case in point. Glen wanted to fly out and give the men a lecture on safety procedures.

On checking around discreetly, Jeff found out more about Glen Morgan. Like many other senior company managers, Glen had an engineering degree. He had been plant manager of a Heartland facility similar to the one at Widefield for 12 years before being promoted to his current job as concrete pipe operations manager six years earlier, in early 1971. Glen understood the pipe operations inside and out and continued to be a hands-on manager after his promotion. Jeff also learned that the wisdom of building a new plant at Widefield had been debated by senior Heartland management for several years and that Glen Morgan had been its chief proponent. About $18 million had been invested in the new facility, but the projected level of sales used to justify this investment had never materialized. As a result, the new Widefield plant had acquired the reputation of a "big white elephant," and Morgan had trouble finding a seasoned replacement for the manager who started up the Widefield plant, and later for the startup manager's successor, Stu Little, when he also failed. Experienced Heartland managers seemed unwilling to be associated with the Widefield plant, and Morgan had finally asked Dick Hill to take over on a temporary basis prior to Jeff's arrival. Jeff wondered how best to deal with his boss, the mystique of spinner magic, the safety issue, and the other problems at the plant.

C a s e   8–2

Bob Galvin and Motorola, Inc. (A)

Mary Gentile, Todd D. Jick

On April 24, 1983, the biennial meeting of Motorola, Inc.'s top 153 officers was drawing to a close, and Bob Galvin, chairman and chief executive officer of the $4 billion company, was about to offer his concluding comments. The theme of the two-day session had been "Managing Change," an appropriate topic, since the 55-year-old producer of electronics equipment had experienced a year of 15% growth—or half a billion dollars between 1982 and 1983. Galvin knew that the message he had in mind was surprising in light of the company's apparent success.

Increasingly as he "walked the halls" of the corporation, Galvin had heard more and more complaints. Managers were upset by longer product development cycles, by too many layers in the management structure, and by ponderous, inflexible decision approval processes. Galvin interpreted these frequently heard complaints in the context of a rapidly changing competitive environment. He recognized the growing threat from Japanese manufacturers to key Motorola products, such as cellular telephones and semiconductors. And much to the annoyance of his senior managers, he often asserted "we haven't even begun to compete internationally yet."

Galvin believed that the firm's current inability to respond quickly and flexibly to the changing needs of the customer could prove fatal in the coming global

This case was prepared by Research Associate Mary Gentile (under the direction of Associate Professor Todd D. Jick), as the basis for class discussion rather than to illustrate either effective or ineffective handling of an administrative situation.

competitive crisis. Still, he kept asking himself if he, as chief executive officer, could make the kind of changes Motorola needed. If he did nothing else in his last years before retirement, he wanted to reposition Motorola on the path toward renewed competitiveness. He knew this would be all the more difficult because many of his managers did not recognize the problems he saw. As he approached the speaker's podium, Galvin reflected that "I suppose I've been preparing for this speech for the last 45 years."

Motorola, Inc.

Galvin Manufacturing Company was founded by Paul V. Galvin, Bob Galvin's father, in 1928. The Chicago-based firm's earliest products were alternating electrical current converters and automobile radios. Paul Galvin dubbed the car radio he developed the "Motorola"—from motor and victrola—and in 1947, this became the company's name as well.

From their firm's modest beginning with less than $1,500 in working capital and equipment, Paul Galvin and his brother, Joe, tried to create a humane and democratic work environment for their employees; everyone, from Paul Galvin himself to the newest production line employee, was addressed on a first-name basis; the Galvins had replaced the typical time clock in the plant with an employee honor system; and by 1947, Paul Galvin established a profit-sharing program for the 2,000 workers the firm then employed. As a result of such efforts, Motorola remained union free.

Over the years, Motorola extended its product base to include home radios, phonographs, televisions, and transistors and semiconductor components. By 1983, however, under Bob Galvin's leadership, the firm had sold many of its consumer electronic businesses and developed other markets based on new technology. By then, the firm was composed of five geographically dispersed sectors or groups:

1. **The Semiconductor Products Sector,** with 1982 net sales of $1.3 billion, produced such products as microprocessors, memory chips, and integrated circuits.

2. **The Communications Sector,** with 1982 net sales of $1.5 billion, produced products such as: two-way radios, paging devices, and cellular telephones.

3. **The Information Systems Group (ISG),** with 1982 net sales of $485 million, produced an integrated line of data transmission and distributed data processing systems.

4. & 5. **The Automotive and Industrial Electronics Group (AIEG)** and **The Government Electronics Group (GEG)** had combined 1982 net sales of $564 million. AIEG produced such products as fuel-injection systems, electronic engine controls and instrumentation, and electronic appliance controls. GEG conducted research in satellite communications technology.

This product-focused organizational structure grew out of Paul and Bob Galvin's emphasis on the customers' interests and their concern that a large, centralized organization might not be responsive enough to those interests. Over the years, Motorola had gradually decentralized. In the 1950s Paul Galvin formed divisions; in the early 1960s Bob Galvin established product lines with product managers who managed specific marketing and engineering areas, but who purchased the centralized manufacturing and sales functions. By the 1980s, the groups and sectors structure was in place, along with a multilayered matrix system of management. At the close of 1982 Motorola had approximately 75,000 employees, with operations in 15 foreign countries as well as the United States.

Bob Galvin

Bob Galvin joined the firm as a stock clerk in 1944, without completing his college degree. He worked in a variety of positions until 1948 when he became executive vice president. He became president in 1956, and chairman/chief executive officer in 1964.

Galvin was an equitable and accessible manager. His leadership style was rooted in humility and an abiding respect for his father's values. He often quoted Paul Galvin when explaining a decision he had made, and in assessing his own influence at Motorola, he pointed to the "privilege" of his long service with the firm, as well as to the "mantle" he had received from his father: "I am fortunate to carry some of his reputation, in addition to what I've earned myself." He was a serious and thoughtful man who defined his role as "leading the institution: I try to be a good listener, to look for the unattended, the void, the exception that my associates are too busy to see."

Over the years he had championed not only various reorganizational efforts and product/market shifts but a variety of participatory management, executive education, and strategic planning programs. For example, in the late 1960s, Motorola developed a technology innovation planning process—the Technology Roadmap—which involved the periodic projection of future technological developments and the subsequent planning and reviewing of the firm's progress against that projection.

In the 1970s, Motorola developed the Participative Management Program (PMP) as a means to enhance productivity and employee involvement in the firm. PMP divided employees into small groups that met to discuss problems and potential improvements in their area of responsibility. Each group sent one member to report its ideas to the group one level up, which thereby enhanced communication in all directions. PMP efforts were also tied to a bonus incentive program.

Galvin's style and the Motorola culture were clearly people oriented. High value was placed on senior service and in fact, no employee with more than ten years' service could be fired without approval from Galvin himself. John Mitchell, Motorola's president, commented: "Bob *is* the culture here."

Some Motorola managers, however, criticized Motorola's "low demand environment" a tone set by Galvin himself. He devoted significant attention to the

I would like to share with you a special selective view of leadership. It finds its expression in a series of paradoxes.

We know so much about leadership, yet we know too little. We can define it in general, but find it hard to particularize. We recognize it when obvious, but it is not always obvious why. We practice leadership, which implies we are still preparing for the real thing.

It is neither necessary to impress on you an elaborate definition of leadership nor is this an appropriate time to characterize its many styles. Let it suffice that we acknowledge that no leader is worthy of the title absent creative and judgmental intelligence, courage, heart, spirit, integrity and vision applied to the accomplishment of a purposeful result through the efforts of followers and the leader. Rather, I elect to share with you some observations on a further series of paradoxes that reveal themselves as we analyze leadership.

When one is vested with the role of the leader, he inherits more freedom. The power of leadership endows him with rights to a greater range of self-determination of his own destiny. It is he who may determine the what or the how and the when or the where of important events.

Yet, as with all rights, there is a commensurate, balancing group of responsibilities that impose upon his freedom. The leader cannot avoid the act of determining the what or the who or the where. He cannot avoid being prepared to make these determinations. He cannot avoid being prepared to make these terminations. He cannot avoid seeing to their implementation. He cannot avoid living with the consequences of his decision on others and the demands these consequences impose on him. Only time will prove the merit of his stewardship. Because he is driven to pass this test of time, he will be obliged often to serve others more than himself. This obligation will more and more circumscribe his destiny. So those who assume true leadership will wonder from time to time if the apparent freedom of the leader adds a greater measure of independence, or whether the dependence of others on him restricts his own freedom.

For one to lead implies that others follow. But, is the leader a breed apart, or is he, rather, the better follower? Leadership casts the leader in many such roles:

- Observer—of the work his associates perform.
- Sensor—of attitudes, feelings, and trends.
- Listener—to ideas, suggestions, and complaints.
- Student—of advisors, inside and out of his situation.
- Product of experience—both his and others'.
- Mimic—of other leaders who have earned his respect.

Is he not the better follower, as he learns more quickly and surely from the past, selects the correct advice and trends, chooses the simpler work patterns and combines the best of other leaders? It is not good leadership to know when not to follow an aimless path? The paradox again: To lead well presumes the ability to follow smartly.

Because a leader is human and fallible, his leadership is in one sense finite— constrained by mortality and human imperfections. In another sense, the leader's influence is almost limitless. He can spread hope, lend courage, kindle confidence, impart knowledge, give heart, instill spirit, elevate standards, display vision, set direction, and call for action today and each tomorrow.

**Exhibit 1
(continued)**

The frequency with which one can perform these leadership functions seems without measure. His effectiveness and personal resources, rather than attenuating with use, amplify as he reuses and extends his skills. Like the tree whose shadow falls where the tree is not, the consequence of the leader's act radiates beyond his fondest perception. Again, we see the paradox of the leader—a finite person with an apparent infinite influence.

A leader is decisive—is called on to make many critical choices, and can thrive on the power and attention of that decision-making role. Yet the leader of leaders moves progressively away from that role.

Yes, he or she can be decisive and command as required. Yet that leader's prime responsibility is not to decide or direct, but to create and maintain an evocative situation, stimulating an atmosphere of objective participation, keeping the goal in sight, recognizing valid consensus, inviting unequivocal recommendation, and finally vesting increasingly in others the privilege to learn through their own decisions. A wiser man puts it thus:

> We measure the effectiveness of the true leader, not in terms of the leadership he exercises, but in terms of the leadership he evokes; not in terms of his power over others but in terms of the power he releases in others; not in terms of the goals he sets and the directions he gives, but in terms of the plans of action others work out for themselves with his help; not in terms of decisions made, events completed and the inevitable success and growth that follow from such released energy, but in terms of growth in competence, sense of responsibility and in personal satisfaction among many participants.
>
> Under this kind of leadership it may not always be clear at any given moment just who is leading. Nor is this important. What is important is that others are learning to lead well.

The complement to that paradox is that the growth that such leadership stimulates generates an ever-growing institution and an ever-increasing number of critical choices, more than enough of which fall squarely back on the shoulders of the leader who trained and willingly shared decision-making with others.

And there are others which, if not paradoxes, at least are incongruities. Have we not witnessed some who have claimed leadership yet never fully achieved it? Have we not observed others who have shunned leadership only to have it thrust upon them?

Each of us here is at once part leader and part follower as we play our roles in life. Fortunately, there is a spark of leadership quality in many men and women, and, most fortunately, the flame of future leadership burns brightly in many who matriculate here. It is this wellspring from which we will draw and which gives us confidence for the continued advance of society.

On this day, you may feel a sense of relief that you have borne your final test. Walter Lippman, for one, would not long have let you cherish this illusion. He once observed:

> The final test of a leader is that he leaves behind in others the conviction and will to carry on.

This, for a few of the best of you here who would be leaders, may be the most personal paradox and crucial test of all.

development of a strong managerial succession at Motorola and consequently was quite confident in Motorola's senior managers—his "family," as he called them. He felt convinced that if he but pointed out a problem to his officers, they would certainly be motivated and capable of resolving it appropriately. From time to time he gave a speech on leadership as he perceived it (Exhibit 1), including the following excerpt:

> Again we see the paradox of the leader—a finite person with an apparent infinite influence.
>
> A leader is decisive—is called on to make many critical choices, and can thrive on the power and the attention of that decision-making role. Yet the leader of leaders moves progressively away from that role.
>
> Yes, he or she can be decisive and command as required. Yet that leader's prime responsibility is not to decide or direct, but to create and maintain an evocative situation, stimulating an atmosphere of objective participation, keeping the goal in sight, recognizing valid consensus, inviting unequivocal recommendation, and finally vesting increasingly in others the privilege to learn through their own decisions.

Galvin hoped to encourage this "privilege" through the variety of innovative programs that Motorola adopted.

Motorola in 1983

Galvin believed, in that spring of 1983, that Motorola was poised on the edge of a new competitive era. The company had just come through a recession in the semiconductor industry which had caused an 8% downturn in earnings between 1980 and 1982. Difficult as that period had been, however, Motorola's losses had been far less severe than those of competitors like Texas Instruments and Intel. "Motorola did see their profits slip by 6% during the worst year of the recession. But their archrivals, TI and Intel, experienced a 49% and 72% drop, respectively."[1] (See Exhibit 2). And Galvin wanted to build on Motorola's strengths at a time when performance was beginning to look strong again. Although the first quarter was a bit slow, sales seemed to be on the upswing as Motorola faced the summer of 1983, and Galvin saw the national economy and his firm gearing up for rapid growth in the next few years. He recognized this growth as a blessing and a threat.

Increases in sales and earnings were welcome, of course, as was the accompanying confidence within the firm. However, rapid expansion brought new structural and managerial challenges and exacerbated existing deficiencies. In addition, confidence could engender a dangerous complacency that made change all the more difficult. And finally, Galvin was all too cognizant of the cyclical nature of the semiconductor and computer industries and the growing threat of Japanese competition in both the communications and the semiconductor sectors of the business.

Galvin was also looking internally. One of Galvin's favored management tech-

---

[1]James O'Toole, "Second Annual NM Vanguard Award," *New Management* 3, no. 2 (Fall, 1985), p. 5.

Exhibit 2
Bob Galvin and Motorola, Inc. (A)

Motorola Financial Information (1979–1982)

Four Year Financial Summary
(Motorola, Inc. and Consolidated Subsidiaries, Years Ended December 31)

	1982	1981	1980	1979
Operating Results (in millions of dollars)				
Net sales	$3,786	$3,570	$3,284	$2,879
Manufacturing and other administrative costs of sales	2,269	2,066	1,895	1,672
Selling, general, and administrative expenses	1,013	985	877	756
Depreciation and amortization of plant and equipment	244	205	173	132
Interest expense, net	48	35	43	27
Special charge	—	—	13	10
Total costs and other expenses	3,574	3,311	3,002	2,597
Earnings before income taxes and extraordinary gain	212	259	282	282
Income taxes	42	77	90	111
Net earnings before extraordinary gain	170	182	192	171
Net earnings as a percent of sales	4.5%	5.1%	5.8%	5.9%
Extraordinary gain	8	—	—	—
Net earnings	$ 178	$ 182	$ 192	$ 171

Sector Performance (1979–1982)

Information by Industry Segment and Geographic Region: Information about the Company's operations in different industry segments for the years ended December 31 is summarized below (in millions of dollars):

	Net Sales				Operating Profit			
	1979	1980	1981	1982	1979	1980	1981	1982
Semiconductor Products	$ 992	$1,222	$1,278	$1,298	$170	$186	$131	
Communications Products	1,272	1,252	1,422	1,527	139	144	162	$97
Information Systems Products	NA	279	358	485	NA	34	42	31
Other Products	7655	683	718	564	14	26	50	44
Adjustments and Eliminations	(61)	(60)	(82)	(88)	(3)	2	(4)	(7)
Industry Totals	$2,713	$3,098	$3,335	$3,786	$259	$274	$251	307

niques was walking the halls of the organization, listening to the ideas and the complaints of Motorola's employees, especially the middle managers. Galvin believed these managers were in touch with "real world" implementation issues that higher level managers might miss because of their need to oversee so many different functions and systems. Galvin was a strong believer in open communications and he encouraged employees at all levels to sit down with him in the company cafeteria at lunch, or to catch him in the halls of the firm to share their ideas and their criticisms.

Structural Issues

The issues he heard about in spring 1983 were disturbingly consistent with concerns that had been building throughout the 1970s. Galvin identified them as "structural concerns." Employees complained of the problems engendered by the sheer size and complexity of Motorola's matrix organization. Objective and methodology conflicts routinely developed between Motorola's customer-oriented functional managers (in sales or distribution, for example) and their product line managers. Although traditionally Galvin had always stressed the importance of staying close to the customer and the customer's needs, the complexity of the firm's products often caused product line managers to be more technology-driven than market-driven in their planning and managing processes.

No single manager was clearly responsible for a particular project through all its cycles, from its origin in customer discussions through design, development, testing, production and into sales. Consequently, project deadlines set by engineers carried little weight with the production staff, and the needs of the sales and distribution managers were poorly integrated into the realities of the manufacturing area. Galvin was alarmed by the ever-lengthening product development cycles.

Motorola's lines of authority were as often dotted as solid and spans of control were narrow. As the company grew and its products multiplied (see Exhibit 3), management layers increased as well. One company study, completed in 1983, reported nine to twelve layers between first-line managers and the executive level, with an average span of control over five people or fewer. Thirty percent managed three or fewer people. Individuals were struggling to preserve their turf and budget and maintain internal performance standards. Long-term competitive strategy and customer needs were obscured by short-term incentives, and employees felt both overmanaged and underdirected.

Top management's efforts to energize the firm and to enhance creative cooperation translated into programs like the periodic technology review and PMP, with their step-by-step procedures and committee-based processes. Such programs involved employee at all levels and kept critical issues before them, but some managers worried that their format was too mechanistic and that they enabled employees to comply with the letter rather than the spirit of the programs.

Finally Motorola's chief executive office was structured as a triumvirate with Bob Galvin as chairman, William Weisz as vice chairman, and John Mitchell as president. Galvin defined their respective responsibilities as follows: "John Mitchell is running the business; Bill Weisz is managing the company; and my job is to lead the institution. And in a way, they are all the same thing." Mitchell elaborated: "Bill Weisz and I share the COO position. I handle the Communications Sector, the Automotive and Industrial Electronic Group, and Japan; Bill handles the Semiconductor Products Sector, the Information Systems Group, and the Government Electronics Group." Galvin saw the chief executive office as a model of democratic

Exhibit 3
Bob Galvin and Motorola, Inc. (A)
Motorola Products

Semiconductor Products Sector

Bubble memories
Custom and semicustom semiconductors
Fiber optic active components
Field effect transistors
Interface circuits
Microcomputer board-level products
Microcomputer systems
Microprocessors
Microwave devices
MOS and bipolar analog ICs
MOS and bipolar digital ICs
MOS and bipolar memories
MPU develop system hardware and
    software
Operational amplifiers
Optoelectronics components
Power supply circuits
Pressure and temperature sensors
Rectifiers
RF modules
RF power and small signal transistors
Telecommunication circuits
Thyristors
Triggers
VLSI macrocell arrays
Voltage regulator circuits
Zener and tuning diodes

Communications Sectors

Base stations
Car telephone systems
Closed-circuit television systems
Communications control centers
Component products
Digital voice-protection systems
Electronic command and control systems
Health care communications systems
Information-display systems
Microwave communications systems
Mobile and portable FM two-way
    radio communications systems
Portable data terminals
Radio paging systems
Signalling and remote control systems
Test equipment

Information Systems Group

Communications processors
Data network analyzers/emulators
Digital service/channel service units
Electronic data switches
Intelligent terminals
Leased-line modems
Limited distance modems
Local area networks

Information Systems Group (continued)

Modems
Multifunction company systems for distributed
    information processing and office automation
    appliances
Multiplexers
Network and management systems
OEM modem cards
Software for data entry, word processing, office
    management
Switched network modems
System processors
Technical control facilities
Video operator stations

Automotive and Industrial Electronics Group

Alternator charging systems
Automotive and industrial digital
    instrumentation (tachometers, speedometers,
    odometers, hourmeters), and electronic
    instrument clusters
Automotive and industrial digital monitoring
    systems
Automotive and industrial sensors
CRT display monitors, color and monochrome
    (5" to 23")
Data and graphics terminals and subsystems
Electronic appliance controls
Electronic engine and powertrain controls
Electronic engine governors
Electronic fuel-handling systems
Electronic ignition systems
Electronic motor controls
Electronic regulators
Electronic transmission controls
Engine management systems
Telecommunications equipment
Vehicle monitoring and recording systems
Wireless systems and devices

Government Electronics Group

Countermeasures systems
Drone command and control systems
Electronic fuse systems
Electronic positioning and tracking systems
Fixed and satellite communications systems
Intelligent display terminals and systems
Missile and aircraft instrumentation
Missile guidance systems
Satellite survey and positioning systems
Secure communications
Surveillance radar systems
Tracking and command transponder systems
Video processing systems and products

practice and open communications for the firm. However, this tripartite structure was one of the other complaints that circulated among Motorola's managers. Mitchell explained: "They call us the three bears and they ask 'why can't you be single in voice, style, and direction?' "

Galvin reviewed the concerns he gathered from Motorola's managers; from his son, Chris, who worked in the Communications Sector; and from his own observations. Taken alone, he believed they were cause for concern. When he also considered the rapid growth Motorola appeared to face as the economy emerged from the last two years of recession, and the growing competitive threat from Japan, Galvin became convinced that it was time for action.

Japanese Competition

Motorola was one of the world's leading producers of two-way radios, cellular telephone systems, semiconductors, and microprocessor chips, and Japan was competing in and threatening each of these markets. The firm faced Japanese market practices such as "dumping" (selling product at less than "fair value" as a way to increase market share quickly) and "targeting" (the cooperative efforts of a group of Japanese firms, supported by Japanese law, to break into and capture a particular international market, such as computer memory chips). In response to these challenges, Galvin worked with federal foreign relations and trade committees, attempting to fight "unfair" trade practices and protectionism:

> Testifying before the Senate Foreign Relations Committee last September [1982], he said U.S. policy on trade in high-technology products should make it clear that this country "will not accept a situation where foreign national industrial policies, based on nonmarket mechanisms and unreasonable trade practices, enable any country to disrupt U.S. markets, prevent reasonable access to its home markets or give unjustified advantage to its firms in pursuing Third World markets."[2]

Galvin also knew, however, that he had to make changes closer to home, within Motorola. His success in obtaining an order from Nippon Telegraph & Telephone Public Corporation for paging devices in early 1982 was a result both of pressure from the United States government and Motorola's efforts to produce 100% defect-free product. And even during the difficult recession years of 1981–1982, Motorola continued to invest in research and development, in order to position itself competitively for the market growth it believed would follow. Galvin thought that effective competition with the Japanese meant not only modification in federal trade regulations but Motorola's investment in R&D, enhanced productivity, and quality control. And he believed the means to this end were through the company's employees. This was consistent with the kind of thinking behind PMP, ten years earlier.

As Galvin considered his company's current condition and challenges, he felt a

---

[2]Grover Herman, "Competing with the Japanese," *Nation's Business,* November 1982, p. 48.

great sense of personal urgency. He was 61 years old, nearing retirement, and he wanted to leave a strong and healthy company to his family of managers. And although he wasn't certain how to implement a process of "renewal" at Motorola, he was quite confident of the need. He remembered his father's advice to "just get in motion" when action was required, confident that he would find his way.

Motorola Biennial Officers' Meeting: April 1983

Galvin came to the Officers' Meeting[3] with his mind full of a recent trip to Japan. He had been impressed by the commitment of the industry employees he saw there and with the cutting-edge production technology the Japanese firms utilized. On the long plane ride back to the United States, Galvin had been reading the current management best seller, *In Search of Excellence*. Its authors, Peters and Waterman, advocated simpler organizational structures with direct ties to the consumer.

With all these observations, conclusions, and influences in his mind, Galvin felt an uncanny, undeniable immediacy in his senior officers' discussion of their efforts to manage change. Every time an individual complained of too many layers of command, Galvin winced, "There it is again." Each time an officer mentioned the absence of realistic and convincing deadlines that made sense across departments, Galvin sighed, "There it is again." He knew he needed no more evidence. He was sure of his message and of its significance.

As the meeting drew to a close, his staff expected Galvin's usual clear, concise concluding summary. Instead he stood up and issued a challenge. He called upon his senior managers to take a fresh look at their organizations and to consider structural changes—smaller, more focused business units. He wanted to decrease the many layers of management and to bring management closer to the product and the market. Galvin spoke with ease and conviction: "My message was spontaneous in tone and mood, but it had been building out of years of experience. I had been hearing this message from my middle managers and I'm a good listener." In his speech, Galvin stressed Motorola's

> . . . constant thrust for renewal. Renewal is the most driving word in this corporation for me, the continual search for ways to get things done better.
>
> As I walk the halls, I keep my ears open and I keep picking up signals. A middle manager might tell me that he can't understand how the business did because we keep aggregating our results into one big number. Or another might tell me he thinks he has a good idea but he can't get the authority to get it done.
>
> I see a welling up of the evidence of need and today I think the window is open. So I decided to express my concern and my conviction to you, confident that you share my insights and that together we will find our way to an organized effort of change. When we come together in two years, we will report and share the changes made and the lessons learned.

---

[3]Officers refer to both business officers and officers of the corporation (appointed and elected VPs). Elected officers are elected by the board of directors, and appointed officers must be approved by the chief executive officer.

Galvin had not discussed this presentation with Weisz or Mitchell beforehand. Nor had he explicitly addressed with his Human Resources staff the issue of structural reorganization as the key method of a change at Motorola. He was confident that he knew his audience, his "constituency," and that they would welcome his challenge.

As Galvin concluded, however, and managers stood and began to move out of the room, the buzzing conversations were colored by surprise and confusion more than eagerness. Suddenly the firm's rising sales were a problem. Was this just another PMP pep talk? Was Galvin serious about restructuring the organization? Who would be responsible for this? Even Galvin's wife, Mary, turned to him later that evening and asked: "What exactly did you have in mind, Bob?"

That was Friday evening. On Monday morning, the calls started coming in to Galvin's office, to Joe Miraglia, corporate vice president and director of Human Resources, and passed back and forth between the various senior managers. Rumors were spreading: people wanted to know what had Galvin been reading, and with whom had he been talking? One senior manager jested that perhaps Galvin was miffed that Motorola had not been mentioned enough by the authors of *In Search of Excellence*. But everyone wanted to know: what did Galvin mean and was he serious?

Responses to Galvin's Challenge

The Chief Executive Office

Responses to Galvin's surprise speech varied according to each individual's position and the implications of this challenge for his or her responsibilities. William Weisz, vice chairman, and John Mitchell, president, for example, did not expect the timing and form of Galvin's presentation. The message itself, however, felt familiar. It coincided with both a long-term trend in Motorola toward decentralization and with Galvin's constant concern for the customer's needs. Mitchell commented:

> Bob Galvin's style is to make strong statements like "the implied solution to the problems of the matrix is to divide the company into small businesses." This took people aback. It sounded simplistic and it sounded like it would start right away.

Both Mitchell and Weisz could place Galvin's comments into a context, knowing and trusting the CEO as they did, and although they may not have chosen the timing and the particular solution Galvin proposed, they agreed with his diagnosis of Motorola's ills. As Galvin explained: "The vice chairman came on board with me on this issue in the spirit of faith and of insight. The president was preoccupied with running the business, but he came on as well."

Operating Officers

For many of the top sector and group officers at Motorola there was an initial hesitancy about Galvin's unexpected spontaneous challenge, according to Robert Schaffer, an external consultant who interviewed these officers. Although they recognized that Galvin was earnest, they asked themselves some questions before considering what their response would be and how serious an effort was involved. Was this another in a string of innovations that arose from the visionary Galvin? Was this a commitment by all three chief executive officers or something Galvin alone would pursue as a reflection of his frustration? Would the head of any unit take this as a commitment to action? Did Galvin already have answers or was he willing and ready to open up the issue for questions?

Many of the firm's top officers did not share Galvin's sense of urgency about Motorola's competitive position. The company had a tradition of market strength and of technological leadership. Employees felt secure there; the culture placed a premium on commitment and length of service. And in the spring of 1983, the outlook looked particularly good for semiconductor products. For despite the threat posed by Japanese competitors, the company had grown by half a billion dollars in the last year and it was still moving. One vice president in the Semiconductor Products Sector explained that Galvin's biggest problem in selling his change agenda was the "status quo: Managers here are scientists. They see themselves and the sector as renegades on the leading edge of technology, but when it comes to management and productivity measures, they stick with 'what worked before.'" Even in the Communications Sector where Japanese competition was posing a very serious threat to the pager business and to the just burgeoning cellular telephone business, much of the blame was placed on "unfair" Japanese trade practices.

Perhaps managerial resistance to Galvin's challenge was all the more prevalent because no one was quite sure what he was proposing. Was this a major and radical call to action or only a proposal for new executive training? Many believed it was the latter and thus, even those managers who shared Galvin's concern for Motorola's competitive position were doubtful that more educational programs would make a difference. If, on the other hand, Galvin was ordering a concrete structural change (an action that would be uncharacteristically directive), then he needed to be more precise. In the meantime, many managers simply waited for the thing to blow over.

Human Resources

In the ensuing days, while top management struggled to understand what Galvin had meant in his speech and what implications it had for them, Galvin himself met with Joe Miraglia, vice president of Human Resources at Motorola, whom he considered his "professional pivot point" within the organization; Galvin took the Human Resources function very seriously. The two promptly set about developing the vision the chief executive officer had introduced. Although Miraglia did not question Galvin's identification of problems in the organization, he commented:

> Bob's idea was to create smaller business units more functionally integrated at lower levels. We in Human Resources disagreed; structure was not the sole answer. We didn't want this to be seen as just a structural solution imposed from above by "those who know better."

Miraglia believed Galvin's vision had to be developed and that his influence had to be focused more clearly. Nevertheless, Miraglia and his staff within the sectors supported Galvin's basic assumptions. Phil Nienstedt, manager, Human Resources Programs for Semiconductor Products, explained:

Business had been good in 1983, but it was something of a false prosperity as the company came off the leaner recession years. The company was growing with little control or discipline. Galvin was hitting some hot buttons in the Officers' Meeting when he said we needed to focus on the customer to develop flexibility, smaller business entities, wider spans, less levels, fewer inefficiencies. The Human Resources staff had discussed these issues with Joe Miraglia before. But Bob Galvin was vague and unclear as to what he wanted to do about these things. I think he did this intentionally, to be provocative, to get people thinking and wondering. The problem with this kind of change, however, is that short-term objectives, like getting the work out the door, get in the way of addressing this kind of long-term problem.

Dick Wintermantel, director, Organization and Human Resources, in the Semiconductor Products Sector, pointed to another inhibitor to change:

It's difficult for managers to make changes at Motorola and many times this difficulty relates to core cultural values that served the company well on its way *up* the growth curve, but which may be dysfunctional now. For example, respect for senior service may run counter to competitive staffing needs. Once you have 10 years of service, you're treated with employment *and* job security. We are constrained to redeploy people even if there are strategic and competitive reasons to do so.

Always responding to the customer's request for new products can result in thousands of products and no coherent and efficient organization. A mentality of "we can do it ourselves" runs counter to the alliances necessary for penetrating offshore markets and resources. And, finally, a mistrust of "systems" and "bureaucracy" can obstruct the development of necessary cost reduction systems or worldwide communications systems.

Although the HR team shared Galvin's sense of urgency and his belief in the necessity for change, they questioned both his structural focus and some aspects of the culture he had built. Miraglia explained: "Bob Galvin is confident that if his senior line managers agree with him, they will be able to assemble the infrastructure necessary to make change happen." The HR staff believed that neither managerial agreement nor an effective change process would be easy to come by.

Case 8–3

Bob Kohler: Creating Change at ESL

Teri Tompkins, Vijay Sathe

In February 1989, Bob Kohler, president of ESL Incorporated, sat at the conference table which he used for a desk and wondered if the reorganization (Exhibits 1, 2 and 3) that he and ESL's top management had implemented would increase focus on business development and improve ESL's capabilities to successfully acquire new business. He thought of the increased competition that ESL was facing and the pressure from the government to become more cost competitive. How could he convince the 2700 employees of ESL that things had to change when in fact current ESL financial results looked good?

Kohler reviewed the charts which summarized a study of ESL's competitive position (Exhibits 4 through 8), which showed that competitors were becoming more effective, increasing ESL's proposal costs and reducing the number of wins. He noted that the cash cows for ESL were maturing businesses, and the sales projections for the "cash cows" were flattening out. The analysis confirmed one of Kohler's suspicions that the controllable costs were only a fraction of the percentage of uncontrollable costs, making cost cutting difficult to manage. The Department of Defense had delayed procurement, and in some cases cancelled programs in 1988.

It had taken considerable time just for Kohler to convince ESL's top management that ESL was never going to grow beyond a medium-size corporation unless something was done. Now that he felt he had persuaded them, he was faced with

This case was prepared by Research Assistant Teri Tompkins under the supervision of Professor Vijay Sathe as the basis for class discussion rather than to illustrate either effective or ineffective handling of an administrative situation. © 1989 by Vijay Sathe.

Exhibit 1
ESL's Corporate Organization Prior to Reorganization

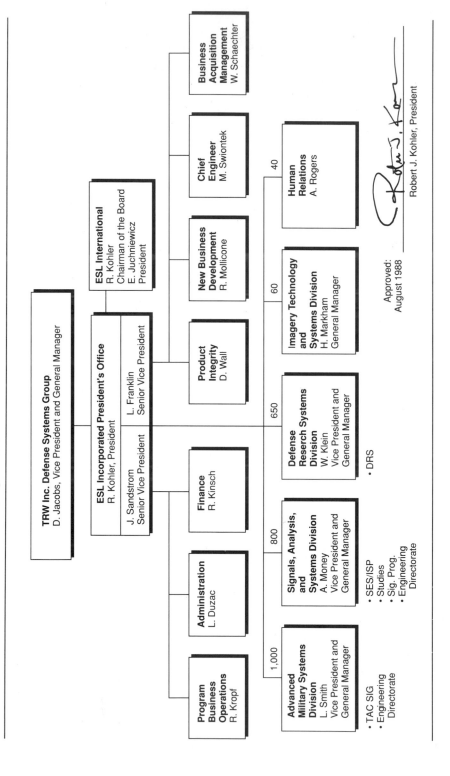

Exhibit 2
ESL's Corporate Organization After the Reorganization

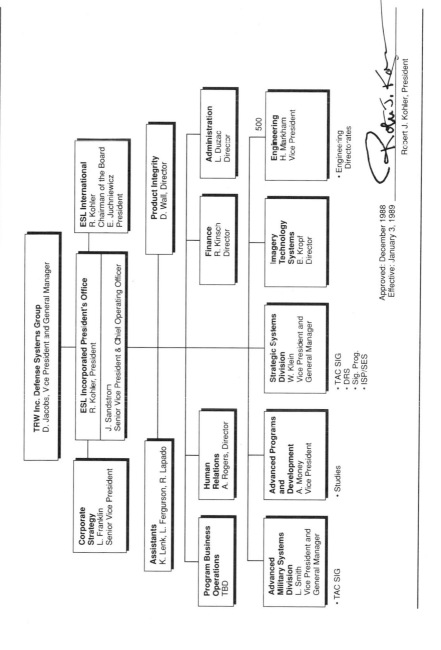

TRW Inc. Defense Systems Group
D. Jacobs, Vice President and General Manager

ESL Incorporated President's Office
R. Kohler, President

J. Sandstrom
Senior Vice President & Chief Operating Officer

ESL International
R. Kohler
Chairman of the Board
E. Juchniewicz
President

Corporate Strategy
L. Franklin
Senior Vice President

Assistants
K. Lenk, L. Fergurson, R. Lapado

Product Integrity
D. Wall, Director

Program Business Operations
TBD

Human Relations
A. Rogers, Director

Finance
R. Kinsch
Director

Administration
L. Duzac
Director

Advanced Military Systems Division
L. Smith
Vice President and General Manager

Advanced Programs and Development
A. Money
Vice President

Strategic Systems Division
W. Klein
Vice President and General Manager

Imagery Technology Systems
E. Kropf
Director

Engineering
H. Markham
Vice President

• TAC SIG

• Studies

• TAC SIG
• DRS
• Sig. Prog.
• ISP/SES

500

• Engineering
  Directorates

Approved: December 1988
Effective: January 3, 1989

Robert J. Kohler, President

499

Exhibit 3
Changes in ESL's Organization

Prior to Reorganization	After Reorganization
1. Advanced Military Systems Division (AMSD) Sigint* Engineering directorate	Advanced Military Systems Division Sigint
2. Signals, Analysis and Systems Division (SASD) ISP Sig. PNL Engineering directorate Studies	Strategic Systems Division ISP Sig. PNL DRS
3. *Studies* under the Signals, Analysis and Systems Division	Advanced Programs and Development
4. Two engineering directorates under AMSD & SASD	Engineering division
5. Defense Research Systems Division DRS	Strategic Systems Division DRS Sig. PNL ISP
6. Imagery Technology and Systems Division	Imagery Technology Systems

*Initials like "Sigint" are used to protect confidentiality of ESL's defense business.

Exhibit 4
ESL Financial Results

($ in Millions)	1986	1987	1988
Sales	268	335	332
Profit (Normalized)	9.9	14.4	12.3
Cash Flow	−7.7	19.4	−17.2
Investment			
Capital Expenditures	33.0	10.8	15.3
Over Ceiling IR&D/B&P	0.7	2.4	2.7

convincing the rest of ESL management and employees that the way ESL did business in the past was no longer going to work.

Kohler thought of the past two and a half years he had been president of ESL. He had often felt that he was fighting an uphill battle. He realized that his ideas were going to take a lot longer to implement than he had first thought. He felt that some of the engineers in certain groups were self-centered and non-responsive to the needs of ESL. He wanted them to control project costs and to stop blaming each other when a project was out-of-control. Accountability was one of Kohler's

Exhibit 5
The Process: Financial Analysis (Sales Growth 1984–1988)

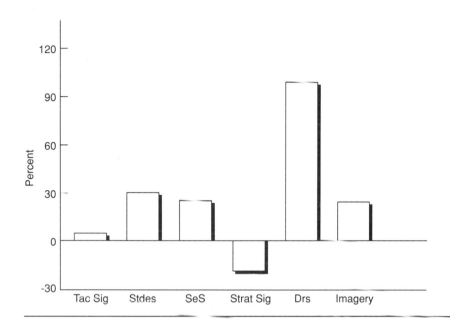

concerns and he told top management that he expected employees to start taking responsibility for their actions. He felt that ESL engineers were so used to working on "fun" projects, that they weren't responsive to the changing customer needs. He had cited numerous examples where engineers had designed and built more than the customer had asked for, exceeding the budget and schedule in doing so. While he admitted that this type of engineering had worked in the past, he felt that the new competitive environment could not allow for it now.

To make his point, Kohler let it be known that "zero-pay raises" would be instituted for those who didn't perform to the new standards. He also began to demand greater accountability and cost control. Accordingly, ESL's top management began to require more reports and assurances that their people were performing.

Kohler felt that in some ways he was like a general held hostage by the troops. He had never imagined when he became president how difficult it would be to manage the bright, creative engineers. It was hard for him to tell if his communication to the "troops" was being heard. There were so many filters. He wasn't even sure if he was receiving full information from the trenches. Some of the engineers were extremely specialized or had an elitist ranking among the other engineers, which made managing them virtually impossible. If these temperamental engineers didn't like what was being done, they'd ignore management, and management wouldn't find out until significant cost overruns had occurred. Said one

Exhibit 6
ESL Status: Profit Analysis (1989 Profit Forecast versus Projection)

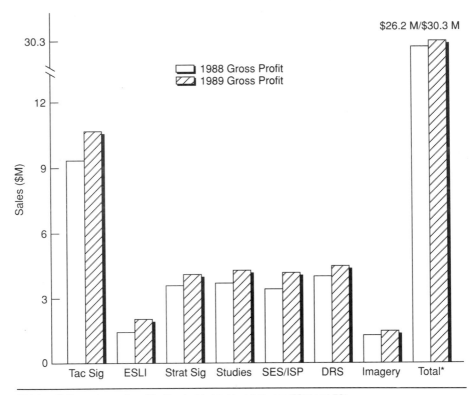

*Total profit figures are reduced by the double bookings between ESLI and ESL

consultant to ESL, "If the "prima donna" engineers don't get what they want (e.g. resources, control) they can threaten to quit because they know they can drive down the road into a new parking lot anytime."

A Strategy for Change

Kohler felt that the core lines of business would not grow substantially; therefore, new business was needed if ESL was to grow. He started two new initiatives, ESL International and Imagery. ESL International was begun in order to expand ESL's existing tactical military products into new markets. Payoff was expected to be rapid. In fact, in 1989, they had booked $100 million in sales. ESL had been in the imagery business for some time but found themselves trailing well behind the two market leaders. Strategically, ESL needed to either let go of the imagery

Exhibit 6 (concluded)
ESL Status: Profit Analysis (1989 Sales Projections)

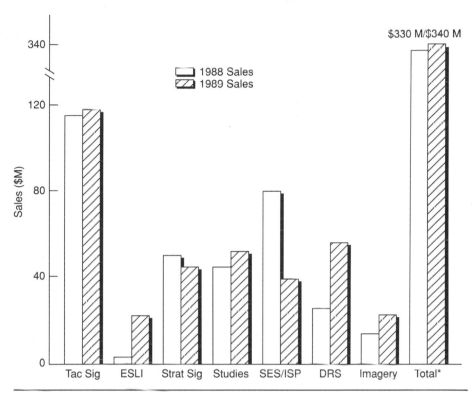

*Includes $7M Reduction for overlap in ESLI

business or try to be number 1 or number 2 in it. Kohler and his top management felt that imagery was a critical part of their reconnaissance and intelligence business and that if they were to serve the market in its totality it was necessary to support imagery. Payoff was expected in 1992 or 1993. Financial resources were diverted to these two initiatives and less money was made available to other lines of business.

Reaction to Kohler's changes were met with approval by some, but were strongly resisted by others. Many engineers felt that resources were being drained from their important programs and their hands were being tied. They felt the company was making a big mistake in not supporting their programs and that this was hurting everything that ESL stood for—providing the best engineering for the customer. A number of engineers, some of them well-thought-of in the company, decided to leave. One engineer, who was disillusioned with the lack of resources, the emphasis on cost control, and the loss of key engineering personnel commented, "Now we're

Exhibit 7
ESL Incorporated Return on Investment

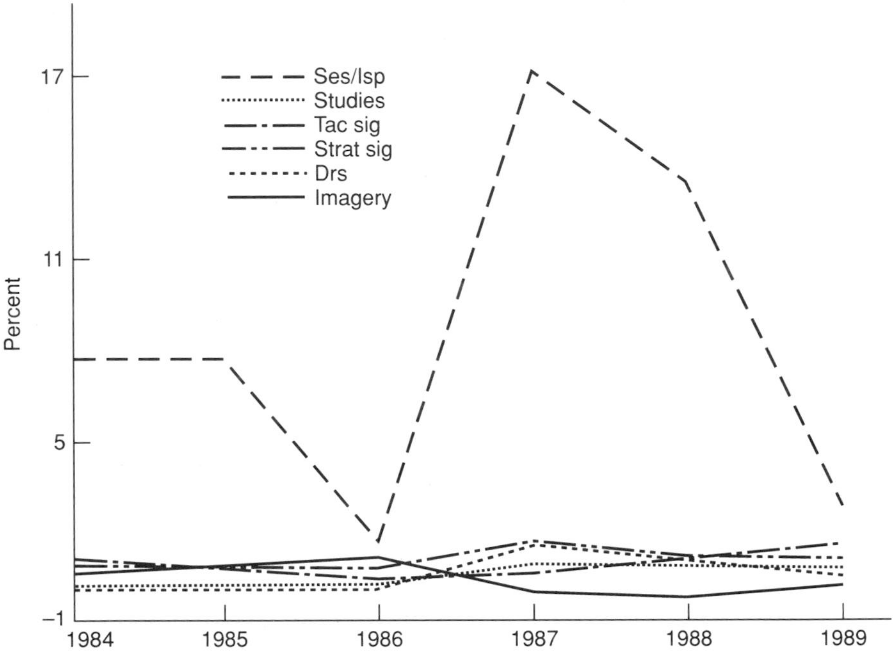
Ses/Isp
Studies
Tac sig
Strat sig
Drs
Imagery
Percent
17
11
5
−1
1984
1985
1986
1987
1988
1989

Exhibit 8
LOB Analysis/LOB Prioritization

LOB	*Priority*	*5-Yr. Awards ($M)*	*Growth ST*	*Potential LT*
ESL International	1 (LT + ST)	724 (.7)	High	High
Tactical SIGINT	1 (LT)	634 (.8)	Low	Moderate
SES/ISP	1 (ST)	177 (.8)	Low	Low
Studies	2	156 (.9)	Low	Low
DRS	3 (ST)	235 (.7)	Medium	Low
Imagery	3 (LT)	212 (.5)	High	High
Strategic SIGINT	4	168 (.5)	Low	Low

LOB = Line of Business
ST = Short Term
LT = Long Term

Exhibit 9
Kohler Explains Bid and Proposal Pool

Every company that does defense business with the government negotiates their bid and proposal pool. The Congress appropriates in effect a percentage of the Department of Defense budget that a company can negotiate as a recoverable expense. The B&P pool is negotiated on the basis of how good a company is at independent research and development

The program gets scored by government people and if you have a program that gets high scores you will tend to get more money than a company whose program gets low scores. How much a company spends on Independent Research and Development versus how much they spend on proposals is their own business, but if they spend 90% on Bid and Proposal and only 10% on IR&D, they will get less for their total budget because they will be judged on the IR&D only. Any dollars spent above what was negotiated with the government comes out of profit.

ESL Incorporated has historically received 6% of sales for bid and proposal. That percentage has decreased slightly in 1987 through 1989. Other companies in the industry had also experienced decreases in their bid and proposal pools.

---

viewed as just another software developer, just like everyone else. We no longer have excellent hardware people working for us because of the poor way this business is operated."

"They give us a lot of lip service about the cost of doing business, but it's clear where the costs have gone up. Top management has added lots of paperwork and report forms which has only resulted in more bureaucracy," one manager bitterly complained. "It's hard to fly like eagles, when you work with turkeys!" said another.

Nature of the Business

Until several years before, ESL's marketplace was characterized as primarily "sole source." Customers were willing to pay a premium to get the performance they desired. ESL had the reputation of being able to solve very difficult technical problems, and customers came to ESL to have such problems solved. They were willing to pay what they perceived to be a higher price for this service.

In 1989, the situation was changing. Many of ESL's lines of business had seen increased competition. The only exceptions to this was in the maintenance, engineering support, and direct follow-on work to ESL-built systems which were already in place.

The move towards greater competition came at a time when the Department of Defense (DOD) was under considerable pressure. The "intelligence budget" was expected to be flat over the next few years. The available money designated for trying to win contracts (known as the bid and proposal pool) was being decreased as a percent of sales. Whereas ESL used to write mostly sole source proposals, they were now required to write mostly competitive proposals with a lower percent of bid and proposal. (See Exhibit 9 for an explanation of Bid and Proposal Pool).

The government was instituting stricter procedures and reporting measures as they became more concerned with issues of waste, fraud and abuse. It was becoming more critical for the CEO to spend more time in Washington in an effort to represent ESL's best interest, and to defuse overreaction. The division of the CEO's time and energy between outside environmental pressures and internal managerial pressures was thus becoming ever more demanding.

There had been significant changes in the marketplace in which ESL operated:

1. Essentially all system development jobs were competitive, with greater emphasis placed on cost in addition to technical innovation.
2. Fewer programs would be greater than $10 million in sales.
3. ESL's customer mix was changing with new customers emerging: a smaller percentage of ESL's customers had prior ESL experience. This meant that ESL could not rely on their excellent historical credibility and reputation to garner business.

Kohler was also concerned with the reputation ESL had acquired with their historical customers. In a report conducted by the Culture Committee, a special task force at ESL that Kohler had commissioned (see Appendix 8–3A, pp. 521–26), ESL's historical customers characterized ESL's problems:

1. ESL places too much emphasis on technical design and innovation and not enough on meeting the budgeted cost and schedule. Customers want balanced performance.
2. ESL is too expensive. They do not effectively reuse previous designs and they tend to develop things instead of buying from better qualified industry sources, including both off-the-shelf products and new designs where another contractor is better qualified than ESL.
3. ESL has used systems engineering poorly and they do not apply systems engineering disciplines in the design and definition stages to their advantage, including not writing good specifications to procure subsystems from ESL or from subcontractors, and not flowing down top-level requirements to the lower levels to hardware and software engineering, and to operations. Customers find that ESL's development process lacks discipline. While they seem to get there in the end, the process is stressful.
4. ESL is "technically arrogant." They design and develop what they believe the customer needs, not what the customer asks for.
5. ESL is slow in staffing jobs at the start, with the result that the remainder of the program suffers.

Kohler agreed with ESL's historical customers. He felt that the lack of discipline and organization was particularly visible in the proposal preparation stage because of the need to effectively organize and mobilize a team in a short period of time. The symptoms could also be seen in other ESL internal processes, especially planning and budgeting.

History of ESL

In February 1989, ESL, a subsidiary of TRW, had one of the largest intelligence analysis capabilities in the U.S. ESL was a leader in building surveillance systems for both tactical and strategic applications. The company delivered on 300 plus contracts totaling more than $300 million in sales.

The five men who started ESL had formerly worked for Sylvania GTE. They became disillusioned with Sylvania after an organizational shake-up in 1963 and started ESL. Perhaps the one who had the greatest influence on the young firm was its first president, Bill Perry.

Perry's leadership set the tone for ESL. In 1964, when ESL was awarded its first contract, he set standards of integrity and a dictum of "the best provide more than the customer asks for" in quality and performance. ESL quickly developed a reputation among engineers as a "fun place to work," a place where an engineer could really put his or her talents to the test. Within a few years, ESL was thought to have the best engineers in the industry.

Bill Perry was the creator of ESL's culture. He was known to be very ethical and he communicated that to his employees. He also communicated trust in his people. He was willing to let ESL employees try new things and he had a high tolerance for mistakes.

ESL was like one big family. Employees and their families would gather for all company picnics. Even the children of ESL employees felt that other ESL employees were like aunts and uncles to them. So it wasn't surprising, when ESL had its first major setback in 1967, that all the employees banded together to save the fledgling company.

It was then that ESL had a chance for a contract bigger than any they ever had. Everyone devoted all their energy to winning this contract and virtually all other efforts were dropped. When the contract was lost, there was not enough work for the seventy to eighty employees, so the company worked out deals with other firms in the area to "rent the employees" out for several months until ESL got new contracts. As a result, no one was laid off during this crisis.

Bill Perry had an orientation which gained ESL a reputation for being responsive to customer needs. He got ESL involved in important national defense issues. He inspired the company toward a peaceful direction, so ESL steered away from weapons and toward reconnaissance projects. "We became a company of doves, not hawks," said one long time employee.

Prior to 1970, ESL employees could invest a portion of their salary in the company's stock. As the company was putting the paperwork together to go public in 1970, the stock market collapsed. As a result the price of ESL stock dropped from $25 to $6. However, ESL stock sold faster than any then available in the venture capital market.

In 1977, President Jimmy Carter was able to convince Bill Perry to come to work for him. His leave-taking was an emotional occasion for the 1700 ESL employees. (480 of those employees were still with ESL in 1989.). Bill made his exit quickly, communicating trust and confidence in the managers that were staying.

Jack Melchor took a short-term position as president while an executive search firm looked for a new CEO. ESL's sales at the time were $55 million.

The position was offered to Bob Bernett of TRW, but he declined the offer. However, Bernett was impressed with ESL and he thought they might be a good buy for TRW. Negotiations began in October of 1977, when most of ESL stock was owned by the employees. The sale was finalized in July 1978 despite the objections of some employees. Gil Decker of ESL was made president and he reported to Burnett. TRW decided to let ESL retain its corporate identity, and to let ESL managers run their own business. Said one senior manager who had opposed the sale, "It was a very successful [sale] because we at ESL decided to take responsibility to run this company well. We decided we'd never be an embarrassment to TRW. Very few employees left ESL as a result of the [sale]."

In 1983, Don Jacobs became president of ESL. Jacobs was promoted to a division manager at TRW in 1986 and the search for a new president for ESL began once more. The transition for Jacobs took about six months, and Lew Franklin was acting president during this period.

Soon after his promotion, Jacobs had said that he was considering Art Money as his successor. In the meantime, one of ESL's major customers called Bob Kohler, who was then Vice President at Lockheed, and asked him if he wanted to be president of ESL. Kohler thought about it and said, "President is better than Vice President; sure, I'm interested." The senior customer said, "I'll take care of it." The next day, Jacobs called Kohler and, after three meetings over a two week period, they negotiated a formal offer. In June of 1986, Bob Kohler became the first president to be selected from outside of ESL Incorporated. Kohler surmised: "I believe I became president due to serious customer pressure."

Bob Kohler

Nineteen Years in Government

Kohler had been with Lockheed Missiles and Space Company, as vice president of advanced programs and development since 1985. Prior to that Kohler had spent 19 years with the Central Intelligence Agency (CIA). Kohler's most recent position with the CIA had been as director of the office of Development and Engineering, Directorate of Science and Technology (ODE/DDS&T) in Washington, D.C. Prior to working with the government, he was with a firm in Boston where he had helped the company acquire patents in photographic science. He was considered an expert in imaging. Kohler had a B.S. degree in Photographic Science (solid state physics) from Rochester Institute of Technology.

Within the government, Kohler had a reputation of getting the job done and keeping his promises. One senior level manager at ESL said, "Kohler had his own set of high standards, and he felt that the government had the right to dictate what they wanted from their suppliers." As an agent of the government, Kohler felt he should do whatever was in the government's best interest. One manager at ESL said, "Kohler would use whatever power he had to keep or get programs on schedule and within cost. Because of this, he delivered what he promised."

If a program was running behind schedule, Kohler would create all kinds of difficulties for the company. He wouldn't tolerate a "trust me" attitude from the contractor. He would use forceful tactics if he felt that the company wasn't doing everything they could to fulfill their contract. For example, he would withhold fee payment or demand that certain company managers be fired in an effort to get the company to fulfill its contract within cost and on-schedule. He would even make sure a company was not granted future contracts if they failed to comply.

First Six Months at ESL

Several of Kohler's key managers said that he came on very aggressively at ESL during his first six months as president. The assertive style that he had used at the CIA alienated him from many of his key managers. Kohler felt frustrated as he tried to get his top managers to respond and to make changes that he believed were critical to the long-term health of ESL. For example, he was unhappy with the lack of analysis with which senior management approached a problem. In his effort to try to get better and clearer information during management briefings, he instructed the human resources department to train managers in the art of presentations. He was adamant that viewgraphs be legible and succinct. If managers presented poor viewgraphs, he would yell at them or embarrass them to try to get them to understand what he wanted.

One incident was particularly memorable to Kohler and many others at ESL. One day, a middle manager was making a briefing for the first time to some TRW people, Kohler and his ESL senior managers. Unfortunately for the middle manager, he was using viewgraphs which Kohler had already expressed displeasure with to another manager. In a rage, Kohler got up from his chair, stormed over to the startled manager, and tore up the viewgraphs. Word of this incident spread quickly throughout ESL.

It was at this point that one senior manager decided he had nothing to lose and went in to talk to Kohler about the incident. After listening to the senior manager, Kohler began to realize that he had made a mistake. He decided he needed to apologize to the manager in question, so when he saw him in the hall he told him: "That really wasn't smart of me, I'm sorry." "That's fine," the manager replied.

A top manager commented on Kohler's first six months at ESL: "Kohler took on too many challenges in the beginning and tried to change too many things at once." Said another, "Probably one of the worst problems for Kohler in the beginning was people's perception of him as egotistical and mean. For instance, if he got mad at someone or got frustrated in a meeting he might throw an empty coke can at the person to make his point," said another. In truth, Kohler had never thrown a coke can at ESL, although he had thrown them while he was working for the government.

Another senior manager said, "Kohler has a reputation for theatrics. He used to wear a whistle around his neck. If he felt that he wasn't being heard, he'd blow it right in the middle of the meeting. If he doesn't like something, he'll make sure that the person knows that he doesn't like it!" He also would ring a ship's bell which hung on the wall in the conference room by his office. "It makes a hell of a loud noise," the senior manager said wryly.

Kohler's Transition

On several separate occasions, different senior managers felt strongly enough about an issue to risk confronting Kohler about it. To their surprise, they found Kohler receptive and willing to listen to their views. Indeed, Kohler was glad to be getting some feedback from his managers.

Kohler began working with Herman Gyr, an organizational consultant affiliated with ESL. Gyr had been brought in by the Human Resources department to help top management understand and work with the organizational changes. Kohler and Gyr talked about methods Kohler could use to bring about change within the organization. Kohler began to sit back at meetings and encourage open discussions. To help ESL's senior managers think beyond their individual responsibilities and look at the whole picture for ESL he would announce, "Okay, you're the board of directors, what's your vote?" At other times, he would stand up and lead the discussion pointing out what he saw as critical flaws or unrealized potentials. His management team began to trust him and appeared more willing to do the needed analysis.

While ESL top management was beginning to understand Kohler, he was still very much resented by most of the employees lower in the organization. Stories would circulate about his can-throwing and whistle-blowing, which gave him the reputation for being egotistical. Rumors circulated that he would only stay at ESL a year or two and then they would get rid of him. Many people resented the changes that he was making and they wanted him out of office.

As one senior manager described the situation: "My sense is that some ESL employees thought of Kohler as an aberration and that he would pass. They would not commit to Kohler's decisions because they felt they could wait him out. Kohler exacerbated the problem by feeling compelled to let the people know whether a decision was supported unanimously by his team. If the decision was unpopular, some ESL employees would delay action hoping that Kohler would be out of office soon. Since they knew some of ESL's top management disagreed with the decision, they hoped that the decision would be rolled back once Kohler was gone."

Kohler described the changes during his first six months: "Basically there were only three changes. One, there was a lot of talk about change which irritated a lot of people. Art Money consistently fought me, wanting to know why we should change. Two, were the initiatives. The ESL International initiative was fairly easily accepted but the Imagery initiative was not. People argued that we shouldn't do the initiative, that we could use the money in other areas. In fact, one senior manager left in protest of this initiative. Three, I made some minor organizational changes. I had eleven people reporting to me, so I made Franklin and Sandstrom Senior Vice Presidents in charge of the support services and I was in charge of the divisions. This was interpreted by some as a demotion, and it had more impact on the organization than was initially realized."

"Prior to my arrival, Jacobs had tried to do a little fixing up. He had basically fired (although the guy stayed with the company) the Vice President of AMSD division and put Luther Smith in charge. Jacobs also combined two divisions into one and put Art Money in charge of the SASD division. So when I came on board, a lot of changes had already occurred. In fact, our organizational consultant, Herman Gyr, was working with Art Money to build SASD division for a year before I started working with him."

In response to Kohler's perception that Art Money "consistently fought" him, Money stated, "I wanted to discuss the changes and get consensus from the Executive staff before "jumping" into changes and then figuring out what we're doing and did do!"

Kohler summarized his activities during 1987 as follows: "I did more walking around, more involvement with the business, more getting down in the organization, and more informal meetings with small groups of people. There was less theatrics on my part, and I tried to communicate that I did not have all the answers."

A Tragedy

One afternoon in February 1988, Toni Rogers, the Human Resources Director, was meeting with Kohler in his office when Kohler's assistant, Les Ferguson, came in and told him that there was someone on the grounds with a gun. "Get away from the window," Les motioned to Kohler.

"What do you mean get away from the window?" Kohler asked

"We don't know who's out there, and you might be a target, so move," he replied.

"Right."

Kohler and Toni moved into the conference room next door, closed the curtains and tried to continue their meeting. Les Ferguson returned a few minutes later saying, "We've called the police and security is on the way. There's a guy loose with a gun in the M5 building."

Kohler and Toni looked at each other. Kohler said, "This is more serious than we thought. Let's figure out what we should do."

Kohler and Toni were meeting in building M1 (see Exhibit 10) and they soon learned that the gunman was barricaded in M5. They also learned that he had shot at least one person in the parking lot who had gotten in his way, as he sought to reach an ESL woman employee who was his intended target.

As events began to unfold, Kohler and some of ESL's top management gathered in building M1. Most of the employees who had been in M5 had escaped to other buildings, primarily M4 and M6. Employees from building M3 had been evacuated to M1. The police would not allow any one to go home. Kohler considered what needed to be done. He turned to Toni, "Have we called CONCERN (the employees assistance group)?"

"It's already been done," she replied.

"Good," Kohler said.

Exhibit 10
ESL

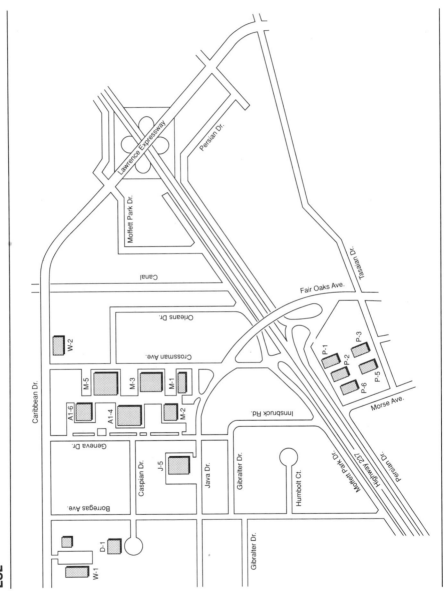

NOTE: There is no exit onto Fair Oaks from 237 westbound and no entrance from Fair Oaks to 237 eastbound.

512

During the next few hours, there was a great deal of confusion. Kohler worked with the police and directed ESL support to the police. People were milling around in the halls, sitting in empty conference rooms, and standing in the central garden area of building M1. Families of ESL employees were also gathering at ESL. Kohler looked around at the crowd of employees and families. "We need to let people know what's going on," he said.

Kohler walked over to a concrete planter in the garden of building M1, stepped up and asked everyone to gather around. He looked at the employees. Some of them looked upset and some worried. They knew some of their friends were missing; friends they had worked with for 15 to 20 years. Kohler knew he had to be factual without unduly alarming them.

He spoke in a loud voice: "We don't know very much but I'm going to tell you what we know. There are still some people in the building, but we don't know how many. Some of them have called in. Some of them are hiding. We know that one person was killed in the parking lot. His name was Larry Caine. There are two SWAT teams here from the police, one from Sunnyvale and one from Santa Clara. We are working closely with the police to figure out what to do next. Please stay here until otherwise notified by ESL. We don't know what's going on and it could be very dangerous. We don't want to risk your life."

Kohler continued to speak, reassuring employees and telling them what he knew. He asked if anyone had any questions.

Someone asked, "Do you know about my wife?"

Kohler asked, "What's her name? We'll try to locate her for you."

Another person wanted to know why the sharp shooters didn't just shoot the gunman. Kohler explained, "Our primary concern is for the safety of those people still left in the building. The police are doing all they can."

Someone else asked, "Is there anything we can do?"

"Sure. Don't panic," Kohler replied. "Help us figure out where people are." People started to put together lists and in some instances were able to locate missing people. After he finished speaking, Kohler decided to go to buildings M2 and M6 and let them know what was going on.

Toni spoke about the incident later, "It wasn't like we had a big command post erected right then and there. Too many things were going on. Kohler would get some data and he'd make a decision. He might say 'Jim (Sandstrom), here's what's going on,' or he'd ask me what I thought we should do. He took action, and he took the right action. I think in a true leadership style he did the things that needed to be done. They were hard things to do. When he personally went around to the outlying buildings, we didn't know what kind of danger he was in. (They found out later that the guy had a high-powered rifle and scope and could have picked Kohler off in the parking lots.) But he went because he felt the people needed to hear from him."

At 9 P.M., the gunman finally surrendered. The police got the people out and found that seven people had been killed. Kohler said to the police captain who was in charge at the scene, "I want to know the names of the people who were killed because I'm not going to let these families wonder all night long about what's going on.

The captain said, "I can't release the names to you."

"Why not?" Kohler asked.

"The rules are that names can only be released by the coroner after the coroner has completed his investigation. It's not a police department prerogative," the captain replied.

"When is that going to happen?" Kohler asked.

"Tomorrow afternoon sometime," came the reply.

"That's unacceptable," Kohler exclaimed. "That's completely unacceptable. Who has the authority to waive this?"

"The Chief of Police," the captain said.

Kohler called the chief of police and the city manager. They asked to speak to the captain and told him, "You are authorized to release the names to Kohler. What he does with them is his business."

Toni explained, "Kohler accepted responsibility if there was a mistake. Then at midnight, Kohler, Lew Franklin, and I divided up the list and called each family."

Kohler continued the story, "We orchestrated the calls ahead of time. We wanted to establish who we were and what our authority level was. We had people from CONCERN with us and they took the call when it got to a place where we couldn't handle it."

Said Toni, "I remember just before he dialed the first number Bob (Kohler) turned to me and said, 'How do I do this (tell them about the murders)'. He really cared how these families felt. Today, I'd trust Kohler with my life."

This traumatic incident caused many employees who had had little contact with Kohler to view him differently. "I really think Kohler showed concern and leadership during this crisis," said one manager. As a result of this tragedy many of the lower level managers began to accept Kohler and to entertain the possibility that the direction he was leading ESL in might be appropriate.

Organizational History

Before 1984, the engineering group had been centralized, with one single organization serving all of the lines of business and the manager of engineering reporting directly to the president. Each of the strategic lines of business (LOB) also had a manager that reported directly to the president. There was competition among the lines of business for good engineering talent. It was up to the manager of engineering to determine how to spread the resource talent to each LOB. If the LOB manager felt slighted, they would go to the president. President Don Jacob found that he was spending a lot of time ironing out difficulties between engineering and the LOB's.

In 1984, Jacobs grew tired of the squabble for engineering talent and decided to divisionalize and give each LOB the engineering resources to do the job. Half of the engineering group went to Luther Smith's division and half went to Art Money's division. Each engineering group consisted of hardware, software, and systems engineering.

Six hundred and fifty people were employed in engineering. There were between 60 and 70 managers. Engineering worked on several hundred projects at any one time, with 75 or so being sizable jobs.

Engineers were expensive to recruit, averaging around $3000 per hire. Not only did they have to be highly skilled, with a background in signal processing and communications, but because security clearance took up to a year, it was helpful if they already had secret or top secret clearances. To work at ESL, one had to be a U.S. citizen. The cost of living was high in Silicon Valley so attracting new engineers, especially from other parts of the country, was difficult.

Program Management

One of the areas in which Kohler wanted to lead ESL was toward excellence in program management. With his experience managing engineering development and operations of a variety of major technical programs, he had earned a reputation throughout the defense industry for his accomplishments in program management.

ESL was organized under a matrix design. Program (or project) managers would request workers from the various functional departments in order to assemble a team for the program. This request was done through an agreement called a Project Work Authorization (PWA) which was like a contract between the functions and the project. It was the job of the program manager to execute the program's requirements. Part of the job was also to provide the functional manager with resource (human and capital) forecasts, so that the resources were available when the program needed them.

Program managers were divided into three levels: Program Manager I (responsible for small projects), Program Manager II (medium-sized projects), and Program Manager III (responsible for very large, complicated projects). There were approximately 50 Program Managers I, 50 Program Managers II, and 15 Program Managers III at ESL. Twenty percent of the Program Managers III were engineers by training and 34% of Program Managers II were engineers by training.

The responsibilities of the functional manager were described in ESL's technical policy PM-1:

> Functional (line) managers are responsible for providing and managing resources for a specific functional activity. They shall provide the resources to support program needs. They will ensure that the technology base, at a minimum, is current, and preferably at the leading edge. They are responsible for the administrative management of the functional group including salary administration, capital forecasting and other resource needs, worker power forecasting, training, personnel needs, and career development. The functional managers shall review the technical content of the work done to support the programs, as well as be responsible for

the budget and schedule agreed on with the program manager. They are expected to cooperate with all program managers in the execution of all program requirements.

In the matrix, the program manager was oriented toward meeting program requirements (e.g. build a box within the predetermined specifications that performs at a predetermined level) as determined in the contract. The functional manager was oriented toward supporting the program's personnel needs, as well as finding staff to support all other programs at ESL that needed the skill or technology of the functional organization.

The nature of the matrix created a situation where a worker had two bosses, one on the program work and one for all other aspects of the worker's life. Performance evaluations (known as the Performance Objective Appraisal Process, or POAP for short) were supposed to be done by the Functional Managers in consultation with the Program Manager. In practice this wasn't always the case. Some managers didn't use the POAP so there was inconsistency in the way a worker was evaluated. The functional manager was supposed to consult with the program or project manager to see how the worker was performing. This didn't always occur, especially if the functional manager didn't use the POAP. Sometimes a worker would get a good evaluation from his functional manager because he had excellent technical skills but the functional manager would completely ignore the problem the project manager was having with the worker in getting the worker to perform tasks on schedule and within cost. The program or project manager felt that they didn't have any teeth in their management responsibilities.

Some program managers depended on their interpersonal skills to accomplish tasks. One manager described his style: "I visit with my workers' boss often. It's important that I establish an excellent communication system. That's the only way I'm going to be able to successfully manage my program. I build bridges so that when I need certain resources, I know the manager understands my needs and is going to give me the best person for the job."

In contrast, another manager commented: "To get work done I need to understand what's going on with a functional organization such as engineering. Beyond that I don't depend a great deal on the organization. I don't really need an engineering manager or his boss."

Concerns of program managers included the constant changing of personnel on the customer side, the lack of training for those who had never worked on a large scale program, the loss of key engineers to other companies in the valley, the lack of a good cost control system, and the lack of direct control of the people assigned to the program. In addition, there was concern about the balance of technical objectives (produce a high-quality, viable product) with the business objectives (produce what was promised in the specifications of the contract within cost and on schedule).

One engineer commented, "The program managers that I've seen have been bean-counter types. They come in strictly with a business background, and with very little experience that is required on the technical side. They've put a lot of

Exhibit 11

Organizational Positions at ESL

President
Vice President
Director
Lab Managers
(This position was eliminated after the reorganization.)
Department Managers
Section Heads

Organizational Levels at ESL

President's Office
Division
Directorates
Labs
(This level was eliminated after the reorganization.)
Departments
Sections

emphasis in cost and schedule and make decisions like 'I can cut 5% here or shorten the schedule here' without knowledge of what they are doing to the technical side of the house. They tend to jump all over the engineers if they aren't meeting cost and schedule because they don't understand the engineering side. This has forced the engineers to come in and report only what that they think the program managers want to hear. The program office doesn't understand what's happening over in the engineering world as far as design and delays. It tends to force an unrealistic picture to be formed over on the program side, which is unfortunate."

On the other hand a lower level project manager with an MBA had this to say, "Lab managers are ex-engineers. They understand the technical side and the customer side. What they don't understand is the business and quantifiable side. Business people should run the labs and technical people should work in the market (with the customers)."

Human Resources Management

The only director level manager to report directly to Bob Kohler was Human Resources (see Exhibit 11 for a description of the ELS hierarchy). "Bob believes human resources is important and he is sending this message to upper level managers by including me in corporate management meetings," said Toni Rogers, the director of Human Resources.

"The biggest complaint we get from people is that the company doesn't take care of them in development efforts, even though we've always spent a lot of money sending people out for seminars and other training. Including tuition, we've probably spent about one and a half million dollars on training. That's a lot for a company this size," Rogers said.

The way in which time taken off for training was charged created problems for ESL. The government would not pay for training as a direct charge to contracts, so people who would normally charge their time directly to their project were required to charge it to overhead. "That creates real budgetary constraints," said Rogers.

Most of the management development courses were offered to first level managers and not many were offered at the program level or above. Training was under the human resources department. Approximately 25% of the first line managers went to a course offered by ESL human resources staff called LAMP (Leading and Managing People). Approximately 10% of the Lab Managers and Directors had taken the LAMP training.

TRW offered a course called Team Advance Management Training. This course was offered to Lab Managers and his or her people. The purpose was to build teamwork and trust.

Consultants on special topics such as "how to deal with change" and "organizational effectiveness" were usually offered at special all-day or several-day meetings for directors, and vice presidents. Very little on-site management development courses were offered to these managers.

In addition to the in-house training courses, educational programs were made available to management. Approximately 50% of the upper level managers had attended some kind of managerial offsite course lasting anywhere from two to eight weeks. Most of these courses were offered through major universities.

Several managers commented about the poor work done by program managers, and attributed this to a lack of training. Said one manager, "The career ladder for technical people needs to be improved. So does the training; someone needs to follow-up on the program managers' skills."

Several managers talked about the lack of managerial skill or training in the levels below Vice President. "There appears to be lack of skill both on the business side and the technical side. The people at the directorate don't know the nuts and bolts of the business, so they don't know when they are being fed a line of bull."

Rogers emphasized the proactive rather than the reactive side of human resources. "I want the H.R. people to work actively with their managers and the people they support. Although we still have to do the basics, like counseling and support, that's not what I want the H.R. people to spend their time on. I want them to help with offsites (training) and to help people with (skill) development—things that will make a difference in the organization."

Organizational Change

Since the summer of 1988, Kohler and the top management of ESL had spent considerable time analyzing and characterizing the business environment, examining the health of their core lines of business, developing strategic objectives, and defining specific action plans to allow them to realize their objectives.

Kohler believed the evidence from these meetings and the analysis (shown in Exhibits 6 through 8) demonstrated that the best they could hope for in their core lines of business was to increase market share. These discussions resulted in an unanimous agreement on the urgent need to change the organization to enable both the company and the divisions to refocus on new business development and acquisition, plus program execution. (See Exhibit 3 for details regarding the organizational changes.)

In addition to his primary concern for new business development, Kohler wanted the new organizational structure to 1) effect significant change in ESL's engineering culture; 2) to challenge workers (e.g. by providing incentives) to do what ESL said it would do, even if they weren't the ones to develop the bid and proposal; 3) to effect the acceptance of accountability to meet commitments to programs; 4) to improve engineering efficiency to help reduce the cost of doing business; and 5) to support the continuing development and commitment to ESL's long-term corporate strategic planning. "The system prior to the reorganization wasn't working very well with two engineering matrixes. Project managers had to draw on staff support from too many areas," said Kohler.

Kohler announced the new organizational structure on December 8, 1988. The significant organization changes were the formation of the Advanced Programs and Development organization, reconsolidation of engineering, realignment of some business areas and key support activities, and the creation of a corporate strategy office. Kohler hoped that these changes would allow ESL to refocus both the company and the operating divisions on new business development, to effect the required cultural changes, and to commit to ESL's long-term corporate strategy.

An operations manager commented about the reorganization, "I think the reorganization was an attempt to become more cost competitive by becoming more streamlined. While I think Kohler's general direction is good, I feel he needs to do more. We have strategic goals but what we need now are more tactical goals with quantifiable measures. For example, what kind of performance in quantitative terms do we expect from ESL International or any other area before we cut off their supply hose? I don't think this necessarily has to come from Kohler. I think it has to come from the finance area and the directorate level. I think this is starting to come through with our POAP's, but people don't look at the POAP's with enough seriousness yet."

Effects on Engineering Personnel

The new consolidated engineering division was composed of four directorates and engineering operations. The four directorates were organized according to functional lines.

1. Electro-magnetic Sub-Systems: focus on analog hardware and mechanical engineering with 120 employees.
2. Data Management and Processing Subsystems: Software emphasis with 200 employees.
3. Engineering Systems: Systems engineering with 100 employees.

4. Signal Processing Systems: Digital Hardware, plus the supporting drafting group and the fifty technicians. A total of 203 employees were in this division.

To consolidate, the organizational position of lab manager was eliminated. This meant that some managers were demoted from positions of lab manager to department manager or from department manager to section head. (See Exhibit 11). The number of managers was reduced by 20. Some of the people who had a power base prior to the reorganization were suddenly confronted with the loss of their support. As one engineer said, "A few empires have tumbled, and these people are pretty shaken." Bob Kohler wanted to communicate to the engineers that there were changes that needed to be made if ESL was going to remain competitive. Kohler felt his challenge was to maintain momentum and to capitalize on the shake-up in order to ensure that the necessary changes occurred.

Hi Markum was moved in to manage the consolidated engineering group and was promoted to Vice President. The main focus of the new engineering division was to avoid duplication of systems which had been occurring. In addition, Kohler wanted to more sharply focus the responsibilities of the engineering division and the general managers. Markum was charged with a focus on quality within the engineering division. Kohler wanted Markum to work closely with the Vice Presidents of ASTD and SSD. He charged them, as corporate officers to take a *corporate view* when allocating the engineering resource talent, rather than divisional interest and passing their problems up to him.

An operations manager said that the reorganization had affected him because the engineers that he had worked with had new bosses. "It's put a hiccup in my work. I've had to go to the new bosses and replay the status of the programs. It hasn't affected my programs financially as most of my programs are beyond the design stage, so I don't need a lot of engineering help."

Other Changes

Kohler also made two changes in his top management team. Art Money, who had been vice president and general manager of SASD, was now responsible for business development. In light of the importance he felt that marketing had at ESL, he was glad that Money had been willing to take the job.

Kohler was a little concerned about moving senior vice president Lew Franklin from a line position to what, in essence, was a staff position. Franklin had been in the company since its inception. ESL issued a badge number for life to each employee and while ESL was up to badge number 7569, Franklin was known around ESL as badge number six. Perhaps Franklin had hoped for the president's job before Kohler was chosen, and Kohler hoped that Franklin didn't feel that he was trying to remove him. Franklin's new job of corporate strategy was vital to the company.

It was still too early to tell how the reorganization had affected ESL, but Kohler had high hopes that ESL employees were taking his concerns seriously now. He wondered what his next steps should be.

Appendix 8–3A

The Cultural Environment at ESL

Donald Sifferman

September 1, 1988

Background and Trends

ESL's marketplace until several years ago was characterized by being primarily sole source, with customers being willing to pay the cost to get the performance they desired. ESL had the reputation of being able to solve very difficult technical problems, and customers came to ESL to have such problems solved. They were willing to pay what they perceived to be a higher associated price for this ability.

That situation is changing. AMSD's business has been competitive for several years, DRSD's business has been competitive from the start, and essentially all of SASD's business is now competitive. In the competitive procurements, the principal competitive criterion is the lowest cost for a system responsive to the customer's requirements. The only exceptions to competition seem to be operation, maintenance, and engineering (OM&E) support for, and direct follow-ons to, ESL-built systems.

The move to competition comes at a time when the DoD budget is under considerable pressure. The intelligence budget is expected to be, at best, flat over the next few years. The available B&P pool is being decreased through aggressive Government negotiations to decrease B&P, as a percent of sales, that is available to industry. Whereas we used to write mostly sole-source proposals, we are now being required to write mostly competitive proposals with a lower percent of B&P. ESL is having difficulty dealing with competitive proposals, a situation that is aggravated by having to do so more efficiently.

In addition, there have been significant customer changes in our marketplace as follows:

1. AMSD

   a. The United States Army, the historical customer, is buying less equipment.

   b. Aggressive expansion into the international arena has culminated in establishing ESL International.

   c. The U.S. Air Force has become a major customer.

2. SASD

   a. BLAZER, one of our best customers, is no longer buying systems.

   b. Classified customers are now committed to competition for new developments.

   c. There are now several new classified customers.

   d. The NSA is asserting itself as a SIGINT czar, but only slowly getting acquisitions underway.

   3. In general, there are few procurements greater than $10M.

3. DRSD

   a. This is a new business area with new customers.

In summary, there have been significant changes in the marketplace in which ESL operates:

1. Essentially all system development jobs are competitive, with the emphasis placed on cost rather than on technical innovation.

2. Fewer programs will be greater than $10M.

3. B&P as a percent of sales will decrease over time, further aggravating the shift from sole source to competition.

4. The portion of the DoD budget that we access is, at best, flat.

5. Our customer mix is changing with new customers emerging; a smaller percentage of our customers have long-term favorable history with ESL.

6. Historical customers characterize ESL's problems as follows:

   a. ESL places too much emphasis on technical design and innovation and not enough on cost and schedule. They want balanced performance.

   b. ESL is too expensive. We do not effectively reuse previous designs and we tend to develop things instead of buying from better qualified industry sources, including both off-the-shelf products and new designs where another contractor is better qualified than ESL.

   c. ESL has used systems engineering poorly and we do not apply systems engineering disciplines in the design and definition stages to our advantage, including not writing good specifications to procure subsystems from ESL or from subcontractors and not flowing down top-level requirements to lower levels, hardware, software, and operations. They find that our development process lacks discipline. While we seem to get there in the end, the process is stressful.

  d. ESL is technically arrogant. We design and develop what we believe the customer needs, not what he asks for.

  e. ESL is slow in staffing jobs at the start, with the result that the remainder of the program suffers.

Our internal experience is similar to that of our customers. The lack of discipline and organization is particularly visible in proposal preparation because of the need to effectively organize and mobilize a team in a short period of time. These symptoms can be also seen in other ESL internal processes, especially planning and budgeting.

Changing Awareness of ESL's Behavior

Since late 1987 there has been an increasing awareness of ESL's cultural difficulties and the fact that they hold us back from responding to the changes in the marketplace. This started with Bob Kohler's presentation at the Director's offsite meeting in December 1987. It was followed by the work of the Culture Task Force at the December 1987 offsite and during January and February of 1988, development work with the Executive Staff, Bob Kohler's letters to ESL members, and the Performance Objectives and Appraisal Process (POAP) flowed down from the President and the Training Task Force.

The Culture Task Force has its roots at the Director's Offsite in December 1987. The group, comprised of nine ESL members who had all been at ESL for more than eight years, concluded that "Our present culture is holding us back now and will cause us to fail in moving to the big time." Their focus at the offsite was directed at identifying behaviors and attitudes that are counterproductive. While action plans to correct the deficiencies were addressed, little time was available for this difficult topic. After the offsite, Bob Kohler chartered the task force to continue its work; the tasking was as follows:

  1. Assess ESL's culture, both good and bad, in the context of going into the big time

  2. Identify specific directions ESL needs to go for ESL to positively evolve its culture

  3. Make specific recommendations to the Corporate Officers by February 22, 1988.

The task force spent considerable time during January and February 1988 in meetings and off-line working sessions. In addition, it conducted a sensing session with nine ESL members, who had been at ESL several years, to ensure that they had a balanced perspective on ESL's culture and cultural issues. Also, because some confusion existed on what Bob Kohler meant by "the big time," they defined big time as follows:

  1. Being a professional, disciplined, and businesslike company that knows itself, its competition, and the business environment, and knows how to deal with them

2. Winning and successfully performing on programs
3. Having a leadership style that involves clear roles and responsibilities at each level and for each function, resulting in effective delegation.

The Culture Task Force identified many desirable ESL qualities that should be retained as we move to improve ESL. The positive qualities they listed include:

1. Informality in how we deal with each other
2. People-oriented family attitude and concern for ESL members
3. Pleasant, but affordable, facilities
4. Entrepreneurial environment
5. Fun and exciting place to work, challenging work
6. Honesty and ethics in our dealings with our customers
7. Pride in ESL, our members, and our accomplishments
8. Broad-based member involvement with customers
9. Responsibility to do a quality technical job for our customers
10. Understanding our customer requirements
11. Technological leadership
12. Encouragement of all sizes of projects.

It is noted that although all of these qualities are present in ESL, there are situations where they are not present. In those cases, they are considered goals.

Cultural Issues ESL Needs to Address

The Culture Task Force identified a number of cultural problems that have been holding ESL back. The three highest priority cultural problems are:

1. Lack of accountability and discipline. We do not follow our own policies, procedures, and rules; projects deliver late and/or overrun at significant personal hardship to the staff involved; and there appears to be a lack of trust in and following the requests of our leadership. In summary, ESL management rarely assigns clear responsibilities to its members and then does not hold them accountable. It is believed that this is caused by a lack of participation in the decision process, an independent attitude (e.g., "If I don't like it, I won't do it, and I won't even tell you so."), and a cultural history that has not penalized our members for not being accountable.

2. Multiple, conflicting cultures. Different cultures are expected, but it is bad if the conflicts are not managed. The conflict between programs and functional organizations in the use of matrix management has received a lot of attention. However, other conflicts exist and need to be addressed, including engineering versus nonengineering, systems engineers versus designers, and large programs versus small programs.

3. Accounting-based measurement of engineering management. Engineering management is incentivized more to achieve ESL internal resource budgets than to do good engineering. A lot of internal staff time and energy and a lot of time in division- and company-level management meetings is spent on budgeting and execution against ESL internal resources including LMOP (e.g., indirect labor, labor to project, director's allocation), B&P, IR&D, capital equipment, and facilities. On the other hand, there is a lack of accountability in meeting commitments to programs, getting technical work done at cost and within schedule. Under pressure to meet ESL internal overhead budgets, the functional engineering organizations have historically understaffed; this has often been the root of program performance problems.

Several related cultural problems consist of:

4. There is a contempt for planning. This seems to be the result of the following attitudes: (a) things change anyway, so why bother to plan, and (b) planning isn't fun. Planning is not treated seriously, except for current-year, ESL internal budgets where managers know they will be held accountable; see item 3 above. The grand plans that have been made in strategic plans and at company offsites have generally been ignored when the managers return to their day-to-day activities. (This is starting to change as Bob Kohler has been holding managers responsible for such action items.)

5. Management sets conflicting priorities. This seems to relate to other culture factors including a lack of long-range planning, a lack of delegation, a focus on ESL internal budgets, and lack of accountability. This seems to be prevalent in assigning engineering staff to programs and proposals (as a result of understaffing or unwillingness to assign the right staff earlier, upper management personally gets involved in moving staff from job to job, depending on what the latest crisis is) and in managing ESL internal resources when budgets are not met in one area so that changes must be made in other areas. An example of the latter is B&P overruns impacting on the IR&D program.

6. Managers get a rush from saving the day. An example is managers several levels up personally exercising control over a situation, such as reassigning staff from job to job or reallocating ESL internal budgets.

7. There is a sink-or-swim attitude; little training or mentoring exists. This is true for new employees who are merely given a job to do and are left to figure out on their own how to get it done at ESL. It is also true in assigning members to key positions of responsibility such as functional supervision, program management, or proposal management. In many cases the member develops his or her own way of doing things since they are not helped or advised, and since there is a lack of procedures on how we do things at ESL.

8. A lack of interorganizational cooperation and mutual respect exists at ESL. This is probably a result of the entrepreneurial culture where individuals personally got the job done, and a lack of understanding of the interdisciplinary efforts necessary to solve complex problems in large programs and within an organization as large as ESL.

These problems are probably a logical result of the entrepreneurial spirit required in the early days of ESL when bright, technical people charged into difficult technical problems. Through sheer energy, intelligence, and enthusiasm, they were able to solve the problems, even though, in retrospect, there was little or no planning and organization. That role model, encouraging a "charge in and do it" attitude, is now serving ESL poorly in an environment where an integrated team effort is required to solve complex programmatic and ESL internal problems.

An underlying factor for the cultural problems discussed above is that we don't take the time to get organized before we get started. We are too anxious to get the job done, and believe we will somehow get to the end. The steps involved in getting organized include:

1. Defining the problem or task before beginning work.
2. Developing an action plan (e.g., what, by whom, when).
3. Negotiating with the people involved in the program to get their help and support; and where appropriate, modifying the plan based on their input and their ability to support it and obtaining their agreement and commitment to the plan.
4. Documenting and publishing the plan to serve as the basis for accountability and communication to the affected parties.
5. Periodically reviewing and, if appropriate, updating the plan.

ESL does this poorly because of our history and culture. We have been unwilling to invest the time and energy at the start of projects. While we recognize that we have to change, we are finding it difficult to break the old molds.

In addition to taking time to get organized, our culture needs to change to incorporate a new management style. This style should include

1. Responding to direction from the top, instead of members doing their own thing
2. Having a sense of mutual dependence and mutual respect. Understanding and believing that all parts of ESL are essential, that "we are all in it together"
3. Taking the time to make and agree to a plan of attack at the beginning of a project and holding each other responsible for meeting the agreed-to plans
4. Leadership at all levels.

Summary

ESL is in a time of change, and we need to be responsive to the changes if we are to remain as successful as we have been in the past. Business as usual will not be sufficient in the future; the negative aspects of our culture will hold us back if we do not change. What is needed, in general, is a professional, organized, disciplined, committed, and accountable approach to every aspect of our business. We must pull together as a company, treating this situation as both a challenge and an opportunity.

Reading 8–1

Evolution and Revolution as Organizations Grow*

Larry E. Greiner

A small research company chooses too complicated and formalized an organization structure for its young age and limited size. It flounders in rigidity and bureaucracy for several years and is finally acquired by a larger company.

Key executives of a retail store chain hold on to an organization structure long after it has served its purpose, because their power is derived from this structure. The company eventually goes into bankruptcy.

A large bank disciplines a "rebellious" manager who is blamed for current control problems, when the underlying cause is centralized procedures that are holding back expansion into new markets. Many younger managers subsequently leave the bank, competition moves in, and profits are still declining.

The problems of these companies, like those of many others, are rooted more in past decisions than in present events or outside market dynamics. Historical forces do indeed shape the future growth of organizations. Yet management, in its haste to grow, often overlooks such critical development questions as: Where has our organization been? Where is it now? And what do the answers to these questions mean for where we are going? Instead, its gaze is fixed outward toward the environment and the future—as if more precise market projections will provide a new organizational identity.

Companies fail to see that many clues to their future success lie within their

*Reprinted by permission of *Harvard Business Review*. "Evolution and Revolution as Organizations Grow" by Larry E. Greiner (July/August 1972). Copyright © 1972 by the President and Fellows of Harvard College; all rights reserved. This article is part of a continuing project on organization development with the author's colleague, Professor Louis B. Barnes, and sponsored by the Division of Research, Harvard Business School.

own organizations and their evolving states of development. Moreover, the inability of management to understand its organization development problems can result in a company becoming "frozen" in its present stage of evolution or, ultimately, in failure, regardless of market opportunities.

My position in this article is that the future of an organization may be less determined by outside forces than it is by the organization's history. In stressing the force of history on an organization, I have drawn from the legacies of European psychologists (their thesis being that individual behavior is determined primarily by previous events and experiences, not by what lies ahead). Extending this analogy of individual development to the problems of organization development, I shall discuss a series of developmental phases through which growing companies tend to pass. But, first, let me provide two definitions:

1. The term *evolution* is used to describe prolonged periods of growth where no major upheaval occurs in organization practices.

2. The term *revolution* is used to describe those periods of substantial turmoil in organization life.

As a company progresses through developmental phases, each evolutionary period creates its own revolution. For instance, centralized practices eventually lead to demands for decentralization. Moreover, the nature of management's solution to each revolutionary period determines whether a company will move forward into its next stage of evolutionary growth. As I shall show later, there are at least five phases of organization development, each characterized by both an evolution and a revolution.

Key Forces in Development

During the past few years a small amount of research knowledge about the phases of organization development has been building. Some of this research is very quantitative, such as time series analyses that reveal patterns of economic performance over time.[1] The majority of studies, however, are case oriented and use company records and interviews to reconstruct a rich picture of corporate development.[2] Yet both types of research tend to be heavily empirical without attempting more generalized statements about the overall process of development.

A notable exception is the historical work of Alfred D. Chandler, Jr., in his book *Strategy and Structure*.[3] This study depicts four very broad and general phases

---

[1]See, for example, William H. Starbuck, "Organizational Metamorphosis," in *Promising Research Directions*, ed. R. W. Millman and M. P. Hottenstein (Tempe, Ariz.: Academy of Management, 1968), p. 113.

[2]See, for example, the *Grangesberg* case series, prepared by C. Roland Christensen and Bruce R. Scott (Boston: Intercollegiate Case Clearing House, Harvard Business School).

[3]*Strategy and Structure: Chapters in the History of the American Industrial Enterprise* (Cambridge, Mass.: MIT Press, 1962).

in the lives of four large U.S. companies. It proposes that outside market opportunities determine a company's strategy, which in turn determines the company's organization structure. This thesis has a valid ring for the four companies examined by Chandler, largely because they developed in a time of explosive markets and technological advances. But more recent evidence suggests that organization structure may be less malleable than Chandler assumed; in fact, structure can play a critical role in influencing corporate strategy. It is this reverse emphasis on how organization structure affects future growth which is highlighted in the model presented in this article.

From an analysis of recent studies,[4] five key dimensions emerge as essential for building a model of organization development:

1. Age of the organization.
2. Size of the organization.
3. Stages of evolution.
4. Stages of revolution.
5. Growth rate of the industry.

I shall describe each of these elements separately, but first note their combined effect as illustrated in Exhibit 1. Note especially how each dimension influences the other over time; when all five elements begin to interact, a more complete and dynamic picture of organizational growth emerges.

After describing these dimensions and their interconnections, I shall discuss each evolutionary/revolutionary phase of development and show (*a*) how each stage of evolution breeds its own revolution, and (*b*) how management solutions to each revolution determine the next stage of evolution.

Age of the Organization

The most obvious and essential dimension for any model of development is the life span of an organization (represented as the horizontal axis in Exhibit 1). All historical studies gather data from various points in time and then make comparisons. From these observations, it is evident that the same organization practices are not maintained throughout a long time span. This makes a most basic point: management problems and principles are rooted in time. The concept of decentralization, for example, can have meaning for describing corporate practices at one time period but loses its power at another.

The passage of time also contributes to the institutionalization of managerial

[4]I have drawn on many sources for evidence: (*a*) numerous cases collected at the Harvard Business School; (*b*) *Organization Growth and Development,* ed. William H. Starbuck (Middlesex, England: Penguin Books, 1971), where several studies are cited; and (*c*) articles published in journals, such as Lawrence E. Fouraker and John M Stopford, "Organization Structure and the Multinational Strategy," *Administrative Science Quarterly* 13, no. 1 (1968), p. 47; and Malcolm S. Salter, "Management Appraisal and Reward Systems," *Journal of Business Policy* 1, no. 4 (1971).

Exhibit 1
Model of Organization Development

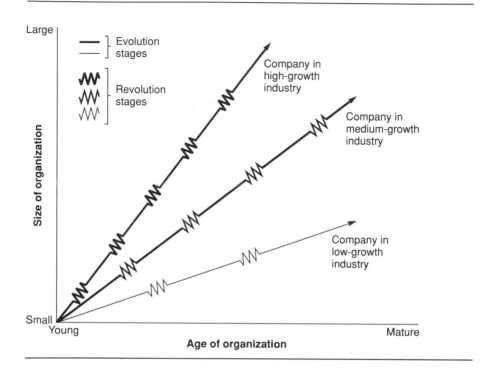

attitudes. As a result, employee behavior becomes not only more predictable but also more difficult to change when attitudes are outdated.

Size of the Organization

This dimension is depicted as the vertical axis in Exhibit 1. A company's problems and solutions tend to change markedly as the number of employees and sales volume increase.Thus, time is not the only determinant of structure; in fact, organizations that do not grow in size can retain many of the same management issues and practices over lengthy periods. In addition to increased size, however, problems of coordination and communication magnify, new functions emerge, levels in the management hierarchy multiply, and jobs become more interrelated.

Stages of Evolution

As both age and size increase, another phenomenon becomes evident: the prolonged growth that I have termed the evolutionary period. Most growing organizations do not expand for two years and then retreat for one year; rather, those that survive a crisis usually enjoy four to eight years of continuous growth without a major economic setback or severe internal disruption. The term *evolution* seems appropriate for describing these quieter periods because only modest adjustments appear necessary for maintaining growth under the same overall pattern of management.

Stages of Revolution

Smooth evolution is not inevitable; it cannot be assumed that organization growth is linear. *Fortune*'s "500" list, for example, has had significant turnover during the last 50 years. Thus we find evidence from numerous case histories which reveals periods of substantial turbulence spaced between smoother periods of evolution.

I have termed these turbulent times the periods of revolution because they typically exhibit a serious upheaval of management practices. Traditional management practices, which were appropriate for a smaller size and earlier time, are brought under scrutiny by frustrated top managers and disillusioned lower-level managers. During such periods of crisis, a number of companies fail—those unable to abandon past practices and effect major organization changes are likely either to fold or to level off in their growth rates.

The critical task for management in each revolutionary period is to find a new set of organization practices that will become the basis for managing the next period of evolutionary growth. Interestingly enough, these new practices eventually sow their own seeds of decay and lead to another period of revolution. Companies therefore experience the irony of seeing a major solution in one time period become a major problem at a later date.

Growth Rate of the Industry

The speed at which an organization experiences phases of evolution and revolution is closely related to the market environment of its industry. For example, a company in a rapidly expanding market will have to add employees rapidly; hence, the need for new organization structures to accommodate large staff increases is accelerated. While evolutionary periods tend to be relatively short in fast-growing industries, much longer evolutionary periods occur in mature or slowly growing industries.

Evolution can also be prolonged, and revolutions delayed, when profits come easily. For instance, companies that make grievous errors in a rewarding industry can still look good on their profit and loss statements; thus they can avoid a change in management practices for a longer period. The aerospace industry in its infancy is an example. Yet revolutionary periods still occur, as one did in aerospace when profit opportunities began to dry up. Revolutions seem to be much more severe and difficult to resolve when the market environment is poor.

Phases of Growth

With the foregoing framework in mind, let us now examine in depth the five specific phases of evolution and revolution. As shown in Exhibit 2, each evolutionary period is characterized by the dominant *management style* used to achieve growth, while each revolutionary period is characterized by the dominant *management problem*

Exhibit 2
The Five Phases of Growth

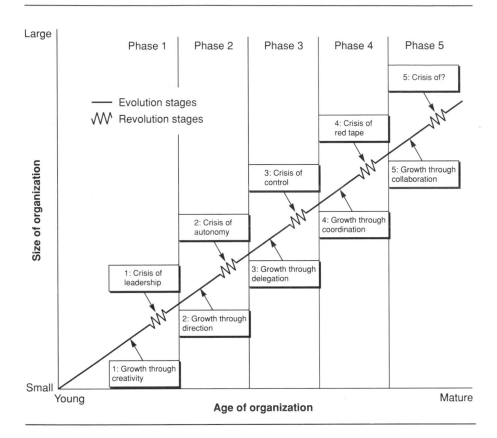

that must be solved before growth can continue. The patterns presented in Exhibit 2 seem to be typical for companies in industries with moderate growth over a long time period; companies in faster-growing industries tend to experience all five phases more rapidly, while those in slower-growing industries encounter only two or three phases over many years.

It is important to note that *each phase is both an effect of the previous phase and a cause for the next phase.* For example, the evolutionary management style in Phase 3 of the exhibit is "delegation," which grows out of, and becomes the solution to, demands for greater "autonomy" in the preceding Phase 2 revolution. The style of delegation used in Phase 3, however, eventually provokes a major revolutionary crisis that is characterized by attempts to regain control over the diversity created through increased delegation.

The principal implication of each phase is that management actions are narrowly prescribed if growth is to occur. For example, a company experiencing an autonomy crisis in Phase 2 cannot return to directive management for a solution—it must adopt a new style of delegation in order to move ahead.

Phase 1: Creativity

In the birth stage of an organization, the emphasis is on creating both a product and a market. Here are the characteristics of the period of creative evolution:

The company's founders are usually technically or entrepreneurially oriented, and they disdain management activities; their physical and mental energies are absorbed entirely in making and selling a new product.

Communication among employees is frequent and informal.

Long hours of work are rewarded by modest salaries and the promise of ownership benefits.

Control of activities comes from immediate marketplace feedback; the management acts as the customers react.

The Leadership Crisis.   All of the foregoing individualistic and creative activities are essential for the company to get off the ground. But therein lies the problem. As the company grows, larger production runs require knowledge about the efficiencies of manufacturing. Increased numbers of employees cannot be managed exclusively through informal communication; new employees are not motivated by an intense dedication to the product or organization. Additional capital must be secured, and new accounting procedures are needed for financial control.

Thus the founders find themselves burdened with unwanted management responsibilities. So they long for the "good old days," still trying to act as they did in the past. And conflicts between the harried leaders grow more intense.

At this point a crisis of leadership occurs, which is the onset of the first revolution. Who is to lead the company out of confusion and solve the managerial problems confronting it? Quite obviously, a strong manager is needed who has the necessary knowledge and skill to introduce new business techniques. But this is easier said than done. The founders often hate to step aside even though they are probably temperamentally unsuited to be managers. So here is the first critical developmental choice—to locate and install a strong business manager who is acceptable to the founders and who can pull the organization together.

Phase 2: Direction

Those companies that survive the first phase by installing a capable business manager usually embark on a period of sustained growth under able and directive leadership. Here are the characteristics of this evolutionary period:

A functional organization structure is introduced to separate manufacturing from marketing activities, and job assignments become more specialized.

Accounting systems for inventory and purchasing are introduced.

Incentives, budgets, and work standards are adopted.

Communication becomes more formal and impersonal as a hierarchy of titles and positions builds.

The new manager and his key supervisors take most of the responsibility for instituting direction, while lower-level supervisors are treated more as functional specialists than as autonomous, decision-making managers.

The Autonomy Crisis.   Although the new directive techniques channel employee energy more efficiently into growth, they eventually become inappropriate for controlling a larger, more diverse and complex organization. Lower-level employees find themselves restricted by a cumbersome and centralized hierarchy. They have come to possess more direct knowledge about markets and machinery than do the leaders at the top; consequently, they feel torn between following procedures and taking initiative on their own.

Thus the second revolution is imminent as a crisis develops from demands for greater autonomy on the part of lower-level managers. The solution adopted by most companies is to move toward greater delegation. Yet it is difficult for top managers who were previously successful at being directive to give up responsibility. Moreover, lower-level managers are not accustomed to making decisions for themselves. As a result, numerous companies flounder during this revolutionary period, adhering to centralized methods while lower-level employees grow more disenchanted and leave the organization.

Phase 3: Delegation

The next era of growth evolves from the successful application of a decentralized organization structure. It exhibits these characteristics:

Much greater responsibility is given to the managers of plants and market territories.

Profit centers and bonuses are used to stimulate motivation.

The top executives at headquarters restrain themselves to managing by exception, based on periodic reports from the field.

Management often concentrates on making new acquisitions which can be lined up beside other decentralized units.

Communication from the top is infrequent, usually by correspondence, telephone, or brief visits to field locations.

The delegation stage proves useful for gaining expansion through heightened motivation at lower levels. Decentralized managers with greater authority and incentive are able to penetrate larger markets, respond faster to customers, and develop new products.

The Control Crisis. A serious problem eventually evolves, however, as top executives sense that they are losing control over a highly diversified field operation. Autonomous field managers prefer to run their own shows without coordinating plans, money, technology, and manpower with the rest of the organization. Freedom breeds a parochial attitude.

Hence, the Phase 3 revolution is under way when top management seeks to regain control over the total company. Some top managements attempt a return to centralized management, which usually fails because of the vast scope of operations. Those companies that move ahead find a new solution in the use of special coordination techniques.

Phase 4: Coordination

During this phase, the evolutionary period is characterized by the use of formal systems for achieving greater coordination and by top executives taking responsibility for the initiation and administration of these new systems. For example:

Decentralized units are merged into product groups.

Formal planning procedures are established and intensively reviewed.

Numerous staff personnel are hired and located at headquarters to initiate companywide programs of control and review for line managers.

Capital expenditures are carefully weighed and parceled out across the organization.

Each product group is treated as an investment center where return on invested capital is an important criterion used in allocating funds.

Certain technical functions, such as data processing, are centralized at headquarters, while daily operating decisions remain decentralized.

Stock options and companywide profit sharing are used to encourage identity with the firm as a whole.

All of these new coordination systems prove useful for achieving growth through more efficient allocation of a company's limited resources. They prompt field managers to look beyond the needs of their local units. While these managers still have much decision-making responsibility, they learn to justify their actions more carefully to a "watchdog" audience at headquarters.

The Red-Tape Crisis. But a lack of confidence gradually builds between line and staff, and between headquarters and the field. The proliferation of systems and programs begins to exceed its utility; a red-tape crisis is created. Line managers, for example, increasingly resent heavy staff direction from those who are not familiar with local conditions. Staff people, on the other hand, complain about uncooperative and uninformed line managers. Together, both groups criticize the bureaucratic paper system that has evolved. Procedures take precedence over problem solving, and innovation is dampened. In short, the organization has become too large and complex to be managed through formal programs and rigid systems. The Phase 4 revolution is under way.

Phase 5: Collaboration

The last observable phase in previous studies emphasizes strong interpersonal collaboration in an attempt to overcome the red-tape crisis. Where Phase 4 was managed more through formal systems and procedures, Phase 5 emphasizes greater spontaneity in management action through teams and the skillful confrontation of interpersonal differences. Social control and self-discipline take over from formal control. This transition is especially difficult for those experts who created the old systems as well as those line managers who relied on formal methods for answers.

The Phase 5 evolution, then, builds around a more flexible and behavioral approach to management. Here are its characteristics:

The focus is on solving problems quickly through team action.

Teams are combined across functions for task group activity.

Headquarters staff experts are reduced in number, reassigned, and combined in interdisciplinary teams to consult with, not to direct, field units.

A matrix-type structure is frequently used to assemble the right teams for the appropriate problems.

Previous formal systems are simplified and combined into single multipurpose systems.

Conferences of key managers are held frequently to focus on major problem issues.

Educational programs are utilized to train managers in behavioral skills for achieving better teamwork and conflict resolution.

Real-time information systems are integrated into daily decision making.

Economic rewards are geared more to team performance than to individual achievement.

Experiments in new practices are encouraged throughout the organization.

The ? Crisis.   What will be the revolution in response to this stage of evolution? Many large U.S. companies are now in the Phase 5 evolutionary stage, so the answers are critical. While there is little clear evidence, I imagine the revolution will center around the "psychological saturation" of employees who grow emotionally and physically exhausted by the intensity of teamwork and the heavy pressure for innovative situations.

My hunch is that the Phase 5 revolution will be solved through new structures and programs that allow employees to periodically rest, reflect, and revitalize themselves. We may even see companies with dual organization structures: a "habit" structure for getting the daily work done, and a "reflective" structure for stimulating perspective and personal enrichment. Employees could then move back and forth between the two structures as their energies are dissipated and refueled.

One European organization has implemented just such a structure. Five reflective groups have been established outside the regular structure for the purpose of continuously evaluating five task activities basic to the organization. They report directly to the managing director, although their reports are made public throughout the organization. Membership in each group includes all levels and functions, and employees are rotated through these groups on a six-month basis.

Other concrete examples now in practice include providing sabbaticals for employees, moving managers in and out of "hot spot" jobs, establishing a four-day workweek, assuring job security, building physical facilities for relaxation *during* the working day, making jobs more interchangeable, creating an extra team on the assembly line so that one team is always off for reeducation, and switching to longer vacations and more flexible working hours.

The Chinese practice of requiring executives to spend time periodically on lower-level jobs may also be worth a nonideological evaluation. For too long, U.S. management has assumed that career progress should be equated with an upward path toward title, salary, and power. Could it be that some vice presidents of marketing might just long for, and even benefit from, temporary duty in the field sales organization?

Implications of History

Let me now summarize some important implications for practicing managers. First, the main features of this discussion are depicted in Exhibit 3, which shows the specific management actions that characterize each growth phase. These actions are also the solutions which ended each preceding revolutionary period.

In one sense, I hope that many readers will react to my model by calling it obvious and natural for depicting the growth of an organization. To me this type of reaction is a useful test of the model's validity.

But at a more reflective level I imagine some of these reactions are more hindsight than foresight. Those experienced managers who have been through a developmental sequence can empathize with it now, but how did they react when in the middle of the stage of evolution or revolution? They can probably recall the limits of their own developmental understanding at that time. Perhaps they resisted desirable changes or were even swept emotionally into a revolution without being able to propose constructive solutions. So let me offer some explicit guidelines for managers of growing organizations to keep in mind.

1. *Know where you are in the developmental sequence.* Every organization and its component parts are at different stages of development. The task of top management is to be aware of these stages; otherwise, it may not recognize when the time for change has come, or it may act to impose the wrong solution.

Exhibit 3
Organization Practices during Evolution in the Five Phases of Growth

Category	Phase 1	Phase 2	Phase 3	Phase 4	Phase 5
Management focus	Make and sell	Efficiency of operations	Expansion of market	Consolidation of organization	Problem solving and innovation
Organization structure	Informal	Centralized and functional	Decentralized and geographical	Line-staff and product groups	Matrix of teams
Top management style	Individualistic and entrepreneurial	Directive	Delegative	Watchdog	Participative
Control system	Market results	Standards and cost centers	Reports and profit centers	Plans and investment centers	Mutual goal setting
Management reward emphasis	Ownership	Salary and merit increases	Individual bonus	Profit sharing and stock options	Team bonus

Top leaders should be ready to work with the flow of the tide rather than against it; yet they should be cautious, since it is tempting to skip phases out of impatience. Each phase results in certain strengths and learning experiences in the organization that will be essential for success in subsequent phases. A child prodigy, for example, may be able to read like a teenager, but he cannot behave like one until he ages through a sequence of experiences.

I also doubt that managers can or should act to avoid revolutions. Rather, these periods of tension provide the pressure, ideas, and awareness that afford a platform for change and the introduction of new practices.

2. *Recognize the limited range of solutions.* In each revolutionary stage it becomes evident that this stage can be ended only by certain specific solutions; moreover, these solutions are different from those which were applied to the problems of the preceding revolution. Too often it is tempting to choose solutions that were tried before, which makes it impossible for a new phase of growth to evolve.

Management must be prepared to dismantle current structures before the revolutionary stage becomes too turbulent. Top managers, realizing that their own managerial styles are no longer appropriate, may even have to take themselves out of leadership positions. A good Phase 2 managers facing Phase 3 might be wise to find another Phase 2 organization that better fits his talents, either outside the company or with one of its newer subsidiaries.

Finally, evolution is not an automatic affair; it is a contest for survival. To move ahead, companies must consciously introduce planned structures that not only are solutions to a current crisis but also are fitted to the *next* phase of growth. This requires considerable self-awareness on the part of top management, as well as great interpersonal skill in persuading other managers that change is needed.

3. *Realize that solutions breed new problems.* Managers often fail to realize that organizational solutions create problems for the future (i.e., a decision to delegate eventually causes a problem of control). Historical actions are very much determinants of what happens to the company at a much later date.

An awareness of this effect should help managers to evaluate company problems with greater historical understanding instead of "pinning the blame" on a current development. Better yet, managers should be in a position to *predict* future problems, and thereby to prepare solutions and coping strategies before a revolution gets out of hand.

A management that is aware of the problems ahead could well decide *not* to grow. Top managers may, for instance, prefer to retain the informal practices of a small company, knowing that this way of life is inherent in the organization's limited size, not in their congenial personalities. If they choose to grow, they may do themselves out of a job and way of life they enjoy.

And what about the managements of very large organizations? Can they find new solutions for continued phases of evolution? Or are they reaching a stage where the government will act to break them up because they are too large?

Concluding Note

Clearly, there is still much to learn about processes of development in organizations. The phases outlined here are only five in number and are still only approximations. Researchers are just beginning to study the specific developmental problems of structure, control, rewards, and management style in different industries and in a variety of cultures.

One should not, however, wait for conclusive evidence before educating managers to think and act from a developmental perspective. The critical dimension of time has been missing for too long from our management theories and practices. The intriguing paradox is that by learning more about history we may do a better job in the future.

Reading 8–2

Problems of Human Resource Management in Rapidly Growing Companies*

John P. Kotter, Vijay Sathe

Rapid growth companies—that is, companies that grow at an average rate greater than 20 percent per year (in number of employees) for at least four or five years in a row—are of considerable importance to managers, investors, and the public at large. They offer managers an exciting place to work and significant career advancement opportunities. It is not uncommon to find young managers in top spots in these companies. They offer the investor the chance for a much greater than average financial return. It boggles the mind to think how much money was made by those who bought large blocks of IBM, Polaroid, or Xerox stock around 1950. And rapid growth companies offer the public at large a significant source of expanding employment. Just a few rapidly growing companies in the same geographic region can sometimes make the difference between a stagnant economy with high unemployment and a robust economy with low unemployment.

Those interested in rapid-growth companies would agree that most of them share a common key to their success—their high rate of growth is sustained by virtue of their position of leadership in a rapidly expanding product/market area. This leadership position is typically achieved and maintained via the aggressive marketing of new and technically sophisticated goods or services. Through good fortune or shrewd calculation, these companies tend to be at the right place, at the right time, with the right set of capabilities.

People interested in rapid-growth companies seem to be much less aware of the

*© 1979 by The Regents of the University of California. Reprinted from *California Management Review* 21, no. 2 (Winter 1978), pp. 29–36. By permission of The Regents.

fact that most of these firms share at least one other important pattern in common. These companies tend to experience similar human resource problems.[1] These problems are important because the way in which managers deal with them typically determines whether or not the company will be able to sustain its rapid growth over time.

In this article we will first identify the common problems that seem to plague rapid-growth companies, and then discuss solutions that some of the more successful ones have used to deal with them. This article is based on our experiences with 12 companies that have grown on the average of 40 percent per year for five or more years.

Problems Caused by the Need for Rapid Decisions

The president of one rapidly growing firm told us the following story, which highlights one of the problems created by rapid growth:

> I was having lunch with an acquaintance of mine who is the president of a company that is about twice our current size. His firm has been growing at between 5 and 7 percent per year for the last 10 years. I was telling him about some of the decisions I had made during the previous two weeks and some of the decisions I had to make in the upcoming week. At one point he stopped me and said something like—"You know, you make as many important business decisions in a month as I do in a year." And while he may be exaggerating a bit, I think he's basically right. Since we grow at about 5 percent per month, I end up making decisions in a month that he gets nearly a year to make.

The speed with which decisions must be made in rapid-growth companies puts a strain on managers that many people simply cannot cope with. Many of us intellectually and emotionally need more time to make decisions that is available in such situations. We need time to get relevant information, to analyze that information, to identify alternative decisions, and to select a decision. Especially when the decision stakes are high, many people need time to emotionally come to grips with their intellectual choice. For some managers, this needed time runs into months or even years.

The required decision-making speed in rapid-growth companies also places the organizational structure under stress. The need for quick new-product design, development, manufacturing, and marketing decisions, which is characteristic of these companies, requires a rapid flow of information across departmental lines and close cross-functional coordination. The traditional functional structure is not designed to cope with these requirements. It is best equipped to handle a more stable set of tasks. When it is small, a rapidly growing company can achieve the necessary cross-functional coordination because of the flexibility afforded by its small size.

---

[1] Two recent articles deal with some of this subject. One is based on a study of five small (100–200 employees) but rapidly growing firms: George Strauss, "Adolescence in Organizational Growth," *Organizational Dynamics* (Spring 1974). The other is based on the experience of one rapidly growing firm: William George, "Task Teams for Rapid Growth," *Harvard Business Review*, (March–April 1977).

As it grows, however, the traditional functional structure will start to cause problems for a rapid-growth company. Decisions will begin to "fall between the cracks." Decisions will not be made. And certain activities will get "bogged down" because the structure cannot cope with the rapidly changing environment.

The need for rapid decisions has a similar impact on informal structure and culture. The informal relationships among individuals and groups in organizations almost always include some distrust, suspicion, bad feelings, and misunderstandings. All of these factors impede smooth information flow, effective collaboration, and rapid decision making. When a company is small, these relationships can be managed so as not to undermine effective decision making. But growth makes such management more difficult because the number of relationships to be managed increases more rapidly than the number of employees.

Problems Caused by Rapidly Expanding Job Demands

Similar organization positions in companies of very different size obviously place quite different demands on the incumbents. The job of the chief financial officer in a $10 million company, for example, is significantly different from that of the person holding the same position in a $150 million company. Internal reporting and control, data processing, financial planning, annual budgeting, and internal auditing all would probably be a significant part of the responsibilities of the chief financial officer of the larger company. Most, if not all, of these functions would probably be absent in the smaller company. Since a rapid-growth company's annual sales could grow from $10 million to $150 million in just a few years, the chief financial officer's job in such a company could change dramatically in a relatively short time period. Some people can adjust to such a change. Many cannot.

Peter Drucker has said that one of the biggest impediments to successful growth is the inability of key managers to change their attitudes and behavior to fit the changing needs of the organization.[2] And while Drucker is talking about all growth situations, we believe this is especially true in high-growth situations.

The problem of people not being able to change as rapidly as their jobs typically creates two more problems. First, it often leads to a shouting match between various levels of management regarding questions of delegation and development. For example:

> **A middle-level manager:** The biggest problem we have in this company is top management's unwillingness to delegate more. My boss is still making the same kinds of decisions in the same ways he did five years ago. But the company today is three times as large as it was then. He should be doing other things today and delegating many of those decisions to me.

> **A top manager:** Our biggest problem today is somehow getting middle management to the point where they can handle their ever-increasing responsibilities. I'm still making some decisions that I should not be making. But I have no qualified person beneath me to whom I can delegate those decisions.

---

[2]Peter Drucker, *The Practice of Management* (New York: Harper & Row, 1954), pp. 246–252.

> **A middle-level manager:** Top management says that we are not ready to handle more delegation. But how are we ever going to get ready if they don't allow us to make some of those decisions. Sure we would probably make a few errors, but we would learn a lot in the process.
>
> **A top manager:** We can't afford mistakes around here. We cannot take chances with the record of success we have had here.

People's inability to grow and change as quickly as their jobs creates a second problem related to unmet career expectations. Managers often join rapid-growth companies for the advancement opportunities. But many of these companies find it necessary to fill between 10 and 50 percent of their nonentry-level openings from the outside because people with the necessary experience are not being developed as rapidly as needed within the company. When an ambitious person sees numerous higher-level jobs filled from the outside, he or she often becomes frustrated.

Finally, people's inability to grow with job demands can place key managers in difficult, guilt-eliciting positions. The following story has been repeated to us in varying forms literally dozens of times:

> Jerry was my fourth employee. I hired him in 1966 to be my first full-time salesman. He worked long hours for us and got two key contracts that saved the company in 1967.
>
> When we hired our seventh salesman, I made Jerry sales manager. And in 1971, I made him vice president for sales. Today, in 1977, we have revenues of 25 million on a yearly basis, the marketing department has nearly 100 employees, and Jerry is way over his head.
>
> In retrospect, I should never have made him vice president of sales in 1971. But he expected the title change since I had just made my engineering manager the vice president of engineering. And I didn't want to hurt his feelings or make him think I didn't fully appreciate the loyalty and long hours he had given the company.
>
> Today his inability to manage his department is hurting us severely, but I have delayed moving him for months. I know I have to act soon. But god, it's hard. I really think that as much as I love my wife, throwing her out of the house would not be as emotionally demanding.

Problems Caused by Large Recruiting and Training Demands

Perhaps the most obvious problems faced by fast-growing companies are recruiting and training. Fast growth requires the recruitment, selection, and assimilation of large numbers of people. And for most rapidly growing companies, satisfying this need at an affordable cost is difficult.

The slow-growing company in a mature industry can often satisfy its hiring needs by waiting for the right people to walk in the door. It can satisfy its assimilation needs by osmosis; the relatively few new people learn the ropes from those they interact with.

Rapidly growing companies, however, cannot rely on such a passive stance.

Such firms often have to hire 5 to 10 times as many people each year as do slow-growing companies of equal size. They are forced to aggressively seek out possible employees. Because they are often in new industries or have new products or services, they may need somewhat atypical combinations of talents, which makes recruiting even more difficult. As a result, the typical high-growth company spends considerable time and energy in recruitment and selection of new employees, but is still unable to hire people as quickly as required. A personnel officer in one such company told us:

> I go through a hundred resumes a day. So do other people here, including some line managers. Our whole department is constantly involved in recruiting and hiring. And that's not necessarily good, because we neglect other duties like training and organizational development activities. But even though we are so focused on just recruiting, we still do not bring people in as quickly as many of our line managers want. To get the kind of engineers we need, for example, it usually takes us six months. In the company I worked for 10 years ago, which wasn't growing very fast at all, six months for hiring was fine. Here it's not. Our engineering vice president says the strain we put on his department by hiring so slowly is enormous.

Assimilating and training new employees is equally difficult in rapid-growth firms. Unlike the situation in a slow-growth company, the new employees are seldom put in a group where they are surrounded by "old-timers" who can informally teach them the job, the company's goals and values, and the structure and procedures. It is quite possible that the average seniority of the people they interact with is a year or less. This situation can cause a number of problems, such as those described by one company president:

> Our new recruits out of college can sometimes get lost in here. We had one last year that nearly cost us a $100,000 order because he was not trained or being supervised closely.
>
> The people we hire with 10 to 20 years of prior experience can cause another type of problem. They bring with them a whole set of ideas about corporate goals, personnel philosophy, how to do things, and the like, which sometimes are quite different from our own. In their cases, we not only have to teach them our ways, we have to get them to unlearn what we consider "bad habits."

The difficulty of achieving quick assimilation is particularly important because of its crucial role in rapidly growing companies. When only 2 or 3 percent of the employees are relatively new, it really doesn't matter much if they are not fully on board for six months to a year. However, when 20 to 50 percent of the employees are relatively new, how quickly they get on board matters a great deal.

Problems Caused by Constant Change

"Change is inevitable in a situation like ours," one president of a rapidly growing company told us, "and it's a fact of life we just have to learn to accept and live with. But that's easier said than done."

Rapid-growth situations tend to be full of uncertainty and ambiguity caused by constantly changing employees, job demands, structures, systems, products, and markets. And uncertainty can create problems. It is not possible, for example, to do career planning, as in a more stable and certain environment. It is very difficult to devise clear rules and procedures to help guide people's actions. Some individuals like this type of an environment, but many do not. If there are too many employees of the latter type in a high-growth situation, the strain they feel will affect organizational performance.

Constant change also means perpetual loss of the familiar, including aspects of it that were valued, and the constant need for readjustment. Psychological research shows that loss and readjustment cause stress, even on people who like change because of the challenge or the material rewards associated with it. And stress, beyond a point, creates its own problems. As one executive in a rapid growth firm told us: "Lots of people around here are on edge. The stress sometimes shows in their work, and in their marriages. The divorce rate in our management group is considerably above the national average."

Finally, change usually creates the need for even more change to keep the organization in balance. Increased revenues require more employees, which requires more recruiting and training. Increased size eventually requires new systems to be developed, which often requires more specialists to be hired and trained. And all of these activities consume resources, which tend to be scarce in high-growth situations.

Problems Caused by a Constant Strain on Resources

Rarely are high-grown companies such a "sure bet" in the long run that investors are willing to run up operating losses in the short run. As such, the stockholders or the corporate management of these companies typically expect them to turn in at least a modest profit every year. But profit generation can be incredibly difficult, for two major reasons. First, because of constant change, these companies cannot realize the efficiencies that are possible in more stable situations. Second, rapid-growth firms typically have to plan for and operate in business environments that are always larger than their current financial resources. As the controller of one company so aptly put it:

> We are currently doing planning and development as if we were a $100 million-a-year company, which we will be in two years. In terms of sales orders and manufacturing capacity, we are operating like a $50 million-a-year company. But the money we are putting in the bank as a result of deliveries is equivalent to yearly sales of about $35 million.

Financial analysts are familiar with this paradox—companies experiencing a substantial revenue growth are frequently cash starved. What is often overlooked, however, is that the simultaneous strain on the company's human resources is often equally or more severe.

It is not uncommon for managers and professionals in high-growth companies to complain of being "burned out," and of being unfairly compensated relative to their contributions:

> We never have enough people. Everybody works 60 to 80 hours a week. After a while it really gets to you, especially since the pay isn't that great.

> I joined the company in 1973, which means I've been here for 10 years! [From an interview in 1977.]

> My wife keeps asking me why I haven't gotten much larger bonuses. Given my contribution to the company and its success, she has a good point.

The relentless resource strain also means that people do not have the time to do anything but what is required immediately. Important activities that are not cloaked in urgency tend to fall by the wayside. Thus, the tasks of assimilation, training, and development of the ever-growing numbers of employees typically receive the short shrift from line managers who are constantly preoccupied with more pressing matters. These tasks also are often ignored by personnel people who are fully occupied with the more urgent demands of recruitment and hiring, and with routine but necessary functions such as employee benefits and payroll. Tasks associated with the design and implementation of new information, control, and operating systems are also easily ignored. And planning of all types gets neglected.

Interaction Effects

The problems already described are difficult in themselves. If unattended, however, these problems can interact to produce a vicious circle in which the situation can get completely out of hand (see Exhibit 1). The following detailed case history illustrates what can happen:

> Three years ago a company we are familiar with was highly effective and growing rapidly. The ability of the professional and managerial employees and the flexibility possible because of its small size enabled the firm to develop and market new products rapidly. As the company grew, so did the job demands. Some people grew with their jobs, but others began to strain under the ever-growing number of responsibilities. Most, however, were satisfied and highly motivated because the company was achieving its objectives in ways that could clearly be related to their own efforts. There was a personnel manager but no formal human resource function. However, human resource problems were generally handled effectively on a personal basis by top management.

> As the company's growth continued, a point was reached at which there was a clear need for considerable human resource development activity. Although many persons were being promoted, an equally large number were being brought in from the outside to fill high-level openings. Those not promoted were skeptical when told they were passed over because they lacked the necessary experience. They felt they deserved a chance and could learn quickly if given the opportunity. Top managers, however, were unwilling to take chances with those who, in their opinion, were not yet ready for promotion. At one point consideration was given to establishing a human resource function to aid in the assimilation of the ever-growing number of newcomers and to help in the training and career development

Exhibit 1
The Consequences of Unattended Human Resource Problems in Rapid-Growth Companies

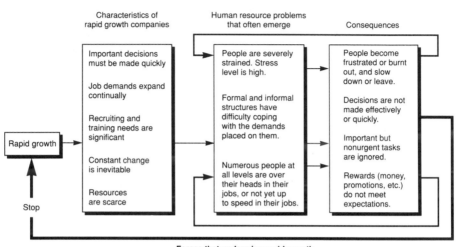

Forces that undermine rapid growth

of all employees, particularly those not promoted. Given the demands on the company's resources that this entailed, however, the plan was "temporarily" shelved.

The situation remained as described for about one year. Those affected waited to see what action management would take. When it appeared that there would be no major change in the handling of these problems, some employees that management considered to be valuable but unpromotable began to leave. Others wondered why they were putting in such long hours without any promotion. They began to cut back their contribution to a level they perceived as equitable with the recognition and rewards received.

The turnover and diminution of effort predictably hurt the company's performance and resulted in a greater strain on its financial and human resources. The high turnover meant that even more people had to be hired from the outside. This, in turn, led to further problems of assimilation, on the one hand, and more frustration for those not receiving promotion, on the other. Turnover continued to increase, and performance fell dramatically. The company was trapped in a vicious circle.

Today this firm's rate of growth has dropped to 12 percent per year. Profitability remains poor. Morale is low. Competition has moved in, and the initial momentum has been lost. A new president has taken over recently and is in the process of deciding how best to get the company fired up again.

Solutions

Successful rapid-growth companies we know rely on some or all of the following solutions to cope with the problems we have described.

Recruiting, Selection, and Training.   Despite the short-run problems created, the more successful rapid-growth companies tend to be very selective in their hiring. They screen large numbers of people, sometimes hundreds for each opening, in order to hire a large percentage of people who (*a*) can perform the job without a great deal of training—as a result, they do not hire large numbers of people right out of college; (*b*) have obvious potential for growth, (*c*) like volatile environments; (*d*) are willing to work long hours; (*e*) are flexible; (*f*) have philosophies and personalities consistent with the company "culture."

To keep the cost of finding these types of people within bounds, a number of firms actively encourage their employees to do informal recruiting and screening whenever they can. As one human resource person told us: "You can always spot our people at cocktail parties. They will have some guy pinned in the corner while they get information about him or while they try to sell him on the company."

To help get these new people assimilated, the more successful rapid-growth firms often hold one- to three-day orientation sessions. These sessions are typically run by line executives—not staff personnel people—who outline the company's history, philosophy, strategy, structure, and compensation system. In one firm, the chief executive officer plays a central role in these sessions.[3]

Team or Matrix Structures, and Team Building.   After they have reached a certain size, most successful rapid-growth companies adopt an organizational structure that relies heavily on teams or a matrix.[4] Unlike most traditional structures, these types of organizational arrangements are capable of successfully handling a volatile, rapid decision-making environment.

Team and matrix structures can be difficult to implement, however. They completely undermine the "authority must equal responsibility" dictum that most managers follow. The resulting ambiguity can be frustrating and difficult to live with. This is probably why some rapid-growth companies try to do without these structures despite the fact that they are needed.

To help make their team or matrix structure work, successful rapid-growth companies usually rely on team-building activities.[5] With the aid of outside consultants or experts within their human resource department, they periodically have managers in natural work teams (which might involve people within or across departments) go away from the firm for a few days to clear up any problems that are hampering the group's effectiveness. Team-building activities help members maintain good working relationships despite the ambiguity inherent in the

---

[3]For a more detailed description of this type of orientation session, see John P. Kotter, "The Psychological Contract: Managing the Joining Up Process," *California Management Review* (Spring 1973), pp. 91–99.

[4]See George, "Adolescence"; and William Goggin, "How the Multidimensional Structure Works at Dow Corning," *Harvard Business Review* (January–February 1974).

[5]For a further description of team building, see Shel Davis, "Building More Effective Teams," *Innovations* (1970), pp. 32–41.

organizational structure and assist in increasing a work team's ability to make effective decisions quickly.

Managing the Culture.   All of the more successful rapid-growth companies we have encountered emphasize the importance of creating and maintaining a certain type of informal company culture. The characteristics of this culture include a shared belief in openness, a shared sense of what the company is and where it is going, a clearly perceived commitment to employee welfare, and norms supporting flexibility and change.

To help keep information flowing efficiently and accurately, an atmosphere of open doors, unlocked desks, and approachability is usually encouraged. "We want no secrets around here," one person told us, "and we work hard to convince people that we mean it."

People we have talked to sometimes refer to their company's "philosophy" or their company's "religion." To create this shared sense of goals and values, one firm spent considerable time and energy communicating a new corporate strategy to virtually all employees. The president of another firm had actually written a paper, which was widely circulated in the firm, on the company's philosophy. Such a shared vision, he believes, helps bind people together and helps coordinate their actions without the need for more formal rules, procedures, and structures.

The employees in the successful rapid-growth companies we know of generally believed that the company really cared about its people. As one person put it: "One of the reasons I've worked as hard as I have and feel as strongly as I do about the company is because I know it really cares about me and others." This belief is created through many different kinds of actions. In two of these firms, job openings are always posted, and insiders are always considered before hiring someone from the outside. In another company, people are given time off whenever the long hours seem to be affecting them physically.

Finally, the culture in these companies tends to be supportive of flexibility and change. This is fostered by the words and deeds of top people. One CEO, for example, has told groups of employees on numerous occasions that he is not sure he will be the right person for the CEO job in four to five years: "If I'm not, so be it. I'll find a more appropriate replacement for myself and try to contribute here in some other way."

Planning.   Successful rapid-growth companies manage to find the time to do organizational and human resource planning. Being aware of the potential problems described in this article, their leaders periodically look into the future and modify current decisions if they see important problems developing. They recognize that change is inevitable and try to plan for it. They work to project human resource needs so as to keep staffing demands consistent with available resources.

This type of planning activity does not have to be time consuming. The key to its success is largely attitudinal; that is, if managers understand the problems of rapid growth and anticipate their potential negative impact, they can devise various means of overcoming them.

Organizing and Staffing the "Personnel" Function. Because of the potential severity of human resource problems in rapid-growth firms, the more successful companies generally have a full-time, formally designated human resource function. The less successful ones seem to resist this. Instead, they cling to the more traditional role of the personnel function—recruitment, hiring, fringe benefits, and so forth.

Even when quite small ($30 million per year in revenues for manufacturing firms), successful rapid-growth companies typically have a head of human resources who is unusually talented and well paid in light of the company's size. This person generally reports directly to the president and often has a very close informal relationship with the president. Because of this relationship and the person's own competence, the human resource function is perceived as powerful and important in these companies.

In many of the more successful firms, the human resource function is also staffed below the director with a very capable group of people. Organizationally, these people are often deployed such that each of the other departments in the company has one or more human resource personnel assigned to it. Each of these staff people then works closely with the assigned department to recruit and train people, to run team-building sessions, to help manage the culture, to plan, and to help people both understand and adjust to the inevitable stresses and strains.

Being Sensitive and Tough at the Top. The top managers of successful rapid-growth companies tend to be unusually sensitive to human resource problems and are willing to deal with them with toughness if necessary.

Without a high level of sensitivity to potential organizational and human resource problems, top management will tend either to ignore them or to relegate them to a low order of priority. And toughness is needed to deal with tasks that can be unusually unpleasant. An example is the frequent need to replace or reassign individuals (including those at the very highest levels) whose jobs have outgrown them. Another example is the willingness to do battle with a corporate management group that may be unfamiliar with, and hence insensitive to, the special challenges and needs of human resource management in a rapidly growing company.

One of the more impressive examples of sensitivity and toughness we have seen was when a CEO replaced himself, long before retirement, with an outsider. He sensed that he was no longer appropriate for the job and that no one who reported to him could handle it then or in the foreseeable future. So he hired an outsider and explained his actions at length to a number of disappointed insiders.

There is no question that it takes a very capable group of people, and one that can absorb a lot of physical and emotional strain, to manage a high-growth company successfully. To maintain its record of success, the management of such a company needs to understand, anticipate, and overcome the problems described in this article. An awareness of the solutions used by companies that have successfully sustained high growth over long periods of time should help in devising remedies that best fit a particular situation.

Reading 8–3

How to Decipher and Change Organizational Culture*

Vijay Sathe

Two basic arguments are presented here. First, behavior change does not necessarily produce culture change. Second, managers can benefit by taking this into account when conceiving and implementing organizational change. The following topics will be covered in this discussion:

1. Definition of culture.
2. How to decipher culture.
3. How to influence culture change.
4. How to know if the attempted culture change is occurring.
5. The alternatives to major culture change.

Accounts from the experiences of several companies and managers who have succeeded or failed in creating culture change will be presented for purposes of illustration. In addition, the case of Cummins Engine Company and its operating head, Jim Henderson, will be used to provide one in-depth illustration of successful culture change.[1] It describes how Jim Henderson, chief operating officer of Cummins Engine Company, managed a difficult inventory situation in the mid-1970s, and succeeded eventually in modifying the company's management culture.

---

*Excerpted from R. H. Kilman and Associates, *Managing Corporate Cultures* (San Francisco: Jossey-Bass, 1985). Reprinted by permission.

[1]A detailed written account of this case, along with two companion video tapes, has been published elsewhere (Browne, Vancil, and Sathe, 1982).

Definition of Culture

There are many definitions of culture (Kroeber and Kluckhohn, 1952). Early authors (e.g., Taylor, 1871) defined culture rather broadly to include knowledge, belief, art, law, morals, and customs. Two major schools in cultural anthropology have influenced later work. The view of culture favored by the "adaptationists" is based on what is directly observable about the members of a community—that is, their patterns of behavior, speech, and use of material objects. The "ideational school" prefers, in defining culture, to look at what is shared in the community members' *minds*—that is, the belief, values, and other ideas people share in common (Keesing, 1974; Swartz and Jordan, 1980).

This is one reason the subject is confusing: Different people think of different slices of reality when they talk about culture. To integrate various views of culture, Edgar Schein (1983) has proposed a three-level model that we will adapt for use here.[2]

The first level of culture is composed of technology, art, audible and visible behavior patterns, and other aspects of culture that are easy to see but hard to interpret without an understanding of the other levels. This is the slice of cultural reality that the adaptationists have been most interested in. We will denote this level by the term *organizational behavior patterns, or behavior*.

The second level of culture reveals how people explain, rationalize, and justify what they say and do as a community, how they "make sense" of the first level of culture. We will denote this level with the term *justifications of behavior*.

The third level of culture goes deeper still and is the level that the ideational school has been most interested in. It consists of people's ideas and assumptions that govern their justifications and behavior. We will denote this level by the term *culture*, which we will define specifically as *the set of important assumptions (often unstated) that members of a community share in common*. Two basic types of assumptions are people's beliefs and values—not what they *say* their beliefs and values are or those they will comply with because of the demands of others, but those beliefs and values they consider to be their own, that is, those they have *internalized*. People may not become conscious of these held true beliefs and values until they are violated or challenged and even then will resist changing them (Bem,

---

[2]This conceptualization is based on the model proposed by Schein (1983), but two points should be noted. First, Schein uses the term *values* to denote espoused values, whereas the terms *beliefs* and *values* are used here to denote those assumptions that people actually hold, that is, the ones they have internalized (Bem, 1970; Rokeach, 1968). Second, Schein focuses on preconscious and unconscious assumptions because these are powerful and people may not even become aware of them until they are violated or challenged. Such assumptions are hard to discover and debate because they are taken for granted. Conscious assumptions have also been included in the definition of culture used here because although these are easier to detect and debate, they too have a strong influence on behavior and are hard to change. People do not easily give up internalized beliefs and values, whether consciously or unconsciously held (Bem, 1970; Rokeach, 1968), as opposed to beliefs and values that they merely espouse or comply with (Kelman, 1958).

1970; Kelman, 1958; Rokeach, 1968). Thus, the effects of culture defined in this way are not only subtle and powerful but persistent as well.

This definition does not imply that the other two levels of culture are unimportant. Rather, the levels are interrelated but sufficiently distinct so that combining them is not analytically advantageous (Geertz, 1973). Managers are interested in how people behave as well as in what they believe, but we know a lot more about how to create behavior change (Beer, 1980; Schein, 1980) than we do about how to create belief change. We will see that behavior change does not necessarily produce belief change, in part because of the intervening level of justification of behavior. These processes cannot be understood and managed if all three levels are included under the culture label. Organizational insight and analytical power are to be gained by using different terms for each level and examining all three levels. Let us now take a closer look at this definition of culture by examining two of its major elements—content and strength.

The content of a culture influences the *direction* of behavior. Content is determined not by an aggregate of assumptions but by how the important ones interrelate and form particular patterns. From the variety of beliefs and values that the people in a community may hold, the important assumptions are those that are widely enough shared and highly enough placed relative to other assumptions in the community so as to be of major significance to the life of the community. A key feature of the pattern of a culture is the *ordering* of its cultural assumptions, which indicates their relative importance.

As Schein (1983) has explained, the content of a culture ultimately derives from two principal sources: (1) the pattern of assumptions that founders, leaders, and organizational employees bring with them when they join the organization (which in turn depends on their own experience in the culture of the regional, national, ethnic, occupational, or professional community from which these people come) and (2) the actual experience that people in the organization have had in working out solutions for coping with the basic problems of adaptation to the external environment and internal integration. In short, the content of culture derives from a combination of prior assumptions and new learning experiences.

The strength of a culture influences the *intensity* of behavior. Three specific features of culture determine its strength: *thickness* (how many important assumptions there are), *extent of sharing* (how widely they are shared in the organization), and *clarity of ordering* (how clearly some are more important than others). The stronger cultures are thicker, more widely shared, and more clearly ordered and consequently have a more profound influence on organizational behavior. Such cultures are also more highly resistant to change.

What makes some cultures stronger than others? Two important factors are the number of employees in the organization and their geographical dispersion. A smaller work force and more localized operations facilitate the growth of a stronger culture because it is easier for beliefs and values to develop and become widely shared. But larger organizations with worldwide operations, such as IBM, can also have strong cultures that derive from a continuity of strong leadership which has consistently emphasized the same beliefs and values, as well as a relatively stable and longer-tenured work force. Under these conditions, a consistent set of enduring beliefs and values can take hold over time and become widely shared and clearly ordered.

Deciphering a Culture

The internalized beliefs and values that members of a community share in common cannot be measured easily or observed directly. Neither can one simply rely on what people say about it in order to decipher a culture. Other evidence, *both historical and current*, must be taken into account to infer what the culture is.

The managers at Cummins seemed to share five important assumptions, ordered as follows:

1. Provide highly responsive, quality customer service.
2. Get things done well and quickly ("expediting").
3. Operate informally without systems.
4. Top management will tell us what to do if there is a problem.
5. The company is part of the family.

The procedure used to decipher this culture is now presented.

Inferring the Content of Culture

Each important shared assumption may be inferred from one or more manifestations of culture, that is, the shared things, shared sayings, shared doings, and shared feelings one experiences in the organization. The aim is to discover a pattern of important assumptions that help "make sense" of the cultural manifestations. The challenge is to ensure that the "making sense" is from the point of view of the "natives," that is, those whose culture is being deciphered (Swartz and Jordan, 1980). With this in mind, three basic questions may be explored to infer the content of culture from its manifestations:

1. What is the background of the founders and others who followed them? An understanding of the background and personality of the founders and others who helped mold the culture offers important clues about the content of culture. For example, Irwin Miller, who had led Cummins for over 30 years, strongly believed in community service and in "rooting out bureaucratic behavior," which led to two important cultural assumptions (the company is part of the family, and operate informally without systems). Also, most of the Cummins employees came from the local community, and many were from families whose members had previously or currently worked at the company, further reinforcing the cultural belief that the company was part of the family.

2. How did the organization respond to crisis or other critical events? What was the learning from these experiences? Since culture evolves and is learned, focusing on stressful periods of an organization's history can provide two types of important clues to help decipher culture. First, this may reveal how particular assumptions came to be formed. For example, the inventory crisis at Cummins ultimately caused the belief in operating informally without systems to get transformed into a new belief in using systems to do the routine work and relying on informal operation to expedite. Second, by focusing on such periods in history, particularly those that were traumatic for the organization, one also has the opportunity to discover the *ordering* of the cultural assumptions, which is hard to decipher because such assumptions may not ordinarily conflict with each other. The organization may be forced to choose between two important assumptions during a stressful period.

For example, although Cummins did not like to lay people off, it did so during periodic downturns. This suggests that the first four cultural assumptions, which were not affected by these traumatic events, were more important than an assumption which was violated to some extent—Assumption 5 (the company is part of the family). Similarly, the 1974 inventory crisis brought Assumptions 3 and 4 into conflict with Assumptions 1 and 2. Since the former were questioned and were eventually modified but the latter were not, Assumptions 1 and 2 must be considered more central than Assumptions 3 and 4.

The people at Cummins had so thoroughly bought into the values of (1) highly responsive, quality customer service and (2) expediting behavior, that these ideals had become more than strategic objectives and operational directives. They had become taken-for-granted, shared assumptions that were a central part of the Cummins management culture. These assumptions were never questioned by the managers at Cummins, even during times of stress such as the economic downturn and the inventory crisis. Indeed, the purchasing managers went so far as to *ignore* higher management directives and ordered extra parts because they believed customer service would otherwise be adversely affected.

3. Who are considered deviant in the culture? How does the organization respond to them? In a sense, deviants represent and define a culture's boundaries. An understanding of who and what is considered deviant in a culture helps in deciphering it. For instance, Cummins hired lots of M.B.A.s from among the brightest and the best in the early 1960s, many of whom didn't make it in the company. Those that survived were culturally compatible. Many of those who disappeared were deviants—people who believed in systems and procedures, and those who believed their talent and professional education gave them special status in the company ("I am a hot-shot M.B.A.; I'll teach these guys how to do it right"). These people violated important cultural assumptions (expedite, operate informally without systems, the company is part of the family) which are revealed by trying to understand why these people were rejected by the culture.

A cultural assumption may be so consistently adhered to and taken for granted

Exhibit 1
How Culture Perpetuates Itself

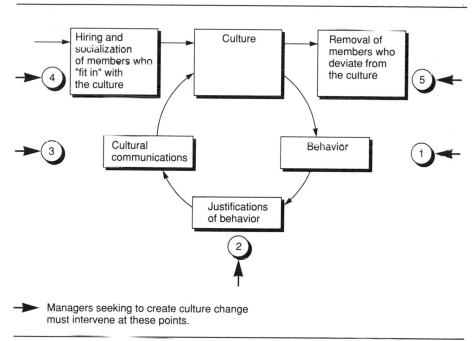

Managers seeking to create culture change
must intervene at these points.

that almost no one ever violates it. Such an assumption may be particularly hard to discover. Its centrality and power may only be revealed on those rare occasions when someone knowingly or inadvertently violates it, incurring the wrath and fury of the entire community. An example of such an assumption in academia is intellectual integrity. A recent case in point is the disbelief and heated controversy surrounding the chairman of medicine of a prestigious school, who has been accused of plagiarism ("Stanford," 1984). Much can be learned about a culture by looking for such infrequent but critical incidents that deeply offend the people in the community. There is no indication of such a critical incident at Cummins.

How to Influence Culture Change

Managers interested in producing culture change must understand and intervene in each of the basic processes that cause culture to perpetuate itself (Exhibit 1). There are two basic approaches for effecting a desired culture change; (*a*) getting people in the organization to buy into a new pattern of beliefs and values, (Processes 1, 2, and 3) and (*b*) adding and socializing people into the organization and removing people from the organization as appropriate (Processes 4 and 5). Let us consider each of these processes in turn.

Behavior

The process by which culture influences behavior is consistent with the conventional wisdom—that is, that beliefs and values influence behavior (Process 1, Exhibit 1). However, the opposite is also true. A considerable body of social science literature indicates that *under certain conditions* (to be discussed shortly), one of the most effective ways of changing people's beliefs and values is to first change their corresponding behavior. The general techniques for creating behavior change are well covered in the existing management literature (Beer, 1980; Schein, 1980), but these methods must be used more restrictively if culture change is to be produced. As elaborated below, the motivation to change behavior must be based on intrinsic motivators rather than relying exclusively, or even excessively, on extrinsic forms. For example, consider the experience of one company and its chief executive officer Matt Holt:

> Buffeted by shifting market forces and management turnover, the corporate business strategy had lacked coherent direction. Matt Holt's mandate was to take a longer-term view of the business and to create a technology-driven organization. Analysis conducted with the help of outside consultants indicated that a "cultural meta-morphosis" was needed to accomplish this. A reorganization followed, including changes in the measurement and reward system to "encourage the required behavior."
>
> Matt realized there would be a "wait and see" period while people tried to figure out "whether they really mean it." He knew that his "true intentions" would be judged on the basis of what he did, not just what he said. Accordingly, he tried to ensure that the management systems inspected and rewarded the required behavior, and he conducted his own affairs (that is, use of his time, visits, "pats on the back") to reinforce and support what the new formal systems were signaling. Two years later, there had been some improvements. People appeared to be "doing the right things," allocating their time and resources as prescribed by the new systems. Missing, however, was the missionary zeal, the sense of commitment and excitement that Matt had hoped to inject into the life of the company as people came to identify with and share his vision of the mission.

Some behavior change had occurred here, but no culture change. The problem was the heavy reliance on extrinsic motivation, as explained below.

Justifications of Behavior

Behavior change does not *necessarily* produce culture change, because of the intervening process of justification of behavior (Process 2, Exhibit 1). This is what happened in the case of Matt Holt. People were behaving as called for by the new formal systems, but they continued to share the old beliefs and values in common and "explained" their new behavior to themselves by noting the external justifications for it (Aronson, 1976; Bem, 1970)—for example, "We are doing it because it is required of us," and "We are doing it because of the incentives." There was behavior compliance, not culture commitment. In a very real sense, people in this case were behaving the way they were because they felt they had no choice, not because they fundamentally believed in it or valued it.

Thus, one reason culture perpetuates itself is that even if behavior is changed (Process 1, Exhibit 1), people tend to rationalize it in terms of external justifications (Process 2) and continue to adhere to the prevailing pattern of beliefs and values. Managers attempting to create culture change must remain alert to this danger and try to counteract it by using each of the following three approaches.

The first recommendation, which may appear counterintuitive, is to minimize the opportunity for external justification by inducing the appropriate behavior change with a *minimal* use of rewards, punishments, and other *extrinsic* forms of motivation (Aronson, 1976, pp. 109–17). This doesn't "feel right" at first for many of us who have become used to offering incentives to get what we want. However, others are likely to be going along just for the incentives rather than because they fundamentally believe in what we are asking them to do. This is exactly what happened in the case of Matt Holt. In contrast, Jim Henderson at Cummins offered no financial incentives and relied minimally on other extrinsic motivators (principally some unannounced plant visits to draw attention to the inventory problem in order to produce the desired behavior). This approach took time and exposed him to personal risk and criticism from his superiors, Irwin Miller and Don Tull, for not acting more forcefully to solve the growing inventory crisis. Henderson understood that the recommended "strong measures" would indeed solve the short-term inventory problem but would not help bring about the new culture he was seeking to create in which his managers would take more personal responsibility for the problem (rather than waiting for directives from the top) and introduce and use the systems required to prevent its periodic recurrence.

The second recommendation follows from the first: To the extent possible, the necessary behavior change should be induced by using *intrinsic* forms of motivation. Essentially, this means that one must get people to see the inherent worth of what it is they are being asked to do. As Schein (1973) has explained, one way to do this is to persuade people to unlearn or question their current pattern of beliefs and values by helping them to see that their assumptions either are not confirmed by reality testing or are actually disconfirmed. This lack of confirmation, or disconfirmation, which is typically accompanied by pain, guilt, anxiety, and lack of self-confidence, provides the necessary intrinsic motivation to learn the new behavior. Matt Holt, for instance, did very little in this area. In contrast, the weekly inventory meetings that Henderson instituted at Cummins provided a forum for joint exploration that led people to see the value of the new approach he was advocating.

Some use of extrinsic motivators may be unavoidable. A third approach, then, that managers interested in producing culture change must use is to *nullify inappropriate rationalizations* of the new behavior. A somewhat drastic technique for doing this is to give people an "out"—those who do not "buy into" the new pattern of beliefs and values may be given the option to leave or transfer to a different organization. If it is perceived as a feasible and a real option, giving people the opportunity to leave can be a powerful tool in producing culture change, not only because it weeds out those who are unlikely to buy into the new pattern of beliefs and values (Process 5, Exhibit 1) but also because those left behind will find it more difficult to come up with inappropriate rationalizations—the perception of choice helps build commitment (Salancik, 1977). This technique is somewhat risky in that some valued people may choose to leave before one has had a chance to convert them. However, such people tend to be marketable and may leave anyway if they feel coerced.

Another technique is to attempt to directly nullify inappropriate rationalizations. Matt Holt made no attempt to do so. In contrast, Jim Henderson helped remove the inappropriate rationalizations used by his subordinates at Cummins ("Why change? Those above will tell us what to do," and "The guy at the top will act sooner or later to get us out of this crisis.") He did so by demonstrating that he was going to operate differently from the way Don Tull had managed the Cummins operations over the past 30 years. Henderson was not going to issue orders in the old way to quickly fix the problem, even if this meant that the inventory problem would worsen and thereby expose him to personal risk and criticism from above for not acting decisively according to the proven methodology.

Managers engaged in culture change must also communicate the new pattern of beliefs and values and get people to adopt them. Let us now turn to this process.

Cultural Communications

Culture is communicated via both implicit and explicit forms (Process 3, Exhibit 1). The former include rituals, customs, ceremonies, stories, metaphors, special language, folklore, heroes, logos, decor, dress, and other symbolic forms of expression and communication (Pondy, Frost, Morgan, and Dandridge, 1983). Examples of the latter are announcements, pronouncements, memos, and other explicit forms of expression and communication. Both forms must be relied on to persuade people to adopt the new cultural beliefs and values.

If the new pattern of beliefs and values in question is more intrinsically appealing to the people in the organization than is the prevailing pattern, the main problem in getting their adoption is the credibility of the communication, as in much political campaign rhetoric ("I like what I am hearing, but is this what the communicator really believes?"). However, if the new pattern of beliefs and values being communicated is *less* intrinsically appealing to the audience than is the prevailing pattern, as it was in the cases of both Matt Holt and Jim Henderson, credible communications about the new pattern of beliefs and values result in their being believed to be true intentions rather than mere corporate propaganda (for example, "I think management is really serious about this"). But this doesn't mean the new pattern will be adopted. The audience may remain aware of the new beliefs and values, and even comply with them, without internalizing them. Let us consider each of these processes in turn.

Credible Communication of New Beliefs and Values. This is a difficult task; explicit communications by managers of the new beliefs and values that they hope the people in their organization will buy into, such as "We believe people are our most important asset," may fall on deaf ears or be seen as mere corporate propaganda. How can communications be made more credible?

First, backing up words with deeds gains credibility, especially for individuals who in the past have consistently lived by what they said. A leader who has lost his or her reputation for credibility cannot reestablish it immediately. A considerable period of demonstrated consistency between the communicator's espoused beliefs and actual behavior must elapse before explicit communications are accepted as true intentions rather than mere fluff.

Second, communications tend to be accepted with less skepticism when they are not apparently espousing something that is in the communicator's self-interest. Explicit communications about new beliefs and values are more credible if their advocates apparently stand to lose in some meaningful way if the organization adopts these beliefs and values, or when they entail significant personal sacrifice for the proponents.

Given these difficulties and limitations of explicit communication, two indirect means exist to get across a new pattern of beliefs and values so that they seem credible. One is to spread the word by more informal means of communication, including reliance on neutral intermediaries (especially those who formerly had been cynical). This is because people receive communications less skeptically when they don't feel that the communicators are *trying* to persuade them (Aronson, 1976). Second, research shows that communications are not only more memorable but also more believable when implicit forms, such as telling stories and anecdotes from company history or individual experience, are used to communicate intended beliefs and values (Martin, 1982).

Why are stories more credible? Essentially, it is their concreteness, as well as the fact that the moral of the story is not explicitly stated. The listener draws his or her own conclusions, and is more likely to believe them. The problem with such communications is that a different moral may be inferred than the one intended. One way to guard against this danger is to pick stories which minimize the potential for misinterpretation. Ultimately, however, the way to increase the credibility of communications is to ensure that they are backed by consistent action that is in keeping with the intended beliefs and values. Both Matt Holt and Jim Henderson did a good job in this area.

Internalization of New Beliefs and Values. If they are credibly communicated, a new pattern of beliefs and values that is more intrinsically appealing than the present pattern will be accepted and eventually internalized. However, to the extent that the new pattern of beliefs and values is *less* intrinsically appealing—that is, perceived as "alien" by the people in question—communications about them must be not only emphatic and credible but persuasive as well. Such "culture persuasion" cannot rely on statistics and other facts alone, for alien beliefs and values are not neccssarily accepted and internalized on the basis of hard evidence. (McMurry, 1963, p. 139; Pfeffer, 1981, p. 325). This was the challenge that both Matt Holt and Jim Henderson faced.

There are two basic approaches for getting people to accept and eventually internalize new beliefs and values, especially alien ones: identification and "Try it, you'll like it."

The first approach relies on the audience's identification with one or more persons who credibly communicate their attachment or conversion to the pattern of beliefs and values in question. Such a person could be the manager directing the culture change, or it could be anyone else whom the audience not only believes but *identifies with*. Here is one example:

> In a company with a long tradition of authoritarian management, a new CEO with a strong belief in participative management was having a great deal of difficulty getting managers to do more than go through the motions. One of the senior executives from the "old school," who was widely respected and admired as a company folk hero who would never say or do anything he didn't really believe in, then began to come around. As word of his conversion spread informally, others began to change their beliefs. It got to the point that his "idol's" department became a model of the intended culture. The belief in participative management began to seep to the rest of the company and gradually became more widely shared.

There was no indication that this mechanism was at work in the case of either Matt Holt or Jim Henderson. The following account of how the "folk hero" just mentioned came to change his belief in participatory management in the first place indicates the second approach (try it you'll like it) to getting the acceptance and eventual internalization of new beliefs and values, especially alien ones:

> He began to try the approach being advocated because he was a company loyalist who had an even stronger value: "I owe the new boss a fair shake." He was skeptical at first, but then came a few fairly dramatic changes having to do with the improved morale of certain valued but difficult employees, changes that he attributed to the new philosophy. Gradually, he changed his mind about participative management. Advocacy followed, and eventually he became a "culture champion."

If people can be persuaded to give it a fair chance and they like the experience that they attribute to it, they may buy into the new beliefs and values being advocated. This is the approach that Jim Henderson used successfully at Cummins. As mentioned previously and as illustrated by contrasting the cases of Matt Holt and Jim Henderson, such persuasion to try the new behavior must not rely too heavily on financial and other extrinsic forms of motivation; otherwise the incentives may serve as external justification for the new behavior and may produce no changes in the prevailing beliefs and values. This is especially important when the beliefs and values in question are alien. Where the intrinsic appeal of the beliefs and values in question is greater, one can rely more on extrinsic motivators to induce the new behavior without increasing the risk of inappropriate rationalizations. Furthermore, both appeals and challenges can be effective tools in getting people to "give it a try" without heavy reliance on extrinsic motivators and their attendant risk of external justification.

In the case just cited, the value of participative management was not intrinsically appealing to the folk hero, but he decided to give it a try because the appeal was to his higher value (I owe the new boss a fair shake). A more general form of this appeal is to ask people to "give it a try" in more tentative, exploratory, and relatively nonthreatening ways, like "Let us try it as an experiment" or "Let us try it; we can always go back if it doesn't work." Another general form of appeal is to show people that the proposed changes are really nothing new ("We have done it before, it is part of our heritage"). One may also be able to get people to try the new behavior without heavy reliance on incentives by challenging them to do so.

Hiring and Socializing Newcomers and Removing Deviants

A final set of processes that are important to consider if culture change is being attempted is (1) the hiring and socialization of newcomers to fit into the intended culture and (2) the weeding out and removal of existing members who do not (Processes 4 and 5, Exhibit 1). Neither of these processes was relied on to any great extent in the cases of Matt Holt and Jim Henderson.

Changes in the *content* of culture (in the number of important shared beliefs and values and the way they are ordered) require appropriate changes in administrative philosophy––changes in human resource management policies and practices that alter the "breed" of people hired and socialized into the company as well as those who are removed.

Strength of culture is increased by adhering to a consistent philosophy to guide human resource management policies and practices over time. Keeping down the rate at which people are brought in and turned over also strengthens the culture. With a more stable work force, there is greater opportunity for the beliefs and values to become more clearly ordered and widely shared.

There is a limit to how rapidly culture can be changed by adding, socializing, and removing people from the organization. It is difficult to effectively assimilate a large member of new people in a short period of time. A large influx of people can also lead to political infighting, ploys, and counterploys in the organization as people jockey for position, especially where large numbers of new people are brought in at higher levels.

How to Know if Culture Change Is Occurring?

If the prevailing culture is fairly open, as it was in the cases of both Matt Holt and Jim Henderson, it will be easier to see whether people are buying into the new beliefs and values. Where the culture is not so open, people may "put on the airs" that they feel they must, making the detection of culture change tricky. Consider the following situation:

> Over a period of three years, Winn Hughes, an innovative division general manager responsible for 2000 people and $200 million in annual revenues, attempted to create an "entrepreneurial division culture." Several new ventures were launched

by the division during this period, and one was highly successful. When Winn was promoted to a different part of the company, he felt he had left behind several promising ventures in the pipeline and, more important he felt, many "product champions." Within one year of his departure, however, he learned that all these ventures had "died in the tracks" or had been killed.

It *wasn't* the case that Winn's replacement had ordered these actions, nor even that his successor was antientrepreneurial. Instead, the new head, who called himself a "balanced asset and growth" manager, said he would fund deserving projects and starve others—it was up to the people who believed in their projects to stick their necks out for them. No one had come forward.

"Where are my product champions?" Winn asked himself with great disappointment when he heard about this. "They have disappeared into the woodwork!" he thought.

The real answer was that there never were any product champions in that division, which had witnessed three general managers in five years. Under Winn's predecessor, a cost-cutting "hatchet man," these managers played the cost and efficiency game. During Winn's tenure, they played the entrepreneurial game. And under Winn's successor, the "balanced" DGM who they perceived was an asset manager deep down, they played the "this year's return on investment" game. In short, these managers believed in playing the game that happened to be in town. That was their principal shared value, along with security consciousness and risk aversion—these were the underlying constants that explained these people's actions under three different general managers over a period of five years. Winn had been fooled because he mistook compliance for commitment.

Behavior change does not necessarily indicate a corresponding culture change, because the organization's leadership and systems (structure, measurements, controls, incentives, etc.) can effect behavior change without any culture change, as they did in the case of Matt Holt. It is also what happened in this case. Culture change can be positively inferred only if the new behavior can be attributed neither to the organization's leadership nor to its systems. A good test of culture change is whether the new behavior persists after the leadership that helped create the culture change leaves or after the systems used to create the culture change are further altered.

Although this is a good test of culture change, it is of little use to current leadership that wants to know if the culture change they are attempting to create is in fact taking hold. That is what Winn Hughes should have asked himself and, in retrospect, says he would have liked to have known. They are not foolproof, but three types of tests may be used to make some reasoned judgments about whether culture change is occurring:

1. Is There Evidence of Intrinsically Motivated Behavior? Would the new behavior persist if extrinsic motivators (administered by the organization's leadership and systems) were somewhat diminished? Winn could have eased off a bit on the bonuses and the public recognition he was giving product championing, to see how many were really committed to the concept. If this is deemed too risky a test ("Let's not mess with what is working well"), one can look for opportunities that impose greater demands on the organization to see if the people respond appropriately *without* a corresponding increase in the extrinsic motivators. In the case cited, the deadlines on two key projects had to be advanced a bit for competitive reasons. The managers involved argued that the new deadlines could not be met without additional resources, resources that were not forthcoming because of a budget crunch. They said they would do their best, but there was no indications that they were stretching themselves to try. No one was putting in longer hours, for example. Both the projects failed to meet the slightly advanced deadlines.

2. Is There Evidence of "Automatic Pilot" Behavior? If a crisis or a novel situation is encountered, do the people involved "automatically" do what seems to be appropriate in light of the desired culture without waiting for directions from the organization's leadership or prodding from the organization's systems? In Winn's case, one of the new ventures was an outdoor product that encountered unexpected breakage on the customers' equipment on one particularly cold winter night during its first year on the market. Rather than acting immediately and offering free replacements, the managers involved took 48 hours to "investigate the problem" and reached a decision only after consulting with Winn (who was on an overseas field trip and was difficult to reach), while irate customers waited. Winn was upset that they had waited to consult with him on this relatively straightforward issue but didn't probe further for the significance of this critical incident. Had they been product champions, these managers would have taken the modest personal risk of acting without the boss's input to do what had to be done.

3. Is There Evidence of "Countermandated" Behavior? Do people behave in ways that run counter to established cultural values and/or organizational directives but that make sense in light of the desired culture? There was no evidence of such behavior in Winn's division. For example, the managers involved might have bootlegged resources from other parts of the company (which would have been counter to the company culture) or ignored certain policy directives (for example, 20 percent of engineering time had to be devoted to research projects rather than development projects) in an attempt to meet the advanced project deadlines.

While it may be infeasible or inadvisable to conduct these tests as planned experiments to determine if culture change is in fact occurring, one can look for occasions and situations that offer the opportunity to learn from such "natural experiments" that provide tell-tale signs of culture change, or of lack thereof. Thus, with detective work and opportunistic testing, a manager can make reasoned judgments about whether culture change is occurring.

The Alternatives to Major Culture Change

Since major culture change is difficult to effect and generally takes a relatively long time to accomplish, why bother to create such change? Why not rely on the organization's leadership and systems instead to create the necessary changes in organizational behavior patterns?

The answer is that, under certain conditions, creating behavior change without culture change may not work at all or may work but at very high costs to the organization. The reason for this is that creating culture change in the organization is analogous to gaining the commitment of the individual. Just as it is possible to secure an individual's compliance without gaining his or her commitment, so also it is possible to secure behavior change without culture change and with essentially the same kinds of costs and risks, of which there are basically three types:

1. *Inefficiency:* The costs of monitoring behavior to secure compliance and the costs of rewards and punishments (administered via the organization's leadership and systems) required to sustain it. These costs rise sharply as the organization gets larger and geographically more dispersed, because monitoring and rewarding/punishing appropriate behavior becomes increasingly difficult. In contrast, these costs are much smaller when behavior change is accompanied by appropriate culture change, because the behavior is self-monitored and the rewards and punishments driving the behavior are at least partly self-administered.

2. *Insufficiency:* Compliance is often characterized by the "just enough" syndrome—people will do just enough to get by. Committed people, on the other hand, will put in the energy, time, and effort to do what needs to be done, not just what they are minimally required to do. Compliance can be a problem also, because the organization's leadership and systems can never fully anticipate every contingency that can arise. When something novel or unforeseen happens, the organization is at the mercy of the individual to do what is appropriate, which may be different from or even contrary to the specified behavior. Thus, where energy and commitment are critical and where novel or unplanned responses are frequently called for, behavior change without a corresponding culture change may be inadequate.

3. *Irrelevancy:* Finally, there are considerations which are simply not addressed by behavior change alone. These relate to mental processes, such as perception and thinking, which are only affected by culture change, not by behavior change. Where changes in such mental processes are an important aspect of the organizational changes being sought, behavior change by itself is not a viable option.

Unless the considerations mentioned above make it essential, a major culture change may not be worth the time, costs, and risks associated with it. Whenever possible, it makes sense to ask whether the desired results can be achieved without a major onslaught on the prevailing culture, especially a strong one. Indeed, this is one of the creative aspects of management. It is recommended that the following questions be seriously considered before embarking to radically transform a strong culture.

1. Can the Desired Results Be Obtained by Behavior Change without Culture Change? This is a particularly attractive option where only temporary changes in behavior are required to deal with a transient situation. It may also be a better alternative where the culture is weak, but appropriately so, because the business environment is unstable and requires abrupt changes in the organization's behavior patterns.

There are also times when the necessary behavior changes must be effected quickly and culture change is less critical. At Citibank in the early 70s, for instance, John Reed converted the operating group from a service-oriented "back office" to a "factory" in order to cope with the rising tide of paper (see Cases 7–1 and 7–2).

Reed had little time to spare and relied on a core group of managers with expertise in production management (many of them recruited from Ford Motor Co.), heavy use of extrinsic motivators (threats and punishments), as well as the removal of several middle managers to effect the required behavioral changes. Culture change did not follow, but this was not essential in this case, as evident from applying the three critical tests just mentioned. Inefficiency was not great, because all the people were located on two floors in one building and behavior compliance could be relatively easily monitored. Insufficiency was not a big problem, because the changes were toward a predictable, routine technology with little room for novelty or possibility of having to deal with the unexpected once the operations were debugged and running. Finally, irrelevancy was not a major consideration, because the important changes involved skills and behavior rather than perceptions and other mental processes.

2. Can the Desired Results Be Obtained by Creatively Utilizing the Existing Potential of the Prevailing Culture? Rather than viewing culture as something to be changed, one can look upon it with the frame of mind that says: "Culture is my friend. How can I rely on it to accomplish the desired ends?" For example, in a professional consulting group with a "Lone Ranger" culture (each on his or her own), several attempts to transform the group's culture into a more collaborative one failed. Finally, the business strategy and organization were reconceptualized as several "independent entrepreneurs," each with his or her own "fiefdom," in lieu of the failed attempts to get them to collaborate and dominate a preferred market segment. Results improved dramatically and were sustained for a longer period of time than ever before.

3. Can the Desired Results be Obtained by Utilizing the Latent Potential of the Prevailing Culture? Rather than look upon culture as something to be changed, one can ask: "What hidden part of this culture can I awaken to achieve the intended results?" If appropriate dormant values can be detected and activated (constituting an incremental rather than a radical change in culture's content, as explained earlier), the desired results may be more easily achieved. For example, the newly appointed head of a demoralized unit ("We are not as good as the competition") decided to challenge the group on what he correctly perceived to be their two hidden "hot buttons": values of self-confidence and pride in the group. The group responded tentatively at first, but these values were strengthened and reinstilled in the group as the new leader repeatedly showed the group how performance improved when these dormant values were adhered to.

In sum, an understanding of these approaches and methods can help managers decide how best to utilize the prevailing culture to the extent possible and how to transform it to the extent necessary to most effectively achieve the desired results.

References

Aronson, Elliot. *The Social Animal*. 2nd ed. San Francisco: W. H. Freeman, 1976.

Beer, Michael. *Organization Change and Development*. Santa Monica, Calif.: Goodyear Publishing, 1980.

Bem, Daryl J. *Beliefs, Attitudes, and Human Affairs*. Monterey, Calif.: Brooks/Cole Publishing, 1970.

Browne, Paul C., Richard F. Vancil, and Vijay Sathe. *Cummins Engine Company: Jim Henderson and the Phantom Plant*. Harvard Business School case 9–182–264, 1982. There are two videotapes accompanying the case: (*a*) "Managerial Philosophy, Personal Style, and Corporate Culture" (Videotape 9–880–001, 28 minutes) and (*b*) "The Phantom Plant" (Videotape 9–880–002, 14 minutes). Both videotapes and the case are available from Case Services, Harvard Business School, Boston, MA 02163.

Geertz, Clifford. *The Interpretation of Cultures*. New York: Basic Books, 1973.

Keesing, Roger M. "Theories of Culture." *Annual Review of Anthropology* 3 (1974), pp. 73–79.

Kelman, H. C. "Compliance, Identification, and Internalization: Three Processes of Attitude Change." *Conflict Resolution* 2 (1958), pp. 51–60.

Kroeber, A. K., and Clyde Kluckhohn. *Culture: A Critical Review of Concepts and Definitions*. New York: Vintage Books, 1952.

Louis, Meryl. "Surprise and Sense Making: What Newcomers Experience in Entering Unfamiliar Organizational Settings." *Administrative Science Quarterly*, June 1980, pp. 226–51.

Martin, Joanne. "Stories and Scripts in Organizational Settings." In *Cognitive Social Psychology*, eds. A. Hastorf and A. Isen, 1982.

McMurray, Robert N. "Conflicts in Human Values." *Harvard Business Review*, May–June 1963, pp. 131–32.

Pfeffer, Jeffrey. *Power in Organizations*. Marshfield, Mass.: Pitman, 1981.

Pondy, Louis R., Peter J. Frost, Gareth Morgan, and Thomas C. Dandridge, eds. *Organizational Symbolism*. Greenwich, Conn.: JAI Press, 1983.

Rokeach, Milton. *Beliefs, Attitudes, and Values*. San Francisco: Jossey-Bass, 1968.

Salancik, Gerald R. "Commitment Is Too Easy." *Organizational Dynamics*, Summer 1977, pp. 62–80.

Schein, Edgar H. *Organizational Psychology*. 3rd ed. Englewood Cliffs, N.J.: Prentice-Hall, 1980.

Schein, Edgar H. "Personal Change through Interpersonal Relationships." In *Interpersonal Dynamics*, eds. W. G. Bennis, D. E. Berlew, E. H. Schein, and F. L. Steele. Homewood, Ill.: Dorsey Press, 1973.

Schein, Edgar H. "Organizational Culture: A Dynamic Model." Working Paper No. 1412–83, Massachusetts Institute of Technology, February 1983.

Seeger, John A., Jay W. Lorsch, and Cyrus F. Gibson. *First National City Bank Operating Group (A) and (B)*. Cases 9–474–165 and 9–474–166, 1975, Case Services, Harvard Business School, Boston, Mass. 02163.

"Stanford Investigates Plagiarism Charges." *Science*. April 6, 1984, p. 35.

Swartz, Marc, and David Jordan. *Culture: An Anthropological Perspective*. New York: John Wiley & Sons, 1980.

Taylor, E. B. *Primitive Culture*. London: J. Murray, 1871.

PART SIX

Part Six consists of a case which integrates all the material presented in the previous text, cases, and readings. All of the concepts of organization design and development presented thus far must be utilized to design, develop, create, and maintain an organization which is both adaptive *and* effective.

The VeriFone Case presents the many, often conflicting dilemmas faced by leaders of dynamic organizations who must manage for short-term positive outcomes while managing for long-term effectiveness. These leaders must be able to use their understanding of the dynamics of organizational design and change to manage for the future.

VeriFone Case

Wendy Wanderman, Vijay Sathe, Sidney Harris

In November 1989, Hatim Tyabji reflected on the developments over the past three years since he took over as President and CEO of VeriFone, a leader in the rapidly emerging Transactions Automation industry. Much had been accomplished during this period to put the company in its commanding marketing position, but the 43 year old CEO was far from satisfied.

With the active involvement of this top management team (see Exhibit 1), Hatim envisioned VeriFone ". . . to become recognized as the creator *and* leader of the 'Fourth Wave of Computers'; placing computers into the hands of people who don't know they are using computers." The following passage was excerpted from a published corporate document. "Wherever transactions can be automated, there exist potential applications and markets for VeriFone products. With the proper economies of scale and cost structures, the company's base technology has virtually unlimited applicability. This is the essence of the Fourth Wave of Computing and its global applications."

In its Centennial Edition (June 23, 1989), *The Wall Street Journal* selected VeriFone as one of 56 "Corporate Stars of the Future . . . for their potential to bring vision and innovation to the marketplace of tomorrow." Also *Business Week* numbered VeriFone as one of 25 "High-Tech Startups to Watch" in its special June 1989 issue, "Innovation in America."

VeriFone's transaction systems could be found in most retail stores which accepted customer payment via credit cards. The Point-of-Sale (POS) "terminal" served as the vehicle by which transactions could be delivered, whether the transaction was a simple credit card authorization or an actual transfer of funds from the customer's bank account to the retailer's bank account. This "fourth wave computer" could be programmed to run many different transaction applications. In addition to the "CPU," a transaction system would include peripherals (printer, pin pad, bar code reader). The appropriate telecommunication capability was built into the CPU; in fact the ability to be certified on as many as 50 different networks was a major "perimeter of defense," largely responsible for the company's success.

VeriFone's original core market had been financial institutions, which provided electronic payment processing services to retailers. A bank would buy (in bulk)

This case was prepared by Wendy Wanderman, Ph.D. student, under the director of Professor Vijay Sathe, in collaboration with Professor Sidney Harris, as a basis for class discussion rather than to illustrate either effective or ineffective handling of an administrative situation. © 1990 by Vijay Sathe.

VeriFone's transaction systems, including the application software specific to its needs and then sell these systems to each of its retail accounts. As of 1989, 78 of the 100 largest banks in the U.S. were VeriFone customers. Transaction systems were also sold to oil and gas companies, and VeriFone now also dominated this market segment. Regardless of the distribution chain, the end users were the retail clerks and gas station attendants, people who were usually not computer literate.

Additional information on VeriFone's market is contained in Exhibit 5, which was excerpted from the company's document, *VeriFone: A Business Overview*.

Exhibit 1—Backgrounds of Corporate Officers

William Melton—Founder and Chairman of the Board, 47 years old. Bachelor of Arts (psychology—Westmar College), Master of Science (Asian Studies and Chinese Language and Philosophy—University of Hawaii). Founded the company in 1981. Prior to VeriFone, he founded Real Share Inc.

Hatim Tyabji—President, Chief Executive Officer, and Director, 43 years old. Bachelor of Science (Poona, India), Master of Science (SUNY), MBA (Syracuse), AMP (Stanford). Joined the company in his present position in November 1986. Prior experience included 13 years in management positions at Sperry Corporation. In his last position at Sperry, he was responsible for all research and development, product engineering, and manufacturing for commercial information systems.

F. Thomas Aden—Vice President and General Manager, International, 39 years old. Bachelor of Science (MIT). Joined the company in present position in October 1987. Prior experience included extensive experience in both domestic and international business, including sales management and product management positions with NBI, a major international supplier of office automation products.

Thomas Hubbs—Vice President, Finance, Chief Financial Officer, 45 years old. Bachelor of Science (business administration—Lehigh), MBA (Santa Clara). Joined VeriFone in present position January 1987. Prior experience included senior finance positions with several high-technology corporations.

Gregory Lewis—Vice President and General Manager, North America, 44 years old. Joined VeriFone in October 1984 to organize a sales function, promoted to current position in October 1987. Prior experience included 13 years in customer service, product management, sales and operations at National Data Corporation.

Ashok Narasimhan—Vice President, Market and Product Development, 41 years old. Bachelor of Science in physics (Madras, India), MBA (Indian Inst. of Mgmt.). Joined the company in December 1988 in present position. Prior experience included 18 years of financial and general management experience in the computer and

Exhibit 1 (Concluded)

automotive industries, and founder and president of Wipro Systems Limited, India's largest producer of commercial software.

Nason (Tuck) Newport –Vice President, New Business Development, 40 years old. Bachelor of Arts (Occidental), Master of Science (management—Stanford). Joined the company in November 1984, and headed the marketing effort before assuming his current position at the end of 1988. Prior experience in the areas of marketing, publishing, computer software development and politics, included six years as editor and publisher of the *Hawaii Observer*.

James Palmer—Vice President, Operations, 53 years old. Bachelor of Science (EE—Drexel). Joined the company in mid-1987, and headed both manufacturing and product development before assuming current position in December 1988. Prior experience included 25 years of technical, manufacturing and engineering management positions at Sperry Corporation.

William Pape—Vice President, Information Systems and Controls, Chief Information Officer, 37 years old. Bachelor of Arts (psychology—Stanford), Master of Arts (psychology & communications—Hawaii). Joined VeriFone in 1983 and was responsible for product development, software development, product marketing, prior to assuming his current duties in May 1988.

Clive Taylor—Vice President, Worldwide Marketing, 49 years old. Joined VeriFone in 1988 and is responsible for product management, product marketing, systems marketing, training and education, technical publications and corporate communications. Prior experience included 25 years of international marketing, sales, support and general management with Sperry Corporation and Unisys Corporation.

Genesis

VeriFone was founded in Honolulu, Hawaii in 1981 by William (Bill) Melton, an entrepreneur who had previously founded Real Share, Inc., a network service provided for TeleCheck check guarantee franchises throughout the United States and Puerto Rico. His original intention for VeriFone was to design and market a low cost, intelligent terminal system for the retail end of the credit card and check authorization pipeline.

Based upon his previous experience in Real Share and his educational background in psychology, Bill wanted to create VeriFone's culture in accordance with his belief that "a corporation's culture should reflect its type of product." Since VeriFone's transaction devices "forward deploy the intelligence from the mainframe to the point of transaction," a compatible culture would further deploy the corporate intelligence to offices located close to the customer. This decentralized structure continued to the present time and was a fundamental part of the Company's operations (modus operandi).

Bill felt that the technical specialist often knew more than his non-technical manager, but just as often the specialist's communication skills were inversely proportional to his or her technical abilities. These specialists were generally more comfortable 'talking' to a computer screen than having a face to face (or phone) conversation with another employee or with a customer. Bill saw the manager's role as that of a translator between the customer and the specialist; he or she could translate the customer's needs to the specialist who would then be able to provide the technical solution to meet those needs. In order to motivate the specialists, Bill determined that he must encourage trust and respect by aiding and supplementing their lack of communication skills and providing "ownership" over projects. Since the technical specialist comprised a large proportion of VeriFone employees, Bill was determined to develop an open, consultative culture. One early employee stated that there were literally no rules and policies at VeriFone because, "Bill had this habitual distaste for bureaucracy and structure."

In order to accommodate the dispersed nature of the organization and the communication skills (or lack thereof) of the technical specialists, electronic mail (E-mail) was installed at the company's formation and had continued to serve as the main communications tool.

The Early Years (1981–1984)

The company's first product was designed to perform only one function—obtain credit card authorization. It had limited intelligence, functionality and flexibility. The first systems, which were shipped in 1982, had a DOA (Dead on Arrival) rate of 50%! Fortunately, the competition's products were just as limited in functionality, and cost twice as much. The market for transaction devices looked promising, but was still in its infancy and had not yet attracted many entrants. These two factors allowed VeriFone to "hobble along" while it tried to resolve some of its design problems.

A major change in the design philosophy occurred in 1983 when William R. Pape joined the organization. Will had just returned to Hawaii following his successful formation of a software company which had produced Spellguard, the first spelling checker for microcomputers. VeriFone's terminal was one of the few high-tech projects in Honolulu at that time; that, combined with Bill's charisma, attracted a small group of bright entrepreneurial engineers and programmers to try and make the product viable. In 1983, Will described VeriFone as a "loose confederation of people working towards a goal."

Will's strong programming background and previous work with microcomputers convinced him that the intelligent and versatile attributes of the computer should be introduced into VeriFone's product. Prior to this time, the entire functionality of the terminal was "hard wired"; even small modifications entailed significant engineering and manufacturing changes. (This type of device was referred to as a dedicated controller.) The mass marketing of the microprocessor and memory chips

(ROMs and RAMs) in the early 1980s dramatically altered the architecture of many products, including VeriFone terminals. The philosophy of general purpose computers could not be applied to the design of these terminals—build a general purpose microcomputer and then develop specific applications (credit card authorization, electronic funds transfer, inventory management, etc.) as software programs to run on these computers. The ability to add to or modify existing functionality, as well as to fix "bugs," would then require a software rather than a hardware change. This significant shift in design philosophy proved to be one major factor in VeriFone's eventual success.

In an effort to provide quicker response to customer needs and in keeping with Bill Melton's philosophy of forward deployment of intelligence, the application programmers were separated from the operating system designers and moved into the sales offices, enabling them to work directly with their customers on specific applications. This also ensured that a specific need of one customer did not alter the "general purpose" nature of the unit's operating system, but rather would be solved within that customer's application software. Subsequent development of proprietary transaction automation software languages enabled even faster turnaround time on new and/or modified applications; these language tools were also available to customers who wished to develop their own software.

Another key contributor during the company's early years was Gregory (Greg) A. Lewis, currently Vice President and General Manager, North American Division. After working informally with Bill for several months, Greg formally joined VeriFone in early 1985, bringing with him 18 years of marketing and sales experience in the credit card and financial transaction industries. Greg had long been convinced of the viability of transaction automation devices; his particular dream was to have the ability to " . . . downline load the application software to terminals at the customer site, via telephone lines."

At this point in time, software changes could only be made by physical interaction with each terminal; either by replacing a memory chip or reprogramming the unit at the customer site. With banks (or service providers) having thousands of retail customer locations, physical interaction was obviously undesirable, and a major impediment to market growth. Greg was convinced that VeriFone had the ability to achieve his dream: "I really believed from what Will had told me that the software was going to be available to change the industry. The platform was already there." (Downline loading ability was accomplished in early 1986.)

When Greg first joined VeriFone, it was one million dollars in debt, had negative cash flow, had borrowed fifty thousand dollars against a VISA order for two hundred terminals and was several months behind in that delivery. Terminals were being manufactured (on credit) in Taiwan, but there was no money to send a VeriFone engineer to Taiwan to oversee the production. With the critical need to obtain orders, the company attended an ATM (Automated Teller Machine) show in New Orleans; this visibility, combined with Greg's extensive industry contacts, served as the catalyst for new orders. In just the last 60 days of 1984, close to one million dollars worth of orders were booked. Revenues that year were $3 million dollars.

New Products and Venture Capital

During 1985 VeriFone introduced their "Junior Terminal"; this smaller, cheaper and "smarter" device helped Verifone in its quest for greater marketshare. Omron, a Japanese company, and GTE were then the industry leaders. While at the end of 1984 VeriFone was either #12 or #13 in a field of 13 competitors, by the end of 1986 it had become the industry leader.

In early 1985, desperate for cash, Bill Melton realized that he had to seek financing with venture capitalists (VCs). He compared this to: " . . . taking that first drug needle; there is no turning back." Bill was grateful that he had been able to run the company without outside financing for its first four years. Because the company was "born and bred" in Hawaii, it had developed an informal, familiar culture very much in tune with the Hawaiian culture. Without interference from VCs and other outside investors, Bill was able to mold VeriFone in accordance with his own "social experimentation concepts." Bill felt that if the company had been started in the Silicon Valley, there would have been considerable pressure for VeriFone to fit the prescribed "formulas" of a typical high-tech, Silicon Valley company with respect to geographical dispersion, number of employees, travel budgets, etc.

The first external funds were provided by a British investor, John Porter, in early 1985. John was introduced to VeriFone by Tuck Newport (Exhibit 1), a fellow Sloan Program alumnus. John took an equity position and active managerial interest in VeriFone, and assumed some of Bill Melton's management responsibilities (Co-Chairman of the Board, and direct responsibilities for marketing and finance. Bill continued running development and manufacturing). John also used his extensive contacts to pursue larger and more long-term financing. He was able to persuade several blue chip Venture Capital firms to invest in late 1985—Kleiner, Perkins, Caufield and Byer, Technology Venture Investors, Sigma Associates, and Morganthaler.

To the experienced VCs (as well as Bill Melton, John Porter, and the key company staff), it was apparent that a successful product alone would not guarantee a successful company; thinly managed VeriFone required structured leadership and business controls to guide it toward a dominant position in the Transaction Automation industry. Thus began a search for a leader who could move VeriFone from a start-up firm (which had never made a profit) to a successful, profitable company. The investments in late 1985 were made with the understanding that a search for a President and CEO would be the first order of business. The investors also insisted that VeriFone move its headquarters from Hawaii to the San Francisco area in order to be closer to the Venture Capitalists, and the majority of its customers. (See Exhibits 2 and 3 for financial information.)

Hatim Tyabji Takes Charge

The CEO search began in early 1986. Several specialized search firms were asked to present viable candidates, with the proven ability to take a profitless start-up

Exhibit 2
Summary Financial Data: 1982–1989

	Actuals—$ millions							Est.
	1982	1983	1984	1985	1986	1987	1988	1989
Revenue	0.3	1.6	3.3	15.3	31.2	44.5	73.2	119.6
Operating Income	(0.1)	0.0	(0.8)	1.4	0.5	1.2	10.5	17.0
Net Income	(0.1)	0.0	(1.1)	0.9	0.1	0.1	6.4	10.0
Headcount	12	25	41	127	265	307	402	745
ROE	NA	NA	NA	19.5%	0.6%	0.7%	12.2%	16.6%
Total Assets				7.6	23.0	32.6	70.7	93.6

company (approximately 30 million dollars in revenue) and grow it to a profitable giant. Bill Melton recalled that he felt like a young bachelor knowing that it is the right time to marry, being presented with a list of suitable brides (many with excellent credentials), but none generating an emotional reaction. Nevertheless, Bill was determined to choose a "good bride" for his company.

While Bill and VeriFone's Board of Directors were looking for its CEO, TVI (one of VeriFone's investors), which also held equity positions in several other companies, was trying to interest Hatim Tyabji, a high-ranking executive at Sperry Corporation, to take a leadership position at one of these firms. Hatim's name had not appeared on VeriFone's list of "potential brides" because the nature of the two businesses (VeriFone and Sperry) were completely different (small, low-cost terminals vs. large, expensive mainframe computers; decentralized, loose management vs. centralized, bureaucratic management; etc.). One day in mid-1986, both Bill Melton and Hatim Tyabji were visiting the TVI offices. Bill (with the Board's approval) had just made his "bridal" selection; Hatim was there to discuss his future involvement with TVI. Bill and Hatim were introduced by Burton McMurtry, TVI's Managing Partner. Casual conversation between the two turned into more serious discussions; it was like "love at first sight," Bill recalled. He told Burt McMurtry to cancel the just agreed-upon "bride." Bill was determined that Hatim would become the next President and CEO of VeriFone. Although Hatim had an excellent position with Sperry, and was promoted again after the merger with Burroughs, he felt the bite of the "entrepreneurial bug" and wanted to take on the challenge. He joined VeriFone in November 1986.

Digging In

Hatim's background in product development, manufacturing, finance and general management proved to be invaluable as VeriFone's financial weaknesses and lack of systems and controls became apparent. Although, by the end of 1986, VeriFone's products had gained a reputation for quality and reliability, with almost 200,000

Exhibit 3
Income Statements and Balance Sheets: 1985–1989

	Years Ended December 31,				
	1985	1986	1987	1988	1989 (Est.)
	(in thousands, except per share data)				
Consolidated Statement of Income Data:					
Net revenues	$15,340	$31,226	$44,454	$73,421	$123,468
Costs and expenses:					
Cost of revenues	7,401	18,468	25,396	36,390	64,904
Research and development	1,176	3,568	5,933	6,669	12,934
Selling, general and administrative	5,381	8,786	12,335	20,842	31,299
Total costs and expenses	13,958	30,822	43,664	63,901	109,137
Income from operations	1,382	404	790	9,520	14,331
Interest income (expense), net	(475)	(382)	(647)	782	1,517
Income before income taxes	907	22	143	10,302	15,848
Provision for income taxes	43	2	37	3,915	5,788
Net income	$ 864	$ 20	$ 106	$ 6,387	$ 10,060
Net income per share	$.13	—	$.01	$.36	$.50
Common and common equivalent shares used in computing per share amounts	6,415	10,725	13,224	17,658	19,930

	December 31,				
	1985	1986	1987	1988	1989
	(in thousands)				
Consolidated Balance Sheet Data:					
Working capital	$ 3,705	$ 8,422	$14,697	$54,094	$49,878
Total assets	7,606	23,191	32,785	72,677	92,847
Long term debt and obligations under capital leases— noncurrent portion	198	596	91	34	1,216
Stockholders' equity	4,648	11,097	18,586	55,305	68,038

Exhibit 3 (Concluded)
Balance Sheet as of 9/30/89

VeriFone, Inc. Consolidated Balance Sheet (Actual to Plan)
as of September 29, 1989

	Actual	Plan	Variance
Assets:			
Cash	$ (414,231)	$ 813,000	$(1,227,231)
Investments—Other	1,616,735	4,000,000	(2,383,265)
Investments Preferred "D"	17,435,000	32,247,000	(14,812,000)
Accounts receivable	25,783,331	21,736,000	4,047,331
Allowance for doubtful accounts	(875,216)	(1,024,000)	148,784
Inventory	23,935,265	19,082,000	4,853,265
Prepaid expenses	2,527,534	307,000	2,220,534
Total current assets:	70,008,419	77,161,000	(7,152,581)
Fixed assets	14,941,275	15,371,000	(429,725)
Less: Accum Depn	(3,755,715)	(4,529,000)	773,285
	11,185,560	10,842,000	343,560
Other assets	10,542,571	1,345,000	9,197,571
Total assets	$91,736,550	$89,348,000	$ 2,388,550
Liabilities:			
Notes payable to bank	$ 1,900,000	$ 3,382,000	$ 1,482,000
Accounts payable	10,023,080	6,837,000	(3,186,080)
Accrued expense	6,240,424	3,189,000	(3,051,424)
Taxes payable	5,689,907	5,214,000	(475,907)
Other liabilities	58,164	0	(58,164)
Long-term debt—current	72,679	0	(72,679)
Warranty reserve	693,651	0	(693,651)
Total current liabilities:	24,677,895	18,622,000	(6,055,895)
Deferred income	1,414,119	0	(1,414,119)
Capital lease obligation	1,147,704	0	(1,147,704)
Long-term debt	(13,075)	7,700,000	7,713,075
Total liabilities:	$27,226,643	$26,322,000	$(904,643)
Stockholders' Equity:			
Preferred stock—Other	$ 149,551	$ 149,553	$ (2)
Preferred stock—Ser "D"	60,000	60,000	0
Common stock	170,817	147,571	23,246
Notes receivable—C/S purchases	(369,951)	0	(369,951)
Paid in capital—Preferred, other	17,836,755	18,278,447	(441,692)
Paid in capital—Preferred, Ser "D"	29,840,569	29,840,000	569
Paid in capital—common	4,480,946	1,593,429	2,887,517
Retained earnings	12,325,349	12,957,000	(631,651)
Currency translation	15,872	0	15,872
Total stockholders' equity:	$64,509,908	$63,026,000	$1,483,908
Total liabilities & equity	$91,736,550	$89,348,000	$2,388,550

systems in the financial/retail marketplace, the financial picture was bleak. The Company's plan projected profit before tax (PBT) and revenue for 1986 to be 3 million dollars and 30 million dollars respectively. Detailed analysis revealed an actual loss of 2 million dollars, due to overvalued, obsolete inventory and a host of other financial control losses. One of the investors, who had to inject more capital into the company said that VeriFone suffered in those years from "profitless prosperity."

Hatim took action to correct the lack of accountability and controls. The Board had a CFO search underway since Fall 1986. Tom Hubbs was hired in January 1987 as Vice President of Finance and CFO. He had extensive start-up experience, and began to assemble a financial team, including a controller, systems specialist and planner. James (Jim) A. Palmer, Vice President of Operations, joined VeriFone in February 1987. Jim had been associated with Hatim during his 25 years of manufacturing management experience at Sperry Corporation. His most recent assignment, as Executive V.P., Manufacturing, Japan, provided VeriFone with the critically important understanding of how to manage a manufacturing operation in the Far East.

Despite the strengths of both Tom and Jim, revenues and profits in the first half of 1987 proved to be abysmal (2.7 million dollar loss by July). Hatim believed that there were two main reasons for this disastrous performance: mismatched and underutilized strengths of the management team; and fratricidal warfare among the organizational groups. The newly hired (by Hatim) Vice President of Sales was not a team player; the Engineering and Manufacturing groups were not "in sync" with each other; there was virtually no Product Marketing. Hatim was also being tested and challenged by the troops: "On top of all the in-fighting we were rapidly running out of money." Hatim felt that 1987 was the lowest point in his professional life. If ever there was a time for him to use his management and leadership skills, it was now!

One of Hatim's strongest allies was, in fact, Bill Melton. Contrary to what many entrepreneurs found very hard to do ("allow their baby to be raised by another") Bill was determined that Hatim's leadership position should be unchallenged. Hatim could then use Bill's considerable talents in the product and customer parts of the business. In mid-1987, Bill moved from Hawaii to one of the sales offices located in the Washington, D.C. area. "If I had stayed in Honolulu, many VeriFone employees and customers might have assumed that the corporate headquarters hadn't really moved. If I had moved to the new San Francisco headquarters, many would have interpreted this as a sign that I was still in charge. I purposely moved to the Washington area to demonstrate my original concept of "forward deployment of intelligence" and at the same time, to make clear to all concerned that Hatim was the one and only CEO of VeriFone." In addition, the VeriFone organization chart at the time clearly showed Bill Melton (Chairman) reporting to Hatim Tyabji (CEO).

Hatim's Second Year as CEO

During his second year at the helm, Hatim orchestrated four major events, two involving personnel and functional reorganizations and two involving outside financing. In October, 1987, he proposed his first major organization, which included: transferring Will Pape from Vice President of Software development in Hawaii to Vice President of Product Marketing at headquarters in Redwood City; firing the recently hired Vice President of Sales and promoting Greg Lewis into that position; placing product development (both hardware and software) onto Jim Palmer's broad shoulders (he still had manufacturing) and also moving Jim from Taiwan to the Honolulu development center. Placing engineering and manufacturing under the same vice president was intended to produce a more coordinated and cooperative effort. The Board of Directors had reservations about the reorganization ("Was Hatim just playing musical chairs?"); however, they went along and the changes were implemented. The end of 1987 did, in fact, show a slight profit.

With a pressing need to obtain more financing, Hatim prepared to meet with some VCs in New York during mid-October, 1987. The latest financing, done in August 1986, had been at $1.10 per share. VeriFone's board told Hatim that, given the poor financial profile of the company, he would be lucky to get $1.20, but Hatim wanted $1.75 per share. His presentation to the financiers, scheduled for October 20th, one day after Black Monday, was postponed to mid-November. Hatim recalled the details of the all-day meeting:

> I presented for six hours, during which time they asked a lot of tough questions. Their decision to do the deal came down to the Management Team's credibility; we were able to obtain a sliding scale deal, based on future results, something unusual in the venture capitalist world. We raised 6.9 million dollars; the number of shares, and therefore, the price per share would depend on the 1988 PBT (profits before taxes). The price would be $1.10 for PBT less than 5 million, 1.45 for 7 million PBT, and 1.85 for PBT greater than 9 million. We actually ended up with 10.3 million PBT. We started moving forward in the 4th quarter of 1987 and have never looked back since!

The Management Team's credibility with the Board of Directors naturally soared. Asked what he thought was responsible for the turnaround starting in late 1987, Hatim said: "I had my team in place, my guys responded, and the Board was behind me."

The second reorganization, which was finalized in May 1988, was the direct result of Hatim's extreme frustration at the inability of the financial group to report revenue and profit actuals in a timely manner. Hatim could not get the actual numbers for almost two weeks following any month end. Will Pape described the situation: "It's like trying to navigate a ship from the back instead of from up front; how can you see where you're going?" At a staff meeting in mid-April 1988, Will proposed the development of an information system which could extract the daily projected sales, invoices, etc. from the present accounting system and then report and predict revenue and PBT estimates on a *daily* basis. Tom Hubbs, CFO, (who had line responsibility over MIS), strongly supported Will's proposal and further suggested that due to Will's strong background in software and information science, the MIS function should be transferred to Will. By the end of May, Hatim had promoted Will to Vice President of Information Systems and Control and CIO, with line responsibility over MIS, Human Resources and Administration. According to Hatim: "This was the single best move I've made. I organize around people; I recognize their strengths, and then restructure and capitalize on those strengths." REVWatch and PBT Flash began in July, 1988 and proved to be accurate within 2 to 3%.

The reorganized management team combined with the 6.9 million dollar financing was contributing towards continued profitability in 1988. Although Hatim was not actively pursuing more financing, he was then presented with an unusual opportunity. One of VeriFone's major oil customers wanted to have a service contract on all of the terminals located at its gas stations, but VeriFone did not have a nationwide field service organization. At their customer's suggestion, VeriFone approached DataCard, with an eye to potentially sub-contracting the field service work to them. In the course of these discussions, DataCard (who also owned Datatrol—one of VeriFone's competitors), became interested in forming an alliance with VeriFone. In June, 1988, a deal was negotiated whereby VeriFone sub-contracted its service business to DataCard and DataCard agreed that VeriFone would develop and manufacture the terminals to be sold by its Datatrol division.

DataCard was also interested in obtaining an equity position in VeriFone. Based on the first six months PBT, Hatim was confident that his previous financing would come in at $1.85 per share; furthermore the company did not need cash per se. At a negotiating meeting in Minneapolis in late June, 1988, DataCard, a privately held company, and its owners, agreed to purchase 6 million shares at $5 per share. The transaction was consummated in mid-August.

Reassignments and New Players

During 1988, Hatim continued to restructure his management team in order to use each person's talents most effectively. Clive Taylor, an associate from Sperry Corporation, with over 25 years of international management experience joined VeriFone in mid-1988, helped administer the joint venture agreement with DataCard, and became Vice President of Worldwide Marketing in January 1989. At the end of 1988, Ashok Narasimhan joined VeriFone as Vice President of Market and Product Development, thus relieving Jim Palmer of his "double duty." Ashok had 18 years of financial and management experience, including the founding and developing of Wipro, the second largest computer company in India. (See Exhibit 4.)

1988 was the first truly profitable year for VeriFone; it ended with a 10 million dollar profit on 73 million dollars of revenue. Hatim felt that the management restructuring which he began in 1987 had been successfully accomplished by the end of 1988.

Developing a New Vision

Bill Melton's motto, "Twice the functionality at half the cost" of the early days was transformed to, "low cost, high value," i.e., holding costs and prices down while bringing quality up, so as to deliver the highest value to the customer. Since this was the strategy that many Japanese firms used with great success, and because

VeriFone had already surpassed its chief rival, Omron (an independent billion dollar Japanese conglomerate), Hatim was fond of saying, "We have out-Japanesed the Japanese!"

Earlier in the Fall of 1987, while in the midst of addressing tactical issues, Hatim had decided that it was also necessary to develop long-range strategic plans. The point-of-sale financial market was still growing rapidly, but that growth would slow in 1990–91. At the time, VeriFone held a 55% market share. What new markets would be compatible with VeriFone's products and expertise? Where could small, powerful, low-cost, user-friendly terminals with embedded telecommunications be used? These terminals were not only small, but their memories were designed to retain information (non-volatile) even when power was removed. This battery-backed feature would be useful in markets where portability was important.

The informal structure of the management team (Hatim, Bill and the vice presidents) encouraged each team member to candidly state his views on the subject under discussion. After full discussion, one member would synthesize the various opinions and try to achieve consensus. Bill Melton used to lead these discussions in the early days, and Tuck Newport later assumed the responsibility for putting this down on paper.

It was at one such meeting, in December 1987, that the vision of "Fourth Wave of Computing" was created. VeriFone's terminals were, in fact, microcomputers; they were presently being used by thousands of (often) computer-illiterate retail clerks. This product line could be modified (mostly through software) to take any type of transaction, automate it and deliver it, via phone lines, dedicated networks, or other telecommunications methods, to any front-end processor or large mainframe computer. The transaction could just as easily be hourly employee attendance records as electronic funds transfer (EFT). According to Hatim: "We are trying to create mass markets, where none now exist, by revolutionizing price points."

New Stars on the Horizon

The Electronic Benefits Transfer (EBT) market was very similar to VeriFone's credit card bank (bank and oil company) transaction (core) market. Washington State had automated their unemployment benefits distribution process with the use of VeriFone terminals. When an individual became eligible for unemployment benefits, he or she would be issued a plastic "unemployment payment" card, with identification information embedded within a magnetic strip (similar to most credit cards). In order to receive his or her unemployment payment, the individual would go to a participating supermarket, where the VeriFone systems would be located at the customer service counter. These systems communicated (via telephone lines) to a mainframe computer which housed all pertinent unemployment information. If the individual was eligible for a payment, the amount would be transmitted back to the VeriFone terminal and a credit slip would automatically be printed on VeriFone's printer. The individual would then be able to cash in this credit slip at the same supermarket. (The supermarkets were quite happy to participate because usually the unemployed individual used part of his or her benefit to buy groceries.) In 1989,

Exhibit 4
Organization Chart—Numbers and Locations of Employees**

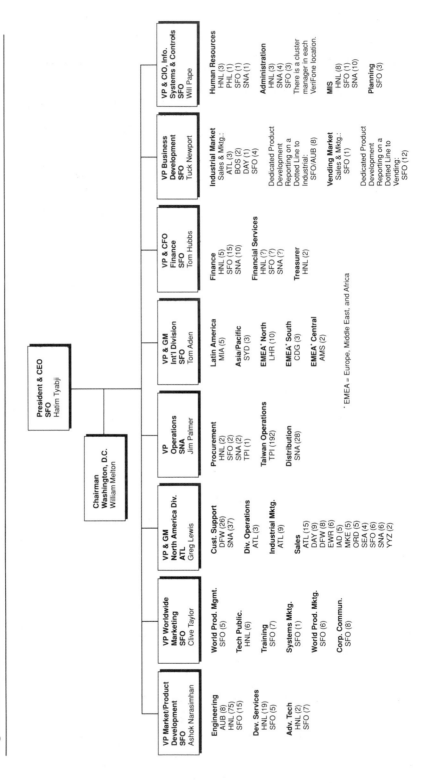

President & CEO
SFO
Hatim Tyabji

Chairman
Washington, D.C.
William Melton

VP Market/Product
Development
SFO
Ashok Narasimhan

Engineering
AUB (8)
HNL (75)
SFO (15)

Dev. Services
HNL (19)
SFO (5)

Adv. Tech
HNL (2)
SFO (7)

VP Worldwide
Marketing
SFO
Clive Taylor

World Prod. Mgmt.
SFO (5)

Tech Public.
HNL (6)

Training
SFO (7)

Systems Mktg.
SFO (7)

World Prod. Mktg.
SFO (6)

Corp. Commun.
SFO (8)

VP & GM
North America Div.
ATL
Greg Lewis

Cust. Support
DFW (26)
SNA (37)

Div. Operations
ATL (3)

Industrial Mktg.
ATL (9)

Sales
ATL (15)
DAY (9)
DFW (8)
EWR (6)
IAD (5)
MKE (5)
ORD (5)
SEA (4)
SFO (6)
SNA (6)
YYZ (2)

VP
Operations
SNA
Jim Palmer

Procurement
HNL (2)
SFO (2)
SNA (2)
TPI (1)

Taiwan Operations
TPI (192)

Distribution
SNA (28)

VP & GM
Int'l Division
SFO
Tom Aden

Latin America
MIA (5)

Asia/Pacific
SYD (3)

EMEA* North
LHR (10)

EMEA* South
CDG (3)

EMEA* Central
AMS (2)

* EMEA = Europe, Middle East, and Africa

VP & CFO
Finance
SFO
Tom Hubbs

Finance
HNL (5)
SFO (15)
SNA (10)

Financial Services
HNL (?)
SFO (?)
SNA (?)

Treasurer
HNL (2)

VP Business
Development
SFO
Tuck Newport

Industrial Market
Sales & Mktg.:
ATL (3)
BOS (2)
DAY (1)
SFO (4)

Dedicated Product
Development
Reporting on a
Dotted Line to
Industrial:
SFO/AUB (8)

Vending Market
Sales & Mktg.:
SFO (1)

Dedicated Product
Development
Reporting on a
Dotted Line to
Vending:
SFO (12)

VP & CIO, Info.
Systems & Controls
SFO
Will Pape

Human Resources
HNL (3)
PHL (1)
SFO (1)
SNA (1)

Administration
HNL (3)
SNA (4)
SFO (3)
There is a cluster
manager in each
VeriFone location.

MIS
HNL (8)
SFO (1)
SNA (10)

Planning
SFO (3)

Location Guide

ATL — Atlanta	EWR — Newark (New York)	SEA — Seattle
AMS — The Hague, Netherlands	HNL — Honolulu	SFO — Redwood City/San Francisco
AUB — Auburn, CA	IAD — Washington, D.C.	SNA — Costa Mesa
BOS — Boston	LHR — London	SYD — Sydney, Australia
CDG — Paris	MIA — Miami	TPI — Taiwan
DAY — Dayton, Ohio	MKE — Milwaukee	YYZ — Toronto, Canada
DFW — Dallas	ORD — Chicago	

New Jersey was looking at such a system; the competitive bidders (VeriFone's customers) were the large system integrators (EDS, etc.) and *all* were specifying VeriFone's terminal systems for the user-end of the system.

The potential size of the EBT market was enormous; welfare benefits could be distributed in the same manner as unemployment benefits. (Ramsey County, Minnesota already had such a system.) The verification and transfer of medical benefits was another large and lucrative market for VeriFone systems. Private or government medical plans could issue each eligible subscriber a plastic "benefit card" and install a VeriFone system in each participating pharmacy or doctor's office. Assignment of benefits would be automatically transacted at the time of the visit, eliminating the need for expensive and time consuming paperwork.

During 1988, VeriFone also began to experiment in two new markets which bore less resemblance to the core market than EBT. Tuck Newport, who had joined VeriFone in 1984, became the Vice President of New Business Development to oversee initiatives in the industrial and vending markets. The industrial market included data collection applications, such as time and attendance reporting and inventory management. The vending market was concerned with unattended POS (point-of-sale) transactions using prepaid cards in vending machine purchases as well as turning parking lots and movie ticket sales into unattended POS transactions by accepting prepaid cards.

The International Division, which was formed in October 1987 when F. Thomas (Tom) Aden joined VeriFone, introduced VeriFone's transactional systems into the financial communities in Europe, Asia, and Latin America. Although the basic process of transaction automation delivery and credit card verification was similar, the telecommunications protocols and hardware safety regulations varied from one country to another. Therefore, VeriFone was developing a modular design concept, including modular telecom boards, so that products could be tailored to each country's standards without any hardware modifications. The market potential was enormous and International's revenue growth reflected that potential.

Problems of Success

Hatim, and his management team of eight vice presidents, started 1989 with a goal of consolidating VeriFone's position as the creator and leader of "The Fourth Wave." However, they were not faced with the types of business issues which many successful companies, especially rapidly growing ones, had to deal with.

Stress

PBT Flash, the daily "state of the company," was sent via E-mail to all involved home office and field personnel. Since this "memo" gave a daily picture of how well the current month's projections were being met, all employees clearly knew when actual revenues fell behind forecasts. Each month-end at the Costa Mesa Distribution Center was particularly stressful, because extra efforts were made to ship every possible order to meet the monthly forecasts. What was unusual about this "end-of-the-month crunch," commonly found in companies trying to meet their monthly targets, was the absence of game playing to meet the numbers. For example, in August 1989, a major shipment was held up because no signed purchase order had been received from the customer, only verbal authorization. Other companies trying to make the monthly numbers might have shipped the order in anticipation of receiving it (the purchase order), or on the customer's assurance that it was forthcoming.

Although Taiwan and Costa Mesa both reported to Jim Palmer, providing smooth product flow and communication, the Costa Mesa employees had no control of when products bulk-shipped by sea from Taiwan would reach the distribution center in Costa Mesa. Although there was four weeks of finished goods inventory on hand in Costa Mesa, a typhoon in Asia could disrupt product flow, and exacerbate the end-of-the-month crunch. In that case, the stress on the Costa Mesa employees was enormous.

E-Mail

Electronic mail (E-mail) had been a major form of communication at VeriFone since the company was founded in 1981. Due to the vastly dispersed work force, it had always been essential to have a communication tool which eliminated time and distance considerations. The first culture shock for most new employees was the fact that VeriFone did not have secretaries and circulated no hard copy memos. Each employee had either a terminal or a PC and an E-mail account. Few companies had such a policy, which represented a major capital investment. With new employee orientation consisting of a series of computerized tutorials, a very strong message was sent to each new employee about the importance of computers and E-mail. Everyone was expected to manage his or her own E-mail messages with no exceptions. Each account was by first name, last initial (i.e., HATIM_T); even the phone book was alphabetized by first name, with the three-letter designation of the home-base airport in parentheses! Thus, everyone from janitor to CEO was on a first name basis, and each employee's travel schedule (flights, hotels, etc.) were accessible to other employees via E-mail. The familial culture was thus reinforced by the E-mail system.

Most managers were comfortable with E-mail and used it extensively. Although unaccustomed to this operating mode when he joined VeriFone, Hatim had no difficulty fitting into this part of VeriFone's culture and learned to type up to 45 words per minute within the first year. As a matter of fact, he had become one of E-mail's strongest proponents. A few managers expressed concern about the amount of time they each spent on E-mail. One manager asked: "Why send an E-mail message to someone at my own facility? Isn't it easier just to walk down the hall and get an answer?"

Since E-mail was the major communication tool, employees who did not stay on top of their mail found themselves outside the loop of decision making. Operational decisions were often put in the form of a default message, for example: "Should I first run report X or report Y? If I don't hear from you within two hours,

I'll run report X." Most of the mid-level managers estimated receiving almost 60 messages per day, while the top executives dealt with over one hundred daily messages. As the company grew from 300 employees in 1987 to 400 in 1988 to over 650 employees in 1989, the amount of E-mail traffic also grew. Would this communication mode continue to be effective as the company grew even larger?

All employees were encouraged to purchase PCs and modems for their home, and an allowance of up to $3,000 per employee was given for this purpose. Most employees appreciated this as a terrific company benefit, but there was some concerned that this tied them to the company on a 24-hour basis. As one senior executive stated: "I think a man's home is his castle, a place for privacy. E-mail can tie you to the company 24 hours per day; you are never free."

E-mail also proved to be a very fast and convenient method for requisition approvals. Tom Hubbs described one such incident: "A capital expenditure request went from the engineering originator in Redwood City, to the Chief Engineer in Hawaii, to the Vice President for Market and Product Development in Taiwan, to myself in Costa Mesa, to Hatim somewhere on the East Coast. The entire approval process was completed within an eight-hour day; this probably would have taken much longer if formal requisition paperwork had to follow the same path." Hatim added:

> We accept electronic signature approvals, something most companies have not come to grips with, not only for capital expenditures but also for personnel requisitions, salary increases, and stock options. I approved the 4.5 million dollar new facility investment in southern Taiwan by pressing a button on my PC. Other managers also have approval levels, which can be pulled up on the computer and reviewed on-line in case there is any question about what the limit for a particular managerial level is. We can do electronic signature approvals because we have a different mind-set. We do not accept truisms; we challenge conventional wisdom. As another example, we do not have personal secretaries. I have insisted on not having one ever since I first came to VeriFone because I believe in leadership by example—do as I do, not as I say. 'Please get one, Hatim', my staff often kid me; they can't very well ask for a personal secretary when I don't have one!

Travel

Although E-mail bridged the time and distance gap for internal memoranda and certain operational decisions, it did not, and could not, take the place of face-to-face meetings. Hatim felt strongly that there was no substitute for face-to-face contact and communication, and this was one of the reasons why he and his management team traveled constantly, to visit customers, facilities, or one another. The management team held regular two-day meetings at various VeriFone offices each quarter; the meeting calendar was established a year in advance in order to avoid any scheduling conflicts, and enabled people to plan their time. The schedule, once established, was religiously adhered to.

VeriFone's internal travel office had a direct computer hook-up to an airline's computer reservation system. Each employee's travel schedule was available to all other employees via computer terminal, so that he or she could always be contacted.

Company Culture

While the E-mail system, the constant travel, the first-name informality, and the absence of secretaries and paper were the most visible manifestations of the VeriFone culture, Hatim had personally crafted a "VeriFone Philosophy" statement (see Exhibit 6) to clearly communicate the beliefs and practices which he deeply felt were fundamental to the company's success. According to Hatim: "We are trying to create and perpetuate a familiar and *honest* environment; a distinctly different place to work. The VeriFone philosophy is our guiding document. Its principles are practiced."

However, due to the company's youth, percentage of newcomers, and the widely dispersed operations, it was not clear to what extent VeriFone managers and employees had understood and "bought into" this statement of philosophy. According to one senior manager: "Hatim is clearly passionate about this philosophy, and so are a few of the managers on his team, but some elements of the philosophy (e.g., 'dedicated to meeting our customers' needs') are clearly more evident than are others (e.g., 'accountability and teamwork')."

Marketing

Marketing had always been a great concern at VeriFone, but there had never been a clear consensus as to what marketing was and how it should be done. Several members of the management team had assumed this responsibility at different times over the past eight years. Most recently (prior to Clive becoming Vice President of Worldwide Marketing in early 1989), it had been split; Greg Lewis had been in charge of product marketing and Tuck Newport had been in charge of "all the other marketing stuff." When Clive assumed his current responsibility, he found that: "No one will disagree with my plans, but they keep grumbling that we're not doing marketing; when I ask then what they think marketing should be, no one can be specific."

What Clive, in fact, found, was that the marketing group was devoting all of its time in direct support of the sales force. "Many of the guys were spending almost all of their time making sales calls with the salespeople rather than: (1) training these salespeople to be independent; (2) creating new product plans, development plans, etc. Clive explained the situation: "When VeriFone first started, there were few products, few distribution channels and really only one market (financial). The objective was to *get market share,* and literally everyone in the company supported the sales group in this goal. Therefore, marketing became synonymous with product management. Now that we are the market leaders, we must refocus our marketing philosophy."

In mid-1989, Clive reorganized his group into three distinct areas: Product Management, which directly supported the products in the field; Worldwide Product Marketing, which developed new markets for VeriFone's products; and Systems Marketing, which dealt with new markets which required direct selling of systems. He was hopeful that the separation of product management from product marketing would allow VeriFone to be more effective in the marketplace, since it called for the former group to provide more direct support to the sales force, thus freeing up the latter group to focus on more strategic and analytical aspects of marketing.

Exhibit 5—VeriFone's Business: An Overview

The following excerpt was taken from the company's document, *VeriFone: A Business Overview*.

Background

Recent advances in microprocessor design and manufacturing technology have created a mass market for powerful, special-purpose microcomputers, making them available to medium- and small-sized retailers. At the same time, the growing number and affluence of U.S. consumers have dramatically increased the volume of electronic transfers that take place every day—and the expectations of consumers initiating those transactions. Meeting those expectations has become an intensely competitive business, and VeriFone has made a commitment to establishing and maintaining a clear worldwide leadership role in the emerging "Transaction Automation" industry.

Just as computer technology has produced major changes in the way business does business, it has made possible a new class of transaction computers that are beginning to significantly change the way people do business. Hardly a day goes by that an American consumer does not deal with these computers in some way—often without realizing it. Common transactions include a cash withdrawal from an automated teller machine, a prescription refill at a pharmacy and even a videotape rental.

The analogies are clear: in the corporate world, the first computers simply automated manual functions such as bookkeeping, transaction posting, sales order entry and record maintenance. After basic automation was in place, business began to look to computers as decision support tools, as a means of holding, sorting and using information about the business for competitive analysis and strategic decision-making.

The same dynamic has now moved computers out of the data processing center and the back office and into the consumer arena—be it the shopping mall or the home—and is particularly visible at the actual point of customer sale. The transaction process evolved from simple verification of credit and checks, to the situation we have today. Transaction Automation has become an innovative, strategic, profitable and competitive application of technology to multiple industries serving consumers and businesses in a variety of ways at numerous transaction points.

Much of the impetus for the evolution in the automation of commercial and industrial transaction processes has come from advances in technology, deregulation of the telephone industry and the phenomenon of a credit card economy requiring safeguards that only computers can provide. While Transaction Automation has its roots in point-of-sale (POS) and electronic funds transfer (EFT) applications, many new capabilities for electronic transaction management and automation are emerging almost daily—in retailing, health care, government benefits distribution, facilities

Exhibit 5 (Concluded)

management and access control, management information systems and other areas. This has created a new industry: the Transaction Automation industry.

VeriFone was established to address these needs and provide these services. The company has carved out a clear market leadership position, initially in the automation of credit authorization and other POS/EFT functions, and it is now committed to establishing a similar leadership role in the automation of the transaction process in a wide variety of markets.

Evolution

Point-of-sale credit authorization devices were originally conceived and designed to address a specific need: to reduce credit card fraud and check losses. While this is still a pressing need—and a large market—the industry has moved rapidly into many other applications requiring much more than a single-function POS system. True Transaction Automation encompasses a much wider range of transactions (not just purchases) that depend on multifunctional devices to capture and process information. And, by doing it in a way that is convenient for the user, Transaction Automation yields a competitive business advantage to the service provider.

So, it comes as no surprise that the first-generation transaction terminals used in the industry's early days are giving way to far more powerful and less costly intelligent devices. Today's Transaction Automation systems offer built-in communications, card readers, data security, multitasking operating systems, networking, and a variety of data capture and reporting capabilities.

Product Development

When VeriFone was basically a one market company (financial institutions), product development was conducted at the central engineering facilities in Honolulu and most tailoring was done with customer-specific software, handled through the local sales office. This worked well because the product was generic enough to be used for several different applications without major changes to the hardware.

Several of VeriFone's new markets required products with different hardware, and this situation was less compatible with a centralized engineering group. It was important to have a group of engineers working closely (and in physical proximity) with the product marketing group and with the customer. One high level manager attributed the delays in product modifications to " . . . a constipated engineering group." Another suggested that the successful franchising techniques of companies, such as McDonald's, be adopted to "clone" these new ventures by establishing a cross-functional team (product development engineers, programmers, and sales and marketing personnel), or even a dedicated "mini organization," for each new venture. Some concern was expressed that perhaps there was not enough "original VeriFone DNA material" (bright, motivated technical specialists and aggressive marketing and sales entrepreneurs with the ability to move very quickly on a new opportunity) to produce these organizational clones. Hatim felt that steps had already been taken to address these issues:

Industrial and Vending already have their own product development groups, and dedicated personnel for International are assigned. In addition to the development groups in Honolulu, Auburn and Taipei, a development group is to be added in Bangalore, India. A worldwide infrastructure of application programmers (55 are already in place) is being put together to continue developing applications based on customer need. Four hundred plus applications have already been developed. In this business, "records sell the record player."

VeriFone had always prided itself on being responsive to its customers. Hatim was known to "bite his lips" rather than reprimand a manager who violated company policies and procedures in order to better serve a customer. But with VeriFone's rapidly growing customer base (currently there were 2,500 active customers), there was some concern about whether needed product development resources would be pulled away from one of the new ventures to address customer requirements in established markets. Hatim responded: "We have developed a reputation of caring for our customers, of being extremely responsive, of delivering high quality. We will never compromise on these points."

Some concern was also expressed with respect to the level of technology being used in the VeriFone products. The company, which had made a major breakthrough in transaction terminals by designing them (essentially) as microcomputers, was still using the eight bit microcompressor, when technological advances in 16 and even 32 bit processors were already in the maturing stage. Hatim put the problem in perspective:

Customers buy from us because we provide system *solutions*. As long as we continue setting price/performance standards, the base technology in our "CPU" has *never* been an issue. As a matter of fact, since our "engine" (the Z-80) costs us only 60 cents, we enjoy a distinct advantage. Our acquisition of ICOT has given us the 16 bit technology. The real question is what mix of the old and the new technologies is most appropriate, and how rapidly should we upgrade our technology.

Taking the Company Public

By Fall 1989, both revenues and profits were continuing to climb; VeriFone projected over 17% pretax profit on 120 million dollars of revenue in 1989. It was anticipated that an initial public offering (IPO) would begin by the mid-1990 time frame. There was some concern about how the proposed IPO would impact both VeriFone employees as well as potential investors.

As was common with IPOs, concern about its impact on employees was expressed at several levels within the company. What would happen to the organization if those with large equity stakes sold their stock and left VeriFone? If this small group decided to stay, would they steer the company differently in order to protect their investments? What about the natural resentments felt by those employees who had either small or no equity? Given the pressure felt by almost all in the product chain, several people wondered why they should be placed under so much stress when they would get no direct benefits from a public sale.

Hatim had worked hard to move VeriFone to a dominant market position. Was it possible that, with all of that hard work, he had neglected to nurture and develop successor talent? He felt that he had an excellent management team, but was there "CEO material" in that group? Hatim knew that he was a very strong and highly visible leader: "Some of my staff are confident enough to frankly state their opinions, but some of the others are not so outspoken. What if I got hit by the proverbial truck tomorrow? I feel strongly that a CEO should be responsible for developing leadership talent around him, so that he can be replaceable. This was my one failing at Sperry. I sure as heck don't want a repeat of that here."

For his part, Bill Melton had withdrawn from day-to-day management responsibilities. He had, in fact, recently announced to the VeriFone senior management team that he would henceforth play the role of an "outside" board member, rather than an "inside" member. He now wanted to see how his "baby" would fare under public scrutiny that awaited the company.

Looking Ahead

Looking beyond the planned IPO, Hatim and his management team were taking steps to position the company for global competitive advantage in the 1990s. A 9-million dollar capital investment had already been made to upgrade the company's information systems, develop its CAD capability, and improve manufacturing productivity. In addition, a new 4.5 million dollar manufacturing facility had been opened in southern Taiwan, and ten million dollars in cash had been invested in the ICOT acquisition. Specific tactical position steps now being planned included the following:

1. Continue to build upon VeriFone's dominant position in the domestic financial marketplace.

2. Open VeriFone offices in London, Paris, and the Hague by the end of 1989. (The market conditions in Europe were viewed as similar to what the U.S. market was in 1985, and VeriFone was hoping to create and capitalize on the expected explosive growth.)

3. Continue installations in the financial marketplace throughout the rest of the world, where the growth prospects were seen as promising. (VeriFone units had already been installed in 40 countries.)

4. Create a fully staffed business unit in 1990 to attack the multi-lane retail, supermarket and fast food markets. (ICOT, acquired by VeriFone in 1989, had a presence in these market segments.)

5. Make major inroads into the international petroleum market. (Shell, Mobil, Exxon, BP, Amoco, Unocal, Citgo, and Total were already customers in the domestic market, and major orders from Shell, Canada were received in 1989.)

6. Invest in the embryonic EBT market. Because of the dependence on state and local government and the long sales cycles, patience would be needed to succeed in this market.

7. Plan for slower penetration into the Industrial marketplace. (Results for 1988 were on plan, but 1989 results were disappointing. With continued investments in 1989 and 1990, major payoff was now expected in 1991.)

8. Plan for payoff in the Vending marketplace during the second half of 1991, with continued investments in 1989 and 1990.

In the manufacturing and development areas, several tactical positioning actions were also being planned:

1. Establish a factory in the EEC in the first quarter of 1991.

2. Open a second distribution center on the east coast of the U.S. in late 1990.

3. Open customer support/repair depot in India for Southeast Asia/Australia in mid-1991.

4. Maintain and grow the product development centers in Hawaii, Auburn and Taipei, with common CAD tools and networking for instantaneous communication.

5. Establish a fully-functioning development center in Bangalore, India by early 1990.

Other tactical positioning steps already in motion included the following:

1. Continue to emphasize *integrated systems solutions* (including the telecommunications interface) in contrast to the competition's "box oriented" approach, which required the customer to be the integrator of the system.

2. Perpetuate the "lean and mean" headquarter staff (VeriFone's productivity in terms of revenues per employee was among the highest in the industry).

3. Continue to vertically integrate the firm by developing and manufacturing peripheral products presently being purchased. (The printer, which was at one time supplied by Epson, was already being manufactured in-house, but Epson still supplied the internal assembly. Such components could be developed and manufactured by VeriFone; other components, such as ICs, could be *designed* internally and farmed out for manufacture.) The rationale for vertical integration was not only to reduce dependence on external suppliers, but also to take advantage of VeriFone's superior development and manufacturing capability. (For example, the margins on printers increased from 32% when supplied by Epson, to 47% currently, to a projected 55%.)

4. Verticalize the sales organization into true lines of businesses in order to achieve the proper focus on the different market segments. (Hatim stated: "This reorganization will not occur until the end of November 1989, when I know that we have met our year-end numbers. I'll announce the changes in early December; then everyone will be ready and energized for the new year."

These specific positioning steps and the strong balance sheet and cash position (Exhibit 3), gave Hatim and his team some confidence that VeriFone could indeed accomplish its mission. Equally important was the loyalty that both VeriFone's customers and employees had exhibited. For example, strong support was displayed by customers at the Advisory Council meeting in Denver on October 18, 1989, and all VeriFone managers based in San Francisco scheduled to attend that meeting had done so despite the great difficulties in getting out of the area the morning after the San Francisco earthquake. Employee loyalty was also demonstrated by VeriFone's employee turnover statistics. A 1987 turnover rate of 26% (compared to 23% and 17% respectively in the computer and telecommunications industries), dropped to 13.5% in 1988 and was 11% in 1989 (compared to industry turnover rates that remained unchanged from 1987 levels).

With the benefit of all these assets, there was a good chance that VeriFone could realize its dream of achieving world dominance in the industry it was trying to create, and thus reach its objective of becoming the recognized creator and leader of the "Fourth Wave." Hatim wondered what else he could do, or do differently, to ensure this success.

Exhibit 6—VeriFone Philosophy Statement

VeriFone Philosophy

Philosophy:

> A system of motivating concepts or principles; the system of values by which one lives.

We are committed to:

- Building an excellent company.
- Meeting the needs of our customers.
- Recognizing the importance of each individual.
- Promoting a team spirit.
- Focusing accountability in everything we do.
- Fostering open communications.
- Strengthening international ties.
- Living and working ethically.

Commitment:

> A pledge to do a specific act or thing; the state of being bound emotionally or intellectually to a course of action.

We Are Committed to Excellence

Excellence:

> The state, quality or condition of excelling; superiority.

As a way of life, excellence is reflected in how we design our products, provide service to our customers and behave toward each other.

Exhibit 6 (Continued)

At VeriFone, "Quality By Design" means:

- We design excellence into our products, projects and processes.
- We do things right the first time, conforming to the specifications of our products or services.
- We correct the root causes of problems.
- We analyze the processes by which we carry out our jobs, constantly seeking ways to improve.
- We pay close attention to detail.
- We take pride in the products and services we provide.

Providing excellent products and services leads to credibility in the marketplace. VeriFone's growth and success will be a natural by-product of the respect and loyalty we earn from our customers.

We Are Dedicated to Meeting Our Customers' Needs

Customer:

> One who buys goods or services.

Our motto is:

- We shall satisfy our customer requirements with on-time delivery of defect-free systems and services.
- Our products are tools for helping customers solve business problems. We provide complete system solutions by working closely with our customers to satisfy their specific requirements. We balance cost, quality and innovation to maintain fair and competitive prices.
- Service is an essential element of product quality. We are committed to providing the best customer service in the industry. We go the extra mile to bring solutions to our customers.
- Excellence begins at home. We provide the same level of support to both internal and external customers.

Each Individual in Our Organization Is Important

Importance:

> Having great value, significance or consequence.

An excellent company needs excellent employees—people who bring productivity, enthusiasm, and excellence to their jobs.

Exhibit 6 (Continued)

To draw on the strengths of our employees, we provide a challenging and exciting environment that nurtures individual growth. To encourage outstanding performance, we:

- Help identify opportunities for personal growth.
- Encourage continuing education.
- Offer competitive compensation.
- Reward, retain and promote those individuals who contribute to the achievement of our corporate goals.

Management is dedicated to providing equal opportunities for employment, development and advancement to all qualified employees. VeriFone employees earn recognition through high productivity and a commitment to excellence in all things they do.

We Are an International Company

International:

> Extending across the boundaries of two or more nations.

VeriFone is not just another multinational company. Our decentralized operations and extensive communications network link customers and employees worldwide; we are truly an international company.

At VeriFone, an international perspective means:

- We design our products to satisfy international requirements.
- We decentralize our development, manufacturing, sales and service centers.
- We endeavor to understand and adapt to cultural norms wherever we operate.
- We encourage open dialogue between employees, regardless of geographical distribution.
- We consider the impact a decision will have on employees in all of our offices.

We Live and Work Ethically

Ethics:

> The accepted principles of right and wrong that govern the conduct of an individual in relationship with others.

The goal of any business is to make a sound profit. Our dedication to quality will help us realize that goal. We do not compromise our integrity in the name of profits.

Exhibit 6 (Continued)

VeriFone is changing the way people do business. Because we truly have an impact on people's lives, we must set a positive example of leadership and credibility in all things we do.

- We fulfill our commitments.
- We treat others with dignity and respect.
- We are honest and fair in all transactions with our customers, suppliers, shareholders and each other.
- We obey the laws of the countries in which we operate.

It is our duty to make a positive contribution to the communities in which we operate. Excellence in everything we do will ratify VeriFone's world citizenship.

We Work as a Team in a Spirit of Trust and Cooperation

Teamwork:

> Cooperative effort by group members to achieve a common goal.

Teamwork is synergistic—together we can do more than we could as individuals working alone. Teamwork creates a productive environment where ideas and initiatives flourish.

At VeriFone, we respect each other's abilities and contributions to the team. That respect is the cornerstone of trust and cooperation. We depend on each other to get the job done. We assist and support each other; we share the rewards together.

We Focus Accountability for Every Assignment

Accountable:

> Answerable; capable of being explained.

VeriFone is a 'Buck Stops Here' company.

By defining responsibility and accountability for each product or task, we:

- Provide a clear local point for both internal and external customers to channel questions or requests for support.
- Eliminate duplication of effort.
- Ensure that all employees are working toward a common goal.

The people who know best how the job should be done are the ones doing it. We involve employees directly in the management of their own areas of responsibility.

Exhibit 6 (Concluded)

We Believe in Open Communication

Communication:

The exchange of thoughts, messages or information.

An open communications policy at VeriFone means:

- We promote informal and open dialogue throughout the company.
- We respect the right to be heard. Every employee is encouraged to offer suggestions, express concerns and voice opinions.
- We communicate responsibly. We direct our comments to the appropriate decision makers and focus on solving problems.
- We answer questions honestly and as fully as possible. We admit when we cannot discuss sensitive or confidential issues rather than give vague or misleading responses.

VeriFone's electronic mail (email) system provides both vertical and horizontal communication links—internationally. Through email, any employee may reach the entire company instantaneously (anonymously, if desired).

The use of electronic tools models the larger application of our products in the marketplace. We invite our customers to communicate with us through email.

This philosophy statement was distributed in the form of a brochure, in English on one side and in Chinese on the other side.